HIS HOLINESS

BY CARL BERNSTEIN

All the President's Men
(with Bob Woodward)

The Final Days
(with Bob Woodward)

Loyalties: A Son's Memoir

HIS HOLINESS

JOHN PAUL II AND THE HIDDEN HISTORY OF OUR TIME

CARL BERNSTEIN

and

MARCO POLITI

Doubleday

LONDON · NEW YORK · TORONTO · SYDNEY · AUCKLAND

TRANSWORLD PUBLISHERS LTD
61–63 Uxbridge Road, London W5 5SA

TRANSWORLD PUBLISHERS (AUSTRALIA) PTY LTD
15–25 Helles Avenue, Moorebank, NSW 2170

TRANSWORLD PUBLISHERS (NZ) LTD
3 William Pickering Drive,
Albany, Auckland

Published 1996 by Doubleday
a division of Transworld Publishers Ltd
Copyright © 1996 Carl Bernstein and Marco Politi

A catalogue record for this book is available from the British Library.

ISBN 0385 405383

Printed and bound in Great Britain by
Mackays of Chatham PLC, Chatham, Kent

CONTENTS

For Jim Hart and Thea Stone
(C.B.)

For Roberto
(M.P.)

PROLOGUE

Professor Henryk Jabłoński, president of the Polish Council of State, watched anxiously as the white Alitalia jet began its descent to Warsaw's airport. Near him a detachment of the People's Army of Poland, in ceremonial regalia, snapped smartly to attention. Around him were arrayed the full diplomatic corps as well as a large contingent of Church and civil dignitaries. Phrases like "great son of the nation," "prestige of the fatherland," "union of all Poles"—chaotic fragments from a flurry of official statements—flashed through his mind. The last of these statements had been drafted on May 29, 1979, only four days earlier, at the conclusion of a meeting between the first secretary of the Communist Party, Edward Gierek, and the primate of the Polish Catholic Church, Cardinal Stefan Wyszyński.

Now that plane was dropping down on Warsaw like a meteorite and no one knew what its impact would be. On board, Pope John Paul II was restlessly reviewing the outlines of his first speeches. His pilot, Giulio Macchi, after entering Polish airspace, had made a detour—"In your honor, Holy Father"—flying the plane over the city of Kraków. On October 1, 1978, at the age of fifty-eight, Karol Wojtyła had left that city as its cardinal archbishop. He stared down at so many familiar sights: the imposing hill of Wawel Castle and its cathedral; the broad bend of the Vistula River where once he had walked with his father; the great Market Square with its Sukiennice, the medieval loggia of the merchants; and the sprawling industrial suburb of Nowa Huta, the new "workers' city" that the Communists had tried in vain to make churchless and godless. From the air he could even see the road to the town of Zakopane and the old Solvay chemical factory, a dilapidated red-brick building where he had toiled as a common laborer during the Nazi occupation. It grew more decrepit every year, like the political regime that had expropriated it.

1

"I'm going back, I'm going to meet the Church that I come from," he had told Italian premier Giulio Andreotti as he left Rome. Beyond that, he had no more idea than Henryk Jabłoński what to expect from this first journey of a pope to Communist Eastern Europe. Speaking in an uncharacteristically flawed Italian, a mark of his anxiety, he reiterated to journalists on board the plane that whatever happened, it would be profound. "For this," he said emphatically, "there had to be a Poland."

"I think that all these differences between Communists and capitalists . . . are in a way surface differences," he commented later in the flight. "Underneath is where the people are. This is a human reality, a reality of the first order for the mission of the Church."

Then, pressed by a German journalist, he turned his thoughts to the other Eastern European nations under Communist rule and the limits he was certain the Communist parties of the bloc would put on their citizens in the week to come: "Perhaps only a few people will be able to get to Poland during these days, but the spiritual effect will be felt."

During the flight, he also glanced at the telegrams that are routinely sent to leaders of the countries the papal plane flies over. They contained some hints: For Marshal Tito's Yugoslavia, where the Church functioned with relatively few restrictions, the pontiff invoked "divine assistance." In the case of Gustav Husak's Czechoslovakia, where the Church endured severe repressive measures, he limited himself to good wishes for prosperity.

From the cockpit the pilot could already see endless lines of people making their way toward Warsaw's center, and massive crowds gathering along the road that the pope would take from the airport. "For me this is a homecoming," the pope told a Polish journalist with a smile. Then, after a long pause, he added: "I'm doing all I can not to let my feelings run away with me."

At 10:07 A.M. on June 2, 1979, the pope's plane landed in the Polish capital. At that moment the bells in all of Poland's churches began to ring out. From the Baltic Sea to the Tatra Mountains, from Silesia to the border of the Union of Soviet Socialist Republics, the country echoed with their peals.

In 1966, the Polish Communist Party leaders in Warsaw, under pressure from the hawks in the Kremlin, East Berlin, and Prague, had refused permission for Pope Paul VI to visit Poland. Now history was taking its revenge. Like a smiling nemesis, John Paul II was knocking on Poland's door. He was returning to his own country like a conqueror and—though the Communist leaders could not know this yet—in the future he would come back any time he wished.

As the pope knelt to kiss the ground at Okęcie Airport and hugged two little girls who came to pay him homage with big bouquets of white and red carnations (the colors of Poland) and white and yellow lilies (the colors of the Vatican), the sound of those bells was lapping against the frontiers of East Germany, crossing the border of Czechoslovakia, hurdling the barriers of Ukraine and Byelorussia in the Soviet Union and of Catholic Lithuania. In the coming days, the meaning of the insistent clanging of those bells would become clearer to millions of people.

Protocol in the first moments of the pope's visit confirmed that the Church in Poland had achieved a status unprecedented in any other socialist country. For one thousand years the Church had remained the embodiment of Polish nationhood through wars, slaughters, partitions, persecutions, and conquests. Angry Politburo leaders in Moscow simply could not grasp that the Catholic Church in Poland was no mere cog in the state machine, like the Russian Orthodox Church. In Russia the Church was tolerated grudgingly by the government and completely subject to the power of the party. In Poland it *was* a power. President Jabłoński began by quoting Wojtyła's predecessors John XXIII and Paul VI and expressing his hope that the new pontiff would continue their policy of "coexistence among peoples." In his official capacity as head of the national Church, old Primate Wyszyński, who had spent three years under house arrest at the close of the Stalin era, responded. He signaled a subtle shift in power occurring at that moment, though he swathed it in ecclesiastical rhetoric: "Holy Father, you have our joyful hearts in your hands, and at your feet the noble soul of ever faithful Poland."

Across the whole of Poland the red flag of communism seemed to have miraculously vanished, and there remained only the banners of the nation and of the Holy See. At the airport a choir of Catholic students burst joyfully into the medieval hymn "Gaude, Mater Polonia" (Rejoice, Mother Poland).

Despite the urgent analyses offered by politicians, diplomats, journalists, and secret agents during the pope's first hours back in Poland, no one fully grasped the enormity of the event, not even perhaps the pope himself. It was probably impossible to do so, for who could plumb what was happening in the hearts of a whole people? For the next nine days the men, women, and, especially, the young people of Poland would live in a sort of trance of sustained, almost erotic excitement, as if they were experiencing not just the visit of a compatriot who had assumed supreme religious authority over one of the world's great faiths, but the coming of an emperor, a messiah. The experience was overwhelming and irresistible.

Zbigniew Bujak, who the year before had taken part in the founding of an unauthorized trade union group, was among the thousands of Poles who thronged the road to the airport to get a look at the pope. He was not quite sure why he had come. He was a leader of the opposition, a marked man. The police were breathing down his neck. Militiamen had recently brought him in for questioning. The secret police had a dossier on him. His wife and the wives of his companions had been interrogated. "We've begun our opposition," he was thinking as he stood there, jostled by the crowd, "but whom can we count on?" He didn't quite know yet what direction opposition to the state should take. Suddenly the pope passed by in a white army jeep and the roar of the crowd became deafening. Bujak was struck by Wojtyła's smile as he blessed and greeted these people who were responding almost deliriously to the deep feelings they read in the pontiff's face. At that moment he realized that "this too was an anti-Communist demonstration," and he felt a great weight being lifted from him. "Both the fears we had when we began our struggle against the totalitarian system and our concern over future developments now disappeared," he recalled years later. His comrades had similar experiences. "We saw that there were many of us. This was very important and put our doubts to flight."

Arriving in Castle Square, at the entrance to Warsaw's Old City, John Paul II appeared almost overcome by the tension, the emotions, and the expectations so evident in the cries of the crowd, in the excited faces and frenetically waving hands. The cobblestones that the pope's car drove across were garlanded with flowers: bouquets of three or four carnations at most, tied together with red or white ribbons, thickened with bits of green. The people of Warsaw had laid these bouquets in two neat rows bordering the pope's route through the Old City to the cathedral of Saint John. Those thin rows of flowers were a revelation of poverty, love, and hope.

At the sight of the cathedral Wojtyła's face lost its purposeful expression, and tears began running down his cheeks. Except for a moment during the conclave that elected him pope, no one had seem him cry since the day his father died, thirty-eight years earlier. He dried his face with the back of his hand.

Some around him were cheering wildly, but many didn't applaud, merely looked at him and, like him, gave vent to their feelings in subdued weeping. Even the rigid features of Primate Wyszyński, at the pope's side, cracked under the strain.

For the first mass that Karol Wojtyła would celebrate in Poland as pope, the bishops had had a huge platform built in the center of Victory Square, where Poland's Unknown Soldier was entombed. Ordinarily, the Communist Party alone used this square for military reviews, rallies, and other displays of its power. Now three flights of stairs led to an altar, surmounted by a wooden cross thirty-six feet high. On the eve of the papal visit that gigantic cross, adorned with a simple red ecclesiastical stole, had become a place of pilgrimage for the citizens of Warsaw. Tens of thousands of them, a few at a time, had come to stare at the cross and at the transformation of the vast square, a symbol of Communist might, into a religious shrine. To limit the crowds at the mass, the Polish government had insisted that only those with tickets (distributed through parish churches) be allowed to attend. The number of tickets to be issued had then become the subject of exhausting negotiations between Church and government.

When John Paul II arrived in the square at four in the afternoon, three hundred thousand people were already waiting, and scores of thousands more, denied admission, had gathered on the perimeter of the city center. Missing were any high-level representatives from the state or the Communist Party. First Secretary Gierek and the members of the Politburo were back in their offices at Central Committee headquarters, glued to their TV sets, nervously following the flickering images on the screen. Under their orders, the cameras of state TV were allowed to focus only on the pope and his entourage, not on the vast crowds attending the largest religious gathering in Eastern Europe since World War II.

A storm of applause greeted the pope upon his arrival, and then silence descended on the square. John Paul II, with Cardinal Wyszyński just a breath away, stopped first to view a half-destroyed portico to one side of the square, on which were traced in bronze the names of the major battles of Polish history. Behind him rose the great cross. In front of him, an honor guard watched over the Tomb of the Unknown Soldier and its eternal flame. Here were the two Polands, the Sword and the Cross, the Nation and the Faith.

Slowly the pontiff approached the tomb. The crowd was motionless. The Vatican and Polish flags barely stirred in the light breeze. John Paul II made a slight genuflection, but Stefan Wyszyński fell to his knees so hard that his bones creaked. Pope and primate, together, were reclaiming possession of Polish history.

John Paul II paused to meditate and then kissed the tomb. A few minutes later, after the playing of Dąbrowski's March, the enduring anthem of Poland's quest for independence, the mass began. Three hundred thousand people listened raptly as, in his homily, the pope recalled Paul VI's unfulfilled desire to come to Poland and noted the special import of his own accession as a son of Poland to the throne of St. Peter. "Don't we perhaps have the right," he asked, "to think that in our day Poland has become a land with a special responsibility to bear witness?"

He stood erect in front of an image of Our Lady of Częstochowa, a revered icon symbolizing the faith of the nation. Then in a throbbing crescendo, he issued his proclamation, the very words that party leaders in Warsaw and Moscow most feared: "To Poland, the Church brought Christ, the key to understanding the great and fundamental reality that is man. . . . Christ cannot be excluded from human history in any part of the globe, from any latitude or longitude of the earth. Excluding Christ from human history is a sin against humanity."

Archbishop Agostino Casaroli, appointed Vatican secretary of state by John Paul II shortly before the trip and now seated in front of the altar, was sensitive to every nuance of the pope's address. With these words, he realized, Wojtyła had abruptly canceled the whole Eastern policy—*Ostpolitik*—promoted by the Vatican for the previous twenty years. John XXIII and Paul VI had worked to reduce tension between the Church and Communist regimes, to make new persecutions less possible, to get more churches built, more priests ordained, more bishops appointed—in short, to bring about peaceful coexistence.

What was taking place now in Warsaw's Victory Square was a breakthrough to unknown horizons. John Paul II never uttered a word that might lead directly to a confrontation between Church and state, between the party and Christian believers, but everything he said marked the beginning of a grand turnabout for the Church—in Poland, in Eastern Europe, in the Soviet Union, in world affairs. Through him the Church was laying claim to a new role, no longer simply asking space for itself. Through him it was demanding respect for human rights as well as for Christian values, respect for every man and woman and for the autonomy of the individual. These demands represented a direct assault on the universal pretensions of Marxist ideology, which by now had become an empty shell in the countries under Soviet influence.

In the square the crowd continued to swell as those without tickets began to find their way in. Perhaps four hundred thousand were there now, and above their heads hovered giant images of the Mother of God and the pope. John Paul II raised his voice: "Jesus Christ will never cease to be a book forever open, on man, on his dignity, on his rights, and at the same time a book of knowledge on the dignity and the rights of the nation. On this day, in this Victory Square, in the capital of Poland, I ask, with all of you, through the great Eucharistic Prayer, that Christ may not cease to be for us an open book of life for the future. For our Polish tomorrow." As he spoke everyone could feel the sort of electrical charge that links great actors and their audiences. Ten minutes of uninterrupted applause engulfed the tiny figure of the pontiff standing at the foot of the enormous cross.

In the square, songs of triumph and determination rang out: *"Christus vincit, Christus regnat, Christus imperat"* (Christ conquers, Christ reigns, Christ rules). And then the chant, repeated over and over, "We want God."

In the United States, among those witnessing the event on television was Ronald Reagan, then campaigning for the Republican presidential nomination. He was sitting in front of a little portable TV on the veranda of his ranch near Santa Barbara with Richard Allen, a Catholic who would become his first national security adviser. As the Polish crowd dissolved in rapture, Reagan's eyes began to fill with tears. What the two men were witnessing, they agreed, confirmed that there was a metastasis in the body of communism.

• • •

The next morning the pope attended a mass for university students in front of the Church of St. Anne. The event, which had been expected to draw about thirty thousand students, quickly swelled into a gathering of two hundred thousand people. Once again, the atmosphere was electric. If the students were searching for a symbol of resistance to the Communist regime in his message, they found it in the crucifix. Almost all of them had brought along small wooden crucifixes, no larger than ten or twelve inches across; many had been crudely fashioned from two pieces of wood. They waved them before the pontiff the way revolutionary Communists used to shake their fists. From his throne, John Paul looked out at a forest of crosses and raised his hand to bless them.

When the sermon was over, two young men and a young woman approached the pope and recited aloud: "We come before you with the cross raised on high. In this sign we shall conquer, and you stand beneath this symbol."

In Moscow the top Soviet leadership was already getting alarming reports from the KGB on these first moments of the papal tour. The potential dangers had been underscored in a recent report to the Politburo from the USSR Council for Religious Affairs: "The Polish comrades characterize John Paul II as more reactionary and conservative in church affairs, and more dangerous on the ideological level, than his predecessors." As a cardinal, the report noted, "he distinguished himself by his anti-Communist views. He was a champion of human rights in the spirit of President Jimmy Carter, and he cooperated with church dissidents."

In Lithuania, the KGB reported hundreds of thousands of believers were listening by radio to programs from Warsaw, and churches were packed for masses in honor of the pope. Many Lithuanians had traveled to visit relatives in cities nearest the Polish border so they could watch the pontiff on Polish television. In Latvia and Estonia, too, citizens of the USSR were watching—on Finnish TV.

All this came at a moment when the Soviets were worried about a surge of Islamic fundamentalism in the Central Asian Muslim republics of the USSR. Four months earlier, Ayatollah Khomeini, an exiled Shiite leader, had entered the Iranian capital of Teheran as a conquering hero after the collapse of the Shah's regime. To the leaders in the Kremlin, the victory of the Ayatollah and the election of the Polish pope, coming at almost the same time, looked like a double sign of peril. Their rise hinted at a nightmare scenario: the USSR besieged from the East and the West, by a gigantic pincer movement of believers. Foreign Minister Andrei Gromyko constantly warned his colleagues not to underestimate Karol Wojtyła's potential to stir up the Polish masses the way Khomeini had incited the Iranian people.

Moscow's foreboding shadowed every step taken by the Polish Communists. On the evening of June 2, when the leaders of the Polish party drew up their balance sheet for the first day, they were relieved that calm had prevailed. There had not been a single incident despite the million or more Poles who had gathered in and around Warsaw. Yet the leaders of the state had the situation in hand only in a technical sense. Catholic Warsaw was behaving as if the Communist regime didn't exist. The only symbols visible in the streets were religious and historical ones that predated Polish communism. The job of maintaining order among the columns of the faithful and in the gigantic demonstration on Victory Square had been assumed by priests and thousands of parish volunteers identifiable by their brightly colored boy scout berets. The militia had stayed on the sidelines, as had been agreed upon by Secretary Gierek and Primate Wyszyński.

For Edward Gierek, John Paul II's repeated invocation of Christ, his exhortations to the Polish multitudes to think of Jesus as a guide for the "Polish tomorrow," sounded like revolutionary cries disguised as prayer. ("May the Spirit descend upon us" was how the pope closed his homily. "May he renew the face of the earth.") What did the secretary of the Polish United Workers Party have in his ideological arsenal to counter that? What answers could he give to the tough questions that the Kremlin and local party hard-liners were already asking? All he could offer was a summary of the polite but unsettling discussion he had had with the pope at the Belweder Palace, in which the pope unexpectedly laid down a list of demands for unparalleled concessions by the Communist regime—for guarantees of basic human rights hitherto inconceivable anywhere in the Eastern bloc.

John Paul II, whose plans in 1979 never encompassed the overthrow of the Communist system, was nonetheless launching a personal policy of pressuring the regime for radical change in the nature of its governance. He based his own program largely on the very principles of equality and justice that the Party was forever glorifying in theory, if not in practice, and on the claim that the Church had a social role to play in achieving those universal goals. As it turned out, *this* was truly destabilizing.

That night, John Paul II recited the rosary at the window of the chapel in the primate's residence, sharing his triumph with hundreds of his compatriots gathered in the courtyard below. In Victory Square, on party orders, teams of street cleaners were quickly dismantling the thirty-six-foot cross, the pretext being that on the following day the pope's helicopter would take off from that very spot. The party could order the cross removed from Victory Square, but it could do remarkably little about removing the Polish pope from the hearts of his people.

·   ·   ·

The pope's trip to Poland was a spectacular public demonstration of his potential power and acuity. But almost as spectacular—in its implications, at least—was a meeting of two men that took place in Rome early in the Reagan administration. At the appointed hour, a bearlike, rumpled-looking man in a gray suit, whose unfamiliar face would have caused few people on earth to take a second glance, was ushered into the pope's modest office in the Vatican. A fervent Catholic who attended mass almost every day, a man whose house was filled with statues of the Virgin Mary, a believer who would soon be engaged in prayerful contemplation with the pope himself, William Casey, the director of the U.S. Central Intelligence Agency, had arrived on a distinctly earthly mission. He was about to hand over to John Paul II a single remarkable photograph, taken by one of America's spy satellites from hundreds of miles above the earth.

At his desk in his private study, the pope examined with infinite care this photo whose details only slowly came into focus—first, the vast multitudes of people, no more than indistinguishable dots on a flat surface; then, at their center, the single white dot that, he saw, was himself in his white cassock addressing his compatriots in Victory Square in 1979. This would be one of dozens of CIA satellite photos that he would examine in the coming years.

In a meeting enveloped in secrecy, a meeting that would not be revealed to the world for another decade, Casey would use that photo to help seal an informal secret alliance between the Holy See and the administration of President Ronald Reagan that would hasten the most profound political change of the age. These two men, one hailed by millions as the prince of light, the other derided by many as a prince of darkness, would meet perhaps half a dozen other times before communism would crumble, first in the pope's beloved Poland, then in Eastern Europe, and finally in the Soviet Union itself. But no meeting would be more significant than this one.

Although the Vatican in the years to come would seek to dispel the impression that these two representatives of such different kinds of earthly power had formed a new Holy Alliance, the pope would thereafter receive virtually every relevant scrap of information the CIA possessed not only on Poland, but on other matters of importance to Wojtyła and the Holy See.

Equally stunning was the religious nature of some of the discussions between Casey and the pope. In addition to talking about events shaking the world in Poland and in Central America (where the United States and the Church were both struggling against priests and political movements they regarded as pro-Marxist) the CIA director and the supreme pontiff entered into a highly intimate, spiritual conversation. As Casey's widow, Sophia, would disclose many years later, "they would ask each other to pray for things"—especially in regard to Poland, according to a papal aide. There is no question that the pope offered Casey his blessing, and that Casey responded with the CIA's temporal equivalent—a wealth of information to which very few people in the world were privy.

Since taking office twenty months after the American satellite photographed the pope in Poland, Casey and his patron, Ronald Reagan, had come to believe that there was a potential third superpower in the world—the twenty-block-square Vatican city-state—and that its monarch, Pope John Paul II, had at his command a remarkable arsenal of unconventional weaponry that might help tip the balance in the cold war, especially with overt and covert help from the United States. That the pope was not then dreaming of the collapse of communism, that his interests were not necessarily congruent with those of the Reagan administration in many different spheres, mattered little to Casey and Reagan. Intuitively, they understood what the pontiff might accomplish and how his acts might push forward their own global policies.

"How many divisions has the pope?" Stalin had asked contemptuously during World War II. To this question, an answer would soon be given, one that would leave the Politburo of the Union of Soviet Socialist Republics deeply surprised and vexed. Karol Wojtyła was both the inspiration for and the ultimate protector of the Solidarity movement—a non-Communist Polish workers alliance within the Soviet empire. Solidarity was receiving funds from the West, and Casey had already taken steps to ensure that these monies would continue to flow. The highest priority of American foreign policy was now Poland, he informed the pope. In Washington, Reagan and Casey had discussed the possibility of "breaking Poland out of the Soviet orbit," with help from the Holy Father. Solidarity and the pope, as they saw it, were the levers with which Poland might begin to be pried loose.

Wojtyła's accession to the papal throne and the ensuing events in Poland were redrawing the strategic map of the cold war. For decades, it had been an axiom that Moscow and Washington were the essential coordinates, with Berlin the critical point between. But now, like a photograph being developed, two other key points were appearing: the Vatican and Warsaw.

In the Kremlin, Mikhail Gorbachev, the newest member of the Soviet

Politburo and the Central Committee's secretary for agriculture, had already taken note of the danger to socialism now looming in both Rome and Poland. A decade later, on the occasion of the first public report of a Holy Alliance between the United States and the Vatican, Gorbachev would write: "One can say that everything that has happened in Eastern Europe in recent years would have been impossible without the pope's efforts and the enormous role, including the political role, he has played in the world arena." By then both Gorbachev and Reagan had departed the world stage, and only the aging pope was left to rail at the new world he had helped bring about.

When John Paul II took control of the Church, its influence and power in the world were widely believed to be declining. But Wojtyła saw himself as a man called upon by destiny, by God, to change the face of his Church and the world. He had been an actor, poet, playwright, and philosopher, and all these aspects of his personality came together in the supreme role of his life—as pontiff. What was wholly surprising was the skill he deployed as a politician on the temporal stage. As pope, he became one of the most remarkable figures of the second half of the twentieth century.

Though a mystic and a solitary by nature, he was energized by perhaps the largest crowds ever assembled before a leader in history. His moral and doctrinal message to the Catholic faithful was a demanding one, and not at all welcomed by many in his Church and outside it. Neither polls nor trends nor the ideas of his critics interested him greatly. With even more fury than he aimed at the Soviets (but with far less success) he would, as the years went by, protest against the liberalism, hedonism, and materialism of his age. Abortion, contraception, and modern sexual ethics were anathema to him.

The roots of all he felt and did as pope, in terms of both Catholic dogma and geostrategic doctrine, were to be found deep in the soil of his native Poland. As a youth, like many of his compatriots, he had steeped himself in the lore of Polish messianism, the idea that Poland was the Christ of Nations that one day would rise again to point the way for all of humanity.

For a decade, his Poland would be the crucible of the cold war and he, the hinge on which history swung. This, then, is his story.

PART ONE

LOLEK

MOTHER

In the telling, there was no pain. At the moment of birth, the mother asked the midwife to open the window so that the first sounds her newborn son heard would be the singing in honor of Mary, Mother of God.

And so the midwife sprang from the foot of the bed to the window and threw back the shutters. Suddenly the little bedroom was flooded with light and with the intonations of May vespers to the Blessed Virgin, from the Church of Our Lady, in the very month dedicated to her. And so the first sounds heard by the future pope, John Paul II, were hymns sung to Mary from the parish church directly across the street from where he was born, in a humble flat owned by Jews in the Galician town of Wadowice.

This was the story told by the old pope himself, as he walked through the Vatican gardens in his seventieth year, contemplating the arc of his remarkable life and describing this great gift from his own martyred mother.

· · ·

Karol Józef Wojtyła was conceived in a time of war between newly independent Poland and Lenin's Soviet Republic. On May 7, 1920, in the last month of Emilia Wojtyła's pregnancy, the Polish forces of Marshal Józef Piłsudski won their greatest military victory over the Red Army: the conquest of the Ukrainian city of Kiev. As the nation was swept up in the news from the front, Emilia engaged a midwife and prepared the tiny bedroom for her child. She was thirty-six years old, a frail woman, both emotionally and physically. Six years earlier she had lost a daughter, Olga, whether stillborn or in infancy is unknown. Her husband, age forty, a lieutenant in Piłsudski's army, was too old to go to the front, so he was able to help watch over their thirteen-year-old son Edmund during her difficult pregnancy.

On May 18, the day Emilia went into labor, Piłsudski made his triumphant return to Warsaw from the Ukrainian campaign. Thousands of Poles lined the streets waiting to greet the conqueror of Kiev as his special train, festooned with flowers, pulled into the station. Honor guards and mounted cavalry accompanied the marshal's horse-drawn carriage to the church of St. Alexander, where a mass of victory was to be celebrated and a magnificent choir would sing the "Te Deum." From the church, joyous students pulled Piłsudski's carriage to the Belweder Palace, passing through a grand arch inscribed "Hail to the Victor." For this was the day on which the Polish nation would proclaim to the world that it had regained its greatness.

It would be fifty-nine years before Poland would again experience a day of such joy and hope: fifty-nine years until the baby being born in the provincial town of Wadowice would return triumphantly to Warsaw as Pope John Paul II.

Emilia's labor was difficult. Her weakened body was tested almost beyond endurance but, according to the midwife, there were no complications. The infant, born healthy, was named Karol Józef—Karol after his father and Józef after Marshal Józef Piłsudski, Joseph of Nazareth, and his uncle. The birth register in the sacristy of the church of Our Lady of Perpetual Help, directly across the street from the room in which Karol Wojtyła was born, records the event: "Natus—18, V, 1920—Carolus Josephus Wojtyła, Catholic, male, legitimate child. Parents: Wojtyła, Carolus—father, military functionary; mother, Kaczorowska, Emilia, daughter of Feliks and Maria Szolc."

Emilia was delicate and sensitive, with compelling dark eyes—sensual, tender, feminine. When she first met Karol Wojtyła in a church in Kraków where, according to family lore, they had both gone to light candles to the Virgin, he had been a young noncommissioned officer in Kaiser Franz Josef's army. She was attracted by the very qualities his Austrian military superiors had noted in their reports: He was "upright, of moral character, serious, well behaved, modest, honorable, very responsible, very good-hearted, and tireless." He was also articulate, orderly, and gentle, qualities that served Emilia well. She needed calm.

Death had long marked Emilia's life: Four of her eight brothers and sisters had died before they were thirty. A beloved older sister, Olga, had died at age twenty-two. Her mother had died at thirty-nine or forty-three (the records are ambiguous) when Emilia was in her teens. The family was of

Lithuanian origin, but she had been born in 1884 in Silesia, a German-speaking province of the Austro-Hungarian Empire, just west of Galicia. She was the fifth child of a saddler married to the daughter of a shoemaker. Her parents had moved to Kraków, the great cultural and Catholic heart of Poland and its ancient capital, when she was an infant. In the pope's telling, it was his mother "who created the wonderful religious life of the Wojtyła family." She had attended a convent school run by the Sisters of Mercy for eight years, until her mother died. Her piety was quiet and deep.

In 1904 Karol and Emilia Wojtyła, newly married, moved to Wadowice, a small but important town on the old imperial highway thirty miles south-west of Kraków. As an administrative center for the region, the town was garrisoned by a prestigious infantry regiment, in which Karol Wojtyła served as a clerk.

Their first son, Edmund, was born in 1906. He was a treasure: uncommonly bright, handsome, athletic, even-tempered—and helpful. After her daughter's death, around 1914, Emilia's health deteriorated. But the birth of Karol—lively, playful, and winsome, with an obvious resemblance to his mother—buoyed her spirit, even as her body grew weaker. She never complained about the way her pregnancies had undermined her health. Rather she took delight and obvious pride in her sons, investing her hopes and aspirations in them.

From the beginning, Karol's mother wanted him to be a priest. "My Lolek will become a great person," she often told her neighbors. She doted on him, calling him "Loluś" (a diminutive of Karol) as an infant, and then "Lolek." With Edmund off at school and her husband, known to townspeople as "the Lieutenant" following a promotion, at work, she bathed her young son in a basin, read to him, and in the summer months sat with him in the courtyard as she sewed. She had been a seamstress in Kraków and now, to help make ends meet, she took in dresses, shawls, and women's coats for mending and repair.

As it had for centuries, life in Wadowice revolved around the market square in front of the Church of Our Lady. On Thursday peasants from the countryside sold produce—beetroot, potatoes, and wheat—from stalls set up there, and when she was able Emilia would take Karol grocery shopping with her. She dressed modestly, though she loved pastel colors, and wore her long hair piled high in the fashion of the day. She was anything but plain. Acquaintances were invariably struck by her charm.

But there were times when she would suffer back pains so terrible that she couldn't even walk as far as the market or sew or look after Lolek. Then she would close the door to her room and take to her bed. On such days, after Edmund came home from school, the Lieutenant would do the cooking and cleaning and attend to his wife. Emilia was also afflicted by dizziness and fainting spells, which Karol sometimes witnessed. She would go on daylong, even weeklong, visits to doctors in Kraków, where members of her family still lived, sometimes taking Karol with her.

Emilia faced her problems with faith and stoic endurance. "Even people who didn't know her recognized her inner calm and her religiousness," one neighbor testified. The word *calm* occurs repeatedly in the descriptions of those remembering both Emilia and her husband, but sometimes her moods could turn melancholy, and she might even obliquely reveal glimpses of her sorrow over the loss of her infant daughter—as she did to Maria Janina Kaczorowa, a teenage girl who lived on her street. "You are so young, but the moment comes when every person has to accept her misfortunes," she told her sadly. She never revealed, however, how or when Olga died. And no baptismal certificate or birth record for her has ever been found. She isn't buried in the family tomb; and when Karol Wojtyła's home was later turned into a museum, her name wasn't listed on the plaque that records his parents' and brother's names.*

Emilia soon taught Lolek how to make the sign of the cross, and she read to him often from the Bible. Just inside the doorway of their apartment was a majolica urn filled with holy water in which Lolek, Edmund, Emilia, and Karol Sr. would dip their fingers and cross themselves before entering or leaving. There was a prie-dieu in the parlor. Though small, the Wojtyłas' apartment was cozy and warm, filled with books, holy pictures, and family

---

* The records of the military parish church where Emilia and Karol Wojtyła were married in Kraków were lost during World War II.

photos. Over a mantel, a portrait of Lieutenant Wojtyła dressed in the uniform of the Piłsudski Legion hung as a proud reminder that he had helped restore Poland's freedom. The second-floor apartment was wholly unremarkable but had a certain petty bourgeois dignity. Each of its rooms—a little kitchen, a tiny bedroom, and a common living-sleeping room—led directly into the other: In short, it was a railroad flat. There was no bathroom, because Wadowice still had no running water. Bathing water had to be drawn from one of two wells in the market square. Each room looked directly out onto the sandstone wall of the Church of Our Lady and on a sundial carved with the adage *"Tempus fugit, aeternitas manet"* (Time flies, eternity remains). Karol would watch the dial's shadow progress as he played and read.

Though Emilia's burdens were eased when Lolek went off to school at age six, her condition continued to worsen. When her sons came down with the usual childhood diseases, she would beg her husband fearfully, "Please don't leave me alone." Sometimes, now, she would lapse into long silences, and she lay in bed half-paralyzed much of the time.

Her sons' accomplishments brought her great joy. Edmund—called "Mundek" by the family—was at the university, studying to be a doctor; Lolek was enrolled at a primary school for boys, a few minutes away. On his first report card, he received marks of "very good" (in religion, conduct, drawing, singing, and games and exercise) and "good" in all other subjects. He was passionate about playing soccer, excelled at reading, and went to mass each morning before school. After school, Emilia and Lolek often read Scripture together, if her health permitted.

On April 13, 1929, while eight-year-old Karol was off at school, Emilia was taken away to the hospital. His teacher and neighbor Zofia Bernhardt met him in the courtyard when he came home. "Your mother has died," she told him bluntly. Emilia had been forty-five years old. Her death certificate cited myocarditis and nephritis—inflammation of the heart and kidney.

As a seminarian, Karol Wojtyła told a colleague that his mother had been "the soul of home." He remembered her bathing him tenderly, getting him ready for mass, and worrying that he wouldn't get to school on time.

But after he had begun his priestly vocation, he opened his heart to a Carmelite priest from Wadowice and spoke in a somewhat different manner of his feelings about Emilia. "My mother was a sick woman. She was hard-working, but she didn't have much time to devote to me." This statement sounds strikingly like a complaint, a cry of deprivation. Through the rest of his life, Wojtyła would almost never speak of his mother, though as a young man he sometimes spoke enviously to his friends of the warm family lives that their mothers provided.

One of the pope's closest aides has described Emilia as "burned" emotionally and physically by the circumstances of her life and her time—by unbearable disappointment at the death of her daughter and by the difficulties of an era of war and economic privation. Certainly, Karol Wojtyła's mother was a very sick woman for much of his childhood, but from his relative silence about her, and the paucity of the historical record on her, today we can only speculate on her effect on him. At the very least, it was not an easy life for Karol Wojtyła either with her or without her.

The role of women, particularly the supreme importance of their devotion to motherhood, would become one of the major pastoral themes of Karol Wojtyła's priesthood, his writing, and, later, on a grand scale, his papacy. His opposition to abortion, his intense desire to protect the unborn, his belief in "a special feminine genius" and in a circumscribed role for women in the Church have all been crucial elements in his thinking—and in his career as pope; and all may reflect the complex feelings and unmet longings that he carried with him from his relationship with his mother, as well as from her early death.

Every time that Pope John Paul II exalts mothers who die giving life to a son or daughter, it is possible to hear a faint echo of the tragedy in his own life. On April 4, 1995, in the seventeenth year of his papacy, John Paul II singled out two Italian women for beatification (the first step toward canonization as a saint), holding them up as "models of Christian perfection." One was a pediatrician, Gianna Berretta Molla, who though sick with cancer in 1962 chose to carry her fourth child to term rather than have the abortion that might have saved her life. The other was Elisabetta Mora, cited by Wojtyła for remaining faithful to an abusive husband who ultimately abandoned her and her children. He praised her for demonstrating "total fidelity to the sacrament of marriage in the midst of numerous conjugal difficulties."

On that day, there were some in the Vatican, including the pope's great friend Cardinal Andrzej Maria Deskur (to whom he had confided the story of his birth), who believed that the life, childbearing, and death of Emilia Wojtyła constituted a powerful exemplary force in her son's pontificate and, through him, in the lives of millions of women—as these most unusual choices for sainthood seemed to indicate.

BROTHER

The great themes of the life and papacy of Pope John Paul II are to be found in the birth, childhood, and youth of Karol Wojtyła: the devotion, the discipline, the drama, the intellectualism, the isolation, the suffering, the mystery, the Marian piety, the fascination with martyrdom; the tormented relationship to womankind, the familial ties to Judaism; the emphasis on death and transfiguration. And always, above all else, the passion of Poland: Poland triumphant, Poland torn asunder, Poland as the Christ of Nations.

The funeral mass for Karol's mother was celebrated in the Church of Our Lady three days after her death. The next day Lieutenant Wojtyła took his grieving sons on a pilgrimage to the Marian sanctuary at Kalwaria Zebrzydowska. Thereafter, at important and difficult moments in his life and the life of the Church, Karol Wojtyła would return to Kalwaria, Poland's earthly Jerusalem where the Great Mother, the Holy Virgin, the Madonna of the Angels, the Queen of Poland, dies every year and enters heaven. There, in the foothills of the Beskid Mountains between Wadowice and Kraków, on the eve of the Assumption, tens of thousands of pilgrims accompany the Virgin to her tomb in an atmosphere of pious exaltation. Amid hymns and prayers they keep watch over her all night, and the next day celebrate her triumph over death and her entry into heaven. Generations of Wojtyłas had guided groups of pilgrims to Kalwaria at the feast of the Assumption each year, intoning hymns in voices that gained the family some renown in the surrounding countryside.

Kalwaria, a place of repentance and redemption, is the holiest site in Poland after the shrine of the Black Madonna at Częstochowa. In the spring it is the living stage for the mysteries of Jesus' Passion (when penitents weigh themselves down with rocks and beat themselves, in a quest for purity, by identifying with the torment of Christ) and in August for the death and passage of the Madonna.

Immersed in the throng of the faithful, which slowly wended its way from chapel to chapel (there are forty of them, scattered through the fields and forests), Karol as an even younger child had already marched in the grand funeral cortège in honor of the Madonna. He had seen the Virgin Mary laid out on her catafalque: a wooden statue with aristocratic features, eyes closed in the sleep of death, carried on the shoulders of proud mountaineers wearing traditional costumes. He had seen the weeping Apostles played by Polish townsmen. He had joined in the prayers and passionate hymns through which the crowd merges with the event and entrusts itself, its loved ones, its own destiny and that of the nation to the maternal embrace of the Virgin Mother. On the night of mourning he had joined the faithful penitents, hiking the paths along the slopes of the mountain, holding candles and torches aloft, a river of burning faith. And the next day, he had partaken of the joyful outburst of choruses, bands, and cannon salvos, observed the parade of regional costumes, of crosses adorned with flowers, of girls dressed in white like little brides. He had joined tens of thousands of believers as they accompanied the procession of the Virgin Mother, ensconced triumphantly on her heavenly throne.

Now at Kalwaria Zebrzydowska, the three males of the Wojtyła family knelt at the great altar in the basilica built in 1658 atop Mount Calvary by Bernardine monks and beseeched the Great Mother to take Emilia with her to paradise. Mourning his own mother, Karol prayed before the painting hanging over the main altar of the monastery, in which the Madonna's head is bowed toward the Child and the Child's nose presses tenderly against his Mother's cheek. Her arms enfold him. *"Totus Tuus"* (I am all Yours) Wojtyła would inscribe on his papal coat of arms half a century later.

> On your white tomb
> blossom the white flowers of life.
> Oh how many years have already vanished

without you—how many years?
On your white tomb
closed now for years
something seems to rise:
Inexplicable as death.
On your white tomb,
Mother, my lifeless love . . .

So the youth Karol Wojtyła would write in one of his first poems, when he was nineteen, privately expressing the grief of his childhood years, the burden of loss that he never confided even to his friends. Even as priest, bishop, and pope, the adult Karol Wojtyła would keep his own counsel and almost never entrust to other mortals the traumas of his life.

His mother's death robbed Karol of his lightheartedness. His teacher Zofia Bernhardt noted the change in his temperament. Formerly an outgoing, seemingly happy, and secure youngster, a "born leader," he began to withdraw into himself, seeking refuge in books and prayer. A classmate, Jan Kuś, often found Karol depressed, and other school friends remarked on his melancholy air. When asked about his mother, he merely said that she had been called away by God. Yet Bernhardt also noted that his exceptional friendliness and helpfulness as well as his rare scholastic talents, evident even in primary school, continued as before.

Lieutenant Wojtyła, who had retired on an extremely modest pension in 1927, when Emilia's health was failing, tried to be a mother as well as a father to both his sons. With Edmund away at the university, he devoted almost all his time to housekeeping and the care of Karol.

At the age of eleven Lolek moved on to the public high school, the Wadowice boys' gymnasium. That same year Karol also became an altar boy, and almost immediately the parish priest, Father Edward Zacher, put him in charge of the other altar boys. Some days he would serve two or even three masses. Karol also developed a close relationship with his religion teacher, Father Kazimierz Figlewicz, who saw in the boy's behavior the "shadow of an early sorrow" as well as almost limitless talent and cleverness.

The single source of great and ongoing joy in Karol's life was his brother, Edmund—Mundek—whom Karol idolized. Fourteen years older than Karol, a medical student at the university in Kraków, Edmund was a robust, energetic young man, with blue eyes, blond hair, and the look of an athlete. He was a thoughtful extrovert with charming manners, a sportsman, a great bridge and chess player, and a soccer star. When he came home on breaks, he taught the boys of Wadowice the finer points of the sport. His love for his little brother seemed boundless. The two of them could be seen dribbling a soccer ball between them through the streets of the town in the summer, or he would carry Lolek on his shoulders through the fields by the Skawa River. He took Karol on his first long hikes in the mountains, sharing his passion for nature and outdoor exercise; he taught him to ski. For Lolek, Mundek was a refuge from depression.

In 1930 Karol was taken by his father to Kraków for the ceremony conferring a medical degree on his brother. It was an inspiring journey for Karol, who walked in awe across the great Gothic courtyard of the ancient Collegium Majus, founded by fourteenth-century Jagiellonian kings. He watched with pride as Edmund was accorded special honors by the professors in their splendid academic robes: "Magna cum laude" was their verdict, acknowledged by his classmates' loud applause. For Lieutenant Wojtyła, Edmund's graduation meant also that the Wojtyła family finally had a financial buttress. Edmund's medical degree pointed toward a more prosperous future, without the deprivations they were accustomed to on Lieutenant Wojtyła's meager pension.

Edmund began his career as a doctor at the Children's Clinic of Kraków, then worked as a resident in a hospital in Bielsko, Silesia, the homeland of his mother's family. Karol visited him there as often as possible, staging little one-man performances in which he read and recited for the patients. Lolek's outgoing confidence and optimism seemed to return when he spent his happiest childhood hours alone with his brother.

So there could have been no crueler blow than the one that struck without warning on December 5, 1932: Karol was told that his brother had died at the hospital, of scarlet fever contracted from a patient he had desperately tried to save. Like his mother, his brother had died alone, with no kiss or caress from those who loved him. That afternoon a neighbor, Helena Szczepańska, who sometimes helped his father with the housework, found Lolek standing dazed outside the gate to the courtyard of their apartment. "In a moment of emotion I took him in my arms and hugged him," she recounts. "Poor Lolek, you've lost your brother," she murmured. With a grave face, Karol looked up and said, with a resoluteness that left the woman stunned, "It was God's will." Then he locked himself up in silence.

Karol experienced Edmund's death, unlike that of his mother, with an adolescent's increasing comprehension. In a rare confiding moment, Pope John Paul II would later tell the French writer André Frossard, "My brother's death probably affected me more deeply than my mother's, because of the peculiar circumstances, which were certainly tragic, and because I was more grown up."

The details of Mundek's death proved particularly painful. During an epidemic of scarlet fever, Edmund had chosen to spend a night at the bedside of a young woman patient to whom he was especially devoted. Not only had he failed to save her, but he quickly realized that he too was infected. Covered with red blotches, suffering excruciating headaches and a fever that climbed to 104, he was shaken by fits of vomiting and angina attacks. He spent the last four days of his life in agony and desperation. To the senior physician, Dr. Brücken, who tried to console his dying assistant, he kept asking, "Why me? Why *now?*"

The idea of the hand of God, in his unfathomable wisdom giving and taking away, the idea of a Judgment awaiting everyone now suddenly, unexpectedly took hold in the consciousness of Karol Wojtyła. From this moment on, the parts of the Bible that would preoccupy him were the apocalyptic accounts of the Four Last Things—death, judgment, heaven, and hell.

Standing with his father alongside Mundek's coffin at the cemetery in Bielsko, he listened to a eulogy delivered by Dr. Brücken: "With your weak, fading glances you sought to find in us some way of escape. I can still see your face, shattered by pain. I can hear your words of bitter lament." Karol remembered, vividly, both his brother's tortured questions and the details of the exquisitely happy hours he had shared with Mundek.

Many decades later, when an Italian journalist presented Pope John Paul II with a little book dedicated to his brother, the pope slowly pressed the photo of Mundek on the dust jacket to his lips and kissed the image. In a desk drawer in his Vatican study the supreme pontiff keeps a beloved treasure which he received from the hospital staff in Bielsko: his brother's stethoscope.

FATHER

By the time he turned fifty, in the year his wife died, Lieutenant Wojtyła's hair had become white. Now widowed, with his firstborn son and daughter dead, he was nonetheless determined that his surviving son would receive all the nurturing, love, and family discipline he could provide.

He made breakfast in the morning and supper at night. At noon father and son ate together at a dairy restaurant run by Mrs. Banaś, down the street from their apartment. Young Karol's day was rigorously structured: wake up at six A.M., breakfast, mass at the parish church, school from eight in the morning till two in the afternoon, two hours of play, church again in the evening, homework, supper, and a walk with his father. He had no difficulty accepting such a rigid routine. "The father who demanded so much of himself," he would say when he became pope, "didn't have to demand anything of his son."

They prayed together. They played together.

Karol's schoolmate Zbigniew Siłkowski was a frequent visitor to the little apartment at number 2 Rynek Street. Some days he arrived to find the Lieutenant washing linen or darning socks. One day he heard a loud racket as he approached the front door—shouts and the pounding of feet, then the cry of "Goal!" Opening the door, he found father and son flushed and sweaty, playing soccer with a ball made of rags in an almost empty front room, all the furniture having been pushed up against the walls.

On days when Karol served mass, his father would invariably be in attendance. He taught Karol to live his intense religious feelings without flaunting them. Schoolmates who stopped by the church to seek divine assistance on their examinations often saw the Wojtyłas kneeling together before the altar of the Sacred Heart, lost in prayer.

Antoni Bohdanowicz, a schoolmate who regularly came to study with Karol in his kitchen, was always curious about why Karol, after finishing his homework in one subject, would excuse himself and disappear momentarily into the next room. Finally, Bohdanowicz peeked through a crack and saw Karol on a kneeler, praying.

A postcard from the period shows Wadowice as a small village nestled at the foothills of the Beskid Mountains, where the swift-flowing Skawa River runs into a broad valley, and, dominating the town, the spire, cupola, and clock of the Church of Our Lady. The view is picturesque: A horse grazes in a wheat field on the other side of the river; a woman and child contemplate the vista. In reality, the town was a far less dreamy, rural, and idyllic place to live.

With a population of about seven thousand, Wadowice served as a little capital for surrounding rural villages. It was a minor industrial center with a steel parts factory, a steam-powered sawmill, and a primitive plant that made fertilizer by treating bones with sulfuric acid in open pits. There were two wafer factories, one of which produced *opłatki*, the unconsecrated communion hosts consumed in Polish homes on Christmas Eve.

Wadowice was also a place of modest cultural ferment. Its provincial dynamism contrasted with the dreariness of the poverty-stricken Galician countryside. Living in close proximity were artisans and workers, peasants and professionals, priests and intellectuals, as well as the officers and soldiers of the town's garrison. The town had three public libraries, a cinema, a theater, and a gymnastic society (Sokół, the Falcon), where Polish patriots had trained body and spirit during the years of Austrian occupation; after independence, its clubhouse continued to serve as a cultural and social center. The renowned state-run gymnasium (high school) for boys, founded in 1866, sent many of its students to the ancient Jagiellonian University of Kraków. The gymnasium's curriculum continued a noble legacy of humanistic studies, at once classical and militantly Polish. There were also two private gymnasiums in the town, one administered by the Pallottine Fathers, the other by the Carmelite monks. Many students from both parochial schools went on to the priest-hood. As a former state employee, Lieutenant Wojtyła was entitled to a fifty percent reduction in fees at the public gymnasium; that and his conviction that his son shouldn't be pressured into entering the priesthood were proba-bly decisive in his choice of this high school for Karol.

Karol had thirty-two classmates in his grade—the sons of manual la-borers, farmers, officers, and local professionals—and formed fast friendships that cut across class and religious lines. Several of his classmates were Jewish. Among his closest friends and neighbors was Jerzy ("Jurek") Kluger, the son of the president of Wadowice's Jewish community, and Regina ("Ginka") Beer, a Jewish girl for whom he had great fondness. About fifteen hundred Jews lived in Wadowice, more than twenty percent of the town's population; most were artisans and shopkeepers, but many were professionals as well. Galicia, like Lithuania to the north, was one of the major centers of Jewish culture and learning in Eastern Europe, and the well-organized Jewish com-munity of Wadowice had developed rapidly after 1819, when the ancient laws preventing Jews from settling freely in urban areas were abolished.

Ever since 1830 there had been a rabbi and a synagogue in Wadowice. The Jewish community soon had its own cemetery and another house of prayer. Karol grew up in an environment where Catholics and Jews mingled with relative ease. While he was familiar with the Orthodox, marked by their side curls and black gaberdines, his friendships and normal everyday dealings were only with those liberal Jews who were more comfortable with the idea of assimilating into Polish society.

The Wojtyłas' landlord was Chaim Bałamuth, a Jew. On the ground floor, below the Wojtyła apartment, Bałamuth had a glass and crystalware shop. He was a well-to-do, thoroughly modern businessman, one of the first merchants in town to sell motorcycles. Since the time of the Apostle Peter, no Roman pontiff has ever spent his childhood in such close contact with Jewish life. (As archbishop, Wojtyła would also preside over the diocese that contains Oświęcim—Auschwitz.) He knew the great festivals of Israel, whose celebra-tions he could follow from the balcony of his house. In the courtyard he saw the Succoth booths set up by Ginka Beer's family, and the menorah in their window during Hanukkah. His father had offered them the use of his balcony for a Succoth booth.

On Saturdays Karol could watch Jewish soldiers accompanied by a sergeant marching in formation to the synagogue to pray. They had been granted the right to absent themselves from the town barracks on the Sabbath. In return, they reported for duty on Sundays. When Karol was a teenager, a new recruit came to the Twelfth Infantry Regiment of Wadowice, Moishe Savitski, a twenty-one-year-old youth with a splendid voice. Attorney Kluger, president of the Jewish community, immediately drafted him as cantor of the synagogue; and on the feast of Yom Kippur, Karol Wojtyła was taken to temple by his father to hear the Kol Nidre sung by Savitski. There were a number of non-Jews in attendance for the same reason. Karol—already awed by the terrible shadow of the God of Job—listened, stirred and yet intimidated by the solemn, heart-rending chants with which Israel confesses its sins and entrusts itself to the Lord.

Karol's ties with Jurek Kluger were very close. They had been in the same class in the gymnasium since they were eleven. Jurek's grandmother was fond of Karol, who sometimes visited their house to play and have a cup of tea, with some fruit or a piece of cake. Indeed, his grandmother teased Jurek because he didn't imitate his classmate's example: "Karol is so well-mannered, such a good student, so hardworking. Couldn't you be a little bit more like him?"

Attorney Kluger had a grand, three-story house on Market Square at the corner of Zatorska Street, with an office across the way and a thriving law practice. He was held in the highest esteem both by his coreligionists and by most of the Gentile movers and shakers of Wadowice. Though Kluger had no personal dealings with Lieutenant Wojtyła, he was quite happy to see his son regularly going to visit Karol, one of the best students in the gymnasium.

Karol and Jurek excelled at soccer. Along with their companions they played down by the river in a grassy clearing between the railroad trestle and the bridge over the provincial highway. Once Jurek had to run all the way into the parish church to drag Karol off to a game; and when a woman expressed her amazement at seeing the son of the president of the Jewish community next to the altar, young Wojtyła remarked, "Aren't we all God's children?"

As a goalie Karol earned the nickname "Martyna," after a famous soccer star, although the best goalie in the gymnasium was his Jewish friend Poldek Goldberger. Christians sometimes played as a team against Jews, but with no obvious racial or religious animosity; and if Goldberger couldn't get to a game, Wojtyła might take his place on the Jewish team.

This placid picture of the Wojtyłas' relationships with Jews, however, was hardly the average Polish experience. Anti-Semitism in Poland, whose prewar population of Jews reached three million before the Holocaust and stood at thirty thousand after the Nazi occupation, was ingrained and widespread, though Wadowice seems to have experienced less of it than many other towns and cities or the surrounding countryside. In 1936, around the time that Karol was playing goal on the Jewish soccer team, the Catholic primate of Poland—the head of the national church—Cardinal August Hlond, wrote in a pastoral letter:

> There will be a Jewish problem as long as the Jews remain. . . . [I]t is a fact that the Jews are fighting against the Catholic Church, persisting in free thinking, and are the vanguard of godlessness, Bolshevism and subversion. . . . It is a fact that the Jews deceive, levy interest, and are pimps. It is a fact that the religious and ethical influence of the Jewish young people on Polish people is a negative one.

Even after the war, hundreds of Jewish Poles returning to their homes from concentration camps in 1945–46 were murdered in pogroms, including forty-five killed in the town of Kielce.

If after the death of his brother Karol became sad and dispirited, he slowly recreated a sociable, self-confident exterior, while letting books shield him from the world and nurture his private, contemplative, even tortured, self. He was fascinated by the language and literature of his homeland. He devoured Sienkiewicz's *With Fire and Sword, The Deluge,* and *Quo Vadis?,* of which he could recite long passages by heart. Among his favorites were books of poetry. Above all, he loved the poems of Adam Mickiewicz, the romantic apostle and champion of Polish independence—an ideal which the sons and daughters of a dismembered land had dreamt about throughout the nineteenth century.

With his classmates Karol also set off on long hikes into the Beskid Mountains, especially in the fall when the days were still gorgeous. These were the mountains where he had first been taken by Mundek. Their solitude would always remain with him and bring him peace.

The only activity that young Wojtyła shunned was fighting. No one had ever seen him in a scrape with another boy. "He's not a coward, he just doesn't get into quarrels," was how Jerzy Kluger put it. Kluger was slightly envious of Karol's ability to make himself liked even by casual acquaintances. The fact that Karol, apart from being a good goalie, could speak Latin, quote Homer, enjoy a joke, and tell interesting stories around a bonfire in the woods made him a boon companion. The single problem was that he wouldn't let anyone copy his classwork. His desire to help seemed to be blocked by the moral imperative not to deceive the professor. Only once did he let somebody copy an algebra assignment, but it caused him such discomfort and embarrassment that it was the last time.

By the end of his first year at the gymnasium, his teachers and fellow students realized that Karol stood apart—marked, in the words of one teacher, by "his great composure, talent, and versatility." He was the perfect pupil, warmhearted, faithful to his friends and his principles, extroverted yet deeply contemplative—all of which reflected the influence of his father.

The bare documentary record of the life of Karol Wojtyła Sr. would suggest a man of modest ambition, retired at age forty-seven from a dull career as a keeper of army records and accounts, content to live on a small pension that minimally supported his family. But the testimony of those who knew him—including his son—paints a more compelling picture of a stern but loving father, pious and cultured, concerned with books, athletics, history, the destiny of his country, his Church, and Catholic life.

He was the son of a tailor—a trade that served him well when he fashioned clothes for Karol from old army uniforms. "Of simple origins, he was a total gentleman in the way he spoke and behaved," says Jerzy

Kluger. Perhaps most important, he was deeply religious but free of any bigotry.

The Lieutenant's family roots were in Galicia, where the Wojtyłas had lived as peasants for several centuries and where he was born and raised. For the son of a tailor, being conscripted into the army offered escape from the narrowness of village life. A career in the military bureaucracy also satisfied his need for order, discipline, and dignity. In Kraków and Wadowice, where he spent his whole army career, he was able to slake his thirst for books and culture. He had no love for military life per se, but his salary was sufficient to marry Emilia and start a family. After Edmund's birth he had asked to be transferred to the civil service, but with the outbreak of World War I that possibility vanished.

In the eyes of many, especially children in the neighborhood, Wojtyła looked like an eccentric retiree, down on his luck, and in uncertain health. But he had a highly developed sense of character and duty to God, especially in the upbringing of Lolek. He had so little social life that some in Wadowice incorrectly thought him not just taciturn, but antisocial. After Emilia's death, the only pleasures he allowed himself were walks along the banks of the Skawa, an occasional swim in the river during the summer, and his daily newspaper.

Alone with his son, he threw off his natural introversion. In the evenings they would engage in long discussions, often about Polish history. He taught his son to speak German, compiling a Polish-German dictionary to help him. This enabled Karol to read Kant's *Critique of Pure Reason* in the original, a feat that left his classmates flabbergasted. Throughout high school, the Lieutenant was his son's tutor, in both academics and ethics. Their household, noted Karol's friend Zbigniew Siłkowski, was "a community of two people."

But there was no disguising the loneliness. For Christmas and Easter father and son sometimes took the hour's walk, following a road that skirted the fields, to Biała Leszczyny to visit the elder Wojtyła's half-sister, Stefania. And there were occasions when Stefania came to Wadowice for the holidays, bringing with her a semblance of normal family life. On Christmas Eve they exchanged *opłatki,* and at Easter the table was heaped with eggs blessed in church. But such familial rites were scarce.

The Lieutenant was not averse to entertainment, and he and Lolek frequently went to the movies together, a pleasure his son was particularly keen on. Once, as the two Wojtyłas were walking home after seeing a light Polish comedy, Karol, with his strong voice, was heard singing the theme song: "Barbara, you see / you're the only one for me. / Barbara, you know / all the boys wink at you so / 'cause there's nobody else like you."

TANGO

At the age of fourteen, Karol Wojtyła discovered the theater. It struck him like a thunderbolt. It was as if he had suddenly come face to face with his destiny. "His life took a new turn," Antoni Bohdanowicz, his schoolmate, recalls. "Lolek now devoted every free minute to the theater."

He had also reached puberty and was changing physically. Where he had been, in the words of a religion teacher, "somewhat plump," now he slimmed down. His face was a bit rounder about the cheekbones; his deep blue eyes had gained a look that was piercing. He was a very attractive young man, and students from the girls' gymnasium took note.

Though as a boy he had been fascinated by the stage, he now began to read plays and, encouraged by his teachers, tasted the thrill of taking the lead part in school productions. This encounter with art, this widening of his world, finally seemed to lift the last shreds of his veil of melancholy. In the parlor of Zbigniew Siłkowski, the stationmaster's son, Karol took part in dramatic readings and afternoons of chamber music and poetry recitations. As he spoke the work of the great nineteenth-century poets Mickiewicz and Słowacki, the future pope found his way fully into the kingdom of the word.

Adam Mickiewicz, the Romantic bard, in particular set strings resonating in Karol, the echoes of which can still be heard in his cadenced speeches from the papal throne. Mickiewicz was a cosmopolitan Slav whose work quivers with his love of freedom and of the natural beauty of his homeland. As a cultural figure he was torn, poised between Polish Lithuania, where he was born, and Russia, where he was confined by order of the tsar; between France (where he later lived) and Turkey (where he died in exile);

between Poland and the sunnier world of Italy (where he tried, in vain, to get Pope Pius IX to intervene on behalf of Polish revolutionaries fighting the Russians). Mickiewicz was a poet who questioned God's indifference to human suffering and whose thought prefigured Christian socialism. He was a prophet who wanted to lead not just Poland but all of humanity toward a new destiny, a voice that powerfully expressed Polish messianism.* All these themes took permanent hold on Wojtyła's imagination.

Mickiewicz was committed to universal human rights, and in his 1848 *Manifesto for a Future Slav State Constitution* he declared that "all citizens are equal—including Israelites." He was also a theoretician of the theater. He believed that a new Slavic drama would fuse Greek tragedy with the medieval mystery plays, the natural with the supernatural. Breathing the heady atmosphere of nineteenth-century Romanticism, Karol and his stage partners would all immerse themselves in his visionary Weltanschauung.

At the gymnasium a troupe of young actors was formed by a teacher of Polish literature. The group's first production, a collage of romantic verse and popular songs, was staged in Wadowice's park. Karol quickly became the star.

Students from the girls' gymnasium took part in such shows. During rehearsals, recitals, and discussions, the adolescent Karol struck up his first friendships with young women. Two girls were to hold a special place in his heart, Halina Królikiewicz, the daughter of the director of the boys' gymnasium, and Ginka Beer, two years his senior.

Extremely gifted at recitation, Ginka became his unofficial drama coach and perhaps a surrogate older sister as well. Jerzy Kluger remembers her as extremely beautiful: "A Jewish girl with stupendous dark eyes and jet black hair, slender, a superb actress." Karol always went along with her to rehearsals and thought up all sorts of tasks (like waxing her skis) that would leave them together.

---

* As Nobel Prize winner Czesław Miłosz, a friend of the pope, has written, "Poland had to redeem the nations with its own sufferings, and the mission of Polish pilgrims was to announce to the materialistic western nations a new, spiritually transformed world."

Halina Królikiewicz was beautiful too and an excellent actress (as she would be all her life). Attracted to each other and yet competitive, she and Karol became the best young actors in Wadowice and the stars of the little theater group. It was obvious to all that Karol was attracted to her. She considered the boy with the thick, dark blond, always unkempt hair "different from the others . . . a tall boy, a handsome boy, with a very beautiful voice, with excellent articulation."

Their bond of friendship became increasingly intense, so close, in fact, that they—unconsciously, it would seem—brushed up against erotic attraction, without ever, according to Halina, acting upon it. Viewed now from a society as hypersexual as our own, their relationship may be hard to understand: a subtle, restrained, pure, and unspoken emotional bond between two teenagers brought up in the most rigid Catholicism in provincial Poland in the 1930s.

After the election of Wojtyła to the papal throne, an iron curtain lowered on all aspects of his private life. In the face of the sometimes crude curiosity of the media, friends and acquaintances closed ranks. Still, some did talk about Halina and Karol's relationship, among them Jerzy Bober, who knew both of them a few years later at the university. He had no doubt that something more than artistic motivation was at work: "There were so many threads mysteriously wound together in the skein of fondness, feelings, youthful flirtations, and even grand affections."

Karol was quickly acknowledged as the theater group's director and set designer. His memory soon became legendary. Two days before the opening night of Juliusz Słowacki's *Balladyna*, the actor assigned to play the part of Kostryn dropped out. As the company panicked, the calm voice of Karol Wojtyła was heard, offering to play both Kostryn and the protagonist, Kirkor (possible only because Kostryn doesn't appear until after Kirkor dies).

How could he ever learn the part in so short a time? he was asked.

"I already learned it during rehearsals," he casually replied. Less than forty-eight hours later *Balladyna* was staged with Karol playing both parts magnificently. He was also enamored of Słowacki's poems, memorizing in particular "The Slavic Pope":

Amid the discord God rings
An enormous bell
For the Slavic Pope
The throne is open.
This one will not flee the sword,
Like that Italian.
Like God, He will bravely face the sword,
For him, world is dust . . .
Look, here comes the Slavic Pope,
A brother of the people.

Many of the shows in the auditorium of the gymnasium were directed by Karol Wojtyła, the future Slavic Pope. They often dealt with patriotic themes, and the group's productions were in great demand at meeting halls around the city. They performed at the Sokół clubhouse and in the parish house of Our Lady. The group won recognition as a repertory company and went on tour through the neighboring villages: Kęty, Andrychów, Kalwaria Zebrzydowska.

The cast was always the same; only the choice of plays varied. Karol had practically all the leading roles; he was the king in Wyspiański's *Sigismund Augustus*, Haemon in Sophocles' *Antigone*, John the Evangelist in an adaptation of the book of Revelation, the terrible Henryk in *The Undivine Comedy*, the frivolous Gucio in Fredro's *Maiden Vows*. Halina Królikiewicz was always his leading lady. A photograph shows her powdered-pale and charming in an elaborate white dress, next to an elegant Karol-Gucio sporting a fake mustache.

When the famous Polish actress Kazimiera Rychter came to Wadowice, the stagestruck youngsters asked her to judge a recitation contest. The evening turned into a duel between Karol and Halina, who won. Karol's interpretation received second prize, but made a deep impression on the spectators: As his choice of material this fifteen-year-old in a blue gymnasium uniform, who leaned slightly forward as he recited, had decided on *Promethidion*, a poem by Cyprian Norwid, a nineteenth-century poet-philosopher with an obscure style and difficult syntax.

The *Promethidion* speaks of work as a means of redemption if it is accepted with love and exalts the supreme function of art as the "banner on the tower of human labor." It was a very long and demanding poem, and the listeners were struck by the "modern, firm, and strong" tone with which Karol recited it. There was no lyrical mawkishness in him, according to Halina Królikiewicz; she remembers being swept away by Karol's style, by his ability to penetrate the text. Karol had "strength of expression without any exaltation and exaggeration." Norwid also powerfully influenced Wojtyła's career as bishop and pope. (John Paul II's encyclical on work and labor, *Laborem Exercens,* reflects some of the ideas of the *Promethidion.*) Among Norwid's poems that Wojtyła knew was "Polish Jews," written after Cossacks on horseback had broken up an anti-Russian demonstration in Warsaw in the 1860s, treating Jews in the crowd with exceptional brutality. In "Polish Jews" Norwid describes Poland's "priceless heritage" of two great and ancient cultures—Polish and Jewish.

These were happy years for Karol. Neighbors often heard him singing as he headed down the stairs to rehearsals. He spent hour after hour discussing poetry with his peers and cementing friendships that would last a lifetime. At fifteen he became president of the Marian sodality, an organization dedicated to veneration of the Virgin, and was reelected the next year. He was chosen to head the Abstinence Society, which advocated a policy of no alcohol and no smoking for young people. He was serious but not fanatical about this commitment. Thus one winter day the class was returning by train from an outing and, inevitably, a bottle of brandy was passed around among the boys. The professor leading the group had the first sip and then others took their turns. Jan Kuś noted with satisfaction that his classmate Karol didn't shrink from the opportunity.

Wojtyła also thoroughly enjoyed dancing. Twice a month the Wadowice Gymnasium reserved a hall for lessons. This was a legacy from the courtly days of the Austro-Hungarian Empire, a time of classical culture and polite manners, of instruction meant to promote a healthy mind and a graceful body. Boys from the gymnasium met their counterparts from the nearby girls' gymnasium. The lessons were given by a woman who patiently led the pupils through the elementary steps, while one of their teachers played the same few bars of music over and over again on the piano. The atmosphere was extremely formal: the boys seated along one wall of the large room, the girls opposite them. A contingent of mothers came to chaperone.

Wojtyła was an enthusiastic participant. To the sound of a gramophone he learned how to invite someone to dance, how to press her lightly in his arms, and how to escort her back to her place with a deep bow. Karol wasn't the least bit bashful with girls. When he became pope he would never display the clumsiness with women that so many priests, raised in the repressive atmosphere of pre–Vatican II seminaries, couldn't manage to hide.

With ease Karol danced polonaises, mazurkas, waltzes, and tangos (though the calm Central European variety, not the fiery Argentinean ones). When the "season" arrived (between New Year's Day and Lent) the students, male and female, including Karol, went to the Sokół Club to dance to piano and accordion accompaniment. Together with Poldek Goldberger, the best piano player in the class, Karol sometimes amused himself and others composing popular and patriotic songs, and even a few romantic tangos.

However, he absented himself from the parties called *pryvatkas*, where boys and girls would get together in someone's house to indulge in a little drinking, listen to music, and flirt. They were a waste of time, he told Halina Królikiewicz, and after a while his friends gave up insisting that he join them.

Toward the end of his high school years he became acquainted with an intellectual who was to have a profound influence on his life. Mieczysław Kotlarczyk was a professor of Polish literature, a man totally dedicated to the theater, always busy with directing and stage design. In 1931 he had founded the Amateur University Theater in Wadowice. He also collaborated in publishing cultural reviews like *The Voice of the Nation* and *The Forge*; spoke on the radio; was in contact with the great director of the Kraków National Theater Juliusz Osterwa; and kept up with the latest dramaturgical developments in Germany.

Kotlarczyk was a scholar of language, a connoisseur of its mystical, magical pulsations. He spoke of the Living Word: Through language, he told his students, the rhythm and rhyme of a theatrical work must become the protagonists of any performance, while costumes and sets should be reduced to the minimum.

In Kotlarczyk's apartment, Karol spent hours discussing the role of the theater and the significance of language in Polish life. Later, as a cardinal, he would praise Kotlarczyk as a pioneer of an extremely original kind of drama, the "expression of deep-rooted Polish and Christian traditions of the art that has been handed down to us by our entire literature." Kotlarczyk was for Karol not just a teacher, but perhaps his only intimate conversation partner, to whom he confided his thoughts on his own life and on the destiny of Poland. Nineteen years older than Karol, Kotlarczyk became almost an older brother, an echo of Edmund.

In those years, his friends from the theater group never doubted that Karol was going to become either an actor or a man of letters as well as a married man with a family. Nothing in his life hinted at any other fate.

On May 6, 1938, the archbishop of Kraków, Adam Sapieha, arrived in Wadowice to administer the sacrament of confirmation before graduation. This was a great event for the city. With the garrison band playing, the mayor and civic authorities welcomed the archbishop's black sedan in Market Square. Born of an aristocratic Galician family, Prince Metropolitan Adam Stefan Sapieha was an important personage in the new Poland—and beyond. Pope Pius X had even kept him in Rome for some years as a member of the papal household. He was a prelate of intense piety, a highly skilled administrator, and a sort of spiritual talent scout.

Sapieha wasn't very tall, but his aquiline nose, his aristocratic features, and his remarkable energy contributed to an impressive presence. Karol was given the job of welcoming him in the name of the students, and he greeted the archbishop with a fluent speech in Latin. Sapieha watched the student's expressive face, framed by a mass of unruly hair. His manner was at once decisive and thoughtful. His eyes revealed sensitivity and sincerity. "What will he do after graduation?" the archbishop asked, turning to Karol's religion teacher, Father Edward Zacher. "Will he enter the seminary?"

Karol himself asked permission to answer. "I'm going to study Polish literature and philology."

"What a pity," the archbishop replied.

·   ·   ·

Every first Friday of the month—a day of special devotion in the Church—Karol Wojtyła went to confession and took communion. This had been his regular practice since entering the gymnasium. He never missed this appointment with the Body of Christ. Every morning he made a visit to the parish church before going to school; and if he didn't serve mass, he still stopped to pray. After classes he returned to church. He prayed after meals and while doing his homework. He prayed before going to sleep and during the special devotions of the sodality of the Blessed Virgin.

His friends became accustomed to his monastic rhythm of prayer. They realized that in his piety there was nothing of the show-off. "Everyone saw that he was different and that he was doing things differently," Jan Kuś recalls. It wasn't just the endless recitation of prayers, it was a gradual pulling away from daily cares and concerns, a slow ascent to a state where his own thought would be annihilated, a plunge into God.

Friends who watched him immersed in prayer left church with conflicting impressions. Some maintained that his face showed "something beautiful, something marvelous." Others claimed that they had seen Wojtyła's face turn pale as a sheet, or ashen, seemingly stripped of flesh. To one girl from his theatrical group he seemed for an instant ugly and frightening. Each of these impressions was correct. For Wojtyła, prayer meant passing through a series of stages from pain to serenity, from concentration to abandon. As pope he would explain that prayer begins in dialogue and reaches a point where God alone is acting: "We begin with the impression that it's our initiative, but it's always God's initiative within us."

In the eyes of his friends this meditative, contemplative behavior always made him a little mysterious. At the gymnasium they defined it as a sort of "holiness." Nobody dared tell dirty stories or use swear words, much less blaspheme, in his presence. One student who snuck up behind Wojtyła and shouted a curse in his ears was seized by classmates, dragged into a bathroom, and thrashed. Even when he was called up for compulsory paramilitary exercises in the summer, his comrades-in-arms shied away from singing the usual crude soldiers' songs. Such anecdotes sound like legend, but his moral standards and his calm, quiet manner had a demonstrably intimidating effect on almost everyone around him.

Father Józef Prus, the rector of the Carmelite high school, often saw him in the convent church, a pseudo-Romanesque red brick building on a small wooded height behind Market Square. The main altar shows St. Joseph with the Baby Jesus holding the lily of purity; to the left is an Italian-style painting of the Madonna. Wojtyła used to sit in front of the altar of the Holy Virgin, praying for hours. He preferred it to the parish church near his home, where more people would be passing by.

Father Prus carefully noted this boy who kept coming back to the empty church to spend seemingly endless hours in silent meditation. As he began to talk with him, he got the feeling that this strange young man, who managed to combine an ambition for the stage with contemplation, who declaimed neo-Romantic poetry and at seventeen—he would confide to Prus—had already read Karl Marx's *Das Kapital* in the original German, was in search of a spiritual guide. In the end the Carmelite priest became his spiritual father and gave him his first books on St. John of the Cross, who would become a theological force in his life.

Wojtyła found himself strongly attracted to the ways of the Discalced (barefoot) Carmelite monks, with their days passed in silence, concentration on God, and penance. Twice in the 1940s he would try to enter the order. Even when he understood that his place was in the secular clergy, he never lost his yearning for the monastic life. When he became archbishop of Kraków, he often went to a wooden hermit's hut built in the garden of the Albertine Sisters. As pope, in his seventies, he invited a group of Carmelite Sisters to open a small convent inside the Vatican.

Under the influence of Carmelite mysticism, his commitment to Christian life became even more rigorous at the very time when his classmates began to have their first amorous adventures. Halina Królikiewicz reports that she never saw him dating, even though all kinds of opportunities were there for such a charming boy.

Through most of his teenage years, Karol's relationship with his neighbor Ginka Beer was a source of real emotional sustenance. So he was especially flustered when, one day in the summer of 1938, Ginka appeared unexpectedly at the door of his apartment. Though they were extremely close and saw each other in the hallway, on the stairs, or outside practically every day, she had never visited him before. As his father invited her in, Karol sensed immediately that something was wrong and was too disturbed even to stand when she entered.

Ginka told him that her father, the manager of a bank in Wadowice, had decided that their family should emigrate to Palestine. Poland, he thought, was no longer safe for Jews. In Wadowice, young toughs were demanding boycotts of Jewish shops and businesses and smashing their windows. Her father had tried to talk other Jews into leaving as well, but none would listen.

Lieutenant Wojtyła tried to persuade her to stay. "Not all Poles are anti-Semitic. You know I am not!" he repeated several times. "I spoke to him frankly and said that very few Poles were like him," Ginka recalled almost forty years later. "He was very upset. But Lolek was even more upset than his father. He did not say a word, but his face went very red. I said farewell to him as kindly as I could, but he was so moved that he could not find a single word in reply. So I just shook the father's hand and left."

Later Karol too tried to persuade Ginka to stay, but it was futile. Again Karol had lost someone he loved. Decades later, at a reunion in the Vatican of Wojtyła's classmates and neighbors, Jerzy Kluger told the pope, "Ginka is here."

"Where is she?" the pope responded, quickly moving on from the group he was talking with to see her. "He asked me all kinds of questions, about my parents and my sister," the now elderly Ginka Beer Reisenfeld recalls. "He was really very nice." Her mother had died in Auschwitz; her father was killed in the Soviet Union, she told the pope. "He just looked at me and there was deep compassion in his eyes," she related. "He took both my hands and for almost two minutes he blessed me and prayed before me, just holding my hands in his hands."

·   ·   ·

As a youth in high school, Karol Wojtyła had opted for premarital chastity; and he decided to remain faithful to this principle, even when his closest friends were having their first sexual experiences. Not that sexual opportunities came easily for students of the gymnasium, both because of the customs of the era and because the headmaster and his staff were very strict. Any student caught going out for a walk alone with a girl in the secluded walkway known as Aleja Miłósci (Love Alley), in a park behind the Carmelite convent, risked serious punishment. Accordingly, some adventuresome teenagers' first sexual relations were consummated on outings or trips to nearby villages.

How do we know that Karol Wojtyła never gave in to sexual temptation? He himself insisted this with papal authority. In the 1990s, when he learned that one of his biographers, a Carmelite priest named Father Władysław Kluz, had defined confession as the means by which young Wojtyła *regained* God's grace, John Paul II became very upset and wrote him: "To regain implies that I had lost, through a grave sin, the grace of God. Who told you that I committed grave sins in my youth? It never happened. Can't you believe, Father, that a young man can live without committing mortal sin?"

MYSTICS AND NAZIS

Following his graduation from the gymnasium, Karol and his father packed up the meager contents of their apartment. Lieutenant Wojtyła had nothing to hold him in Wadowice. In August 1938, he would move to Kraków with his son, who was enrolled at the Jagiellonian University, just as Edmund had been. Together father and son rented a tiny basement apartment on Tyniecka Street in a quarter of Kraków known as Dębniki, along the Vistula River. The apartment was so small and ill-lit that it made the old railroad flat in Wadowice seem luxurious by comparison.

Karol quickly adjusted to a heavy course load at the university—Polish etymology and phonetics, medieval Polish literature, eighteenth-century Polish drama, and contemporary lyric poetry—approaching his studies with characteristic confidence and concentration. Socially, however, he initially found it hard to adjust to life at a great university in the heart of a cosmopolitan city. Quiet and intense, he still dressed in the shoddy clothes, including a pair of crude drill trousers and badly patched shoes, that he had worn at the gymnasium. In the sophisticated atmosphere of Kraków, he looked out of place.

In the evening, Karol studied, prayed, and spent time talking with his friends. He wasn't interested in going to parties, drinking, or stopping at student haunts like the Green Balloon cabaret on Floriańska Street. Despite his worn clothes and modest demeanor, he soon made friends with a gregarious, self-assured set of aspiring playwrights and poets. Through an introduction from his new friend Juliusz Kydryński, he gained entry to the home of the worldly Szkocki family where, in the evening, he talked about Romantic literature and listened to piano sonatas sublimely played by Mr. Szkocki, a noted musicologist. Karol visited there regularly and came to call Mrs. Szkocka* "Granny."

But the idyll was short-lived.

Germany had invaded Czechoslovakia, and the Poles at the university shared a pervasive sense that war was on its way. Anti-German demonstrations were commonplace on campus (as were anti-Semitic rallies). Some students hung Hitler in effigy. While Wojtyła was opposed to the Nazis, he generally avoided the subject of exactly how to oppose them. Krystyna Zbijewska, a fellow student, sensed a streak of radicalism in his beliefs, a cross between socialism and Christian humanism. He spoke often of the immorality of the gap between rich and poor, something that then concerned few students in his circle. But mainly he talked about the theater and his classes. "Perhaps that's why we got on so well . . . because the two of us just concentrated on our studies," said Zbijewska many years later.

• • •

Wojtyła was in the ancient cathedral of the Polish kings when German bombs first hit Kraków. It was September 1, 1939. As on every first Friday of the month, he had gone to church to make his confession and receive commu-

* In Polish, family names ending in *ski* or *cki* take a final *a* in the feminine.

nion. Suddenly Luftwaffe pilots were targeting the barracks on Warszawska Street. The city resounded with bomb blasts and screaming sirens. Civilians ran desperately to their houses and took refuge in cellars.

On the Wawel Hill, site of the cathedral and the royal castle, Wojtyła found himself alone in the deserted church with a priest he knew and trusted: Father Kazimierz Figlewicz, his old religion teacher from Wadowice, who had heard Karol's first confessions. From him Karol had learned to be an altar boy, and even now, at the height of the Nazi attack, Father Figlewicz instructed him to serve mass: "We have to celebrate mass, in spite of everything. Pray God to spare Poland."

Wojtyła obeyed. The main altar, carved of black marble, which supports the massive silver sarcophagus of St. Stanisław, the martyred bishop of ancient Kraków and the patron saint of Poland, is like a rock. Over the sarcophagus hangs a golden canopy upheld by gilded columns. The cathedral made a glorious shelter, and the tombs of Stanisław and of various Polish kings bore witness to Poland's tenacity and its great gift for surviving aggression. "Kyrie eleison, Christe eleison, Lord have mercy, Christ have mercy," the young university student recited, kneeling before the altar of the crucified Christ, as the stained-glass windows shook from the explosions.

History, which Wojtyła had generally ignored, nonetheless erupted in his life. The boy who had once abandoned the high school history club to concern himself with poets and writers, who avoided political debates and maintained a studied ambiguity on the Spanish Civil War, that dress rehearsal for World War II (he stood with the pro-Franco bishops against the Republic but was also disturbed by the merciless display of Hitler's power in Guernica) was now caught literally in the cross fire.

The Germans had chosen Poland as their prey, and the life of this model student was about to be transformed and all his private projects suspended. Until then, he would write to his friend Kotlarczyk, "for us life consisted of evenings on Długa Street, with refined conversation until midnight or beyond, but now . . ." Now the most profound questions, practical as well as moral, would press upon them.

As soon as mass was over, Wojtyła ran to his father's house. Then he helped his friend Juliusz Kydryński drag a cart with the Kydryński family's belongings to the outskirts of Kraków. On the way they were overtaken by a new air raid and took shelter in the archway of a house, where Wojtyła prayed in silence while the German dive bombers passed overhead.

German troops were advancing on the city. Wojtyła decided that he and his father should leave Kraków and again hurried back to their apartment. Father and son left on foot, carrying only a valise between them. Old Lieutenant Wojtyła hobbled along exhausted amid a flood of refugees heading east. Taking the train was too dangerous. The streets, strafed periodically by German planes, were the only path of escape. A truck driver gave the Wojtyłas a brief lift, but soon they were on foot again. On the heights of Tarnobrzeg, 120 miles east of Kraków, his father gave up. Meanwhile, word had spread that the Russians were about to enter eastern Poland. The Wojtyłas decided to return to Kraków.

The collapse of Poland was swift and horrifying. By September 6, the Germans had occupied Kraków. On September 17, Soviet troops crossed the eastern border, and the Polish government took refuge in Romania. On September 27, Warsaw surrendered. On the 29th, Archbishop Sapieha celebrated the last pontifical mass in the cathedral on the Wawel. (The Nazis would permit no more.) On November 1, the Germans annexed Gdańsk and enormous chunks of western and southern Poland (including Wadowice). The rest of the country—with the exception of a Soviet zone in the east—was transformed into a Nazi colony known as the General Government, with its capital in Kraków. The swastika now flew over Wawel Castle.

For Karol Wojtyła life in occupied Poland had begun: bread lines, the quest for a bit of sugar, complicated deals to get a little coal for the winter. Apart from such privations, in the first few weeks there was still an appearance of normality. On November 2, Karol registered for his second year at the university. In his free time he went to the last theater performances allowed by the Germans. At the house of his friend Juliusz Kydryński people continued to meet for readings of Polish literature.

Mieczysław Kotlarczyk, his theater teacher, whom he called "brother," was forced by the country's division to remain in Wadowice. They corresponded frequently. Wojtyła was still trying to grasp the unforeseen and incomprehensible collapse of independent Poland: "I did not see her in a fully truthful light," he confessed in an early letter to Kotlarczyk. "The idea of Poland was alive in us, just as it had been in the generation of Romanticism. But this Poland was not living in the truth, because the peasants were beaten and imprisoned on account of their just demands for political rights, because they felt their hour of destiny approaching, because they were in the right. But the nation was deceived, and lied to; and her sons, just as in the times of the Partition, were dispersed around the world. Why? So they wouldn't rot in the jails of their own country."

Wojtyła understood that Poland's end was not due simply to the German invasion but to the authoritarianism and egoism of the Polish ruling classes. Free Poland had lasted barely twenty years. "Did we really achieve liberation?" he asked on November 2, 1939, the day after the new partition of his country was made official. (Almost exactly fifty years later, he would ask the same penetrating question following the collapse of communism in Poland.)

For the moment Karol Wojtyła found the answer to these conflicts in a vague Christian-Romantic ideal: "I think that our liberation lies at the door of Christ. I see an Athenian Poland—but more perfect than Athens, thanks to the boundless immensity of Christianity," he wrote to Kotlarczyk. The ideal society was the one envisioned by the bards and prophets. In the final analysis Poland had fallen because, like Israel when it was conquered by the king of Babylon, "she failed to recognize the messianic ideal, her own ideal, which was held high like a glowing ember, but never realized."

On October 26, the Nazis ordered compulsory labor for all Polish adults (and for all Jews twelve years and older). On November 6, a trap was sprung on the professors at the Jagiellonian University. As Wojtyła learned from classmates, faculty members were summoned by the German authorities for a discussion of their academic programs. One hundred and eighty-six professors showed up and were immediately deported to the concentration camp at Sachsenhausen-Oranienburg. In the wake of international protests and interventions by the dictators of three Catholic countries—Mussolini of Italy, Franco of Spain, and Horthy of Hungary—about 120 of them were released. Among those who perished was a professor who was hosed down with ice-cold water and left outside to die in subfreezing temperatures.

The first winter of occupation brought the Poles face to face with the question of how to resist Nazism. The Third Reich was already carrying out plans for the cultural annihilation of Poland. The secondary schools, the universities, and the theaters were all closed. The Church was barred from celebrating the feast days of Polish saints. For the Nazis, the Poles were *Untermenschen*, subhuman, and had to be made to feel that way.

It was during those early months of national humiliation in 1940 that Wojtyła met a strange character, a sort of magician of souls.

•　　•　　•

On the surface there was nothing commanding about Jan Tyranowski. He looked awkward: thin, slightly stooped, with combed-back grayish hair. His voice was high-pitched, almost like a girl's. He lived in the same neighborhood as Karol. His neighbors, however, knew little about him. Some thought him freakish. He worked as a tailor, living by himself. No one knew if he had ever been married. It was rumored that he had been a patient in a mental hospital.

He had set up shop in a one-room apartment at 11 Różana Street, where he made and altered men's suits and overcoats. But he spent most of his time tirelessly recruiting young men for a secret religious society. He observed them when they went to mass at St. Stanisław Kostka Church in the neighborhood. He watched them while they prayed and noted how often they returned to the church.

Tyranowski subjected Wojtyła to this silent examination, keeping an eye on him as he went to a retreat organized by the Salesian Fathers, listening in on him during afternoon Bible readings run by a professor from the university. Then one day, in a muted voice, he said: "May I have a word with you, sir?"

That winter seventeen-year-old Mieczysław Maliński, who would become a close friend of Wojtyła's, was also approached at the church door in the same well-bred but insistent manner: "I have been watching you for some time now," Tyranowski told him. "You come to mass almost every day. I would like to propose that you join the Living Rosary."

The Living Rosary was a strictly clandestine organization, because the

Nazis—who had already begun to obstruct the operation of the seminaries and otherwise restrict Church activities—would never allow the formation of any group of religious activists. The Living Rosary began where the normal recitation of the rosary ended: The fifteen mysteries of the rosary were to be embodied in fifteen young men who pledged to follow Christ's commandment "to love God and neighbor" day by day in every aspect of their existence. Tyranowski personally oversaw each one of them, meeting them individually so as not to arouse the Germans' suspicions.

Like the others, Wojtyła met Tyranowski once a week in the tailor's ill-lit second-floor room, at the end of a narrow corridor, where three sewing machines were practically buried in an indescribable mountain of books. The Master, as he was called, recommended particular volumes on religion, encouraged his protégés to read up-to-date theological manuals, and tutored them in the thinking of great mystics like St. John of the Cross and St. Teresa of Ávila, to whom Karol had already been exposed. Now, under Tyranowski, he delved deeply into mystical practice.

For Wojtyła the appointments on Różana Street became a pilgrimage to a spiritual fountainhead. More and more often he was seen taking slow walks with Tyranowski along the banks of the Vistula, directly across the river from Wawel Castle. Tyranowski was a molder of personalities. Wojtyła found in him a patient guide, gentle but tenacious. His whole day came to be punctuated by the directions of the Master, whose motto was "Every moment has to be put to use." Wojtyła took on the job of minutely regulating his daily existence. He began to precisely schedule his work as a clandestine university student and as a waiter in a restaurant owned by his mother's brother—as well as his religious activities: spiritual exercises, Bible readings, the study of religious texts, prayer, meditation, and mass. This represented for him a continuation—and intensification—of the regime imposed by his father. The notion that "every moment has to be put to use" became perhaps the most salient feature of Wojtyła's life and work.

Tyranowski demanded that all his disciples keep a careful diary to show whether they had fulfilled their daily obligations. In their notebooks, next to each subject—from sacred Scripture to afternoon nap to evening prayer—there was a blank space to put a little cross certifying that the obligation had been met. Every time Wojtyła went to his weekly session with the Master, he had to reread his notes and render an account of his actions.

Many of the characteristics that Wojtyła would later manifest as a professor, as a bishop, and as pope seem to derive directly from experience with Tyranowski. (Even in his frail old age, he would continue to exhibit an indefatigable willpower and a tireless appetite for work that left even his most dedicated Vatican aides gasping for breath.)

Tyranowski, one witness says, "knew how to convince people and bind them to himself." He spoke very quietly; he was never strict or overpowering. As Franciszek Konieczny recalls, "If he wanted to get access to a man and win him over, Tyranowski wouldn't try to use power, but persuasion. And he cared a great deal about everyone." He took to heart the personal problems of his followers. Later as a bishop, Wojtyła would do the same with his priests, convinced that bishops and priests had to form a living community—an extension of the male "community of two" that he had long ago experienced with his father.

As pope, Wojtyła would refer to Tyranowski as "one of those unknown saints, hidden like a marvelous light at the bottom of life, at a depth where night usually reigns." Tyranowski brought him "the revelation of a universe," John Paul II would say. "In his words, in his spirituality and in the example of a life given entirely to God alone, he represented a new world that I did not yet know. I saw the beauty of the soul opened up by grace."

Part of this new world was to be found in the works of St. John of the Cross, the impassioned Spanish monk whose writings now shone across the ages to the young Wojtyła. This Carmelite mystic taught in his poems and commentaries about a way to God through lengthy contemplation and an almost brutally austere stripping away of all one's worldly attachments— commonplace human sentiments and affections as well as material things. He spoke of creating a void at the center of the self through rigid self-denial, an emptiness that God would rush to fill with a great and beautiful infusion.

This practice St. John called "the way of negation" and if it forced one through times of absolute desperation and blindness—"the night of the senses" and "the dark night of the soul"—it also promised at journey's end a direct and lasting awareness of God.

"Strive always to bend yourself not to what is easiest, but to what is most difficult, not to what you find most pleasurable, but most disagreeable . . . not to consolation but to what leaves you disconsolate," St. John taught. And "Those who pass for the friends of Jesus Christ know little of him for we see them going in search of solace rather than of his bitter sufferings. God values your readiness to face suffering and deprivation for love of him more than all the consolations, spiritual visions and meditations which you may have."

If there was one thing that the young Wojtyła could relate to, it was suffering. A passionate mystical vein now burst forth in his verse:

> To drown, to drown! To bend and then
> slowly arise without feeling in that flow the steps
> down which went, running and trembling,
> only the soul, the soul of man immersed,
> the soul swept away by the current.

In the year he met Tyranowski, Wojtyła began frenetically to write three plays at once: *David, Job,* and *Jeremiah.* They expressed all the thoughts seething in the mind of a young man who still felt that the theater in the dark night of Poland's soul was "like a church in which the national spirit will bloom." There are constant references in these dramas to the situation of Poland. The mystique of sacrifice and the recognition of the moral decadence of Israel/Poland are underscored in these plays with soliloquies on the value of suffering and the longing for a new national liberation. Israel/Poland in its time of trouble, Wojtyła warned, had to be defended not only with the sword but above all through spiritual renewal.

The theater would now become a weapon in the defense of Polish culture and the Polish homeland in the face of a relentless Nazi onslaught. In this spirit of religiously inspired resistance Wojtyła began to put on clandestine performances of plays with a group of friends who called themselves Studio 39.

Meanwhile, Nazi pressure was intensifying. Anyone without a regular job certified by the German authorities ran a high risk of being deported to

Germany. In October 1940 Wojtyła found work as a manual laborer for the German-run Solvay chemical firm on the outskirts of Kraków. The job supplied him a work permit, thereby exempting him from forced labor in the Reich. It also guaranteed him a nighttime pass, a salary, and increased food rations (because Solvay's operations were war-related). In short, his job, which he got through connections, offered indispensable protection from the whims of the occupying power.

A myth has grown up about Wojtyła's work as a stone breaker in Solvay's Zakrzówek quarry and, later, as a worker in its factory at Borek Fałęcki. After his election as John Paul II, the flowering of a cult of personality in the Roman Catholic Church led to the growth of the legend of the worker-pope. *"Papa obrero,"* cried Latin American workers from Mexico to Brazil every time John Paul II met with impoverished masses organized by the unions. And in Italy, when the pope first visited the steel mills of Terni, workers placed a foundryman's helmet on his head, as if he were "one of them."

In reality Wojtyła did heavy labor in the quarry for only a few months, after which he was transferred to lighter work. Contrary to legend, he wasn't forced to do slave labor; and there were no Nazi taskmasters in the factory armed with whips (as in some accounts published after his election). In 1940 many students from the Jagiellonian University found a safe haven at Solvay. Edward Görlich, a co-worker of Wojtyła's, confirms that the German director of Solvay, a certain Herr Pöhl, "paid the Gestapo to turn a blind eye to the high concentration of young Polish intellectuals in the Solvay plant." Wojtyła could have gotten an office job, but to be on the safe side he preferred the inconspicuous role of a common worker.

The fact remains that his experience in the quarry and the factory, like his earlier association with Jews in Wadowice (many of whom were soon to die in nearby Auschwitz), gave John Paul II an education that no Roman pontiff before him had ever had. His years at Solvay lent him an immediate awareness of the condition of workers that would serve him well in his future struggle against a Polish Communist regime and would lead him to consider the alienation and exploitation of workers in ways unexpected for a pope. John Paul II would feel no hesitation in occasionally using Marxist language, convinced that it was necessary to give a Christian response to a real problem: the relations of workers to the product of their work.

In 1982, during one of his trips to Africa, John Paul II called it "a great grace of my life to have worked in a quarry and in a factory. This experience of working life, with all its positive aspects and its miseries, as well as, on another level, the horrors of the deportation of my Polish compatriots to the death camps, have profoundly marked my existence."

The Zakrzówek quarry where Wojtyła began working in the fall of 1940 was a canyon with walls more than sixty-five feet high. Beyond the masses of granite were wooded hillsides from which the bell towers of Kraków were visible. But for those working in the quarry, the world was reduced to looming rock walls bounded on top by a fence. Wojtyła watched ill-clad men, numb with fatigue, set off dynamite charges, smash rock, and drag the rubble toward the tracks of a little "railway" that transported it for processing in the plant. During his first days on the job he was in charge of checking the trolley rails; then he was handed a pickax and told to break up large blocks of limestone for loading onto the trolleys that took them to the kiln. This physical labor jolted the young intellectual. For eight hours at a stretch he was forced to stay outside in below-zero temperatures. The other workers called him "the student" and watched as he learned to endure the cold dressed in a shapeless jacket of blue cloth, blue trousers, and a sweat-soaked cap with a frayed ribbon. On his feet he wore wooden clogs, and his whole "uniform" was streaked with calcium dust and machine oil stains.

Wojtyła, familiar only with the world of clerks, peasants, and intellectuals, began to experience the brutalization brought on by hard labor and rote work and the poverty of unskilled manual workers. He shared with the others as well the wretched pleasure of stealing away for a few minutes to drink fake coffee in a heated hut. The day shift ran from six A.M. to two P.M., the swing shift from two P.M. to ten P.M., and the graveyard shift from ten P.M. to six A.M. Once a week the shifts were rotated.

Tyranowski had explained to him that everyone's personality must be modeled on Christ, and Wojtyła now accepted his work as a Christian trial. Witnesses agree: He complained only a few times when the pain in his hands, unused to a pickax, became excruciating. He worked in silence, conscientiously, methodically. He listened a lot and had little to say in a situation utterly new to him. One day he witnessed a companion die as a rock fragment pierced his temple while he operated a stone saw. He experienced the pain and rage of the other workers, the agony of the man's grief-stricken wife and the confused face of his child. "They lifted up the body," he wrote at the time in a notebook for his poetry. "They filed past it in silence. Exhaustion and a sense of injustice still emanated from it."

Under the impact of the work in the quarry and the privations of the war, Wojtyła changed physically. His face became thin and bony. He hunched over when he walked, as if his whole body were being quite literally crushed by poverty. Wartime rations were dismal, a constant diet of potato soup or gruel. When by luck the Solvay kitchen managed to get some horse meat, it was cooked up as a kind of goulash, and the workers made a banquet of it. As a supplement to the daily menu a slice of bread would be served. Wojtyła was privileged: Every now and then the women in the kitchen would cut him an extra large slice because he had a reputation for being a well-bred, modest, intellectual, and pious young man.

At Solvay, Wojtyła exchanged his monthly vodka coupons for contraband meat, bacon fat, and other foods; or he used the coupons to buy clothes. He had a family to provide for: At home on Tyniecka Street waited his depressed father, who seemed to be losing interest in life.

Word of young Wojtyła's unusual ways soon spread. One day some people saw him come to work pale and freezing from the cold, without his jacket because he had given it away to a poor wretch he met on the road. Józef Dudek, a co-worker, tells how Wojtyła persuaded the other employees not to punish too severely a colleague who had signed up with the Nazis as a *Volksdeutscher*—a citizen of German origin—to get better treatment during the occupation. Even at work Wojtyła never gave up saying his prayers or crossing himself before and after meals.

At the canteen he was courted with particular insistence by Irka Dąbrowska, the eighteen-year-old daughter of one of Solvay's managers and a cook's helper. "Mr. Józef," she begged Józef Krasuski, a co-worker of Wojtyła's, "please, talk to Lolek, he is such a handsome and nice man." Irka badly wanted Karol to come to her birthday party, and Krasuski urged him to accept the invitation: "Lolek, don't be silly, everybody's hungry. Go there, you'll get a nice meal."

Out of politeness Wojtyła finally agreed to attend the party, but he showed up wearing his work uniform and wooden clogs. "These are my clean overalls," he explained, "the ones I keep for big occasions." When Irka, a very tall, skinny girl, insisted on knowing what the young man really thought of her, Krasuski hid her in a clothes closet and lured Wojtyła into the room under the pretext of offering him a cup of tea.

"Do you like her?" Krasuski asked.

"She's very nice, but she has only one fault," Wojtyła replied.

"What's that?"

"If only you could cut a little bit off her feet, so she wasn't so tall; and if only she were a little bit rounder."

. . .

On February 18, 1941, the weather was freezing cold. His father, who had fallen gravely ill a few weeks after Christmas, was bedridden at home and unable to take care of himself. Around midday Wojtyła stopped at a dispensary to pick up some medicine and then went to the Kydryńskis' house where the mother of his friend Juliusz had prepared a lunch for him to take to his father. Mrs. Kydryńska had the tin with the food ready; Juliusz's sister, Maria, decided to come along and help.

Arriving at the basement flat, Maria went to the stove to warm up the meal. Karol walked into the next room, only to come out a moment later sobbing. His father was dead.

His emotional defenses shattered. He embraced Maria, his face bathed in tears, and cried out: "I wasn't there when my mother died, I wasn't there when my brother died, I wasn't there when my father died." Each time, God had struck without giving him a chance to share the last moments of the dying. A few months before, in his dramatic poem *Job*, he had written:

> I know I am small—
> but there are others even smaller than I,
> He chooses me, he hurls me into the ashes.

He can do this—but why?—
Why do this to me?—He is the Dispenser.

After the last rites were administered, Wojtyła kept watch over his father's body all night with his friend Juliusz. "Karol prayed a little, then he talked a little with me about life and death," Kydryński recalled. "I'll never forget that night. I think it was extremely crucial in Karol's life."

During this vigil Wojtyła pondered his destiny and vocation. Witnesses unanimously agree that the shock brought on a crisis. "The powerful calm and serenity" of this man, who had apparently been so insignificant, had illuminated Karol's life. Now Wojtyła was deprived of his main source of emotional warmth and support. Of his family, nothing was left. "These days I often think about my parents and Mundek," John Paul II would write to his cousin on the eleventh day of his pontificate. And later he would tell the writer André Frossard: "At twenty I had already lost all the people I loved, and even those I might have loved, like my older sister who, they said, had died six years before I was born."

His father's death drove him still deeper into mystical and philosophical reflection. At the Kydryńskis' house, where he moved for six months and called Mrs. Kydryńska "Mama," Wojtyła was often seen praying stretched out on the floor with his arms extended in the form of a cross.

·   ·   ·

In the same house, Maria Irmina Woltersdorf, the young fiancée of his friend Wojciech Żukrowski, also found a welcome. To get her work permit, the girl had taken a job at the Typhus Institute for medical research, run by the Nazis. Żukrowski told Wojtyła that the Germans "hire young girls to breed lice. They put little cages on the girls' thighs, and the lice drink the blood." The research was used to produce vaccines, and, as Żukrowski stressed, "Polish girls go there to give blood to the lice." In exchange they got a triple ration of food. Wasn't it obligatory to fight against such people? Żukrowski certainly thought so.

As he and Karol sat one afternoon on a bench by the banks of the Vistula, a coal barge passed downstream. "Tonight we're going to rob some coal," Żukrowski told him. Żukrowski belonged to a resistance group, and his apartment served as a support base for escaped Allied prisoners fleeing from the Nazis.

"How can you hope to pull it off?" Wojtyła asked.

"I've got a revolver."

"But they've got so many more weapons, tanks, planes."

"It doesn't matter," Żukrowski insisted.

"Prayer is the only weapon that works," Wojtyła replied.

That was his position, one he never changed through all the years of occupation. Prayer and trust in God were the only way to combat evil and violence.

Early in 1941, on the recommendation of his former French professor, the directors at Solvay gave him a different assignment. No more splitting rocks; three months of that was enough. Wojtyła would work in the quarry counting and keeping track of the dynamite charges needed to explode the boulders.

Żukrowski, whose job was to insert the fuses, took advantage of his position to steal explosives for the resistance, but at no time did he inform Karol of his activity. His friends understood that Wojtyła wasn't cut out for conspiracy. His nonviolent attitude didn't change even when on May 23, 1941, the Nazis arrested the Salesian Fathers from his parish church, St. Stanisław Kostka, and shipped them off to a concentration camp. One novice and twelve Salesian priests, including the superior, Father Jan Świerc, died in that camp. Still, when some partisans contacted the young men from the Living Rosary to urge them to become part of the armed resistance, Wojtyła succeeded in persuading most of the boys not to join the underground.

The Living Rosary had expanded. Tyranowski had transformed the first fifteen disciples into leaders of new groups of fifteen. He advised them to get ready and save themselves for the future, when Poland would once again be free and prepared to realize the ideal of a society inspired by Christian principles.

When the Nazis arrested his dear friend Juliusz Kydryński and sent him to Auschwitz (he was released after a couple of months), Wojtyła consoled and helped his mother, but his reaction was the same: You just had to pray. It was the same when the Germans imprisoned his friend Tadeusz Kwiatkowski, the director of a clandestine magazine, *The Literary Monthly.* Wojtyła repeated to Żukrowski: "Remember, we have the duty to pray God to give them the strength to endure all this." Wojtyła believed in the power of prayer: Prayer could actually mold or change events.

Especially painful to the circle of persons closest to him was the arrest of the seminarian Szczęsny Zachuta, with whom he had attended meetings of the Living Rosary. Zachuta belonged to a resistance movement and had helped Jews seeking baptismal certificates to save themselves from deportation and death. Finding out about his activities, the Nazis shot him. Even then Wojtyła continued to maintain that the best way to resist was to simply call upon God.

When it came to giving support to others, however, he did his part every time collections were taken to aid the family of an arrestee or to raise money for a bribe to liberate someone fallen into the hands of the Nazis. Although he was well acquainted with the writer Zofia Kossak-Szczucka, a member of Żegota, a secret organization that helped Jews, he never engaged in any direct resistance against the Nazis or in activities to rescue Jews. To the Polish Jew Marek Halter, who asked him decades later whether he had helped to save any Jews, John Paul II answered: "I cannot lay claim to what I did not do."

In his friends' houses Wojtyła sometimes followed the progress of the war on a map, but in general he didn't discuss political affairs at any length. When in June 1941 the Germans began their lightning advance into the Soviet Union, his first reaction seemed ambivalent. Now that the former allies were enemies, "Communism has no chance, no possibility of expanding under these circumstances," he told Żukrowski. No sooner had the Nazi assault bogged down on the Russian front than he and Żukrowski recalled the old Polish saying "When the Black Eagle [of Prussia] heads east, he returns with broken wings." But, in truth, Wojtyła was more interested in the religious situation in Russia than in the events of the war there. He was already taken with the idea that the Russian people had to rediscover the path to Christianity. As he told Żukrowski, "Russia is spiting God. But this battle against God is also creating a hunger for God."

In the tragic year of 1941, Wojtyła's theatrical activity continued without missing a beat. In August his idol Mieczysław Kotlarczyk, the director whose dramatic theory of the Living Word had once inspired him, managed to bring his family to Kraków from Wadowice and moved into the two-room Wojtyła apartment. The two friends proceeded to explore theatrical reality together, and so the Rhapsodic Theater, specifically conceived to help save the Polish spirit from annihilation by the Nazis, was born.

The Living Word, the Living Rosary: Running on these parallel tracks, Wojtyła's inner search intensified. Both concepts nurtured his mystical tendencies. The Living Rosary refined the soul to bring it closer to God, the Living Word refined the actor's articulation to give clearer expression to the great questions of life.

Kotlarczyk aspired to create a theater of the inner depths "where, more than just attending the performance, one listens to it." The actor, Wojtyła learned, must follow the verse, not smother it in pathos. His goal must be to etch his character into the consciousness of the spectators.

Someday, such thoughts, nurtured in the horror of wartime Poland, would grow into Pope John Paul II's remarkable religious theater, in which— seated alone on a stage, a huge crucifix behind him—he would hold hundreds of thousands, even millions of people spellbound with his finely tuned "performance."

In Kraków the work of the Rhapsodic Theater was considered an important part of the spiritual resistance to Nazism; Kotlarczyk also maintained ties with Unia, a clandestine Catholic movement. Rehearsals were held on Wednesdays and Saturdays in the "catacombs," the basement apartment where Wojtyła and Kotlarczyk lived. On the way there the young actors would see posted on walls and lampposts lists of persons wanted or already shot. "We had friends of ours on those lists," one of the group recalls. Every time they got together, fear of a Nazi raid or roundup was in the air. Along with Karol Wojtyła, the theater's members included Krystyna Debowska, Halina Królikiewicz, Danuta Michałowska, and set designer Devi Tuszyński, a Jew. "Those Wednesdays and Saturdays were unforgettable despite the terror and the arrests," Kotlarczyk remembered. "The rehearsals of works by the greatest Polish writers and poets went on, often in a dark, cold kitchen, sometimes with just a candle or two. But we firmly believed in our survival; we were sure we would reach the frontiers of freedom." The performances took place in private houses before audiences of no more than ten to fifteen people. One day, during a performance, the loudspeakers on the street began to boom out a war bulletin from Wehrmacht headquarters. Wojtyła went on delivering his lines in a calm and deliberate duel with the metallic voice of the occupying power. Actors and spectators realized that they were engaging in a dangerous kind of cultural opposition for which they could be deported. Despite that, between 1941 and 1945, the Rhapsodic Theater managed to organize twenty-two performances. A remark by Halina Królikiewicz gives some sense of the charged atmosphere of the recitals: "It sounds like a paradox. For me those years were something wonderful. I wasn't afraid, I was happy with what I was doing. We had a feeling that whereas others were fighting with the Home Army [the partisans], we were fighting with words."

The first production of the Rhapsodic Theater, in November 1941, was of *King Spirit* by the Romantic poet Słowacki. Wojtyła distinguished himself in the role of Bolesław the Daring, the king who orders the murder of Bishop Stanisław, the latter declared a saint—and the single person in Polish history with whom Pope John Paul II would most identify. The style of Wojtyła's performance revealed the anguish of his inner journey in those years. Halina Królikiewicz felt that "in each successive performance the way Wojtyła played his part became more ascetical, more profound." Danuta Michałowska recalled that his was a "performance full of tension, in which Karol didn't miss a single accent, a single pause that could be exploited to heighten the listeners' emotions." Juliusz Osterwa remarked that "a great actor was born." Like the others, Kotlarczyk was convinced that the only possible future for Wojtyła was a career in the theater.

In the fall of 1942, however, after a long discussion with his confessor, Father Figlewicz, Karol Wojtyła went to the residence of Archbishop Sapieha to announce, "I want to become a priest." The decision caught his friends by surprise. Before taking this step he had gone to the Carmelite hermitage at Czerna, in hopes of joining the order. But the novitiate had been closed by the Nazis, and the abbot, Father Alfons, could only tell him to wait till it reopened.

Wojtyła asked Kotlarczyk, the director of the Rhapsodic Theater, not to assign him any new roles. Now he would be dedicating himself entirely to the Living God, and the only drama he would reenact would be the sacrifice of Christ. "Mr. Mieczysław Kotlarczyk," he said later, "thought that my vocation would be in language and the theater, while the Lord Jesus thought that it would be the priesthood, and somehow we agreed on this." Tadeusz Kudliński, in whose house the Studio 39 theater group gathered, spent a whole night trying to convince him not to give up his acting career. Kotlarczyk too tried to talk him out of his decision, quoting the parable in Matthew 25 about the man who hid his talent in the ground. He reminded him of the words of the poet Norwid, also paraphrasing the Gospels: "Light isn't meant to be kept under a bushel basket." All the entreaties were in vain.

Although he too was astonished, Juliusz Kydryński seemed to understand Karol better than the others. Later, he summed up the personality of his friend: "Karol Wojtyła was like all of us. But at the same time was different, because he was chosen."

MENTOR

Adam Sapieha, the prince metropolitan of Kraków, was a patrician, a patriot, and a politician.* He took pride in his aristocratic origins, remembering with pleasure his childhood years spent learning to fence and ride a horse with nonchalant ease. His father and grandfather had taken part in rebellions against the tsar, and at seventy-two, he remained resolutely at his post when Hitler's armies entered the city. He hadn't followed the example of the primate of Poland, Cardinal August Hlond, who had fled abroad with the Polish government in exile. He took charge of the Committee of Civilian Assistance and became a guiding light for the people of Kraków in their suffering.

His relations with the Nazi occupying forces were cold and distant;

---

* His title dates to the Middle Ages, when many metropolitan bishops also had feudal titles.

he met Governor General Hans Frank only once. To the German leader, who proposed a joint crusade against Bolshevism, he offered an unequivocal rebuff. Sapieha had no intention of fighting any battle side by side with the swastika.

In the early days of the occupation the archbishop established an underground seminary to ensure the Polish Church a flow of candidates for the priesthood: The Nazis had decreed that only seminarians already registered by 1939 could continue training. His strategy was inspired by a clear-eyed realism. He had already sensed that when the war was over, the death list of members of the clergy and religious orders might be a long one. In fact, 1,932 priests and clerics, 850 monks, and 289 nuns would die in the war years.

Sapieha was in contact with various resistance groups and with the Polish government in exile in London. He personally aided Jews by distributing baptismal certificates to protect them from Nazi searches; he supported the clandestine cultural initiatives of Unia; he worked to find refuge for the few prisoners able to escape from the concentration camps, and, in 1944, for Polish Home Army fighters from the Warsaw insurrection. During the war five of his close relatives were murdered by the Nazis.

When Wojtyła entered the ranks of Sapieha's secret seminarians in October 1942, he found himself plugged in to a carefully organized system. Each student was assigned a professor who supervised him individually. Classes were held in convents, churches, and private houses. Students were instructed to keep their studies secret from acquaintances and to maintain outwardly secular routines. Sapieha kept special watch over him, inviting him to serve mass in the chapel of the archbishop's palace. After morning mass they often had breakfast together. Sapieha liked the skinny, meditative young man, and Wojtyła looked upon the archbishop as his third master, after Kotlarczyk and Tyranowski.

Wojtyła continued to work at Solvay and to live at home. At Solvay, Wojtyła's job sometimes required him to haul great quantities of "lime milk" for softening the water from the kilns, toting the liquid on his shoulders with a yokelike harness in two wooden buckets, each weighing sixty-six pounds.

"Why did you come here, sir?" a worker, Franciszek Pokuta, asked him.

"To avoid being deported to Germany," Wojtyła frankly replied.

His co-workers often found him seated behind the pipes or perched on the tank platform of the boiler room studying or praying. He preferred the night shift, which provided more calm and solitude in the factory. Władisław Cieluch, a co-worker, frequently saw him on his knees around midnight. If a colleague arrived, Cieluch recalls, "he would throw down his book and pretend he was doing something."

Some mockingly called him "the little priest" and pelted him with oakum or other refuse during his prayers. He remained unruffled. He read his breviary and a book that would be a major influence on him: *The Treatise on Perfect Devotion to the Most Holy Virgin Mary* by St. Louis Grignion de Montfort. More difficult was the bulky manual of philosophy that his director of studies, Father Kazimierz Klosak, had given him to study: *Natural Theology* by Father Kazimierz Wais. The book seemed like a granite wall to him. "I sit by the boiler and try to understand it," he told his friend Maliński. "I actually wept over it." For two months he struggled and finally could declare: "In the end it opened up a whole new world to me. It showed me a new approach to reality, and made me aware of questions that I had only dimly perceived before."

A philosopher-pope was born amid the pipes and boilers of Solvay.

Every day he took a long walk to his father's grave, and at night he often threw himself down on the damp floor of his room to pray for hours.

On February 29, 1944, not for the last time, Wojtyła had a brush with death. It was shortly after three in the afternoon. He was returning home from a night and morning double shift at the factory, when a German truck coming around a curve hit him.

His head struck violently against the truck's side and he was hurled to the ground unconscious. The driver didn't even slow down, much less stop. A woman named Józefa Florek came running to help him, but at first glance the young man in work denims and wooden clogs appeared to be dead. A passing German official stopped and determined that Wojtyła, despite his blood-covered head, was still alive. Moved to compassion, the official flagged down a truck and ordered the driver to take the young worker to the hospital, where doctors diagnosed him as suffering from a concussion and serious head wounds.

A fellow seminarian, Franciszek Konieczny, who went to visit him in the hospital, found Wojtyła in a room with his bed turned toward the window, facing the Carmelite monastery grounds. "Didn't you want to enter the Carmelites?" Konieczny joked. "Well, look, they brought you here." After thirteen days he was released from the hospital, spent the remainder of his convalescence at the house of the Szkocki family, and then returned to the factory.

On August 6, 1944, "Black Sunday"—while Hitler's armies drowned the great Warsaw uprising of the Polish Home Army in blood—Nazi forces conducted a giant sweep of Kraków. The revolt in the capital, which had begun on August 1, took the Nazis by surprise. Hitler's orders were to smash any concerted Polish resistance. Soviet troops were on the offensive and approaching the Vistula, near Kraków. The SS and the Gestapo combed the streets of the city. No one forgot the terror of that day. "The Germans were sure there would be an uprising in Kraków to support Russia. So they rounded up all the men, house by house," Maliński, also a student in the clandestine seminary, recalled. More than eight thousand men and boys were taken into custody, many of whom were then transported to prisons and concentration camps. Maliński escaped only because he was playing soccer outside the city with fifteen boys from his Living Rosary: "We were waiting for Wojtyła and his group, but they didn't come."

Wojtyła was in his apartment on Tyniecka Street when he heard shouts and the pounding footsteps of German soldiers. He began to pray in his little room: first on his knees and then stretched out on the floor. The Kotlarczyks were also in the basement apartment, paralyzed with fear. Overhead they heard the soldiers charging up the stairs, but in their haste the troops never found the door leading down to the basement flat. Wojtyła and the Kotlarczyks remained motionless for what seemed an eternity—until long after the Germans left.

Prince Metropolitan Sapieha decided to gather his remaining seminarians forthwith in the archbishop's palace. The next day, Monday, he sent priests to notify them, one by one. "Outside, the city was deserted," one witness recalls, its inhabitants shut up in their houses or in hiding. From the Dębniki neighborhood, on the other side of the river, Wojtyła made his way to the palace, moving cautiously through empty streets. Mrs. Szkocka went ahead of him, checking the intersections for German patrols. Father Mikolaj Kuczkowski, a native of Wadowice, followed them.

They finally got to Franciszkańska Street, where Wojtyła found he had to approach the palace under the eyes of a German sentinel, watching over nearby police warehouses. Fortunately, the guard ignored him as he passed through the sixteenth-century gateway into Sapieha's palace. All he had with him were two notebooks.

In the chapel, Sapieha assembled seven young men and three other seminarians who had begun their training before the war. "I am your rector," said the prince archbishop. "We shall put our trust in God's providence. No harm will befall us." The seminarians were given old cassocks, too big or too long or too tight; everyone made do, including Mieczysław Maliński, whose cassock gave off a stench of tobacco. Later Sapieha also provided them with false documents; he saw to it that Wojtyła's name was crossed off the list of workers at Solvay to avoid searches by the Gestapo.

The archbishop was counting on a rapid Russian advance and the liberation of the city. In a few weeks, he told his protégés, the Russian army would be entering Kraków. He was wrong. On Stalin's orders, the Red Army halted on the eastern side of the Vistula, purposely allowing the Germans to finish the destruction of the Polish resistance fighters allied with the exiled government in London (thus preparing the way for Stalin's anointed proxies to take control of a postwar Poland). Wojtyła and his brethren had to get used to long months hiding out in the archbishop's palace. If there was a search, they were to say that they were priests. The windows were draped, and it was absolutely forbidden to part the curtains. The only breath of fresh air came during an afternoon stroll in the courtyard. Volleyball was the students' only distraction.

Sapieha came every day to take part in academic and practical discussions. There was little tension, no envy, none of the cliques that might have arisen under normal conditions. The memory of the little community on Franciszkańska Street would remain deep in Wojtyła's heart as an example of brotherly life together, and Sapieha would always serve as his model of what a bishop should be. Kazimierz Suder, who was a seminarian during the same period, noted: "Sapieha was informed about everything that was going on in the country. He knew and solved our problems. . . . He was very friendly to the priests, very friendly to the novices, very interested in their lives, in their studies, very concerned that the priests should receive a high level of preparation." Finally Wojtyła had put on the clerical robe that his mother had wanted to see him wear from the moment she first held him in her arms. Now he was living in contact with a man of action and piety who knew the world and knew how to draw upon hidden energies from long hours of prayer. "He awakened me for the priesthood," Wojtyła would say twenty years later, as he entered the cathedral on the Wawel wearing the insignia of the archbishop of Kraków.

Though Wojtyła confided to the archbishop his continuing desire to join the Carmelite order, the prince metropolitan was against it; and by his own example he would show Wojtyła that an intense, mystical relationship with God is not reserved exclusively for those who lock themselves within the walls of a monastery.

On November 13, 1944, Wojtyła received the tonsure, the medieval rite of having one's hair clipped to symbolize submission to the Lord.

With the arrival of the new year German resistance to the Allies broke down. On the eastern front the Red Army launched a major offensive on January 13. There were fears that the Germans might turn Kraków into a last line of defense, a "fortress," almost certainly resulting in the city's destruction. On January 17 Soviet planes appeared for the first time in the skies over Kraków. The inhabitants, shut in their houses, were uncertain whether the Nazis would turn Kraków into another piece of scorched earth. From the windows they could see convoys of trucks heading for Germany loaded with the last bits of plundered Polish property, mostly works of art.

Sapieha sent his seminarians into the cellar and began his wait for the Red Army by praying in the chapel, while machine gun fire crackled around Wawel Castle. In the end, Kraków was saved. A few Russian bombs fell and some bridges were destroyed, but the Polish Florence, as Kraków has been called, remained intact. The liberators came by night, crossed the city in search of Germans, and asked for admittance to the archbishop's palace. The ensuing encounter read like a page out of Gogol. "Who lives here?" asked the two Soviet army majors arriving at the gate. "The metropolitan," answered the archbishop's driver. The two officers inspected the cellar, found the seminarians and nuns awaiting the verdict of history, and saluted them grandiloquently. "You have been liberated," they announced. "The Polish government is right behind us." Then came the crucial question: "Have you got any vodka?" At that point the archbishop's driver pulled out a bottle. The first officer took a swallow—then another. Half the bottle was gone before the other officer finally intervened. "Stop it," he ordered. "Now, I'll drink and you'll do the talking."

The much-feared Russian liberators didn't look nearly as terrible as the seminarians had imagined. They were ragged, tired, sometimes crude, but not especially aggressive. Little episodes stuck in their minds: the young soldier who had found a bicycle and rode it around the streets in childish exuberance, soldiers shooting deliriously into the air, others who went hunting for watches and alcohol with infantile greed.

In Wojtyła's mind this moment would always be associated with the Russian soldier he met who asked him about God and religion: "The soldier knocked on the gate of the seminary, which at that time was still partially in ruins. I asked him what he wanted, and when he asked if he could enter the seminary, I spent several hours with him."

The soldier had been taken to church as a small child. At school and at work he had heard over and over again that God didn't exist. " 'But I always knew anyway'—he kept repeating—'that there *is* a God. And now I want to find out more about him.' " Wojtyła recorded this singular conversation in a notebook, commenting: "During our long talk I learned a great deal about how God impresses himself on human minds even in conditions that are systematically negative."

•   •   •

The war now over, Wojtyła went back to the reopened Jagiellonian University, where he was elected vice president of the student body and devoted himself to completing his third- and fourth-year theology studies. From April 1945 until August 1946 he also worked as a teaching assistant. His marks, as usual, put him near the top of his class. The balance sheet of the twenty-six exams he took gave him "excellent" in nineteen subjects, "very good" in six, and "good" in only one, psychology. As usual the people he met continued to twit him gently about his impeccable piety. "Karol Wojtyła, future saint," said a card he found pinned to his door one evening.

Among his colleagues and friends, as everywhere else in Poland, conversations were focused on the country's future. After Yalta it was clear that being consigned to the Soviet sphere of influence would sooner or later mean a loss of real independence. But Wojtyła took no active part in these discussions. He certainly felt no sympathy for the pro-Russian Poles, especially those who were clerics, but the important thing, he asserted on walks with Maliński, was that they should always remember to be "Poles, Christians, humans."

When he learned that the Carmelite novitiate of Czerna had reopened its doors, he applied for admission. Father Alfons, the abbot, had been murdered by the Germans and Father Leonard Kowalówka, a friend of Wojtyła's, was now head of the novitiate. He explained, however, that permission from the archbishop was required for admission to the order, and Sapieha was adamantly against the idea. Wojtyła doggedly tried again in 1948, after two years of studies in Rome. But again Sapieha refused. "I have given permission a hundred times for all kinds of candidates who wanted to join the monastery," the prince metropolitan explained. "I denied it only twice. Once I turned down Father Koslowski, who is also from Wadowice. This is the second time I'm going to say no." When the order's provincial persisted, Sapieha offered a hint of where Wojtyła fit in the archbishop's plans. "With the war over we have only a few priests, and Wojtyła is badly needed in the diocese." Then he added: "And later he will be needed by the whole Church."

On November 1, 1946, the feast of All Saints, the archbishop personally ordained Wojtyła a priest six months ahead of his classmates in the chapel of the archbishop's palace. On the next day, All Souls Day, in the Wawel Cathedral, Father Karol Wojtyła celebrated his first mass. His former teacher Father Kazimierz Figlewicz served him as *manuductor*, the elder confrère who guides a new priest during the celebration, steadying him as, for the first time, he experiences the tremendous power involved in the transformation of bread and wine into the Body and Blood of Christ.

Thus the circle was closing. Lolek had learned to be an altar boy with Father Figlewicz. He had served mass with him on the day the Nazis invaded Poland and bombed Kraków. In this same cathedral, amid the tombs of kings and Polish heroes, Karol Wojtyła became a priest in liberated Poland. During the service he prayed for the souls of all his dead family members.

On November 3 he said mass in the Salesian church in his old neighborhood of Dębniki with Jan Tyranowski looking on, and on the 4th he celebrated a solemn inaugural mass at the Wawel. His former co-workers from Solvay presented him with a cassock; and his colleagues from the Rhapsodic Theater were all on hand for the occasion. They listened to Wojtyła as, now an actor in a greater mystery, he proclaimed the Word of the Living God.

"Fecit mihi magna" ("He has done great things for me," Luke 1:49), Wojtyła wrote on the holy card that he distributed to his friends during a brief reception. Then he went to Wadowice to say mass in the parish church of his childhood. On November 11 he administered baptism for the first time, to the infant daughter of his old friend Tadeusz Kwiatkowski and his old recital companion Halina Królikiewicz.

PART TWO

FATHER KAROL

LOVE

The Stalinist consolidation of Eastern and Central Europe was brutally swift. In June 1948, Karol Wojtyła returned from two years of Roman studies (concentrated on the philosophies of St. Thomas Aquinas and the Spanish mystics) to a Poland that was undergoing a different kind of transformation than its socialist neighbors. Fitting communism to Poland, Stalin had said, was like putting a saddle on a cow, and the realities of postwar Poland reflected this.

Containing the Catholic Church was among the first orders of business for the Communist parties as they came to power in Europe. In Yugoslavia, the bishop of Zagreb was sentenced in 1946 to sixteen years of hard labor on charges of wartime collaboration with the Fascists. The day after Christmas in 1948, Cardinal József Mindszenty, the primate of Hungary, was arrested on trumped-up charges of treason and condemned to life in prison. In Czechoslovakia that same winter, Archbishop Josef Beran received a sentence of fourteen years. In Hungary and Czechoslovakia thousands of monks, priests, and nuns were arrested.

But in Poland, in both the religious and the economic spheres, the process was less severe—and less successful. For centuries, through wars and partitions, Polish culture and its peasantry had become inextricably bound up with the Church: The Church was a force that the Communists had to treat with a measure of respect. It had always stood its ground against invaders as well as indigenous infidels. With an overwhelming 95 percent of its population Catholic, Poland was unique. As a result, though the activities of the postwar Polish Church were circumscribed, it was allowed to exist and to continue to practice its faith. Soon it became the muted voice of whatever opposition persisted. The number of Polish priests and nuns who went to jail was a fraction of the total in neighboring nations. A semblance of dialogue, however stilted and precarious, continued between the state and believers. Stalinist terror, whether measured by show trials or the mass eradication of any opposition, was not nearly so intense in Poland as elsewhere behind the iron curtain. In Poland, only a halfhearted attempt was made to collectivize the land, and many peasants were initially given their own patches of ground by the regime.

Wojtyła showed no particular concern for the political situation in his country as he began his pastoral life. On the contrary, his awareness of the Communist suppression of civil rights in Poland or elsewhere seems to have taken hold slowly, and in a peculiarly Wojtyłian manner.

Archbishop Sapieha chose the rural parish of Niegowić to give his favored young priest a taste of pastoral experience: performing baptisms and hearing confessions, officiating at weddings and funerals, calling on the sick and infirm, saying mass, tending to the lives of country parishioners who for centuries had been the principal clientele of the Polish clergy.

Niegowić, to which the twenty-eight-year-old Wojtyła was assigned in July 1948, was an isolated, primitive village in the Galician countryside, thirty miles from Kraków. It had two hundred inhabitants, a wooden church, and a cluster of houses with no electricity, running water, or sewage system. Here Wojtyła arrived in a threadbare cassock and shapeless shoes, a skinny, bespectacled priest carrying his belongings in a battered briefcase, hunched over, trudging slowly along the unpaved road from the railroad station five miles away.

The accommodations accorded him and the other young curate who assisted Niegowić's pastor were quite decent, however—more spacious than his former lodgings in Kraków. The rickety *wikariówka* (rectory) had two rooms for each man and a small kitchen garden behind it. Meals were substantial and good. Until Communist agrarian reform was implemented, the pastor of Niegowić owned 120 acres of land, 120 cows, two teams of horses, and abundant poultry. He employed a cook, an assistant cook, a groom, a cowherd, and a girl to run errands.

Wojtyła's daily schedule was rugged: He rose about five A.M., said mass, then made the rounds of the parish on a horse-drawn cart (usually reading a book) to teach religion, celebrate mass in outlying hamlets, and serve his parishioners. Maria Trzaska, who still lives in Niegowić, remembers the young vicar helping her brother dig ditches and thresh wheat. The threshing was done as in biblical times, by beating the grain with a flail made of two pieces of wood bound together.

It was a healthy life. The vicar's parishioners often saw him taking solitary walks after lunch in the orchards behind the church. Sometimes he prayed as he walked. Then, finding a quiet spot, he would stop and meditate. For a modest fee Father Wojtyła employed young Stanisław Wyporek, the son of a local farmer, to type with two fingers his thesis on faith in the writings of St. John of the Cross, which would complete his Roman degree. Stanisław understood not a word of it because the manuscript was in Latin. Meanwhile, he tried, without much success, to teach the future pope to ride a bike. "He used to tell us there was something wrong with his balance."

During the seven months he spent in Niegowić, Wojtyła distinguished himself by his dedication to young people. He organized them into theatrical performances; helped them in their studies and trades; took them on trips to Kraków or hiking in the woods; and played volleyball and soccer with them in the meadows. As the sun set, a bonfire would be lit, and the priest and his young flock would join hands, swaying back and forth, singing popular songs, then communing in prayer. It was an unusual enterprise for a cleric in the 1940s, and one which attracted the attention of the authorities.

Here, in a tiny rural village, Wojtyła first experienced how the Stalinist machine functioned. The secret police wished to disband the local Young Men's Catholic Association and replace it with a section of the Socialist Youth Group. They began by persuading a member of Father Wojtyła's circle to inform on him and tried to blackmail others into doing the same. Stanisław Wyporek, his hunt-and-peck typist, was among those visited by an agent who asked for reports on the doings of young Catholics, but he refused to collaborate. One evening the police picked Wyporek up in a car, took him to a nearby village, gave him a beating, and accused him of belonging to a clandestine group. The boy returned to Niegowić at nine the next morning, cowering and in a state of shock.

Wojtyła, who met him on the road, soothed and consoled him. "Don't worry, Stanisław, they'll finish themselves off," he said of the Communists.

Later to others from the group he said, "Socialism isn't against the Church's teachings, but the Communists' methods run contrary to the Church. Communism imposes materialistic conceptions on the people, it tortures the nation." Years later, when Stanisław Wyporek visited Wojtyła in his Kraków apartment, he found on his bookshelf works by Marx, Lenin, and Stalin. "Are you converting to another ideology?" he asked jokingly. "Stanisław," Wojtyła replied, "if you want to understand the enemy, you have to know what he wrote." Such overtly political comments by young Father Wojtyła were extremely rare.

He advised his youthful typist to tell the truth to the secret police about what the boys in the parish were up to. There was nothing to hide. Wojtyła's special pedagogy was taking shape: "He never told us to resist," says Wyporek. "The bad things, he said, should be overcome by goodness. We should set a good example. We should show our humility."

.   .   .

In March 1949, Archbishop Sapieha recalled Wojtyła to Kraków and transferred him to the university parish of St. Florian. Almost a half century later, John Paul II would acknowledge that the most memorable experience he had at the beginning of his pastoral work was the discovery of the *fundamental importance of youth.* "It is a time in life given by Providence to every person and given to him as a responsibility," he said in his book of interviews, *Crossing the Threshold of Hope.* "During that time he searches, like the young man in the Gospel, for answers to basic questions; he searches not just for the meaning of life, but also for a concrete way to go about living this life. . . . He desires to be his own person." Every pastor must identify this characteristic in every girl and boy. "He must love this fundamental aspect of youth."

And Wojtyła did.

Karol Tarnowski, a university student in this period, recalls the distinctive manner with which Wojtyła heard confessions. Some might last as long as an hour. "He knew how to listen, and he was ready to do it and answer our questions nonstop. Time meant nothing to him." Though others might be waiting to enter the confessional, the seventeen-year-old felt unhurried and secure in the company of the priest whose pensive profile he glimpsed behind the confessional grille. The timbre of Wojtyła's voice was normal; he didn't whisper, but rather spoke as if he were meditating out loud.

Wojtyła explained to his fellow seminarian Maliński:

> When we talk about confession, . . . you can't play at being woodpeckers, one pecking from one side, the other responding from the other side. You can't settle matters with a smooth word. You have to establish a dialogue and treat it seriously from the heart. Confession is the crowning moment of our apostolic activity. . . . So the question is whether we can preserve the apostolic values. In the absence of deep inner life, a priest will imperceptibly turn into an office clerk, and his apostolate will turn into a parish office routine, just solving daily problems.

Old Archbishop Sapieha had intuited that St. Florian's would be a perfect assignment for Wojtyła. Here he could expand his unusual rapport with young people and develop new pastoral methods while keeping in contact with Kraków's vibrant cultural and intellectual life. Here, too, he could pursue his own literary and philosophical efforts.

When Wojtyła began going on trips to the mountains or lakes with the young university men and women from St. Florian's, his goal was to try out a new kind of education. The hikes and outings were intended not as a mere occasion for healthy fun. Nature was a way to get closer to God, to stir the soul through meditation, to reach toward and bring together the essential human being and the essential God.

The "boys and girls" in his company—for that was how he addressed them—felt a special warmth toward him and his unusual ways. Later they would give their group a somewhat self-important name, the Wojtyła *Srodowisko* (Milieu), but he preferred another term, *paczka* (the pack).

The group began the day by building an altar from an upended kayak or a pile of stones, on which the sacrifice was celebrated. Then, after mass, a long line of campers would leave to hike over the mountains or to cross a lake in their kayaks, with Wojtyła in the lead, often dressed casually in a polo shirt and shorts, which helped keep him from being recognized as a priest by the police. (Clerics were forbidden to lead groups of young people outside of church.) The young men and women called him *wujek* (uncle), partly out of affection, partly to avoid suspicious entanglements with strangers. Several times the militia arrived to scour the campsite shortly after the group had left, but they saw no priest among the hikers in the distance. Wojtyła usually chose a boy or girl to spend the day with, devoting hours of personal conversation to each one. Every evening he ate with people from a different tent. The young opened up to him, sometimes frankly discussing problems in their love lives. Many of them were engaged, but unmarried men and women slept in separate tents.

For Karol Wojtyła attention to sex, love, and marriage became basic elements in the pastoral care of young people. Many years before the Catholic reevaluation of marital relations by the Second Vatican Council, Wojtyła worked out his vision based on a belief that marriage was a genuine *vocation*, just as the choice of priesthood was. His way of not just pointing out the norms laid down by Church dogma, but confronting the practical and sexual problems in relationships was attractive to young people. His attitude was highly unconventional. The young chaplain seemed to feel no embarrassment in talking about sexual relations. Sex, he believed, took on a heightened intensity and a specific *loving* importance—beyond procreation—in the context of a monogamous couple bonded in marriage for life. (This was almost exactly the revision of doctrine the Council adopted.)

The advice he gave to men and women differed. "The moral question concerning relations with women," recalls Karol Tarnowski, who like others in the Milieu turned to Wojtyła for help and advice, "was a kind of primary thing for him. He wanted to help us understand that giving birth to a child is a participation in the act of Creation."

Wojtyła, as one of the group put it, was "less intellectual in the way he treated girls." He taught women that they had a special gift, in addition to childbearing: the capacity to form men. "Would you like to educate him?" Wojtyła asked Maria Bożek, a young student who told him she didn't want to be with a certain young man. As Wojtyła felt this particular person was the right choice for her, he was insistent. "Would you like to make a man of him?" he asked again.

"Yes," Maria answered, not very confidently. Eventually, however, she married Karol Tarnowski, a young man whom Wojtyła had thought an inappropriate choice for her.

Wojtyła "is fatherly and extremely loving," she reflected many years later. "He is extremely patient." Even after he became an auxiliary bishop, she continued to seek his counsel, and he welcomed her at his residence to discuss family problems or simply to sit silently with him when she was overcome by grief.

In Wojtyła's vision, time and patience were the crucial elements in any developing relationship between a man and a woman. Steadily paddling a kayak with his "sailor-boy" or "sailor-girl" (as he called his rowing partner of the day), he would explain that a man and a woman "should learn to be together a lot before they enter into a more intimate relationship. They should learn how to deal with one another, how to be patient, how to put up with one another, how to understand each other." Since sex could have meaning only within the context of an indissoluble bond of marriage, to make marriage last it was essential to learn to come to terms with the negative traits of one's partner.

"The surface of love," he would go on, "has a current whirling beneath it: swift, flickering, changeable. This current is sometimes so overwhelming that it sweeps men and women away. Love isn't an adventure, it can't be a single moment. It has the taste of the whole man." The eternity of the human being, Wojtyła told the students, passes through love.

The point was not to repress sexual desire and feelings, but to direct them toward a union that guaranteed the dignity of both partners. "Sexual relations outside of marriage," he would later write, "always cause objective harm to the woman, even if she consents to or positively desires them." The same was true for men, he felt, but more often he saw women as victims of male disrespect. He educated men about the positive value of tenderness, without which, Wojtyła said, "A man will simply tend to subject a woman to the demands of his body and mind."

To reinforce the idea of self-discipline Wojtyła directed some engaged couples not to see one another continuously, to space out their meetings at two- or three-day intervals. But his suggestion had little success, usually because the women—not the men—rebelled at the idea.

In this way, the hikes and canoe trips turned into schools of marriage and counseling sessions. The conversations and reflections from these hours spent in the outdoors would reappear in *The Jeweler's Shop*, Wojtyła's play about the troubles of married couples, and in his remarkable treatise *Love and Responsibility*, both published in 1960, when Wojtyła was already an auxiliary bishop.

Love and Responsibility would cause a sensation in Church circles because no one had ever heard of a bishop dealing in print with subjects like sexual excitement, unsatisfied wives who faked orgasms, or the fundamental importance of a man's making sure that his mate climaxed. Even his advocacy of "the equality of man and woman in marriage" seemed somewhat shocking at the time. In his years as a university professor, his students became so captivated by this unusual priest that, according to his former pupil Zofia Zdybicka, many of them wondered if Father Karol hadn't once had a fiancée or perhaps even a wife. In fact, much of his information came from the confessional.

Although his footnotes in *Love and Responsibility* cite few sources other than his own philosophical writings, it is apparent from the text that Wojtyła had done his research on human sexuality, especially on matters of anatomy and physiology. The views of "sexologists" are frequently mentioned, as are the "teachings of sexology." As for his audacity in creating a theory of sexual relations without any direct experience, his whole life had been stirred by questions about love, of which sex is so much a part: the miracle of love between man and woman, love of one's fellow human beings or of the parent for a child, love as the basis of societal values; love as Christ's dowry to his disciples. His audacity—a trait he had in abundance in any case—lay foremost in his willingness to speak bluntly and with feeling about what occupied his mind in a time when such language was considered daring in a priest.

A representative passage from this pope-to-be went thus:

It must be taken into account that it is naturally difficult for the woman to adapt herself to the man in the sexual relationship, that there is a natural unevenness of physical and psychological rhythms, so that there is a need for harmonization, which is impossible without good will, especially on the part of the man, who must carefully observe the reactions of the woman.

If a woman does not obtain natural gratification from the sexual act there is a danger that her experience of it will be qualitatively inferior, will not involve her fully as a person. This sort of experience makes nervous reactions only too likely, and may for instance cause secondary sexual frigidity. Frigidity is sometimes the result of an inhibition on the part of the woman herself, or a lack of involvement which may even at times be her own fault. But it is usually the result of egoism in the man, who failing to recognize the subjective desires of the woman in intercourse, and the objective laws of the sexual process taking place in her, seeks merely his own satisfaction, sometimes quite brutally.

Such was the stuff to which the young men and women in Wojtyła's pack were introduced during their kayak tutorials. Even after becoming pope, Wojtyła maintained his ties with these fifty or sixty men and women. (None of them has ever been divorced.) Later, one of these protégés—Tarnowski, who eventually married Maria Bożek—argued with his mentor, now pope in the Vatican, that the Church's ban on contraceptives for a Catholic couple who had honestly done their duty of bringing children into the world might be untenable. Suggesting to Tarnowski that he look for another confessor, the old pope, who had spent so much of his young manhood constructing what he thought was a humane theory of Catholic marriage, then told him: "I can't change what I've been teaching all my life."

LUBLIN

In October 1954, the government of Poland shut down the Theological Faculty of the Jagiellonian University where Karol Wojtyła was a lecturer in Christian ethics. The Catholic University of Lublin (KUL), where he arrived later that month to teach ethics and philosophy, was endowed with unique importance: It was the only university run by the Catholic Church in the immense territory under the dominion of Stalin's heirs and Mao Zedong. The head of the Polish Church, Cardinal Primate Stefan Wyszyński, had taken his degree in canon law from the university; and from 1946 to 1948, while the Communists solidified their power, he had served as the bishop of Lublin, dedicating himself to the reorganization of KUL, a former monastery which the Nazis had turned into a barracks.

At Lublin University Wojtyła affected a poetic manner, wearing a jaunty purple beret, horn-rimmed glasses, and a black cassock that was clean but frayed from all the time he spent on his knees. As in his own university years, however, there was little occasion for lightheartedness. The political and religious climate in Poland had turned much grimmer: The government had only recently arrested the university's rector and nine priests on the faculty. Archbishop Eugeniusz Baziak, successor to Archbishop Sapieha upon the latter's death, was imprisoned, as was Wojtyła's friend the pastor of St. Florian's. A priest in charge of the Kraków Women's Living Rosary and the Catholic Young Men's Association had been condemned to death along with two lay co-workers (their sentences were later commuted to life imprisonment). In September 1953, Cardinal Wyszyński himself was arrested: He had vigorously opposed the new Polish constitution that deepened the imprint of communism on the state and eliminated many rights long accorded the Church. Even *Tygodnik Powszechny,* Kraków's Catholic weekly newspaper, which had printed Wojtyła's poems since 1949, had been closed for refusing to run an obituary on Stalin, who died on March 5, 1953.

Wojtyła soon joined a small circle of professors who gathered secretly around the dean of the Faculty of Philosophy, Father Jerzy Kalinowski, to discuss their predicament as it related to that of the university, the nation, and the Church. They became intellectual conspirators, seeking subtle ways to undermine communism spiritually and philosophically.

"The Catholic hierarchy thought that the task of a Catholic university was to defend Catholicism in a hostile communist world," said one of the circle, historian Stefan Świeżawski. "By contrast we thought our fundamental role was to do good scholarly work. . . . The second thing was to enhance the role of philosophy in the communist system, to sharpen the dialectic between Christian philosophy and the communist system."

Karol Tarnowski recalls Wojtyła arguing that the Marxist ethic overlooked the reality of man. The Marxists, said the young philosopher-priest, considered "man as something that will be, shall be, must be created in communism—but there is no place for an individual man, nor for the essence of Man. Because the essence of Man is concretized in every human being."

For Wojtyła, the Christian approach to life and society was extremely realistic, while the Marxist approach wound up being "purely idealistic, because no concrete Man could be found in Marxism, only the idea of Man." Many years later, returning to Poland for the first time as pope, Wojtyła would echo this theme. The confrontation with communism was "not about fighting against communism," Wojtyła declared, "but advancing the positive task of deepening Christian life."

"Wojtyła's attitude," says Świeżawski, "was to use each moment to strengthen your orientation, to expand your knowledge, to concentrate on positive work—not wasting your time on political issues and conflicts."

This stance remained Wojtyła's even during the historic events of 1956, when the Communist world was shaken by a workers' revolt in the industrial city of Poznań, setting the stage for an anti-Communist rebellion in neighboring Hungary. Tens of thousands of Polish demonstrators demanding pay increases were met by a wall of security forces as they marched on Poznań's Freedom Square that June. The security forces attacked: Fifty-three people were killed and more than two hundred injured. In the rage that followed the massacre in Poznań, a reformist faction of the Communist Party, led by Władysław Gomułka (an anti-Stalinist who had been under house arrest for eight years) came to power. Many of Poland's political prisoners, including Cardinal Wyszyński, were released; and a triumphant Gomułka announced that Polish Communists were "taking their place at the head of the process of democratization." However, in Moscow, Soviet party secretary Nikita Khrushchev declared that the actions of the new Polish government were "menacing the whole socialist camp," and troops of the Russian-led Warsaw Pact advanced on the capital. Gomułka warned Khrushchev that the Poles would fight, as government forces blocked a Soviet armored column sixty miles west of the capital. At two A.M. on October 20, Khrushchev caved in. (There is no record that Wojtyła ever addressed these events either publicly or privately.)

In Hungary, however, Khrushchev didn't back down, and Soviet troops and tanks crushed the Hungarian revolution with enormous loss of life. Cardinal Mindszenty, freed from prison by his fellow citizens in Budapest, fled to the American embassy when Russian troops reentered the city. He would remain there—"free" yet imprisoned—for fifteen years. Wojtyła often commented that Mindszenty shouldn't have sought asylum in the embassy, but should have remained with his flock. His own models were Cardinals Sapieha and Wyszyński, who had stayed at their posts in moments of danger, even at the risk of martyrdom.

Twenty-four winters later, the men in the Kremlin worried that Karol Wojtyła might return from the Vatican to Poland to be with his flock and personally confront a Soviet invasion.

A LETTER FROM ROME

The primate of Poland, Cardinal Stefan Wyszyński, glanced perfunctorily at the tanned young priest who, even in his cassock, projected vigor and athleticism. He knew the priest's age, thirty-eight, but little else about him except that he was interrupting his vacation, at the Mazurian Lakes, where he had been on a retreat with a group of young people. A telegram sent on July 4, 1958, had urgently summoned him to the primate's residence on Miodowa Street in Warsaw.

For ten years Wyszyński had been the senior official, and the personal symbol, of the Polish Catholic Church. In his shrewd, stubborn dealings with the Communist authorities he had diplomatically defended the Church's independent tradition. In 1948, when only forty-seven, he had become the youngest primate in Polish history.

In 1950, Wyszyński had angered the reigning pope, Pius XII, by signing an accord with the Communist government that recognized its supreme authority in the temporal sphere, while allowing the Church limited rights in the spiritual realm. "The Episcopate will be guided by Polish raison d'état," the agreement declared, while the pope "is the competent and highest church authority [in] matters of faith, morality and Church jurisdiction." The government interpreted this as giving it veto power over the appointment of bishops.

After signing the agreement with the government, the primate explained his rationale: "Martyrdom is always a grace and an honor, but when I weigh the present great needs and demands of Catholic Poland, I want martyrdom only as a last resort. I want my priests at the altar, at the pulpit, and in the confessional—not in prison."

Nonetheless, he himself had spent more than three years—from 1953 until the winter of 1956—in a monastery under house arrest, because of his persistent assertion of the rights of the Church and his protests against Stalinist strictures on clerical activity.

"Are you a prelate or a canon?" he now asked Wojtyła in his customary tone of imperious courtesy.

"Neither, Your Eminence. I am a priest and apart from that an assistant at the Catholic University of Lublin."

The cardinal lifted a sheet of paper from his desk with his bony hand and looked again at the priest, who was waiting in silence, without a trace of nervousness: "This is an interesting letter that we have received from the Holy Father. Listen, please: 'At the request of Archbishop Baziak, I am appointing Father Karol Wojtyła auxiliary bishop of Kraków; kindly express your approval of this appointment.' "

The primate paused to study Wojtyła's reaction. Later that evening Wyszyński would jot down a description of the scene in his private diary, a routine of his for years. Sometimes an intimidated candidate for apostolic office in Wojtyła's situation would babble, "I have to consult with my spiritual director about this decision." Then the primate would say, "If you are a mature person, you should know what you want to do."

Other priests might try to gain a little time by saying, "I have to ask Jesus about it in my prayers." At which the primate would point to the door.

"There's a chapel right behind that door there. Please, say your prayer. But please don't take any more than fifteen minutes, because I don't have the time, and neither does Jesus."

Wyszyński asked Wojtyła, "Do you accept the appointment?"

"Where do I sign?" the priest replied without hesitation.

That July 8 remained fixed in the primate's memory: It was the first time he had been bypassed in the appointment of a Polish bishop. Since the authorities made it so hard to conduct Church business, Pius XII had granted Wyszyński the extraordinary privilege of selecting and keeping on hand a list of future bishops already formally approved by the pope. When Wyszyński wanted to appoint someone, he would send a secret message to Rome, and as soon as he got a coded signal from the pontiff, would go ahead with the appointment. Karol Wojtyła's name was not on Wyszyński's list.

In Wojtyła's life there had always been a guardian angel to guide and push him forward at just the right moment: first Archbishop Sapieha; now his successor, Eugeniusz Baziak. Later that role would be taken by Pope Paul VI, and—finally, during the conclave that elected him pope—by Cardinal Franz König.

Half an hour after the "conversation" in the primate's palace, a priest arrived at the convent of the Grey Ursuline Sisters (the name comes from the color of their habit) on the bank of the Vistula River. He asked the nun who opened the door where the chapel was and entered it without saying another word. He strode quickly toward the altar and sank to his knees in the front pew.

An hour passed, and another. A sister, then several more, came and went in silence. Around suppertime, a rumor began to circulate that the silent priest was Professor Wojtyła, and the nuns decided to invite him to eat. But the priest wouldn't leave his place. The mother superior went to look in the chapel and found Wojtyła still immersed in meditation, his head clasped in his hands. That evening he ate nothing. When the nuns went to bed, he was still in the chapel. He continued praying for eight hours.

On September 28, 1958, Karol Wojtyła was consecrated a bishop in the Wawel Cathedral in Kraków. On October 9, Pope Pius XII died at the age of eighty-two, and on October 28 the cardinals elected as pope Angelo Giuseppe Roncalli, seventy-seven, who took the name John XXIII. Less than three months later the new pope called an ecumenical council. One of the letters of invitation, which were sent to all 2,594 bishops around the world, went out to young Karol Wojtyła.

THE COUNCIL

The Second Vatican Council—Vatican II—was a revolution.

The Catholic Church as an institution always tends to stress elements of continuity, as if an evolutionary pattern had been inscribed in its destiny from the time of Christ. Not surprisingly, a close reading of the documents of Vatican II shows clear evidence of compromises struck between traditionalists and supporters of innovation: The Roman Catholic Church has always managed to absorb original impulses by linking them to its oldest traditions.

But in the eyes of millions of contemporaries, Catholic and non-Catholic alike, the Council was rightly seen as revolutionary, a radical break with the past. At Vatican II, the absolutism of the Curia—the papal bureaucracy of congregations, tribunals, and pontifical offices (in Rome and beyond) that for centuries had dictated and enforced the rules of Catholic life—was curtailed, and an extremely Rome-centered concentration of Church power was eased. John XXIII's Council seemed to open the Catholic community up to the world.

Any number of developments soon confirmed, for Catholics, that a break with a model of the Church inherited from the anti-Protestant Council of Trent (1545–63) was taking place: Vatican II brought liturgical reform, use of the vernacular in the celebration of mass, an affirmation of freedom of conscience, rapprochements with Protestant and Eastern Orthodox communities, openings to other religions, dialogue with nonbelievers, the disavowal of anti-Semitism, and, above all, the presentation of the Church not as a static institution but as the People of God making their way through history, a new Israel on pilgrimage.

Almost four years of preparation preceded the convocation in Rome of 2,381 bishops, superiors of religious orders, and cardinals—the "Council Fathers"—in October 1962. It is instructive to reread the seven-page memorandum that Karol Wojtyła sent to Rome in response to the questionnaire received by the bishops prior to the Council. In fact, his expectations for Vatican II were modest indeed, and the central concern he urged on his fellow Church leaders bore little relation to the concerns of more farsighted participants. In his opinion, the Council's purpose should be to deliver a clear statement on the importance of the transcendence of the human person* against the growing materialism of the modern age. Not until his own papacy would this concept—a central element of the philosophy of St. Thomas Aquinas—again guide the Church so forcefully.

With respect to the essential unity of all Christians in the Church, an ideal close to the heart of John XXIII, Wojtyła stood for reaffirming the traditional doctrine (enunciated by Pius XII) of the Church as the Mystical Body of Christ: There could be only one Body, a single Church of Christ, thus making unity with other Christian churches dependent on fealty to Rome. The young bishop, in answer to other questions, held that it was necessary to give laypeople a greater role in the Church. Among subjects he hoped to see discussed were the importance of priestly celibacy, the pastoral utility of athletic and theatrical activities, ecumenical dialogue, and reform of the breviary and the liturgy.

On the occasion of the Council, Wojtyła left Poland for the first time in fourteen years. A few months earlier Archbishop Baziak, his patron, had died; and on June 15, 1962, Wojtyła at the age of forty-two had become capitular vicar, or temporary head, of the diocese of Kraków. Within the Polish Bishops Conference he had also been appointed national chaplain of the "creative intelligentsia"—in recognition of his links to the world of culture.

But within the larger Church he was an unknown quantity—a Bishop Nobody—when on October 11 he entered the basilica of St. Peter for the inaugural session of the Council. Along the sides of the immense central nave, platforms had been set up with ten sloping rows of seats. All around Wojtyła rustled a forest of white miters, interrupted here and there by the bulging

---

* In Catholic theology, the term "human person" refers to the whole human being of body, reason, and soul.

black headgear of the Oriental patriarchs of the Eastern Orthodox Churches. Seated in a separate section were 101 "observers" from other Christian denominations, an absolute novelty, plus several hundred theologians and other "experts" who were to assist the Council in its deliberations.

Wojtyła, with his brand-new bishop's miter, did not have to walk far because, in keeping with protocol, the episcopal greenhorns were assigned places at the entrance to the basilica. From his seat Wojtyła could watch the Council Fathers as they prepared to plunge into the unknown. "As far as the Council goes," Pope John XXIII had joked on the eve of its opening, "we are all novices. The Holy Spirit will certainly be present when the bishops gather, and we'll see what happens."

In summoning the Council, the old pope had called for *aggiornamento*— renewal, an effort to bring the Church up to date. Wojtyła was stirred by the greatness of the moment. To be a Catholic bishop in Rome at this time in history was like being an American at the Second Continental Congress in 1776, or a Frenchman at the opening session of the Estates General in 1789. "I set out on this road with the deepest emotion, with a great tremor in my heart," Wojtyła said as he took his leave from the faithful of Kraków.

The basilica of St. Peter echoed with the chant of the "Veni Creator," and Wojtyła watched the solemn progress of Pope John XXIII borne aloft on his gestatorial chair, accompanied by assistants bearing the *flabella,* or ceremonial fans. In contrast to those he called the "prophets of doom" in the Church hierarchy—in large part, his own Curia—Pope John had a sturdy confidence in a Council of renewal. He had convened the largest gathering of elders in the history of the Catholic Church. He had called to Rome bishops from 141 countries, more than triple the number of bishops who had taken part in the First Vatican Council ninety years earlier. At that time there hadn't been a single African among them. Now there were more than a hundred black bishops. The Europeans made up barely a third of the Council Fathers; and the Italians found the French, German, and English-speaking bishops pressing on their heels. For the first time there was a Japanese cardinal, as well as a Chinese, an Indian, and an African one.

Greatly moved, Wojtyła wrote a poem, perhaps more heartfelt than accomplished (as was generally the case with his poetry):

We shall be poor and naked
transparent as glass
which not only reflects but cuts
and may the world thus split open
recompose itself beneath the lash
of the consciences that have chosen the backdrop of this temple.

Given the poet-prelate's ways of thinking and of experiencing the life of the Church, the Council was also a personal revolution for Wojtyła. He came from a culture of bishops where the rules of secrecy and episcopal solidarity were in full force. The Polish Bishops Conference met every two months behind closed doors. No whisper of dissent or clash of opinions ever leaked out. In the face of relentless pressure from an atheistic state, the bishops presented a front of total unanimity. Above them all, Primate Wyszyński reigned like a monarch.

The average Polish bishop had never known any other way. But from his seat in St. Peter's Wojtyła was now witness to the flaring up of angry disputes, to voting by mutually hostile blocs, to verbal duels, triumphant applause, murmurs of protest, sarcastic thrusts, outbursts of rage—a Church version of parliamentary democracy, including petitioning, lobbying, and behind-the-scenes maneuvering by the conciliar "parties," members of the Curia, and even the pope himself.

Wojtyła's sensibility was shaken by a memorable revolt of the Council Fathers, who at the very start of business overwhelmingly decided to cast aside all seventy-two schemas, the preservationist agenda drawn up by the Curia. This meant virtually throwing out four years of preparatory work, in order to begin discussion of the most far-reaching changes. Wojtyła listened spellbound to the harsh attacks on the inquisitorial Holy Office—the curial congregation responsible for fighting heresies and therefore the pernicious doctrines of modernism—by the cardinal of Cologne, Joseph Frings, and the furious reply by the prefect of the Holy Office and its grand inquisitor, Cardinal Alfredo Ottaviani. He noted how the traditionalists invoked Article 222 of canon law to argue that it was the pope's prerogative to dictate the Council's agenda, while the reformers—eventually backed by the pope—

claimed the right to reject any imposed draft agenda in the name of the freedom of the Council.

The preparatory schemas were ultimately rejected because they reflected an old vision of the Church as a monarchy in which all power was concentrated in the hands of the pope and in which the transmission of the faith followed a dogmatic and deductive path to the believer: The Church had all the truth and so every practical decision in life involved only the application of some infallible principle already enunciated by the hierarchy. Pope John was prodding the Council to start over, to recognize that the era of "Christian states" or of "Christendom"—a society completely formed by Christian inspiration—was over.

Back in Poland, Wojtyła had witnessed attacks on the hierarchy by the atheistic authorities, in other words, by "enemies." But in Rome the harshest critiques came from within the Church. He wasn't at home with this mode of debate. "He was never a man to criticize the Church," recalls Karol Tarnowski. As the hour of the Council approached, some of the young people Wojtyła was closest to in Poland had joined in the harsh judgment of the hierarchy. They found it liberating to criticize the Church's past, but Wojtyła wasn't at all happy with such criticism. Wojtyła had had tense moments even with some of the editors of *Tygodnik Powszechny,* who tended toward a reformist interpretation of Pope John's *aggiornamento.* "I remember very well," Tarnowski stresses, "that he didn't approve of my—or anyone else's—critical attitude toward the Church."

This was—and is—an essential element in Wojtyła's character. He has always been ready to listen, but listening isn't the same thing as real tolerance. In the final analysis, his philosophical method does not allow for any genuine and open conflict between opposing truths. To him, it is a simple matter: Others have to be lovingly led by the hand, like children, onto the path of "truth," which they will then come to see for themselves. Even in his "pack," as Tarnowski notes, "he didn't stir up in our group any sort of intellectual discussion in a critical sense." Unsurprisingly, the parliamentary climate of the Council proved out of sync with Wojtyła's temperament. As pope, John Paul II would prevent the triennial meetings of the bishops in Rome (the synods) from taking the same independent path as the Council Fathers were to take.

Yet the conciliar sessions were a great school for Wojtyła. He looked, he listened, he learned, and he often approved of the results, however unaccustomed he was to the way things got done.

The young capitular vicar from Kraków was also completely unused to the press and public opinion intervening in the affairs of the Church. In Rome, sooner or later everything ended up in the newspapers—closed-door meetings, secret communications, supposedly confidential agreements. For a bishop from Poland, this was unimaginable. Wojtyła mistrusted the way the media influenced internal debate in the Church (and when he became pope his Secretariat of State would issue an order prohibiting executive officers in the Curia from giving interviews without special permission).

Neither did Wojtyła like the leading role that theologians were assuming in the conciliar debate. In a certain sense the revolution of Vatican II was their doing—the work of the men of the "French school" like Yves Congar, Henri De Lubac, Jean Daniélou; and of the "German school" like Karl Rahner, Hans Küng, Bernhard Häring, Hans Urs von Balthasar. The theologians, not the bishops, prepared the terrain for renewal of the liturgy, for ecumenism, for unprejudiced biblical studies, and for a new era of ecclesiology. Catholic Poland, locked behind the iron curtain, had contributed little, if anything, to these developments.

During Wojtyła's reign as pope, some of these great conciliar theologians would be marginalized or even forbidden to teach, while others more sympathetic to the pope's views would be appointed cardinals. Either way, the authority of the bishops would be jealously guarded, for as John Paul II, Wojtyła has remained deeply suspicious of excessive interference by theologians in Church business. In his eyes such men should be subordinate helpers, if not mere instruments, of the bishops and the popes.

· · ·

Once Karol Wojtyła became John Paul II, some writers couldn't resist the temptation to exaggerate his impact on the Council. There is, however, no evidence that he ever played a crucial role at Vatican II, even if, as the sessions went on, he did emerge as an extremely active participant, and his thoughtful speeches earned him notice and respect among his peers. Only as *Gaudium et*

Spes (Joy and Hope), the Pastoral Constitution on the Church in the Modern World, was hammered out, did he directly enter into the circle of decision makers—but on the losing side.

The arrival in Rome of Cardinal Wyszyński and eleven Polish bishops, had been preceded by a report in the influential French journal *Informations Catholiques Internationales* that depicted the Polish Church as an institution well behind the times. By and large the Polish bishops had not come to Rome with great plans for reform. The feeling expressed by the French article was so widespread that Wyszyński felt obliged to decry the lack of understanding that surrounded his delegation: "Our bishops have been accused of being reactionary, as if they wished to hold on to rights from the feudal era. The question, however, is not one of feudalism nor of privileges, but of the Church's right to live."

The energies of the reform process came from the West—from France and West Germany, with contributions from Belgium, Holland, Switzerland, Italy, and the United States. On the eve of the Council, when John XXIII felt he needed help in working out a global plan of renewal, he had turned to Belgian Cardinal Leo Suenens; and the first trend-setting speeches about how to enhance the Church's mission in the contemporary world were delivered by Suenens himself and by the cardinal of Milan, Giovanni Battista Montini, the future Pope Paul VI.

Even if Poland wasn't considered a leading force at the Council, Wyszyński still enjoyed enormous personal prestige because of his battle against communism. In addition, on certain key issues in the conciliar debate—such as religious freedom and a strong voice for the bishops conferences—the primate came down strongly on the side of reform. Similarly, his views on social issues were almost universally regarded as quite advanced, equally critical of Marxist *and* capitalist materialism—demonstrating (once again) that, in the Church, flatly distinguishing between "conservatives" and "liberals," or between ideological majorities and minorities, usually distorts the truth. The frontiers waver and blend, depending on the issue at stake.

A series of votes resoundingly demonstrated that an overwhelming number of the bishops were in favor of thorough renewal and of an end to the Curia's suffocating power. Wojtyła joined with the bishops who wanted to reform the Church. Years later he described his perception of the event: "The Second Vatican Council was nothing less than a *Magna Carta*, a great charter designed to make the Church available for the preaching of the Gospel in the world of today."

.   .   .

Between October and December of each year from 1962 through 1965, the Council was in session. When Pope John XXIII died on June 3, 1963, he was succeeded by Paul VI, who carried on his conciliar legacy after removing from the Council's agenda the questions of birth control and clerical marriage. Ultimately, the Council produced four constitutions, nine decrees, and three declarations.

One of the ground-breaking documents of Vatican II was *Lumen Gentium* (Light of the Nations), the Dogmatic Constitution on the Church, devoted to the nature, structure, and mission of the Church. In *Lumen Gentium*, the principal aim of the reformers was to stress the role of the Church as a community rather than as a juridical, monarchical society.

In this vein, Wojtyła took the floor to argue that the community was indeed the foundation of every structure of the Church, because "every Christian participates in a special, unique, and irreplaceable way in the mission that the Church has received from Christ." According to Wojtyła, that essential horizontal dimension of the Church intersects with but does not in any way nullify its vertical dimension—the priests and bishops—which is deeply rooted in the sacrifice and mystery of Christ.

Lumen Gentium provoked intense debate as the reformers succeeded in reevaluating the role of the bishops, whose power over Church policy had diminished almost to the vanishing point after Vatican I: The First Vatican Council, in 1869–70, had put forth the dogma of the infallibility of the pontiff while reducing the bishops to little more than papal functionaries, something on the order of Napoleonic prefects. Vatican II enthroned them as successors of the Apostles, indeed as the "vicars of Christ."

Invoking the example of the company of the Apostles gathered around Peter, the reformers sought to assert a collegial view of Church power and proposed that an international assembly of bishops help the pope to govern the Church universal. No one has yet indicated that Wojtyła took any position on the bitter disputes provoked by this issue. In reports on the Council that he sent back to the bishops and the faithful in Kraków or gave to the young priests of the Polish Institute in Rome, where he was staying, he always papered over any dramatic outbursts or serious conflict in the affairs of the assembly.

Eventually Paul VI resolved the problem of power sharing by fiat: He first suggested to the presiding chairmen of the assembly that the question be studied by a special committee. Then, without ever letting that committee be formed, he established a new entity, the Synod of Bishops, as a consultative, not a power-sharing, body, which would convene in Rome only every three years. At the same time, he subjected the Curia to partial reform, assigning to its various departments residential bishops (those who actually headed a diocese) who would be involved in curial matters while continuing to oversee their dioceses at home. All this proved far less substantive than what the reformers had had in mind. They wanted a body of bishops to *control* the Curia and to rule with the pope.

For Wojtyła, the whole episode was a lesson in the art of government. Despite their very different temperaments, Paul VI became another of Wojtyła's spiritual fathers, offering him a living model of how a pontiff might make his way among the Church's pressure groups and affirm his own supremacy at an opportune moment.

Paul VI cleverly alternated measures that placated the traditionalist minority and encouraged the reformist majority. On issues of power or doctrine that he considered essential, however, the pope made his own decisions. In one instance, to appease the Polish bishops, he imposed a definition of Mary as the Mother of the Church, even though the Doctrinal Commission of the Council had explicitly rejected such a proposal, fearing that an "overestimation" of Mary's role would widen the gap between Protestants and Catholics. After the debate on *Lumen Gentium*, Paul VI appended to the text an "Introductory Explanatory Note" that underscored the supreme, unmediated power of the pope and the nonfunctional nature of the assembly of bishops, should it ever try to act without the pope.

At his seat in the basilica, Wojtyła took notes on the debates, marking the upper right-hand corner of every page (as he still does) with a cross and the letters *AMDG*—for *Ad majorem Dei gloriam,* To the glory of God. The feeling of a universal flock gathered around its shepherd for this exceptional occasion completely absorbed him, and sometimes on the blank pages he would sketch out poems. From the earliest sessions, Wojtyła made friends with the African bishops, men from a culture quite alien to his own but to which he seemed irresistibly drawn. The African bishops appeared to him to be animated by a fresh, living, physical faith and inspired one of his poems during the Council. As pope, John Paul II would hold a particular affection for Africa, which he regards as the continent of hope for Catholicism.

In Rome an old friend, Monsignor Andrzej Maria Deskur,* with whom Wojtyła had attended Archbishop Sapieha's seminary, introduced him to key figures in curial circles. At the large round table in Deskur's dining room, from which the apse of the basilica of St. Peter could be seen, Wojtyła made his first important acquaintances outside Poland. Deskur, a member of the Council's press office who had been at the Vatican for ten years, was well connected with both the monsignors and the cardinals of the Curia as well as with bishops from abroad.

"Every Monday I asked him whom he wanted to meet, and Karol gave me a list," Deskur recalls. Others at the table included the Polish American Bishop John Krol and the rector of the Polish College, Bishop Władysław Rubin, one of the secretaries of the Council's preparatory commission, both of whom were to become cardinals and play a part in his future.

.   .   .

At the Council, the Poles were the most important delegation from the Communist world, and so they had a certain authority on questions affecting the Church behind the iron curtain. Once a week the Polish bishops met under the chairmanship of Wyszyński to ensure precise coordination on every initiative important to them. As always, the delegation approached conciliar

---

* The title "monsignor" is reserved for bishops and Church officials (especially in the Vatican) of special importance, such as the head of an office.

questions from the standpoint of believers whose religious traditions were threatened by a Communist regime. Hence the Polish bishops were invariably unnerved by critical attacks on Church tradition, above all out of fear that these might play into the hands of the Communists. Wyszyński expressed constant concern that what was going on in the Council should be useful for the preparation and observance of the thousandth anniversary of Christianity in Poland, scheduled for 1966. A rededication of the Polish nation to its Catholic roots was the best way, he felt, to strengthen the power of the Church in its ongoing struggle with the authorities.

Before long Wojtyła became the spokesman for the Polish delegation, and he often negotiated on its behalf with the French and German bishops; after Wyszyński, he was the Polish bishop who attracted the most attention. Seven speeches by Wojtyła to the full assembly appear in the Council record, and he submitted thirteen written statements. Bishop Karol Wojtyła was beginning to make a name for himself.

The one person who initially refused to acknowledge Wojtyła's stature was the primate of Poland. After the death of Archbishop Baziak in 1962, Cardinal Wyszyński had to resolve the problem of appointing his permanent successor as metropolitan archbishop of Kraków. According to procedure, he was obliged to present the Polish government with a list of three candidates (previously approved by the pope) and to await a green light from the Warsaw authorities. Karol Wojtyła's name wasn't among the three on Wyszyński's list—all of whom were rejected flatly by the government. And Wyszyński didn't insert Wojtyła's name into his second list of three—all of whom were also summarily rejected by the regime.

Between these two strong-willed priests there had always been some sort of barrier, a continuing discomfort. For Wyszyński in the early years of their acquaintance, this bordered on a sense of distrust toward Wojtyła. Emotionally and temperamentally, they were strangers to one another. Wyszyński was a sociologist, Wojtyła a philosopher. Wyszyński's origins were peasant class; Wojtyła's were lower middle class. Wyszyński had been active in the resistance as a chaplain for the partisans; Wojtyła had remained, at best, on the margins of that movement. The primate was more at ease with the masses; the bishop of Kraków was more on the wavelength of intellectuals.

The two men lived in different worlds. Even the way they dealt with the reality of Communist Poland differed. The primate was a true politician; the bishop seemed to be a man of abstract principles, far removed from politics.

The fact remains that Wyszyński considered at least six candidates better suited than Wojtyła to occupy the archbishop's chair in Kraków, even though Wojtyła was then serving as acting archbishop there. Eventually this reluctance on the part of Wyszyński wound up helping Wojtyła. The Communists were looking for a candidate whom they could use to undermine Wyszyński's supremacy. They decided that Wojtyła, who had always seemed reticent about politics and more interested in intellectual problems, was the man for the job.

Father Andrzej Bardecki, the religion editor of *Tygodnik Powszechny*, recalls that Zenon Kliszko, the powerful number-two man in the Communist regime, made it known that he hoped Wyszyński would name Wojtyła as archbishop. "Wyszyński has already named six candidates to succeed Baziak in Kraków, and I didn't approve any of them," Kliszko boasted. The Communist leader thought Wojtyła would be more open-minded, more willing to engage in dialogue, than the prelates on Wyszyński's lists. The comrades were fascinated by Wojtyła's intellectual qualities. Bardecki noted later, "Both the Primate and Kliszko were wrong. What Kliszko regarded as an asset in Wojtyła, Wyszyński regarded as a drawback. The communists thought that they could handle Wojtyła quite easily, and Wyszyński was afraid they could, too."

In the end the primate gave in to pressure from a delegation of senior clerics in the archdiocese, known as the chapter of the Kraków cathedral. Bardecki has a vivid recollection of the satisfaction that swept over the Communist Party when Wojtyła was named archbishop.*

Wojtyła became archbishop of Kraków on December 30, 1963; on March 8, 1964, he made his triumphant entrance into Wawel Cathedral. For the

---

* At the time a religious dissenter, the Benedictine abbot Piotr Rostworowski, was imprisoned in Gdańsk. One evening the prison commander entered the abbot's cell after roll call and announced, "We've got very good news. Wojtyła has been appointed metropolitan of Kraków." Three months later the commander returned to the cell, complaining, "This Wojtyła fellow has cheated us."

occasion he chose vestments whose symbolism filled the crowd in the cathedral with stunned admiration. He was wearing a chasuble donated to the archbishops of Kraków by the medieval Queen Anna Jagiellon, and on top of that a pallium given by Queen Jadwiga in the sixteenth century. His miter came from the seventeenth-century Bishop Andrzej Lipski, and the crozier went back to the time of King Jan Sobieski, who conquered the Turks in the Battle of Vienna in 1683. His ring was from the fourth successor to St. Stanisław, Bishop Mauritius, who died in 1118.

Wojtyła's splendid vestments represented almost one thousand years of Polish history. This wasn't mere respect for tradition; it was a way of reminding the faithful and the "infidels" in power that the Church of Poland was the nation; that without the Church the history of Poland did not exist.

Now in the Gothic cathedral where he had heard the first Nazi bombs bursting upon Kraków, he became a successor to St. Stanisław, the medieval bishop murdered by his king, like Thomas à Becket in England. Celebrating the sacrifice at the tomb of the martyr-bishop that day bound Wojtyła by precedent to be ready to shed his blood, like Stanisław, for the cause of the faith.

ARCHBISHOP

With his appointment as archbishop of Kraków, Wojtyła gained stature and so, when the discussion at Vatican II turned to the issue of freedom of conscience and religion, his speeches became more authoritative. *Dignitatis Humanae* (Of the Dignity of the Human Person), the Declaration on Religious Freedom, was bitterly resisted by traditionalists, who remained wedded to Pius IX's *Syllabus of Errors* (1864), which damned many of the trends of recent theological research as "pernicious modernism." They considered the concept of religious freedom totally unacceptable. Cardinal Ottaviani, prefect of the Holy Office, maintained that it was impossible to grant any "rights" to error, that mistaken doctrine could not be elevated to the sublime level of the Church's everlasting truth. (Most Curia members knew the joke about Ottaviani asking a taxi driver to take him "to the Council," and the cabbie responding, "You mean Trent?") To the cardinal, of course, virtually all non-Catholic teaching came under the description of "error."

The reformist wing of the Council responded by insisting on a distinction between *error* and the *person in error.* John XXIII had used this approach in reference to Marxism and its adherents, thereby justifying dialogue with representatives of Communist regimes: Error was always wrong, but the person in error always had to be respected.

For the Catholic bishops of Western countries, a proclamation of freedom of conscience was an essential prerequisite to the opening of any real dialogue with other Christian churches. In the West, religious freedom assumed the neutrality of the state and respect for all religious denominations. By contrast, for the bishops of the East, religious freedom was a principle to be wrested from an atheistic state—and a matter of human rights.

Through Wojtyła's speeches a bridge began to be built between the two schools of thought. He carefully avoided the concept of indifferentism, with its notion that all doctrines are equally valid, while defending the draft of *Dignitatis Humanae* against the accusations of the traditionalists. He insisted that the text contained both a concession and a claim: If the Catholic Church was ready to admit religious freedom where it was strong, then the Church was in the position to demand freedom from governments that infringed on the rights of believers.

Wojtyła was deeply convinced that personalist ethics—which stress the uniqueness and inviolability of the human personality—would never allow the imposing of ideas on anyone. He took the same line when the Council discussed the problems of atheism—a question that vexed the Council Fathers from almost the beginning to the end of Vatican II. "It is not the Church's role to lecture unbelievers," Wojtyła declared on taking the floor on October 21, 1964. "We are involved in a quest along with our fellow men. . . . Let us avoid moralizing or suggesting that we have a monopoly on the truth." Wojtyła didn't want the Church to be seen as an authoritarian institution. He explained that instead of dictating the truth, one had to use the heuristic method, just "as you allow the pupil to find the truth, as it were, on his own."

Talk at the Council of actual "relations with atheism" meant dialogue with Marxists. In his 1963 encyclical *Pacem in Terris* (Peace on Earth), John XXIII had laid down a new principle: Ideologies, he had said, are immutable, but the historical movements they inspire are subject to change, and in any case an effort must be made to distinguish between ideological error and its adherents. The good had to be sought in *all* men of goodwill. For the Polish bishops, dialogue (as opposed to negotiations) with Marxists didn't make much sense. Wojtyła stuck to this line. He had brought to the Council a lot of baggage from those long evening discussions with his professor friends in Lublin. As Professor Świeżawski says: "We tried to avoid a dialogue with Marxism, because we thought it was a political road going nowhere. There was no way we could have a sincere and honest discussion with the side that had all the power. This put us in a different position from that of western Catholic intellectuals."

Wojtyła and his friends thought that Western intellectuals were naive and ignorant, even downright stupid, when it came to the realities of communism. Wojtyła's attitude on this never changed, nor as pope did he ever seek to learn what Marxism in the Western world was actually about.

At the Council he concentrated once more on human beings, not on movements. Atheism, he said in addressing the issue again on September 28, 1965, should be considered mainly as an internal state of the human person; and it should be studied using sociological and psychological criteria. "The atheist is persuaded of his 'ultimate solitude,' because he thinks God doesn't exist. Whence his desire to become immortal in a certain sense through the life of the collectivity. And so we have to ask whether collectivism favors atheism or vice versa." For this reason dialogue with Communists was very difficult.

Still, Wojtyła didn't believe that classic anti-Communist rhetoric— purveyed by many cardinals and bishops—was useful. As Świeżawski put the matter: "We never attacked Marxism; that wasn't the point. We didn't want to get entangled in those matters." When a group of bishops asked at the Council that an explicit condemnation of communism be included in the Constitution on the Church in the Modern World (*Gaudium et Spes*), Wojtyła opposed the move as counterproductive.

Gaudium et Spes is one of the pillars of Vatican II and the "conciliar revolution." It proclaims that the Catholic Church lives and acts *within* world history and that in its relations with society it not only gives but receives. The document declares its respect for the autonomy of civil society. All this signaled a desire that the Church turn to the world more openly than ever before.

The first words of the document, which provide its title, have a poetic élan that captures the reformist atmosphere of the moment: "The joys and hopes, the sorrows and agonies of men today, especially of the poor and the suffering, are also the joys and the hopes, sorrows and agonies of the disciples of Christ. And there is nothing human here that doesn't find an echo in their hearts. Their community, in fact, is made up of men who, gathered together in Christ, are led by the Holy Spirit on the path to the Kingdom of the Father; and they have received a message of salvation to be proclaimed to one and all. The community of Christians therefore sees itself in real and intimate solidarity with the human race and its history."

It is noteworthy that in the entire paragraph the word "Church" is never mentioned. Pride of place is awarded to the "vocation of man." Only after the Church has lent an ear to society and tried to read the "signs of the times" in history is the problem posed—in paragraph four—of the mission of the Church in the world today.

From the beginning, Wojtyła and the Polish bishops were in disagreement with such a stance and soon became full-fledged protagonists in the debate over the document. As far back as May 1964, Wojtyła had presented the chairmanship of the Council with a text, drawn up in the name of the Polish bishops, that proclaimed the Church's relation to the modern world to be based on the concept (dating from the Counter-Reformation) of the Church as a perfect society, founded by Christ and above history. A glance at the final version of *Gaudium et Spes* reveals the abyss between the thinking of the Poles and that of the reformist wing, led in this case by French bishops and theologians.

For Wojtyła, then and now, the Church is the only guardian of God's truth; and though the pope's philosophy exalts the dignity of the human being and his or her freedom of conscience, each person must follow the precepts of the Church to reach the truth. In the name of the Polish bishops

Wojtyła had already addressed the Council on October 21, 1964, attacking a basic concept in what became *Gaudium et Spes:* dialogue with the world. "The situations," he said, "in which the Church finds itself in the various countries of the world are diverse and contrasting. In some of them the Church can freely teach the truth. In others, however, it is blocked and persecuted. It is not possible to speak at the same time to all people, Catholics and non-Catholics, believers and non-believers. It's not possible to speak to those who are outside the Church, those who are fighting against it, and those who don't believe in God, using the same language that one speaks to the faithful."

No real dialogue can be established, he added, "unless we reflect that the Church, while being part of the world, is above it." During his speech Wojtyła couldn't resist one cutting remark: Those who embark on dialogue, he said, often end up delivering monologues.

What particularly worried Wojtyła was the affirmation that the Church shouldn't simply teach the world, but should learn from it too. Didn't that run the risk of confusing people's minds on the specific mission of the Church?

Wojtyła and the Polish bishops weren't the only critical voices. The German bishops, ordinarily a driving force in the reformist wing of the Church, took a hostile stance toward the draft, finding it too optimistic, too inspired by trust in technological progress, too little attentive to sin and the importance of the Cross.

On November 14, 1965, however, the final draft was presented and on December 6 approved by a vote of 2,333 in favor and 251 against. The latter was the highest rate of opposition registered in a final vote on any conciliar text, in sharp contrast to the near unanimity that generally characterized such votes. Paul VI sided decisively with the optimists. In closing the Council on December 8, 1965, he exclaimed, full of enthusiasm: "No one in the world is a stranger, no one is excluded, no one is far away."

In the debates over *Gaudium et Spes* a strong bond was forged between Wojtyła and the German bishops. That was strengthened by a November letter sent from the bishops of Poland to the bishops of Germany, calling for reciprocal forgiveness and reconciliation between the two nations. The final appeal of the document—*"We forgive and beg forgiveness"*—prompted an impassioned response from the Communist government and incomprehension from many Polish citizens, even anti-Communists. After the horrors of the Nazi occupation and the ovens of Auschwitz, what was there to ask pardon for? The Communist Party called for a public protest. Among the signers of a letter of protest printed in the official party newspaper were the workers of Solvay.

From Wojtyła's point of view, the letter of reconciliation was, in practical terms, a farsighted act. It prepared the German episcopacy to acknowledge the postwar western boundaries of Poland at the Oder-Neisse line, and it brought Wojtyła closer to his German confrères in the name of rejecting nationalism and undertaking a joint defense of European values against communism.* The German cardinals would later be part of the alliance that would elect him pope.

Karol Wojtyła emerged from the Council as a figure esteemed for his philosophical learning, for his pastoral commitment, and for his ability to listen. He had distinguished himself in the Council hall for his personality and principles, which defied labeling. Attached to tradition but keen on Church renewal, he was a positive-minded activist who was nonetheless convinced of the impact of sin on human history and society. He never questioned the authority of the Church, yet he avoided obvious clerical narrow-mindedness. At the center of all his concerns was the concrete human being and his or her salvation.

On November 30, 1964, he had had his first private audience with Pope Paul VI, who had closely followed the speeches of the new metropolitan archbishop. To Paul VI, Wojtyła seemed to be the leading personality among the Polish bishops, capable, unlike Cardinal Wyszyński, of bringing conciliar renewal to the Church of Poland. On December 13, 1965, when Wyszyński was received by the pope in a farewell audience with the Polish bishops, the primate had the gall to set conditions for introducing the conciliar reforms into Poland: "We are aware that it will be difficult, but not impossible, to put the decisions of the Council into effect, given our situation. Therefore we ask

* After World War II, the borders of Poland were shifted westward into former German territories, because Poland had to cede eastern parts of its territory to the Soviet Union.

the Holy Father for one favor: complete trust in the bishops and the Church of our country."

Timid by temperament, Paul VI was also a hypersensitive man. In the face of such lack of tact and respect, he listened in icy astonishment as Wyszyński continued: "Our request may seem highly presumptuous, but it is difficult to judge our situation from afar."

From that moment Wojtyła became the Vatican's point man in Poland. With Wyszyński the pope limited himself to saying that he expected the Council's decisions would be implemented in Poland as everywhere else— "energetically and willingly." But to Archbishop Wojtyła he gave a stone from the early Vatican basilica of Emperor Constantine to serve as part of the foundation of a church Wojtyła was planning to build in Nowa Huta, outside Kraków.

Archbishop Wojtyła returned to Kraków renewed and strengthened. He considered the Council a fundamental event for himself and for the Church, a great impulse for preaching the Gospel and stimulating the Church to make man more humane.

However, in his subsequent writings about the Council, Wojtyła focused almost wholly on the texts of Vatican II and the effect of the Council on the bishops who attended, "as though it had not aroused expectations among most everyone in the Church," as Peter Hebblethwaite, a biographer of John XXIII and Paul VI (and a frequent critic of Wojtyła), put it.

Halina Bortnowska, a Polish theologian and personal friend of Wojtyła who edited a version of his 1972 book *Sources of Renewal*, felt it necessary to note in her introduction that "there is no appeal to post-conciliar . . . discussions. One has the feeling of great abstractness and remoteness from the world of people seeking some guidance for their lives."

As for postconciliar developments, Archbishop Wojtyła never doubted that in its voyage through time the Church still had a few course corrections to make.

A CARDINAL APART

Cardinal Wyszyński had to rethink his position on Wojtyła. In 1966, when the celebrations in honor of the first thousand years of Christian Poland reached their peak, the primate discovered that in the archbishop of Kraków he had a trusted and loyal ally in the struggle against communism.

Poland really was a special province of Christianity. After the Council, bishops all over the world were looking to the future and trying to introduce reforms, but in Poland the bishops were looking to the past. The country had some reason to do so, quite apart from Cardinal Wyszyński's reluctance to pursue a reformist agenda. ("You don't restructure your army during a battle" was the primate's credo.) The glorious past served to remind the Communist authorities that down through the ages the Church had represented the unity of the nation even when the Polish state had been wiped off the map. In concentrating on the thousandth anniversary rather than on the Council, the Polish Church was sanctifying tradition. It was a question of "roots" versus "change."

The centerpiece of the millennial observance was an emotional mobilization of tens of millions of Catholics around the "Queen of Poland," the Black Madonna of Częstochowa. A copy of the revered painting of the Virgin, blessed by Pius XII, was sent on pilgrimage to every one of the eleven thousand parishes in the twenty-seven dioceses of Poland. This was an unprecedented referendum on faith in a country behind the iron curtain. The painting went from church to church and was received with great pomp and euphoria by unending delegations of parishioners. Millions of others headed for the shrine of Częstochowa, where the original painting was kept.

This tumultuous response to an icon that for centuries had symbolized the triumph of the Church over the sovereign state alarmed the Communist regime. Party chief Władysław Gomułka was now just another fossilized leader of the Communist East, his reformist impulses long since overcome by his desire to stay in power. Vexatious, even ridiculous, episodes began to occur as the government tried to thwart the Church. Competing events, such as soccer matches, were ham-handedly scheduled to coincide with ceremonies organized around the image of the Black Madonna. Efforts were made to block the passage of the icon from one city or parish to another. Finally, in Silesia, the government ordered the copy sent back to the monastery of the Pauline Fathers in Częstochowa.

But banishing the painting from sight did not suppress the wave of popular feeling among Poles using the Madonna's pilgrimage to express their yearning for independence. As a sign of protest, thousandth-anniversary masses continued to be said in front of empty picture frames placed on the altars of churches throughout the country. Archbishop Wojtyła presided over fifty-three special millennial masses and on May 3, 1966, celebrated a pontifical mass at Częstochowa in the name of Paul VI, whom the regime had forbidden to travel to Poland for the anniversary.

The government had for several years been slowly coming to the realization that the archbishop of Kraków was not a tool in its hands. In July 1965, Zenon Kliszko, Gomułka's right-hand man, had arranged to meet the archbishop at Wawel Castle privately, supposedly for a joint review of state-Church relations. An earlier incident in which Wojtyła had acted independently of Wyszyński in relations with the party gave Kliszko hope that he might develop a special rapport with the archbishop. Shortly after the death of Archbishop Baziak the authorities in Kraków requisitioned the diocesan seminary building for use by the state as a teacher's college. The young auxiliary bishop had then gone personally to the regional secretary of the Polish United Workers Party, Lucjan Motyka, to protest.

This was an unprecedented move. No Polish bishop had ever set foot in a Communist Party committee room. Motyka had shown himself willing to strike a compromise: The Teachers College of Kraków would be installed on the fourth floor of the building, while the other floors would be left to the seminarians.

Kliszko's hopes of developing a cozy relationship with Wojtyła, however, proved wishful thinking. After an hour of discussion in the archbishop's office, he left in disappointment. Gomułka was informed that Wojtyła had rigidly hewed to the line taken by the primate. Wyszyński, through his own private channels, came to know this too, and never forgot it.

Yet the authorities continued to believe that Wojtyła was more inclined to make compromises with the state than Wyszyński, whom they regarded as "the standard-bearer of the anti-communist front." That description is contained in a confidential 1967 Polish secret police report which also noted:

It can safely be said that he [Wojtyła] is one of the few intellectuals in the Polish Episcopate. Unlike Wyszyński, he deftly reconciles traditional popular piety with intellectual Catholicism, both of which he knows how to appreciate. . . . He has not, so far, engaged in open anti-state political activity. It seems that politics is not his strong suit; he is over-intellectualized. . . . He lacks organizing and leadership qualities, and this is his weakness in the rivalry with Wyszyński.

The police document then outlined a strategy for dividing the two cardinals, based on its belief that

the model of Catholicism and coexistence with socialist countries proposed by Wojtyła . . . corresponds to the future line of the Vatican. . . .

We must observe and study every feature of the relations between the two cardinals, and conduct an elastic policy, to fit the changing circumstances. . . . We must use diplomatic channels to determine whom the Vatican is the most likely to support and to see whether Wojtyła has any real chances of becoming the head of the Polish Episcopate. We must not hit the archdiocese too hard—although we must occasionally apply "administrative measures"—in order to defuse suspicions toward Wojtyła on the part of groups at home and abroad [who are] not sympathetic toward him. . . . We must encourage Wojtyła's interest in the overall problems of the Polish Church, and assist him in handling problems with his archdiocese. For this reason, we should initiate high-level meetings between Wojtyła—for example, with Premier Cyrankiewicz and with Kliszko—to discuss general questions.

. . . And we must continue to demonstrate our ill-will toward Wyszyński at every opportunity, but not in a way that would force Wojtyła to show solidarity with Wyszyński.

"Wojtyła was heroically loyal to Wyszyński," Father Andrzej Bardecki of Kraków recalls, despite the primate's dictatorial style. Once, in Rome, Wojtyła was told that no Italian cardinals skied. Wojtyła responded, "That's funny. In Poland forty percent of all our cardinals are skiers." He was reminded that there were only two Polish cardinals. "In Poland," he replied without batting an eyelash, "Wyszyński counts for sixty percent."

When it came to dealing with the Communists, Wojtyła and Wyszyński were divided by a generation gap. For Wyszyński, the question of whether a real Polish Church or nation could exist was hardly academic; for Wojtyła, the more relevant questions were what kind of Poland would exist and how the Church and religious rights in Poland could actually flourish.

Whatever their private differences, Wojtyła was convinced that it was necessary to join forces with Wyszyński because he shared the primate's view that under Communist rule the Church could survive only if its unity was unshakable. In 1967 when the Communists denied the primate the passport he needed to go to Rome for the Synod of Bishops, Wojtyła refused, out of solidarity, to attend the meeting.

SEX AND THE *PAPABILI*

In the history of the Church it is seldom possible to say with certainty why a particular cardinal was elected pope. The exceptions prove the rule. But a careful observer can retrace the reasons that have brought the candidate into the limelight of the *papabili* (likely candidates).

Cardinal Andrzej Deskur, a man with a profound knowledge of the Curia, believes that in some mysterious way every pope chooses his own successor. Pius XII, he claims, recommended John XXIII by appointing him to the patriarchal see of Venice, one of the most prestigious Church posts in the Latin West. The ailing John XXIII clearly considered the cardinal of

Milan, Giovanni Battista Montini, the right man to finish the work he had begun at Vatican II.

In turn, Paul VI indicated his preference for two men, Albino Luciani, patriarch of Venice, and Karol Wojtyła, archbishop of Kraków. To the first he made a gift of his papal stole, before a cheering crowd, while on a visit to Venice. To the second he offered special attention, which became quite evident to insiders soon after the Council.

In 1967 Paul VI made Wojtyła a cardinal. The letter of appointment is now kept at Wojtyła's birthplace in Wadowice. Karol Wojtyła was forty-seven years old—the second youngest living cardinal—when, in the basilica of St. Peter, he received the red cap from the hands of the pope. "I know that I must prove myself as I go along the road of my new calling, and that I must demonstrate my worth anew," he said, characteristically blending humility and an underlying pride.

Thereafter the collaboration and affection between Paul VI and the archbishop of Kraków intensified. Wojtyła was named to four Vatican congregations: Clergy, Catholic Education, Liturgy, and Oriental Churches. The pope also appointed him a consultor to the Council for the Laity.

And then there was their special cooperation on the landmark papal encyclical *Humanae Vitae* (On Human Life). If ever there was a moment when the Catholic Church seemed poised to adopt a new attitude toward contraception and artificial birth control, specifically banned under Church doctrine, this was it. On June 24, 1966, after seven years of study, Pope Paul VI's commission on the subject submitted a majority report stating that the Church's opposition to contraception "could not be sustained by reasoned argument"—and that the practice of artificial birth control was not "intrinsically evil." Nine bishops voted in favor of the report, three against, and three abstained. Wojtyła was a member of this commission, and, though not present on the day of the vote, he had argued strongly against any change in Church doctrine on the question of birth control.

Wojtyła's views had already been enunciated in his book *Love and Responsibility*, namely that the use of contraceptives devalues the dignity of the conjugal act and of the woman (by presuming that she is merely an object for male pleasure); and a year before the commission's vote, Wojtyła had begun work on a paper about contraception, based on his long-held views and the findings of his own study commission from Kraków, composed of laypeople and clergy. These materials, which took four months to prepare, were sent directly to the pope.

Paul VI empathized deeply with Catholics who wished to plan their families. Yet he was extremely uncomfortable with the recommendations of his commission. He did not want to be the pope who set the Church on a new approach to sexuality whose effects were hard to imagine. The pressures on Paul VI were immense—from the laity (mostly in favor of relaxing the Church's ban), from Cardinals Ottaviani and Wojtyła, both of whom had supplied extensive theological documentation in support of the ban, and from the majority of his own commission, whose co-chairman, Cardinal Julius Döpfner of Munich, had convened a working group that submitted materials urging liberalization of the Church's rules.

It was Wojtyła's arguments and materials that proved decisive in helping the pope decide what his heart had been telling him all along: that the ban on artificial contraception must be upheld. After studying Wojtyła's submissions, he went ahead with his decision and issued *Humanae Vitae* in mid-July 1968. Upon reading it Cardinal Wojtyła commented with satisfaction, "We helped the pope." According to Father Bardecki, Wojtyła's colleague from *Tygodnik Powszechny*, sixty percent of the text of *Humanae Vitae* can be traced back to the work of Wojtyła's Kraków's commission and his paper. Thus the sexual philosophy of Wojtyła and his flock of Polish Catholics became the rule for the Church universal.

Humanae Vitae provoked a firestorm of protest in the Catholic world. But Wojtyła, immensely pleased, defended it strenuously in public. To promote it among Catholic families in his diocese, he founded special "marriage groups," which undertook to follow the precepts of the encyclical and what he called its "expression of the unchanging truth, always proclaimed by the Church."

This episode bound Paul VI yet more closely to Cardinal Wojtyła, whom he regularly entertained in private audiences. Between 1973 and 1975 alone, the archbishop of Kraków entered the pope's study for private audiences eleven times. Then, in 1976, Paul VI honored Wojtyła with an extraordinary invitation: He asked him to deliver the Lenten spiritual exercises at the

Vatican for members of the Curia and the papal household. That same year, the *New York Times* placed the cardinal on a list of the ten most frequently mentioned candidates to succeed Pope Paul VI.

·   ·   ·

Dressed in a black cassock with vermilion buttons, the preacher entered from the little door to the sacristy, made a dignified genuflection, slowly stood up and nodded toward an invisible presence to the right of the altar. Then he turned his back to the great marble altarpiece and bowed to his audience in their red and purple caps. Near the altar was a little table with a microphone. The cardinal sat down and began his sermon: "May God grant me the grace to speak as I desire and to formulate thoughts worthy of the good things given me, since He is the guide of Wisdom" (Wisdom of Solomon 7:15).

Before him sat the leading figures of the Catholic Church—the distilled essence of curial power, a lay observer might have said. For the man at the microphone, these hundred or so men were simply the pope's closest and most faithful co-workers, among them the cardinal secretary of state, Jean Villot, a detached and aristocratic Frenchman; Monsignor Sostituto Giovanni Benelli, the powerful number-two man in the Secretariat of State; the Yugoslavian Franjo Seper, prefect of the Congregation for the Doctrine of the Faith (previously the Holy Office); the American John Wright, prefect of the Congregation for the Clergy; the strong-willed Sebastiano Baggio, prefect of the Congregation for Bishops; Cardinal Bernardin Gantin of Benin, president of the Pontifical Council for Justice and Peace; and Sergio Pignedoli, president of the Secretariat for Non-Christians.

For a moment, the preacher's eyes fell on the small and lively figure of the pope's foreign minister, Monsignor Agostino Casaroli, the secretary of the Council for Public Affairs. He was the promoter of the Vatican's dialogue with Communist countries, a tireless diplomat engaged in guaranteeing the churches of Eastern Europe not so much a *modus vivendi* but, as he ironically put it, a *modus non moriendi* (a way of not dying). The Italians had given him the nickname "Lagostina," from the brand name of a pressure cooker that can handle the highest temperatures.

As during every year in the first week of Lent, the Mathilde Chapel of the Vatican was full. In the square hall by the second loggia, the floor of the Apostolic Palace ordinarily devoted to official audiences with the pontiff, there now gathered prefects, secretaries, and sub-secretaries of the sacred congregations who had come to make their spiritual exercises.

"In the days to come we shall be accompanied in a special way by the prayers of the Church of Poland, from which I bring here the expressions of the deepest communion in faith, hope, and love," Wojtyła continued. "This is like an invisible foundation by means of which we are always bound together with the Successor of St. Peter."

He spoke in a firm, clear voice, trying to give his Italian the most authentic inflection possible. Whatever tension he was experiencing did not show. Wojtyła had not had much time to prepare. He had been caught off guard by the papal invitation, which usually went to a renowned theologian, and had hastened off to a rest home run by Catholic nuns in the Tatra Mountains where, on more relaxed occasions, he liked to take long, solitary walks. This time, however, he locked himself in his room to write, asking to be left absolutely undisturbed. He took his meals there, leaving only to visit the chapel or the bathroom.

Members of the Curia now observed Wojtyła with great interest. This was one of the few times a pope had chosen a member of the College of Cardinals to deliver the Lenten exercises. His personality, so far as it was known, pleased many people in the Vatican, but no one present, with the possible exception of Archbishop Deskur, could be said to know him intimately. Even though he was always ready to engage in conversation, the Polish cardinal remained something of a closed book. He seldom talked about himself despite the breadth of his experience as a scholar, a dramatist, and a witness to all too many of the horrors of history. Some people in the chapel knew that he had lost his mother, brother, and father in his early years, but he never mentioned it, not even on All Souls Day, when Catholics ordinarily visit the graves of their relatives. Although he found it easy enough to make contact with people in ways that intrigued them, he had nothing of the easygoing, hail-fellow-well-met character sometimes encountered in high-ranking churchmen. He was warm in personal interchanges, but rarely jovial, eager to hear what people had to say, yet a loner. He had many acquaintances and a few friends, but—except perhaps for his personal secretary—no real confidant.

He was known to have a charismatic power over young people. He could touch the hearts of both the humble and the more sophisticated. Some were quite swept away when they met him face to face and spoke of his capacity to look into a person's eyes in a special way. Uncharacteristically for a man of the Church, he treated women with absolute ease and a sense of friendliness that held no trace of embarrassment or inappropriate familiarity. Some, however, noticed in him a certain defensiveness when challenged, a tendency to locate his interlocutors at a given point on the theological or ideological spectrum and to speak not to their personality or individual beliefs but to the label he gave them. Sometimes he seemed to be choosing in advance those people who he felt would yield to his charm and rejecting out of hand those who might not.

People who met him were often struck by the extreme simplicity of his manner, by his modest demeanor. He owned practically nothing except for his books and ecclesiastical robes, a few family mementos, skis (which he stored in the episcopal palace), and hiking clothes. One might have called him humble, if he hadn't revealed occasional flashes of intense pride and, it would seem, a highly developed sense of self.

In the Vatican Wojtyła was known not just as a philosopher but as a polyglot. Even if his accent was sometimes a bit flawed, the archbishop of Kraków moved easily among various European languages: German, Russian, French, English, Italian, Spanish—a linguistic facility complemented by a growing propensity for travel. He had been to the Holy Land, to North America, to Australia, to New Guinea, to any number of European countries—participating in congresses, visiting Polish communities abroad, following an inner impulse that no one could completely explain.

His capacity for meditation was tireless. He had written a book on conjugal love and the meaning of the sexual act; he had written a book on the fundamental principles of Vatican II; he had published a long anthropological work called *The Acting Person*.

These were not easy books, especially the last, which was humorously characterized by the priests of Kraków as a penitential exercise for souls in Purgatory. One thing that pleased a number of the curial bishops and cardinals was Wojtyła's seeming capacity to see beyond the cultural and ideological trends shaking society and the Church all over the Western world. The archbishop of Kraków wasn't a frightened defender of the establishment; he didn't give the impression of clinging to the past out of a spirit of reaction. Nor did he let himself be swept away by the progressive, leftist impulse then sweeping some Church circles, in which many curial cardinals sensed the fierce undertow of secularization and Marxism.

His was a voice that sounded just the right note in the ears of curial princes worried about a world where alien forces antithetical to the Church seemed to be triumphing. The 1970s, instead of hastening the spiritual springtime John XXIII had prayed for, had brought turmoil. In Italy the Vatican was shell-shocked by the passage of a divorce law in a national referendum in 1974. That defeat for Catholic traditionalism had come as a complete surprise to the Curia, revealing how weak the Church hierarchy's grasp of changing realities actually was.

The following year, 1975, had looked even more alarming. In Italy the Communist Party won a record number of votes in local elections, almost as many as the Christian Democrats. In Portugal a putsch brought a leftist military junta to power. In Greece a socialist left-wing party was voted into power. The United States had lost the war in Vietnam, defeated by a Marxist regime in Hanoi with help from the Soviet Union and Communist China. In Africa the former Portuguese colonies of Angola and Mozambique seemed to be heading onto the path of Marxism, while in Latin America a new liberation theology was drawing inspiration from class struggle at the expense of the established Church.

What Wojtyła offered these princes of the Church was the possibility of a seemingly original way out of the crisis now agitating society and the Church. As he preached to them that Lenten day, social and political systems must simultaneously allow self-determination to the individual, yet there must exist higher community interests and norms to which the individual will is subsumed.

In the Mathilde Chapel Cardinal Wojtyła proceeded with his sermon, his Italian coming ever more easily as he spoke. He could sense alongside him the presence of Paul VI, though the pope himself was in the little anteroom to the right of the altar. Suffering from prostate cancer, Paul further chastened his body by wearing beneath his robes a hair shirt with iron points that tortured his flesh. Wojtyła too wore something underneath his shirt: a Carmelite scapular to remind him of his mystical dedication to God.

"During these weeks numerous spiritual exercises are being held in the Polish Church," he continued, "not just in parish Lenten retreats, but also exercises designed exclusively for young people, who have made it clear that they want and need them. Often enough the number of those who wish to take part in such retreats exceeds our rather modest powers of organization. That is what happened this year, for example, in my diocese, with the students in the senior year of high school: There were only two thousand seats, but the number of requests greatly exceeded that."

A gust of consolation swept through the crimson and violet. In the West young people were moving further and further from the Church. Even among students who remained devout Catholics one often met ferocious critics of the ecclesiastical system. To some, though not all, of the bishops and cardinals of the Curia, the Polish Church looked like a happy island in a turbulent sea, despite the atheistic state that threatened it. In Poland the churches were packed, the seminaries overflowing with aspirants to the priesthood. The dioceses were exporting missionaries all over the world; and the young were proud to call themselves Catholic, if only by way of contesting Marxist-Leninist ideology and proclaiming Polish identity in the face of Moscow's hegemony.

Down through the ages, Poland had been a bulwark of Christianity against both Orthodox schismatics and the Turkish devil. Couldn't it be a bulwark against the new Satan, Muscovite communism and its international offshoots?

In the Curia there was widespread admiration for Cardinals Wyszyński and Wojtyła, but also an awareness of the crucial differences between them. Wojtyła neither represented the traditional anticommunism of the Church, nor, like Wyszyński, was he identified with an anticommunism continually forced to make difficult compromises with a hostile state. It seemed as if the archbishop of Kraków was living in a transcendent dimension. His confrontation with communism took place in the context not of a specific religious denomination or ideological issue, but of the rights of man, pure and simple. Jerzy Turowicz, editor of the Catholic weekly in Kraków, was on target when he ventured this definition of Wojtyła: "He's not a leftist; he's not a rightist; and he's not a nationalist either."

The Polish cardinal also knew how to act decisively to utilize the power of symbolism. For example, from his earliest days as a bishop he had tried to obtain a building permit for a long-promised church at Nowa Huta, the vast new industrial quarter built by the Communists on the edge of Kraków as a socialist model city. So he had spent Christmas Eve after Christmas Eve celebrating midnight mass outdoors in the snow and subzero cold at the site where the regime had reneged on its promise of a church. Once during the Mass of Resurrection on Easter he had proclaimed amid the huge cement housing blocks of Nowa Huta: "Many a time since those days, people have decreed the death of Christ . . . many a time they have announced the death of God, saying: 'There is no God.' But they didn't realize that if that is true, Man and his intellect become meaningless."

In his anteroom the pope, pale and ill, could hear the preacher's voice rising as he launched into his peroration. The pope especially appreciated the young Polish cardinal's initiative in convoking a diocesan synod at Kraków to implement the Council's teachings. Beginning in 1971 three hundred working groups had set almost eleven thousand people studying with an enthusiasm equaled in few countries of the Christian West.

Paul VI felt drawn to Wojtyła for many reasons. His resoluteness served as a counterweight to the hesitant character of the pope; his warm loyalty helped compensate for the sharp criticism he had received from the faithful and from dissenting theologians (notably on the question of birth control and other sexual issues). Wojtyła's meditations on the power of love—his words now enveloping the little Mathilde Chapel—matched the reflections of a pope who dreamt of a civilization of love.

When Wojtyła affirmed that the more love a person wants to give to others, the more he must renounce the love directed toward himself and the more he must forget about his personal concerns, he touched a profound chord in Paul VI. The pope, whose Curia thought of him as a closed and reserved person, felt within himself an immense need for joy and love. A German painter who had made a portrait of him once said that Paul VI was like an oyster, whose pearl remained always hidden.

One must try always to give more love than one receives, the preacher was saying. For the man seated on the papal throne, these were precious words indeed.

.   .   .

The spiritual exercises in the Vatican lasted a week. The sermons were given three times a day. For Karol Wojtyła they were a unique occasion for showing the curial cardinals his vision of the Church. Paul VI had suggested that he speak in Italian, not Latin; and this advice proved to be psychologically astute. Addressing the cardinals in their everyday language, the archbishop of Kraków was able to guide them better along the pathway of his ideas. Christ, the Gospel, the Church were signs of contradiction in the modern world, he said. All too often, modern society sought to shape the Gospel according to the distortions and diversions of consumerism, while in other places, the Church was simply persecuted. Surprisingly, he declared that the greater risk came from systems that appeared to be free and tolerant yet constantly undermined Christian values through materialism and hedonism. This too was a kind of programmatic persecution, he insisted, one fostered by liberal individualism.

When on the morning of March 13 Cardinal Wojtyła spoke for the last time in the Mathilde Chapel, Monsignor Andrzej Deskur looked with satisfaction on the Kraków Wunderkind whose rise in Vatican circles he was relentlessly supporting. His ascent had been gradual and remarkably unhindered. It had been helped considerably by Wojtyła's membership on the council of the Synod of Bishops, the body that did the preparatory work for the triennial assemblies. First elected to the council in 1971, he had come in third among the European candidates. In 1974 he moved into second place. Three years later he was elected again, but with fewer votes—perhaps a sign that some bishops were anxious to slow down his steady rise in the Church hierarchy.

Cardinal Secretary of State Jean Villot followed Wojtyła's Lenten sermons with particular attention. As a keen student of human nature, Villot noted the appeal the archbishop of Kraków had even for men as shrewd as the heads of the Curia. There was an aspect of his personality that didn't reveal itself at first blush, a hard, hidden core that sustained him: an iron will and an unlimited belief in the power of that will. "It is through the will that man is lord of his actions," Wojtyła had noted in one of his essays, adding that self-control is the most fundamental manifestation of the value of a person.

Anyone who ignored his winning smile, and instead looked him straight in the eye, knew this already.

THE POLISH LEGACY

In his heart, Cardinal Wyszyński had already designated Wojtyła the future primate of Poland. He discussed the matter in 1974 with his aide and confidant Romuald Kukołowicz: "I would like to strengthen the Polish Church as much as possible before my departure." Much more than Wyszyński, Wojtyła was able to reach the next post-Yalta generation of believers who were Poland's future. There was a real battle under way with the Communist Party for the souls of young people. Wojtyła understood their problems: low living standards, boring work in factories and offices, the blankness of the huge housing projects, their need for idealism, for personal achievement and freedom—and, not least of all, their attraction to a materialism and hedonism largely suppressed by the Communist system and equally disapproved of by the Church.

Since the Council Wyszyński had seen Wojtyła reluctantly mature as a political figure. "He quite obviously didn't want to get into politics," remembers Jacek Woźniakowski, a leading spokesman of the Catholic group Znak*

---

* Znak (The Sign, in Polish) was the name of a group of Catholic intellectuals gathered around the Znak publishing house, its monthly journal (also called Znak) and its weekly Catholic magazine Tygodnik Powszechny. After the war, Wojtyła began to write articles and poems that Tygodnik published under his pen name of Andrzej Jawień. Later, many of his contributions were under his own name.

in Kraków. "He thought he should stick to church matters; he thought that political problems should be left to laymen or to Cardinal Wyszyński." Wojtyła's refrain was always "I'm not very interested in politics." His friends, almost in desperation, repeatedly had to urge him not to be so standoffish because as archbishop of Kraków there was no way he could avoid politics.

Beginning in 1968, however, Poland became engulfed in a series of crises—both internal and with its Soviet neighbors—from which no one, not even Wojtyła, could long remain aloof. The party's hold on Polish society, always shaky, began to break down. In the spring of 1968, students went into the streets shouting anti-Soviet slogans after the cancellation—at the behest of the Soviet ambassador—of a performance in Warsaw of Adam Mickiewicz's patriotic (and anti-Russian play) *The Forefather's Eve,* a work Wojtyła had greatly admired since his acting days. Students were beaten and arrested, universities closed, and—as if to blame Jews for the unrest (though only thirty thousand remained in the country, from a prewar population of three million)—the interior ministry launched a hysterical anti-Semitic campaign. Virtually all Jews in the government and teaching professions were fired, those in the party were purged, and most left the country.

Wojtyła responded by publicly defending the students, and, as a further gesture, he invited the Jewish philosopher Roman Ingarden, his former professor at the Jagiellonian University, to hold a conference in the Kraków archdiocese.

Anti-Soviet feelings in the country were fanned that August, when Polish troops joined other Warsaw Pact forces in the invasion of Czechoslovakia and the suppression of the reformist Prague Spring. Sixteen months later, events in Poland took an irrevocable turn when the government raised food prices during the Christmas season. In that "Bloody December" of 1970, Polish workers went into the streets demanding better working conditions,

---

Between 1956 and 1976 a number of intellectuals affiliated with Znak decided to seek seats in the Polish parliament under the Znak banner and received permission from the Church hierarchy. Once elected, they became a small minority faction that was the voice of Catholicism in the parliament. Members of Znak also founded Poland's Klub Inteligencji Katolickiej (KIK—Clubs of Catholic Intellectuals).

higher wages, and a rollback of the price increases. In Gdańsk and other Baltic cities, as well as in Łódź, tanks fired on workers, and hundreds were killed.

Shaken by the specter of Poles killing Poles, Wojtyła hewed to Wyszyński's course, remaining at once politically cautious yet strongly supportive of the people. "When people are injured and suffering," he said during his Christmas sermon in Kraków, "the Church comes to their aid without any political motivation, solely out of Christian love and Christian solidarity." That New Year's Eve, however, he seemed to cross a political Rubicon when he called openly for the "right to food, the right to freedom . . . an atmosphere of genuine freedom, untrammeled . . . unthreatened; an atmosphere of inner freedom, of freedom from fearing what may befall me if I act this way or go to that place."

Eleven days earlier, responding to the crisis, the Communist Party had replaced Gomułka with Edward Gierek, the party chief of Silesia, who had worked in the coal mines in Belgium and France during the Nazi occupation. Leaning on his experience in the West, the former engineer promoted himself as one of a new breed of economic managers—a technocrat, not just another Communist *apparatchik.* He embarked on a course aimed at ensuring better relations with the West, the granting of loans by the United States and Western Europe to modernize Polish industry, and a resolute policy of appeasement toward the Vatican, marked by a spasm of church building.

Paradoxically, Gierek's interest in Western capital and his relative liberalism contributed to the country's economic crisis (his excessive borrowing mired Poland in debt). As it became increasingly apparent that the Communist Party wouldn't be able to maintain hegemonic power within society, Wojtyła learned to exploit this fact to the Church's advantage. He flooded the authorities with petitions and requests for new seminaries, churches, and public processions. He protested the government's attempt to prevent the teaching of the catechism to children; he demanded respect for the provisions of the 1950 accord between Church and state which exempted seminarians from the draft. He fought to affirm the freedom of Christians to express their faith without suffering discrimination. When the state cut the supply of newsprint to the dioceses and to *Znak,* the Kraków Catholic monthly, as a means of censoring the Catholic press, he objected loudly. From the pulpit and through his contributions to *Tygodnik Powszechny*—articles, speeches, homilies, poems, and essays—he defined his positions, which were carefully worked out, principled, unusually devoid of empty rhetoric, and always based on his personalist Christian philosophy.

He began to work side by side with militants from the only clandestine Catholic group directly sponsored by Cardinal Wyszyński: Odrodzenie (Rebirth), which had been founded in the 1920s as an association to promote a Catholic renaissance in Poland. After conspiratorial activities during the war, it had continued under the Communist regime as a clandestine training ground for a Catholic lay elite. Its members, in Wyszyński's view, could pursue the agenda of the Church's hierarchy in situations where the clergy preferred to stay behind the scenes. Little groups of Odrodzenie could be found in every Polish diocese. Wojtyła was regularly invited to address Odrodzenie gatherings (disguised as pilgrimages) in the sanctuary of the Black Madonna in Częstochowa, where he spoke about religious and social problems.

"Once he decided that he would have to get involved with politics after all," says Woźniakowski, "I was struck by what a quick study he was, how rapidly he assimilated information, how he reshaped it to his way of thinking, and how, especially after following a long political discussion in silence, he had this extremely interesting way of summing things up."

During meetings with his Znak friends in the archbishop's palace in Kraków, Wojtyła often seemed far away. While they were discussing the Church and the regime, religion and civic life, he sat at his desk, reading documents, writing letters. Then almost effortlessly he would produce a statement, focusing precisely on the key points under discussion.

Watching how easily Wojtyła took on political responsibilities, Woźniakowski had an intuition: "Given this unsuspected talent of his, I thought for the first time that he might become pope, though in the very distant future."

Wojtyła's meetings with intellectuals became a method of governing the diocese of Kraków. In his residence he met not just with the editors of *Tygodnik Powszechny*, but with historians, mathematicians, philosophers, scientists, writers, actors, musicians. He questioned them about Poland, about the world beyond. In a break with traditional church bureaucracy, his office door was always open—literally—to the priests of the diocese; and he expended great care on his pastoral visits to all his parishes.

Józef Mucha, his chauffeur during these years, still recalls with astonishment the archbishop's exhausting daily schedule. "At half-past five he was already in the chapel at the residence. Around seven he went to the Franciscan church across the street, where he prayed for a long time. He was back at eight for breakfast. Afterwards he went to the chapel again, closed the door, and worked, prayed, and read till eleven."

On the left side of the chapel, not far from the altar, Archbishop Wojtyła had a seat built for himself with a kneeler and a little table of dark wood. That way he could write and pray at the same time. He could also look out a window onto the garden courtyard where he used to walk as a clandestine seminarian, or he could seek inspiration in the tabernacle.

"After eleven," Mucha goes on, "the archbishop received in his study anyone who wished to speak with him." Lunch—the principal meal of the day—was at one-thirty, and afterward Wojtyła took a ten-minute nap in his armchair in the bedroom. "If his nap lasted a quarter of an hour, he would jump up shouting, 'Oh dear, I overslept five minutes.' "

In the episcopal palace, Wojtyła maintained the spartan style he was most comfortable with. Though his study and bedroom were relatively large, they were furnished very simply. The varnish on his desk was peeling, and his plain bed was covered with a worn bedspread. On the wall were a Renaissance Madonna and a wintry Polish landscape. His rosary lay on a bedside table. He owned seven cassocks—four red and three black—and three pairs of shoes, all black.

Afternoons were often devoted to visits to the 329 parishes in the archdiocese. Evenings were spent discussing the Church's problems in Poland with his friends from Znak and *Tygodnik Powszechny*. Occasionally he would drink a little wine or a beer with them.

Even while riding in his car the archbishop continued to work virtually nonstop. Mucha had built him a wooden book rest with a lamp, so that

Wojtyła could read when it was dark. "When he traveled by car he always had four briefcases with him," his chauffeur reports, "and two of them were full of books."

One thing Karol Wojtyła rarely did then (or does today) was read newspapers; nor was he particularly interested in watching the news on television or hearing it on the radio. Every two weeks Father Bardecki, the religious editor of *Tygodnik*, came to his study in the archbishop's palace and gave him a summary of the news from the heavily censored newspapers of Poland and state-run TV. In the era of mass media Wojtyła has refused to be personally connected to this seemingly essential feature of contemporary life—even while making as potent use of it as any figure in history.

.   .   .

June 1976 brought a new outburst of anger and hatred toward the Communist regime in Poland. Bloody clashes between workers and police took place in Radom, Ursus, and other urban centers after the government again raised food prices. It was the same situation that had led to the fall of Gomułka.

Poland and the Church were propelled to a new level of conflict when a general strike was declared. The primate and Wojtyła supported the workers' grievances but urged them to return to their jobs and successfully prevailed upon the government not to bring charges against, or otherwise punish, any of the strikers.

"We cannot afford to be irresponsible, for we are in a very difficult geographical position," declared Cardinal Wojtyła in his New Year's Eve sermon in 1976. But for the archbishop of Kraków, recognizing the reality of Yalta—Russian domination in Eastern Europe—didn't mean that Poles had to surrender their sense of nationhood. "The past year has shown that we had to take up the fight for the basic truths of our existence as a nation and a state. We had to repeat again and again that the state exists for the nation, and not the other way around. After so many struggles, so many wars on various fronts, after so much suffering, this nation deserves to be free and independent."

Seizing the momentum from the strike, in November 1976 a group of intellectuals, among them the dissident former Marxists Jacek Kuroń and Adam Michnik, formed a Committee for the Defense of the Workers, known by its initials, KOR. Many of KOR's leaders had been leftists, but now they gravitated toward the Church. The Catholic Intellectual Clubs (KIK), of which Wojtyła was chaplain, became more openly involved in defending the rights of citizens. "Flying universities"—underground seminars to counter official propaganda—were encouraged by the arch-bishop, who allowed Kraków's churches and monasteries to be used for classes.

After June 1976, Wojtyła perceived a new vulnerability in the system, a real opening for the Church and the people to win basic rights and freedoms that the Communists had heretofore been adamant in suppressing. From 1976 to 1978 Wojtyła delivered a body of homilies that stirred a movement of spiritual resistance. Reading them is, in some ways, not unlike reading the great sermons that Martin Luther King Jr. delivered during America's moral and political crisis a decade earlier. Increasingly he directly criticized the government's abuse of moral authority in its treatment of workers, dissenters, intellectuals, students, and believers. Inevitably, he invoked the example of St. Stanisław:

> St. Stanisław has become the patron saint of moral and social order in the country. . . . He dared to tell the king himself that he was bound to respect the law of God. The age-old veneration of St. Stanisław is, in fact, a confession of the truth that moral law is the foundation of social order. He was also the defender of the freedom that is the inalienable right of every man, so that the violation of that freedom by the State is at the same time a violation of the moral and social order.

He persistently attacked censorship of the press (his own sermons were often excised by the regime from Catholic periodicals) and proclaimed the right of all citizens to voice their opinions. "We want the climate of truth to be core of our social life," he said in another sermon in 1977. "We want to see a true picture of ourselves in newspapers, in the radio, on television. We do not want an artificially contrived truth, a manipulated public opinion. . . . We do not want an authority based on police truncheons."

"We sometimes hear it said that there is to be a second Poland [a reference to Gierek's economic reforms]," Wojtyła declared in his Christmas sermon that year. "But there is only one Poland, and this second one, if it is to be Poland, must spring from the first. It may not deny any element of our national and cultural heritage."

Wojtyła's most impassioned, extensive, and carefully reasoned declarations on human rights were delivered before many thousands of young people who in the Corpus Christi processions of 1977 and 1978 thronged the area of Wawel Hill, partly in tribute to a student opposition leader, who they believed had been murdered by the authorities. (The regime claimed he had died accidentally.) To the assembled young people in 1977 the cardinal said:

> Human rights cannot be given in the form of concessions. Man is
> born with them and seeks to realize them in the course of his life.
> And if they are not realized or experienced, then man rebels. And
> it cannot be otherwise, because he is man. His sense of honor
> expects it.

As Wojtyła spoke, a military jet roared overhead in an effort to drown out his words. This produced derisive laughter from the crowd, which applauded and cheered rapturously when the cardinal looked upward and greeted the "uninvited guest." The jet having completed its flyover, he resumed: "And it is impossible to resolve these problems by means of oppression. Police and prisons provide no answer either. They only raise the price that will ultimately have to be paid. . . . There is only one road to peace and national unity, and that is through unfettered respect for the rights of man, for the rights of citizens and Poles."

He praised the students—"the mature and independent youth"—for the peacefulness of their protests throughout the spring. "They are capable of thinking about basic issues like social justice and peace, the rights of the human person, the rights of the Nation." He concluded by addressing the crucified Christ: "I apologize to the Lord Jesus Christ, because I didn't—at least apparently—speak about Him. But only apparently. Actually I spoke so that we all may understand that He, who is living in this Sacrament, lives our human life."

.   .   .

Thus, Cardinal Wyszyński could rest assured that his office would be in good hands. Wojtyła was to be primate of Poland. Wyszyński had clearly said so to his trusted aide Kukołowicz.

On August 26, 1978, the College of Cardinals, including Wojtyła, met in conclave at the Vatican and chose a new pope to succeed Paul VI. He was sixty-six-year-old Albino Luciani, the patriarch of Venice. People liked his smile and the obvious humanity of his manner. He took the name John Paul I, from his two immediate predecessors. Non-Italian cardinals were heartened by the election of a man who hadn't been part of the apparatus of the Curia. Everything seemed settled for years to come, perhaps even for the rest of the century.

MME. TYMIENIECKA

In 1974, a vivacious, cosmopolitan Polish aristocrat entered the cardinal's office convinced she had found a kindred philosophical spirit. Her name was Anna-Teresa Tymieniecka, and for the next four years she and the cardinal embarked on a philosophical dialogue that resulted in a recasting and definitive English-language edition of his most important written work, *The Acting Person.*

Later, after he was elected pope, reporters would scour the earth looking for women who had been Karol Wojtyła's lover, wife, or companion. They found none because there were none.

But in the process, they overlooked the crucial role of Dr. Anna-Teresa Tymieniecka in his life: her influence on his philosophy and thus on his papacy. They missed the fact that she helped to make him prominent—and *papabile.*

Until Mme. Tymieniecka, the major figures in the adult life of Karol

Wojtyła had been men. Her interaction with the cardinal—weeks spent writing together, taking walks, laboring over the text of *The Acting Person*—and her introduction of Wojtyła first to the European philosophical community and then to American audiences were formative experiences for the young cardinal.

The story of their remarkable collaboration is recorded in their correspondence, more than ninety pieces of which are under lock and key in a Harvard University library; in Tymieniecka's uncontroverted written account, in her interviews with the authors of this book; and in the personal testimony of Dr. George Hunston Williams, a professor at Harvard Divinity School, author of *The Mind of John Paul II: Origins of His Thought and Action* (1981), and a friend of Tymieniecka's.

Dr. Williams is a Protestant minister who was an official observer at Vatican Council II, where he befriended Bishop Wojtyła. In his book he briefly notes Tymieniecka's role as co-author of the English-language edition of *The Acting Person*, but never mentions the personal relationship that developed between the two or the extent of their collaboration. Nonetheless, he and others say that the Vatican became extremely unhappy with his book solely because of its mention of her work with the cardinal and sought to disavow it in Catholic circles. Elsewhere the book was widely praised.

There were two primary reasons for the Vatican's reaction, according to both Dr. Williams and Mme. Tymieniecka: First, the Vatican feared news reports that a woman personally known to Wojtyła had influenced the future pope's thinking and writing; and second, the project on which they collaborated, a massive reworking of the original Polish edition of *Osoba i Czyn* (literally Person and Act), embraced the modern philosophy of phenomenology at the expense of Thomism—the teachings of St. Thomas Aquinas which for centuries have guided Catholic philosophy.

In 1977 Cardinal Wojtyła profusely acknowledged his debt to Mme. Tymieniecka in a handwritten introduction reproduced in the book, and a year before he signed over to her the world rights for this new English version, which he proclaimed the only "definitive" and authorized edition. He directed that all future editions of the book be translated from it rather than from the original Polish.

However, when Wojtyła became pope a papal commission appointed to consider how to handle the suddenly valuable literary output of Karol Wojtyła urged the new pope to disavow the work he had done with Mme. Tymieniecka, get back the rights to *Osoba i Czyn*, and redesignate the original Polish edition as the authentic text. Representatives of the Vatican tried—unsuccessfully—to stop both publication and distribution of the Tymieniecka version of the book.

John Paul II did not question the recommendations or actions of the commission, and a period of estrangement followed between the new pope and Mme. Tymieniecka—although he continued to write to her regularly (almost every month, she says) and, less often, to members of her family. Meanwhile, she engaged lawyers and considered suing the supreme pontiff of the Roman Catholic Church or his representatives for copyright infringement. She began assembling a meticulous record of their collaboration and correspondence and turned it over to various persons and institutions for safekeeping and eventual release upon her death. Against the wishes of the Vatican, she persisted in publishing their joint effort, and it remains in print as the standard English edition. When it was published, the Vatican launched a campaign in the Catholic press against Tymieniecka's work on the book, intimating that her thoughts had usurped Wojtyła's, resulting in an overly phenomenological interpretation of his ideas.

She has characterized the pope's public silence in the dispute as a peronal "betrayal," though she and the pope have since reconciled. In the papal entourage, however, there is no question about the authenticity of either their collaboration or the philosophical content of the resulting book.*

"He was an incomparable philosophical partner," says Tymieniecka,

---

* Dr. Joaquín Navarro-Valls, the pope's spokesman, concedes that the commission was "overprotective" in its handling of the Tymieniecka matter. He also praises her work: "The book is more phenomenology than Thomist but this is the beauty of the book," he says. "From a philosophical and literary point of view, it is an outstanding analysis. . . . I think this is the last outstanding book written on phenomenology." He explains the commission's behavior as follows: "Imagine the situation of a new pope with a certain amount of literary and philosophical production, and he is a non-Italian pope and most people didn't know the works of Wojtyła; and they [the commission] felt they must be protective of the image of the pope. . . . The confusion with those circumstances could be

who was born in the late 1920s. "Ours was a philosophical partnership. He said so too, but whether he really meant it is another question. He expressed it very vividly."

In one of his letters to her, dated February 8, 1979, Pope John Paul II reminisced about their relationship: "In this respect I have myself to a considerable degree relied upon your competence, experience or—as I nevertheless believe—your intuition. Do not defend yourself against it, because it is intuition (and not only some 'erudition') that is your enormous strength precisely as a philosopher."

It is her contention—and Dr. Williams supports it, as do many other experts on the Wojtyła papacy—that there is a direct connection between *The Acting Person*, particularly the English edition, and the encyclicals, pronouncements, and philosophy of Pope John Paul II. "Their work together was extremely important," says Williams. "And afterward the Vatican and the pope behaved rather badly in trying to suppress knowledge of their collaboration."

Discussing the encyclical *Veritatis Splendor* (The Splendor of Truth), perhaps the pope's masterpiece, Dr. Williams says: "It is part of the relationship. He cannot be understood, even as pontiff, without this encyclical; he couldn't have done what he's done without that relationship [with Tymieniecka]. It cannot be wiped out of the biographical, intellectual account."

The original Polish text of *Osoba i Czyn*, never formally edited by anyone but Bishop Karol Wojtyła, was a much less developed, imprecise, and (by

---

huge, the situation was so new, [that the response would have been] 'let us take care how this can be interpreted.' "

Meanwhile, the commission was under pressure from some Polish academics as well, who contended that the English translation used by Tymieniecka and Wojtyła in their joint edition was faulty.

However, Dr. Rocco Buttiglione, a protégé of Wojtyła's and the author of a book about the pope's philosophy, also praises Tymieniecka's work, and calls her Wojtyła's "partner in a philosophical dialogue" in *The Acting Person*. "I think that it was a very positive dialogue between Tymieniecka and the Holy Father. . . . [T]he dialogue with Tymieniecka helped the Holy Father to further some aspects of [his own] thought. . . . I would say that Tymieniecka helped Wojtyła to consider the possibility of recasting his own thought in more phenomenological terms, and giving a phenomenological form to some concepts he had acquired through Thomist metaphysics. So she may have helped Wojtyła to reach the idea of a more intimate contact between phenomenology and Thomism."

many accounts) almost impenetrably dense work than the version produced through their collaboration.

The pope's friend and philosophical protégé Tadeusz Styczeń wrote in December 1978 in *Tygodnik Powszechny* that, "due to the care of Professor Teresa Tymieniecka, director of the World Institute for Advanced Phenomenological Research and Learning, this work . . . is not a translation in the ordinary sense of the word, for the work has been enriched with new reflections by the author, contains a series of new analyses and a new precision . . . so much so that we could talk about a new book worthy to be translated into Polish."

Dr. Tymieniecka does not maintain that the underlying philosophy of the English edition of *The Acting Person* is hers rather than Wojtyła's. Her role in his thought, she says, was "influential." She and other experts maintain that her work enabled Wojtyła to articulate and refine his ideas through what she has described as the development of the cardinal's "philosophical style." Eventually Cardinal Wojtyła wrote in his preface to the English-language edition that Dr. Tymieniecka was responsible for the book's "maturation" and "its final shape."

In essence, she was a collaborator and editor. Until her presence in the cardinal's life, he had been ignored and even rejected by the philosophical community.

" 'You know, the Polish Catholic philosophers didn't think very much of this book,' " Tymieniecka says the cardinal told her at their first meeting. "He was very discouraged about his book. He was discouraged in general with this reception of his book—and his philosophy."

But perhaps just as important as the contents of the English-language edition is the story of the collaboration itself. The cardinal and his philosophical partner spent countless hours together, and in the process Tymieniecka—the wife of a distinguished Harvard professor who served on President Richard Nixon's Council of Economic Advisors—became one of the few witnesses to his character outside the narrow ecclesiastical circle of his Polish milieu.

During a period of four years, they worked together on the manuscript in Kraków, in Rome, in Vermont, in Switzerland, and in Naples and maintained a regular dialogue and correspondence that turned, by her account, for the most part on philosophy. On at least two occasions during their collaboration, she says, they quarreled seriously—though she will not say about what. Theirs was "a philosophical dialogue between two independent minds," Dr. Williams observes.

She promoted him, helped plan his first extended visit to the United States, and arranged for Harvard to invite him to deliver his first American lecture. Working with the apostolic delegate to the United States, she secured speaking engagements in Washington. She managed to get him an invitation to tea with President Gerald Ford in the White House (the cardinal had to decline because of a schedule conflict), and she flooded the media with press releases announcing the visit to America of the distinguished Polish cardinal who some Europeans were saying might be in the running for the papacy.

Wojtyła and his private secretary, Father Stanisław Dziwisz, stayed at the Vermont country home of Mme. Tymieniecka in the summer of 1976. The cardinal celebrated mass each morning at a picnic table in the backyard; he borrowed her husband's shorts to wear beneath his swimming trunks when they swam in a neighbor's pond; and they took long walks (usually in the company of Dziwisz) to discuss philosophy and their work.

She devoted herself totally to the project for four years, visiting him six times each year in Kraków and Rome, working with his secretary and with the cardinal, and then returning to her home in New England to work alone on the manuscript.

Meanwhile, during the period of their collaboration many of Cardinal Wojtyła's philosophical reflections and papers—previously published only in Poland—were translated into English and published in the *Analecta Husserliana*, the hardbound publication of the International Husserl and Phenomenological Research Society, of which Dr. Tymieniecka was the director. He also presented papers at many philosophical congresses in Europe, as arranged by Tymieniecka.

•   •   •

When asked whether she had developed a romantic attachment to the cardinal archbishop—however one-sided it might have been—Tymieniecka, a

Catholic, says, "No, I never fell in love with the cardinal. How could I fall in love with a middle-aged clergyman? Besides, I am a married woman."

But Dr. Williams, who has spent hundreds of hours in conversation with her has no doubt that such an attachment did develop. "Yes, of course there was that. Eros is the basis of philosophy in a way. You have to love. She is a passionate human being. Hers was a catholic passion towards Wojtyła, that is to say, it was restrained by his ecclesiastical dignity and her own understanding of what restraints there would be. But there would be a lot of emotion, within those limits, on her part."

Having observed Wojtyła in her presence and discussed the situation with Mme. Tymieniecka, Dr. Williams concludes, "I don't think he understands what she's coping with when she's in his presence. . . . A magnet pulls steel particles. He doesn't know that."

Dr. Tymieniecka, small, pixyish, blond, has described Wojtyła as sexually naive, both in his manner and in his writing in *Love and Responsibility*. "The cardinal was modesty itself" in their relationship, she says. "He is a man in supreme command of himself, who has elaborated this beautiful, harmonious personality." She adds:

> To have written [as he has] about love and sex is to know very little about it. I was truly astounded when I read *Love and Responsibility*. I thought he obviously does not know what he is talking about. How can he write about such things? The answer is he doesn't have experiences of that sort. *Love and Responsibility* is not only about sexuality. Its philosophy is linked to *The Acting Person*.
>
> He's innocent sexually, but not otherwise. To be a cardinal under the Communists he had to be extremely shrewd. There is no naiveté. This is a very clever person who knows what he is doing.

To an inquiry about a sexual component or attraction in her relationship with the pope, Tymieniecka replied: "I will be extremely personal and tell you that I am not interested in sexuality. In any way. I am an old-fashioned Polish lady who considers that this is not a matter for conversation of any sort."

.　　.　　.

Anna-Teresa Tymieniecka was born on an estate in Masovia in Poland and was educated at the Jagiellonian University in Kraków, where she studied in 1945–46 under Roman Ingarden—the phenomenologist whose work also influenced Karol Wojtyła around the same time.

She left Kraków in 1946, the year she got her bachelor's degree, as the Communist government began dividing up the large estates of the old Polish nobility. Thereafter she made her home in Paris and Fribourg, Switzerland. She received her M.A. from the Sorbonne in 1951 and her Ph.D. from the University of Fribourg in 1952, where for six years she had been working on her doctorate under the direction of Professor Ignacy Bochenski.

Bochenski, an authority on Marxist philosophy, was a Polish priest who had been chosen by Archbishop Sapieha to carry a letter to Pope Pius XII seeking the Vatican's aid in working against the Nazi occupation of Poland. The letter fell on deaf ears.

In 1954, Mme. Tymieniecka came to the United States and subsequently taught philosophy as an instructor at the University of California at Berkeley and mathematics at Oregon State University. She completed postdoctoral research at Yale, became an assistant professor of philosophy at Pennsylvania State University, and lectured at Bryn Mawr College.

.　　.　　.

The story of the relationship between Karol Wojtyła and Anna-Teresa Tymieniecka begins in 1972, when Tymieniecka, then in her mid-forties, acquired a copy of *Osoba i Czyn*, published in 1967 by Karol Wojtyła. "At the time the author [was] completely unknown to me," Tymieniecka has written.

A brief perusal quickly showed that this work displayed certain affinities with my own work in phenomenology, as evidenced in [Tymieniecka's] *Eros and Logos* (published in 1962). In my book I had argued forcefully for the priority of action over cognition as *the key to an understanding of human being*—in opposition to the prevail-

136

ing emphasis in phenomenology upon the priority of the cognitive character of intentional constitution. . . .

I was astounded, and not a little excited, by the thought that another philosopher had arrived at a point of view so compatible with my own. My interest in this book was, therefore, understandable. . . . Here, at last, was a kindred spirit.

In 1972 and 1973, she kept talking to her students about "a book of genius" by Cardinal Wojtyła. When in the spring of 1973 she was invited by the Seventh Centennial International Thomas Aquinas Congress to represent American scholarship on its Scientific Committee, she went to Poland to invite the cardinal to present a paper in the phenomenology section, which she was to moderate.

"The cardinal, whom I had contacted by mail, answered my invitation by granting me an audience on July 29 at [his residence] in Kraków," she has written. "He was surprised to find such admiration for his philosophical thinking, since his work had been severely criticized on all points by a number of Catholic philosophers in the course of a symposium in Lublin devoted to the discussion of his thought. However, after a further audience, I was able to overcome his reluctance to take part in an international forum of professional philosophers, and he promised to contribute a paper."

Their first conversation was in one of the drawing rooms of the archbishop's palace, where they sat and chatted for about an hour. Wojtyła, she says, told her he "was startled by my visit. He said he was definitely amazed that I came from abroad to tell him I considered *Osoba i Czyn* a great book."

The cardinal's secretary, Sister Eufrozja, was delighted that someone had taken a positive interest in Wojtyła's philosophy, and when the two women had tea and cookies together in the sisters' refectory she encouraged Tymieniecka to return the next day. "That's when I gave the speech [to Sister Eufrozja]," says Tymieniecka. "I wanted to work on her to convince him. I said I was inviting him to address the Thomas Aquinas conference in Naples. I wanted him to represent Catholicism—I had a Jew and a Protestant. I saw him as having ideas very congenial with my own. . . . I gave her an enormous speech—on the theme that we needed a leader of Christianity in the world because everything was falling apart—that I came there because I'd read his book. I said I needed him because I am a laywoman, a freethinker, and I needed someone [in the conference] to represent Christianity."

In their subsequent correspondence, the cardinal and Tymieniecka agreed that he would appear in Naples and Rome for the Aquinas congress, deliver a paper at the plenary session on "Self-Determination as the Constitutive Structure of the Person," and then participate in her phenomenology colloquium. At the conference itself, held from April 17 to 24, 1974, Cardinal Wojtyła also accepted her invitation to contribute future papers to the scholarly journal *Analecta Husserliana.*

According to Tymieniecka, they had by then started discussing the possibility of an English edition of *Osoba i Czyn* on which both would work and which she would have published by the phenomenology society.

> This was on my part a labor of love, to make him known and to bring him proper recognition as a philosopher. . . . My condition was that we do it together. He wanted me to do it alone [edit the work], and I refused. I said, "Only if we do it together."

In November, after receiving a letter from the cardinal responding positively to her suggestions for more undertakings like the one at the Aquinas congress, Tymieniecka traveled to Kraków to visit Wojtyła again. During this visit, which lasted more than a month, they agreed that she would publish an English translation of *Osoba i Czyn* in volume 10 of the *Analecta Husserliana,* and a contract was drawn giving Tymieniecka exclusive worldwide publication rights. Meanwhile the cardinal commissioned a professional translator in Poland to begin work on an English version of the manuscript. Tymieniecka has recalled:

> [M]y very first discussion with the prospective translator on July 13, 1975 did suffice to bring out the enormous difficulties involved in rendering the book into English. The criticisms delivered by the Polish scholars did appear to be justified in many respects. When questioned by me on this point the author admitted that he had

never edited his book for publication, and that after he had committed it to paper the typewritten text was simply printed.

This had always been Wojtyła's method, and it appears to be one of the reasons that so many of his writings are considered vague, difficult, or inaccessible. In addition to "innumerable deficiencies in the text," the original included "unfinished sentences, improper grammar, vague expressions, a profusion of repetitions, and unfinished analyses," Tymieniecka has said.

At this point, according to Tymieniecka and others, their collaboration began in earnest: an undertaking that stretched over the next three years, in which she arranged other appearances for him at European philosophical conferences (in Rome in March and September of 1976, for instance), usually of a week or more duration. In 1975 she began working on arrangements to bring him to the United States for a speaking tour the following summer, in conjunction with his participation in the Eucharistic Congress in Philadelphia. Her purpose was "to introduce this great thinker to the international community."

Meanwhile, the pattern of their collaboration on the book was established during the conferences in European cities, around the table at the Collegio Polacco when Wojtyła was in Rome on ecclesiastical business, and on the visits she made to Poland.

I went to Poland three times a year, and Rome three times a year. Five weeks to Poland each visit, and two to three weeks to Rome each visit, for four years. In Poland, I would stay at least three weeks in Kraków during which we worked together any time he had the time. . . . He would send me a note or Sister Eufrozja would call.

I stayed with my friends, usually university people—sometimes in a hotel. . . . He would send a note on the day before [they would meet]. For five weeks I was available whenever he was available: two weeks in Warsaw and three in Kraków. An absolute dedication. We had enormous discussions, the most fascinating philosophical discussions, about his book and his other writings. And my writings, he was reading all my writings at this time—not all of them, but whatever I gave him.

A picture from around this time on the piano at her house in Vermont shows her as a fetching, diminutive woman in a miniskirt, her blond hair pulled back in a short ponytail.

During each five-week period of work together in Europe, they would usually be able to meet six to eight times, she says:

> Sometimes [for] one hour, sometimes for lunch or for dinner, or for breakfast, or when he could find a little time. . . . Once for three hours in a car ride to Bologna and then back, just to discuss the book. He had no time. He was traveling all the time through the diocese. We met once or twice [during each of her stays in Kraków] for a day's outing during which we went for six hours to discuss philosophy. These were walks in the woods—he was a dedicated walker. I managed. I was rather on the weak side. These would be with Dziwisz. The three of us. . . . Often we went to the mountaineering part of the countryside, and the [Communist] secret service would follow the cardinal. Mucha [the cardinal's chauffeur] would try to lose them.

This point has an interesting footnote: After Wojtyła became pope, Polish Communist sources and police documents were the basis for some of the unfounded suppositions and rumors that Karol Wojtyła had had a relationship—presumably sexual—with a Polish woman while a prelate. In fact, the woman that undercover agents apparently *had* seen him with on several occasions was in all likelihood Mme. Tymieniecka.

They talked about literature, nature, poetry, anthropology:

> We had a dialogue all the time between two philosophers—it went far beyond the book; that was the whole charm of this work. Had we not done this, I probably would not have developed such

a devotion to the book. He was an incomparable philosophical partner.

As for *The Acting Person* itself, the broad themes were "already articulated in the book in Polish. We were concentrating on smaller philosophical points; there were very unclear formulations to be addressed, sentences had to be finished. But the big themes were clear."

These were the same broad themes that would become the basis of his philosophy as pope:

> In *The Acting Person* are found most of his politics of the Church as pope. These were the reasons why he was capable of leading Christianity, and why I went to Kraków the first time. They went against the tendencies of the Church culture of the time. He stressed the self-determination of a human being: that it is in the hands of an individual to delineate his life, to work out his life; and consequently a society and political system have to give the individual the opportunity for self-determination.
>
> If, on the one hand, the social-political system does not give this self-determination its proper rights—as in totalitarianism and communism, which suppress the self-determination of the human being—then the state is pernicious. On the other hand, if societies and cultures allow the individual to become strictly individualistic and oblivious to the community ties which self-determination both calls for and establishes—then social cooperation disintegrates.

. . .

Wojtyła's visit to the United States in 1976 was a triumph. It was also the first time he caught the attention of a large and influential American audience. "I wanted to introduce him as a great personality, a great statesman, but nobody would accept that at first," says Tymieniecka. "He came from an inconsequential country, and nobody knew him. I got him a dinner at the Harvard president's house—two hundred fifty people—and the university gave him a car and driver, and all the Polish professors were to receive the cardinal at his arrival." The formal invitation for Wojtyła to speak at Harvard had been extended by Dr. Williams.

At Harvard his lecture was extremely well received by both academics and leaders of the Church and was accorded extensive news coverage, including an article in the *New York Times*. Indeed, at a luncheon at Harvard attended by university officials and the press, Tymieniecka's husband, Harvard Professor Hendrik Houthakker, a Dutch-born Jew who had spent time in a Nazi internment camp, introduced Wojtyła as the next pope.

During the three weeks between the Eucharistic Congress and Cardinal Wojtyła's lectures and meetings with American Catholic leaders in Washington and other cities, he stayed twice at Tymieniecka's house in the Vermont woods—six or seven days in all. (In Washington, she acted as hostess for both a dinner and reception in the Cardinal's honor.)

This period, Mme. Tymieniecka says, was the most intense of their collaboration, an impression shared by Professors Williams and Houthakker. The situation, says Tymieniecka, "was beautiful; we were doing marvelous things, an incomparable philosophical dialogue. He would work in the kitchen. When he sits at the table he concentrates extremely intensely and does not get up until he finishes. . . . Then he reflects on it."

She had decided to receive the cardinal in "the most American way possible." Breakfast was Quaker Oats. "Everybody went swimming in the neighbor's pond. Mass was under the tree, on a picnic table at seven-thirty A.M., so my son could assist [before work]. Father Dziwisz was the altar boy. We had animals—a horse, a goat, a donkey—and they approached during the mass to see what was going on."

Sometimes she and Wojtyła worked for sixteen hours a day, she says, often taking long walks, discussing "philosophy, society, literature, poetry. We had enormous discussions. . . . He was planning after *The Acting Person* another volume of what he considered to be anthropology, a treatise on ethics, which eventually became the basis for *Veritatis Splendor.*"

She found him "the most elegant man . . . the most elegant actor. There is an ingredient of perfect composure and a very smooth—this is the key—self-control in his behavior. It should not be forgotten that he was trained as an actor." She continues:

> He has developed in himself an attitude of modesty, a very solicitous way of approaching people. He makes a person feel there is nothing else on his mind, he is ready to do everything for the other person. . . . Due to his innate personal charm, which is one of his greatest weapons, he has in addition a poetical nature, a captivating way of dealing with people. These are all evidences of his charisma—even the way in which he moves, though now it is no more, now that he is an old gentleman. He had a way of moving, a way of smiling, a way of looking around that was different and exceedingly personal. It had a beauty about it.

Gradually, listening to the cardinal express his thoughts and working with him over a long period in intellectually intimate circumstances, Tymieniecka reached some other conclusions about him.

> The greatest power of the pope, this special calling, is Christ-like. What does it consist of? He sees someone for the first time in his life and he is able to open to this man a hidden treasury of brotherhood. Christ himself could not do it better. This is why people are so mesmerized by him. By his smile, by his warmly emotional attitude, which is so solicitous, as if [the other person] were the closest brother, the closest kin to whom the pope gives himself entirely. This is beyond the question of pose or reality. It is essence.
>
> People around him see the sweetest, [most] modest person. They never see this iron will behind it. That *is* the pope. His is the most relaxed manner. The incredible work going on in his mind, you don't see it. . . . His usual attitude [with others] is suavity. His iron will is exercised with suavity and enormous discretion. It doesn't manifest itself directly. To some extent this is the pose.

But it is a second nature, not altogether a pose. Probably he was always like this. You look at his pictures [as a youth]: a very sweet type of a boy—very thoughtful, even slightly sentimental.

If there is one trait of character which I can observe in him it is love of contradiction. . . . Perseverance is another primary characteristic. He never sees an obstacle. Nothing is an obstacle.

"He's extremely proud," she learned, "terribly sensitive to pride. This is an extremely multifaceted human being, extremely colorful. He is by no means as humble as he appears. Neither is he modest. He thinks about himself very highly, very adequately."

Does he ever change his mind? Tymieniecka was asked.

I have the impression he does not. He's very interested in new ideas. He's open to new ideas when they are consistent with his. He is a very systematic person. This is not a man who acts by trial and error. He's not experimenting. He entered the papacy as a mature man in possession of a system. The rest of his life is about implementing it.

·   ·   ·

Mme. Tymieniecka found Wojtyła wise, except when discussing the West and the United States. Tymieniecka concluded that many of the cardinal's impressions were wrong and his lack of knowledge disturbing. And she got the impression that he saw Communist rule in the East as impregnable. She discussed these subjects with her husband—though not much else about the details of the time she spent with Wojtyła. Dr. Houthakker recalls:

She felt that he considered the Communists to be more powerful than they really were. My wife had the impression that Wojtyła thought that in the long run the Communists would prevail, so that in a way he was fighting a losing battle. He was very much aware of the power of the Soviet system. He was not aware of the power of the Western system.

. . . My wife was certainly concerned about his lack of understanding for the West. She talked to him about the nature of this society which is so different from the society in which he was brought up. . . . He tended to regard Western countries and especially the United States as immoral, amoral perhaps. He had no real appreciation of the virtues of democracy. She on at least two occasions was instrumental in telling him that he was going to sound like Savonarola in the United States, and she told him that it's a wonderful country; and of course there are things that she may not like, but there are certain things that he can't say. She persuaded him not to express his disdain or alarm about the decadence in the West and in the United States in particular. This is very important, because he could have spoiled his reception in the United States by the things he was going to say.

Later, in a conversation with Houthakker in the Vatican after Wojtyła became pope, the impression was intensified: "I tried to talk to him about the merits of capitalism and democracy," Houthakker says, "but I had a feeling I wasn't getting anywhere."

During the Wojtyła papacy, more than a few American bishops would have the same experience.

. . . .

Observing the relationship between his wife and Wojtyła over the years, Dr. Houthakker says:

You have to realize that my wife and I have somewhat different spheres of interests. We don't see each other except on weekends, when there's always plenty to be done.

My wife is very feminine, and I'm sure she thought of Wojtyła as a man as well as a priest. No doubt about it. My wife is always classifying people as handsome or otherwise. She must have made the same judgment with respect to him. The fact is that I don't think she was especially attracted by him. She just was not unaware of the fact that he was a man, as she could not help but be. . . . I think that my wife found and still finds the pope on the whole quite congenial. And so she finds she can discuss with him what she can't with many other people, because he's Polish and because on the whole she doesn't get along with other Poles.

What did the cardinal find in the relationship?

"Maybe a sort of window to the outside world," Houthakker speculates. "Because I think he wasn't aware that he had spent his life in a sort of circumscribed environment."

Describing Tymieniecka as "a very outspoken and straightforward person" (Dr. Williams uses almost the same words), Houthakker says, "She has not treated him with undue deference, with more respect than is due the pope; she talks with him quite freely." Perhaps, he believes, this is another reason for her influence with him.

· · ·

Williams notes, "She has told me more about her relationship with him than I felt appropriate—surely for him, and for me to be hearing." However, during the period when he was writing his book *The Mind of John Paul II*, in the first years of Wojtyła's papacy, she was extremely circumspect—and of virtually no help, he says.

Later, after listening to her at length, he concluded (as he had thought all along) that Tymieniecka felt a powerful sexual attraction for the cardinal, but that this was "sublimated" by the reality of his office and replaced by "an intellectual passion . . . in which she was excited by ideas. I believe it was a kind of collaboration in which her own sense of being a universal Catholic was enhanced by this winsome, mysterious scholar, who was not a standard product of a theological seminary, a phenomenologist rather than a Thomist. And I think she found that was frontier-crossing in terms of the intellectual history of her Church.

"Oh, I think they laughed and joked and swam and did everything together—in company of course," he says.

Williams has no doubt that Tymieniecka, in her way, fell in love with the cardinal and that Wojtyła did not return her love: "There's the question of whether he was emotionally engaged. I find there's quite a disequilibrium even when they're together and they're also looking at the same scenery, picking the same grapes and so forth." Wojtyła, he surmises, was attracted to her on an intellectual level:

> The heart has its reasons, and the mind has a heart. His mind does have a passion, a kind of passion that may have been uniquely experienced in the sharing of *The Acting Person*. And that is *Person and Act*. If you just get the title of his book, the original conception, there's a duality there—the person and the act—and I believe that that is a paradigm of the relationship. . . . And you might say that in reversing his original intentions he's *Czyn* and she's *Osoba*.

PART THREE

CONCLAVE

A POPE IN PAJAMAS

Sister Vincenzina entered the pope's bedroom a little after five A.M. She pulled back the curtains from the bed and discovered a corpse. John Paul I was curled up on his right side, clutching a handful of papers, his face stiffened into a half smile. Every morning at four-thirty the nun was accustomed to leaving a cup of coffee just outside the pope's bedroom door; when she saw that it hadn't been touched, she became alarmed. So she decided to go inside and check for herself. It was September 29, 1978. The life of the Apostolic Palace was thrown into utter disarray.

At seven forty-two A.M. Vatican Radio made the announcement of the pope's death, but it also lied. To reveal that Sister Vincenzina had seen even a dead pope in his pajamas was unthinkable. Thus in the official version Monsignor John Magee, the pope's Irish secretary, discovered the body. Cardinal Jean Villot, the Vatican secretary of state, had issued strict instructions: "The world cannot be told that a woman was the first person to enter the pontiff's bedroom."

Another widely disseminated pious lie was that the pope had been reading *The Imitation of Christ* by the fifteenth-century mystic Thomas à Kempis when he was stricken. Later Vatican authorities would say that John Paul I had been holding in his hand the rough draft of a homily he was preparing. But soon enough, word got out that the pope had been involved in a harsh discussion with his secretary of state about forthcoming personnel changes in the Curia and the Italian Church and that on the night of his death, he had phoned Cardinal Giovanni Colombo, archbishop of Milan, to ask his advice.

This led some monsignors in the Curia to whisper that the sheaf of papers found in Luciani's hand dealt with appointments and transfers—notes for reshaping the balance of power within the Church. Pope John Paul I's notes were never published. In keeping with the usual practice, Secretary of

State Villot ordered the removal of every personal item belonging to the pontiff, including his glasses, his slippers, and above all the medicines on his night table. The examination by the pope's physician, Dr. Renato Buzzonetti, was thought by some to be slapdash, but it was used to draft a bulletin stating that John Paul I had died on the evening of September 28 of a heart attack (myocardial infarction). The pope's intimates, especially those most familiar with his mental and physical state, thought the real cause of death was probably a pulmonary embolism.

A few hours after the announcement, rumors began circulating in Rome about the "mysteries" surrounding the death of Albino Luciani. The decision by Vatican authorities not to have an autopsy only inflated these suspicions and gave rise to the legend that the pope had been poisoned, an incredible hypothesis even to the most paranoid observers in the Vatican. One man who found this theory especially ridiculous was a priest who knew Albino Luciani extremely well, having been his personal secretary in Venice for seven years. "He broke down," the priest said, "under a burden too great for his frail shoulders and from the weight of his immense loneliness." On the night before his death, as he was finishing dinner, John Paul I had said to Monsignor Magee, "I've made all the arrangements for the spiritual exercises next Lent." Then he added, "The retreat I'd like to make now is the retreat for a good death."

The key to the end of John Paul I would seem to lie in this premonition. His soul had already been mortally wounded by stress, by isolation, and by his profound desire not to be pope. A few days before his death, he had told Secretary of State Villot at dinner, "Another man better than I could have been chosen. Paul VI already pointed out his successor: He was sitting just in front of me in the Sistine Chapel . . ." It was, of course, Wojtyła. "He will come, because I will go."

•　　•　　•

In Kraków word of the death of John Paul I came over the radio on the morning news. Father Mieczysław Maliński was listening to the program in the rectory of the parish church of St. Anne. His first thought was to alert the cardinal. He hurried to the archbishop's palace. In the courtyard he met

Wojtyła's chauffeur, Józef Mucha, who was rushing to see the cardinal for the same reason. Together they entered the kitchen on the ground floor. There was a pleasant warmth there, in contrast to the first autumnal chill in the streets. They could smell the bread, eggs, and coffee. Cardinal Wojtyła was in the adjoining room, seated at a long, narrow table, discussing the day's agenda with his closest aides.

He had just finished celebrating mass in his chapel and was taking his short morning break. He regularly ate breakfast not in the palace's historic apartments on the second floor, but on the ground floor next to the kitchen.

Mucha tried to persuade one of the nuns working in the kitchen to bring the news to the cardinal.

"You have to go tell him the pope has died in Rome."

"But he died a month ago." The nun's expression was dazed.

"No, the new one."

"I can't tell him that. If you want to, tell him yourself."

Irritated, Mucha poked his head into the food delivery passageway and asked the cardinal's secretary, Stanisław Dziwisz: "Father, have you heard that John Paul I is dead?"

Wojtyła had just spooned the sugar into his teacup. He froze and turned pale, his right hand still raised. In the silence the only sound to be heard was the spoon dropping onto the table.

"No," Wojtyła murmured.

The first effect of the news on the cardinal, as Mucha recalls, was a migraine headache. Wojtyła shut himself up in the chapel for several hours, then followed his usual work schedule and, as planned, went to visit a parish.

All day long he was tense. He knew he wouldn't be going to the next conclave as a spectator. That August during the balloting that had led to the election of Luciani, he had already gotten a handful of votes—nine, according to Romuald Kukołowicz, Primate Wyszyński's aide.

These pro-Wojtyła votes were a signal. The archbishop of Kraków had taken them so seriously that when John Paul I was elected he felt enormously relieved. "He was very happy," recalls Sister Andrea Górska, former superior of the Ursuline Sisters of Warsaw, at whose convent the cardinal stayed when visiting the Polish capital. "Cardinal, you look so much younger," the nun told him when Wojtyła returned from the August conclave. "Because we elected a magnificent pope," Wojtyła replied. "He's a truly believing person, very simple, but believing."

But not very sturdy. Pope John Paul I, as a cartoon in *Le Monde* portrayed him, had been crushed beneath the weight of the dome of St. Peter's after a pontificate of just thirty-three days. It was a sign to the cardinals that a man of simple faith was no longer enough to steer the bark of Peter.

On October 1 Wojtyła celebrated mass for the dead pope in the church of St. Mary in Kraków. On the 2nd he left for Warsaw. Mucha, who drove him to the airport, found him sad and depressed: "Everyone was saying he wouldn't be coming back."

Once again the cardinal stopped at the convent of the Ursulines in Warsaw. In the coal-gray building erected in the 1930s Wojtyła kept a little two-room apartment that he used during his frequent visits to the capital. He spent the day trying to occupy his mind with normal business. He attended a board meeting of the Polish Bishops Conference and spent the last hours of the evening reading the Ph.D. thesis of his Lublin student Andrzej Szostek.

The next morning, as he took his leave of Sister Andrea, he was pale and distracted. "Eminence, I don't know what to wish for you—to come back or not to come back," the nun said. "Sister," Wojtyła gravely replied, "there are so many things we don't know. Our life is such that only God knows everything."

THE CAMPAIGN

While only God knew everything, the Polish bishop Andrzej Deskur was among the best informed people in the Roman Curia. He had been an intimate friend of Karol Wojtyła ever since they were theology students together. On October 4 after the Vatican funeral mass in honor of John Paul I, the archbishop of Kraków went to dinner at Deskur's. Deskur, the president of the Pontifical Council for Social Communications, was the right person to brief him on the situation.

The leading cardinals were deeply divided and deeply worried by the upcoming election. Once again they would have to count friends and enemies, build alliances, turn minorities into majorities. It was exhausting work, particularly because it all went on behind the scenes. Officially everything was entrusted to the Holy Spirit, but the process of electing a pontiff called for all the perseverance, cunning, and even rancor of which human beings are capable. Cardinal Bernardin Gantin of Benin had summed up the general disorientation when he said, "We are groping in the dark."

The almost instant election of Pope John Paul I on August 26 seemed a genuine miracle, though it had backstage assistance from the powerful curial cardinals Sebastiano Baggio and Pericle Felici. In barely four ballots a compromise had been worked out between the most reform-minded cardinals, who wanted a "pastoral" pope unfettered by the curial power structure, and more tradition-inclined cardinals, who demanded absolute guarantees of orthodoxy. Albino Luciani, the patriarch of Venice, had been the ideal man for such a trade-off: a new man in the eyes of the world, humane in manner, rigid in doctrine.

Now another name had to be found, and once again the Italians were likely to push one of their own. But first the cardinals had to thrash out the meaning of the Second Vatican Council and decide whether to continue the reform process within the Church.

Cardinal Pericle Felici, the prefect of the Supreme Tribunal of the Apostolic Segnatura (the high court of the Roman Catholic Church), was the central figure mobilizing the cardinals labeled "conservatives" by the secular press of Italy and the world. His was a coalition with a long list of complaints: a clergy in crisis, vocations decreasing, seminaries adrift, theologians in rebellion, Catholic sexual ethics abandoned, the principle of authority challenged, communism on the offensive in Europe and Latin America.

Karol Wojtyła shared these concerns; and many in the Curia were well aware of that. But he was less pessimistic than they were. He didn't feel that the Church had to turn its back on Vatican II. He didn't agree with the pathetic description of Pope Paul VI so often uttered by contemptuous right-wing cardinals: the engineer of a locomotive who had no idea where his train was going.

On the contrary, the archbishop of Kraków appreciated Pope Paul's intelligent faith, his patience, his "gradualism," his capacity to mediate, his will to safeguard the Church's teaching, his desire to engage in a dialogue with the modern world. Many cardinals in both the moderate and the so-called progressive wing of the conclave were aware of Wojtyła's balanced attitude toward Paul and his pontificate.

Wojtyła left Bishop Deskur's apartment certain that he was on the list of candidates. This time he didn't have with him Father Mieczysław Maliński, his friend from Kraków who had the habit of bluntly speaking his mind. Before the August conclave as he drove Wojtyła to a meeting of the cardinals in the Vatican, Maliński had remarked, "The next pope is supposed to be a poor man; and you, you buy a round-trip ticket when you know you're going to stay on as pontiff?"

Wojtyła had a faraway look, as he always did when he was listening and thinking. Maliński insisted: "You'll be the pope, because you're a pastor, not a bureaucrat. You're neither a Cardinal Siri from the right, nor a man from the left, like Cardinal Suenens. You're from the center. People want a man from the center." However, everything depended on one condition, Maliński added: "So long as the Italians don't find a cardinal to identify with. But they don't have one. Aside from Bertoli, Baggio, and Benelli, they have no respected candidates. So they'll have to choose a foreigner."

"Why not someone from the United States? From France? From Germany?" Wojtyła asked.

"Nobody from France and nobody from Germany, because then everyone in the Vatican would have to speak German or French; and all the monsignors in the Curia would quit," Father Maliński replied mockingly.

It was an unwritten rule of the conclave that no cardinal from a powerful country would ever be elected pope. "The pope must be a man from a small country," Maliński commented.

"Cardinal König comes from a small country too," Wojtyła objected. König was from Austria.

"Why you and not König? Since the Council there have been several bishops synods, and at every one of them you were elected to the synodal council. Nobody in the world has been on it so many times."

Wojtyła didn't answer.

From August to October there had been nothing to change Maliński's perceptive analysis.

On October 5, after the visit to Deskur, Wojtyła went to lunch at the house of another important Polish prelate in Rome, Bishop Władysław Rubin, a member of the Vatican Congregation for Catholic Education. Among his various assignments Rubin was a consultant to the Pontifical Council for the Pastoral Care of Immigrants, presided over by the influential Cardinal Sebastiano Baggio. Working on that council as a minor official was another Pole, Father Ryszard Karpiński, who around the middle of September (when Pope John Paul I was alive and seemingly well) had stumbled on a surprisingly candid indication of curial inclinations. He was driving in a car with his boss, Archbishop Emanuele Clarizio, vice president of the council, and in the course of the conversation Clarizio had said, quite out of the blue: "Cardinal Wyszyński is too old to be pope, but Cardinal Wojtyła would make a good one." This report reached Rubin, who now shared it with an increasingly uncomfortable Wojtyła.

In the Church of Rome, the eve of a conclave is a unique moment for the cardinals to try their hand at real democracy. It's the brief season when they are adults, not the sons of the Holy Father, but citizens of the Church endowed with a basic right: one man, one vote. They are entitled to grant power and, in so doing, they make decisions about how power will be used in their Church in the future. This time they had to decide who would lead the Church toward the third millennium, and many of the cardinals were determined to fight to the end for their own vision of the Church.

Being a candidate in a papal election is perhaps the most unusual thing that can happen to a leader. It calls for a large measure of humility, self-control—and schizophrenia. The candidate knows he is *papabile*, but he can't say so. He can't present his platform; he can't even acknowledge that he's in the running. He has to entrust everything to the Holy Spirit while joining in, or being witness to, classic maneuvers for reaching consensus behind his candidacy and trying to block his opponents.

The fundamental rule is to stay out of the spotlight. Everything has to be said in velvety, allusive language, molded by centuries of diplomacy. People feel each other out in an arcane pas de deux where they never mention the issues. Hyacinthe Thiandoum, the cardinal of Dakar, has described the meeting he had in a Roman convent with the patriarch of Venice, Albino Luciani, just one day before the opening of the August conclave.

"My Patriarch," Thiandoum said when supper was over and the nuns were bringing in the coffee.

"I am the patriarch of Venice," Luciani replied.

"We're waiting for you," the African cardinal insisted.

"That's none of my business," the future pope concluded.

Everything had been said before they so much as stirred the sugar in their espresso cups.

So the candidate bent on success lets others take care of his business and stays as outwardly calm as possible, keeping a low profile. In October, as the partisans began to line up their votes, this was the posture Wojtyła assumed; in any case, it suited his temperament.

But he couldn't plug his ears. His friend Archbishop Deskur was expert in organizing useful meetings for him. One evening he set up a dinner with the seventy-five-year-old Cardinal Mario Nasalli Rocca, a curial veteran and powerful wire-puller. During supper at the convent of the Felician Sisters on the Via Casaletto, Nasalli Rocca broke the taboo by flatly declaring: "For me there's only one candidate—Cardinal Wojtyła."

Wojtyła was embarrassed. "Supper isn't the right place to discuss this sort of thing. Let's leave something for Providence to decide," he said, in his very best papabile manner. Deskur glowed with approval.

Such support for Wojtyła from an old curial fox was critical at a moment when political maneuvering had gone into high gear. The most varied occasions were put to use: dinners at the homes of prelates, conversations in restaurants, walks around St. Peter's Square, meetings in the Apostolic Palace—while in the bars near the Vatican, the wildest rumors and the most insinuating slanders made the rounds.

In the week before the conclave Wojtyła witnessed the effort by Cardinal Giuseppe Siri of Genoa to seize his last chance of being pope. Siri had been the heir apparent to Pius XII, but the conclave that followed Pius's death had surprisingly elected John XXIII. Then came Paul VI, then John Paul I. . . .

Siri was one hundred percent anti-Communist; in the 1960s Nikita Khrushchev had called on him to serve as a secret conduit between Moscow and the Holy See. The cardinal was also well known since the days of Vatican II for fighting tooth and nail to slow down any reform movement. Now the implementation of the Council reforms was at stake. While paying lip service to the memory of John Paul I, he permitted himself a few heavy-handed ironies: "You can't just govern with smiles or protestations of humility and simplicity." The rudder of St. Peter's bark, he hinted, urgently needed his own firm guidance.

The cardinals who considered the Vatican II reforms a prelude to chaos were ready to support Siri as the man to restore order—or at least as a candidate who might scare the reformist cardinals into dropping any candidate of theirs too committed to change. The great game of preconclave jostling for position was approaching its moment of truth.

Wojtyła knew that Siri's candidacy struck terror into the hearts of the more progressive cardinals. They felt that his was a challenge to the very essence of Vatican II: openness to the modern world, liturgical reform, freedom of theological research, serious encounter with the other Christian churches, and dialogue with other religions, even the "religion" of Marxism.

On Wednesday, October 11, more than a dozen notable cardinals gathered in the French Seminary; they wanted to form an anti-Siri front and pick an alternative candidate. It was a summit conference with an eye to Saturday, the 14th, when the conclave was set to begin. Among the participants were the Frenchmen Paul Guyon and François Marty, Canadians George Flahiff and Maurice Roy, Brazilians Evaristo Arns and Aloísio Lorscheiter, Basil Hume of England, Bernardin Gantin of Benin, Stefan Kim of South Korea, Leo Suenens of Belgium, and the Italians Giovanni Colombo of Milan and Salvatore Pappalardo of Palermo.

The participants favored a united front to defend the achievements of Vatican II. They didn't end up proposing any specific name, but on the lists of the *papabili* the stock of Cardinal Giovanni Benelli shot up. He was archbishop of Florence and had been for ten years the powerful Monsignore

Sostituto, that is, vice secretary of state for the Vatican. He had also been one of Paul VI's most loyal co-workers and, before Montini's ascent to the throne, his secretary. This *papabile* clearly intended to keep the Church open to the modern world.

But outside observers who thought that there were only two factions at war in the Catholic Church were mistaken. The battle lines of the struggle were much more jagged. Cardinals Joseph Höffner of Cologne and Joseph Ratzinger of Munich didn't like the extreme dogmatism of a man like Siri, but they were also worried that cardinals labeled as "liberals" by public opinion might become too influential. So Cardinal Ratzinger used an interview in the *Frankfurter Allgemeine Zeitung* to sound an alarm over the risk of Communist influence on the conclave. Denouncing the dangers of "pressure from the forces of the left," Ratzinger reminded the voters of the criticisms voiced by John Paul I against liberation theology—the theological movement in Latin America that opposed capitalism and often identified with revolutionary struggles against entrenched dictatorships.

Wojtyła shared Ratzinger's concern. For some years now the archbishop of Kraków had increasingly valued his younger and more combative confrère from Munich. The fifty-one-year-old Ratzinger was a brilliant theologian who early in his career had been highly critical of the Roman Curia and supportive of another theologian strongly opposed to Vatican authoritarianism, Hans Küng. During Vatican II Ratzinger had fought the traditionalists, pleading the cause of renewal in the Church. In the 1970s, however, he had become frightened by the postconciliar earthquake. He worried about the Church becoming too left-wing, too immersed in social and political issues, too sensitive to the secular forces unleashed in Europe in 1968.

While taking part in the official preconclave gatherings of cardinals at the Vatican, Ratzinger stressed that in the Catholic Church there must be "no historic compromise" like the alliance forged between the Italian Euro-Communists and the Christian Democrats in Parliament. In using the phrase "no historic compromise," Ratzinger stressed to his listeners that he was quoting the words of John Paul I. Wojtyła understood. This meant that a group of cardinals from Germany and other countries would block the reactionary bid by Cardinal Siri and his friends in the Roman Curia but that they weren't ready for a "leftist" pope. "Committed to the Council, but firm against the left" began to strike many moderate cardinals as a description of the ideal candidate.

Wojtyła knew that one of the influential cardinals he was in frequent contact with was campaigning for him: Franz König of Vienna, an unusually broad-minded prelate who liked mountain climbing even more than the archbishop of Kraków did. He could easily climb thirteen-thousand-foot peaks. He had also managed to climb over the iron curtain in the frostiest years of the cold war.

This tall, imposing figure, who bore an uncanny resemblance to the late German chancellor Konrad Adenauer, spoke fluent English, French, Russian, Italian, and German. John XXIII had chosen him in the early 1960s as an icebreaker in the Communist countries of Eastern Europe. He had been the first Western Catholic Cardinal sent to Tito's Yugoslavia and later to Budapest to meet with Cardinal Mindszenty, trapped in voluntary exile in the United States embassy. Paul VI had entrusted König with the leadership of the Secretariat for Non-Believers because he could handle Marxists, both culturally and politically.

By 1978 Franz König had had twenty years' experience in the College of Cardinals. He and the archbishop of Kraków knew each other very well and Wojtyła would regularly stop at the episcopal palace in Vienna en route to Rome. They often had long talks about the situation in Eastern Europe, especially in the countries where the Church was largely forced underground. "The iron curtain was always on Wojtyła's mind," König recalls. "He believed it would stand a long time."

In Rome König explained to many of the cardinals his conviction that the next pope would have to be young, healthy, and non-Italian. After the death of Paul VI he had declared that the cardinals from Eastern Europe had a right to have their candidate too. Now if anyone asked for a name, he would suggest Karol Wojtyła. When he met with Wojtyła himself, König never discussed strategy—there was no need to. But neither did he conceal his goal; in fact he joked about it. One evening, as he dragged his friend Wojtyła to the exclusive Eau Vive restaurant, run by African and Asian nuns dressed in native costumes, König told the taxi driver: "Careful—you've got the next pope on board."

Except for such small, almost intimate encounters, Wojtyła avoided unofficial meetings, especially of the large, conspiratorial variety like the one at the French Seminary. Nor had König himself attended that one. Though he was a personal friend of many of those present and fully shared their reformist position, he preferred to act even farther behind the scenes. The headquarters of his discreet campaign to elect a Polish pope was in the Salvator Mundi Clinic on the Janiculum Hill, his Roman residence. When entertaining cardinals he told them why Wojtyła would be acceptable to a broad spectrum of electors: "Cardinal Wojtyła is not an Italian, and he comes from a Communist country—those are two points in his favor. Beyond that he's made a good impression with his public statements at Vatican II and at the synods. When he speaks, people like what he has to say; and they like his winning personality."

There were practically no substantive arguments against him. From time to time König also let slip the words that Paul VI had once said about the bishop of Kraków: "He's a brave, magnificent man." And there was no over-looking the fact that Paul VI had chosen Wojtyła to preach the Lenten retreat for the pope in 1976.

But as he sounded out his brethren, König found no immediate consensus. The Germans had mixed feelings, and the Italians committed to conciliar reforms were split. A few names of other foreign candidates, such as Cardinal Marty of Paris, were also being bruited about.

The farther he went, the more König realized how hard it would be to break down the stereotype that for a half a millennium had demanded an Italian pope. Cardinal Raul Silva Henríquez of Santiago de Chile, known for his courageous opposition to the dictatorial regime of General Pinochet and sometimes mentioned as a candidate himself, was not opposed to the idea of a non-Italian *papabile*, but he hesitated. "We're still disposed to electing an-other Italian," he confided to the vice director of *L'Osservatore Romano*, Father Virgilio Levi, "but they ought to tell us who their candidate is."

Among the most enthusiastic supporters of Wojtyła's candidacy was

Brazilian Cardinal Aloísio Lorscheiter, bishop of Fortaleza. He was one of the most junior members of the Sacred College. Only two years had passed since Paul VI placed the crimson cap on his head. Nevertheless he already wielded a good deal of influence as the head of the Brazilian bishops conference and chairman of the Latin American bishops conference, the authoritative voice of the Catholic Church in Latin America. He was an enemy to all dictators, a defender of the most liberal clergy, and a protector of leftist "base communities" inspired by the new Marxist-tinged liberation theology.

Lorscheiter hoped to see 1978 as a great turning point in the governance of the Church. He wanted "a Good Shepherd, sensitive to social problems, patient, willing to engage in dialogue and look for common ground." He was searching for someone who favored more collegiality, more communication between the bishops conferences and the pope, more participation by the local churches in the decision-making process in Rome. Beyond that, he suggested, "frequent trips by the pontiff to various continents would be useful."

Lorscheiter had supported the election of John Paul I; now he shifted his support to Cardinal Wojtyła. He had appreciated Wojtyła's speeches at the synods, his commitment to preaching the Gospel, his attentiveness to different cultures, his balanced position in the debates, his sensitivity to problems of social justice, his openness to people from other nations and continents. The Brazilian cardinal immediately began campaigning among the Third World cardinals for the archbishop of Kraków, little realizing how few of his positions were actually shared by Wojtyła. Even a well-known candidate can disappoint his most fervent supporters once he becomes pope.

While Wojtyła stayed discreetly out of the limelight, his indefatigable countryman Bishop Deskur had taken on the role of campaign manager. He now sought to bring the American faction to Wojtyła's side by organizing a small dinner at his apartment on October 11 with Cardinal John Patrick Cody of Chicago and Bishop Rubin—as well as Wojtyła—in attendance. Cody was a member of two key Curia departments: the Congregation for the Propagation of the Faith (which has economic control over the churches in many parts of the Third World) and the Congregation for the Clergy, directed by another American, Cardinal John Wright of Pittsburgh.

The mood at the table was cheerful. As always, Deskur—a quick-witted and gregarious intellectual—was a stimulating talker. Cody (who soon after would be accused of financial improprieties) was chattering away almost nonstop, full of energy and enthusiasm. The guests tiptoed around the subject of the conclave, but every now and then there was an allusion to Paul VI and John Paul I. A pensive Wojtyła concentrated on his meal and didn't join in the flow of conversation. The guests included Monsignor Virgilio Levi. Observing Wojtyła, Levi thought: "What a strange dinner companion. He says only a few words while the others are beaming."

That same day Cardinal König decided the time had come to approach the primate of Poland. At the end of a routine meeting, König offered the Polish cardinal a lift. It was a beautiful day, sunny and mild.

"Your Eminence," the archbishop of Vienna asked tactfully, "do you see any good candidates on the horizon?"

"No outstanding ones, as I see it."

"Perhaps Poland has a candidate?"

"What? You mean I'd have to go to Rome?" Wyszyński snapped. "If I left my country, that would be a triumph for the Communists."

"There's also another man," the cardinal from Vienna prodded.

"No, that's out of the question. He's not well known enough."

König dropped Wyszyński off at his residence with the clear feeling that the primate didn't consider Wojtyła's candidacy a real possibility. Up till the last moment the two great men of the Polish Church were keeping their distance. In Rome they lived apart: Wyszyński at the Polish Institute on the Via Cavallini not far from the Vatican, Wojtyła amid the greenery at the Polish College on the Aventine, the hill that looks down on the roofs of Rome, the banks of the Tiber, and Michelangelo's dome. There was no danger that Wojtyła's visitors would ever meet Wyszyński's.

The primate continued to be convinced that the Italians wanted an Italian pope, that they would never tolerate a foreigner on the throne of Peter—and he repeated that to anyone who would listen.

Still he was struck by König's boldness. The next day Wyszyński unexpectedly summoned his countrymen Deskur and Rubin to the Polish Institute. "We had absolutely no idea what he wanted from us," Deskur recalls.

"We got there, and he asked us who would be the next pope. Both Bishop Rubin and I gave the same answer: Wojtyła."

"How do you know?" Wyszyński asked, almost in shock.

"Your Eminence," Deskur replied, "I've been living in Rome for thirty years."

At that moment Deskur was already sure that Wojtyła's electoral base was broadening. The Polish American Cardinal John Krol had begun to campaign actively for him. And there was another pivotal player who had Karol Wojtyła in mind: the Vatican's French secretary of state, Jean Villot.

Wojtyła knew this too. Five months before, on May 18, he had celebrated his fifty-eighth birthday in Deskur's Vatican apartment. The guest of honor was Cardinal Villot, along with Bishop Rubin and Luigi Poggi, the special papal nuncio for Eastern Europe. During lunch that spring afternoon, as talk turned to the future of the Church, the secretary of state had said that Wojtyła was the only man who could win the two-thirds majority needed for election. "I remember poor Poggi looking at Rubin," Deskur recalls. "He was wondering whether the cardinal secretary of state was crazy. Talking about the next pope in the pope's own house, when the pope himself was apparently in reasonable health, came as a complete surprise to us."

Afterward Cardinal Villot sent Deskur a brief note, as if to counter Deskur's surprise and Poggi's incomprehension: "I stand by what I said during lunch. It wasn't a slip." Deskur still has that card.

Only days before the conclave was to begin, however, Deskur, stressed beyond his limits in his self-appointed role as Wojtyła's campaign manager, suffered a massive stroke from which he would never fully recover. Karol Wojtyła paid him a tender, solicitous visit at the Gemelli Clinic. Then, to relieve his own stress, Wojtyła took off for the beach on the last two afternoons before the conclave convened. The chilly autumn water was warm enough for this man of the North, who swam vigorously just outside Rome.

Before the cardinals were locked into the conclave, one more drama would be played out, a Renaissance drama of pride, intrigue, and treachery, starring, in his last great performance, the would-be pope and lion of the right Giuseppe Siri.

On the very eve of the conclave Italian journalist Gianni Licheri, an old acquaintance of Siri's, contacted the archbishop of Genoa for an interview. Siri knew that the men about to elect the pope were hypersensitive, so he stipulated that the story not be published until October 15, when the doors of the conclave would already be shut and none of the cardinals could read it.

The reporter apparently agreed, and Siri spoke frankly. He made no secret of his hostility to the democratization of the Church. He mocked collegiality, one of the principal doctrines of Vatican II, which called for responsible power sharing between Rome and its bishops. "I don't even know what episcopal collegiality is," he declared, indifferent to the fact that his every word was being taken down by the tape recorder. "The synod can never become a deliberative body."

On October 14, a few hours before the cardinals headed into the Sistine Chapel, a copy of the interview was delivered to the Roman residence of every member of the Sacred College. The trap, it seemed, had been sprung. Siri was mortally wounded, even though his supporters decided to fight for him till the bitter end. In the Curia, where tigers are used to disguising themselves as doves, rumor had it that the man who set the trap was Giovanni Benelli, the cardinal from the city of Niccolò Machiavelli. True or not (Benelli denied it firmly), in the poisoned atmosphere of preconclave maneuvers, many believed it.

On October 14, at half-past four in the afternoon, having concluded the Mass of the Holy Spirit in St. Peter's Basilica, 111 cardinal-electors entered the conclave in solemn procession. Wojtyła took the risk of arriving late, because he had decided to pay a final visit to Deskur. Only a few hours earlier, a prophecy had been passed along to him by Bishop Bronisław Dąbrowski, who had just arrived from Warsaw: The Communist minister for religious affairs, Kazimierz Kąkol, after learning that Wojtyła had received a clutch of votes at the August conclave, had had a dream that the archbishop of Kraków would become pope.

Now there was no more time for forecasts and worldly maneuvers. Marching in procession behind a crucifix carried by the master of ceremonies, the crimson-robed cardinals were now plunged into an atmosphere of meditation and contemplation. The image of Christ on the Cross reminded the electors of their enormous responsibility. The choir sang the "Veni Sancte Spiritus"—Come, Holy Spirit.

In the Sistine Chapel the cardinals assembled beneath another image of Christ, the powerful figure in Michelangelo's *Last Judgment*. They listened in silence to the reading of the rules binding them to absolute secrecy and forbidding communication with the outside world. New regulations, promulgated during Paul VI's reign, called for up-to-date technology to prevent spying or news leaks. Vatican security forces had already combed the area, using electronic detectors to search for bugs. Two-way radios were forbidden, as were ordinary radios, tape recorders, and portable telephones.

After the gathering in the Sistine Chapel the cardinals all went to their cells, assigned in advance by lot. Karol Wojtyła looked for number 91 and carried his suitcase in. The cells were formed by installing partitions in the old apartments of the Borgia popes. The archbishop noted his simple camp bed, night table, and small desk. There was no sink. To get to the common bathroom he had to pass by the cells of the other cardinals. His own living conditions had never been a concern. All his life he had been used to spartan arrangements. Even in the archbishop's palace his room was more like a monk's. Whenever she packed his luggage for him, Maryśka, his housekeeper, didn't put in much more than socks and underwear, a few shirts, and two pairs of shoes. When he went to the country to stay with his friend Father Franciszek Konieczny, he sometimes asked to borrow an old-fashioned night-shirt.

According to witnesses, Wojtyła seemed serene on the eve of the balloting. Some noticed him sitting in his cell reading a journal on Marxism. Later that evening a young American priest, Donald Wuerl, who was accompanying the nearly blind Cardinal John Wright, walked out onto the only open space within the conclave precincts, the large courtyard of St. Damasus. Suddenly Wuerl felt a strong hand grasping his arm and turned to see Karol Wojtyła.

"You're walking, we'll walk together," the archbishop of Kraków said. As the priest looked at him in some surprise, Wojtyła added: "I'll speak English so I can practice, and you'll speak Italian so we'll know what we're saying."

Striding back and forth across the square, the two launched into a bilingual conversation: the Pole in his harshly accented English, the American in his hopelessly flat Italian. Wojtyła seemed completely relaxed. Wuerl thought of a cryptic remark by Cardinal Wright: "This conclave is going to elect a successor to John Paul I, not to Paul VI." What did that mean? Paul VI had been elected to see Pope John XXIII's ecumenical council to its conclusion. John Paul I had been elected to hold the doctrinal line within the Church while presenting Catholicism's human face to the world. Would his successor have to carry out this unenacted program?

On the following day, Sunday, October 15, the battle began. In the morning two rounds were fought out between Siri and Benelli. On the first ballot, as the story has been pieced together, each got about thirty votes. On the second, the number of their supporters increased. In the afternoon, however, the two rivals lost ground; and Cardinal Ugo Poletti, chairman of the Italian Bishops Conference, received a bloc of about thirty votes. With the fourth ballot, a new curial candidate arrived on the scene: Cardinal Pericle Felici. Wojtyła received five votes, which was a sort of warning signal. At this news, a look of unhappiness appeared on his face.

The harshness of the contest at the ballot box contrasted with the atmosphere of unreal quiet that permeated the conclave. "People think we're having the fiercest sorts of discussions in the conclave," Cardinal König recalls, "but that's not true. Everything is proceeding very calmly. Two or three people talk with one another; then everybody goes back to his cell."

Silence was the true protagonist of the event. Wuerl, now a bishop, recalls, "It wasn't unusual to see the [Pauline] Chapel half full of people praying one hour before they went into the Sistine Chapel." The only sounds to be heard were steps in the corridor. The cardinals prayed in silence, rose in silence, and returned to their cells in silence. At table, conversation was minimal. In the Sistine Chapel one could say that the only sound to be heard was the rustling of the ballots, which were folded twice and then deposited in the chalice that served as a ballot box.

Still, the battle for the future of the Church was being fought in earnest. It was clear that the Italian candidates were blocking one another, creating a logjam. While Siri's candidacy showed no sign of giving way, his adversaries weren't inclined to concede defeat either. Nor were any alternative candidates succeeding in capturing anything close to a majority.

Franz König's hour had arrived. On the night of October 15 he felt ready to launch his offensive. He spoke with the German cardinals, with the French, with the Spaniards, with the Americans, always in a soft, casual manner, as if this were the most matter-of-fact issue: a few words exchanged in a corridor, a conversation while leaving the dining room, a brief visit to someone's cell. Then the conclave slipped back into its great silence.

At one point, however, König felt the need for a discussion with the whole German-speaking group, in which he included the Dutch and a few cardinals from elsewhere in Central Europe. There for the last time the archbishop of Vienna pleaded the cause of Karol Wojtyła. He was cautious and convincing. Now a current of tension began to ripple through the conclave, as though history were in the making, as every elector began to consider seriously the possibility of voting for a non-Italian.

On Monday morning, October 16, there were two more ballots. Siri began to lose ground, while many of the other votes were divided among Cardinals Giovanni Colombo, Ugo Poletti, and the Dutchman Johannes Willebrands. The results indicated that the Italian candidates were finished. On the sixth ballot, the last before the midday meal, the votes in favor of the archbishop of Kraków abruptly surged.

At lunch Karol Wojtyła looked so tense that some of his supporters feared he might refuse to accept election.

That afternoon, as the whispery silence thickened, Karol Wojtyła was glimpsed in the cell of Cardinal Wyszyński, agitated and weeping. The archbishop of Kraków had collapsed in the arms of the primate of Poland. There was no more doubt what would happen next.

"If they elect you," Wyszyński said, "you must accept. For Poland."

Wojtyła composed himself. Two ballots later he heard his name announced. Ninety-nine cardinals out of one hundred and eight had given him their vote. They had done the unimaginable: They had chosen a pope from a country subject to the Soviet Union, a country with a Marxist and atheist government. He was the first non-Italian pontiff in 450 years, a young pope, at the age of fifty-eight. Outside of Poland and the Sacred College, few knew much about this Slav who had become shepherd to a flock of eight hundred million Catholics, who as a schoolboy had once told Prince Archbishop Sapieha that he wasn't interested in being a priest.

Amid the silence the voice of the cardinal president could be heard asking: "Do you accept? What name will you take?"

Wojtyła accepted. The tension vanished from his face, which took on a solemn expression. Not only did he say "Yes," as tradition demanded, with a clear voice, but he added: "With obedience in faith to Christ, my Lord, and with trust in the Mother of Christ and of the Church, in spite of the great difficulties, I accept." He had written this out after leaving Wyszyński's cell.

Now to express his commitment to the legacy of the last three popes and his affinity to Albino Luciani, he took as his name John Paul II.

As he spoke, a stirring of joy passed through the conclave. One by one the cardinals went to do him homage on their knees. When it was Wyszyński's turn, John Paul II rose from his chair and, as the Polish primate started to kneel, the pope flung his arms around him and lifted him up. The hard, imperious cardinal of Warsaw clung to the pope like a child. John Paul II held him firmly. Never in its history had Poland been so honored as it now was in the person of Wyszyński's loyal deputy, whom the old man had always kept at arm's length.

Only the vein that pulsed on Wojtyła's forehead betrayed the storm in his heart as he prepared to leave the chapel. Calmly, he allowed himself to be escorted to the antechamber with scarlet-covered walls known as the *camera lacrimatoria*—the "crying room"—where the new pope sits alone for a few moments to await the pontifical tailor, who fits him with one of three white cassocks—small, medium, and large—already waiting on a chair. Nowhere is it recorded whether, as legend has it, the new pope proceeded to cry—either in joy or despair. What is known is that Pope John Paul II put on the largest of the three cassocks and purposefully made his way out onto the great loggia of St. Peter's to greet the Romans and the world.

In the early evening darkness the crowd was impatient, but when they heard the Polish pope readily speaking Italian ("He's a Negro," someone had shouted upon first hearing his exotic name announced), surprise gave way to pandemonium. The new pontiff exhorted the Romans: "If I make mistakes in speaking your language—I mean, our language—you will correct me."

Night had come. Following the example of his predecessor, Albino Luciani, the pope asked the cardinals to remain in conclave to dine together. Wojtyła moved about in a very relaxed manner, spoke with his colleagues in the same friendly fashion as before, joking with the nuns who served at table.

His Polish secretary, Stanisław Dziwisz, began to weep quietly. The pope embraced him like a mother comforting a frightened child.

PRIDE AND FEAR IN WARSAW

The officer flung the door open and, ignoring both protocol and discipline, shouted: "Comrade General, sensational news! Wojtyła's been elected pope."

The man at the desk had a pale, almost ghostly white face. Hidden behind dark glasses, his eyes were invisible. The back brace he was strapped into made him sit stiffly. In his olive-green uniform he looked like a manne-quin. He thanked the adjutant correctly and acknowledged the message: In two hours members of the Politburo and other state officials would meet in extraordinary session.

At the age of fifty-seven, Wojciech Jaruzelski, minister of defense of the People's Republic of Poland, had already had his share of life's shocks and surprises. He had survived the collapse of independent Poland, invaded by the Nazis and then the Soviets. During the brief period of the Hitler-Stalin pact, he had been deported to Siberia (where his eyelids had been severely damaged from the sun, and his back nearly broke from chopping wood). Then he had fought his way back home alongside Russian soldiers as a member of the People's Army of Poland, forged at Stalin's behest. Following the peace of Yalta, he had come through the Stalinist era miraculously unscathed. He had methodically risen through the ranks during the reformist regime of Władysław Gomułka and the short-lived "Polish springtime" when the coun-try, although bound to the Warsaw Pact, opened up to the West and its markets. Now Poland's socialist economy was reeling, and in some factories workers were attempting to form semi-independent trade unions.

Jaruzelski seemed almost overwhelmed with ambiguity: How to handle this news from Rome? Wojtyła as pope meant trouble. Relations between the cardinal of Kraków and the Communist authorities had been strained. Yet the general allowed a wave of patriotism to sweep over him. For the first time in the thousand-year history of Catholic Poland, a son of the motherland was ascending the loftiest throne in the world. It was as if this day—October 16, 1978—had conferred a magnificent prize on the entire nation. Perhaps a bit of the splendor would shine on the government too, undoing the sense of defeat and indignity that scarred the national conscience. Poland had once been a European power, but that had been a long time ago.

The streets of Warsaw were filling up with people on their way to church to pray and light votive candles. Their joy seemed close to rapture—as if Easter, Christmas, and Independence Day had all come at once. Government-controlled Polish radio and television had incongruously broadcast the historic news in the form of a brief bulletin. Since the party hadn't issued any official response, no one had dared flesh out the report with so much as a thumbnail biographical sketch of the new pope.

Yet across the capital the bells were booming like an autumnal cloudburst, as each church rang out in celebration of the news. Jaruzelski thought the choice of a pope from Kraków was a master stroke. From the great cathedral on the Wawel Hill and his episcopal palace, Wojtyła had systematically and ostentatiously ignored the party hierarchy. With philosophical contempt, he had denied any legitimacy to Marxist-Leninist ideology; and with his considerable influence on the Catholic intelligentsia, he had built up a front of spiritual resistance to the country's political leadership. Indeed, Wojtyła's election *was* dangerous. Jaruzelski was worried that the Polish Church would become a model for all of Eastern Europe, that its influence, hitherto held within the borders of Poland, would now reach Christians in the USSR.

Jaruzelski felt swamped by confusion. He picked up the phone and tried to get some guidance—and commiseration—from the chief Communist overseer of the Catholic Church in Poland, Stanisław Kania, head of the party's Administrative Department.

"You already know the whole story. What's your political appraisal?" As usual, Jaruzelski, speaking in a flat, bureaucratic tone, kept his emotions under wraps. He had the sense that this event, for all its glory, would cast a disturbing shadow over the People's Republic. He saw difficult times ahead with the Soviet Union.

"There's a broader view from the Vatican than from the Wawel," Kania replied, half-jesting. The papacy would have a tempering effect on Wojtyła.

As administrative chief, Kania's most difficult mission was to maintain the party's supremacy over the episcopal establishment. Kania too was deeply ambivalent. He had stored in his memory details from the files on the Polish bishops that had piled up in his Office of Religious Affairs after years of spying on the clergy. The reports described Wojtyła as a man of great intellectual gifts, but increasingly distant and unfriendly in his dealings with the Communist *apparat*. There were frequent mentions of a "Kraków line" in the Church that was hard to control. The cardinal was too cosmopolitan, they said; he had too many contacts with the outside world, and he had traveled to the West.

Now Kania had to draft a congratulatory telegram to the new pontiff: something warm and friendly, to salute the triumph of a "son of the Polish nation."

Shortly after nightfall, the top government and party leaders—the Polish Politburo—began to arrive at the fortress of the Central Committee on Jerozolimskie Avenue. In their black limousines they had seen the brightly lit churches full of people. From Kraków to Gdańsk, from Wrocław to Lublin, the whole nation was having a blissful seizure. All over the country telephone lines were clogged as people rushed to tell their relatives, friends, and colleagues the story of how Karol Wojtyła had become pope. For devout Catholics it was a gift from God and the Holy Virgin to faithful Poland.

But these men had a different view: Many of them believed that the choice of Wojtyła had been engineered by the United States. The Americans and West Germans had conspired to fix the election in the Sistine Chapel.

The puppet master, the chief wire-puller behind the whole thing was Zbigniew Brzeziński, the fiercely anti-Communist national security adviser to U.S. President Jimmy Carter. Brzeziński too happened to be a native son of Poland.

"Wojtyła will give us a talking to," complained the secretary of the party's Economic Council, Stefan Olszowski, but, as his comrades took their seats, no one offered a reply.

First Secretary Edward Gierek opened the session. He seemed still in shock as he yielded the podium to Kania.

Kania was a big man, broad and paunchy with a peasant's face. The most important thing for Poland, he said, was to maintain the policy of rapprochement already agreed on with the Vatican. The government was letting new churches be built; Polish bishops were free to travel in the West. All this had to go forward. The first secretary himself had visited the late Pope Paul VI to pave the way for a concordat with the Holy See and full normalization of diplomatic relations. The state was already negotiating such an accord with Primate Wyszyński to define the rights of the Polish Church. For the government, it was fundamental that the Church—and its new pope—treat communism in Poland with respect.

"What is there to build on?" Kania asked tentatively. He conceded, of course, that past relations with the archbishop of Kraków offered little ground for optimism. But Communist rhetoric required that every negation be followed by an affirmation. The Church of Rome, he declared, had learned the value of cooperating with the Communist authorities. "We can expect the Holy See to stick to the path of reconciliation, of *Ostpolitik.*"

But that wasn't enough to calm the assembled leaders, now beset with visions of a grand conspiracy. Was a Polish pope a threat to the socialist system in Poland? That was the crucial question.

"What if the new pope decides to come to Poland?" one of the ministers asked Kania. The weight of the question settled oppressively over the entire room.

The government, warned the minister of internal affairs, has to focus immediately on the risk of a wave of pilgrimages by the Polish faithful to Rome. "Those trips alone might pose a danger to the stability of Poland."

In the very first hours of his pontificate, the election of the first pope from a socialist country had raised the specter of destabilization. Suddenly the Vatican had become an ominous, unknown quantity to the Communist world.

The next day, October 17, the Soviet ambassador in Warsaw drove to Central Committee headquarters. The man from Moscow was already agitated as he studied the reports in his briefcase. Once inside the building, he put aside his impatience and listened to the hopeful explanations from Comrade Kania. Finally the Russian spoke.

"If you haven't been on good terms with Wojtyła up till now," the Russian brusquely noted, "you can only expect relations with the Vatican to get worse."

This time, Kania's supply of orthodox optimism had run out, and he said nothing.

"—much worse," the Russian warned.

Kania's mind drifted to the moment when he had telephoned Gierek with the news.

"Holy Mother of God," the first secretary of the Polish Communist Party had exclaimed.

PART FOUR

IL PAPA

THE GENERAL TAKES COMMAND

Poor Albino Luciani: Staying in his conclave cell for one more night among the other cardinals had allowed him to pretend that he was still just another cardinal, that he had yet to accept the job of spiritual leader of eight hundred million people all over the globe. Such thoughts were not on the mind of Karol Wojtyła. His 175-pound frame gave him a convincing air of sturdiness, tempered by an athlete's agility. From the moment the cardinal chairman announced his election in the conclave, his presence of mind had been astonishing. To his confrères in crimson he had seemed perfectly self-possessed as he received their congratulations. He appeared free and easy as he drank the glass of champagne served in the Borgia apartments after his public blessing of the Romans. He seemed calm as he chatted with the cardinals, calm too as he joked with the nuns waiting on him (he invited them to sip a glass as well). He was up to the job.

For Pope Wojtyła spending the night with the cardinals meant binding them to him in brotherhood, sealing a pact with them that went beyond obedience, facing with manly solidarity the arduous tasks that awaited them. Now these hundred-odd men from five continents had to become as cooperative a body as his co-workers in Kraków, a little army with an intimate sense of a common destiny, like the friends who had joined him on long hikes in the Tatra Mountains.

Before falling asleep he wrote a homily for the mass he would celebrate the next morning with the cardinal-electors. His predecessor had had almost his entire speech written for him by Monsignor Giovanni Coppa, an expert Latinist from the Secretariat of State. Its contents reflected the ideas of the pontiff, but still more those of Secretary of State Jean Villot, who was hoping for greater collegiality in the administration of the Church universal. Karol

Wojtyła wrote his own sermon. The secretary of state and the curial *apparatchiks* would have to get used to it: From now on many things would come directly from his own hand.

On the morning of October 17, again beneath Michelangelo's Christ, the pope from Kraków, speaking in Latin, expounded his strategy: Fidelity to the Council above all, and collegiality—these were the issues close to the heart of those who didn't want to give up on Church renewal. And then, as requested by the majority of the cardinals, who were frightened by the all too rapid changes of the postconciliar period, John Paul II insisted on obedience to the pope's teaching, respect for liturgical rules, and discipline. Finally he stressed the need to carry on ecumenical dialogue and the Church's commitment to peace and justice in the world. This was exactly the program that had gotten him elected.

When on October 22 he appeared in St. Peter's Square to celebrate the mass inaugurating his pontificate, he seemed fully invested with the mission entrusted to him by God. He had the serenity of an actor who had already memorized his part. The square was full of people, two hundred thousand of them. About four thousand pilgrims had come from his native Poland. Seven hundred had come from the Polish diaspora. The president of Poland, Henryk Jabłoński, was on hand, along with King Juan Carlos of Spain; the presidents of Lebanon, Austria, and Ireland; and scores of delegations, including one from the Soviet Union led by Ambassador to Italy Nikolai Ryzhov. There were patriarchs and heads of the other Christian churches. Above all there were the people, there was the world. As he made his way to the altar, John Paul II had already realized that in this extraordinary square, whose colonnade spreads out as if in a great embrace, the whole world always has its eye on the pope.

Watching him by satellite, believers and nonbelievers alike from a hundred nations assisted at the solemn ritual by which the Roman Church raises a man to its post of supreme dignity, transforming him into a splendid monarch like the emperors of Byzantium. For the first time, Karol Wojtyła sat on his throne, the papal *cathedra*. As the strains of the ancient litany of the saints faded away, amid clouds of incense enveloping the altar, the first cardinal deacon, Pericle Felici, approached the new pope, placing on his shoulders the sacred pallium, a white wool stole interwoven with little black crosses, the emblem of papal power.

Felici was a witty Church traditionalist, a man equally in love with Latin and the latest video systems, a Roman to the core. With his sonorous voice, buoyed by the force of a centuries-old tradition, he turned to the pope from Kraków and pronounced the Latin formula of investiture: "Blessed be God, who has chosen you as Pastor of the whole Church, entrusting you with the apostolic mission. May you shine forth gloriously during long years of earthly life until, called by your Lord, you are clothed with immortality as you enter the Kingdom of Heaven. Amen."

"Amen," repeated all 117 cardinals of the Holy Roman Church.* Then they rose from their seats and marched up in a long line to kiss the pope's ring as a sign of obedience. John Paul II gave them all the fraternal embrace. But when Stefan Wyszyński knelt down to do him homage, the pope bent down too, crushing the old primate in a passionate hug. Wyszyński personified the heroic history of the Polish Church, its resistance to invaders, its struggle with atheism. This second embrace, this public singling out of Wyszyński, was a signal, for anyone who wanted to read it, of what was coming next. Henceforth John Paul II would be the global master of symbols.

There was only one leitmotif in Wojtyła's sermon: Christ.

"Brothers and sisters," the new pope exclaimed, "don't be afraid to welcome Christ and to accept his power. Help the pope and all those who wish to serve Christ and, with the power of Christ, to serve man and the whole human race." John Paul II had a boldness that was very different from the tortured reserve of Paul VI and the smiling timidity of John Paul I. Here was someone who really sounded like a herald of God, someone who wanted to shake the Church out of its inferiority complex vis-à-vis the world, someone who wanted to rattle the foundations.

John Paul II spoke with a professional's rhythmic intonation, measuring the pauses, breaking off for moments of applause. This too contrasted

---

* Cardinals over age eighty do not participate in the conclave itself; thus only 111 were present in the Sistine Chapel.

with the singsong rhythms of Paul VI and the unassuming patter of John Paul I.

"Be not afraid!" he declared, all but shouting. "Open up, no, swing wide the gates to Christ. Open up to his saving power the confines of the state, open up economic and political systems, the vast empires of culture, civilization, and development." In the VIP stands and among the people thronging the square and the adjacent streets, the pontiff's words flashed like an electric charge. Here's a pope, the audience sensed, who's ready to reconquer the world.

In Poland people were riveted to their TV sets. An entire nation had come to a halt. Warsaw was a spectral city where even the buses had stopped running. The bishops had put off mass until evening to allow the people to watch their Polish pontiff.

Out on St. Peter's Square the pope's voice grew more and more excited. "Be not afraid! Christ knows what we have inside. Only He knows." This wasn't so much a mass as a call to arms. John Paul II spoke in Italian, Polish, French, English, German, Spanish, Portuguese, and—turning toward the lands of the East—Russian, Slovak, Ukrainian, and Lithuanian. In his mouth the lines in foreign languages didn't sound like polite little snippets, but like arrows aimed directly at every corner of the earth.

When the final notes of the "Te Deum" fell silent, Karol Wojtyła, the supreme pontiff, couldn't stand still. With long strides, his green vestments aflutter, and grasping the crozier like a pilgrim's staff, he sped across the colonnade as the cardinals looked on in amazement. This wasn't the delicate gait of a cleric used to negotiating seminary corridors: He strode like a mountaineer. He didn't submit to the crowd, he dominated it. He embraced a group of handicapped persons in their wheelchairs. He spoke to Polish pilgrims, he shook hands, kissed babies, patted bouquets of flowers that people proffered to him. Then, heading back to the center of the parvis, he fixed his glance on the delirious crowd, and, wielding the crozier in both hands like a sword, he traced a powerful sign of benediction.

·   ·   ·

In the first hundred days of his pontificate John Paul II pointed out the path he would take. Audiences and meetings showcased his new agenda for the Church. He exhorted the clergy of Rome not to water down their priestly charism with exaggerated interest in social problems. He championed the cause of celibacy. He invited the American bishops to keep a watchful eye on Christian doctrine and Church discipline. At one conference with nuns he insisted on the necessity of wearing the religious habit: It was an important outward sign, he emphasized, "to remind you of your commitment, which sharply contrasts with the spirit of the world." With the Canadian bishops he spoke of the need for individual confession. He reminded members of the Vatican Secretariat for the Union of Christians that the ecumenical movement couldn't make progress by compromising the truth.

He extolled mothers who refused to have abortions when their lives were at risk. He reaffirmed the indissolubility of marriage and criticized the Italian government, which had recently introduced legal abortion. When a woman journalist asked him about the ordination of women, he shot back: "The Virgin preferred to stand at the foot of the Cross."

During a meeting with young people, he outlined his portrait of the ideal Catholic: "One must above all have certitude and clarity about the truths to be believed and practiced. If you are insecure, uncertain, confused, and contradictory, it will be impossible to build."

For the journalists accredited to the Holy See he put on a show that ignored all the rules of protocol. He received them in the Apostolic Palace on October 21 even before the inaugural mass. He got up from his papal throne and mixed with them all, giving interviews in various languages, touching on all sorts of subjects—Marxism, ecumenism, Poland, Lebanon, skiing, and his life in the Vatican. "Five days have passed," he joked, "and if things go on like this, I think I can stand it." As he was about to conclude, he was asked if a press conference like this would ever be repeated. "We'll see how you treat me," he replied. It was a glimpse of how *he* would treat the press throughout his pontificate: The press was a guild to be hypnotized with his personal charm, an instrument to be used for his benefit. With few exceptions journalists as human beings didn't interest him.

On November 5 he took his first official trip outside the Vatican, to Assisi, the city of St. Francis, the patron of Italy. For the Polish pope this was a way to gauge the sympathies of the Italian people. The response he got surpassed all expectations. The enthusiasm was frenetic. Wojtyła was welcomed as *their pope.* The squares and alleys of the medieval city were jammed with crowds. To see and applaud his arrival some townspeople, including nuns, climbed out on rooftops (risking a fall because of powerful downdrafts from the blades of the pope's helicopter).

John Paul II pleased the crowd because he proved a man of flesh and blood, pious but virile. He didn't have a clerical face. He spoke spontaneously. He wasn't reluctant to say that Christ was the most important thing in the world. He presented the Gospel as a way to confront the difficulties of contemporary life—from terrorism to political instability. Nineteen seventy-eight in Italy was the year that saw the Red Brigades assassinate Christian Democratic leader Aldo Moro, an act that seemed to threaten the stability of the state. Western diplomats feared that the country was slipping into the chaos of armed conflict sparked by aggressive bands of extremists. Amid this storm Karol Wojtyła appeared as a pope who was prepared to leave his palace behind to boldly and publicly announce his faith in plain, straightforward language. It was no accident that Italy was the country where people soon began to call the pope by his family name—Wojtyła, as if he were one of the great figures of history: Washington or Garibaldi, Churchill or de Gaulle, Gandhi or Lenin.

At Assisi the faithful listened to John Paul II speak with St. Francis almost as if they were equals. The pope prayed for the resolution of all social and political problems by means of the Gospel—all the sufferings of man today, his doubts, his negations, his confusions, his tensions, his complexes, his anxieties. The pope turned to the saint: "Help us so that Christ himself can be the Way, the Truth, and the Life for the men and women of our time. Holy son of the land of Italy, Pope John Paul II, a son of Poland, asks this of you. And I hope you won't refuse him." Then, with the jubilation of the crowd ringing in his ears the pope heard a cry: "Don't forget the Church of Silence!" Without missing a beat John Paul II replied, "It's not a Church of Silence anymore, because it speaks with my voice."

THE POLISH POPE

In the mouth of the pope the phrase "the Church of Silence"—the Church suppressed behind the iron curtain—regained all its significance. During the long pontificate of Paul VI the Church of Silence was no longer used as a descriptive term. The phrase was left to little groups of traditionalists nostalgic for the preconciliar period. Referring to the situation in the socialist bloc countries, the Holy See preferred to talk about "steps toward normalizing relations" or at most about "obstacles."

Now a pope formed by his Polish experience was ready to remind the Communist regimes that there were Christians who had no freedom of speech or worship. If he had remained the cardinal of Kraków, during those same weeks he would have met with Adam Michnik, one of the most active dissidents in Poland, the cofounder of the Committee for the Defense of the Workers (KOR). The meeting had already been scheduled for October and seemed to point to a major leap in the pastoral-political career of the archbishop of Kraków. Although the papal election had intervened, Karol Wojtyła had only moved to higher ground. From now on his thunderbolts against Communist ideology would be hurled from the chair of St. Peter.

For the new pontiff the job of improving conditions for the Church in the Communist countries could not be left to Vatican diplomacy alone. Change had to come from above *and* from below. John Paul II quickly set to work lighting a fire under the Catholic hierarchy of the Eastern European countries. The cardinal archbishop of Prague, František Tomášek, was the first Eastern prelate to be received in an audience by the pope on the day of his inaugural mass. The cardinal was trying to survive the repressive dreariness of the regime led by party leader Gustav Husak, and the pope wanted to give him outspoken encouragement. He also promised support to the bishops of Latvia and Lithuania, who had come to Rome for the celebration. To the bishops of Hungary, who were content to live with concessions from the regime of János Kádár, the pope sent a letter subtly spurring them on to bolder initiatives: "May the Catholic Church spiritually illuminate Hungary!"

The spiritual illumination of Hungary could only mean considerable change in the status quo.

This was also a way to get the Kremlin and the Communist countries to pay attention to Karol Wojtyła's new version of *Ostpolitik*—and to remind them that the pope was, and continued to think of himself as, Polish. From the very first day John Paul II publicly showed his attachment to his ethnic identity. He asked the president of Poland, Henryk Jabłoński, if he could keep his passport; and for their part the Polish authorities never took Karol Wojtyła's name off the electoral rolls in Kraków. The pope thought of his origins as a sign of Providence.

On October 21, by way of a thank-you for the good wishes from the authorities in Warsaw, the pope sent a telegram to the Polish Communist leader Edward Gierek stressing that the history of Poland "has been bound up for a thousand years with the mission and service of the Catholic Church." On the 23rd, in a message to his compatriots, he exalted the special role played by the Church of Poland in the Church universal and in the history of Christianity. The Polish Church, he added, had become a sign of special witness "that the eyes of the entire world are watching." Without waiting for negotiations with the Polish government, the pope noted, "I very much want to come to you on the nine-hundredth anniversary of St. Stanisław's martyrdom"—May 8, 1979.

That same day he received the four thousand Polish pilgrims who had come to Rome. In so doing he mentioned his predecessor in Kraków, Eugeniusz Baziak, calling him "the great exiled archbishop," showing that the pope hadn't forgotten that Baziak had presided in 1944 over the diocese of Leopoli in his native western Ukraine—then part of Poland. That see was vacant because the Soviet government wouldn't let it be filled. During the meeting with his countrymen, which swept up everyone present in a wave of tears and joy, the pilgrims saw John Paul II and Primate Wyszyński embrace once more. "This Polish pope would not be on the chair of St. Peter," John Paul II told the primate, "had it not been for your faith, which did not flinch at prison and suffering, had it not been for your heroic hope and your limitless trust in the Mother of the Church." Emotion forced the pontiff to interrupt his speech. His voice cracked when his thoughts returned to his homeland.

"It's not easy to renounce going back," he said, "but if such is the will of Christ, one must accept it and I do. I pray only that this distance may unite us still more. Don't forget me in your prayers."

But even when his feelings overflowed, the pope didn't fail to send some political signals: "The love of the fatherland unites us and must unite us above and beyond all differences," he preached. Therefore everyone's faith and convictions were to be respected. With a word of subtle support for the resistance, he said, "Oppose everything that goes against human dignity and that degrades the customs of a healthy society."

．　　．　　．

From the very first the Polishness of John Paul II became a central part of policy—to the great surprise, wonder, and irritation of some members of the Curia. Secretary of State Jean Villot remained puzzled and dismayed that on the first day after the inaugural mass, instead of setting to work on the curial dossiers, the pope had devoted almost all his time to his compatriots.

What some monsignors in the Vatican thought of as sentimental folklore—the new pope's attention to Poland—proved to be a strategy pursued with tremendous tenacity. On November 4 the pope met a delegation from the Catholic University of Lublin and took the occasion to reaffirm that his election was a gift from the Lord to Poland. On December 6 along with a group of Polish priests he sang the traditional songs for the feast of St. Nicholas. On January 7, 1979, he celebrated a mass for his fellow Poles living in Rome. He extolled the sacrifice and martyrdom of St. Stanisław, whom he called a source of the spiritual unity of Poland.

The sensitive ears of the men in the Curia and of Vatican watchers elsewhere pricked up at this persistent repetition: Poland . . . Poland . . . Poland. When the pontiff spoke of his homeland, they realized, he was thinking of *all* the countries of Eastern Europe. At a reception for the diplomatic corps after his election, John Paul II defended the right of believers to freedom of religion and equal treatment. On behalf of all people everywhere he invoked respect for human rights and openness to spiritual values. A few weeks later he gave an audience to the foreign minister of Bulgaria, Petar Mladenov, and told him: "You know that the Catholic Church isn't looking for privileged treatment. In Bulgaria, as everywhere else, it needs living space to fulfill its religious mission."

He rarely missed a chance to insist on freedom of religion as the foundation of all other freedoms. On December 11, 1978, the thirtieth anniversary of the United Nations Declaration of Human Rights, he demanded that "freedom of religion for everyone and for all peoples must be respected by everyone everywhere." During a general audience at year's end he denounced atheism, which "brutally obstructs the quest for God in social, public, and cultural life." This was a picture of life in Eastern Europe, where religion was under harsh ideological constraints and, even when tolerated, was banned from the circuits of career and power. "Such an attitude is contrary to human rights," the pope proclaimed to Kurt Waldheim, then UN secretary general.

. . .

In the Curia John Paul II's approach shook up a policy that had seemed likely to go on indefinitely. One young monsignor, just beginning his career, found himself thinking, "this pope is not just saying, the way we always have, 'Let's try to keep up with these Communists step by step.' No, this pope is here to bring down communism at the altar." The impression began to spread that the pope was getting ready for an ideological battle—and the Vatican would have no choice but to go along.

Monsignor Achille Silvestrini, who worked in the Council for Public Affairs, the Vatican's department of foreign policy, clearly recalls that the pope's "priority was to affirm the rights of religious conscience. Diplomacy was all very well as a tool, but its purpose was to open the doors to Christ."

When Paul VI died, the Polish minister for religious affairs, Kazimierz Kąkol, had gone to the funeral and afterward met Archbishop Agostino Casaroli, the Vatican's foreign minister. According to Kąkol's report to the Polish leadership, Casaroli had assured him: "We are not going to change our policy toward the socialist countries." And then he explained why. The popes don't govern the Church directly, he said, they just make policy. "Decision making results from collegial work by the Vatican departments. It comes out of analysis, out of studying the issues. That's where we get the political line we follow. The pope merely gives it the final touch."

This was to be a dead letter in Wojtyła's pontificate. John Paul II instructed his representatives that henceforth in their negotiations with the Communist states, they should not minimize the irreconcilability of Marxism with the truth, but should highlight it. Silvestrini realized that this approach was more ethical and religious in nature than coldly political. For the pontiff, there was a sharp divide between *us* and *them*. Silvestrini took John Paul II's mode of speaking and acting to mean that for *them* truth didn't exist. The only thing that counted for *them* was what served the interests of power, of the party. But the Church had to respond, "No, truth exists in the conscience of men and women, it exists in society, which has to have this freedom of truth." Thus the pope's rigid philosophical distinctions were destined to have real effect in the world of politics.

Meanwhile in Moscow, *they* were accurately sizing up the new pope. Immediately after the election of Wojtyła the Politburo ordered a detailed portrait of the successor to John Paul I. They entrusted this job to the Institute for the World Socialist System, which had ties with the Soviet Academy of Science.

As early in the new pontificate as November 4, 1978, Oleg Bogomolov, director of the institute, submitted to the secretary of the Central Committee a report that is striking even today for the way it foresees many of John Paul II's moves. "According to high-ranking Catholic officials," Bogomolov wrote, "the election of a Polish cardinal will promote the *universalization* of the Church—that is, its activity in all social-political systems, above all in the socialist system. . . . It is likely that this dialogue [with the socialist countries] will have, on the part of the Vatican, a more aggressive and systematic character than under Paul VI. Wojtyła will apparently be less willing to compromise with the leadership of the socialist states, especially as regards the appointing [of bishops] to local churches."

The report stated that John Paul II would counterbalance his insistence on human rights in Eastern Europe with denunciations of repression in the Western Hemisphere, especially in Latin American countries such as Nicaragua and Chile. Bogomolov repeatedly emphasized that the Soviet Union had to expect a "new aggressiveness" in the Vatican policy toward the socialist countries and linkage between questions of co-existence with the Church and human rights. In Latin America, Bogomolov observed, the Vatican was facing a difficult problem: how to halt the radicalization of the national churches as well as the inclination of some Catholic clergy in these countries to cooperate with forces on the left, especially the Communists. Since John Paul II had briefly been a laborer himself and the problems of the worker were close to his heart, the assessment predicted that he would try to "expand the Church's influence not only in the socialist countries, but also among the working class in the capitalist world."

The assessment described Karol Wojtyła personally as a cardinal who had always taken right-wing positions, but who had urged the Church to avoid frontal attacks on socialism. He preferred instead a gradual transformation of socialist societies into pluralistic liberal-bourgeois systems. Initially "the new pope will be dependent on the Curia which, without a doubt, will try to subject him to its influence. But the independent temper and energy of John Paul II suggest that he will be fairly quick to get the hang of things and break free from the guardians of orthodoxy in the Curia."

The report advised the Soviet Union to support John Paul II's peace initiatives as well as the Vatican's position on the "internationalization" of Jerusalem. Furthermore, it suggested an effort to improve relations between the Soviet government and the Catholic clergy in Lithuania and in the western regions of Ukraine and Byelorussia.

Finally the members of the Politburo read a last recommendation meant especially for them: not to neglect a more attentive approach to the moral and spiritual needs of individuals. "Not infrequently," the report stressed, "an oversimplified and mechanical attitude toward the spiritual sphere of human life . . . creates a basis for strengthening the position of the Church." The hint was prophetic, but too refined for the Brezhnev-era leadership. For the Politburo of that moment it made more sense to talk (as Bogomolov dutifully went on to do) about an increase in atheistic propaganda and closer coordination of religious policies with the other socialist countries.

One thing Bogomolov failed to foresee was how quickly John Paul II would throw down the gauntlet to the Communist leadership with a trip to Poland. When Leonid Brezhnev, the Soviet leader, heard that the Polish leadership was negotiating the terms of such a visit, he angrily telephoned General Secretary Gierek in Warsaw. Gierek described the conversation in his memoirs:

> Brezhnev said he heard that the Church had invited the pope to Poland: "And what is your reaction?" he asked. I said, "We'll give him the reception he deserves."
>
> "Take my advice, don't give him any reception," Brezhnev said. "It will only cause trouble."
>
> "How could I not receive a Polish Pope," I answered, "when the majority of my countrymen are Catholics? They see his election as a great achievement. Besides, what would I say to people about why we're closing the border to him?"
>
> "Tell the pope—he's a wise man—he can declare publicly that he can't come due to an illness."
>
> "I'm sorry, Comrade Leonid," I said, "I can't do this. I have to welcome John Paul II." Then Brezhnev told me: "Gomułka was a better communist [than you], because he didn't receive Paul VI in Poland, and nothing awful happened. The Poles have survived the refusal to admit the pope once; they'll survive it a second time."
>
> "But political reasons dictate that I admit him," I declared.
>
> "Well, do as you wish," Brezhnev said. "But be careful you don't regret it later." And having said that he ended the conversation.

"The pope is very personal," Secretary of State Jean Villot commented to a friend, even as the pontiff was taking his first steps in the Vatican. And the cardinal added prophetically, "No doubt we will have a great pontificate. The new pope is a man who dares to confront problems and persons. We'll end up smelling the smoke of the bombs."

French to his fingertips, especially in the refined, calm, and lucid way he administered the affairs of the Church, Cardinal Jean Villot had been a confidant of Paul VI. His balance compensated for the tormented intelligence of Pope Montini. It was to his advantage that he felt radically detached from the Italian political quarrels in which all the twentieth-century popes had been personally involved.

But Villot soon learned how far apart his and John Paul II's notions of how to lead the Church of Rome actually were. Like Wojtyła, Villot had been one of the participants in the Second Vatican Council. Unlike his Polish confrère, however, he came from a French Catholic culture that, together with its German counterpart, had supplied the Council with its theological elite and had profoundly influenced its results.

One of the most urgent concepts to emerge from the Council was *collegiality.* "The Church has been entrusted to Peter and the Apostles, not to the Curia!" Eastern patriarch Maximus IV had protested to the Council Fathers.

Paul VI had taken a small step forward by instituting the Synod of Bishops. But its powers were strictly consultative and, in any event, it met as a rule only every three years to discuss a single issue, or at most two, chosen in advance by the pope. Indeed, by structuring the synod in this way Paul VI had actually moved to shore up his supremacy, while doing little more than nod in the direction of collegiality. That was why the cardinal-electors had gone back to talking about collegiality during the first meetings of the conclave.

Cardinal Villot wanted to test the pope's intentions in this area: "Is Your Holiness thinking of giving permanent representation to the Synod Council?" he asked. In ecclesiastical jargon to speak of "permanent representation" meant to make provision for the election of a group of bishops by the bishops conferences all over the world who could work together with the pope like a sort of cabinet or limited crown council to govern the Church.

John Paul II unhesitatingly rejected the idea. "No, that would be a synod in the style of the Eastern Churches." That is, it would be a democratic organism, as in the Orthodox Churches, where the synod is a true parliament of bishops that passes laws and makes decisions. "The pope will remain supreme and sole legislator, with the ecumenical council"—the assembly of all the bishops that can be convoked only at the pope's express command. John Paul II offered assurances that he would consult more frequently with the synod on specific problems. But, he added, "There's no need to make this consultation obligatory."

Thus the game of Church democracy was lost before it began; and the hopes of many of Wojtyła's most fervent supporters in the conclave, such as Cardinals Lorscheiter and König, were irrevocably dashed. Whether the new pope realized that he would cruelly disappoint so many people is uncertain. He had never lived in a democracy; and for him the word *collegiality* meant little more than the feeling of clerical togetherness—the solidarity of brothers, who are nonetheless subordinate to the same father, a man with all the discipline and peremptoriness of a monarch.

As for *Ostpolitik*, Villot didn't think the pope's plan of traveling to Poland for St. Stanisław's anniversary was "urgent," but John Paul II paid not the slightest heed to his reservations. The pope was indeed acting in a "highly personal" way. To his friend the French priest Antoine Wenger, Villot remarked: "The new pope has a great deal of willpower and decisiveness. In the course of the first week of his pontificate he has made decisions in which some careful advice wouldn't have been out of place."

· · ·

Even physically Wojtyła couldn't be fenced in. On the first day after the conclave, he began the practice of going outside the walls of the Vatican, being driven to the Gemelli Clinic to visit his old friend Andrzej Deskur. A week later he went by helicopter to the sanctuary of La Mentorella, thirty miles from Rome, where he had gone to pray in the days before his election.

The monsignors in the Curia were forced to realize that he was doing things entirely on his own, in his own style. On his way to take possession of the papal basilica of St. John Lateran, the pope had unabashedly hugged the mayor of Rome, Giulio Argan, who was an art historian—and a Communist. He received French bishop Marcel Lefebvre, who had been suspended from all his religious functions by Paul VI for rebelling against the Council and who was under orders not to ordain priests who had been trained in accordance with preconciliar rules. He also received the Mexican bishop Méndez

Arceo, a notorious leftist. "Most Holy Father," Cardinal Villot glumly murmured, "he is a member of Christians for Socialism." "Socialism is something I'm quite familiar with," John Paul II answered with a smile.

No one had told the secretary of state about it, when *L'Osservatore Romano* announced on November 5 that the pope would be going to Puebla, Mexico, for the Conference of Latin American Bishops at the invitation of Cardinal Salazar López, archbishop of Guadalajara. Mexico had an anticlerical constitution. Priests weren't even allowed to wear their cassocks on the street, and the country had no diplomatic ties with the Vatican. The government took no official interest in the papal visit.

Cardinal Villot had his doubts and voiced them to the pope. He was afraid the pontiff wouldn't be received with the honors due his rank. He hoped that at least one representative of the chief of state would come to welcome him briefly at the airport. But John Paul II wasn't interested in the qualms of his secretary of state or in the niceties of protocol. What he had in mind was something undreamt of by any *curiale*, something as revolutionary as the Council itself—the remaking of the papacy for Christianity's Third Millennium.

ABROAD

Twenty-four hours before leaving for Mexico City, Pope Wojtyła held a two-hour audience for the Soviet foreign minister, Andrei Gromyko. Gromyko was a seasoned visitor to the Vatican, having been there in 1967, 1974, and 1975; but this was the first time John Paul II found himself face to face with a Kremlin elder and a member of its Politburo. Gromyko was a stiff, glacial man, intelligent to be sure, but used to masking his thoughts with soulless bureaucratese. Any observation or objection bounced off him without prompting the slightest reaction, except perhaps for a few propagandistic clichés.

Wojtyła realized that his charm was useless here, and he adopted a very formal manner as he studied the man from Moscow. At the same time, he knew that he too was being observed. Gromyko was struck, first of all, by the pope's robust physique. "This man," he noted later, "knows a thing or two about sports."

John Paul II began with a generic political formula, stressing the importance of contacts with the Soviet Union in order to consolidate peace. He spoke in Russian and later in English. Gromyko replied that every effort had to be made to spare the world the threat of war, especially nuclear war. He cited some initiatives by the Soviet Union and praised the efforts of the Church "on behalf of peace, disarmament, and the liquidation of armaments of mass destruction. We greatly appreciate this." Then Gromyko listed the most pressing areas of conflict around the globe. "As far as ideology is concerned," he said, "religious convictions and the general problems of differing world views must not pose an obstacle to cooperation" between the USSR and the Vatican.

"I share the view that there is no more pressing concern in world politics right now than the task of removing the threat of war," Wojtyła responded. "The Catholic Church acts for the good of peace in the world."

With great caution, the pope confronted the issue that was closest to his heart. "It's possible," he prodded, "that the factors which limit the freedom to practice one's religion haven't been eliminated everywhere. According to some sources"—the pope measured every word—"something like that is occasionally met with even in the Soviet Union."

Gromyko's response was ice-cold. "In the West, such false reports are often disseminated . . . [and] turn common criminals into martyrs. There isn't a grain of truth in the rumors about restrictions on freedom of religion. Ever since the beginning of the Soviet state freedom of religion has been, and is, guaranteed." Gromyko was shameless in repeating such ancient, discredited formulas of Soviet propaganda. No wonder that back in Washington they had christened him "Mr. Nyet." Yet telling the supreme pontiff of the Catholic Church that religious freedom was alive and well in the Soviet Union was a stretch even for Gromyko. "In the hard years of the Second World War the Russian Orthodox Church stood alongside the Soviet state," he continued, "and led its own struggle against fascism. Would this have been possible if the Church in our country had found itself in an abnormal condition?"

The pope's face remained impassive.

"We have religious people," Gromyko said, "but this causes no problems, either for them, for our government, or for the life of Soviet society."

As Wojtyła had always said, *they* lied, *they* had no respect for the truth: In the USSR anyone who openly admitted to being a believer wasn't allowed to become a teacher, have an army career, or hold a position in the Communist Party—though the pope kept his own counsel, for now.

.　.　.

At seven-twenty on the morning of January 25, John Paul II left the Vatican for Fiumicino airport with the happy look of someone heading off on a long excursion. During his first one hundred days the atmosphere of crisis that had weighed on the Church in the last years of Paul VI had been swept away. The papacy was becoming relevant again, a dynamic factor on the global scene. The figure of John Paul II had captured the collective imagination. People rooted for this pope. The more physical a presence Karol Wojtyła was, the more charismatic a symbol he became. People paged through magazines with old photos of Wojtyła canoeing, hiking in the mountains, or just shaving. People said that this was the first pontiff whose shoes you could see—and they looked like big peasant shoes, like the shoes of a fisherman.

At audiences, nuns went crazy. They screamed that he was handsomer than Jesus, and they threw themselves at him in hopes of touching him. People ideologically remote from him were willy-nilly enthralled. Carlo Benedetti, a Vatican reporter for *Paese Sera*, a pro-Communist newspaper, had a strange dream, worthy of being recounted to Dr. Freud: He was walking through a large apartment and, as he entered the last room, he got a glimpse of a woman. "She had her back turned to me. She was standing in front of the mirror, combing her long hair, something like Rita Hayworth. Suddenly she turned around and I saw the face of Wojtyła. Damn it, I thought, he can be everything: even a woman!"

The new pope gave off an air of omnipotence.

On his special plane (the *Dante Alighieri*), 140 journalists, technicians, and Alitalia employees were waiting for the pope and his retinue of twenty-five cardinals, monsignors, and Swiss Guards in mufti. Among the pope's baggage were trunks with John Paul II's speeches already printed and translated into various languages. Except for last-minute changes, every remark, every excla-mation point had already been planned in the Vatican after a flurry of drafts between the pope's study and the offices of the Curia. There was only one speech the pope was still working on, and that was the most important one of all: to the bishops of Latin America gathered for the conference in Puebla.

On the eve of his departure John Paul II got word from his foreign office that Chile and Argentina had officially accepted the mediation of the Holy See in their dispute over the Beagle Channel. The two governments, both run by military dictators, had asked the Vatican to intervene "with the goal of guiding and assisting them in the quest for a peaceful resolution of the dispute." But many Catholics in Italy and Latin America were taken aback when *L'Osservatore Romano* published a large photograph of General Pinochet of Chile. To them Pinochet was a brutal dictator, the leader of a bloody coup d'état, responsible for the torture, death, and disappearance of thousands of members of the Chilean opposition. The archbishop of Santiago, Cardinal Raul Silva Henríquez, was an opponent of Pinochet; he had prompted the foundation, near the archbishop's palace, of the Vicariate of Solidarity to assist the victims of the regime and defend human rights.

John Paul II supported the cardinal's humanitarian action, but he thought that when the Holy See was involved in initiatives for peace and justice, it had to deal with even the most antipathetic regimes. The question of the Beagle Channel, over which the Chileans and the Argentineans had nearly come to blows some weeks earlier, was important to the Vatican because after a century of diplomatic insignificance the papacy was once again being called upon to play a role in international negotiations. To be sure, this was small potatoes compared with the Treaty of Tordesillas (1494), in which Pope Alexander VI divided the map of the world between Spain and Portu-gal, tracing a line in the middle of the Atlantic Ocean and assigning all the lands west of it (except Brazil) to the Spanish monarchs Ferdinand and Isabella and those east of it, from the Azores to Ceylon and beyond, to the king of Portugal. Territorially the dispute over the Beagle Channel was a peripheral matter; what counted for John Paul II was the signal it sent: The Church had to make its voice heard on the international scene.

In preparing for the journey, the pope was well aware that from Washington to Moscow, from London to Rio de Janeiro, his trip was being closely monitored. Latin America was a sore point in relations between the United States and the Soviet Union, but it also had—and has—an immense relevance for the Church. By the year 2000 practically one-half of all Catholics would be Latin Americans. Furthermore, in that region a contest was being played out between military dictatorships and democracy, as well as between Marxism and capitalism. From Cuba, Fidel Castro had intensified his support for guerrilla movements in Central America. The Church had to choose whether to continue backing brutal antidemocratic regimes or to accept the adventure of revolution. John Paul II would have preferred to see the formation of reformist political alliances, but that required a social foundation lacking in the highly polarized Latin American countries.

Nicaragua was a typical example. There the Sandinista guerrillas, some of whom were members of Catholic movements, were fighting the dictatorial rule of the Somoza family, which had been backed for decades by the United States. There seemed to be no other way to turn the country away from oligarchy; and so the Catholic hierarchy of Nicaragua, led by Archbishop Obando y Bravo of Managua, who for years had steered a wary course between the regime and the opposition, was now moving toward support for the Sandinistas. Even the pope's old friend from Kraków Father Mieczysław Maliński wondered: "Whom will the pope align himself with—the military regimes or those fighting against them?" The battle lines were forming inside and outside the Church. The progressives were waiting for the pope to speak out against the dictatorships and to commit the Church to action against "structural injustices perpetuated by the ruling classes." Ten years earlier, the Latin American bishops conference (CELAM), meeting at Medellín, Colombia, had said that one of the Church's tasks was to support the "liberation" of downtrodden peoples. The word itself was thick with ambiguity.

As he headed for Latin America, John Paul II had to confront a "Church of the People," organized around so-called base communities— innovative, politically committed to social change (with arms if necessary), fanned by the winds of liberation theology. In these communities, groups of Catholic laity came together as a living Church but largely independent of established Church structures: They prayed together, administered the sacraments to one another, and acted to alleviate oppressive conditions in behalf of the poor. Now the poet-pope would find himself facing other poet-priests who took their inspiration from Christ the Worker rather than from St. John of the Cross. The base communities in Nicaragua celebrated a peasant mass composed by Carlos Mejía Godoy, whose Credo went like this:

"I firmly believe, Lord, that this whole creation was born from your prodigious mind, that from your artist's hand your beauty blossomed: the stars and the moon, the little houses, the lakes, the little boats sailing on the rivers that flow to the sea, the immense coffee plantations, the white expanses of cotton fields, and the forests butchered by the criminal axe. . . .

"I believe in you, Christ the Worker, the only begotten of God, I believe in you, companion, the human Christ, conqueror of death. . . . You are rising from the dead in every hand that is raised to defend the people from domination and exploitation."

Ultimately the progressives in the church were expecting the new pope to encourage people to follow "the road of Medellín," inviting Catholics to break off all complicity with the ruling classes. Those regarded as "conservatives" in the Latin American Church and in Rome were hoping for exactly the opposite. They knew that the Church had to distance itself from the military regimes, but they wanted order. They were for reforms if possible, but they rejected the idea of overthrowing the establishment. They firmly believed that the Church had to defend itself from "Marxist infiltration," that it should concentrate on dispensing the sacraments and maintaining traditional doctrine.

Within the Church's hierarchy a real political struggle was going on and, for once, the labels of "progressive" and "conservative" actually fit. The Colombian archbishop Alfonso López Trujillo, secretary of CELAM, was a bitter enemy of liberation theology. After the pope's election he went to the Vatican to put pressure on John Paul II to fight the leadership of the Brazilian bishops, who were close to the base communities and the progressive theologians. Brazilian cardinal Aloísio Lorscheiter, a key supporter of Wojtyła's papal candidacy, was the president of CELAM, which made the Church's internal struggle still more complicated.

Even before the pope's journey, Archbishop Trujillo began to maneuver with an eye to the March elections of the directors of CELAM. Trujillo had a military mentality. "Prepare your planes and your bombers," he had written to a bishop who shared his views. "We need you today more than ever; and you have to be in the best shape possible. I think you have to train the way boxers do before they go into the ring for the world championship. May your punches be evangelical and well thrown."

In 1976 Trujillo had presided over a conference in Rome of fifty theologians seeking to analyze and combat "the worldwide expansion of Latin American liberation theology." Trujillo had accused French, German, and left-wing American Catholics of furnishing "logistical support" to Christians for Socialism. "The danger goes far beyond the frontiers of South America," he claimed. "It has reached the entire Catholic world."

Analyses such as these, and others more measured, were sent directly to the Vatican. The pope also knew that some German bishops had been mobilized to help the Latin American hierarchy opposed to liberation theology. In one way or another Catholics on various continents were swept up in the struggle. All of them were waiting for a decisive word from John Paul II.

In France the writer Michel de Saint Pierre, leader of the traditionalist group Credo and a personal friend of Marcel Lefebvre, the rebel bishop who had rejected Vatican II, announced, "This new pope, with his saint's eyes, is God's lumberjack. He is getting ready to cut down the dead wood in today's Church. He won't allow the dogmatic and doctrinal truth to be trampled down again. The new pope's Church will be a Church of discipline. We will assist at the rebirth of a militia of Christ."

Such was the atmosphere as John Paul II embarked for Mexico. "I am not afraid of facing the situation in Latin America," the pope told a journalist. Before going up the ramp of the plane, he placed himself under the protection of the Madonna of Guadalupe. *"Totus tuus sum ego"*—I am all yours—he proclaimed in the presence of the Italian and Vatican authorities who had come to see him off.

·   ·   ·

Hardly had the papal jet reached cruising altitude than the Holy Father showed up in the journalists' compartment. His presence came as a complete surprise: The idea of an in-flight press conference was utterly unknown. To get a closer look the reporters stood on their seats or thronged the first rows. But there was no need. Courteous and patient, John Paul II slowly walked down one aisle and then the other, all the way to the rear of the cabin, taking questions as he went.

The pope immediately attacked his central topic: faith and revolution. Asked whether it was legitimate for Latin American Catholics to choose socialism, he replied: "We have to begin to study what socialism is and what sorts of versions of it there are. For example, an atheistic socialism, which is incompatible with Christian principles, with the Christian vision of the world, with the rights of man, with morality, would not be an acceptable solution."

Someone asked: And if there is a kind of socialism that recognizes the religious dimension and guarantees it in the life of the state?

John Paul II bent his head a bit, as he does in reflective moments. "There is a lot of talk about guarantees, but you don't get to see them till later." His tone was calm, with a touch of irony: "Yes, yes . . . you don't see the guarantees until after the fact."

On the subject of liberation theology his comments were biting. "It's not a true theology. It distorts the true sense of the Gospel. It leads those who have given themselves to God away from the true role that the Church has assigned them. When they begin to use political means, they cease to be theologians. If it's a social program, that's a matter for sociology. If it refers to the salvation of man, then it's the perennial theology, which is two thousand years old."

In talking to the journalists, the pope repeatedly reflected on his homeland. "Poles and Mexicans love the Madonna in the same way, because they have suffered so much," he said. What was the role of the Church? "It looks to the common good. The Church is a reality that lives in the real world. If it's true to itself, it must serve all people, in Italy as in Poland and Mexico."

What would he be bringing to Latin America? "I bring faith. Isn't that enough?" he rejoined, with characteristic self-confidence. Giusi Serena, a flight attendant who had accompanied Paul VI nine years before on his trip to Australia, was fascinated. "He's really friendly," she said. "He gets along with everybody. He's not like the other pope; that one who was always standing on a pedestal."

Karol Wojtyła seemed to be a man happy with his job. That too was a novelty for the successors of St. Peter. "I'm happy to work," he told the journalists. "I'm happy that this is my job. I'm happy to fulfill my mission."

. . .

On January 26, after stopping for the night in Santo Domingo, John Paul II arrived in Mexico City. At 1:05 P.M. when he stepped out of the aircraft, with a big smile, he saw a crowd of ten thousand people. The customary display of the flags of the host nation paired with those of the Vatican was missing. There was no honor guard, nobody from the diplomatic corps, no cannon salvos. In a corner of the airport there was only one surreal placard, proclaiming "Welcome." Welcome to whom? It didn't say.

Official, anticlerical Mexico didn't want to acknowledge the visit. The day before, the newspapers spoke contemptuously of "the visit of the Catholic pope." They carped about the political intentions of the clergy; they confirmed the appropriateness of the pope's being received as an ordinary citizen in the presidential residence. The government had decided that no flags would be hung out on public buildings. The archbishop of Mexico City, Ernesto Corripio Ahumada, felt obliged to deny that the arrival of the pope was designed as one more challenge to the Mexican constitution and the Church's lack of public status. "The Holy Father is not coming here to raise questions that belong to past epochs," he declared. The bishops also assured everyone that the pope would not call for the reestablishment of diplomatic ties between Mexico and the Holy See.

Nevertheless the mass media accused the Church hierarchy of wanting to end the separation of Church and state dating from the second half of the nineteenth century. Some papers, with a condescending air, characterized the pope as "a fifty-eight-year-old Pole."

If he was concerned about all this, John Paul II did a good job of hiding it. He walked down the ramp of the airplane, flung himself onto the tarmac, and fervently kissed the soil of Mexico. When he got up, he found standing in front of him the president of the republic, José López Portillo, and his wife, Carmela, disguised as private citizens. "Welcome, señor, to Mexico," said the president as he shook the pope's hand. "I hope that your mission of peace and harmony, and your efforts on behalf of justice, will be successful. I leave you in the hands of the hierarchy and the faithful of your Church, and may all this promote the welfare of humanity." "That is my mission and my ministry," the pope replied. "I'm very happy to be in Mexico." End of performance. As if in a film by Buñuel, President López Portillo turned his back and left.

The Mexican people paid no attention to these political barriers. Their profoundly Catholic soul swept away the question of nonrecognition. All the church bells in the city began to ring; and at the airport, as a little orchestra blasted out "Cielito Lindo," the crowd broke through police lines, surging around the pope, swamping him and his entourage. A child ran up to hug him; a huge man opened up his poncho in front of the pope and flung out a cascade of roses. Dozens of hands pushed a wide-brimmed sombrero toward him. John Paul II put it on his head: with that little gesture he conquered Mexico—and much of the world.

His car took two hours to get to the Zócalo, the central square of Mexico City nine miles from the airport. The crowd was delirious. Millions of Mexicans thronged the route, waving hundreds of thousands of little white and yellow flags. Wherever the papal motorcade passed, offices emptied out and female staff rushed to the window shrieking, *"Viva el papa, viva México."* A deafening roar accompanied the popemobile. Astonished and intoxicated, everywhere he turned the pope saw tens of thousands of posters with his picture. Buildings were blanketed with Vatican flags. People stuck photos of Wojtyła in the middle of the national tricolor. Every time the pope raised his hand in blessing, the crowd's enthusiasm swelled even higher.

·　　·　　·

For six days the atmosphere would be one of total exaltation. The newspapers, so critical on the eve of the visit, were now filled with triumphalist headlines: "He came, he conquered," proclaimed one Mexico City daily. In pages and pages of special inserts the directors and employees of companies and corporations shouted "Hosanna" to the pope.

The rhythm of the papal TV spots was relentless. The television announcers and the popular personalities who entertained the faithful waiting for the pope spouted wild hyperbole: John Paul II was one of "the great rulers of humanity" and "the incarnation of Christ among us." He was credited with exercising "the most terrific power in the world."

Surrounded by a worship that went beyond anything even he could have imagined, John Paul II didn't neglect the subject that made the trip so controversial. Entering the cathedral of the City of Mexico, the pope took a hard look at the boundaries of his Church: "The Church's faithful are not those who cling to the accidental aspects that were valid in the past but are now outdated. Nor are the faithful those who have launched into the adventurous and utopian construction of a so-called Church of the future."

The tour of Mexico would become the paradigm for all subsequent papal trips. In six days the pope gave twenty-six speeches and homilies. He met with priests, diplomats, bishops, nuns, seminarians, peasants, workers, Indians, families, doctors, patients, militant members of Catholic organizations, monks, students, slum dwellers, government spokesmen, and reporters. Every meeting was separate. This nonstop round of appointments was impressive, even breathtaking. The pope's secretary, Monsignor Stanisław Dziwisz, was forever opening and closing the red leather briefcase containing the pope's speeches. John Paul II entered and left various buildings, he got into and out of the helicopter or the car, composed himself and prayed, then dove into the bubbling cauldron of another jubilant crowd. He celebrated masses and witnessed the dashing maneuvers of the *charros* (Mexican cowboys). The whole schedule was exactly what he had wanted: It was designed to allow the Roman pontiff to encounter every single social and ecclesiastical milieu. The trip was supposed to let various groups experience directly the words and authority of the pope, to present him in different situations so that everyone could return to his or her house, convent, or workplace with news of personal contact with the head of the Catholic Church, who had provided guidance on how to live and act in society.

There is no other institution in the world, now that the Soviet-styled Communist parties have disappeared, where the word of the leader is so radically important and binding as the Catholic Church. From the beginning of his pontificate John Paul II has been aware of the need to bring the "pope's words" to the greatest possible number of people, to point out the correct line to be followed, and to reinforce the spiritual power of the center of the Catholic Church—Rome.

Pope Paul VI, near the end of his pontificate, had expressed his concern about the slow drift of the national episcopates away from the Vatican. Echoing the old slur "banana republics," he groaned, "We will end up having 'banana churches.' " Karol Wojtyła's response to this was to bring the papacy directly into every corner of the world, reaffirming the authority of Peter and binding the bishops to the Roman throne.

John Paul II introduced another novelty during his first trip abroad that would become a regular habit: meeting with representatives of the Polish community. When he visited Uganda in 1964, Paul VI had refused to grant an audience to a group of Italians working there. "I am here for the Africans," he remarked stiffly.

John Paul II took a totally different stance. Wherever he went, he highlighted the presence of his compatriots to reaffirm before the world his bond with his homeland and its destiny. In Ecuador, amid a crowd of 100,000 dark-skinned Indians, he picked up and hugged a blond Polish child. On every one of his trips abroad, Polish voices and Polish flags would be part of the picture. And often those flags would feature the crowned Polish eagle, from the days before the Communist regime.

Just a day after arriving in Mexico John Paul II granted his first audience, at nine A.M., to the Polish community. He reminded them that all Poles scattered throughout the world maintained their ties to the fatherland through the Church and the Black Madonna of Częstochowa. Then John Paul II invited his compatriots to pray for the "Polish pope," that he might pass the test as a truly catholic (that is, universal) pope.

·   ·   ·

On January 25, the day the Latin American Bishops Conference was to open in the basilica of Our Lady of Guadalupe in Puebla, the pope was awakened by *mañanitas,* a brief serenade played in his honor. One-third of Mexico City's thirteen million inhabitants poured out into the streets, lining up to cheer the pope as he passed by. Perhaps there were four million, perhaps five. An army of 100,000 policemen tried to protect their guest, a titanic task. As the bells of the capital pealed over and over, the white and yellow popemobile crawled through the streets. John Paul II would often stop the open car to shake hands and greet people. The cult of the personality, on which the papacy of John Paul II would feed, was born amid his triumphs in Mexico.

Our Lady of Guadalupe is a black Virgin. The Mexicans call her la Morenita. The title comes from a painting that recalls the appearance of the Madonna to an Indian shepherd named Juan Diego in 1531. The Virgin appeared to him brightly shining, but brown-skinned and dressed like an Indian noblewoman. Juan Diego told the story to his bishop, who didn't believe him. Then the Madonna made a rosebush blossom in stony ground. The shepherd gathered the roses and hid them in his cloak to show them to the skeptical bishop. But when Juan Diego opened the fold in his cloak, instead of the roses the image of the Virgin had been imprinted on the cloth. This mysterious image is the chief treasure of the basilica.

The pope liked the story because it showed that ordinary people can have a stronger spiritual grasp than an intellectual bishop. Many years later when a spate of Marian apparitions broke out at Medjugorie in Yugoslavia and the local church was split—the Franciscans for and the bishop against— John Paul II would tacitly support the advocates of the apparitions. His faith in the Mother of God is as unshakable as his support for the faith of ordinary people. After the trip to Mexico the pope would almost always try to include a stop at a Marian sanctuary whenever he went abroad. It was his way of emphasizing the freshness and vitality of popular piety, in contrast to the skepticism of industrial societies and Protestantized Catholics.

For the Virgin of Guadalupe John Paul II composed a prayer that was almost a poem: "I greet you, Mary! With immense love and profound respect I utter these words at once so simple and so wonderful! *Ave Maria, gratia plena, Dominus tecum.* [Hail Mary, full of grace, the Lord is with thee.] I repeat these words that so many hearts treasure and so many lips pronounce all over the world. I greet you, Mother of God!"

In a new basilica of reinforced concrete, with its marble floor, red velvet armchairs around the altar, and chandeliers gleaming from a hundred bulbs, John Paul II issued a series of warnings by way of prologue to the conference of the Latin American bishops. In the ten years since the conference in Medellín, he stressed, "interpretations have been heard that at times are contradictory, not always correct, and not always well intentioned toward the Church." The pope cited one of the key concepts advanced by the Medellín conference—"preferential love for the poor"—but he immediately added that this love must not exclude any class. This papal dictum, endlessly repeated in the following decade, would be used to block any Marxist interpretation of the Church's commitment "to the complete liberation of persons and peoples."

That afternoon, at a reception held in the same basilica for ten thousand priests and members of religious orders from Mexico and the rest of Latin America, John Paul II hammered away at his listeners, urging them not to be swayed by alluring calls to political commitment. "You are spiritual guides," he exclaimed, "not social leaders, not political executives or functionaries of a secular order." Priests and others under monastic vows had to obey their bishops. They were not to work out their own set of doctrines. They had to observe celibacy and chastity. They had to practice frequent confession, daily meditation, and devotion to the Virgin by means of the rosary.

It was a loud and clear call to order and, in the context of Latin America, an admonition to the clergy to stay away from leftist movements. In his head he carried his own Polish model of the Church, and he used the trip to Mexico to preach it to the world.

·   ·   ·

The next day, January 28, the opening sessions of the bishops conference began in Puebla. It was in theory a true parliament of the Latin American Church. On hand were 32 cardinals, 66 archbishops, 131 bishops, 45 priests, 51 members of religious orders, 4 permanent deacons, and 33 laypeople. But the three chairmen of the assembly, Cardinals Sebastiano Baggio and Ernesto Corripio Ahumada, both of whom opposed liberation theology, and Aloísio Lorscheiter, who favored it, had been personally chosen by the pope—not the bishops. The deck was already stacked.

Before coming to Mexico John Paul II had carefully read the books of the Peruvian Jesuit Gustavo Gutiérrez, the founding theoretician of liberation theology. His central thesis was that the proclamation of the Gospel must not become disembodied, abstracted from the real conditions of the people. Faith in Christ had to be an active force that helps to free hundreds of millions of Latin Americans from the oppressive conditions in which they live. To eliminate the structures of injustice, liberation theologians argued, the method of Marxist social analysis could be applied without accepting the materialism of Communist ideology.

To the Vatican all this was heresy; and the Latin American Jesuits who professed sympathy for liberation theology and its historical context were viewed with suspicion. John Paul II had no sympathy for such contamination of faith by politics.

When it came to Marxism, there was always a total lack of understanding between the Eastern European intellectuals, who were formative in Karol Wojtyła's development, and liberal intellectuals from the West. The dissident intelligentsia of the Soviet bloc countries could never comprehend what Marxism meant for so many men and women in the industrialized countries or the Third World: namely, left-wing social democracy, radical reformism, utopia and hope, national revolution, a lever to move the poor out from under crushing social conditions. For the intellectuals of Eastern Europe the whole phenomenon of Western Marxism generally came down to a Soviet conspiracy or to the naive illusions of hopeless romantics abroad in the service of the Kremlin.

For their part, decade after decade, many pro-Marxist Western intellectuals refused to acknowledge the profoundly oppressive nature of the so-called socialist regimes of Eastern Europe. They closed their eyes to the daily violence of systems in which any thick-headed bureaucrat or policeman exercised the sort of absolute power that leftist intellectuals wouldn't have tolerated for a moment in their own countries. With the election of Karol Wojtyła the divergence between the two visions extended to the highest levels of the Vatican. Arriving in Puebla, the pope was spurred less by the will to understand than by the intention to fight an enemy in ambush.

Every faction in CELAM had its lobbies exerting pressure on public opinion. The anti-Communist Latin American Confederation sent the pope a telegram calling for the expulsion from the Church of "Marxist bishops and guerrilla priests." The progressive clergy was accused of pushing the continent toward "Communist tyranny." The telegram, which also appeared as a paid ad in the newspapers, listed the bishops considered most dangerous: Casaldiga (Brazil), Méndez Arceo (Mexico), Obando y Bravo (Nicaragua), and Proana (Ecuador). The blacklist also contained some internationally prominent names, such as Cardinal Silva Henríquez of Chile and Dom Helder Camara, bishop of Recife in Brazil.

On the other side, Christians for Change in Colombia criticized the preparatory document of the Puebla conference for "turning a blind eye to the current history of the persecution and martyrdom, the slow death of democracy in Latin America." Amnesty International prepared a report on seventeen thousand Latin American political prisoners and thirty thousand "disappeared."

Everyone was calling on the pope to pass judgment. John Paul II had come to cut the Gordian knot.

His speech in the old Palafox Seminary, before a subdued audience of cardinals, priests, members of religious orders, and laypeople, marked a turning point in the Vatican's approach to Latin America. The bonhomie and smiles seen by millions of Mexicans vanished from John Paul II's face when he told the bishops, "We must keep watch over the purity of doctrine." That meant avoiding false interpretations of Christ or theories that pass over his divinity in silence. The pope was almost ferocious in his denunciation of any revisions of the Gospels that deviated from Church doctrine. "They make an effort to show Jesus as politically committed, as someone who fought against Roman domination and the powerful, indeed as someone implicated in the class struggle." No, the pope affirmed, wading in with all his authority and rock-solid determination. No, the Roman pontiff would not allow these currents in the Church. "This notion of a political Jesus, a revolutionary, the subversive from Nazareth," he proclaimed, "is not in harmony with the Church's teaching."

His voice swelled proudly, his look never wavered, as he claimed: "The Church has no need to resort to systems and ideologies in order to love, defend, and do its share for the liberation of man." The Church finds in its own message the inspiration to work for brotherhood, justice, and peace "against all forms of domination, slavery, and discrimination, against violence, assaults on religious freedom, and acts of aggression on man and on human life."

It was an unequivocal message to the tense and eager audience in the hall, a crystal-clear signal that immediately got through to the Kremlin and the White House. The pope from Kraków would never let Catholics align themselves with Marxist movements in a battle for social justice and democracy. The Polish pope would never approve of what the Italian pope Paul VI, in his encyclical *Populorum Progressio* (Progress of Peoples) had declared permissible in extreme cases: revolution against deeply entrenched dictatorships. The Polish youth who under Kraków's Nazi occupation had prayed for deliverance but never joined the resistance was now imposing his method on the clergy of Latin America.

Aloísio Lorscheiter, who had played a key role in the election of Karol Wojtyła as pope, swinging many Third World votes his way, now listened, gauging every word. Among the cluster of papers in Lorscheiter's hand was the text of the speech he would give at the conference the next day to introduce the sessions. His emphasis was different, more attuned to existing conditions and the feelings of the poor. "To proclaim the Gospel today and tomorrow to our Latin American brothers," he would argue, "who are driven by hope and at the same time tortured in the depth of their souls by the offense to their dignity, is not just a fraternal and noble thing to do. It is our mission, our duty; it is our life."

At the bishops conference the pope spoke for an hour. The first part of his speech had been written to prevent the Church from turning to the left. In the second part he showed his passion for justice. At Puebla John Paul II used the word *liberation* twelve times. He didn't forget to say that private property has a social dimension and that there has to be a more just and equitable distribution of goods, not only within nations but also on the international level, to prevent the stronger countries from oppressing the weaker ones. "The Church has the duty to proclaim the liberation of millions of human beings," he declared. But lest he be misunderstood, he added that that liberation primarily meant freedom from sin and the Evil Spirit.

The liberation theologians present at Puebla tried to put the best spin possible on the pope's speech—which wasn't easy. The Brazilian Franciscan Leonardo Boff noted that in the first part the predominant features seemed to be "reservations and suspicion," while the second part had "an explicitly liberational vision." Gustavo Gutiérrez, the author of *Theology of Liberation,* had followed the pope's remarks in Mexico. "It strikes me as important," he said, "that the pope announced the evangelical value of the defense of human rights, not as a temporary operation but as an intrinsic mission of the Church."

In the following decade, the Church in Latin America would become an important factor in that region's transition to democracy. But, in keeping with the directives from Wojtyła, the Church's hierarchy in almost every country would systematically be at odds with leftist movements.

John Paul II had spoken to the lords of the Church, the bishops. Now a totally different audience was awaiting him: an ancient people, steeped in suffering, victim of the Christian *conquistadores.* The organizers of the trip had expressly scheduled an encounter with the native Indians of Mexico. The place selected was Cuilapán, in the state of Oaxaca, where indigenous tradition was still very strong.

The pope made his entry from on high, in a helicopter, and took his place outdoors on a little throne surmounted by a canopy. Twenty-five thousand people had gathered on the dry open fields of Cuilapán, with its scorched mountain range serving as a backdrop. The *Indios* were dark-skinned, silent, timid, dignified. They had arrived at dawn and had been waiting patiently for hours. The women squatted on the ground with their babies tied to their backs. The men strolled among the stalls of an improvised market where, beneath a few rags for shade, vendors hawked tortillas and little pastries.

At noon Archbishop Bartolomé Carrasco presented John Paul II to the audience. "His Holiness," he said, "wanted to meet with the poor, with the sick, with the excluded, in whom the Church, as part of its task of evangelization, discovers the suffering face of Christ. From this material reality, which gives birth to a great spiritual wealth, our joyful greeting goes forth to the Father and Shepherd of the universal Church."

The man chosen to extend his "joyful greeting" to John Paul II was a Zapotecan peasant named Esteban Fernández. He was a thickset little man with a face like a piece of wood hollowed out by wind and rain. He was forty-eight years old, with a wife and seven children. *"Datu ganibanu eneuda,"* he pronounced in his guttural native tongue: We welcome you and we greet you with joy. Then he stared at the pope and burst out: "We're suffering a lot. The cattle are better off than we are. We can't express ourselves, and we have to keep our suffering locked up inside our hearts. We don't have jobs, and nobody helps us. But we're putting what little strength we have at your service. Holy Father, ask the Holy Spirit for something for your poor children."

The crowd, cordoned off from the pope by a wire netting, listened to John Paul's response in silence. Not everyone could understand his Spanish, and some people were beginning to walk away.

"Dearest brothers," he replied, "my presence among you is meant to be a living sign of the Church's universal concern. The pope and the Church are with you and love you. We love your persons, your culture, your traditions. We admire your marvelous past, we encourage you in the present, and we have high hopes for your future." Only when they realized that he was advocating the return of their land did they applaud. John Paul II spoke gently, with feeling and empathy. "The pope wants to be your voice," he said, "the voice of those who can't speak or of those who have been silenced. The peasants whose sweat waters even their own dejection can't wait anymore. They have the right to be respected. They have the right not to be deprived of what little they possess by schemes that at times amount to downright plundering. They have the right to see the barriers of exploitation fall, barriers often made up of the most intolerable kinds of egoism."

The pope wore a sombrero to shield him from the hot southern sun, as he spoke of reforms—bold, thorough, and urgent. He said there could be no more waiting. He passionately affirmed that "the Church defends the legitimate right to private property. But it also teaches no less clearly that there is a social mortgage on all private property. And if the common good demands it, we shouldn't hesitate even if it comes to expropriation, rightly carried out." Then the pope raised his voice. "I call upon those of you who control people's lives, you powerful classes who sometimes keep land out of production, land hiding the bread that so many families lack. The conscience of humanity, the conscience of the nations, the cry of those who have been abandoned, above all the voice of God, the voice of the Church, all repeat with me: It is not fair, it is not human, it is not Christian to go on maintaining situations that are clearly unjust."

·　·　·

Over the years John Paul II always nourished a special love for the Indians of the Americas, as he did for many indigenous peoples, whom he considered defenseless children in need of protection and help.

In Mexico John Paul II's first trip abroad was a triumph. In a country where anticlericalism is prescribed by the constitution, uniformed policemen were seen on their knees in front of the pope, kissing his hand. When he left Mexico City, millions of people beneath his flight path raised little mirrors skyward to flash a greeting to his plane.

But there were many in his own Church who believed that the Polish pope's cries for change through faith, absent any political commitment by the Church, could never have the transforming effect on Latin America that they would have on the pope's own homeland.

·　·　·

In the wake of his trip to Mexico, Pope Wojtyła plunged into a burst of activity such as the Curia had never seen. He continued to travel the world and to make decisions at a pace more suited to the CEO of a multinational corporation than to a reigning Roman pontiff.

In 1979 he went to Poland, Ireland, the United States, and Turkey. He wrote his first encyclical and promulgated documents on the reorganization of the pontifical Catholic universities and the training of catechists. He transformed the Wednesday papal audiences into a lecture series on human destiny, original sin, sexuality, and the theology of the body. He went abroad once again in 1980, flying to Africa, France, and Brazil. He called a meeting of the College of Cardinals to take a worldwide approach to reducing the Vatican's huge deficit; and he convoked two special synods, on the Dutch Church and on the Ukrainian Uniate Church (Catholics accepting Rome's authority but practicing the Byzantine rite, i.e., the Eastern Orthodox liturgy).

He used the first synod to block all further postconciliar experimentation by the Church in the Low Countries, which had introduced radical changes in the liturgy and promoted lay participation in functions usually reserved for clergy. The synod on Ukrainian Catholicism, attended mainly by exiled Ukrainians living in the United States and Canada, was an emphatic signal to Moscow that Pope Wojtyła would never accept the obliteration of the Uniate Church, which had been forcibly dissolved by Stalin at Lvov in 1946 and annexed into the more malleable orthodox patriarchate of Moscow. Uniate priests who had protested were jailed.

The cornerstone of the first phase of John Paul II's pontificate was his encyclical *Redemptor Hominis* (The Redeemer of Man), published five months after his election. Starting with its title Pope Wojtyła showed his determination to put Christ and his message of liberation back into the center of world history.

When he set out to write this encyclical, the world situation didn't look good for Catholicism. In the countries of Eastern Europe—with the sole exception of Poland—Communist regimes had succeeded in marginalizing believers from public life. Meanwhile in the West, the hierarchy worried about a drop in priestly vocations and the systematic spread of hostility or indifference to the Church and religious practices.

A profound spiritual malaise, affecting both religious institutions and secular society, was felt in the West as well as in the Communist East. The Third World was growing more and more destitute. With his encyclical, which he expressly aimed at all human beings, not just believing Catholics, John Paul II sought to confront the pains and anxieties of everyone. Is progress, he asked, really making life more humane? Is it being matched by an equally vigorous moral and spiritual development?

The pope described the human condition in the contemporary world as "far removed from the objective demands of the moral order, far from the demands of justice, and farther still from charity." He blamed *all* economic systems for damaging the environment and for widening the areas of poverty in the world.

The originality of the encyclical lay in its accent on the extraordinary importance of every single individual, his or her own dignity and greatness. In the pope's view, political systems had to be continuously reformed in both the East and the West. "Otherwise," he stressed, "even in time of peace human life is condemned to suffering, as different forms of domination, totalitarianism, neocolonialism, and imperialism inevitably arise."

He wrote like a man who had come to heal the planet in the name of Christ. He presented himself as a herald of God's supreme love. "Man cannot live without love. Without love," the pope wrote, "he remains incomprehensible to himself. His life is devoid of meaning, unless love is revealed to him, unless he encounters love, unless he experiences it and makes it his own, unless he has a lively sense of participation in it."

On the religious level *Redemptor Hominis* introduced something unheard of into the Catholic Church. For the first time John Paul II presented himself as the defender of *all* religions. If anywhere in the world there were men or women suffering in the name of God the torments of discrimination and persecution, the Roman pontiff was ready to intervene: "By virtue of my office I desire, in the name of all believers the world over, to speak to those on whom the organization of social and public life in some way depends. I fervently ask them to respect the rights of religion and of the activity of the Church."

Having published this manifesto on the rights of man, Pope Wojtyła got ready to penetrate the iron curtain.

YALTA

The first day of John Paul II's triumphant return to his homeland on June 2, 1979, had left the Communist authorities in Warsaw and Moscow shaken. More than a million Poles had converged on the airport road, on Victory Square and in the Old City during the first hours of his visit. Students had taken up the crucifix as the symbol of resistance to the regime. Just as disturbing were the pope's words in private to First Secretary Edward Gierek. In the course of their meeting in the Belweder Palace John Paul II had voiced his hopes for the kind of agreement between Church and state that Gierek himself badly wanted. But the pope had laid down a list of conditions designed to convince a Communist power that it would have to make unprecedented concessions if it was to coexist peacefully with the Church.

Gierek had spoken about international detente. The pope replied that "peace and rapprochement among peoples had to be based on the principle of respect for the objective rights of the nation," among which he included its right to "shape its own culture and civilization."

Gierek had spoken about Poland's security obligations and its position in the international community—a clear allusion to the alliances of COMECON (the Council for Mutual Economic Assistance) and the Warsaw Pact, both of which were thoroughly dominated and run by the Soviet Union. John Paul II had responded that "all forms of political, economic, or cultural imperialism contradict the needs of the international order." The only valid pacts could be those "based on mutual respect and on the recognition of the welfare of every nation." His boldness took the Communist leader by surprise. Gierek was disposed to reach a generous settlement on the place to be assigned the Church in Polish society for its religious activities. The pope wanted an acknowledgment that the Church "serves men and women in the temporal dimension of their lives," that is, in the social and political spheres. All this was deeply disturbing to the hierarchy of the Polish Party and—more significant—to the men in the Kremlin.

The next day, Pentecost, June 3, John Paul II arrived in the city of Gniezno like a modern incarnation of the Spirit, by helicopter. The million people who had turned out in Warsaw proved not an exception, just a prelude. Enormous throngs awaited him in the field where his helicopter touched down. "We want God," they chanted, taking up the same cry as the crowds in Warsaw the previous day.

Gniezno is the burial place of St. Adalbert, a martyr like St. Stanisław and, like him, a patron of Poland. The whole subject of religious martyrdom was, for the doctrinaire Communists in the Kremlin and in Warsaw, getting more and more troublesome. In the weeks preceding the pope's visit a historical exhibit had been organized in Gniezno displaying an X-ray of the skull of St. Stanisław. The X-ray was eerie technological testimony to religious lore: On the top of the skull a deep wound from the assassin's sword was plainly to be seen.

Tribuna, the ideological weekly of the Czech Communists that often echoed the Kremlin line of the month with even greater harshness, had accused John Paul II of coming to Poland to render homage to Bishop St. Stanisław, who spent his whole life "implementing the principles of, and demands for, the total dominion of the world by the pope and the Church, as formulated in the Middle Ages by the Pope Gregory VII."

It was no accident that, in the preparatory negotiations for the visit, the Polish authorities had successfully fought to prevent the papal trip from coinciding with the May 8 anniversary of the martyrdom of St. Stanisław, who died fighting for the rights of the people. But John Paul II had no notion of pressing for a direct confrontation with government forces, as Stanisław had, against a despotic Polish King—who later repented. The pope had come to breathe hope into the lives of the frustrated, discontented masses, to bring them a new message. At Rome, he had carefully planned the speeches for every stage of his trip, choosing a different point of attack at each venue.

God had chosen a Slavic pope, he suggested at Gniezno's cathedral of St. Adalbert—softening the edge of his remark with a "perhaps"—so that the Church, which was accustomed to "Roman, Germanic, Anglo-Saxon, and Celtic voices," could now hear the languages that resounded in the temples in this corner of the world.

"Is it not the will of Christ, is it not a disposition of the Holy Spirit, that this Polish pope, that this Slavic pope, should at this precise moment be manifesting the spiritual unity of Christian Europe? Although there are two great traditions, Eastern and Western, to which Christian Europe is indebted, through both of them it professes one faith, one baptism, one God and Father of us all, the Father of our Lord Jesus Christ."

With this language the pope sought to cancel, in the face of the Soviet pharaoh, the boundary between the Catholic and the Orthodox Church. Though the Kremlin might regard it as outrageously presumptuous, he had just pronounced himself the voice of the one hundred million Orthodox believers from Bucharest to Vladivostok who, until now, had never had a powerful advocate to defend them from a suffocating dictatorship.

Slavs and Christians: In response to the imposed unity of the socialist camp, the pontiff tacitly offered another kind of unity, based on blood, language, culture, and religion. One by one he recalled in his homily the baptism of the peoples of the East: Poles, Croats, Slovenes, Bulgarians, Moravians, Slovaks, Czechs, Serbs, and the ancient Russians of Kiev, before ending with Lithuania. "Pope John Paul II, a Slav, a son of the Polish nation," he concluded, "feels how deeply rooted he is in the soil of history. He comes here to speak before the whole Church, before Europe and the world, about those oft-forgotten nations and peoples. He comes here to 'cry with a loud voice.' . . . He comes here to embrace all those peoples, together with his own nation, and to hold them close to the heart of the Church."

The audience held its breath.

Then another thought came to him. As he had ridden along the streets of Gniezno he had sighted a banner with the inscription "Holy Father, don't forget your Czechoslovakian children."

"How could I forget them?" he now declared. "This sign confirms the immense historical and cultural brotherhood that binds our two peoples together. Brothers cannot be forgotten." The Church of Czechoslovakia had been one of the most persecuted in Europe. The Husak regime still subjected the clergy to harsh and burdensome controls. Many dioceses had no titular bishop. The government in Prague was fearful of the reaction that might be triggered by contact between the Czechoslovakian bishops and the pope during his visit to Poland. Although he had an invitation from the Polish Church for the pope's whole visit, Cardinal Tomášek was delayed by Czech authorities until June 6. Ordinary laypeople had to put up with restrictions on traffic at the normally wide-open Czechoslovak-Polish border. Usually the only condition for crossing the frontier was to have in one's possession a certain amount of Polish currency. During the pope's visit to Poland the Czechoslovakian banks announced that they were out of Polish *zloty*.

But it took only one banner—"Holy Father, don't forget"—for John Paul II to improvise with the readiness of a great actor and a great politician in front of the whole world, to devastating effect. The crowd was an enormous help. At Gniezno the faithful were much more spontaneous and passionate than the citizens of Warsaw, who had followed instructions from Church authorities and shown restraint. At Gniezno the crowd repeatedly cried, "Long live the pope!" There was no end to the banners; and groups of boys stripped off their shirts to run joyfully along the streets with the papal cavalcade. That afternoon, after the mass, groups of young people began to shout exultantly: "Karol, come with us. Karol, God has called you to captain Peter's boat. We won't abandon you. You can count on us."

Among this joyous crowd, his presence personifying centuries of Polish messianism, John Paul II again pointed to his election as a sign of divine Providence. He implied that the election ended the division of Europe symbolized by the Yalta conference and reaffirmed at Helsinki in 1975.* In his own cunning way, the pope was offering a vision of European Christian unity that transcended political-military blocs. With his dramatic flair John Paul II proposed a covenant with all the peoples of Eastern Europe, a treaty that promised an exodus from the dull gray world they lived in. The new Moses thrilled his listeners: "Thus, my dear fellow countrymen, this pope, blood of your blood, bone of your bone, will sing with you, and with you he will exclaim: 'May the glory of the Lord endure forever.' We shall not return to the past. We shall go forward to the future."

.   .   .

By Sunday evening, June 3, John Paul II had already succeeded, through the prophetic vehemence of his speeches, in challenging the ideology of the regime, the role of the state, the nature of Poland's alliance with the Soviet Union, and the geopolitical arrangements in Europe resulting from the Second World War. General Jaruzelski, who was following the pope's moves from a command center in the Ministry of Defense, could see that his comrades in the Polish Politburo were extremely disturbed, even fearful—

---

* The Helsinki accords both reaffirmed existing borders in Eastern Europe and pledged signatories, including the USSR, to respect human rights, including speech, press, and conscience.

both of the responses the pope was eliciting and of reaction from the Kremlin. The party hierarchy didn't like the crowds' attitudes, which struck them as "beyond normal behavior," almost cult-like. Worse, many passages in the pope's speeches went dangerously beyond the expectable tame religious formulas. Gierek, the party secretary, and Premier Piotr Jaroszewicz were already expressing their concerns about "destabilization."

Stanisław Kania, responsible for party ideology and negotiations with the Church, was alarmed by the next phase of the trip. Kazimierz Barcikowski, the party chief in Kraków, was afraid of what the pope might say in the city where he had once been archbishop. The speech in Victory Square in Warsaw, where the pope had invoked the descent of the Holy Spirit, was "a sort of programmatic speech," Jaruzelski thought, and it had set off warning bells. "We were afraid that this was announcing an escalation."

Gierek was the most nervous of all. For the reformist, technocratic wing of the Polish leadership, of which he was the chief representative, the whole policy of cooperation, however limited, with the Catholic Church was at stake. That policy, he believed, cemented national unity and safeguarded the unique identity of Poland vis-à-vis the Soviets. On the one hand, he had argued to his colleagues that his conversation with John Paul at the Belweder Palace was a kind of papal benediction on the Polish regime and on Gierek's personal policy of détente between Church and state. On the other hand, like all the party leaders, he was aware that the Church was putting on a fabulous show of its power and organizational skills. "The stronger the Church was," Jaruzelski recalled, "the more the members of the Politburo feared that this would undermine the stability of the ruling circles."

To make matters worse, every gesture, every allusion of the pope was immediately rebroadcast throughout the world by the more than a thousand journalists who had come to Poland to follow the story. In turn, echoes of the trip from the outside world were having negative reverberations in the USSR, Czechoslovakia, and East Germany, whose leaders eyed Warsaw's every move with suspicion and skepticism.

Gierek consulted with the members of his Politburo, and their assessment was unanimous: It had been a devastating weekend for the Polish leadership. The problems created by the pope and his message after only two days in his homeland were unacceptable. Someone had to intervene.

Stanisław Kania, who for years had handled relations with the Church, was charged with getting word to the pope of the party leadership's discontent. Kania decided to use the new archbishop of Kraków, Cardinal Franciszek Macharski, as his go-between. Macharski was a person who had the pope's confidence—in fact, he was Wojtyła's handpicked successor. Toning down the Politburo's criticisms, Kania began to list (as diplomatically as possible) some reasons for their displeasure: The pope hadn't clearly pinned the responsibility for the occupation and ruin of Poland on the Nazis. He had never mentioned the 600,000 Soviet soldiers who had died liberating Poland. And he had expressed no public appreciation for the achievements of socialist Poland, beginning with the country's reconstruction after the war.

Given the crisis Poland was stumbling through, it was crucial for the Polish leadership and the country's path of modernization that the pope's visit not become a destabilizing factor and a cause of tension with Moscow. This was the point the pope had to be made to understand: Hadn't he told Gierek at the Belweder Palace, "I shall continue to take to heart everything that could threaten Poland, everything that could hurt her, that could be to her disadvantage, that could mean stagnation or a crisis. . . . The man speaking to you is a son of the same motherland as yours?"

Kania summed up the arguments in a letter. To stress its confidential nature, he wrote it out by hand and had it delivered personally to Cardinal Macharski, certain that it would be read by the pope. A period of anxious waiting began.

• • •

The arrival of John Paul II in Poland's national sanctuary at Częstochowa for a three-day visit coincided with a change of tone in his speeches. Religious themes now took over from political ones, though critical allusions to the Communist system continued. The papal entourage noticed that, in the wake of the two strikes launched at Warsaw and Gniezno, John Paul II had chosen to intervene in a quieter voice, turning his many meetings with all sorts of citizens into a "living catechism." Few of the pope's aides were aware of the letter Cardinal Macharski had handed him when he reached Często-chowa.

From the third day on, his trip began to look more and more like a triumphant pilgrimage by the pontiff among his people—and an enthusiastic march of millions of Poles toward the pope, their compatriot. All the regime's precautions for limiting the impact of his visit proved futile. On the contrary, every restriction was turned into formidable counterpropaganda against the regime. The roadblocks set up by the police eighteen miles from Częstochowa to screen the pilgrims served only to remind Poles of the vexations inflicted on them by the totalitarian system. The restrictions imposed on television programs—people in Warsaw or Poznań were barred from seeing what any-one in Częstochowa could see—only increased the desire for the free flow of information. The tricks in TV camera coverage, which during religious cele-brations tended to show only the pope and persons next to him at the altar, instead of the vast crowds, only added to the drama of his words and the shouted responses from the unseen masses.

The state authorities had haggled with Wyszyński over the sites to be included on John Paul II's tour, hoping to reduce the number of people who could see the pope in person. But the Polish Church took it upon itself to thwart this maneuver by organizing convoys of pilgrims from all over the country. A case in point was Silesia, once a political fief of Gierek's. The government had refused to allow John Paul to make a stop in Katowice, a large Silesian industrial and mining center. But the bishops responded by making a tremendous effort to bring to the pope hundreds of thousands of Silesian workers and miners, the shock troops of the Polish working class. Many miners arrived at Częstochowa immediately after working the night shift; among the ocean of banners was one proclaiming, "We are with Christ, despite everything."

The pope spoke to the huge throng about justice and the "rights and duties of every member of the nation so as to avoid granting privileges to some and imposing discrimination on the others." When the voices were heard shouting affectionately, "God help you," he turned to the crowd and replied, "I wish the people of Silesia would send me that greeting, 'God help you,' from nine hundred miles away. . . . If you shout loud enough, the pope will hear you and will reply, 'God reward you.' " Then, as if taking an oath the crowd roared, "God help you! God help you! God help you!"

From June 4 to 6 Częstochowa became something like one of the traveling capitals of the medieval emperors. The whole country looked to the sanctuary of Mary as if to its very center. John Paul II welcomed everyone—workers, students, peasants, intellectuals, white-collar workers, nuns, priests, seminarians, old people, and children—through a system of well-planned meetings and liturgical celebrations. And even when the pope himself wasn't talking or couldn't be seen, the continual celebration of masses for the legions of pilgrims served to strengthen his pact between the Church and the nation.

At Jasna Góra, the sanctuary-fortress of Częstochowa, the bishops of Poland had arranged an imperial scene for John Paul II. Jasna Góra, where the Black Madonna is venerated, is the heart of the Catholic Polish nation and the symbol of its resistance to foreign invaders. When, as Sienkiewicz's *The Deluge* recounts, the Swedes invaded Poland in the mid-seventeenth century, the imposing walls of the fortress had stood fast. Even the Black Madonna was in her own way a warrior. Two blows from the saber of an enemy soldier had slashed her right cheek, but the scar merely underlined her invincibility.

The first papal mass celebrated here seemed almost a coronation in a setting of national-religious exaltation. The faithful had massed by the hundreds of thousands in the field outside the walls in a joyous explosion of religious flags, placards, and pictures. An altar had been set up on the bastions of the fortress, and a grand wooden staircase was built to link it to the crowd below. The pope celebrated the mass beneath a canopy: a figure in white raised on high, reachable only by the stairs, which, as in medieval legends, seemed to join heaven and earth. At night, long columns of people could be seen in the moonlight making their way on foot to the sanctuary. A great many of them slept at the foot of the walls or camped out as best they could in the surrounding woods.

An enormous billboard, hung on the walls by the Catholic students of

Lublin, summed up the general feeling: "Holy Father, we want to be with you, we want to live a better life with you, we want to pray with you." When the pope met the miners from Silesia, the underground monthly *Głos* commented: "The millions of working people gathered to meet the pope would seem to prove that the official thesis of the natural atheism of the working class and its progressive de-Christianization is utterly false." The dissident journal added prophetically: "At present the authorities are afraid that the pope, who used to be a worker himself, and whose sensitivity to exploitation is well known, might act as a spokesman for the Polish working class."

In the face of the intense expectations focused on his person, John Paul II was careful to act with great calm and balance, avoiding confrontational tones. Speaking freely with a group of a thousand university students from Lublin in a closed-door meeting, the pope said: "The cause of Christ can also be furthered or harmed by the choice of a worldview diametrically opposed to Christianity. Everyone who makes this choice with innermost conviction must have our respect." Some students were perplexed by these remarks. By way of explaining his thoughts the pope added: "There is a danger for both sides, both for the Church and for the others, in the attitude of the person who makes no choice at all." Thus, in keeping with his philosophical vocation, John Paul II had returned to preach personal commitment and respect for those who think differently.

His discussions with the bishops were just as calm and deliberate. At Jasna Góra John Paul II wanted to give a public tribute to Primate Wyszyński *and* to the new Vatican secretary of state, Agostino Casaroli. It was a political gesture designed to end the ecclesiastical guerrilla warfare that for years had put the intransigent Polish bishops at odds with the architect of Paul VI's *Ostpolitik.* This was a way of letting both insiders and outsiders know that from now on the pope would personally take charge of such matters.

During the pope's stay at Częstochowa, elsewhere in Poland, especially in the countryside, people looked for ways to show their loyalty to him and the Church, to offer visible proof of their militant piety. For miles and miles, all across the land, in provinces never touched by the papal procession, the chapels, the newsstands, and roadside icons were adorned with bouquets of flowers. Whole villages were covered with little Vatican flags, and the windows of houses were decked with the picture of the Black Madonna, a photo of Wojtyła, or a large *M* (for Mary) surrounded by lilies and surmounted by a crown.

This silent vote by Polish Catholics, all the more striking in its festiveness and in the absence of any competing symbol of Communist ideology, shocked the nation's leadership.

As he was getting ready to move on to Kraków, the pope could reflect with satisfaction on the fact that thus far he had managed to maintain a difficult balance between two conflicting needs: to awaken people's consciousness and not to stampede the faithful into rash action. The boundary between the two was slender, and popular enthusiasm was forever threatening to overflow. On the evening of June 6 the pope's white helicopter landed on the Błonie meadow in Kraków. Despite the rain, another enormous crowd was waiting for him. John Paul II was driven to the Wawel Cathedral in an open car. Later when he went to his old residence, hundreds of torches lit up the route.

AUSCHWITZ

The bishop of Rome knelt down and stared at the cement floor of the death cell. He had with him a small bouquet of white and red carnations, which he delicately placed on the ground. Then he bent down to kiss the rough cement on which the Franciscan priest Father Maximilian Kolbe had lain in agony.

That kiss could be seen summing up many things: the martyr's death, which represents the authentic vocation of a Catholic priest; faith in the love of one's neighbor, which is stronger than human cruelty; horror at the organized extermination of human beings; the sinister echo that Auschwitz (Oświęcim in Polish) sent through the minds of Karol Wojtyła's friends and fellow citizens of Kraków during the war years; the memory of his Jewish friends from Wadowice who had seen their families destroyed by the Holocaust. Ginka Beer, his childhood friend, had managed to escape in time, but her mother had perished at Auschwitz; and Jurek Kluger, his classmate, had made it to safety with his father; but Kluger's mother, grandmother, and sister had died in the gas chambers.

As archbishop and cardinal, Karol Wojtyła had gone to Auschwitz several times to pray and meditate on this same spot. But now his name was John Paul II, and as pope he had to speak to the world. Three ministers had come from Warsaw in the name of the government: from the ministries of religious, veterans, and foreign affairs. For the leadership of the Polish state, Auschwitz was a place for reaffirming the spirit of national unity that had animated the Poles during the occupation and the resistance.

Paul VI had beatified Kolbe at Archbishop Wojtyła's insistence. But John Paul was convinced that the Franciscan friar had to be canonized as soon as possible. It wasn't just that the pope was fascinated by the figure of this "martyr for charity," prisoner number 16670, who on July 30, 1941, had asked the camp commandant to let him die in the place of a poor father of a family, Franciszek Gajowniczek. Beyond that, the pope firmly believed that a place of horror such as Auschwitz had to be symbolically redeemed by a Christian's sacrifice. It was important that wherever evil manifested itself in human history, the Church could point to one or more genuine Christians who had fought for goodness, love, and faith. Kolbe, however, was a complex figure, whose extreme nationalism was regarded by many Jews as part of an anti-Semitic tradition of the Polish Church.

The pope emerged from the cell, which was dimly lit by a small grated window too high on the wall for a prisoner to look outside. There, locked up with nine other persons to die of starvation, Kolbe had spent sixteen days before being finished off with a lethal injection. His destiny, his will to spread the Gospel, which had taken him as far as Japan, and his faith in the Virgin Mary had always captured the imagination of Cardinal Wojtyła.

Making his way down the paths alongside the brick sheds into which condemned human beings had been packed, the pope arrived at the Wall of Death, a cement wall covered with tar, where prisoners were beaten and shot. Once again John Paul II fell to his knees. He evidently felt that this camp, the product of an inhuman ideology, should be sanctified by constant prayer. He wanted Cardinal Macharski to build a little convent for Carmelite Sisters on the grounds of Auschwitz. It would be a place of supplication, of silence, and of redemption. He had no intention of announcing this, either today, June 7, or in the years to come. But it wasn't some sudden or unexpected notion. It was a project that had ripened during his years as archbishop of Kraków; and he hoped that his successor in Kraków would bring it to fruition.

Unlike the sanctuary of the Black Madonna at Częstochowa, Auschwitz and nearby Birkenau, to which a helicopter now carried the pope, were sites of worldwide importance, sacred ground for believers and nonbelievers alike. Here, where torture and extermination had been revered, two destinies had crossed paths: that of the Jews who experienced in the Holocaust—*shoah*—the final result of centuries of bestial persecution and anti-Semitic hatred (by the Church among others), and that of Poland. With the Nazi occupation, Poland had suffered the most terrible of all invasions, one that didn't simply erase national boundaries but sought to wipe out the very identity of a people. The pope went to put on his vestments in one of the sheds where prisoners had been kept. Two hundred priests, former prisoners in the camp, were ready to concelebrate with him. They had on blood-red chasubles embroidered with leafy white olive branches, twisted like barbed wire. Together with them the pope headed in procession toward an altar, built along the tracks where the sealed railroad cars had stopped. Over a million—perhaps as many as four million—men, women, and children had been massacred in this camp. For the first time ever a Roman pontiff was going to render homage to the victims of the Holocaust, to all the victims of Nazi persecution, entering the place to which the wartime pope, Pius XII, had closed his eyes.

The afternoon was mild, the sun was shining, the meadows in the death camp were green and flowering. The pope glanced at the altar of unseasoned wood, surmounted by a tall cross, also of wood. As in the time of the Romans this Christian symbol now reacquired its meaning as an instrument of torture. On top of the cross was a crown of barbed wire, and from the arms hung a cloth with gray and white stripes like a prisoner's uniform. On the cloth those present could make out Father Kolbe's number, 16670.

"*Mea culpa, mea culpa, mea maxima culpa,*" the pope recited in a low voice, and the crowd repeated the Confiteor in a deep murmur. At the foot of the platform stood ex-prisoners in striped uniforms. There was also a delegation of women from the concentration camp at Ravensbrück, with white hair and weary eyes.

"I come here as a pilgrim," John Paul II announced during his homily. "I have gone down into the death cell of Maximilian Kolbe many times before. I have stopped at the wall of extermination, and I have made my way amid the rubble of the crematory ovens of Brzezinka [Birkenau]. As pope I had no choice but to come here. Now that I have become a successor of Peter, Christ wants me to bear witness before the world to what constitutes the greatness—and the wretchedness—of humanity in our time. To bear witness to man's defeat and his victory. So I have come, and I bend my knee on this Golgotha of the contemporary world, on these tombs, most of which are nameless, like the great tomb of the Unknown Soldier. I kneel down before all the stone tablets lined up one after another. The message carved on them recalls the victims of Auschwitz in the following languages: Polish, English, Bulgarian, Romany, Czech, Danish, French, Greek, Hebrew, Yiddish, Spanish, Flemish, Serbo-Croatian, German, Norwegian, Romanian, Hungarian, and Italian."

Once again the pope mentioned the sacrifice of Father Kolbe. Then he spoke of himself and of how he understood his own role as pontiff. He recalled his first encyclical, *Redemptor Hominis*, which was dedicated to "the cause of humanity, to the dignity of man, and finally to his inalienable rights, which are so easily trampled on and annihilated by his fellow men." Here he raised his voice slightly: "Is it enough to put man in a different uniform? To arm him with the apparatus of violence? Is it enough to impose on him an ideology in which human rights are subjected to the demands of the system, completely subjected to them, so as in practice not to exist at all?" The crowd, silent until now, applauded. Many sobbed, and some translators were unable to continue.

When the pope began to speak of the stones commemorating the victims, the silence again became absolute. "In particular I want to pause with you before the inscription in Hebrew. The inscription awakens the memory of the people whose sons and daughters were marked for total extermination. This people draws its origins from Abraham, our father in the faith. This very people who received from God the commandment 'Thou shalt not kill' itself experienced in a special measure what is meant by killing. It is not permissible for anyone to pass by this inscription with indifference."

Sustained applause swept over the expanse of people, some of them painfully aware of Poland's own long history of anti-Semitism.

"Once again," the pope continued, "I choose to stop at another memorial stone, the one in Russian. I will not add any comments. We know what country it speaks of. We are aware of the part played by this country in the last terrible war for the freedom of the nations. No one can pass by this stone unaffected." That was the gesture the government in Warsaw had been looking for, the conciliatory sign to Moscow. But the pontiff measured his words. Like de Gaulle, he didn't speak of the "Soviets," but of the "Russians," and he referred to the merits and sufferings of the country, not the state.

Having paid these debts to history, John Paul II could devote himself to the Polish memorial stone. Six million people (half of them Jews), one-fifth of the nation, had lost their lives during the war: "This is one more stage of the centuries-long struggle of this country, of my country, for its fundamental rights among the nations of Europe, one more loud shout for the right to one's own place on the map of Europe." An old song of independence began slowly to swell among the crowd. "May God Bless Our Free Fatherland." Past and present joined hands. Once again the pope was searching for the right political chord.

"The successor of John XXIII and Paul VI speaks in the name of all the nations whose rights have been violated and forgotten," said the pope, as his glance swept across and beyond the barbed wire.

The speech at Auschwitz was broadcast all over the world. The image of John Paul II kneeling in the shadow of the gas chambers was a powerful incentive—as the following years would show—to Catholic reflection on the Holocaust and on the shared responsibility of the Church for the crime of anti-Semitism.

Some observers, however, remained perplexed by the fact that John Paul II couldn't resist the temptation to baptize almost everything, virtually any contemporary reality or dramatic event whatsoever, by incorporating it into his Christian-Polish vision. "I have come to this special shrine," the pope said, "to the birthplace, as I may say, of the patron [a reference to Kolbe] of our difficult century, just as nine centuries ago Skałka [in Kraków] was the birthplace, at the sword's edge, of St. Stanisław, patron of Poland." He also spoke about Edith Stein, the Jewish student of philosopher Edmund Husserl who became a nun and was then murdered in Auschwitz, whom he also beatified.

Could the complexity of the tragic experience of Auschwitz, could its undeniably unique role in the Jewish Holocaust, be reduced to its being the birthplace of one Catholic's sainthood? Did Auschwitz equal the experience of a Jew converted to Catholicism? Didn't invoking the religious nationalism suggested by the name of St. Stanisław amount to "co-opting" a place that belonged to the conscience of the whole world? This ambiguity would eventually lead to many bitter misunderstandings and a sharp conflict with the worldwide Jewish community when the Polish hierarchy, completing plans initiated by Archbishop Karol Wojtyła, installed the Carmelite convent within Auschwitz. Eventually the pope chose to order the nuns to move.

· · ·

John Paul II's homecoming in Kraków was tumultuous, its implications historic. At night young people organized continuous serenades of patriotic songs beneath the windows of the archbishop's palace. In Market Square, the statue of Adam Mickiewicz, the poet of independence, was permanently blanketed with flowers; and all night long there was a continuous succession of celebrations and of protests against the regime. At an open-air ceremony one afternoon in front of the church at Skałka, the site of the martyrdom of St. Stanisław, the young people once again began to wave their new symbols of resistance—little wooden crosses.

On the penultimate day of his trip, the pope chose a meeting with workers near the monastery of Mogiła, in the Nowa Huta district, to seize ground traditionally claimed by the Communists and deliver a direct blow to Communist ideology. "Christianity and the Church have no fear of the world of work," he proclaimed. "They're not afraid of any system based on work. The pope isn't afraid of the workers." Many times, of course, popes *had* feared worker movements. John Paul II recalled his personal experience working in the rock quarry and the Solvay factory; and he extolled the Gospel as a guide for the problems of work in the contemporary world. Amid an ecstatic crowd, waving thousands of flags and banners, and flanked by eight cardinals—Poletti of Rome, Höffner of Cologne, König of Vienna, Tomášek of Prague, Bengsch of Berlin, Jubany Arnau of Barcelona, Gray of Edinburgh, Macharski of Kraków—and Casaroli, the secretary of state, the pontiff defiantly declared that people couldn't be demeaned as a mere means of production. "Christ will never approve of it," he exclaimed. "Both the worker and the employer must remember this, both the system of labor and the system of remuneration must remember this. The state, the nation, and the Church must all remember this."

The audience cheered and applauded frenetically. For the workers this was pouring oil on the flames. They were already outraged at the government's latest price increases and eager for higher salaries; and they remembered the regime's violence against the workers' protest in 1976 at Ursus and Radom. Now the Polish leadership took the rebuff, powerless to fight back. In the final analysis the requests made of the pope by the government were having no effect at all. Not on John Paul, not on the people. Monitoring his speeches day by day, General Jaruzelski noted both the force of the pope's words and the subtlety of his approach: John Paul II was not only addressing the present state of affairs, "he was consolidating hope and courage" for future struggles, for the long term.

A similar thought occurred to Wiktor Kulerski, who would join the ranks of Solidarity activists barely a year later. "We're living in a different country," he told himself as the pope traveled around Poland. "Communism doesn't matter anymore, because nobody submits to it." Kulerski felt that the pope's stay in Poland was a moment of relief, a moment to gather one's energies: "The pope is here, and he's beyond the reach of the Communists. He can say and do the things we can't. They can't get him. People repeat the pope's words, and they know that he's their bulwark."

During the pope's visit, historian Bronisław Geremek, an intellectual destined to become one of the chief advisers to Solidarity, came to the conclusion that "free people can organize themselves," that "society can do without the party and the state."

Throughout the visit the members of the Polish Politburo felt like twigs dragged along by the current. To speak of the "party's leading role" was now an absurdity. Kazimierz Barcikowski, the first secretary of the Kraków party organization, realized that his main duties during the pope's visit were simply to make sure that the Church was capable of maintaining order and to arrange adequate transportation, food supplies, first aid, and toilets.

On June 10 more than a million faithful arrived at the meadow at Błonie on the edge of the city. Some spoke of a million and a half or even two million. A Catholic publication went so far as to venture three million—a foretaste of legends that would crop up surrounding the pope's visits on every continent, especially in the Third World.

Merely to draw a million people was incredible, even revolutionary in a country of the socialist bloc. John Paul II spent almost three-quarters of an hour riding back and forth in his popemobile along the lanes separating the sections into which the crowd had been subdivided.

The cardinals and bishops, in a group larger still than the one at Nowa Huta—they now included two Hungarian cardinals, a Yugoslav, and three more from the West—were stunned as they watched the gigantic throng acclaiming the pope. And they were stirred: So the Church really wasn't on the decline; and the Roman pontiff still did have a great deal to tell the world. It was something of a revelation.

That day, June 10, was chosen to honor St. Stanisław during the papal trip, and it turned into a celebration of the new power of John Paul II as, brandishing Christ like a battle standard, he announced that the nine-hundredth anniversary of the death of St. Stanisław would be a turning point for the nation and the Church.

That was all the crowd needed; they understood perfectly. As he left, the pope could bestow a new blessing on his people. He could entrust them with a new mission. "You must be strong, dearest brothers and sisters!" he cried. "You must be strong with the strength that flows from faith! You must be strong with the strength of faith!"

For one last time he addressed—without naming them, but in a way obvious to everyone—the peoples behind the iron curtain. "There is no need to be afraid. The frontiers must be opened. There is no imperialism in the

Church, only service." Catching sight of a group of pilgrims from Czechoslovakia, he insisted: "Oh how I would wish that our brothers and sisters, who are united to us by language and the fortunes of history, could also have been present during the pilgrimage of this Slavic pope. If they are not here, if they are not here in this vast expanse, they are surely in our hearts."

The pope and the Slavic nations versus the Soviet empire. The battle lines were now drawn. In his native land, almost one out of every three citizens had been able to see him in person. Not even Marshal Piłsudski, in his days as a conquering hero, had been so enveloped by his people. When the pope went to the altar, two balloons drifted up to the sky bearing the symbol of Polish resistance during World War II: a *P* on top of a pair of *W*'s. It meant "Poland struggles on."

PART FIVE

SHAKING THE EMPIRE

Every major strike in Poland's Communist era had ended in a violent stalemate—in 1956, 1970, and 1976. Each time, the authorities suppressed demonstrations and strikes with brutal force and then promised economic and social reforms. But the promises were never kept, and living standards in Poland continued to plummet. Poland staggered on, and its workers seethed.

By early 1980, with Poland's foreign debt mounting and the country facing shortages that left millions without coal to heat their homes, the government turned once again to its familiar formula of wage freezes and price increases to solve its economic problems. So it came as no great surprise when railroad workers struck in the eastern city of Lublin in July, or when the strikes quickly spread to factories across the country. At his vacation resort in the Crimea, First Secretary Edward Gierek reacted calmly to the news and decided against a prompt return to his country.

From the beginning, the Soviets were troubled. Soviet General Secretary Leonid Brezhnev summoned Gierek to his own villa in the Crimea to express concern about the railway strike in particular: The USSR maintained an army of half a million men in East Germany who were wholly reliant on the railroad corridor through Poland for their supplies. Gierek assured Brezhnev that the strikes were ending. But unlike his predecessors, he and his defense minister, Wojciech Jaruzelski, were unwilling to use military force to compel the strikers back to work.

.   .   .

On Thursday, August 14, Pope John Paul II spent the day in the papal villa at Castel Gandolfo, twenty miles from the Vatican. The air in the Alban hills was more breathable than in the scorching streets of Rome. Ever since the late 1600s the villa had been a refuge for popes during the hottest months of the year.

That Thursday, the pace at Castel Gandolfo was more languid than usual. It was the eve of the Assumption, *ferragosto*, the summer's most sacred holiday for Italians, when everything stops running, even the buses.

While the pope worked in his study, Lech Wałęsa, a square-shouldered, unemployed electrician with a distinctive mustache, was clambering up a steam shovel at the Lenin Shipyard in Gdańsk, Poland. All summer the workers at the shipyard had declined to join the strikes that were sweeping the country. But on this morning, some of them formed into an unruly procession within the gates, demanding pay raises and the rehiring of the shipyard's crane operator—a defiant critic of management who had been transferred to a job outside Gdańsk.

Poland's economy was devastated. Millions of factory workers across Poland were by now thoroughly disgruntled. The spontaneous strikes that had begun in July had spread to more than 150 enterprises. The government was reacting with the usual promises of change and salary increases—so far without violence. This time the protests continued. The sun was setting on the decade of Gierek. The country now found itself mired in debt; productivity was sinking; basic items like spare parts for industrial equipment were in short supply. Bankruptcy loomed.

The workers in the naval shipyard, the most important in Poland, where police in 1970 had killed forty-five striking employees, had shown little enthusiasm for a new confrontation. The director of the Gdańsk shipyard, Klemens Giech, was promising a pay raise if workers would go back on the job, and many were ready to agree. But Wałęsa, who had scaled the yard's twelve-foot-high chain-link fence that morning, now stood next to the shipyard manager atop the steam shovel and denounced his offers.

He was a popular figure who had taken part in the uprisings of 1970 that had brought down Gomułka. After the bloody repression of the demonstrations in Radom and Ursus in 1976, he had devoted himself to creating an independent labor union, and he had often been arrested for these activities. Now he called for a sit-down strike: To protect themselves from security forces, workers would lock themselves inside the factory. The crowd heeded his call.

The next day, August 15, the pope dispatched his secretary, Father Stanisław Dziwisz, to Poland for a discreet "rest period" that lasted a week.

• • •

The truth was that the strikes that shook Poland in the summer of 1980 were not merely strikes. They were political insurrections—"counterrevolution," as Brezhnev correctly put it. This movement, like all historic social revolutions, united a constellation of formidable political forces—labor, the intelligentsia, and the Church—that had never before come together so decisively.

In the previous economic crises, which had ended in violence, the workers had been disorganized and had lacked any national forum for expressing their grievances. In 1980, though there was still no centrally organized political opposition, there *was* a loose alliance of forces prepared to challenge the whims of an imperious state. These were the Workers Defense Committees (known by the acronym KOR) that had been formed by intellectuals to assist workers arrested or fired after the violent crackdown in 1976; the Catholic Intellectual Clubs (KIK); and the bishops who, backed by the Polish pope, now tentatively preached a gospel of human rights as well as of salvation.

In the summer of 1980, the most aggressive of these elements was KOR, led by its charismatic founders, Jacek Kuroń, a former party member whose writing had galvanized the opposition in the early 1970s, and Adam Michnik, a young historian and student of Kuroń's, who was Jewish. KOR's platform called for an independent labor movement and liberation from the stifling guardianship of a one-party system. The committee published its own newspaper, *Robotnik Wybrzeża* (Worker of the Coast), which in turn had inspired the appearance of other antigovernment publications in intellectual circles, in the universities, and even among peasants. KOR had the potential to become a real opposition movement, not least because of its close ties to the Catholic Church.

The intellectual activists of KOR, who had come to appreciate Archbishop Karol Wojtyła in Kraków, numbered only a few hundred, but with feverish enthusiasm they traveled around the country, holding rallies and giving lectures. From the seeds they sowed, an independent trade union movement began organizing in major cities during 1978; and by April of that year volunteers were handing out the first bulletin of a united movement called Free Trade Unions of the Baltic Coast.

In August, as the nationwide strikes of 1980 entered their sixth week, Jacek Kuroń said, "The struggle will continue until there are free unions and truly representational social organizations. There is no alternative. The government doesn't have the consensus needed to get out of the crisis." At the beginning of the month he had come to Gdańsk to discuss with leaders of the Free Trade Unions of the Baltic Coast the possibility of staging a strike at the Lenin Shipyard. But despite widespread discontent among workers there, the activists had had a hard time finding a platform everyone could agree on.

Then Wałęsa took matters into his own hands. On Saturday, August 16, the workers again seemed inclined to call off their strike, in exchange for the promise of a 1,500-złoty raise and a guarantee that a monument would be built at the shipyard to honor the victims of December 1970.

But Wałęsa, emboldened by these concessions, issued a sixteen-point list of demands, the most important of which was government recognition of free trade unions. His proposal was not especially popular, and a day later, when management offered a heftier pay raise, many older workers filed out of the yard, giving up the strike. This was perhaps Wałęsa's greatest moment: Circling the yard in a small motorized vehicle, he rallied the workers back to the cause. When the strike finally resumed in full force on the 18th, Wałęsa issued a new, more radical list of twenty-one demands, including alleviation of censorship and the release of political prisoners. It showed the hand of KOR advisers who had infiltrated the shipyard.

All negotiations were broadcast by loudspeaker through the yard, so word of the strike and the workers' audacious new demands spread rapidly across the Baltic seacoast. That day work stopped in 180 more factories from Gdynia, Gdańsk, and Sopot on the coast to Tarnów (near Kraków) and Katowice in Silesia. Now the avalanche was unleashed.

At Castel Gandolfo, John Paul II received confidential reports on the events in Poland from Dziwisz and from his Secretariat of State, which was in touch with the Polish episcopate. Breaking habit, Wojtyła eagerly watched television reports of the sensational events in his homeland. With him was Sister Zofia Zdybicka, his ex-student who was staying at the summer residence as a guest. Sister Zdybicka, like the pope, was a philosopher, and first as a student, then as a teacher, finally as a friend, she had often discussed such matters as the nature of Marxism and the destiny of man with Karol Wojtyła. "This," she declared as she watched the TV news, "is a lesson for the whole world. Look at the contradiction: The *workers* are against communism."

The pope readily agreed, but at first he seemed less confident, less enthusiastic. "Except that the world doesn't understand anything," he replied. "The world doesn't get it." He said this three times. He didn't seem entirely surprised by the remarkable doings in Poland. Sister Zdybicka remembered being with the pope on another occasion when he had told a visiting professor from the Catholic University in Lublin, "You have to be ready." Ready for what? she and the professor had wondered, but now she thought she understood. This was what the pope had been waiting for.

Wałęsa, said the pope, had been sent by God, by Providence. On the screen they watched Wałęsa and the workers praying. "So serious, so young, those intent faces," she noted. In his lapel Wałęsa wore a pin with a picture of the Black Madonna of Częstochowa. On Sunday and now on Monday, mass was celebrated by the strikers in the shipyard, led by Wałęsa's parish priest, Father Henryk Jankowski, of St. Brygida's in Gdańsk.

Photos of the pope and large pictures of the Black Madonna were posted on the gates of the shipyard. John Paul noted with ironic satisfaction that Western politicians, especially those on the left, were amazed that throngs of strikers were flocking on bended knee around improvised outdoor confessionals and that they had chosen religious symbols for their battle standards. Sister Zdybicka sensed that the pope saw the hand of God lifted up against the Communists, as the workers turned their rulers' weapons against them.

Spontaneous demonstrations were now breaking out along the coast under the leadership of the Inter-Factory Strike Committee in solidarity with the strikers at the Lenin Shipyard. Workers all over the country, spurred into action by KOR, were joining forces with the Catholic intelligentsia, while secular-minded intellectuals too were making common cause with the Church.

The strikers expressed their opposition to the regime by singing hymns and patriotic songs and by flying the Polish national flag over the striking factories. Self-governing strike committees proliferated.

The workers' revolt seemed to be following the scenario of all Marxist revolutions, except that there was no Marx. An Italian cartoonist, Giorgio Forattini, summed up the situation with a stroke of his pen: a strapping Karol Wojtyła, in mechanic's overalls, was laying down his tools and refusing to work.

Bishop Kazimierz Majdański of Szczecin, one of the cities where the strikers' movement was strongest, told a monsignor from the Curia, "The seed sown by the Holy Father is flowering."

On August 18, in a televised speech, Gierek promised reforms and muttered threats: "The destiny of the country is bound up with the socialist system. . . . Anarchical and antisocialist groups are trying to exploit the situation, but we will not tolerate any demand or action that aims at destroying the social order in Poland."

Military units and columns of police vehicles began to stream toward the Baltic coast, but the ports of Gdynia and Gdańsk remained paralyzed. The number of strikers soared to 300,000; the strikes spread to Łódź, Wrocław, and even Nowa Huta.

John Paul II kept silent for a week. Like the heads of the European community who cautioned Gierek and the Polish leadership not to take repressive measures, like U.S. President Jimmy Carter, and like Moscow, which was trying to figure out how the Polish Communist Party could maintain control of the country, the pope was prudent.

As the tension mounted, John Paul II left it to Primate Wyszyński to state the Church's position. The old primate intervened the way he had many times before in moments of national crisis: He moved slowly, kept in check by his constant concern that the crisis might provoke Soviet intervention. On August 16, the anniversary of Piłsudski's final victory over the Red Army, the primate voiced his gratitude to the Holy Virgin. Thanks to her, sixty years ago, Poland's borders had been preserved. He prayed for freedom, peace, and self-determination in Poland—a little hint to the Communist party and to Moscow.

But the situation couldn't be handled with the methods the primate had been using for thirty years. The strike in Gdańsk wasn't just a workers' revolt against miserable economic conditions. The Communist Party in Poland and in the USSR was ready for problems like that. Rather, the platform that Wałęsa had gotten the workers to adopt questioned radically the whole structure of the regime. The call for independent unions stripped away the Communist Party's pretense of being the only legitimate and historical representative of the working class. The demand regarding censorship and access to the mass media for the free unions and the Church denied the party its most efficacious tool (after the army and the police) for exercising a monopoly on power.

Polish workers no longer wanted, as they once had, just a "humanization" of the Communist regime. They were insisting on a real democratization through autonomous power unfettered by the Communist Party. They wanted an independent labor movement that would keep a watchful eye on the government.

Precisely because of this, the Warsaw authorities had for days flatly refused to go to the Lenin Shipyard and negotiate directly with the Inter-Factory Strike Committee (which now had the representatives of 281 state-owned enterprises on board).

On Wednesday, August 20, as the strike movement threatened to provoke long-term political paralysis, the pope said two brief prayers to a group of Polish pilgrims in St. Peter's Square: "God, grant through the intercession of Mary that religion may always enjoy freedom and that our homeland may enjoy security. . . . Lord, help this people, and always defend it from every evil and danger." Rumors abounded that the pope had sent a personal letter to Brezhnev assuring him that the events in Poland were not aimed at undermining the interests of the USSR, but the Vatican denied the existence of any letter.

"These two prayers," said the pope, "show that all of us here in Rome are united with our compatriots in Poland, with the Church in Poland, whose problems are so close to our heart."

Thus did the pope do something that Cardinal Wyszyński couldn't and wouldn't do: He publicly blessed the strike. This was a turning point. Now the bishop of Gdańsk, Lech Kaczmarek, presented Wałęsa and the other fourteen members of the strike committee with medals of Pope John Paul II.

Wałęsa, in turn, sent a reassuring message to Moscow and the Polish

Communists: "Our struggle is about unions; it's not a political effort. . . . We have no intention of calling into question Poland's international alliances."

With the world's attention focused on the extraordinary events in Poland, President Carter privately wrote to the pope that the United States shared the aspirations of the Polish workers and that it would use its diplomatic channels to urge Soviet restraint.

By August 23, a bitter dispute was flaring within the Polish Communist Party between the orthodox pro-Muscovites, who wanted to impose a state of emergency—martial law—and the Gierek reformists, backed by Stanisław Kania and Wojciech Jaruzelski, who favored compromise and avoidance of military force.

That day the pope sent the primate a delicately nuanced letter: "I am writing these brief words to say how especially close I have felt to you in the course of these last difficult days." Then, after the affectionate flourishes and invocations of the Madonna, the letter gave a precise political order: "I pray with all my heart that the bishops of Poland . . . can even now help this nation in its difficult struggle for daily bread, for social justice, and the safeguarding of its inviolable rights to its own life and development."

Bread, social justice, independent development. With these words the pope gave his complete support to the strikers' goals. The Church, observed the Catholic writer Stefan Kisielewski, with only a touch of oversimplification, was managing the first democratic strike in the history of Poland.

That evening the government made a historic concession, agreeing to enter into direct negotiations with the strike committees in Gdańsk, Gdynia, and Szczecin.

With the beginning of negotiations, which turned into a dramatic week-long test of strength, a group of advisers made an appearance alongside Lech Wałęsa. The group included intellectuals, professors, and members of the Polish Academy of Sciences. Two of its leaders were closely associated with Wojtyła: Tadeusz Mazowiecki, editor of the Warsaw Catholic periodical *Więź*, and historian Bronisław Geremek. With the arrival of this group, the strategic leadership of the movement—eventually to be known as Solidarity—passed largely into the hands of the Church. Now the Black Madonna in Wałęsa's lapel was a sign that Solidarity had taken its inspiration directly from Karol Wojtyła.

At the most intense moments in the crisis (between August 24 and 25, when the party was disposed to allow the right to strike, but not the creation of an independent union), First Secretary Gierek succeeded in driving most of the die-hard Stalinists out of the Polish Politburo. He then appeared on television to deliver a self-critical speech, which failed to create any consensus for ending the strikes whatsoever. Fearing that the situation might get out of the government's control and that Moscow would abandon its wait-and-see attitude, Gierek turned to Primate Wyszyński. He asked for "the help of the Church" in avoiding "incalculable consequences for the country." Gierek gave his word not to use force against the strikers, and Wyszyński agreed to intervene.

The most important parts of the speech that the primate delivered on August 26 at the shrine of Częstochowa (and the parts most favorable to the government) were replayed on state television. "You can't demand everything at once," the primate said. "It's better to set up a timetable. No one should put the nation at risk." Wyszyński said that everyone involved had to examine his conscience: "Let's not just point the finger at others. We all have faults and sins that need to be forgiven." Everyone, he preached, must show a sense of responsibility and respect for his everyday duties in social and civic life, "maintaining calm, poise, and circumspection."

Even though his speech contained an attack on state-supported atheism and defended the principle of "free association," the primate's remarks were taken by the strikers for what they were: an invitation not to insist on the immediate creation of an independent labor union. But other Poles balked. The Catholic intellectuals of Znak showed their dissent by an embarrassing public silence; Wałęsa paid no attention; and many bishops openly criticized the primate's position. The pope responded with irritation and disappointment: "Oh, this old man . . . this old man," he sighed to two Polish priests who were passing through Castel Gandolfo. The primate had lost touch with the people.

John Paul II wanted no appeasing of the Communists. He felt that the workers, by reassuring Moscow of their belief that Poland should stay in the

Warsaw Pact, had won the right to organize an independent union. Hadn't he demanded the same thing the month before in Brazil, where 150,000 workers, many of them on strike, gathered at the soccer stadium in São Paulo and exploded in a fifteen-minute ovation shouting, *"Libertade, libertade!"?* The metal-workers of São Paulo had gone out on the longest strike ever against the military regime—forty-two days of resistance—with the support of Cardinal Paulo Evaristo Arns.

There, in the heart of the Brazilian military dictatorship, the pope had stood with the workers and proclaimed "the right of the workers to unite in free associations, with the goal of making their voice heard, of defending their interests, and of contributing responsibly to the building up of the common good."

Could he do less for Poland?

The firm stance taken by John Paul II resolved the Polish crisis. On August 27, at the pope's instigation, the Polish bishops approved a document that explicitly claimed "the right to independence both of organizations representing the workers and of organizations of self-government." The pope's will had become the national will. Now the government had little choice but to give in. Wałęsa knew he had the pope's backing.

On August 31 the historic Gdańsk accords were signed, ratifying the establishment of the first independent union behind the iron curtain. The accords set the standard for subsequent agreements that would be made throughout Poland as the Solidarity movement swept the land. Free trade unions, wage increases, health care improvements, curtailment of censorship, release of political prisoners—virtually everything was now negotiable.

At the signing ceremonies for the accords, Wałęsa dramatically pulled an oversized, brightly colored pen out of his pocket. TV cameras recorded the moment: The pen was a souvenir from John Paul's trip to Poland, and on it was a picture of the pope.

On September 5, Edward Gierek lost his job as secretary and was replaced by Stanisław Kania. That same week, in Rome, the pope instructed Cardinal Casaroli to represent him in an extraordinary meeting requested by the Soviets with one of their diplomats. The message conveyed to Casaroli was mixed: On the one hand, the Soviet leaders in the Kremlin were asking that the pope restrain Solidarity in its demands and thus ease tensions; on the other, they warned they would intervene with troops if the union threatened the USSR's vital interests. As throughout the Polish crisis that would dominate the first decade of his papacy, the pope sought a delicate balance: how to simultaneously support the workers and keep the Soviets out, avoiding a bloodbath that he feared above all other consequences; prevail on the Polish authorities to deal in good faith with Solidarity; and keep the union from overreaching in its demands and provocations. For now, the Soviets seemed satisfied with his assurances, John Paul II felt, and both the Vatican and the USSR agreed to keep the "Casaroli-Kremlin channel" open. But a lot might depend on his ability to influence the workers.

. . .

Top Secret
One Copy only
NOT FOR PUBLICATION
THE CENTRAL COMMITTEE, COMMUNIST PARTY
OF THE SOVIET UNION POLITBURO SESSION OF
29 OCTOBER 1980

Chairman: Comrade BREZHNEV L.I.

Participants: Comrades Andropov I.V., Gorbachev M.S., Grishin V.V., Gromyko A.A., Kirilenko A.P., Pelshe A.Ia., Suslov M.A., Tikhonov N.A., Ustinov D.F., Chernenko K.U., Demichev P.N., Kuznetsov V.V., Ponomarev B.N., Solomentsev M.S., Dolghikh V.I., Zimianian M.V., Rusakov K.V.

Grimly, Chairman Brezhnev opened the meeting. "In fact, the counterrevolution in Poland is in full flood. . . . They are already beginning to take over the Sejm [parliament] and they keep claiming the army is on their side. Wałęsa is traveling from one end of the country to the other, to town after town, and they honor him with tributes everywhere. Polish leaders shut up and so does the press. Not even television is standing up to these antisocialist elements. . . . Perhaps it is really necessary to introduce martial law."

"I think, and the facts bear me out," said Yuri Andropov, head of the KGB, "that the Polish leadership does not fully understand the gravity of the situation which has arisen."

"Our Polish friends talk a lot but they make no sense," complained Defense Minister Ustinov. "It has come to this: Wałęsa and his myrmidons have occupied the radio station in Wrocław."

"There has been a small strike in Yugoslavia," Brezhnev noted. "But small as it was, they took it seriously there, three hundred persons were arrested and put in prison."

"Unless martial law is introduced," warned Ustinov, "things will get more and more complex. There is some wavering in the army. But our North Army forces are prepared and in full fighting readiness."

Finally, Foreign Minister Gromyko voiced the greatest fear: "We must not lose Poland! The Soviet Union lost six hundred thousand soldiers and officers in the fight to liberate Poland from the Nazis. We cannot allow a counterrevolution. . . ."

But how *not* to lose Poland?

"We have to speak firmly to our Polish friends," Gromyko continued. "Comrade Jaruzelski is of course a reliable man; but now for some reason he is beginning to sound rather lukewarm. He is even saying that the army wouldn't fight the workers. I think it's necessary to send the Poles a loud and clear message."

Gorbachev, elected to the Politburo only the previous year, agreed. "We should speak openly and firmly with our Polish friends. Up till now they haven't taken the necessary steps. They're in a sort of defensive position, and they can't hold it for long—they might end up being overthrown themselves."

∙ ∙ ∙

Top Secret

 . . . [R]adio transmissions receivable in the Soviet Union about events in Poland show that these events are being actively exploited in order to compromise the principles of socialism and, above all, to question the leading

Mass during second Polish trip.
Warsaw, Poland, June 17, 1983.

John Paul II flying to Poland in 1987.

The Basilica of Our Lady of Chinquinquira. Colombia, July 3, 1986.

Canonization mass for
Maximilian Kolbe.
St. Peter's Square, Rome,
October 10, 1982.

Yellow Knife, Canada,
September 18, 1984.

Third African trip. Kara, Togo,
August 9, 1985.

Meeting with Aborigines.
Alice Springs, Australia, November 29, 1986.

Meeting with miners and *campesinos.*
Oruro, Bolivia, May 11, 1988.

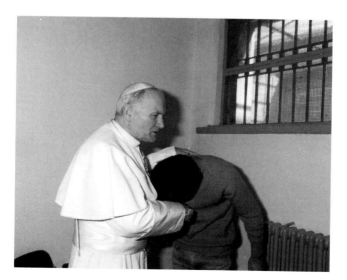

Meeting with
Ali Agca in prison.
Rome,
December 27, 1983.

Meeting with General Jaruzelski during second Polish trip.
Belweder Palace, Warsaw, June 17, 1983.

Meeting with Ronald and Nancy Reagan.
The Papal Library in the Apostolic Palace, Rome, September 20, 1990.

First meeting with Mikhail Gorbachev.
The Vatican, Rome, December 1, 1989.

Blessing a new church.
Rome, March 1996.

role of the party in the construction of socialism and communism, to over-throw the political system of socialism and its social-economic structure.

Arguing that each socialist country has a specific character, [these broadcasts] strongly promote the adoption of the Polish experience of devel-opment, and in particular the creation of "independent trade unions," limita-tion of censorship, reinforcement of the Church's position, etc.

Several weeks later, the danger to Soviet citizens from Polish magazines, newspapers, and other "undesired materials" was judged so threatening that all mail from Poland to the USSR was henceforth to be intercepted. Many of the "undesired" periodicals were Church-related. Special vigilance was to be directed to correspondence passing through the post offices of Leningrad, Kiev, Minsk, Vilnius, Riga, Kishinev, Lvov, and Brest: gateway cities with either large numbers of believers or populations expressing strong nationalist tendencies.

By the fall of 1980, the comrades in Berlin, Budapest, and Prague were already horrified by what was happening in Poland and were regularly com-plaining to Moscow. In East Germany, party leader and president Erich Honecker publicly threatened joint military action by the Warsaw Pact na-tions; and on October 28, his government imposed severe restrictions on travel to and from Poland, after nine years of visa-free transit between the two nations.

"This strange inactivity of Kania is becoming more and more incompre-hensible to the leaders of the socialist countries," Andrei Kirilenko told his fellow members of the Soviet Politburo at the difficult session on October 29. "For instance, when I talked with Husak and other Czech comrades, they were amazed at such conduct. They quoted the example of the time they took a firm hand with the instigators of a strike in one of their enterprises. It got results."

The following day—October 30, 1980—the two leading Polish Com-munists, Prime Minister Józef Pinkowski and Secretary Stanisław Kania, were due in Moscow to discuss matters with the Politburo's emergency commis-sion for Poland.

"The antisocialist elements have lost all restraint," Brezhnev thundered at the Politburo meeting. "As to the introduction of the state of emergency," Gromyko advised, "one has to regard it as a measure to safeguard the achievements of the revolution. Of course, it might be best not to introduce it at once, and especially not right after the return of comrades Kania and Pinkowski from Moscow." It was better "to wait a little bit, but they should be made aware of it. It is necessary to fortify them."

So concerned were the Soviets that as of October 29, only ten weeks after the birth of Solidarity, the Kremlin leaders were determined to get their "Polish friends" to begin preparations for the introduction of martial law and to move with finality against Solidarity and its supporters.

The next day Kania and Pinkowski came and went, pleading the special circumstances of their dilemma, asking for more time, but pledging a new, stiffened resistance to Solidarity's provocations.

Four weeks later, however, the Polish authorities had still not delivered on their promises and the country was in an even deeper crisis as the economy tottered and Solidarity carried out another round of strikes.

On December 5, an extraordinary meeting of the leaders of the Warsaw Pact countries was convened in Moscow to discuss the next step. Again Kania was summoned and heard his policies castigated by Brezhnev, by the Czechs, the Hungarians, the East Germans: They all insisted on a crackdown on both Solidarity and the Church. Otherwise, they made it clear, the joint forces of the Warsaw Pact would be called in to solve the Polish problem. Eighteen divisions were already on the border, and the Polish leaders were actually shown the military plans for intervention and the occupation of Polish cities and towns.

For a full hour Kania talked. Then he and Brezhnev met privately. Intervention, he told Brezhnev, would forever stain the image of the USSR with blood.

"OK, we don't march into Poland now," Brezhnev finally declared, "but if the situation gets worse we will come." Then he headed off to India.

·   ·   ·

For once, Kania's words to the assembled rulers of the Communist states had hit home; they had satisfied even the Soviet chief of ideology,

Mikhail Suslov, which wasn't easy. Presiding over the Politburo on December 11, Suslov sensed a change: "The main thing is that the Polish comrades do understand the great danger hanging over Poland, that they have recognized the great damage done by the activities of antisocialist elements which represent a great menace to the socialist achievements of the Polish people. Comrade Kania is now talking more reasonably about the economic situation of Poland, its indebtedness to the capitalist countries, and the need for help."

Kania was renowned among Polish Communists for his ability to play competing factions off against each other, to say the right thing at the right time to the right elements. This had been the key to his rise through the party ranks, and to his political survival. He could pick up the phone and discuss a given situation with, say, Brezhnev, the primate, a hard-liner in his own party, or someone from Solidarity. His ear could always find something to agree with and his tongue would plead the difficulty of his own position. He could even admit his own mistakes and then spell out the steps he would now take to preserve the primacy of the party, nation, socialism—whatever the occasion called for. Whatever it took. His hands had spent a lifetime cradling telephones, shuffling papers, and slapping backs. This was how he got the job done. And this time he had said the right things.

> One must note [Suslov continued] that in his speech Comrade Kania informed us about a more vigorous offensive against the antisocialist elements. He observed that there will be no more conniving with or yielding to the antisocialist elements. At the same time he said that the Polish United Workers Party, the Polish people, and its healthy forces, the army, the security services, and the militia that support the PUWP [the Polish Communist Party], are able to deal with the situation and to normalize it using their own means.

The comrades from Moscow and Prague and Berlin were understandably relieved to hear this from Kania. The key word had been unmistakably uttered right in front of not just Brezhnev and Suslov but Husak, Honecker, Kádár, and the rest. That word was "normalize," which in the Communist

251

lexicon referred to the period *after* the application of repressive military action, the time when conditions are restored to what they were before the rise of a political opposition. "Normalization" was what had happened in Hungary after 1956 and in Czechoslovakia following the Prague Spring of 1968, which is to say a return to the status quo ante.

And toward this goal, Kania in Moscow on December 5 had been offered plenty of suggestions by those with the requisite experience. Suslov noted:

> Comrade Husak, for instance, quoted many examples of their experience in 1968, when the Communist Party of Czechoslovakia had to fight tenaciously against the right-wing elements. Also Comrade Kadar spoke about the activities of counterrevolutionary elements in Hungary in 1956, when he had to adopt severe administrative measures to crush the counterrevolution.

The Politburo session of December 11 ended on a rare note of optimism regarding Poland: "In my opinion," observed Foreign Minister Gromyko, "the Polish comrades, like the other participants in the meeting, went away highly satisfied with the results of this meeting. They got the charge of energy they needed and the proper directives on all questions regarding the situation in Poland."

· · ·

The Kremlin's optimism was, to say the least, short-lived. Five weeks later Wałęsa was on his way to Rome to meet with the pope and be treated as an international hero.

Through the rest of December 1980, the Church, the party in Poland, and Solidarity used the respite from Moscow (and the coming of Christmas) to coalesce in the name of national unity. In solemn celebration, hundreds of thousands of people gathered outside the Gdańsk shipyard on December 16 to dedicate a huge monument—three steel crosses and three anchors, spanning 140 feet—to the memory of the workers who had been slain in the anti-government riots ten years earlier. The president of the Polish Republic was on hand, along with the chiefs of the party and the princes of the Polish Church.

The ceremony was in fact the defining moment in the five-month-old workers' movement. Lech Wałęsa's remarks were echoed by the speakers from the party and the Church.

This could not have been what the leaders of the Warsaw Pact had had in mind.

"I call on you to maintain peace, order, and respect," Wałęsa said. "I call on you to show reason and common sense in all endeavors for the good of our fatherland. I call on you to be vigilant in defense of our security and to maintain the sovereignty of our fatherland."

A telegram was read from the pope, thanking God that the strikes of August had ended in peace. There was no need for the former archbishop of Kraków to mention that the strikes had transformed the balance of political power in Poland: That much was apparent from the event itself. Wojtyła's successor as archbishop, Franciszek Macharski, blessed the huge steel symbol of Christ's presence in the shipyard ("a monument of reconstruction and a sign of the victory of hope and love over hate"); and mass was then celebrated by the bishop of Gdańsk, who concluded with the words "Let the sun of justice rise above us."

·   ·   ·

Top Secret

January 13, 1981

The Decision of the Secretariat of the Central Committee of the Communist Party of the Soviet Union: Comrades Suslov, Kirilenko, Chernenko, Gorbachev, Ponomarev, Kapitonov, Zimianian, Rusakov "in favor"

About the instructions given to the Soviet Ambassador in Italy regarding the journey to Italy of L. Wałęsa. . . .

Please meet Comrade Berlinguer [the head of the Italian Communist Party, which in December had publicly opposed Soviet intervention in Poland] or his substitute and say the following:

". . . The leaders of *"Solidarność"* and those who stand behind them aim at further aggravating the social-political situation in Poland [and] . . . weakening the position of the party and its leading role in the country. . . .

"This union at present constitutes a real force. . . .

"Despite [Wałęsa's scheduled] meetings with the pope in the Vatican . . . [and] the Italian Communist Party's original decision to refuse to meet L. Wałęsa, the leadership has maintained a vacillating position up till now and does not exclude the possibility of some kind of contacts with him.

"We would consider it advisable to appeal to the leadership of the Italian Communist Party . . . to the need for taking all possible steps to prevent the visit of L. Wałęsa from taking on the appearance of support for a policy of antisocialist tendency."

The appeal failed: Like some visiting movie star, Wałęsa captivated Rome, the media, and many Italian Communists. Wojtyła celebrated a private mass for all fourteen members of the Solidarity delegation who had come to the Vatican. He and Wałęsa met twice.

"The son has come to see his father," Wałęsa said upon being received by John Paul II on January 15. They then retired for a private talk in the pope's study.

The pope seemed particularly joyous and expansive, aware that much of the world now looked to him as the authentic leader of the Polish nation. When it came time for the official ceremony of greeting in the Consistory Hall, he delivered a long speech on the rights of labor.

Some thirty years before, he had written about labor in his first published article. Now he was writing an encyclical on the subject, *Laborem Exercens* (On Human Work), which would incorporate many of the ideas expressed in his impassioned defense of workers' rights before Wałęsa and his colleagues, including Anna Walentynowicz, the crane operator whose firing had spontaneously launched the strike, and Henryk Jankowski, the priest who had celebrated mass in the shipyard throughout the strike.

"I believe that the cornerstone of your venture, which began in August 1980 in the coastal region and in other great centers of Polish industry, was a joint impulse to promote the moral good of society," the pope told his visitors. Part of Wojtyła's genius lay in his exquisite sense of balance, which was much in evidence now: He signaled the Polish authorities that there should be "no contradiction between this kind of self-governing social initiative of working people and the structure of a system that considers human labor a fundamental value in social and national life." And without mentioning them by name, he told the Communists in Moscow that

> after what Poland suffered in World War II and the other great trials in our history . . . it can claim the right to progress just like any other country.
>
> What is at stake here has been, is, and always will be a strictly internal matter for the people of Poland. The immense efforts which were made during the autumn, and which must continue, were not directed against anyone. They were directed *toward*, not against, the common good. The right (which is in fact a duty) to make similar efforts is something that every country has. It is a right that is recognized and confirmed by the law of nations.

With this he left no doubt that he would be the champion of Solidarity's cause, and its philosopher as well. To emphasize his dedication, he invited Wałęsa, his wife, and his colleagues to morning mass three days later in his private chapel.

In Rome, Wałęsa also sat for an interview with the Italian journalist Oriana Fallaci, telling her that "without the Church, nothing could happen" in the Polish resistance movement. He called the work of the Church "ongoing," "obstinate," and "smart." Front pages of newspapers around the world were dominated by pictures and stories of the electrician from Gdańsk and the pope from Wadowice.

It was in this atmosphere, on January 22, that Comrade Mikhail Zimianian returned to Moscow from a fact-finding mission to Poland. He delivered to the Politburo his startling evaluation that an unprecedented threshold had been crossed: Solidarity was actually becoming the dominant power in Poland. There was a new entity in the heart of the Communist world, "a

great force . . . represented by Wałęsa's group and backed by the episcopate." Comrade Zimianian continued:

> The complexity of the situation in Poland derives from the fact
> that not only do we have an active . . . enemy, but also, owing to
> past mistakes, the party has lost a true creative link with the
> people. The working class has many reasons to be dissatis-
> fied. . . . This fact has been carefully exploited by *Solidarność*.
> . . . In Wałęsa's opinion, there are about ten million people in
> *Solidarność.*

This was four times the number in the Communist Party—and many of
the party's members were Catholic. More than 750,000 members of the party
were by then also members of Solidarity.

Even as Wałęsa's delegation met with the pope in the Vatican, in Warsaw Solidarity was demanding negotiations with the government over the
issue of a five-day work week; workers already were refusing to work on
Saturdays, and another big strike was planned to support private farmers who
wanted to form their own "rural Solidarity" union.

Zimianian's analysis got even gloomier:

> There is a growing sense that, should the party lose all its control
> over the mass media, the fight for public opinion will be lost. . . .
> Most newspapers are still not under party control. The situation
> is particularly bad in television. . . . The problem is that, even
> after management was changed, the main working force, i.e., peo-
> ple who directly prepare information materials, sympathize with
> *Solidarność.*

The Politburo, now treating every development in Poland as a crisis,
acted more and more often like so many orthodox Communists from central
casting. At various times in late 1980 and early 1981, the Kremlin leaders
pinned their hopes on undercutting Solidarity through propaganda campaigns
("We must make our Polish friends understand how to deal with the mass

media; it is their weakest spot, and so we have to help them"); flooding Polish factories with copies of Lenin's writings on how to organize trade unions; ordering the Soviet Council for Religious Affairs to produce further studies on the scientific bases of atheism (to counter the pope); shuffling the deck of *apparatchiks* in the Polish party in hopes of finding the right blend of popular appeal and party discipline (a constant refrain); sending cadres of Komsomol Youth from Russia to indoctrinate Polish teenagers; keeping young conscripts out of the Polish army (almost all were Solidarity supporters); and requiring old conscripts to remain in the ranks for extended duty.

The Politburo records, many hitherto secret, also reveal that by 1981 the Kremlin was aware of the deteriorating economy of the USSR and its neighboring states and what a disastrous strain the war in Afghanistan was on the bloc's resources, causing shortages of fuel, food, and raw materials for consumer goods. The situation in Poland was forcing the mobilization of Soviet troops on a second front, the Polish border, and further depleting stores.

Brezhnev was furious with Kania.

"It must be said," noted Konstantin Rusakov on January 22, "that Leonid Ilych [Brezhnev] talks with Comrade Kania almost every week." He tries to "make him understand how to act."

WASHINGTON

When Ronald Reagan took office on January 20, 1981, the first strategic contacts between the United States government and the pope of Rome had already occurred. Zbigniew Brzeziński, the Polish-born national security adviser to President Jimmy Carter, had represented the United States at Wojtyła's accession to the throne of St. Peter.

In 1976, Brzeziński, then a college professor, had attended Archbishop Wojtyła's lecture at Harvard and was impressed. "Why don't you have tea with me?" he said afterward. They had what Brzeziński recalled as "a wonderful conversation" about Poland and world affairs, and later they corresponded regularly, in handwritten letters, exchanging opinions with the knowledge and ease of men who had known the same history and intuitively understood the nuances of Polish life.

By late 1980, Brzeziński, a Catholic, had begun an official dialogue with an important papal emissary, Czech bishop Józef Tomko, in which Poland and the infant Solidarity movement figured prominently. Brzeziński wanted John Paul II to know that there were sources of money, equipment, and organizational support in the United States—particularly from the American labor movement—that were committed to Solidarity's cause. This was a crucial signal for the new pope, who now knew that the fragile, nascent force represented by Solidarity could call on help from the West and count on America as the movement became more of a threat to Communist orthodoxy.

Without revealing many specifics, Brzeziński informed Tomko of a covert CIA operation, secretly authorized by Carter, to smuggle anti-Communist books and literature into Eastern Europe and parts of the USSR, such as the Ukraine and the Baltic states, where dissident nationalism was spreading.

Brzeziński and Tomko discussed various ways the United States and the Vatican could use propaganda and pressure to promote basic human rights—economic, political, and religious—in Poland without provoking Soviet-ordered repression. This had been the focus of the pope's own meeting with President Carter on June 21, 1980, in the Vatican (although Solidarity had not yet been founded), a session that led Brzeziński to make a half-joking observation: "It became clear to me that Wojtyła should have been elected president and Carter should have been elected pope."

Then in the first week of December 1980, Brzeziński telephoned the pope to warn him of the threat of an imminent Soviet invasion of Poland. Speaking in Polish, he outlined the extent of the vast military buildup taking place on Poland's borders.

The pope was shocked at Brzeziński's conclusions and asked him how reliable his information was. The pontiff had already secretly sent a letter to Brezhnev asserting the principle of Poland's right to noninterference in its internal affairs. Moreover, he had thought that the ongoing dialogue through the Casaroli-Kremlin channel had already succeeded in averting such an intervention.

Without going into an elaborate explanation, Brzeziński said there was

satellite intelligence and precise data from "Eastern European sources"—
good sources: "We have various ways of knowing in great detail what the
Soviet high command is doing." As Brzeziński spoke, he was looking at
satellite photos of tents being unfolded next to Russian field hospitals on the
Polish border. What made Brzeziński's diplomacy so urgent was the certainty
of the data: For eleven years, Colonel Ryszard Kukliński, a senior officer on
the Polish general staff, had been providing the United States with sensitive
information about the workings of the Polish government and military—and
hence about the regime's internal security plans and, most recently, its responses to Solidarity. Kukliński's information even encompassed Moscow's
orders to Warsaw Pact forces and the Red Army.

Now Brzeziński asked the pope to use his bishops to get Western
European governments with large Catholic populations to support an ultimatum threatening the Soviets with economic, political, and cultural isolation if
they intervened in Poland. The pope agreed without a moment's hesitation.
Neither man had to elaborate on the reluctance of most of the Western
European nations to confront the Soviets over events in the USSR's "sphere
of influence"—or to jeopardize their lucrative trade with the Russians.

The Soviets were, meanwhile, being given a series of dire warnings by
both President Carter and President-elect Reagan, lest they conclude that the
interregnum between the election and Reagan's inauguration could be exploited in Poland. Brzeziński had also been in touch with Indian Prime
Minister Indira Gandhi, whom Brezhnev was soon to visit, asking her to
"register strongly U.S. concerns" to the Soviet leader. The United States was
also prepared to sell advanced weapons to China if the Soviets invaded Poland.

"If I need to call you back, how do I reach you directly?" Brzeziński
asked the pope. He could hear the pontiff asking someone in the background,
"What's my private phone number?"

Brzeziński, it turned out, didn't need to phone back, as the Soviets
retreated, for reasons that only now are becoming clear. To reassure the pope,
the Soviet Politburo sent Comrade Vadim Zagladin to Rome to say that, for
the present, there would be no intervention.

"Once the Soviets were deterred from invading," Brzeziński observed a decade later, "there was a second period [phase] after Reagan came into power. Efforts were made to support Solidarity, to support a big underground—and the whole thing took on a different meaning. It meant if the Soviets were determined to persist, you could have a long-term political action designed to destabilize the regime. And that's what we did; and the Reagan administration did it."

Upon taking office in January 1981, Reagan asked to be kept up to date on everything that was happening in Poland, especially with regard to Solidarity. In the first week of the new presidency, Richard Allen, Reagan's national security aide, and CIA Director William Casey came up with a formula for keeping the question front and center in the Oval Office: They redesigned the president's daily intelligence brief, the PDB, inserting a separate section, unusually detailed, with extensive reportage devoted to Poland. Kukliński's reports and, increasingly, information from the Vatican and its apostolic delegate in Washington were an essential part of it. Brzeziński had kept his White House credentials and was retained by the Reagan administration as a consultant on Poland, a position that by its nature involved dealing with John Paul II. He later noted:

> We involved the pope directly; and I don't want to talk about it. I
> can't go into details, not as long as he is alive. Casey ran it. . . . I
> got along very well with Casey. He continued everything we did
> [in the Carter administration] and expanded it . . . and led it; he
> was very flexible and very imaginative and not very bureaucratic. If
> something needed to be done it was done; to sustain an under-
> ground effort takes a lot of effort in terms of supplies, networks,
> etc. And this is why Solidarity wasn't crushed. . . . This is the
> first time that Communist police suppression didn't succeed.

Bill Casey had summed up his philosophy in the first weeks of the Reagan administration, in a speech to the Friendly Sons of St. Patrick—of whom he was decidedly one: "Some things are right and some things are wrong, eternally right and eternally wrong." The Catholic Church, which had shaped him, was eternally right. Communism, which he had railed against since his days as a high school orator, was eternally wrong.

Ronald Reagan's basic view of both the Vatican and Catholicism was quite different from that of previous twentieth-century presidents, including John F. Kennedy, the only Catholic to be elected to the White House in the nation's history. Since its inception the United States had been a "Protestant country," where the Catholic Church, until the later decades of the twentieth century, was viewed with suspicion by many Americans. The so-called foreign policy elite, the eastern U.S. "establishment," which until the Nixon adminis-tration dominated the cabinets and counselors of the American presidency, included relatively few Catholics. Previous presidents, including Kennedy, had gone to considerable lengths to put distance between the government and the Church—not simply out of respect for the Constitution, but also because of the broad strain of anti-Catholicism that, until the 1960s, flourished in America.

But Reagan, the son of a working-class Irish-Catholic father and a Protestant mother, was serenely unconcerned by such historical taboos. He had won the lion's share of the Catholic vote. He was extremely comfortable with and drawn to men from working-class Catholic backgrounds, self-made men like Casey who shared many of his own values. Almost invariably they were, like Reagan, the first in their families to attend college, and they weren't Ivy Leaguers. Because of this congeniality and partly by coincidence too, almost all the men Reagan appointed to the most important or visible foreign policy positions early in his administration were Catholics: Casey; Secretary of State Alexander Haig (whose brother was a priest); retired General Vernon Walters, the president's ambassador-at-large; Richard Allen and his successor as national security adviser, Judge William Clark (who had once considered becoming a priest). And they all saw their Church as the crucible of anti-Communist conviction.

Like Reagan, their basic view of the Marxist-Leninist canon was theo-logical: Communism was *spiritually* evil. And whereas Kennedy had done every-thing possible to insulate himself from the Church, Reagan sought both openly and covertly to forge the closest of ties with the pope and the Vatican. "I wanted to make them an ally," he explained years later. Toward that end he successfully shepherded legislation establishing diplomatic relations with the Holy See, something none of his predecessors had been willing to do.

"There was a significant level of careful cultivation of courtesy in this relationship with the pope," said Jeanne Kirkpatrick, Reagan's ambassador to the United Nations, "and this is one of the reasons why it is important to bear in mind the serious Catholic character of Casey and Walters; these are people who go to mass every day. And the way I saw it, and I think the way Ronald Reagan and Cap Weinberger [Caspar Weinberger, the secretary of defense] also saw it, was that this pope was a spiritual force with a lot of human embodiments as well, with whom we had a strong harmony of interests and a shared perspective on some important, strictly temporal affairs. While it's significant that Casey and Clark and Walters and others were serious Catholics, it's also significant that Reagan himself and Cap and I and so forth were not. . . . There was no Catholic cabal."

Solidarity, it was clear, represented an unprecedented internal threat to Moscow, an "infection" that already was spreading dissent within the Communist system, especially in the Baltic republics. The idea of an independent union in a Communist country was anathema to the leaders of Poland's neighbors. The Soviets would do everything within their power to crush Solidarity, Brzeziński had warned, while the new administration should do everything within its power to ensure Solidarity's survival. "If you were able to shake and disrupt Poland, then the shock waves would radiate out in many directions: into the Ukraine, the Balkans, in Latvia, Lithuania and Estonia, Czechoslovakia," said Richard Allen. Reagan fastened on the situation in Poland as evidence for his own belief that a revolution within the Communist empire was inevitable.

On January 30, 1981, only ten days after his inauguration, Reagan met with the senior members of his national security team: Vice President George Bush, Allen, Casey, Haig, and Weinberger. According to Weinberger, "It was there that we decided [on] the need to make a stand on Poland—not only to prevent an invasion, but to seek ways to undermine [Communist] power in Poland."

"Well, thanks to a man named Lech Wałęsa and Solidarity I really seized upon that as Poland's making the move," Reagan said in a self-congratulatory moment in 1991. "Here was literally a common worker or workingman who suddenly found himself leading a great majority of his Polish citizens. And in this thing that was created called Solidarity they were doing the thing I had said that we would look forward to, that the people would bring about that change within their own country."

Though Reagan and Casey and presidential deputy William P. Clark later spoke to each other about "breaking Poland out of the Soviet orbit," Reagan said, "We did not envision ourselves as moving into a country and overthrowing that government on behalf of the people. No, this thing had to be internal people themselves. . . . We could just try to be helpful. Solidarity, of course, was the very weapon for bringing this about because it was a development of laborers, and an organization of the labor of Poland. And this was quite different than what took place in a great many countries [within the Soviet bloc]; and certainly it was contrary to anything that the Soviets, the Communists, would want."

Meeting in the White House on January 30, Reagan and his advisers discussed the new administration's broad foreign policy goals: reversing the Soviet advantage, which they perceived as overwhelming, in nuclear weaponry and delivery systems; covertly confronting worldwide Soviet support for leftist and Communist insurgencies and intensifying the Carter administration's clandestine aid to rebels fighting the Soviet invasionary force in Afghanistan; confronting terrorism; pursuing arms control from a position of increased American might; and fostering the inseparable "linkage" between human rights and American policy toward the Soviet Union and the countries of Eastern Europe, a principle also established in the Carter years.

But the atmosphere of the meeting became most animated—"electric," said one participant—when the president spoke of the pope and the aspirations of the Polish people, which were clearly evident even as their country was being threatened by troops of the Warsaw Pact. Reagan wanted to know what was being done to help Wałęsa and Solidarity, and what could be done that hadn't been tried already.

Reagan spoke now, as he often did, about the Nazis. He drew parallels between the 1980s and the 1930s. "He felt that if democracy had stood up to Hitler there would have been no war," Clark noted later. "He felt that if he didn't stand up . . . it was incumbent on him to do that. His politics were formed in the 1930s. And to him the Soviets were continuators of the Nazis."

At the January 30 meeting, the possibilities of both internal repression by the Polish authorities (raised in Kukliński's latest reports) and a full-scale invasion by the Soviets were discussed. In addition to the tough political and economic actions threatened against the USSR in December, retaliation against the Polish regime, should it move to suppress Solidarity, was now agreed upon. The most serious measures would include economic sanctions in the form of harsh terms for rescheduling Poland's huge debt to the U.S., cutting off agricultural credits, and making it virtually impossible for Poland to obtain further loans in the West.

In the wake of the meeting, a decision was also reached to ensure that Solidarity would continue to get help, no matter how hard the Soviets or the Polish regime tried to suppress it. The goal was to encourage the union by providing more aid and organizational support for clandestine newspapers, propaganda, broadcasting, as well as advice to opposition forces in Poland— "all of the things that are done in countries where you want to destabilize a Communist government and strengthen the resistance to that," commented Illinois Congressman Henry Hyde (one of the few people outside the administration aware of what was happening).

Ever since the birth of Solidarity, its principal American financial support had come from the AFL-CIO: The American labor movement was working with European labor organizations and Social Democratic Parties to channel funds, equipment, and advice to the new union. Haig, Casey, Brzeziński, Clark, and members of the NSC senior staff began meeting frequently with Lane Kirkland, president of the AFL-CIO (a Democrat adamantly opposed to the administration's domestic policies), and Irving Brown, director of the federation's International Department. Brown had been an AFL representative in Western Europe in the early days of the cold war and had helped channel covert American funding to non-Communist parties in the Italian elections of 1948.

At first, "Solidarity wasn't going to be done as a classic covert operation," said Admiral Bobby Inman, who became Casey's deputy director at the CIA. "A decision was made early on that the union relationship with Solidarity was so good that most things that were instructive or helpful could be gotten to Solidarity through that network. Huge financial support wasn't what they needed initially. They needed organizational support, logistical support, good information, communications equipment"—almost all of which could be channeled through the labor movement, working closely with the administration, or through the Polish-American community, which in turn worked closely with the Polish Church.

Meanwhile, Richard Pipes, the director of Soviet and Eastern European affairs for the National Security Council (NSC), appointed Jan Nowak, head of the Polish-American Congress, as a special consultant to advise the administration on questions relating to Solidarity, the Polish Church, and U.S. policy toward Poland in general. "I was not involved in organizing the covert channels," says Nowak. "That was left to Casey and other people. I was trying to get money for the secret press, illegal media, for printing presses and Xerox machines." Much of Nowak's fundraising was done through Polish-American churches. Nowak began meeting with Reagan early in the administration; he found that the president was "very responsive, he was an extremist, an anti-Communist to the extreme. Without the policy of Reagan there would be no victory of Solidarity."

"Casey in particular understood the opportunity to separate the Poles from the rest of the Warsaw Pact," says Richard Perle, an assistant secretary of defense under Reagan. Radio Free Europe and the Voice of America became primary conduits of policy; their broadcasts to and about Poland ensured that the Poles, Germans, Czechs, Hungarians, Latvians, Lithuanians—all the Eastern and Central Europeans living under communism—were aware that in Poland a bold challenge to Communist orthodoxy was taking root. "The depth of animosity between the Poles and Soviets and the East Germans and Soviets was all clear enough," Perle noted. "Yet we had war plans that forced the Poles into a combatant role, whether they wished it or not. We thought it would be good to find ways to encourage them not to fight in support of the Soviets"—to mutiny or even fight against an invasion force. This was the origin of psychological operations—"psy-ops": radio broadcasts, leafleting, disinformation—aimed at the Polish army and security forces and developed by the CIA and the Pentagon.

.   .   .

The first year of the Reagan presidency was, virtually everyone involved agrees, a disaster with respect to establishing a coherent, functioning American foreign policy—except in the case of Poland. Otherwise, Reagan's strongest ideals were incapacitated by feuding among his own inner circle and by a belief, bordering on contempt, among some aides that the president had to be saved from his own zeal and ignorance, especially vis-à-vis the Soviet Union.

In this atmosphere, two men, both of whom had basic views and a style of working that Reagan was comfortable with, achieved a primacy that Haig and others could only wonder at: Bill Casey and William P. Clark. More than any other individual in the administration, Clark understood both the process and the president. In Sacramento he had been chief of staff to Governor Ronald Reagan. Now he had been named by the new president to be his personal troubleshooter at the State Department—Haig's deputy, in fact, with the title of counselor to the secretary.

And the two issues that took up much of Clark's and Casey's time and attention (and their discussions with the president)—Poland and the anti-Communist crusade in Central America—increasingly became enmeshed in dealings with the pope. By the spring of 1981, Casey and Clark were frequently dropping by the residence of the pope's apostolic delegate to Washington, Archbishop Pio Laghi, for breakfast, coffee, and consultation; Laghi was coming to the White House through the "back door" at the southwest gate for secret meetings with Casey, Clark, and, later, the president.

"They liked good cappuccino," Laghi says of Casey and Clark. "Occasionally we might talk about Central America or the Church's position on birth control. But usually the subject was Poland. By keeping in such close touch, we did not cross lines."

"Reagan wanted special briefings on the intelligence aspects of Poland and his feeling [was] that this was an early crack in the iron curtain—a popular uprising," Clark noted. "Casey understood that. And so I asked the State Department and NSC and CIA for special emphasis on a daily basis, not just about what was happening in Gdańsk but in the totality of Poland

and Eastern Europe. Especially in regard to Solidarity and the reaction [in the Communist bloc]."

Clark could see that Reagan was overwhelmed by issues that had never appeared on his mental horizon before he entered the White House. It was true that he didn't know one missile from another. His conversations with Reagan about Poland were extremely short. "I don't think I ever had an in-depth, one-on-one, private conversation that existed for more than three minutes with him—on any subject," he said. "That might shock you. We had our own code of communication. I knew where he wanted to go on Poland. And that was to take it to its *n*th possibilities. The president and Casey and I discussed the situation on the ground in Poland constantly: covert operations; who was doing what, where, why, and how; and the chances of success." And the role of the Vatican.

Allen, Casey, and the president began meeting regularly with the member of the American Catholic hierarchy closest to Pope John Paul II, Cardinal John Krol of Philadelphia. More than any other churchman, Krol kept the White House informed of Solidarity's general situation, its needs, and its relations with the Polish episcopate. He served as an intermediary between the White House, Poland, and the Vatican; and, perhaps most important, he and the president developed a strong personal rapport.

Allen called Krol, inelegantly but with absolute accuracy, "the pope's big buddy." Edward Derwinski, a Polish-American congressman from Illinois dispatched by the White House to Poland in 1981 to survey the situation, was amazed at how rapidly the relationship between Reagan and Krol progressed: "From the start he hit it off well with the president; it was one of those things where the vibes went well. They were the same age. And he really understood the situation in Poland, he had an ability to interpret the situation in Poland properly. And he was consulted not only by the president, but by the State Department, the NSC, and the CIA." He also offered public prayers at two Republican national conventions.

Derwinski sensed that Reagan related to Krol in much the same way he did to his old California friends from the business world: They were at ease with each other; they were affable types, powerful and successful men who liked to tell jokes and took a certain delight in the company of men. (Krol loved few things more than a day on the golf course and a good cigar.)

Tall and athletic, Krol had first gotten close to Karol Wojtyła at Vatican II, where he served as an undersecretary of the Council and spent many of his spare hours conversing—in Polish—and walking with the bishop from Kraków. At the conclave that elected John Paul II, Krol made sure from the beginning that the North American Church was solidly behind Wojtyła.

Thanks to their friendship, from the first day of the Wojtyła pontificate Krol had a uniquely important place in the American Church hierarchy—which enhanced his already dominant role among American cardinals. His bond to the Holy See was intensely personal, going deep into Polish soil: Krol's father had been born in Siekierczna, near Wadowice; he and Wojtyła had been elevated to the cardinalate together on June 21, 1967. In his speech accepting the red hat, Wojtyła had asked that special prayers be said as well for the other new Polish cardinal—Krol. Six months later Wojtyła traveled to the parish church of Krol's father to deliver a homily and recall that "once upon a time, scores of years ago, the ancestors, the parents of Cardinal Jan Krol, departed from this country to the New World, bringing to their new homeland . . . these values from the dowry of Poland."

Ten years older than the pope, Krol was also very much in the tradition of the "older brothers" who loomed large in Wojtyła's life. Both as a cardinal and later in the Vatican Wojtyła experienced a special childlike delight in Krol's company. They sang Polish songs together, danced, swapped tall stories from Polish folklore, joked across the table in a local Polish dialect they shared.

Thus Krol was in a position to do what no other prince of the Church, no other American for that matter, could do: convince Wojtyła that the interests of Poland, the Vatican, and the United States were in many ways parallel and overcome whatever unease Wojtyła might have about forming such a close relationship with an American presidency.

· · · ·

The historic relationship, rooted in anti-Marxist belief, that grew up between the United States and the Vatican, between a temporal and a spiritual superpower, held out the possibility of great rewards for both parties, especially with regard to Poland and Central America. Beginning in the spring of 1981, the Reagan administration maintained an intelligence shuttle at the highest level between the White House and the pope, who was regularly briefed by Casey and by Vernon Walters, a former CIA deputy director. Between them, Walters and Casey secretly visited with the pope about fifteen times over a six-year period to discuss matters of mutual interest.

The pope's judgments, especially concerning Poland and Central America, came to carry real weight in the White House, the CIA, and the NSC, and above all with Ronald Reagan himself. He eagerly awaited reports from both Walters and Casey whenever they visited the Vatican. Other presidents had waited anxiously at their desks for bombers to return from their missions: Reagan waited for reports from the pope.

Meanwhile, the pope was the beneficiary of some of America's most carefully guarded secrets and sophisticated political analysis: information from satellites, from intelligence agents, from electronic eavesdropping, from policy discussions at the White House, State Department, and CIA. Between 1981 and 1988, General Walters says he met with the pope at approximately six-month intervals, briefing Wojtyła on virtually every aspect of American policy and providing intelligence assessments—military, political, economic—on any and all subjects of interest to the Vatican.

The range of subjects discussed by Walters and the pope, as revealed in the classified cables he sent to the White House, State Department, or CIA after each visit, was wide indeed: Poland, Central America, terrorism, internal politics in Chile, Chinese military power, liberation theology, Argentina, the health of Leonid Brezhnev ("We think he's a little gaga," Walters told the pope in 1982), Pakistani nuclear ambitions, conventional force levels in Europe, dissent in the Ukraine, negotiations in the Middle East, violence in Sri Lanka, American and Soviet nuclear weaponry, submarine warfare, Lithuania, chemical weaponry, "new Soviet technology," Libya, Lebanon, the African famine, Chad, the foreign policy of the French government—to name only a fraction of the more than seventy-five topics mentioned in the classified cables.

Meanwhile, from the earliest months of the Reagan presidency, William

Casey and the pope secretly embarked on what the CIA director called an ongoing "geostrategic dialogue," focused on Poland, the USSR, and Latin America.

From the perspective of the administration's policy objectives, the more American intelligence information the pope had, the better. "Reagan had a deep and steadfast conviction that this pope would help change the world," Richard Allen noted. In fact, it was Allen who first characterized the Reagan-Vatican relationship as "one of the greatest secret alliances of all time." Hyperbole aside, the description contained essential elements of accuracy as both powers pursued their individual goals along parallel tracks: keeping each other informed, always taking each other's sensibilities into account, consulting, searching for common moral and political ground, plugging regularly into each other's enormous intelligence capabilities, but never formally undertaking clandestine activities together.

"One of the things you learn about the Catholic Church is that it is set up to collect information on the faithful," Allen had explained to candidate Reagan. "It is excellent information. An ideal intelligence agency would be set up the way the Vatican is. Its intelligence is absolutely first-rate."

During this extraordinary period of Vatican-U.S. collaboration, the pope's unrelenting opposition to abortion was reinforced by the Reagan administration in the most meaningful way: Millions of dollars in American aid to family planning programs around the world were blocked on orders from the president, in deference to the pope, according to the administration's ambassador to the Vatican at the time. The cutoff continued through the Bush administration. Casey, Walters, and the ambassador regularly discussed moral as well as political questions with the pope.

Meanwhile, on the single most important arms control issue of the era—the introduction by NATO of a new generation of cruise missiles into Western Europe—the pope, through his purposeful silence, appeared supportive of U.S. policy. Despite the public opposition of his American bishops, he took this path after lengthy briefings by Walters and Casey and the president's own appeals to Archbishop Laghi, Cardinal Krol and himself.

From Walters and Casey, the Vatican also received definitive intelligence information—some of it based on intercepted telephone communications—about priests and bishops in Nicaragua and El Salvador who advocated liberation theology and were active in opposing U.S.-backed forces there. On Casey's orders, secret payments were made by Colonel Oliver North of the NSC staff and others to "establishment" priests in Central America who were loyal to the pope, though there is no record indicating that Wojtyła knew of the payments. President Reagan, however, was aware of them.

WARSAW

From where he sat in Warsaw, General Jaruzelski saw one problem that was even worse than Solidarity: Moscow. The men in the Politburo didn't understand Poland, its history, or the situation in which Jaruzelski and the country's leaders now found themselves. Most of all, he worried, they didn't understand the Church or its role in society. Solidarity might be a calamity for socialism; but the Kremlin, he was convinced, could bring about a catastrophe for Poland and the world.

On March 4, 1981, he and Kania had been summoned to the Kremlin and dressed down by Brezhnev and the senior members of the Politburo: Gromyko, Andropov, Suslov, Ustinov, Rusakov, and Tikhonov. It had been brutal. When, he was asked, would they impose martial law? Why weren't the hooligans being arrested? Didn't they understand that the party was losing all its authority with the people? That their allies were in an uproar? How could they cave in to the Church? Didn't they realize that the pope was an instrument of the Western powers, that the pope *was* the opposition?

Afterward, a communiqué was released to the Polish and Russian press announcing unanimous agreement that the defense of communism in any one country—such as Poland—was a matter not only for that country, but for the "entire socialist community. . . . The socialist community is indissoluble." This was an implicit restatement of the Brezhnev doctrine, Jaruzelski recognized, an echo of the formula that had been used to justify the invasion of Czechoslovakia in the spring of 1968.

In virtually every discussion Jaruzelski had ever had with Brezhnev since the birth of Solidarity, the Soviet president had complained about the role of the Church and of the pope.

"Brezhnev, Gromyko, Ustinov, and the Soviet establishment saw ideological ties between the Vatican and the West," Jaruzelski reflected later, "and that was always the context of our conversations. They had a very primitive perception." Every time he picked up the phone, it seemed, one of the "fraternal allies" or somebody from Moscow was on the line demanding to know why he had made this or that concession to the Church. Why were church services allowed to be broadcast on the radio? (The government had agreed to this as part of the settlement of the August strikes.) Why were priests in the factories? Worse, Jaruzelski now had an endless succession of politicians, generals, and other representatives of the Warsaw Pact staff looking over his shoulder at every moment. Invariably, they saw the Church as an inexplicable puzzle: If the Church was known to be allied with Solidarity, why let it flourish? Control the bishops, restrict their authority, throw the priests out of the factories, refuse to engage in dialogue with the Church, shut down the seminaries.

Jaruzelski knew that things weren't that simple, but in Moscow, in Berlin, in Prague, and in Budapest, the comrades seemed to be pushing him toward a simple solution that could only result in bloodshed, Poles fighting Poles, a civil war within the Polish army, or—worse—Russian soldiers and Warsaw Pact troops fighting Poles in the streets. The Soviet elders seemed to have no idea that it was impossible to maintain peace in this situation *without* the Church.

Jaruzelski and Kania had repeatedly tried to explain such matters to Brezhnev, Gromyko, and the delegations the Politburo kept sending to Warsaw. Now, as spring 1981 came to Poland, new demonstrations broke out and Solidarity even called a general strike. Never had Solidarity had such strong popular support. Soviet troops were again on "maneuvers." Units from the Warsaw Pact were staging landings along Poland's Baltic coast and holding war games at several other sites on Polish territory. The West was again threatening the USSR with the consequences of intervention. Jaruzelski believed that he and Kania had to meet again with the Politburo to restrain the Soviets and explain the most recent actions of the Warsaw government, particularly with regard to the Church, which in the past two weeks had assumed a larger role in negotiations between the state and the union.

Not surprisingly, Jaruzelski had given a lot of thought to the individual members of the Politburo and their particular antipathy to the Church. Ustinov (who called Jaruzelski "General Liberal"), Suslov, Chernenko, and Ligachev were particularly aggressive in their attacks on the pope and the Church. Western politics, not the Holy Ghost, had made the bishops vote for Wojtyła: That was an article of faith in Moscow, and those four never stopped reminding Jaruzelski of it. They believed that Zbigniew Brzeziński, with help from Cardinal Krol, had engineered John Paul II's election.

As for Brezhnev, Jaruzelski pointed out,

> he had participated in the revolution as a young boy. So in his youth he was one of those engaged in the most severe and most sharply ideological struggles against the Church; and it was very brutal. He also fought the Church in the Ukraine where he had worked for many years. So he was one of those Bolsheviks who imbibed atheism and anti-Church attitudes with their mother's milk. If he spoke about the Church, he was speaking about it as an enemy . . . not just an ideological enemy, but a political enemy as well.

Nor did the "fraternal comrades" understand the unique position of Polish Catholicism.

> They were not aware of the underlying strength of the Church in Poland. The Church in Russia was practically destroyed. The Church in Czechoslovakia was weak and divided; . . . The Church in Hungary had been, one might say, pacified. . . . In Bulgaria, there was no problem and in Romania even less so. Romanian bishops would bow to Ceausescu. So in this respect

Poland was an exception; and therefore our allies in Moscow and elsewhere didn't understand us. They kept asking: "How come everybody else can deal with the Church and not you?"

Jaruzelski particularly remembered one of Brezhnev's statements in this context:

He said the Church was expanding its influence and making matters more difficult in Poland, yet we were giving so many building permits for churches that we were surrendering to the Church. And the Church, after all, was our enemy, Brezhnev said; sooner or later it would *gag in our throats, it would suffocate us.*

.   .   .

On March 30, Poland and the pope were very much on Ronald Reagan's mind. At his nine o'clock meeting in the Oval Office, he reviewed the latest intelligence in the special section of the president's daily brief devoted to Poland: Polish airspace had been closed two days before to facilitate further maneuvers by troops of the Warsaw Pact. In East Germany, all railroad flatcars had been requisitioned by the military. Along Poland's borders, 150,000 soldiers from the USSR, East Germany, and the other nations of the Communist bloc had again taken up positions portending invasion. Defense Secretary Weinberger had publicly implied that the United States would not rule out the use of military force if Poland was invaded—an assertion that had greatly disturbed Secretary of State Haig because armed American retaliation was not a real possibility.

That afternoon the president was scheduled to address an audience from the AFL-CIO's Building and Construction Trades Department, one of the routine political chores that presidents do. Given the AFL-CIO's role in conveying American aid to the Polish workers' movement, he especially wanted to use this appearance to say something about Poland and its workers. Just then Poland was a tinderbox, its situation unprecedented: Tens of millions of Polish workingmen and women had held a four-hour nationwide strike on March 27, the largest organized protest against a Communist government since World War II. The country had come to a standstill. Reagan's deeply held belief about communism collapsing from within seemed to be coming true in Poland.

Through the back channel between the White House and the papal apartments, Reagan knew that on February 23 the pope had written a letter to Brezhnev, admonishing him to respect the sovereignty of Poland and the rights of Solidarity. There were rumors (probably unfounded, but widely believed in Poland and encouraged by some in the Vatican) that if Soviet troops intervened, the pope would hasten to his homeland and thrust his own body between the people and Russian tanks.

That afternoon, as the president neared the end of his address to the building trades workers' meeting in the Washington Hilton, he appealed for support for his plans to rebuild the American military. Then he paused and saluted the workers of Poland. "Their courage reminds us not only of the precious liberty that is ours to nourish and protect, but of the spirit in each of us, everywhere." There were cheers and loud applause. "The Polish workers stand as sentinels on behalf of universal human principles," he continued, "and they remind us that on this good Earth, the people will always prevail."

A few minutes later, as he was about to enter his limousine outside the hotel, the president was shot in the side and critically wounded by John Hinckley Jr. Pushed into his car by Secret Service agents, Ronald Reagan was rushed to George Washington University Hospital.

In Rome, upon hearing the news, the pope stopped to pray for Reagan's recovery and almost immediately sent him a personal message with his prayers and hopes.

At the hospital, Reagan underwent surgery for removal of a bullet that had penetrated his lung and lodged within an inch of his heart, missing the aorta—and certain death—by the same distance.

It was "a miracle" that he had survived, the doctors said.

MOSCOW

Chairman Brezhnev opened the April 2 meeting of the Politburo with a tirade.

"We all have huge worries about the outcome of events in Poland," he said. "Worst of all is that our friends listen and agree with our recommendations, but in practice they don't do anything. And a counterrevolution is taking the offensive on all fronts."

The latest agreement between the government and the union, reached three days before under pressure from the pope and brokered by the bishops, was very much on Brezhnev's mind. "Our friends succeeded in averting [a second] general strike," Brezhnev noted. "But at what price? At the price of capitulating once more to the opposition." The government had agreed to recognize a new farmers union under the banner of Rural Solidarity and to investigate and punish police who had attacked workers in the city of Bydgoszcz during a demonstration. Still, many members of the union were disturbed that their leadership had agreed to call off the general strike at the zenith of Solidarity's power and had dropped other demands, including the release of prisoners arrested for antigovernment activities between 1976 and 1980.

Now Brezhnev angrily informed the comrades of his latest phone conversation with Kania, who was feeling hurt because the recent 26th Congress of the Soviet Party had been sharply critical of his government's policies and its constant giving of ground to Solidarity.

> I promptly told him [Brezhnev recounted], "They did right. You should have gotten more than criticism, they should have given you a sound thrashing. Then maybe you might have understood." These were literally my words. Comrade Kania acknowledged that they had acted weakly, that they needed to be tougher.
>
> In that regard, I told him: "But how many times have we told you you needed to take decisive measures, that you mustn't forever

be giving in to 'Solidarity.' You all insist on the peaceful way, not understanding or not wanting to understand that the sort of 'peaceful way' you support can lead to bloodshed."

The assessment to his fellow Politburo members by Defense Minister Ustinov was chilling:

I think that bloodshed is unavoidable: It will happen. And if we are afraid of this, then of course we will be forced to surrender one position after the other. *But this way, we could lose all the achievements of socialism.*

And so on April 2, 1981, sixty-four years after the Bolshevik Revolution and scarcely eight months after the Vladimir Lenin Shipyard had been seized by workers of Gdańsk, the men in the Kremlin were discussing the unthinkable: that all the achievements of socialism, of Lenin's revolution, might be lost.

This was far worse than any other revolt or opposition the Soviets had faced in the postwar era. Unlike the situation in 1956 and 1968, the Soviets' options were limited: by Afghanistan; by the way Solidarity's cause had been embraced around the world, even on the left; by the loss of any element of surprise in the event of military intervention; by deteriorating economic and social conditions in the USSR. The West was poised to invoke truly draconian sanctions against the Soviets if they intervened: There would be economic, political, social, and moral punishment. For weeks Margaret Thatcher, the British prime minister, had been on the phone with other Western leaders saying that they had to have a coordinated plan. The United States had warned the Soviets not to take advantage of Poland while Reagan was recovering. The pope was another factor, a huge factor, beginning with the question of whether he would really dare come to Poland and interpose his body against an invading army.

On March 28, the Soviet ambassador to Rome had met urgently with the pope for two hours. Afterward John Paul II told Cardinal Casaroli that the USSR had pledged not to intervene for six months if the Vatican could keep a lid on events in Poland, presumably by finding a way to dissuade Solidarity from calling further crippling strikes. The pope was already moving in this direction, having written a letter to Cardinal Wyszyński that appeared in that morning's *L'Osservatore Romano:* "The common opinion of nations who love peace is shown by their conviction that the Poles have the undeniable right to resolve their problems by themselves and with their own resources." There was no missing the reference to the Soviets.

The "vast masses" of Polish working people, the pope declared, "are conscious of the necessity to devote themselves fully to their work in order to overcome the country's economic difficulties. They desire to work and not to strike." He urged "an agreement . . . between the state authorities and representatives of the working people to strengthen internal peace and a renewal of those principles which were agreed upon by everybody last autumn."

The settlement reached a few days later, which had so outraged Brezhnev, had met the pope's criteria by reaffirming the Gdańsk accords and giving Solidarity even more power. In exchange, the union had called off its plans for a general strike and the possibility of another violent clash.

Those "principles" mentioned by the pope, as everybody in the Politburo knew, meant acknowledging Solidarity's legitimacy as the representative of the working classes: an anti-Communist alliance of workers in a workers' state. Yuri Andropov, whose information on the situation inside Poland was probably the most precise of anyone's in the Politburo—by virtue of both his membership on its emergency Polish commission and his job as head of the KGB—enunciated the problem at the April 2 meeting:

Solidarity is now starting to grab one position after the other. If an extraordinary session [of the Polish parliament] is called, then there's no excluding the possibility that it will be completely in the hands of the representatives of Solidarity, and at that point, in a bloodless coup, they will take power into their hands.

Meanwhile, the situation in the Polish army, reported Ustinov, "has somewhat deteriorated. The fact is that they have replaced a significant number of old draftees with new ones, the majority of whom sympathize with Solidarity and in that way the army slackens. We believe that we need to keep the old draftees in the Polish army and not let them be discharged. However, the Poles don't want this."

"We'll have to tell them what it means to introduce martial law and explain it all," said Brezhnev.

"Right," echoed Andropov, deferring as always to the waxen-faced man in charge, the man he would succeed the following year. "We have to tell them that martial law means a curfew, limited movement in the city streets, strengthening state security in Party institutions, factories, etc. The pressure from the leaders of Solidarity has left Jaruzelski in terribly bad shape, while lately Kania has begun to drink more and more. This is a very sad phenomenon. At the same time," he continued,

> I want to point out that Polish events are having an influence on the western areas of our country, too. In particular, in many Byelorussian villages where Polish-language radio and TV come in clearly. . . . [I]n some other areas, particularly in Georgia, there are spontaneous demonstrations, groups shouting anti-Soviet slogans in the streets, as happened not long ago in Tbilisi [in Georgia]. Here too we'll have to take tough internal measures.

. . .

Ever since his appointment, at the behest of the Soviets, as prime minister in February, Jaruzelski had been spending practically all of his days and nights in the building of the Council of Ministers in Warsaw. This had been true during the crisis of the past two weeks. He had a small bedroom set up near his office and had not seen his wife or daughter for days.

The strain from incessant Communist criticism of the Polish leadership was beginning to show: Even behind the dark glasses that masked Jaruzelski's eyes, fatigue was evident. The latest attacks from Moscow, Prague, Berlin, and the hard-liners in the Polish party had been the most severe yet. Solidarity's strength and stature had not only taken hold in Poland, the movement had captured the imagination of the world. This too, he sensed, was something the Kremlin found intolerable. Earlier that week, Kania told him, Brezhnev had called back, demanding action against Solidarity and suggesting that the government "go discover" some secret ammunition depots of the unions.

This reminded him of the Czech scenario in 1968, when the Soviets had invaded under the same sort of pretext, which "probably explains the spiritual condition I was in on that April 3," he said later. That afternoon Kania informed him that they were to meet within hours with "one of Brezhnev's deputies: an absolutely secret meeting, the place and time of which would be announced at the very last moment."

With the experience of Czech President Alexander Dubček, who had been summoned to Moscow and arrested, running through his mind, Jaruzelski called his friend General Michał Janiszewski and asked him to take care of his wife and daughter if necessary.

> I couldn't tell him any more, but I think he understood what my request meant because when we parted—after he had tried in vain to convince me to take him with me—he allowed himself an unusual gesture: He embraced me without saying a word.

Accompanied only by an aide, whom Jaruzelski had entrusted with a pistol and a hand grenade containing poison gas, Jaruzelski now went to Kania's office and they drove together to the military airport at Okecie.

It was approximately seven P.M. A single plane was on the runway, a Tupolev 134 without any identifying marks: neither the red star of Red Army planes nor the "Aeroflot" inscription on planes normally used by the Soviet government. A single general staff officer of the Warsaw Pact was waiting at the foot of the ramp.

The flight, which lasted a little less than an hour, took an evasive course to preserve secrecy before heading for the Brest-Litovsk region over the Soviet border.

> When the plane landed [Jaruzelski recalled] I noticed only that we were very far from the airport buildings, whose lights were barely distinguishable. Three cars were waiting for us, three Volgas, with

curtains but no license plates. No one wore a uniform; they were civilians who didn't need to show their papers to prove they belonged to the KGB. We got in the first car (my aide refused to leave us), and we left immediately. I had no idea where we were. The absence of road signs only enhanced the feeling I was traveling toward some unknown planet. At a certain moment our cars took a small unpaved road that led us to a huge, red-brick building—halfway between a fortress and a prison. In that moment I told myself: this could be a one-way trip. Without saying one word I turned toward Kania who was clearly having the same thought.

In the beam of the car's headlights, Jaruzelski could make out three Soviet railway carriages. The motorcade pulled up nearby, and, as the doors were opened for Kania and Jaruzelski, two men got out of the first carriage to greet them.

They were Andropov and Ustinov, the head of the KGB and the minister of defense. "In a system where everything in the picture has its own significance, the message was clear," Jaruzelski reflected. He and Kania followed their "hosts" into the railway car.

The location of the railroad siding itself, near the city of Brest, straddling the Soviet border, could not have been more symbolic of their predicament: Poland was not only the largest of the countries ceded to the Soviets at Yalta, both in population (37 million in 1981) and in sheer size (120,725 square miles). But it was also the Soviets' western corridor to East Germany and, beyond, to Western Europe. When Gromyko had so urgently insisted, "We cannot lose Poland," he left the obvious unstated: Without Poland, and the thousands of Soviet troops garrisoned there, the USSR's unquestioned hegemony over Communist Eastern and Central Europe could not exist.

All four of the participants in that night's secret meeting—Kania, Jaruzelski, Ustinov, and Andropov—were acutely aware of Poland's other distinction: The Eastern bloc's weakest Communist party (as a historian observed) was being overwhelmed by Europe's strongest Church.

The two senior Polish officials now followed their hosts into a luxuriously appointed railroad car, specially designed for important meetings, with a large rectangular table covered in green baize. There were armchairs and sofas and, because the session would be long, a sumptuous buffet.

"Piles of sandwiches, tea, coffee and beer, sandwiches with caviar, fish, and some meat," Jaruzelski noted later. "It was good food, and the atmosphere was very nice."

The conversation was far less pleasant.

For six hours—until three A.M.—Ustinov and Andropov recited a litany of sins committed by the Polish authorities and insisted that there was only one way to get absolution: by imposing martial law in Poland.

No matter how he and Kania kept resisting, the Russians were adamant. Didn't the Polish comrades comprehend that the antisocialist forces, backed by the pope and the West, were actually preparing to take power? Solidarity must be declared illegal; the military must be mobilized against the enemies of socialism; strikes and protests must be outlawed; the party must be rejuvenated; the Church must return to its proper role, to serving the faith, not getting involved in politics. "They said we had disregarded our commitments and pledges and that we had done hardly anything to stop the counterrevolution . . . [that] we had allowed the Church to have an ever increasing role," Jaruzelski later noted.

"In many countries," Ustinov told them, "no sooner does an uprising flare up or some kind of confusion start, than extraordinary measures are taken or martial law introduced. Take Yugoslavia: There was a demonstration in Kosovo, they introduced martial law, and nobody said a word about it. We don't understand why the Poles are afraid of introducing martial law."

Repeatedly, the Polish leaders tried to explain why. Kania conceded that recent events, particularly the general strike and events in Bydgoszcz, had shown that the counterrevolution was at that moment stronger than the forces of the party. But both he and Jaruzelski pleaded for time, arguing that intervention by troops of the Warsaw Pact was "absolutely impossible" and that it was equally unthinkable for the Polish government to impose martial law on its own people. The government would be "misunderstood" and eventually left "powerless." "Yes, it was true that the Church had a great deal of influence," Jaruzelski recalls conceding, "but that was as a peacemaker: It had no wish to challenge the socialist powers. We asked our interlocutors to leave us the time to solve our problems by ourselves, with our own means."

Andropov and Ustinov heard the Polish comrades out, listening patiently as Jaruzelski and Kania argued for their unique circumstances. The Russians' tone—especially with Jaruzelski, whom they addressed as "General," as opposed to the more familiar "Stanisław" for Kania—was respectful, however unpalatable their message. But, Jaruzelski recalled,

> these old guys didn't realize the sacred flame was beginning to sputter. They couldn't understand that the Polish people, or other nations, had begun to question the dogmas of the system. The concept that the trade unions were no longer just a transmission link of the party was heresy to them. We tried—and when I say we I mean the leaders who were committed to putting life into the Gdańsk accords and the new political party line—we tried to explain to the Soviets Poland's particular situation. But they didn't want to understand.

Now, in the ornately furnished railroad car, Jaruzelski listened very carefully as Ustinov and Andropov again threatened military intervention. The tone was flat, the words precise.

"The key words were 'preparing intervention,'" recalled Jaruzelski. "I had my own experience, from the previous December, which I studied very carefully, [and] from the Soviet intervention in Hungary and Czechoslovakia. I knew that decisions are made in the last five minutes, and nobody foresees them. I felt that the most important thing now was to properly judge the situation, the circumstances, the logic of events. 'We cannot agree to the dismantling of a state which is part of the Warsaw Treaty,' they said."

Meanwhile Jaruzelski's strategic sense, his instincts as a general, not as prime minister, were focusing on one ominous detail: As in December, "the Russian hospitals near our borders were emptied to put up army reservists who spoke Polish; there were two headquarters of the Warsaw Pact where such special troops were located, special recognition troops"—an advance guard that would prepare the way for other, non-Polish-speaking forces to invade the country. "You have to remember that we had no borders with Western countries," he continued. "We were surrounded by socialist nations. You have to remember that Czechoslovakia and Hungary were bordered by NATO states. . . ."

He realized that "if at that time I were a Russian general looking at the map of Europe and the world, I would be for intervention." Finally, between heaping portions of caviar, fish, and sandwiches, after six hours of tortuous arguments back and forth, Andropov and Ustinov

repeated the remark of Brezhnev that his representatives in Poland always repeated and that he made for the first time in December 1980: "We aren't coming into Poland now, but if necessary, if the situation gets worse, we will come." They repeated another important remark by Brezhnev: "A friend would never leave our Polish friends alone in the lurch."

By the end of the meeting, "we were at the end of our strength," Jaruzelski wrote in his memoirs. "But we were steadfast, and we were convinced that we had gotten a respite." Neither he nor Kania ever informed the Polish Politburo of the meeting.

• • •

Six days later Andropov and Ustinov reported back to the Soviet Politburo on their meeting with the Polish leaders. Jaruzelski and Kania, they said, had agreed at Brest to sign documents that would eventually be used to decree martial law. Jaruzelski, they added, repeatedly sought Soviet approval during the meeting to submit his resignation.

"The draft of the document for the introduction of martial law was prepared with the help of our comrades and these documents must be signed," Andropov said he and Ustinov had explained in the railroad car. "The Polish comrades said: 'How can we sign such documents when we must have them approved by the Sejm, etc.?' "

Finally they agreed to sign the documents later in the month, after the Sejm had adjourned, according to the Politburo minutes.

We said that it wasn't necessary to go through the Sejm, that "This is the document on the basis of which you will act, when you introduce martial law. But now you personally, Comrade Kania and Comrade Jaruzelski, must sign so that we know that you agree with that document and that you will know what needs to be done at the time of martial law."*

"The general impression of the meeting with our comrades is that they were tense and nervous, and we noticed how worn out they were," Andropov reported. "Comrade Kania said straight out that it was very hard for them to go on, that 'Solidarity' and other antisocialist forces were pressing on them. . . . Comrade Jaruzelski again expressed his wish to be released from the post of premier. We explained to him very simply that he had to remain in that post and worthily meet the obligations that went with it. We emphasized that the enemy was preparing its forces in order to seize power."

The Russians were as anxious as the Poles to keep the meeting secret.

"Maybe we should prepare some information for the 'fraternal parties,' " Suslov suggested at the subsequent Politburo meeting.

"But in no way should we allude to the meeting that took place," interjected Gromyko.

Andropov shut the door. "Any talk about this meeting is completely out of the question."

On April 7, four days after the Brest meeting, Brezhnev announced that "military exercises" around Poland were ending and that the Poles were capable of solving their own problems.

"On the one hand, we should not pester them unnecessarily," Brezhnev advised, or they might "feel their heart sinking into their boots. On the other hand, we must keep up the constant pressure."

---

* Jaruzelski later said he never actually signed the documents.

On April 23, as Suslov arrived in Warsaw to remind the Polish comrades of their duty, the Politburo's Polish commission issued another implacable report:

Proletarians of all countries—unite!

TOP SECRET
SPECIAL FILE

. . . Solidarity, as a group and in its separate factions, is preparing to blackmail the authorities once again by advancing various demands of a political nature. . . . Wałęsa and the extremists of KOR-KOS [the Committee for Social Defense], the same Wałęsa and the Catholic clergy that stands behind him, have no intention whatsoever of slackening pressure on the PUWP. We should also not ignore the fact that the extremists can take control of "Solidarity" with all the obvious consequences.

SPOOK

The director of Central Intelligence had long been an important figure in the modern American presidency, but William Casey turned his position into one of unprecedented power, shaping American policies every bit as much as the secretaries of state and defense and the national security adviser to the president. In the strange epoch that was the Reagan administration, Casey held two portfolios—clandestine minister of state and of war, in the unexaggerated phrase of a biographer.

Following most of his visits with the pope—probably six or seven in all—Casey generally summarized the substance of their talks in confidential letters to the president. They were usually two or three pages long and dealt primarily with Poland, the Soviet Union, Eastern Europe, and Central America. Parts of Casey's visits were intensely private: He and the pope discussed religious matters, engaging in an intimate, spiritual conversation. According to Casey's colleagues, he shared the details of these colloquies with no one except perhaps his family. His widow, Sophia, confirms that the pope and the CIA director asked one another to pray for various matters of individual and mutual concern.

Flying in a camouflaged air force transport, Casey often made it a point to go first to Rome—and the Vatican—on his world tours of American intelligence missions. He also met with senior members of the Roman Curia—usually Cardinal Secretary of State Casaroli—before or after seeing the pope. It was in his various capacities—clandestine minister, anti-Communist, and Catholic communicant—that Casey arrived at the Vatican on April 23, 1981.

"I'd characterize the focus of their discussions on Poland," said Casey's deputy and successor, Robert Gates, "as how do you keep Solidarity and the underground alive and the Soviets out in a way that allows the natural political and economic forces to come to the fore, and to eventually create the 'breakout' that Reagan and Casey and others talked about. This was an evolutionary process, not a revolutionary one: a process that would allow Poland to put greater and greater distance between itself and the Soviet Union."

The gains made by Solidarity were enormous, the pope said to Casey on this day; they had changed the very nature of Polish society. The essential question was, How could the Vatican and the United States work to protect them?

John Paul II, with Casaroli, was also meeting that week with the Soviet ambassador—three times, it developed, between April 19 and April 25—and Casey was apprised of the substance of these discussions. The Soviets thought the situation in Poland had improved from their perspective—there were no strikes at the time—and the pope pledged to continue urging moderation on Solidarity.

Of urgent concern to Wojtyła and Casey were the most radical of the movement's cadres, which they now discussed. The pope and Casey then turned to an extremely worrisome—and sensational—matter. In early April, these "extremist elements" of Solidarity had begun preparations for a violent campaign against the regime. They were stockpiling Molotov cocktails and planning to occupy and destroy Communist Party offices and government buildings throughout Poland. Kania and Jaruzelski, fearing disaster, had come to Cardinal Wyszyński for help. Wyszyński had warned the pope and at the same time tried to convince Wałęsa to cancel a scheduled general strike.

When Wałęsa and other Solidarity leaders refused, the cardinal, who was dying of cancer, fell to his knees in front of Wałęsa, grabbed the coat of the Solidarity leader, and threatened to remain kneeling in prayer until death. The gesture—"this emotional blackmail," Wałęsa supposedly called it—succeeded and Wałęsa agreed to call off the general strike. This, in turn, had enabled Kania and Jaruzelski to tell the Soviets that they had the situation under control and that the Soviet intervention they believed to be forthcoming was unnecessary.

Now the pope told Casey that he was certain Moscow could not tolerate much more pressure from Solidarity. Thus, in early April, the Church had urged the union to "fall back"—to begin a "tactical withdrawal" that would preserve the union's achievements and perhaps keep the Soviets at bay.

Their discussion turned to the Soviet Union and the decline of communism. The conversation was part spiritual and part secular. In talking with the Holy Father, Casey reported to the president, it was sometimes difficult to tell where one began and the other ended, because the pope focused on the absence of *truth* in Communist society, not just the truth of God, but the truth of human nature. That was why Solidarity had taken such a firm hold in Poland: It was a way for the workers to express the truth of their lives and beliefs. Jews, atheists, and many Communists belonged to Solidarity too; not all its members were Catholics.

The Communist authorities in Poland, the pope told Casey, were under unrelenting pressure from Moscow. John Paul II thought that some kind of repressive response by the authorities was probably likely. What mattered was how repression would be imposed, if it came—by whom, on what terms, and how prepared the Church and Solidarity would be.

The pope's caution was born out of fear that everything gained thus far could be lost if the Soviets and their allies invaded. Food was becoming scarce, and that would probably spark further strikes.

The CIA had interpreted the appointment of Jaruzelski as prime minister in February as an acknowledgment of the bankruptcy of the Polish Communist Party. After all the Communist rhetoric about the dangers of "Bonapartism" and such, the Soviets had been forced to turn to a military man to subdue Poland: a leader whom the Soviets hoped they could trust to keep the situation under control because the people still respected the army.

Casey believed that unless the Soviets were prepared to use troops in Eastern Europe, they couldn't hold on to the region indefinitely. Still, only sixteen months earlier the Soviets had made the decision to invade Afghanistan. The Soviet leadership, he noted, had shown its willingness to use force there. The CIA director was not contemplating the imminent demise of the Soviet empire. Only the president talked in such terms, and Reagan's certainty seemed based less on fact than on hope, conviction, and more than a little faith. But Casey didn't disagree that, perhaps sooner than later, Poland might break out of the Soviet sphere of influence. It was clear to everyone that Poland was the most vulnerable of the Communist states in Europe—and John Paul II was a force that the Communists had no idea how to fight. Casey doubted that Moscow would be quite so intimidated by Solidarity or the situation inside Poland without the protection and encouragement of the pope.

Casey realized that the pope was the only person who had access to all sides of the equation in Poland—what Solidarity was doing, what Jaruzelski and Kania were thinking, and what the intentions of the USSR might be. Casey was mightily impressed. The United States had first-rate information about Soviet and Polish *military* planning from Kukliński, but it understood little about the Polish government's relations with the Soviets and what the men in the Kremlin were apparently saying.

Casey knew something about Poland from his experience as an OSS officer in World War II. He had organized sixteen teams of Polish exiles who made night parachute jumps into Germany and set up sabotage missions behind enemy lines. Then in February 1945, at Yalta, the Allies had in effect ceded Poland to the USSR. Instead of favoring the democratic Polish government in exile in London, the agreement had conferred power on the Lublin provisional government, made up of Stalinist proxies. "The morale drained right out of our Poles," Casey had recalled. "I could see it happening before my eyes. After that they just went through the motions. They weren't worth a damn. I never forgot what caving in to the Russians did to those people."

Three decades after Yalta, in reporting to President Reagan, Casey didn't hide the extremely strong emotions he felt in the presence of the pope. He and the pope shared an intense devotion to the Virgin. As a Fordham University upperclassman in the early 1930s, Casey had been asked to give a talk on one of the titles in the litany of Loreto. He chose "Mary, Mother Most Pure." His wife, Sophia, collected statues of the Virgin, which were prominently placed in niches and on shelves all around Mayknoll, their home on Long Island.

Of the Jesuits who had educated him, Casey had written as a young man, "They are brilliant; I'm absolutely convinced that they have the right dope on this world." In the Spanish Civil War he supported Generalissimo Francisco Franco and his Phalangists. Though the Phalangists were fascists, they were Catholic and anti-Communist. The same logic, along with his experience working in the OSS during the war and on the Marshall Plan in postwar Europe, informed his enthusiasm for the Catholic Senator Joseph McCarthy in the immediate postwar years. "This isn't patty cake we're playing with the Russians," he'd said. "You need a McCarthy to flush out the enemy." Some of this experience found its way into the CIA director's discussions with John Paul II.

Casey also had some specific messages that he and the president wanted to convey to the pope. The most obvious one was an absolute American commitment to Solidarity. But he and the president also hoped the pope would become more sympathetic to U.S. positions on the threat posed by Soviet activities around the globe. In particular, the CIA director discussed Central America, where Casey said five hundred Cubans were helping to train the Nicaraguan military and assisting the Sandinistas with their intelligence service and communications systems. Nicaragua was an asylum for the rebels in neighboring El Salvador. The Soviets, the East Germans, the Bulgarians, and the North Koreans were all involved there. In both El Salvador and Nicaragua the Church was under attack from the left, including criticism from priests who advocated liberation theology. The United States hoped that the Vatican would publicly disavow their aims, especially in Nicaragua, where the Church's hierarchy at times had seemed on the verge of embracing the Sandinista movement. Surely the pope didn't wish his pontificate to support the Marxist regime, or permit his priests to imply Rome's approval of it.

Before arriving at the Vatican by car from the U.S. embassy, Casey had received a briefing on terrorism from the CIA station in Rome and a curious—and perhaps important—piece of information that he passed on to the Holy See: When Lech Wałęsa had visited the pope in January, his host had been Luigi Scricciolo of the Italian Labor Confederation. Scricciolo had traveled to Poland in 1980 in the early days of Solidarity to advise Wałęsa and others on organizational matters. He had also helped provide equipment—printers, copying machines, typewriters—for Solidarity. But the CIA had been told by Italian counterintelligence officials that Scricciolo was, in fact, working for Bulgaria. This could mean that Solidarity's plans were compromised, or that Wałęsa was in physical danger.

The pope invited Casey to return—anytime he wanted. And he blessed the CIA director.

THE SECOND HAND

To Italians in the Curia, the most vexing figure in the entourage of the new Polish pope was his chamberlain and private secretary, Monsignor Stanisław Dziwisz.

Curial cardinals and monsignors wondered just how far his power went and whether this slight, boyish figure—known to intimates in the papal household as "Staś"—was the pope's Svengali (he wasn't), his messenger (he was), his confidant (he was), his intellectual sounding board (he wasn't), or simply a young man who was like a son to the Holy Father (he was).

From the first days of his pontificate, Wojtyła was uncomfortable with the personal secretaries that he inherited from his predecessors. Thus Don Stanisław, as he came to be known in the Vatican, rapidly took over many of their most important functions.

"In the *appartamento* there's the pope and Don Stanisław—and then there's everybody else," explains a curial monsignor accustomed to dealing with both. "Only Cardinal Deskur knows him as well and enjoys an equal measure of trust."

But whereas Deskur would become the one person who might be called a true counselor to the pope, Dziwisz's influence was of a different order. He was everywhere.

The monsignor from the Polish hill town of Rabka, just south of Kraków, had been at Wojtyła's side since 1966, three years after his ordination, when the archbishop spotted him working at the seminary library. He became the bishop's chamberlain. Simple, modest, taciturn, he won Wojtyła's affection and trust for exactly those qualities and for his ability to control Wojtyła's habitual tardiness and his overloaded schedule. More than anyone else, he came to know the mind and habits of Karol Wojtyła and could almost unerringly anticipate them. Except for one-on-one meetings with important visitors, Dziwisz was with the pope all day. It was always Dziwisz who knocked on the door to remind the pope of his next appointment, no matter how exalted the visitor.

His role, far more important than that of any curial counselor or aide, even the secretary of state (whose traditional decision-making duties were largely appropriated by Wojtyła himself), included gatekeeper (all appointments with the pope were made through him), conveyor of the pope's orders ("The pope wishes . . ." Don Stanisław would intone whenever he called the heads of curial congregations), and judge of character, ability, and loyalty to the pope.

"I have seen cases where after discussions with Dziwisz the pope has reversed decisions made by the secretary of state," says a senior papal aide. "And Monsignor Stanisław is the one who announces the decisions. He's very much aware of the fact that he is a power."

Dziwisz also has a keen sense of humor, which the pope appreciates, and a tenacious memory. Along with the Polish nuns who attend to the pope's cooking and housekeeping, Dziwisz is family to Wojtyła. In addition to scheduling the comings and goings of cardinals, ambassadors, and presidents, he arranges frequent visits from Wojtyła's old Polish friends, who enter by way of the papal apartments' back stairs.

He is so faithful and attentive that the pope's friend Mieczysław Maliński describes him as "loyal as a watch dog." The pope's love and fatherly regard for Staszek, as he calls him, is one of the basic facts of Vatican life in the Wojtyła pontificate.

• • •

"On May 13 [1981] the Holy Father had lunch with Professor Lejeune, his wife, and another guest," Monsignor Dziwisz recalls. Dr. Jérôme Lejeune, a French physician, was working closely with the pope to promote the rhythm method of "natural" family planning—the only kind of birth control approved by the Church.

At five P.M., the pope emerged from the Apostolic Palace for his Wednesday general audience in St. Peter's Square, which was to include a ride around the square to wave to the crowds, followed by an address from his throne. The audience, Dziwisz remembers, "began punctually at five o'clock, in a perfectly orderly fashion. Nothing foreshadowed what was going to happen" as Wojtyła entered his open popemobile.

As he rode around the colonnade, the pope appeared at ease, "his face pink and smiling," Dziwisz recalls. "How young he looks," thought a Polish nun as he passed in front of her. He went around the Egyptian obelisk once, then a second time. As always, Don Stanisław was just behind the pope, who was standing.

Suddenly Dziwisz heard a deafening noise and recoiled as the pigeons all over the square took flight. "I didn't understand immediately what had happened, for until then no one thought that such a thing was possible"— that someone would try to kill the pope.

But the pope himself and his security team must have known he was courting danger. In Karachi, on February 16 of that same year, an hour before the pope was to visit the municipal stadium, a bomb exploded, killing the man who was carrying it. On November 26, 1979, Mehmet Ali Agca, a Turkish terrorist, had publicly vowed to kill the pope during his visit to

Turkey. In January 1980, Alexandre De Marenches, head of the French secret service, had sent an emissary to warn the pope of a Communist plot on his life. "I had been warned," De Marenches disclosed. "The information was important because [in the context of Eastern Europe] it was credible."

"The Holy Father replied that his destiny was in the hands of God," the intelligence chief wrote in his memoirs. "We never spoke about that again. One would think that, given the close relations between Italy and the Vatican, the Vatican Secret Service would inform Rome about the situation." But apparently that never happened.

And indeed the gunman who fired several shots—two of which struck the pope—was the same Mehmet Ali Agca, whose Browning 9mm automatic pistol was less than twenty feet from the pope when the trigger was pulled.

The report, said Dziwisz, was deafening. The nun who is the pope's housekeeper was looking down at the square from high up in the Apostolic Palace, and she heard it too. The pope, dressed in his white cassock, slumped against his chamberlain.

"I saw that the Holy Father was hit. He was tottering, but there was no sign of blood or a wound on him. Then I asked him, 'Where?' He replied, 'In the stomach.' I asked him again, 'Does it hurt?' He answered, 'Yes.' Standing behind the Holy Father, I supported him so that he wouldn't fall. He was half-sitting, half-leaning on me in the car."

The pope had been wounded in the stomach, the right elbow, and the index finger of his left hand.

As soon as the driver of the popemobile realized what had happened, he sped toward the nearest ambulance stationed by the Bronze Door to the Vatican. But it had no oxygen equipment, so the pope was transferred to a second ambulance, which did.

"The Holy Father wasn't looking at us," remembers Dziwisz. " 'Mary, my mother! Mary, my mother!' he kept repeating. His eyes were closed, he was in great pain."

The trip to the Gemelli Clinic took eight minutes. Dziwisz couldn't tell if Wojtyła was still fully conscious. "He uttered no word of despair or resentment; simply words of profound prayer springing from great suffering," his aide recalls. "Later, the Holy Father told me that he had remained conscious until we reached the hospital, that only there had he lost consciousness and that the whole time he had been convinced that his wounds were not fatal."

"At the very moment I fell in St. Peter's Square," the pope confided to journalist André Frossard, "I had this vivid presentiment that I should be saved, and this certainty never left me, even at the worst moments."

With his blood pressure falling and his pulse almost imperceptible, the pope was taken first to an eleventh-floor room reserved for a papal emergency and then to the hospital's operating room. Don Stanisław went in with him and administered the last rites: "Extreme unction had to be given . . . just before the operation. But the Holy Father was no longer conscious."

The operation lasted five hours and twenty minutes. Wojtyła had lost sixty percent of his blood to internal hemorrhaging.

"Hope gradually returned during the operation," said Dziwisz. "At first it was agonizing. Then it gradually became clear that no vital organ had been hit and that he just might survive."

A 9mm bullet is an extremely destructive projectile, but this one had followed an exceptional trajectory in that it caused no irreparable damage to the pope's body. Like the bullet that almost killed Ronald Reagan, it had passed a few millimeters from the central aorta.

"If it had hit it, death would have been instantaneous," Dziwisz observed. "It did not touch the spine or any vital point. . . . It was really miraculous." The pope and his doctors agreed.

In fact, the pope came to believe that his life had been saved through a miracle performed by the Virgin of Fátima, whose first apparition and feast day, May 13, was the date of the attempt on his life. The shrine of the Virgin of Fátima—Our Lady of the Rosary is her formal name—in Portugal, north of Lisbon, is one of the most revered in the Catholic world. There, in 1917, the Virgin is said to have appeared for the first time to three shepherd children—one of six such sightings by the children. In the apparitions Mary issued three prophecies: that Russia would be "reconverted" after sowing "errors" throughout the world; and, as happened, that two of the three shepherd children would die young. Her final prophecy was described as a terrible secret, kept subsequently in a sealed envelope in the Vatican and known only to the Roman pontiffs.

"One hand fired," the pope said later, "and another hand guided the bullet."

The medical personnel present for the operation, in which twenty-two inches of the pope's intestine were removed, included three surgeons, an anesthetist (who broke one of the pope's teeth while inserting a breathing tube), a cardiologist, and the Vatican physician. It was necessary to cleanse the abdomen, staunch the hemorrhage, sew up the colon in several places, and insert a temporary drainage system—a colostomy.

Then the pope was taken to intensive care, and the wait began.

•   •   •

The attempt to murder the pope remains one of this century's great mysteries. The pope's response to the shooting and its aftermath has only deepened the mystery.

"It is the last great secret of our time," says former CIA director Robert Gates. William Casey, Gates's boss at the time of the shooting, was convinced (and tried to prove) that the Soviets were behind the attempt on Wojtyła's life.

In support of his view, Casey (like the Italian prosecutors of the pope's alleged would-be assassins and like many in the Vatican) cited the so-called Bulgarian connection, a body of tantalizing but controverted evidence that Agca was hired and protected by the Bulgarian secret service, an organization notoriously subservient to the Soviet KGB.

Yet for reasons that are unclear, the pope has said to Deskur, his closest friend in the Vatican, "I was always convinced from the beginning that the Bulgarians were completely innocent, they had nothing to do with it." He has never explained the basis for this statement or mentioned any independent sources of information he may have had.

Whoever was responsible was literally doing the work of the devil, Wojtyła declared to Deskur.

"I asked him," Deskur recalls, " 'Why aren't you following the trials [of

Agca and his alleged coconspirators]?' And the pope said, 'It doesn't interest me; because it was the devil who did this thing. And the devil can conspire in a thousand ways, none of which interest me.' "

One papal source of information might have been Giulio Andreotti, the powerful leader of the Italian Christian Democratic Party, a man with excellent connections in the Italian secret services. (Andreotti had previously served as minister of the interior, of defense, and of foreign affairs as well as premier of Italy.)

Following public reports of the Bulgarian connection, Andreotti met with the pope and expressed "reservations" about the idea that the Bulgarians—either expressly on behalf of the Soviets or not—were involved. "I told him the evidence I had was such to exclude a Bulgarian connection and therefore we had to search for the truth somewhere else," says Andreotti. However, he refuses to say what that evidence might be. The pope responded that "we must be very cautious and wait for some evidence," Andreotti says.

In any event, a few days before the trial of Agca's alleged Bulgarian and Turkish coconspirators began, the pope met with the vice president of Bulgaria to mark the feast of St. Cyril, Bulgaria's patron saint. In that audience, the pope said he hoped the trial's outcome would be one that would not "weigh on a Slavic country or people."

Nonetheless, many of the pope's closest aides and acquaintances (including Deskur) became convinced that the Soviets or their allies were behind the attempt. An informal group meeting in the Vatican, which included Secretary of State Casaroli, argued secretly that the Soviets wanted the pope killed because his death seemed to be the only way to decapitate Solidarity. With the pope dead, this reasoning went, Solidarity could have been smothered by the Polish authorities without the Soviets incurring the lasting international opprobrium that military intervention by the Warsaw Pact would have brought.

"Surely the assassination was not an isolated attack," Casaroli stated publicly in January 1995.

Cardinal Achille Silvestrini, who was Casaroli's deputy at the time, says, "It was clear to us that it was not a random accident . . . not simply the act of a madman. It was something aimed at a goal, there was something behind the killer. . . . We have to keep in mind the situation in Poland and Eastern Europe at that time. If the assassination attempt had succeeded, it would have been the gravestone for Poland and for those who were challenging the control of the [Soviet] system." But Silvestrini is skeptical about the Bulgarian scenario and believes the trail heads somewhere else in the former communist East.

The minutes of the Politburo of the USSR, obtained by the authors of this book, demonstrate the increasing Soviet preoccupation with the pope and the Church—and the Soviet leaders' frustration with Polish authorities for not cracking down on the Church—in the weeks and months preceding the assassination attempt. The head of the KGB at the time of the shooting was Yuri Andropov, who was the Soviet official most familiar with the situation inside Poland and with the dire threat that Solidarity posed to communism.

But such suggestion of motive hardly proves that the Soviets—either through the Bulgarians or in some other way—were behind the assassination attempt. The most potent argument against Soviet involvement is the risk: Had a Soviet hand been found in the assassination attempt, the diplomatic isolation and moral condemnation of the USSR would have been overwhelming. And at the time of the attempt on the pope's life, the Soviets were engaged in a dialogue with the pope to restrain Solidarity. No illuminating documents relating to the assassination attempt have been found in either Bulgaria or Moscow since the fall of communism—though Western intelligence professionals ridicule the notion that a paper trail to the Kremlin might exist.

Deskur and others suggest that by choosing to visit his would-be assassin in prison on December 23, 1983, the pope was sending the Soviets a signal of "forgiveness" and indicating that he didn't wish to see the matter pursued further. Some in the papal entourage maintain that if John Paul II had expressed a belief that the Soviets were behind the attempt, it would have seriously set back efforts toward world peace and put the USSR in a dangerously isolated international position.

Though Casaroli and others met informally in the Vatican to discuss the evidence, Deskur says that the pope would not tolerate a formal internal investigation or analysis. Deskur's own belief is that the Soviets somehow infiltrated the Italian secret services, which (at a time when they were obsessed with terrorist activity in Italy) failed spectacularly to note the presence of Agca—a known terrorist who had already threatened to kill the pope—in their country.

.   .   .

During his visit to his would-be assassin's cell in a Roman prison, the pope conversed with Agca in Italian for twenty minutes. As the audience ended, Agca knelt down and kissed the hand of John Paul II. Afterward, Agca said in interviews that "the pope knows everything." Few intelligence professionals believe that at the time of the assassination attempt Agca would have known the full extent of any conspiracy he was involved in—including the real identities of some of his alleged coconspirators, who worked at the Bulgarian embassy in Rome.

"Ali Agca," says the pope's spokesman, Dr. Joaquín Navarro-Valls, "knows only up to a certain level. On a higher level he doesn't know anything. If there was a conspiracy, it was done by professionals and professionals don't leave traces. One will never find anything."

Though papal aides are loath to discuss this, John Paul II may harbor the deep suspicion that Muslim radicals were responsible for his shooting, or at least that Agca was acting on behalf of an Islamic cause. In private, Wojtyła is hostile to certain aspects of Islam, particularly as interpreted by those he considers radical Muslims. Part of his hostility stems from his belief that the Qur'an condones violence. The shooting of the pope, say some close associates, left its mark on him. Apart from a legacy of sheer physical and mental pain, he continued for many months to ponder the mystery of the act that was meant to kill him, knowing he could be a target again.

Agca's own contradictory confessions and rantings have at various times laid the blame at the door of both the Bulgarian government and an Islamic conspiracy. (He has also claimed to be Jesus Christ.) But Italian investigators insist his actions have been lucid and rational throughout and that his various statements and attitudes, however bizarre they may seem, have often had ulterior motives. Among other things, they may be attempts to send different signals to his possible coconspirators.

One intriguing theory of the assassination that many intelligence professionals in the West take seriously is the so-called Becket scenario: The leaders of the Soviet Union and the Eastern bloc kept uttering the equivalent of King Henry II's "Will no one rid me of this meddlesome priest?" until finally "someone"—the Bulgarian or another Eastern European secret service—acted, but without specific orders from anyone.

One of the reasons for the continuing uncertainty about the assassination attempt was the initial reluctance of Western intelligence agencies—particularly the CIA—to commit their resources to a thorough investigation of the shooting. This may or may not have something to do with (1) the CIA's prior knowledge about an agent for Bulgaria—the same Italian labor official whose name Casey passed on to the Vatican when he visited the pope in 1981—used by Italian unions as a contact with Solidarity, and the agency's fear of embarrassment by disclosure of its knowledge; (2) the desire to downplay the failure of the CIA and other agencies to pick up on the activities of Agca and his accomplices and so prevent the assassination attempt; or (3) the fear of some Western leaders that the Soviets were indeed responsible but that confronting them (and the world) with evidence of their complicity would isolate the USSR and throw international relations into a hopeless crisis. Despite Casey's belief that the Soviets were, and should be held, responsible, many experts in the State Department and the National Security Council were terrified by the possibility of Soviet involvement.

Meanwhile, when the Western press and then Italian prosecutors suggested publicly that the Bulgarians and/or the Soviets had ordered the assassination of the pope, the Soviets responded with a massive disinformation campaign. They alleged, among other things, that the United States had been behind the plot to kill Wojtyła (in order to demonize the USSR and halt the Vatican's campaign for peaceful coexistence with the Kremlin). The Soviets also claimed that the CIA and other Western intelligence services had actually encouraged the Red Brigades to terrorize Italy as a means of marginalizing the Italian Communist Party—a preposterous supposition in the view of non-Italian leaders and governments in the West.

. . .

On May 6, a week before he was shot, the pope addressed a new corps of Swiss Guards, the brightly attired Swiss soldiers who have guarded the popes since 1471: "We pray to the Lord that violence and fanaticism may be kept far from the walls of the Vatican."

His words had a logic rooted in recent events. Political terrorism was sweeping Western Europe, and nowhere was it more threatening than Italy, where the Red Brigades in 1978 had accomplished their most spectacular coup: the kidnapping and murder in Rome of Aldo Moro, the chairman of the Christian Democratic Party.

Upon the arrest of Ali Agca in St. Peter's Square, a picture soon emerged of a fascist thug acting either alone or on behalf of Turkey's neo-Nazi Gray Wolves (a terrorist band associated with the far-right National Action Party) or perhaps of a lone Islamic fundamentalist, though there was little in his background to suggest any intense faith. Born in a village in eastern Turkey torn by rival Muslim groups, Agca had a long record of association with the "Turkish mafia." He had been paid large amounts of money to bring contraband guns, cigarettes, and narcotics across the border from Bulgaria into Turkey.

Described in police reports as bright and articulate, he also displayed a ready self-confidence bordering on arrogance. Though he initially told Italian investigators that it was his own idea to kill the pope, he also bragged of getting help from various terrorists abroad—"Bulgarians, English, and Iranians."

"I make no distinctions between fascist and Communist terrorists," he told his interrogators. "My terrorism is not red or black." Instead he described himself as an "international terrorist," dedicated to an anarchic ideal in a decade of worldwide terrorist violence. To Italian investigators, this description seemed plausible. In Turkey, the easternmost outpost of NATO and one of the few Islamic democracies, this "nonaligned terrorism" took the form of attempts to dismember the state through urban violence, kidnapping, and assassination.

On February 1, 1979, Agca was one of a band of terrorists who took part in the murder of Abdi Ipekci, a liberal and Turkey's most influential commentator, the editor of Istanbul's leading newspaper, *Milliyet*. Arrested five months later, Agca quickly confessed, then escaped that November 25, 1979, by simply walking out of a military prison wearing an army uniform and passing through a series of eight heavily guarded doors. This would seem to have been impossible without high-level help.

The day following his escape, he sent a letter to *Milliyet* about the pope's planned visit to Turkey, scheduled to begin that November 28:

> Western imperialists, fearful that Turkey and her sister Islamic nations may become a political, military, and economic power in the Middle East, are sending to Turkey at this delicate moment the Commander of the Crusades, John Paul, disguised as a religious leader. If this visit is not called off, I will definitely kill the Commander-pope.

On the face of it, this announcement would seem to confound conspiratorial explanations of Agca's subsequent attempt to kill the pope as a means of undermining Solidarity. In November 1979, Solidarity didn't even exist. The Soviets and Polish Communists were believed still to be debating among themselves what kind of pope Karol Wojtyła would be, though his trip to Poland in June of that year portended ill for them. Agca's explanation to the Italian authorities was that the letter was intended to throw the Turkish police off his trail in the days after his escape and force them to concentrate on protecting the pope. Meanwhile, the pope's visit to Turkey came and went without incident.

But Agca's letter has only led certain proponents of the Bulgarian connection to feel even more convinced of Soviet complicity: They contend that Agca was recruited by the Communists because of his proven skills as an assassin, his right-wing connections, and the fact that his threat to kill the pope, for reasons unrelated to Poland, was already on the record.

•　　•　　•

Agca had confessed to the crime upon his arrest, saying he had acted alone, and was sentenced on July 22, 1981, to life imprisonment. In May 1982, when (he claims) he realized that he was not going to be ransomed from jail as his "handlers" had supposedly promised, Agca identified three members of the Bulgarian embassy staff in Rome and four Turks as his coconspirators. (Their lawyers claimed Agca was fed the information in jail by the Italian secret services.) Agca also told Italian authorities that there had been a plot to murder Lech Wałęsa when he came to Rome to visit the pope in January of 1981, although the plan—to detonate a car bomb near his hotel—had to be abandoned because security was too tight.

Luigi Scricciolo, the Italian labor official arrested for his alleged espionage activities on behalf of the Bulgarians, apparently confirmed the existence of such a plot. His lawyer is on the record as saying, "I can tell you for sure that there was [also] a Bulgarian connection in the murder plot against the pope, although my client was not involved." Scricciolo and Agca each identified the same three Bulgarians—indicted for the attempt on the pope's life—as participants in the plot to kill Wałęsa.

Around the same time that Agca began making allegations of a Bulgarian connection, the Italian defense minister disclosed that coded radio traffic between Bulgaria and Italy had risen sharply within weeks of the attempt on the pope's life. The National Security Agency (NSA) of the United States—the most technically advanced intelligence agency in the world, which monitors coded and noncoded radio, telephone, telex, and microwave signals around the globe—ran a "sweep" of all communications between the embassies of Communist countries and their home countries in the months surrounding the assassination attempt. In March and April 1981, the NSA determined, coded cable messages between the Bulgarian embassy in Rome and the headquarters of the Bulgarian secret service—the Durzhavna Sigurnost—in Sofia conspicuously increased. Then, in the two weeks preceding the assassination attempt, exchanges between the embassy in Rome and the Bulgarian headquarters suddenly dropped off.

Agca told Italian investigators that plans called for him to be driven away from St. Peter's Square immediately after shooting the pope and then smuggled from Italy to Yugoslavia in a truck cleared for diplomatic passage at European frontiers. Such a truck, filled with furniture and believed to be carrying Agca's closest Turkish accomplice, evidently did leave the Bulgarian embassy that night, according to the Italian prosecutors. Agca also claimed that he had traveled to Sofia in July 1980, where a Turkish underworld leader/businessman and an accomplice hired him to assassinate the pope for a fee of $400,000. This too would have been before the Gdańsk strikes and the formation of Solidarity in mid-August, but during the period of widespread strikes that began on July 1 over rising food prices in Poland. Agca said he learned later that the two men were acting on behalf of Bulgarian intelligence.

Hotel records confirm that Agca—and the men he described—stayed at expensive hotels in Sofia that July. Over the next nine months Agca traveled in relative luxury through Western Europe, spending at least $50,000, with stops in Vienna, Zurich, and Palma de Mallorca. Much of his time was spent in Rome and then, just before the assassination, in Milan, where he says the Browning 9mm pistol was delivered to him by a member of the Gray Wolves.

On the afternoon of May 13, Agca claims, two Bulgarians and a Turkish partner went with him to St. Peter's to check out how the crowds in the square would be massed and policed; one man was to stay behind and create a diversion to facilitate his escape. With the man alleged to be his principal accomplice, Oral Celik, a Turk, he remained in wait for the pope. Agca fired his pistol at 5:17 P.M. and was then grabbed by a nun and wrestled to the ground by the crowd.

With his immediate capture, the chances of his being spirited away by accomplices—and perhaps killed to keep him silent—sank to nil.

. . .

Many facts about the attempt on the pope's life are contradictory or open to interpretation, and the failure of intelligence agencies around the world to tackle the case immediately and pool their knowledge has helped make it impossible to piece together a definitive record.

"We were very constrained in the first few years of investigation because of concerns from Casey on down not to get in and mess up the Italian case," says Robert Gates. The Italian secret services are famously resentful of interference in their work. "I worried we'd do something clumsy that would absolutely torch the relationship with the Italians. There was concern from Casey on down that we ought to be pretty damn careful about this thing; our gumshoeing around could make a mess of things in the criminal investigation of theirs."

Some of the most important parts of the record suggesting a Soviet-inspired conspiracy through the Bulgarians were publicized first in a *Reader's Digest* article in September 1982 by the late Claire Sterling, a journalist who had the cooperation of Italian prosecutors and already had written a controversial book about terrorism in Europe and the Middle East, including Bulgaria.* Three months before Sterling's article appeared in *Reader's Digest*, Agca picked out photos of three Bulgarian embassy officials from an album of pictures of fifty-six Bulgarian nationals working in Rome and said they helped him carry out the crime.

Several books and long articles were subsequently written challenging the theory of the Bulgarian connection, some by independent journalists, others commissioned or encouraged by the Bulgarian and Soviet governments.

The CIA station chief in Rome concluded that there was no evidence to contradict Agca's statement upon arrest that he was a lone gunman. After a cursory examination of the evidence, most CIA professionals in Washington believed that Agca was a "nutcase" acting on his own, even after he began alleging a conspiracy. The shooting, in their view, did not have the look of a classic KGB "wet"—that is, assassination—operation.

"After the assassination attempt," an internal CIA report later noted, "[CIA] analysts tended to conclude that John Paul II's role as an aggravating force in the Polish crisis was outweighed by his moderating role and that Moscow had little to gain from removing him, particularly given the risk of detection. Killing the pope would not have solved Moscow's Polish problem but could instead have exacerbated it by causing further unrest." Politburo documents from the same period, which nowhere mention the dialogue at the time of the assassination attempt between the Soviets and the pope, might seem to contradict this view.

Contrary to professionals on his staff, CIA director Casey was impressed with Sterling's account. In 1984 he met with her in New York, where

---

* Some of the book's assertions, apparently unknown to Sterling, were based on CIA disinformation.

he complained about the CIA's reluctance to embrace her conclusions and the information from Italian prosecutors.

Others who believed that the Soviets were probably behind the assassination attempt included Zbigniew Brzeziński and Henry Kissinger, then a member of the president's Foreign Intelligence Advisory Board. The FIAB had also done its own limited examination of the case and concluded that a preponderance of circumstantial evidence suggested that the Soviets—through the Bulgarians—were probably responsible.

All this led Casey to belittle his own analysts. "So we put a dragnet out across all of Europe, unparalleled in my experience, and came up with nothing definitive," Gates says, "but it was suggestive."

"The more they looked, the more the stuff checked out," says Herb Meyer, a Casey confidant and deputy. "The professionals at Langley [CIA headquarters] were now in high dudgeon, because they were being bypassed by a special group Casey appointed, headed by two woman analysts. And at this point events began to get ahead of the whole thing; the Italians were moving real fast and going public."

Then, in the winter of 1984–85, the agency began receiving information from a clandestine source in Eastern Europe alleging a definite Bulgarian role. Even the so-called agnostics at the CIA came to suspect that if there really was a Bulgarian role, then the Soviets must have been behind the attempt. That was because the Bulgarian secret service was regularly used by the KGB for dirty tricks the Russians didn't want to be associated with. But the CIA's new source, though judged reliable, was not someone with firsthand knowledge of the alleged plot.

At this point, Gates suggested that a paper be written "assessing the possible Soviet role in the attempted assassination in light of the latest agent reporting from Eastern Europe."

The draft paper, entitled "Agca's Attempt to Kill the Pope: The Case for Soviet Involvement," Gates later maintained, "was a compelling study, though clearly identifying the tenuous nature of our sources, gaps in information, and the circumstantial nature of much of the information." It argued that, from the time of the pope's trip to Poland, the Soviets recognized that he would fan the flames of Polish nationalism and that—even before the rise of Solidarity—they feared this would provoke popular reactions elsewhere in Eastern Europe and even in the USSR. The contrary view, based largely on the CIA's knowledge of the pope's secret dialogue with the Soviets, was that he was a stabilizing influence on the situation in Poland. Only seven people outside the CIA received the paper: the president, the vice president, the secretaries of state and defense, the chairman of the Joint Chiefs of Staff, the national security adviser to the president, and the chairman of the president's Foreign Intelligence Advisory Board.

· · ·

In July 1981, the deputy commercial attaché at the Bulgarian embassy in Paris defected and told French intelligence agents that the plot to kill the pope had been undertaken by the Bulgarian secret service at the behest of the KGB. The defector, Iordan Mantarov, told the French he had learned of the plot from a close friend, Dimiter Savov, a high-ranking official in the counterintelligence division of the Durzhavna Sigurnost, the Bulgarian intelligence service.

What gives particular resonance to the details concerning a motive for the crime supplied by Mantarov in 1981 is their consistency with documents that came to light in the West only after the fall of communism in the USSR and Eastern Europe.

In 1979 Savov supposedly told Mantarov that the KGB thought Wojtyła's selection as pope had been engineered by Zbigniew Brzeziński: The Soviets believed the election of a Polish pope was meant to exploit the growing unrest in Poland over corruption and mismanagement and to strike at the Communist system as a whole. "Eastern European intelligence agencies" became concerned that the KGB's initial fears might be justified. So the KGB—or one of the Eastern European services—began discussions with the Bulgarian intelligence service about a way to eliminate John Paul II.

Mantarov quoted Savov as saying that Agca was selected as the assassin because he was known as a rightist for his role in killing the liberal Turkish newspaper editor and had no links to any Communist country.

Though this account came from a secondhand source, French intelligence agents believed it because other information Mantarov had gotten from

Savov checked out. At the time, neither the Italians nor the French (nor the pope, for that matter) were aware of just how much hostility and fear Wojtyła's ascension to the papal throne had inspired in the Kremlin even in his first year in the Vatican.

The earliest evidence of this is contained in a top-secret document dated November 13, 1979, when the full secretariat of the Central Committee of the Soviet Communist Party approved a multifaceted "Decision to Work against the Policies of the Vatican in Relation with Socialist States." The "Decision" consisted of six points drafted on November 5 by a subcommittee of the secretariat that included Andropov and Viktor Chebrikov, then the deputy chairman of the KGB. The document instructed all Soviet departments and political organizations, from the KGB to the state organs of propaganda, to undertake specific assignments in an anti-Wojtyła campaign, mostly in the area of propaganda.

Summaries of the "Decision" memorandum were sent to the Communist Party leadership and security services throughout the Eastern bloc.

A related document from the same period defined "the problem": The Vatican "now use[s] religion in the ideological struggle against Socialist lands" and seeks "to increase religious fanaticism against the political and ideological principles of the socialist societies. The Vatican, above all, disseminates this new propaganda, which constitutes a change in policy."

With the election of Pope Wojtyła, the document continues, "the characteristics of Vatican and Catholic Church policies in different regions of the Soviet Union have become more aggressive—above all in Lithuania, Latvia, western Ukraine, and Byelorussia."

All this was before the explosion in Poland.

·   ·   ·

Four days after the shooting of Wojtyła, on May 17, President Reagan, who had only partially regained his strength but seemed in the midst of a vigorous recovery, made his first trip since being shot: to deliver a long-scheduled commencement address at the University of Notre Dame—*Our Lady*—in South Bend, Indiana.

By now, Reagan's speechwriters knew his priorities: As on the day he was shot, Reagan again turned his thoughts to the pope and the Evil Empire. Wearing a black academic gown and a black mortarboard with a yellow tassel, the president looked out over a vast audience; he could see that it included a small number of students wearing white armbands and white mortarboards to protest administration policies in El Salvador and budget cuts that hurt the poor. Then the president of the United States made his own prophecy:

> The years ahead will be great ones for our country, for the cause of freedom and for the spread of civilization. The West will not contain communism, it will transcend communism. We will not bother to denounce it, we'll dismiss it as a sad, bizarre chapter in human history whose last pages are even now being written.

He was deadly serious, though the reporters traveling with him mistook his words for mere rhetoric and blind hope. But he had confided to his wife and his closest aides that he was certain this was why he and the pope had been spared.

The previous day, in Kraków, 300,000 people had attended an open-air mass to pray for their former archbishop John Paul II and for the recovery of Cardinal Wyszyński, whose grave illness had been announced by the episcopate the day after the pope was shot. Reagan continued:

> It was Pope John Paul II who warned last year, in his encyclical on mercy and justice, against certain economic theories that use the rhetoric of class struggle to justify injustice: that "in the name of an alleged justice the neighbor is sometimes destroyed, killed, deprived of liberty or stripped of fundamental human rights."
>
> For the West, for America, the time has come to dare to show to the world that our civilized ideas, our traditions, our values are not—like the ideology and war machine of totalitarian societies—a facade of strength. It is time the world knew that our

intellectual and spiritual values are rooted in the source of all real strength—a belief in a supreme being, a law higher than our own.

Not only had he quoted the pope, but in the religious cadences of his rhetoric, Ronald Reagan had begun to *sound* like the pope.

Shortly thereafter, Reagan's national security adviser Richard Allen wrote on White House stationery to William A. Wilson, the president's new envoy to the Vatican, who had recently presented his credentials to the pope.

Dear Bill:

> Your discussions with the Vatican on the situation in Central America are of the highest importance. We need the closest possible cooperation with the Church in securing democracy, stability, and social justice in the region.
>
> You may wish to convey to Secretary of State Casaroli and others that the president places the highest priority on achieving a working relationship with the Church in securing our mutually shared goals for Central America.

WORKERS UNITE

Both Ronald Reagan and the pope subsequently endured major complications from their bullet wounds and spent much of the late spring and summer painfully convalescing—and thinking about Poland.

Both the pope and Reagan were talking to their more skeptical aides as if the Communists had already lost the battle in Poland: a conclusion based less on hard evidence than on their respective notions of history, faith, and spirituality—and, in Reagan's case, congenital optimism. Reagan's remarks at Notre Dame were only the beginning.

On September 6, using highly charged language (though his voice was still weak), John Paul II told a group of Polish pilgrims at Castel Gandolfo that the "right of our nation to independence is a condition for world peace," an assertion certain to inflame sensibilities in the Kremlin. Now the pope was speaking less of universal Christian principles than as the secular leader of a country.

The pope's declaration came as Solidarity was opening its first national congress, at which Lech Wałęsa tactfully urged caution and respect for the state. He warned that Solidarity was "seriously underestimating the government" and that the union had become "far too self-confident." The union called on other Eastern European workers to set up their own independent unions modeled on Solidarity. Strikes in Poland were causing shortages throughout the Eastern bloc. In response, the Soviets began a massive nine-day naval and military exercise in the Baltic and around Poland, with six warships and more than 100,000 troops.

"Yesterday I familiarized myself with the 'Appeal to the People of Eastern Europe' which was issued at the congress of Polish 'Solidarity,'" Brezhnev told the Politburo on September 10. "It is a dangerous and provocative document. There aren't many words in it but they all harp on one point: Its authors would like to cause disturbances in the socialist countries and incite various groups of renegades."

The Solidarity congress had reelected Wałęsa head of the union with only fifty-five percent of the vote; more radical elements of the union were moving in an increasingly brazen direction. They made no bones about their desire to wrest control of the crumbling Polish economy from the Communists and to supplant the party as the leading force in the government.

"Polish citizens profane the memorials to our soldiers, they draw different kinds of caricatures of the leaders of our party and of our government; they offend the Soviet Union. . . . they laugh at us," Tikhonov complained to his fellow Politburo members. "From my point of view, it's inadmissible not to react."

On September 17, the new primate named by the pope, Bishop Józef Glemp, a canon law professor anointed by the dying Wyszyński as his successor, met in secret with Kania and Jaruzelski. "This was an unprecedented meeting," Jaruzelski noted later. "We met in a situation which looked very dangerous at the time because it was soon after the end of the first Solidarity congress. That congress was very belligerent. There was a homily by the pope, read in his name, that fell flat, because many participants in the congress were feeling very aggressive and turned a deaf ear to it."

That some sort of crackdown, perhaps martial law, was likely had become a working hypothesis in Washington and Rome. But people were less sure about it in the factories and streets of Poland, where Solidarity still felt confident enough to flex more political muscle. In early August, through a complicated series of drops and signs, Colonel Ryszard Kukliński had passed on to his American handlers plans for the declaration and implementation of martial law. The cache of documents included leaflets printed in Moscow—in Polish—ordering citizens to remain calm and listing regulations for life under military rule. The pope had been told by Washington of Kukliński's information.

"At the end of our meeting," Jaruzelski recalled, "the primate asked, 'What are we supposed to tell the Holy Father?' Because the next day he was leaving for Rome. So we told him, 'Just share our anxieties and at the same time stress that the authorities are ready for compromise, for understanding, for an agreement—but they won't permit the disintegration of the state.' "

•   •   •

The pope's principled but careful approach found expression on September 14 in his encyclical *Laborem Exercens* (On Human Work), which was devoted to the dignity of the worker and issued in conjunction with the Solidarity congress. The encyclical defended in absolute terms the right of workers to organize into unions, yet it also spoke of their responsibilities in the social and economic life of a nation. Trade unions, the pope wrote, had to put national concerns above those of any individual or group. They had to take into account the problems of their nation's economy—an obvious reference to the situation in Poland.

The Polish-language draft of the encyclical, Wojtyła's fourth, had been ready in the spring, at a time when Solidarity was at its most powerful. But with the assassination attempt, the appearance of the final version had been postponed.

The encyclical was John Paul II's ambitious attempt to forge a worker's manifesto inspired by Christianity rather than by Marxism. This was the first time any pope had dedicated an entire encyclical to work. In it John Paul II called for radical limits on private property in a way none of his predecessors had ever done. "The right to private property," he said, "is subordinate to the right of common use. . . . The only legitimate title to the ownership of the means of production, whether in the form of private property or public, collective property, is that they serve to advance work."

Ever since Leo XIII in the late nineteenth century, popes had criticized capitalist laissez-faire economics as well as Marxism; and even in Poland Primate Wyszyński had used harsh language to condemn materialism, both of the liberal and Marxist variety. But John Paul II went a step further by proclaiming the absolute priority of work over capital—whether in capitalist or socialist systems.

Other passages alluded to the events in Poland, as if the pope wanted to provide a theoretical foundation for the first Catholic-inspired union in history to battle a Communist ruling class. The word *solidarity* was frequently repeated. The role of the unions was extolled as an "indispensable element in social life," although, as the pope made a point of saying, they weren't the same as political parties.

In *Laborem Exercens* John Paul II made his usual effort to put everything within the framework of a Christian anthropology. Work is hard; it is the punishment for original sin, he wrote, but it is above all the capacity to create: "By means of his work man participates in the work of his Creator. . . . Christ belongs to the world of labor."

At the same time, the encyclical contains certain obvious parallels to the thought of Marx, as in the pope's rejection of any doctrine that degrades the dignity and subjectivity of man or in John Paul's conception of the social value of work. "Work brings with it a particular sign of man and of humanity, a sign of a person working in a community of persons," the pope declared. "And this sign determines his internal character: It constitutes, in a sense, his very nature."

Laborem Exercens soon came to be known as the Gospel of Work, and in many Third World countries it strengthened the Church's social commitment. In Poland, Solidarity now had a papal document tailored for its struggle.

By mid-October, the situation there was on the brink of chaos. No one seemed to be in control of the country; uncompromising factions in both the Polish Communist Party and Solidarity were demanding harsh, almost apocalyptic action. Riots and clashes between civilians and security forces were spreading. The Polish economy was in ruins, and the crisis was aggravated by hundreds of strikes, by everyone from coal miners to transport workers. In the stores, even toothpaste and soap had disappeared from the shelves.

On October 13, Jaruzelski hastily dispatched the Polish foreign minister, Józef Czyrek, to meet with the pope at Castel Gandolfo. "The pope was still weak but . . . expressed his desire for a compromise solution, for understanding," Jaruzelski later said. "But it was clear that he hadn't yet recovered, that . . . he didn't have the capability to influence the situation in Poland directly, for example by asking a delegation from Solidarity or Lech Wałęsa to visit him or by writing a letter to them. He just wasn't strong enough."

This seems doubtful, and the pope's aides paint a different picture. Though unquestionably weak, Wojtyła had been able, some weeks before this, to receive two Soviet cosmonauts and engage them in an animated conversation about weightlessness. He hoped that Moscow would see the visit as a gesture of goodwill. Czyrek said later that the pope had questioned him at length about the likelihood of a complete collapse of the Polish economy and the dangers of Soviet intervention.

Before visiting the pope, Czyrek had met with Soviet foreign minister Gromyko at the United Nations, in New York. "You're in Lenin's party, aren't you?" Gromyko roared. "Poland is crawling with counterrevolution. What do you propose to do about it? Don't you know counterrevolution has to be smashed? They'll have you hanging from the lampposts if you don't settle accounts as we did in 1917. And what are you Poles doing? Tell me, what are you doing?"

On October 18, at the behest of Moscow and of all of the "fraternal" Communist Parties, the Polish party finally removed Kania from office for, in Brezhnev's phrase, "inadmissible liberalism" and appointed Jaruzelski the new party secretary—effectively putting the military, the most trusted institution in the country after the Church, in control of both the party and the government, which Jaruzelski also headed.

The following day, Brezhnev telephoned Jaruzelski:

"Hello, Wojciech."

"Hello, Leonid Ilych." There was very little banter.

"It's important not to waste time [by delaying] the firm actions that you've planned against the counterrevolution," Brezhnev counseled. "We wish you good health and success!"

"I'll do everything I can, both as a Communist and as a soldier, to improve things, to turn the country and the party around," Jaruzelski said. "I'm going to outline the appropriate steps. We'll get the army deeply involved in every sphere of the life of the country."

It was exactly what Brezhnev wanted to hear.

Jaruzelski obviously didn't want to discuss the subject of martial law on the telephone. He cryptically informed Brezhnev that he would be meeting later that day with the Soviet ambassador, "to discuss in more detail certain questions; and I will ask your ambassador for advice on questions that he will, of course, convey to you."

. . .

On the evening of November 4, Jaruzelski, Wałęsa, and Primate Glemp gathered at the prime minister's official residence for the first working meeting ever held between the three powers of the Polish nation: Church, state, and union. Jaruzelski proposed the formation of a "Front of National Accord" to end the chaos and serve as a permanent forum for dialogue among political and social forces, in keeping with "Poland's constitutional principles." Though not willing to empower the front with decision-making authority, Jaruzelski said it would have a broad mandate to find a consensus among all parts of Polish society. He proposed that its members represent the Church, the government, Solidarity, the Communist Party, and an assortment of other unions and splinter political parties—all aligned with the Communists.

Jaruzelski had already sounded out Glemp, on October 21; after consulting with the pope, the primate was ready to agree. Wałęsa, however, argued that Solidarity alone should represent Polish workers. Under Jaruzelski's formula, Solidarity would be swamped by the official unions.

According to Jaruzelski, Glemp tried three times, on November 5, 7, and 9, to prevail upon Wałęsa to join the front. The primate, said Jaruzelski, repeatedly "pointed out the necessity for Solidarity to curb its belligerence" and commit to the plan, but to no avail.

With his stamina returning, John Paul II was now becoming directly involved in the Polish crisis almost daily. In the first week of November he met with a group of Polish intellectuals visiting Rome, among them prominent advisers to Solidarity, leading Catholic writers who had opposed the regime, and old friends: Jerzy Turowicz, the pope's editor from *Tygodnik*; Tadeusz Mazowiecki; Jerzy Kłoczowski; and Bronisław Geremek, now one of Wałęsa's principal advisers.

In the course of their discussion, John Paul II astounded his visitors by flatly predicting that the Communists would lose the battle in Poland. Geremek, who later would go to jail twice, said that the pope's words that day inspired him and others with a sense that, despite all the difficulties, their cause would triumph:

Finally [said the pope] something has happened in Poland which is irreversible. People will no longer remain passive. Passivity is one of the tools of authoritarianism. And now this passivity is over; and so their fate is settled now. They will lose.

Wojtyła's visitors were likewise startled by his view of the likelihood of Soviet invasion: He was much less intimidated than the Polish bishops. According to Geremek, "The pope said, 'It should be seen as a possibility and we have to do everything possible to preserve Poland from such an intervention. But we cannot act merely in response to such a feeling.'" The Soviet threat, Wojtyła added, should not lead to the abandonment of Solidarity's basic achievements or principles.

The Polish bishops regularly spoke of limits, of boundaries to demands for dignity and the fundamental rights of workers; Geremek had noted that they were always ready to compromise when they sensed the threat of Soviet repression. "Fear of Russian intervention was always a decisive argument." But the pope was speaking about nonnegotiable principles, about the immutable rights of the Polish people.

.   .   .

Jaruzelski's proposal for the Front of National Accord had caught Brezhnev by surprise and infuriated him. He was so disturbed by the general's meeting with Glemp and Wałęsa that, on November 21, he dispatched a five-page letter to Jaruzelski through the Soviet ambassador to Poland, warning of "the consequent dismantling of socialism" if Solidarity and the Church were accorded meaningful roles in the front:

> Lately in Poland, much has been written about your meeting with Glemp and Wałęsa. Some call it a historical meeting and see in it the beginning of a change of direction from chaos to social or-der. . . . [But] class opponents will surely try to give the "Front of National Accord" the sort of political content that would at the very least strengthen their notion of power-sharing between [the Party], "Solidarity," and the Church with the consequent dismantling of socialism.

The same factors that upset Brezhnev were the reasons the pope had been willing to embrace the Front for National Accord.

"Now," concluded Brezhnev, "it's already absolutely clear that there's no way to save socialism in Poland without a decisive battle against the class enemy. The question in essence is not will there be a confrontation or not, but who will start it, how it will be carried out, and at whose initiative?"

Jaruzelski spent the middle of November trying to suppress wildcat strikes around the country. The strikes had been called to protest the degen-erating conditions of work and life in Poland in general. What little meat there was came mostly from the USSR in filthy wagons that Polish workers often refused to unload. During November, according to one count, there were 105 strikes of indefinite duration, with millions of workers participating; and 115 more were being planned. None was sanctioned by the Solidarity leadership. On October 30 Solidarity's national commission had called for an end to all strikes because they had taken on "an uncontrolled character" that "threatened destruction of the union."

Jaruzelski ordered the army onto the streets in many cities. Armed soldiers could be seen patrolling in groups of three, intervening wherever violence broke out. The government was sending Geremek signals that, if Solidarity could discipline its unruly elements, a larger confrontation could be averted. Wałęsa went so far as to propose that wildcat strikers in the union be disciplined.

Jaruzelski says that around this time he personally warned Solidarity's leaders and the Church that martial law was inevitable if the union didn't agree to three conditions: an effective ban on all strikes through the winter, cancellation of a public commemoration on December 17 of the anniversary of the 1970 Gdańsk uprising, and the resumption of some form of structured dialogue between the government and the opposition.

Jaruzelski said he looked despairingly to the Church to help win Solidarity's support for a law banning strikes for the winter and granting him emergency powers. Instead, Glemp (after consulting with the pope) criticized the bill in a letter to the parliament, warning that it would cause "commotion."

"With this letter," Jaruzelski claimed, not too credibly, "the primate tied our hands, so we couldn't make a move."

Actually, the pope had instructed the Polish bishops not to support any measures repealing the basic stipulations of the 1980 accords between Solidarity and the government. The right to strike, Wojtyła seemed to be saying, was part of the essential liberty and dignity of the workers, though they had a higher responsibility not to invoke it against the national interest.

THE WALTERS MISSION

Before leaving for Rome on November 28, 1981, Vernon Walters drove to CIA headquarters in Langley, Virginia, following the George Washington Parkway alongside the Potomac, to meet with Bill Casey.

"We talked about the fact that the Church was the key to the emergence and survival of Poland as a free country," Walters recollected later. "What we did about it is still classified."

Although events inside Poland were now driving American policy on the Soviet Union and its European empire, Walters's visits to the pope originated elsewhere—in the same set of intertwining policy decisions that came to be known as the Iran-Contra scandal.

When Alexander Haig was designated secretary of state, he felt it would be extremely useful to undertake a limited number of "strategic conversations" with leaders around the world who could lend significant help to American aspirations: in Israel (where the "conversations" led to Iran-Contra), in Morocco, in Central and South America, in France, in Pakistan, in China, in Greece, and in the Vatican.

"It goes back to the beginning of '81 and maintaining a very secret dialogue," explains a Haig deputy who once worked on the concept. The purpose of the dialogue was to convince these selected leaders to move closer to the policy goals of the United States by sharing with them information that would convince them of threats to their own security: whether from Communists, terrorists, neighbors, internal opposition, Islamic fundamentalists, nationalist movements, or liberation theologians.

The Israelis were briefed initially by Michael Ledeen, then an assistant to Haig and four years later an agent in the arms-for-hostages deal. Ledeen, a self-described historian with ties to both Israeli intelligence and European Social Democratic parties, also undertook some early meetings for Haig with officials in the Vatican Secretariat of State, including one of the pope's two secretaries, Archbishop Emery Kabongo. Ledeen describes these discussions as "exploratory," aimed at learning more about the pope's political thinking, especially with regard to the strength of dissent in Poland.

Before Walters went to Rome the first time, Haig had dispatched the retired general to Morocco (King Hassan was indebted to the CIA and well connected in most major Arab capitals); to Argentina, Chile, and Mexico (where the administration was opposing leftist movements); to Greece (whose socialist government might be made to fear Soviet military maneuvers in neighboring Bulgaria); and to France.

Part of the briefing process was often unapologetically designed to promote what Haig's staff called the "gee-whiz factor"—dazzling supposedly less sophisticated foreign leaders with America's intelligence-gathering prowess.

Walters—big, bejowled, loquacious (or bombastic, depending on one's point of view)—could come across to some people as a bumbler, even a self-promoter. "But for certain kinds of audiences," a colleague noted, "for statesmen, for leaders—they loved him. He's got this style about himself, he's good at languages. And seventy-five to eighty percent of the time he was very effective. Especially with the pope. Dick Walters is a very ardent Catholic; he goes to mass every day. And he loved this idea of establishing a strategic dialogue with the pope." Poland was hardly the only reason. Wojtyła, noted the Haig deputy,

> was very important in other regions, like Central America. He was a guy who was deeply popular in Western Europe, in Catholic countries like Italy, Spain. Remember, we wanted to deploy these new [Cruise and Pershing II] missiles in Europe. His American bishops were against it, and against the Reagan military buildup. If he'd gotten up one Sunday and said he'd decided it was a bad idea to put cruise missiles in Italy, that could have blown up the whole INF [Intermediate-range Nuclear Force] deployment issue. If we hadn't deployed INF, we would never have gotten the zero-option INF treaty—arguably that was the major accomplishment of Reagan and Gorbachev. There would have been a major strategic setback. Who knows what would have happened to the end of the cold war? So he was an important asset, a very influential person, and we saw him in those terms.

And what could the United States offer the pope?

"Something he probably wanted more than anything else," says the deputy—a man admittedly more cynical in his views of the relationship than many of his colleagues. "I think he is a very political man—what this gave him . . . was that he felt he had a high-level intimate relationship with the world's most powerful country. He was a player. That's what it gave him."

. . .

On the morning of November 30, 1981, as he did almost every day when he was in the Vatican, the pope rose at five o'clock, shaved, dressed, and walked to his private chapel a few steps from his bedroom. There he prayed for more than an hour. Sometimes the intensity of his praying was such that he would cry out or groan. On other occasions, aides would enter the chapel and find John Paul II lying prone on the cold marble floor, deathly still, his arms extended in the form of a cross. Even the Polish Communists remarked on his mystical nature. Their reports to Moscow noted he often spent six to eight hours a day in prayer and meditation.

The psychological profile of the pope prepared by the CIA also touched on Wojtyła's "mystical essence."

Vernon Walters had read the profile shortly before his arrival at the Vatican that morning, accompanied by the chief of the U.S. mission to the Vatican, William Wilson. In fact, Walters did not much like the profile: He thought it made the Holy Father sound weird—like a cultist or clairvoyant, a fanatic. Walters, born in 1917, was three years older than the pope, a lifelong bachelor who often described himself as "an old-fashioned, orthodox Roman Catholic."

Walters too was fierce in his faith—in God, Church, and country. He had been educated, briefly, by the Jesuits in New York City. He liked to say he was the only U.S. army general without a high school or college diploma. He was certainly the only one who could speak eight languages. He was the unlikeliest of diplomats or warrior-chiefs: a son of the working class who had climbed the military chain of command through his facility in foreign tongues. Walters had served as an interpreter for Presidents Roosevelt, Truman, and Eisenhower and, most famously, Vice President Nixon, whom he had been accompanying in Venezuela in 1958 when an anti-American mob had almost killed Nixon, his wife, and Walters himself. When Nixon was elected president, he named Walters deputy director of the CIA. He didn't trust the agency and wanted a loyal presence near the top.

Ronald Reagan, with whom Walters had met in the Oval Office just before leaving Washington for Rome, had designated Walters his ambassador-at-large, entrusted with the nation's most closely guarded secrets and most sensitive missions. This was certainly one of them.

Walters's visit was especially urgent for the most disturbing of reasons: Washington had recently lost its best source of strategic information about the situation in Poland, Colonel Ryszard Kukliński. On November 2, Kukliński had been called to a meeting in the office of the deputy chief of the Polish army division that had developed plans for martial law. Three other men were in the room. "The Americans know our latest plans," the Polish general said. Indeed, Kukliński had passed on to the United States detailed but undated plans for the imposition of martial law. He kept calm during the meeting in the general's office, but he felt he was under suspicion. Shortly after, taking a circuitous route, he fled to the Canadian embassy in Warsaw, where he stayed in hiding until false credentials could be manufactured and an opportune moment arose to spirit him out of the country in disguise. But his services had been lost at the worst possible moment—just when it was vital to learn definitively if and when martial law was to be imposed.

Upon entering the pope's library with Wilson, Walters had noticed the pope's shoes—tan loafers, not the traditional red slippers—peeking from under his cassock. Except to say he was pleased to see the pope back in good health, Wilson didn't speak.

"Your Holiness, what language should I do this in?" Walters posed his question in English. No interpreters were present.

"I work in Italian every day, I'm more comfortable in Italian," Wojtyła replied—in English.

The pope, like the general, reveled in his capacity for languages. Between them the two men were capable of speaking in a dozen different tongues, sharing a command of English, German, Italian, Latin, Spanish, French, and Russian.

"Holy Father," Walters began, in Italian, "I bring you greetings from the president of the United States."

Walters had also brought an envelope, which he now placed on the table and opened. Inside were satellite photographs.

He passed the first across the polished mahogany surface of the pope's desk, bare except for a few books.

"The president believes you should know what we're doing and why we're doing it." Walters added solemnly, "We have told the Russians to stay out—or else there will be a very grave crisis in Russian-American relations. This has been communicated by our ambassador in Moscow *and* to the Soviet ambassador in Washington. Just in case somebody is afraid to report something."

As he talked, Walters's eyes fixed momentarily on the pope's large gold ring, the Fisherman's ring, in the shape of a cross, placed on the fourth finger of Wojtyła's right hand at his investiture. When he had greeted the pope, Walters had kissed the ring. In his pocket he was carrying several rosaries to be blessed by the Holy Father for relatives and friends.

Now, for fully a minute it seemed, the pope examined the satellite photograph. He immediately recognized the Lenin Shipyard at Gdańsk, crystal-clear in the picture, taken less than forty-eight hours earlier from space. He was less certain about the solid, dark circle some distance away from the familiar complex of brick buildings with their huge smokestacks, which had been caught by the cameras spewing ugly gray billows of smoke.

"What is this?" asked the vicar of Christ. He pointed to the circle.

"Heavy equipment, Holy Father"—military vehicles, personnel carriers, tanks, for use by the Polish security forces.

The general handed the pope another picture across the table.

This satellite photograph—and others that Walters now produced from his envelope—showed the deployment and subsequent movement of Warsaw Pact forces toward the Polish border, tens of thousands of troops diverted from their barracks in the USSR, East Germany, and Czechoslovakia toward the pope's homeland.

Other photos showed missiles, programmed to reach the heart of Western Europe in minutes.

The pope expressed no emotion, which surprised Walters. "From how high was this taken? . . . What is this? . . . What is that?" Most of his questions were matter-of-fact.

"This is a fuel vehicle," Walters explained. "This is a silo, this is a pointed tractor cap that can plow its way through snow and ice—used for military assault, not for agriculture."

This was the pope's usual way of doing business, temporal or spiritual (though he usually made no distinction between the two): to ask the questions and wait for answers, whether from God or man. He wanted to learn as much as possible about what the United States knew, especially concerning Soviet intentions. Nonetheless, Walters was supposed to gather information as well as to give it. He noted later, "We were interested more in what the pope could tell us than in what we could tell him about the internal situation in Poland." Wojtyła had what Walters called "the oldest intelligence service in the world, unless you count the Israelis, but his never stopped functioning for a thousand years."

Walters passed John Paul II another photograph, this one of troops inside Poland—Polish troops. Poland had an army and reserve force of eight hundred thousand troops, Walters told him, including two airborne divisions. Three armored divisions were equipped with the same tanks that the Soviets had, T-72s, made in Poland. Walters expressed his view, shared by American intelligence, that most would fight against the Warsaw Pact forces if the latter were ordered into Poland by the Soviets. This would not be like Czechoslovakia in '68, or even Hungary in '56. "They cannot crush Poland in a night."

The pope nodded, the expression on his face grim.

The general continued: "There will be a war if the Soviets invade. It will be a small war, a short war, but it will be a war. Fought by Poles. And no one knows what the consequences will be."

The pope did not challenge Walters's view that the Poles would fight if Moscow's troops invaded. It had, after all, taken one million troops to subdue Czechoslovakia—where all resistance was of a nonviolent nature.

Briefly the general told the pope how many divisions had moved toward Poland and how they were equipped. Satellite photos showed where they were bivouacked. The Soviet North Army also maintained a force in Poland.

"Our indications are that it will be difficult to get a consensus among the Soviet leadership to invade," Walters said. The Soviets were already stretched thin militarily. They were being bled slowly in Afghanistan, and there might be opposition from some key military leaders to another adventure in which many Russian lives might be lost. They had backed away the previous December and again in April, at the height of Solidarity's power. "They know this will be nothing like Czechoslovakia in '68."

Wojtyła nodded. He knew his people, and he seemed relieved at the intelligence estimate. The CIA made much of the Soviet pullbacks in December and in April, when Solidarity's power was at its height.

Like Reagan, Casey, and Haig in Washington, Walters was convinced that the real power inside Poland was Wojtyła, even as he sat at this desk behind the ancient walls of the Vatican.

Yet this pope also had a deep distrust of the United States, its values, its goals, its capitalism. Above all, he was determined to pursue the interests of his Church, his country, and his conception of Christian destiny, which was quite different from Ronald Reagan's narrower political mind-set. But he didn't articulate this to Walters.

The discussion turned to the principals inside Poland and their ability to control the situation. Wałęsa, said the pope, is a good and holy man, a devout Roman Catholic who can be counted on not to do anything rash, a man of peace. There were other restraining forces in place as well, people known to the pope and to the Polish bishops who backed the Solidarity leadership. Still the situation was very tense and both sides were losing patience.

As for Jaruzelski, both Walters and the pope were inclined to believe that he thought of himself, above all, as a Polish patriot, a devout Communist yes, but a Pole who would do everything he could to convince his comrades in Moscow to stay out. Of late, the pope noted, Jaruzelski had been talking to the Church and, indirectly, to Solidarity's leaders as if martial law was inevitable unless the union and the episcopate were willing to renounce some of the civil and religious rights they had won since the signing of the Gdańsk accords.

Meanwhile, at the State Department, Haig was so focused on keeping the Soviets out that (to Reagan's later chagrin) he was never willing to threaten the Polish authorities with any consequences for imposing repression on their own. His reasoning was that American threats might encourage Solidarity to violently resist martial law, just as Hungarian rebels had fought in the streets in 1956 under the mistaken impression that they would receive help from the United States.

The pope stressed that his primary concern was spiritual: making sure the Catholic church in Poland wasn't forced into the kind of submission it had endured elsewhere in the Soviet empire. Priests were already being threatened for aiding Solidarity. Under no circumstances would the Church go back to the conditions of the Wyszyński era.

Briefly Walters told the pope that the Reagan administration was already doing a number of things to ensure that Solidarity would continue receiving financial and logistical aid from the United States—even to help it operate underground, if necessary. Casey had informed Walters in the broadest terms that such efforts were under way, and Walters hadn't pressed him for details.

"I said to the pope that obviously there was a large Polish-American community that was lobbying us to do something more to help Solidarity," Walters recalled later, "and obviously we—the government—were trying to be responsible and taking appropriate action. And we didn't go into details, and he didn't ask me who, where, when. He's a very sophisticated man for somebody who grew up and spent most of his life in Kraków."

Walters explained the larger framework of his mission in terms worked out beforehand with Secretary of State Haig: The United States was embarking on a historic intensification of the cold war against the Soviet Union, intent on challenging Communist hegemony and leftist insurgencies wherever it could—though that was hardly the way Walters phrased it. Poland was a big part of the picture, but only part of the whole: "Holy Father, you are entitled to know why the United States is spending this enormous amount of money—three hundred billion dollars—on defense." For the next quarter hour the pope and the general discussed the nature of the Soviet threat and the rationale behind the administration's desire to deploy a new generation of intermediate-range missiles throughout Western Europe. Later, the general would return with more satellite photos and charts and descriptions of Soviet hardware and force levels, briefing the pope in great detail for hours.

Walters had mentioned to the pope that he had taken recent trips to South America as well as Africa. Now Wojtyła asked for his assessment of the political situations in Argentina and Chile, both under military dictatorships and on Wojtyła's future travel itinerary.

Walters replied that the United States wanted to see a peaceful transition to democracy in both countries, but sought to prevent leftist forces aligned with Cuba or the USSR from taking advantage of the situation. The same applied to El Salvador and Nicaragua.

Walters spoke of U.S. "efforts to improve the human rights situation in the Americas without causing counterproductive embarrassment to governments by shouting out their faults from the rooftops." This was especially true in El Salvador, he said. In the years when the United States had publicly condemned governments in an effort to change their behavior—a reference to the Carter administration—violence, he claimed, had actually intensified. "In El Salvador," Walters continued, "we have only fifty military security personnel; the Soviets have over three hundred in Peru alone—more than the U.S. has in all of Latin America, excluding the base at Panama."

The real crunch was going to come in Nicaragua, which was where the administration intended to draw the line in Central America. "The Nicaraguans have 152-millimeter guns, Soviet-built tanks; their pilots undergo training in Bulgaria. We seek a peaceful solution that will not endanger the lives and freedom of the Latin American people." He did not tell the pope that even as they spoke, the administration was training a force of "Somozistas"— the Contras—in Argentina or that many more American advisers were headed for El Salvador and Honduras. Casey would do that later.

Liberation theology was "rampant" in the region, said Walters, and the pope agreed; both the United States and the Holy See would use their respective powers to marginalize it.

Walters and the pope had been together for slightly less than an hour, and Walters had resisted every impulse to ask leading questions. Still, he felt that John Paul II was becoming more sympathetic to the broad goals of American policy and more cognizant of the common interests of the Church and the United States. When a monsignor came to the door to remind the pope that it was time to move on to his next appointment, Wojtyła had waved him away.

John Paul II was dressed in a plain white woolen cassock; he sat slightly hunched behind his desk, handsome, but looking fatigued. He had the build of a former athlete. At times his face danced with animation, yet it was serene in a way that Walters had never witnessed in anyone, not even the three other popes he had dealt with on official U.S. business. There was a certain grace in his gestures, an ease of movement that matched the deliberate, sonorous cadence of his carefully chosen words. Walters knew that Wojtyła had been an actor and a poet; and his pale blue eyes, which gazed into Walters's own so deeply that at first it unnerved him, seemed to offer intimacy. Walters's experience in this regard was hardly unique. On orders from Leonid Brezhnev, the Soviet ambassador to Italy had also met secretly with Wojtyła several times. His impressions could only have jolted the party chiefs: "When you greet him you are struck by his look; it's very penetrating, but at the same time it's benevolent and gentle. . . . Every sentence of his generates a great sense of trust and enchants you. . . . The sweetness of his words. . . . He doesn't hurry when he speaks; every sentence is refined and precise. He never says empty words."

Now Walters shared a personal moment with the pope: He had been in St. Peter's Square when the white smoke had risen and the name of the cardinal of Kraków, Wojtyła, had been pronounced as the new successor to Peter. At the time Walters had commented to an acquaintance, "I have just heard the beat of the Holy Ghost's wings."

The pope looked into Walters's eyes and said slowly, "We need the Holy Spirit now in our difficult times." His eyes never left the general.

"Our Church has a sure and steady guide, Holy Father," responded Walters.

Walters's visit with the pope strengthened his belief in the importance of the Vatican in global affairs.

"First of all," Walters reflected at the time, "he understands communism to a degree that none of his predecessors did. Then he has a Church in Poland relatively untouched by the social and religious convulsions that occurred in the Western world after the war." Walters could foresee how the pope might be helpful to the United States in virtually all areas of vital interest to the Reagan administration: Eastern Europe, Central America, the

Middle East, terrorism, arms control, basic moral issues in the public sphere. The pope, Walters concluded, was "powerful jet fuel."

At the conclusion of their meeting, the pope had asked Walters to "talk at length" with the Vatican secretary of state, Cardinal Casaroli. In the presence of that particular prince of the Church, however, the general felt little of the warmth and encouragement he had gotten from the pope. He had the impression that Casaroli had a very different worldview from Wojtyła's, especially with regard to the Soviets and the Vatican's willingness to challenge them. The cardinal kept using the word *prudenza*—prudence. "I'm not sure he totally approves of everything in this papacy," Walters concluded.

As Walters saw it, Casaroli accepted Soviet control over its satellites in Eastern and Central Europe as practically immutable, whereas Wojtyła thought that the Church and its Gospel had the power to bring fundamental change, and would welcome help from the United States in doing so. Casaroli's diffidence, Walters thought, was one more reason to deal personally with Wojtyła and to share more information with him directly.

MARTIAL LAW

Looking at Polish life in the winter of 1981, it would sometimes be difficult not to confuse the images with pictures of Poland emerging from the devastation of World War II. In Warsaw, tens of thousands of freezing men, women, and children huddled in lines, ration cards in hand, for minuscule allotments of the few staples left in the country—even less, old people said, than in Nazi times. The base unit of Polish money, the złoty, had become virtually worthless. Around the cities, people bartered for the necessities of life: coal and wood for fuel, hoarded soap powder, matches, cigarettes, vodka. The presence of drunken men, women, and youths on the streets was depressingly constant. Fistfights and clubbings were too frequent an element of daily life. Factories had closed for want of parts; machinery was rusting because oil was scarce. Babies were malnourished from lack of milk or infant formula. The pharmaceutical industry had shut down, and people were suffering and dying for lack of medicine. Thousands were attempting to emigrate. Solidarity, the authorities, and the Soviets fired speeches and statements at each other, while the Church desperately sought compromise.

On December 2, soldiers backed by helicopters stormed the Firefighter's Academy in Warsaw (part of the Polish military system) and removed three hundred striking cadets dressed in their khaki uniforms. In Radom, in central Poland, Solidarity's leaders responded to the assault with a call for a general strike. This time Wałęsa agreed. He was under enormous pressure; the union rank and file, not just its leadership, was growing more radical.

In the first ten days of December, Primate Glemp met several times with Wałęsa and his top advisers, imploring them to reach a settlement and admonishing them for abusing their power. Their call for a general strike and their refusal to negotiate further had exceeded Solidarity's mandate from the workers, Glemp claimed.

The union, Wałęsa replied, "cannot retreat any further" in the face of unrelenting assaults by the government. Later, in his memoirs, he wrote that at Radom he had lost control over the situation and was forced to take "a hard position, against my convictions, in order not to be isolated."

On December 10, the Soviet Politburo met in emergency session.

Nikolai Baibakov, just back from Warsaw with other comrades, warned that Jaruzelski "has turned into a highly unbalanced person who is very uncertain of his own forces." The general "was in a very downcast state" because of Archbishop Glemp's refusal to back his demands for extraordinary powers. That very morning, the Soviet government had accused the Catholic Church of "stirring up anti-Communist sentiment." Baibakov characterized Glemp's letter refusing to endorse an antistrike law as a "holy war."

"The country is falling apart," Jaruzelski had told Baibakov. "As to the party, in essence it doesn't exist . . . all power is in the hands of Solidarity."

In the view of his Soviet visitors, Jaruzelski was wavering—and making little sense. Still worse, from Moscow's standpoint, he actually seemed to be *asking* for the intervention of Warsaw Pact forces if his own uncertain plans for martial law were to lead to serious division within the Polish army or armed struggle with Polish citizens.

"He says that if the Polish forces cannot manage with the opposition of

'Solidarity,' then the Polish comrades hope for the other countries' help, up to the intervention of armed forces in Polish territory," Baibakov reported.

But there were absolutely no circumstances under which the USSR would permit direct military intervention by the Warsaw Pact, as one member of the Politburo after another now proceeded to make clear—first Andropov, then Gromyko, then Ustinov, Suslov, Grishin, and Chernenko.

What the Politburo members had failed to grasp was that they had threatened intervention so long and so often that not only Jaruzelski but much of the world believed that the Soviets were willing to commit the forces of the Warsaw Pact to the struggle. In fact, their great secret was that they could not and would not.

"We can't risk it," Andropov declared. "We don't intend to bring in troops in Poland. This is the right position, and we must stick to it to the end. I don't know how things will develop in Poland. If Poland falls under 'Solidarity's' power, that's one thing. But if the capitalist countries fall upon the Soviet Union—and they already have an appropriate agreement with different types of economic and political sanctions—then it will be very hard for us. We must be concerned with our country and with the strengthening of the Soviet Union. This is our main position."

There was nothing left for them to do except protect the military and transportation corridor running west from the USSR. "As for the communications from the Soviet Union to the GDR through Poland," Andropov said, "we must, of course, take some measures to protect them." He made it sound like an autobahn reserved for Soviets.

Gromyko was forthright: "Somehow we will have to cool down the way Jaruzelski and the other Polish leaders feel about military intervention. There cannot be any military intervention in Poland. I think that we can entrust our ambassador to visit Jaruzelski and inform him about this."

There was a wistful note in Gromyko's words, as if he knew that Poland was already lost.

Today we are discussing the question of the situation in Poland in a very pointed fashion. Perhaps we have never discussed it so pointedly before. This is because now we too don't know how events will develop in Poland. . . . Either it will surrender its position, if it doesn't take decisive measures; or it will take decisive measures, introduce martial law, isolate the extremists of "Solidarity" and bring the necessary order. There is no alternative.

Suslov, the ideologist, was in his seventy-ninth year. "During the whole period of events in Poland, we have shown self-control and sangfroid," he insisted. "We are carrying out a great work for peace and we shouldn't change our position now. World public opinion won't understand us."

The USSR had launched its "peace offensive," seeking (with considerable success) to convince Western Europeans and Third World governments that its policies were defensive in nature and posed no threat to anyone. The real threat, the Russians maintained, was from Ronald Reagan's saber-rattling and military buildup. "Through the UN," continued Suslov,

we took such huge actions for the strengthening of peace. Look at the results we got from L. I. Brezhnev's visit to the Federal Republic of Germany, and many other peaceful actions. This made it possible for peace-loving countries to understand that the Soviet Union stands strongly and consistently for a policy of peace. That is why we shouldn't change the position that we took from the very beginning with regard to Poland. Let the Polish comrades decide what to do.

"Now everything rests with Jaruzelski," noted Defense Minister Ustinov. "As for our garrisons in Poland, we will reinforce them. I'm inclined to think that the Poles won't risk a confrontation unless 'Solidarity' takes them by the throat and forces them to."

On Friday, December 11, General Viktor Kulikov, the commander of the forces of the Warsaw Pact, returned to the Polish capital with word that under no circumstances would the Soviets intervene.

On the 11th and 12th, Solidarity's national commission met in Gdańsk. Despite reports of military preparations by the Polish army, Solidarity's leaders continued to press for their ambitious agenda as an alternative to confrontation: free elections to the Sejm and to local government councils, control by the workers of factory management and decision making, and a plebiscite on Communist rule.

Wałęsa sat in stony silence through the meeting. When asked to admit that negotiating with the regime was now pointless, he replied, "I'm just sitting here trying to figure out what it is you guys ate today that makes you talk like you do." He continued to defend the idea of a real tripartite national alliance and threatened to go on fighting for it, with or without the committee's consent. The meeting broke up around midnight on the night of December 12. Within two hours, most of the national commission would be under arrest.

.   .   .

Jaruzelski had compelling reasons to choose December 12 for the introduction of martial law. First of all, he was expected in Moscow on December 14 (though he has never acknowledged this "invitation" publicly), and the memory of Dubček's similar visit—and arrest—in 1968 remained strongly with him. By now, given Solidarity's increasing radicalization, the general had little doubt about the necessity of martial law. If Solidarity actually came to power, he could be imprisoned or executed. Beyond that, the general was ultimately a faithful Communist, committed to communism and to Poland as a socialist state. Solidarity's success, he knew, would be the end of communism in Poland, and would have fateful repercussions beyond. Jaruzelski has said he timed the declaration to follow the meeting of Solidarity's national commission, hoping for a conciliatory sign from the union. Solidarity had refused to call off the huge commemorative demonstration it had scheduled for four P.M. on December 17. "The same kind of demonstration in Budapest in 1956," Jaruzelski later wrote, "set off a chain of tragic and bloody events."

Others have suggested that he was waiting for Solidarity's leaders to gather in one place where they could be arrested in one fell swoop. The time chosen for imposition of martial law, Saturday at midnight, had long been designated and the operation rehearsed during war games in February. The list of detainees, eventually totaling more than ten thousand, had been drafted in March, when tensions were at their height. Citizens would wake up on

Sunday to find tanks in the street and no place to gather except in church for mass. Factories would be closed. And in the small hours of a Sunday morning, the detainees would be easy to locate—at home, in their beds.

At the stroke of midnight, tanks and soldiers stationed across the country moved into the streets and forests as Operation X got under way.

At six A.M., Jaruzelski addressed the nation on television.

He was seated stiffly at his desk, in uniform, wearing nontinted glasses. A huge Polish flag was behind him.

"Citizens and lady citizens of the Polish People's Republic! I turn to you as a soldier and chief of government! Our motherland is on the verge of an abyss." By the time he read his prepared statement, thousands were already in jail. The prisoners, he said, were guilty of "growing aggressiveness and an attempt to dismantle the state. How long will our outstretched hand be met with the fist?" he asked.

His speech, twenty-two minutes and fifty-three seconds long, was broadcast over and over through the morning and afternoon, alternating with film footage of a pianist playing Chopin polonaises and patriotic melodies.

For the foreseeable future, the nation would be governed by a Military Council of National Salvation. The new rules of governance, ending sixteen months of hope and excitement, suffering and disappointment, were pasted on lampposts, street corners, and trees throughout the cities and across the countryside. They had been printed months before—in the Soviet Union.

The civil society that Solidarity had been building brick by brick under the protection of the Church was gone. In its place was a declaration of a "state of war." A nightly curfew was in effect indefinitely. Except for those of the military and security forces, every telephone in Poland was dead (even at local Communist Party headquarters) and would remain so for a month. All civilian communications with the outside world were severed. All schools except nursery schools were closed, as were theaters and movie houses. Except for religious services, public gatherings were now illegal. Travel outside one's city of residence could only be undertaken with official permission. All mail was subject to censorship. "Tourism, yachting, and rowing . . . on internal and territorial waters" were forbidden.

During the sixteen months of Poland's great experiment, more than two thousand clandestine books and newspapers had been published, with help from the West. As many as 100,000 Polish citizens had been involved in their preparation, working as printers, writers, or distributors. Now the Military Council of National Salvation forbade the purchase of typewriter ribbons and typing paper without official permission.

The military would henceforth be responsible for running railroads, highways, mail service, broadcasting, distribution of petroleum products, firefighting, importing and exporting, and the manufacture of strategic goods. Polish borders were sealed and the country's airspace, closed. The newscasters on television now wore military uniforms.

Arresting thousands of people and promulgating and carrying out the more draconian strictures of martial law were not Jaruzelski's most difficult tasks. They were accomplished with military precision and authoritarian dispatch.

"The fact that martial law in Poland was [established] without causing enormous protest or bloodshed, without active opposition," former Party Secretary Kania later commented, "was due to the peculiar way that people consented to martial law. People were very tired of the dismantling of the economy, with the permanent strikes. There was no market at all. Shelves in the stores were empty. At its meeting in early December, Solidarity declared that this was going to be their definitive struggle. This created a condition of great fear in society, but not so much that the people began to support the authorities. It would be truer to say that for the moment the support for Solidarity was checked."

For Jaruzelski the essential task now was to win over the bishops. He wanted to leave the Church with no choice but to accept the new reality of a Poland subdued, of Solidarity disbanded, of the Communist state supreme once again and the Church its ultimate guarantor of legitimacy with the people.

Jaruzelski wasn't hoping for miracles—he didn't expect the primate in Warsaw or Wojtyła in Rome to cheer what he had done. But he did expect their reluctant acquiescence and a commitment to the new order of things: to calm, to a recognition of the inherent limits of membership in the Warsaw Pact, and at least to a formal commitment to socialism.

Jaruzelski, on the other hand, did not imagine a complete return to the situation before August 1980. There could be a place in Poland for self-governing trade unions, but not for a trade union movement that aimed to eclipse the party and threatened the existence of the state itself. Economic reforms were essential for Poland, and efforts at renewal had to go forward. But all the elements of Polish society—the government, the unions, the people, the party, and above all the Church—had to acknowledge that there were limits.

Shortly after two P.M. on Saturday, Jaruzelski summoned Kazimierz Barcikowski, secretary of the Polish Central Committee who also served as president of the Joint Commission for the State and the Episcopate, and asked him whether he agreed with the "state of war." Barcikowski did—so now Jaruzelski entrusted him and the minister of religious affairs, Jerzy Kuberski, with the duty of informing Glemp. The last thing the regime wanted was for Glemp to learn about martial law by running into tanks on the street.

When Kuberski arrived at the primate's residence at three A.M. on Sunday, everyone seemed to be sound asleep. A patrolman outside the palace gate rang three times and finally suggested, "Minister, if you climb over the fence, you'll probably be able to get in." Instead, Kuberski returned to the Belweder Palace, where he was ordered to go back and keep trying. "The whole thing," Barcikowski later noted, "was a bit theatrical."

At last a light went on inside when the minister, joined now by Barcikowski and a general, returned and rang again. A nun came to the door. A few minutes later, the three men were greeted by Glemp's chaplain, who took them into a room where they met the primate.

Calmly and succinctly, Barcikowski informed him that a "state of war" had been declared, that no other alternative seemed possible. But he added that this would not affect Church-state relations, that all previous arrangements would be respected. Moreover, martial law—or some of its features— would be abolished as soon as circumstances warranted.

Barcikowski could see the primate's distress. "This is a sad thing," Glemp said. Word that such a declaration might be coming had already reached him, but he hoped that the nation could limp along until Christmas. Then maybe the spirit of Christmas might avert the "state of war."

Though not surprised, Glemp was worried about the future. But neither he nor Barcikowski was prepared to discuss matters in detail. Thus the talk ended abruptly after a few minutes.

Next Barcikowski went to inform Archbishop Dąbrowski, secretary of the Polish Bishops Conference. His phones too were dead. Dąbrowski and Barcikowski met three times in the next few hours, as the archbishop voiced his adamant opposition to martial law and Barcikowski tried to keep him informed of ongoing developments and convince him that the declaration was necessary.

Barcikowski and Dąbrowski knew each other well: As secretary of the Polish Bishops Conference, the archbishop was in charge of relations with the government. At meetings of the Joint Commission for the State and the Episcopate, they had often discussed whether a particular course of action involving Solidarity might make the Soviets more likely to intervene.

"The myth is that there was a Communist state and an anti-Communist Church, and then came Solidarity," Barcikowski would say years later. "In short, three parts with no connection between them. But in the state-Church relationship there was always space for personal contacts on different levels. When Dąbrowski felt the need to have a talk, he would call me, or I would go to the Office for Religious Affairs, where he would meet me. In such talks we discussed virtually everything—including, many times, the question 'Will they invade or not?' Going back to 1980." Sometimes, when there were sharp disagreements, Minister of Religious Affairs Kuberski would throw up his hands and say, "This will be settled by Captain Ivanov." And everyone knew what he meant.

That Sunday afternoon, December 13, from the altar at the Jesuit church of Mary Mother of God in the Old City, Glemp gave a homily on the new condition in Poland. The note he struck could not have pleased Jaruzelski— or even Brezhnev—more: It was broadcast on Polish television—over and over again—printed in the party daily and even on leaflets posted in army barracks.

On Sunday morning [Glemp began] we were astounded to find ourselves under martial law. By the evening we are getting accustomed to the idea and we are coming to see that it is something dangerous, and we ask ourselves: What next? What is going to happen tomorrow? How should we behave? . . . A representative of the Church cannot teach differently from what the Gospel says. In his teachings he has to shed light on the new reality. In our country the new reality is martial law. As we understand it, martial law is a new state, and a state of severe laws which suspend many civic achievements. . . . Opposition to the decisions of the authorities under martial law could cause violent reprisals, including bloodshed, because the authorities have the armed forces at their disposal. We can be indignant, shout about the injustice of such a state of affairs. . . . But this may not yield the expected results.

For the Polish people, who had been shocked and frightened by the regime's actions and the harsh measures of martial law, the message was obvious: The head of the Polish Church was telling the faithful, "Don't resist, because you may be killed." Though the popularity of the government had plummeted in the fall of 1981, Jaruzelski's personal stature remained considerable. The Polish army was still revered for having saved Poland from Soviet invasion in the 1920s: Many citizens still refused to believe—in the face of reality—that Polish soldiers had fired on the workers at Gdańsk in 1970.

Then Glemp used an even more striking choice of words in his homily:

The authorities consider that the exceptional nature of martial law is dictated by higher necessity, it is the choice of a lesser rather than a greater evil. Assuming the correctness of such reasoning, the man in the street will subordinate himself to the new situation. . . . There is nothing of greater value than human life.

"It is not for the historian to judge," commented Timothy Garton Ash, the British chronicler of Solidarity's struggle, "whether the sentence 'there is nothing of greater value than human life' accurately reflects the teachings of Jesus Christ, or whether the late Cardinal Wyszyński or Karol Wojtyła would have spoken in precisely this manner in this critical and incomparably difficult moment. [The historian] can only record that the sermon seems to have played a part in reducing the immediate resistance to martial law, and that the Primate's words were bitterly resented by many Christian Poles who were, at that moment, preparing to risk their own lives for what they considered greater values. A week later the Episcopate would come out with a much clearer defense of Solidarity; but that week was decisive."

Wojtyła had approved the choice of Glemp as Wyszyński's handpicked successor. This endorsement gave even more weight to the primate's words. Shortly after Glemp's message had resounded through the country, members of Solidarity who had gone underground took to calling the primate "Comrade Glemp."

Within two days, other Polish bishops had convinced the primate that his initial reaction had struck exactly the wrong note. The bishops' statement of December 15 began with an expression of grief for "a nation terrorized by military force," but great damage had already been done.

The Church's confusing reaction to martial law was partly the result of the pope's inability to speak with his bishops, and divisions within the episcopate persisted until John Paul II began laying down clear policy for the Church in Poland. Thus in the earliest days of martial law a pattern emerged that was generally to hold true through the five years of Solidarity's underground struggle: that Solidarity drew its strength from the pope and his pronouncements but saw Glemp as hopelessly weak and subject to manipulation by the martial law regime.

Zbigniew Bujak, the seniormost Solidarity leader to escape his captors on December 13 and go underground, later explained some of the reasons why the union was caught so unprepared: "The authorities were evidently planning a sizable operation against the union. But we never thought it would be as serious as this." So many people had spoken in the previous months about the "powerlessness" of the government that the Solidarity leadership had been lulled into believing its own rhetoric. They had also put their trust in the army; many were confident that Polish soldiers would never move against Polish workers, much less fire on them.

Limited preparations for resistance had been made in a few regions: Printing materials had been hidden and in Łódź at least rough contingency plans drawn up to continue operating after the arrest of the national and regional leadership. But there were no such plans nationally, nor had any attempts been made to set in place an alternative radio communications network between factories and regions, though the experience of August 1980 showed how crucial communications were in a strike situation. Finally, the leaders of Solidarity were so overwhelmed with immediate problems that they never got around to detailed technical planning for a contingency they did not seriously anticipate.

Wałęsa was among the first to be arrested. As he wrote,

> This state of martial law took no specific political form at first, but seemed rather like a large-scale military operation. Its full significance became clear only later on, and then it exceeded all expectations. Its consequences weren't just political; it unleashed a cataclysm that totally disrupted social and personal life and called into question the very idea of a national community. . . . It became increasingly obvious that we were in a state of civil war. The "dialogue for Poland" was over; the "war for Poland" had just begun.

Now, with Solidarity's leaders under arrest or underground, a new field marshal would take command: the pope.

.　　.　　.

At the Vatican, the pope's secretary, Monsignor Dziwisz, had heard the news on the radio at dawn and rushed to tell John Paul II. But after this initial word, the pope heard nothing of substance for the rest of the day. Even Washington knew nothing. Poland and Eastern Europe were covered by dense clouds (and would remain so for days), making satellite photography useless. The White House had called the Vatican Secretariat of State to learn if the pope had any information. All communications had been cut between Rome and Warsaw, between Poland and the outside world.

Wojtyła's first instincts were to pray—for guidance and for his people. His greatest fear was that Pole would turn against Pole, that there would be a bloodbath. If Poles took to the streets in a rampage, that would give the Soviets an excuse to intervene—and provoke even more bloodshed and irreversible repression. He wanted to identify with the Polish people in their moment of greatest crisis since the Warsaw uprising of 1944, but he also wanted to send a signal that would reach—and influence—the whole Polish nation: the military as well as Solidarity, ordinary citizens and leaders of the party. As on almost every Sunday, a group of Polish pilgrims gathered in St. Peter's Square, and after the Angelus prayer at noon, John Paul II appeared on his balcony to pray for their homeland—in Polish.

Wojtyła knew that millions of Poles, hungry for news from outside, would be listening to Radio Free Europe, the BBC, the Voice of America, or Vatican Radio. All through the crises of 1980 and 1981, Polish citizens had tuned out the state-sponsored media and turned to these alternative sources just as they had abandoned the Communist press for the hundreds of underground papers and magazines published under the auspices of Solidarity, along with dozens of increasingly bold Catholic journals.

"Too much Polish blood has already been shed, especially during the last war," the pope said. "Polish blood must no longer be spilled. Everything must be done to build the future of our homeland in peace." He then entrusted Poles and Poland to the Madonna of Jasna Góra, "who has been given to us for our defense." Within the hour, the Polish-language services of Western radio stations were broadcasting his message. His words—hours before Glemp spoke—may well have influenced the primate's unfortunate statement.

In his first private discussions with Casaroli, Dziwisz, and his confidant and friend Cardinal Deskur, the pope expressed his continuing concern about possible Soviet intervention. He laid out a four-point policy: first, to get as much information as possible from inside Poland and elsewhere and to reach the episcopate; second, to discourage acts of provocation; third, to open up lines of communication with the new martial law regime; and, finally, to signal to Poland and the world that the pope and the Church stood unequivocally "in solidarity with the Polish nation"—words he used the next evening as he addressed a huge crowd praying for Poland in St. Peter's Square.

"This solidarity with the Polish people serves also to bolster certain values and inalienable principles such as the rights of man and the rights of the nation . . . values and principles that must create, now in our times, great solidarity with a European and worldwide dimension." The contrast with Glemp's words could hardly have been more striking.

To those who saw him up close in those first hours, the pope seemed profoundly saddened but intent on establishing his role as the supreme player in his nation's destiny. His next opportunity came on Tuesday with the arrival in the Vatican of a diplomat sent at the request of the president of the United States and in the name of UN Secretary General Kurt Waldheim.

At the White House, the first news flash from Poland had arrived Saturday evening, Washington time—a bulletin from the American embassy in Warsaw that tanks had taken up positions in the capital. From the basement situation room of the White House, a duty officer had notified the president and vice president, as well as Richard Pipes, the Polish-born senior National Security Council aide who advised the administration on Soviet and Eastern European affairs. Secretary of State Haig and Defense Secretary Weinberger were both out of the country: a sign of just how unprepared the administration was.

Almost immediately Pipes contacted Bogdan Lewandowski, an undersecretary general of the UN, at his New York residence. A Polish citizen, Lewandowski had represented Secretary General Waldheim at John Paul II's inauguration. Pipes had hoped that Lewandowski, who maintained ties with the Warsaw government, might have further information on the coup, but he didn't. The United States was now almost completely in the dark, with neither satellite intelligence nor—since Kukliński's exit—highly placed human sources.

Shortly thereafter, Lewandowski and Zbigniew Brzeziński talked by phone, a conversation in which the idea developed of the UN diplomat undertaking a visit to the pope. Lewandowski's credentials, they agreed, would be extremely useful as a bridge between the pontiff and Warsaw, where Lewandowski had a close relationship with Jaruzelski's deputy prime minister, Mieczysław Rakowski, a member of the liberal wing of the Communist Party. The Vatican too had virtually no information and, like Washington, John Paul II's first priority was to find out what was happening in Poland. Brzeziński then made arrangements with the Vatican for Lewandowski to be received by the pope. In Washington, Pipes and Brzeziński were hopeful that Lewandowski, officially a representative of the UN and thus responsible not to the Polish government but to the secretary general, would share whatever he learned from Rome or Warsaw with the White House—which he did.

Lewandowski arrived in Rome on Thursday morning, December 17, and was taken immediately to meet Wojtyła in the pope's library. "There was still almost a total blackout of information," he recalled. "With all modern communications, even via the Italian embassy in Warsaw, His Holiness had practically no information." What little was known was that thousands of people were being arrested and that citizens were frightened and confused.

He found the pope tense and melancholy, fearful of a "holocaust" with Poles slaughtering Poles. Of particular concern was the possibility that the regime might seek to execute Solidarity's leaders.

During their discussion, which stretched over several hours, the pope spoke eloquently not just about the immediate situation and his fears of bloodshed, but also about the political and social freedoms that had been gained in the past sixteen months. "I also detected," Lewandowski said years later, "concern for the future prospects of his cherished hope to open the Soviet Union to Christianity and to have his . . . homeland serve as an example of true Catholicism, a 'people's catholicism' for the materialistic and permissive West."

During dinner, at which they were joined by Dziwisz, the conversation ranged over John Paul II's hopes and fears, as if the whole purpose and mission of his papacy was now being tested. Yet the pope continued to talk about Poland's "inspiration to the world" and his desire that Lewandowski convey to Jaruzelski this vision, as well as the urgency of his concerns for the safety and security of his countrymen. He wished to open a dialogue immediately between the Church and the government, Wojtyła said, but he was insistent that Jaruzelski understand that the principles established since the Gdańsk accords could not be abandoned.

Between twenty and thirty people had been killed in the early days of martial law, most of them murdered by security forces. Hundreds of others were injured and arrested at the shipyard at Gdańsk, the birthplace of Solidarity, where thousands of workers had rushed when they first heard of the "state of war."

The most serious violence occurred at a coal mine near Katowice, where miners called a sit-down strike. By Tuesday, December 15, more than two thousand men were barricaded inside and threatening to blow up themselves and the mine if the government responded with force. The miners were armed with truncheons, bottles of gasoline, dynamite, and tools fashioned into spears.

At ten A.M., the ZOMO security police, backed by forty tanks, blocked the mine's entrance and began firing rubber bullets at the strikers, while helicopters dropped tear gas into the mine. Nine miners and four ZOMO policemen were killed, and the security forces then attacked civilian doctors and ambulance drivers trying to treat the injured. More than forty persons were wounded.

The violence at Katowice, which was reported by Polish state radio on the next day, Thursday, prompted John Paul II to begin writing a letter that afternoon to Jaruzelski. Written without consultation or assistance, the letter identified the Church (and, unmistakably, Wojtyła himself) as "spokesman" for the cause of his country and for moral justice. It unambiguously condemned the state of martial law, yet it passed no moral judgment on Jaruzelski, even as it bade him uphold loftier principles than might have hitherto occurred to him. Copies of the letter were sent to various heads of state around the globe, to the leaders of the Polish episcopate, and to Lech Wałęsa under house arrest.

> Recent events in Poland since the declaration of martial law on December 13 [wrote the pope] have resulted in death and injury to our fellow countrymen, and I am moved to address this urgent and heartfelt appeal to you, a prayer for an end to the shedding of Polish blood.
>
> During the last two centuries, the Polish nation has endured great wrongs, and much blood has been spilled in the struggle for power over our Fatherland. Our history cries out against any more bloodshed, and we must not allow this tragedy to continue to

weigh so heavily on the conscience of the nation. I therefore appeal to you, General, to return to the methods of peaceful dialogue that have characterized efforts at social renewal since August 1980. Even though this may be a difficult step, it is not an impossible one.

The welfare of the entire nation depends upon it. People throughout the world, all those who rightly see the cause of peace furthered by respect for the rights of Man, are waiting for this return to nonviolent means. All humanity's desire for peace argues for an end to the state of martial law in Poland.

The Church speaks out for this desire. Soon it will be Christmas, when generation after generation of Poland's sons and daughters have been drawn together by Holy Communion. Every effort must be made so that our compatriots will not be forced to spend this Christmas under the shadow of repression and death.

I appeal to your conscience, General, and to the conscience of all those who must decide this question.

The Vatican 18 December 1981
John Paul II

This letter, like all of the pope's responses to martial law, stemmed in part from a central premise. However repugnant, martial law, in the pope's phrase, was a "lesser evil" than civil war or Soviet intervention. The pope correctly assumed that Jaruzelski would eventually need the Church's cooperation to find a way out of the terrible situation in which he and the nation now found themselves. Since Jaruzelski had only two choices—to turn toward the Church or toward Moscow—the pope believed that Jaruzelski would ultimately seek the protection of the Church.

A charter flight from Warsaw that arrived in Rome on Thursday was expected to bring a representative of the Polish episcopate with a message for the pope. But no priest was on board the plane. Frustrated by his continuing inability to make contact with his bishops, the pope instructed the Vatican

Secretariat of State to ask the Polish government's representatives in Rome for permission to send a papal emissary to Warsaw to visit Jaruzelski.

For this mission, the pope chose Archbishop Luigi Poggi, who held the rank of papal nuncio for special assignments and who since 1973 had undertaken other missions in Eastern Europe. On Saturday, bearing the pope's letter in an envelope embossed with the papal seal, Poggi left by plane for Vienna, where he boarded the Chopin Express train to Warsaw.

That same weekend, UN Undersecretary Lewandowski met with Jaruzelski and immediately conveyed the pope's concerns. The general readily assured him that there would be no further bloodshed initiated by the government. It was extremely important, the general said, that the pope fully understand why the regime had acted: Radical elements were dragging the country into an economic abyss and provoking social chaos that would have resulted in intervention by the Soviets. In response to Lewandowski's presentation on behalf of the pope, Jaruzelski pledged to move ahead with the social and economic reforms announced before the "state of war." He never mentioned—then or afterward—his own request for possible aid from Warsaw Pact forces, or his information that the Soviets would not intervene.

"General Jaruzelski at that time was probably the most disliked person in Poland," Lewandowski noted later. Yet Lewandowski judged him "one of the most Christian persons I met in Poland—and not only because of his Catholic upbringing and education . . . He appeared to me as a person believing that he must carry the Cross—of popular hate, of eternal guilt, of no chance of redemption in this life." The diplomat elaborated:

> Jaruzelski never tried to defend the past—that of Communist rule, which he—at least in the eyes of all in Poland and outside— was supposed to defend. The only past we talked about . . . was the Warsaw uprising of 1944 and all the other Polish upheavals of the nineteenth century and after. It was all about Russians, not even Germans. He made no bones about it—he feared another Polish-Russian confrontation, with Poland most certainly being the loser.

Lewandowski also met with Rakowski, the deputy prime minister and perhaps Jaruzelski's most trusted adviser. This was a lengthy "sum-up" of the situation in Poland, Lewandowski said, and (with permission) he tape-recorded the conversation to present to both the pope and the White House. Notwithstanding Jaruzelski's emotional appeal for the pope's understanding, Lewandowski saw little to be hopeful about in Warsaw. Soldiers were everywhere, there was no indication that the "state of war" would be a short one, and people were disillusioned and confused.

On December 21, Lewandowski returned to the Vatican for mass in the papal chapel and then for breakfast with the pope. Before sitting down at the table, he handed the cassette tape of his meeting with Rakowski to Monsignor Dziwisz.

For several hours, Wojtyła questioned Lewandowski about his impressions of conditions in Poland (very depressing but calm), how Jaruzelski had responded to his appeal for dialogue (positively), and about several KOR leaders who were advisers to Solidarity and about other intellectuals who were close to the pope.

The members of KOR, the Workers Defense Committee, had been among the first arrested. For sixteen months they had been the obsessive focus of the Soviet Politburo's fears, as well as of surveillance by Polish internal security. Yet the KOR advisers to Solidarity had not been radicals pushing the union toward the edge. They had urged Solidarity and Wałęsa to exercise restraint, lest the Soviets or the Polish army come in to crush their movement.

Wałęsa was being held in a villa outside Warsaw belonging to the former secretary of the Polish Central Committee. In the first hours under martial law, Barcikowski, the head of the state-Church commission, had tried to prevail on him to meet with Jaruzelski for negotiations.

Wałęsa refused, demanding that all those arrested must first be released. Two days later, he was allowed to meet with two representatives of the episcopate and, soon after that, with his friend and counselor-confessor from Gdańsk, Father Henryk Jankowski.

"Despite the imposition of martial law," Wałęsa later wrote, "the

Church continued to play the role of mediator. Though in complete sympathy with the ideals of Solidarity, the Roman Catholic hierarchy in Poland avoided all overtly political actions and pronouncements, for which the authorities were grateful."

But not Wojtyła in Rome; his public statements expressed more and more outrage as it became apparent that his homeland would remain under martial law for the foreseeable future. Privately, he told his aides that Poland had become "a vast concentration camp"—an interesting choice of words for a Polish prelate whose diocese had once included Auschwitz.

The regime was calculating that the bishops could convince Wałęsa to begin negotiating on its terms; then it would begin releasing Solidarity's leaders in exchange for political concessions. With this in view, Father Alojzy Orszulik, a spokesman for Primate Glemp, was granted easy access to Wałęsa.

In his rage and despair at the authorities, Wałęsa shouted at the priest, "They'll come to me on their knees!"

Not surprisingly, the priest took offense. He "disapproved of my lack of Christian humility," Wałęsa said, "and it took us some time to get used to each other." Their first meetings were tense and uneasy, as Wałęsa advanced one idea after another and Orszulik rejected each as "unrealistic."

More important, Orszulik kept Wałęsa abreast of communications between the pope and the Polish bishops in the first weeks of martial law; and the pope got reliable news about Wałęsa's latest negotiating position. In the first hours of his arrest, the authorities had told Wałęsa that the "state of war" would probably last at least a year—a piece of information that was immediately passed on to representatives of the episcopate.

At times Wałęsa feared that the Church, its importance now enhanced, would sacrifice the gains of the past sixteen months in exchange for concessions from the regime. The primate, Wałęsa later wrote, was urging from the pulpit that negotiations be opened, and "I abandoned all my initial conditions one by one, finally aligning myself with the Church's position. But that didn't produce any tangible results either. That must have been their plan from the beginning: to use the Church simply for the sake of appearances."

Still, Wałęsa came to a new realization about the objectives of the Church:

Later on, I often wondered why the Church, with all its experience, agreed to take part in such an empty charade, and I came to understand that therein lay its wisdom. Accepting the rules of the game imposed upon it, the Church plays for its own stakes in order to exist as an unaligned force within the society. . . . This was the policy of Stefan Wyszyński, a policy followed by the Church in Poland since the end of the war: taking suspect promises and agreements at their face value and building on them to become a moral force the state had to recognize. I realized the Church was taking the same approach in dealing with the situation under martial law.

John Paul II spent a forlorn Christmas, his suffering plain to see. Since becoming pope he had never encountered a situation so unyielding to his will and prayers. Or so it seemed to those around the pontiff, who had never seen him so unhappy, preoccupied, and frustrated.

For sixteen months his country had been the symbol of a new era in Europe, and he had shared in and rejoiced over this era's birth. Now Poland resembled the behemoth on its eastern border—joyless, hungry, vanquished.

On Christmas Eve, as a sign of "solidarity with suffering nations," the pope lit a candle in the window of his Vatican apartment, a sign that millions of others around the world would soon appropriate. It had been the idea of a Protestant minister in the United States.

He tried to keep his words measured—even the Italian Communist Party had thus far been more publicly critical of the regime—as day after day more evidence reached Rome that Jaruzelski's coup had succeeded in overwhelming the country and conquering its spirit. The pope's first direct report from the episcopate had been depressing in the extreme. Bishop Dąbrowski, secretary of the Polish Bishops Conference, had arrived at the Vatican on Monday night, December 21, and had drawn a grim picture of Poland under siege. Solidarity members were being forced to sign loyalty oaths and renounce the union. *Tygodnik Powszechny*, the weekly that had published Karol Wojtyła's articles, and Znak, his book publisher, had been shut down. Jaruzelski was considering huge price increases for food, consumer goods, and services. Though Wałęsa was safe and sound, the general refused to negotiate meaningfully with him, despite Dąbrowski's plea that Wałęsa was the person best equipped to represent the interests of Polish workers.

"Deadly shadows," said the pope, were darkening the prospects for peace. He nonetheless continued to speak about reaching a principled consensus, telling the Christmas convocation of the curial cardinals and prelates that there must be a "peaceful solution in the mutual collaboration between authorities and citizens, in the full respect for the civil, national, spiritual, and religious identity of this country."

He declared, "The Church is on the side of the workers," but he refrained once more from direct criticism of the Polish military authorities. Perhaps nothing symbolized the seeming weakness of the Church's position so much as the sight of the pope's emissary, Poggi, together with Jaruzelski on Polish television. Having been kept waiting for days to see the general, he was nonetheless smiling diplomatically. It was Christmas Eve, and the inference of a papal blessing was all too obvious. Put on a train home without an answer to the pope's letter, Poggi arrived back in Rome on the 27th with the gloomiest of reports. Though Jaruzelski had expressed hope that the Vatican would play a "historic role" in Poland's renewal, he'd said nothing to indicate he was ready to release the thousands now in custody—some in freezing jail cells, others, like Wałęsa, under house arrest. In fact, more arrests were being made each day.

Poggi also tried to instill in Primate Glemp the papal line of principled resistance, but Glemp was afraid of the consequences for the Church. He described Wałęsa as "inflexible," an "inexperienced politician." He took deep offense at the Solidarity leader's outraged words to Father Orszulik. He worried that Jaruzelski would be swept aside by a Stalinist coup if provoked too severely by the Church or the remnants of Solidarity. He had little faith that Solidarity or its guiding ideas could survive.

Conversely, Dąbrowski believed that Solidarity had sent down such deep roots into Poland that it was impossible to destroy it. Unlike the parochial Glemp, he was convinced of its international importance. He thought Wałęsa had both the stature and the ability to represent the workers in negotiations with the government. He saw the events of the past sixteen months in a historical context of which Glemp appeared ignorant. Dąbrowski doubted that the Soviets would be willing to shoulder the burden of governing a country that had so resolutely resisted the Communist saddle for so long, even after it was molded to fit Poland's peculiar form. And that was what the USSR would have to do if it intervened: It would have to govern the country itself. Even the Polish Communist Party, except for its most militantly Stalinist faction, would resist such an intervention, Dąbrowski felt.

Still, the pope was now reluctantly concluding that both the Polish Church and Solidarity had lost much of what they had fought for in the past sixteen months. To Poggi, Dąbrowski, Casaroli, and others, Wojtyła spoke of *"salvare il salvabile"*—saving what was savable. Patience and caution—and faith—were essential. Casaroli instructed the papal nuncios in Western Europe to urge their host governments not to cut off economic aid to Poland in protest. Wojtyła's analysis, supported by American intelligence, held that Jaruzelski would come to resemble the late Marshal Tito of Yugoslavia rather than the typical Moscow puppet, particularly if the Church did not back him into a corner. Wojtyła also believed that Jaruzelski, who as a child had attended a school run by the Marian Fathers, was a secret believer. Over the next few years, this would prove a powerful element in the pope's calculations.

After meeting with Poggi on the 27th, at the close of his traditional Christmastide blessing to Rome and the world, the pope sent his special Christmas wishes to "you, my beloved fellow-countrymen":

> I express to you good wishes from the crib at Bethlehem. I pass on to you the good wishes of the newborn Child. . . . I embrace you one and all, the whole of Poland . . . especially those who are suffering, who have been taken away from their dear ones, those who are afflicted by depression, or even by despair.
>
> So many men in the world are praying for Poland. . . . And I say to you in our native language: "Raise your hand, Child Jesus, and bless—You, who showed the way to the shepherds of Bethlehem and to the Wise Men—show the sons and daughters

of Poland the way toward a better future for their country, in peace, justice, freedom."

This was no mere ritual gesture. Faith and prayer, the pope was certain, could change the course of destiny. On January 1, in his first Angelus message of the new year, the pope entrusted his prayers "in a special way to our Mother's heart. For six hundred years this Mother has been present on Polish soil through her image at Jasna Góra. The year 1982 is the year of the great Jubilee. Before the Mother of Jasna Góra I repeat . . . May the Lord spare you violence, spare you martial law, and grant you peace!"

Poland, he declared from the balcony of his study, "is an important problem not only for a single country, but also for the history of man." He took note of the *Solidarność* banners fluttering in the square below. "This word," he proclaimed, "is the expression of a great effort which the workers in my country have made to ensure the real dignity of the working man. The workers . . . have the right to set up autonomous trade unions to protect their social, family, and individual rights. . . . Solidarity belongs to the present heritage of the workers of my country, and I would say of other nations too."

On January 6, Jaruzelski finally replied to the pope's letter of December 18. His response, which ran to three long-winded, single-spaced pages, was officious, presumptuous, and self-serving. It included a litany of Solidarity's sins, a history of the government's concessions, compromises, patience, and persistence, a recapitulation of the ways in which "we were trying to inform the Holy See about the dangers threatening Poland," and the "many times . . . we asked" the bishops to moderate Solidarity's demands.

Jaruzelski acknowledged that "the introduction of martial law was a shock to society" and that Polish citizens "feel disillusioned . . . crushed by circumstances, embittered." He promised that "all disciplinary measures [will] be of a humanitarian nature"—presumably ruling out torture—and he implicitly demanded that the Church and Poland's intellectuals embrace the coup's rationale in order for martial law to be eased. Not a word was said about negotiating with Wałęsa or the Solidarity leadership.

He then voiced the hope "that Your Holiness will support us in those strivings and efforts" and signed off, "With the highest respect, General of the Army Wojciech Jaruzelski."

To the pope's mind, the signature was the only hopeful aspect of the letter. Jaruzelski had not signed the letter as prime minister, as the head of a Communist state or of the party, but rather as chief of the institution that, with the Church, had protected Poland in its most difficult moments.

Since the imposition of martial law, the pope had been muted in his response, still hoping for some tangible gesture from Jaruzelski that repressive conditions would soon be relaxed. Clearly, the general's letter held out little hope and tried instead to co-opt the Church.

The pope wrote back that the fear and resentment of the people were deepening as a result of conditions "stemming from the prolongation of the state of war." As an example, he cited the two hundred to four hundred percent price rise announced by the government in the first days of January. People couldn't afford to buy food. The pope told the general that the "shock" (as Jaruzelski had phrased it) triggered by martial law was also due to the "internment of thousands of leading Solidarity activists, including Lech Wałęsa, along with a number of painful sanctions in relation to the worlds of labor and culture. . . . It is not only necessary to remove the shock, but, above all, to rebuild trust."

Wojtyła had refrained from directly criticizing the regime until the arrival of Jaruzelski's letter. On January 10, in a Sunday address broadcast by Vatican Radio and its Polish shortwave service, the pope denounced the coup in terms that the people, Jaruzelski, and Glemp could all understand. The pope seemed perturbed by the way in which the primate had invoked the Savior on the day martial law had been declared. And nothing the regime had done had so offended the pope as forcing interned Solidarity members to sign loyalty oaths and renounce their union membership.

"Under the threat of losing their jobs," he declared, "citizens are forced to sign declarations that go against their conscience and convictions." This violation "does grave damage to man. It is the most painful blow inflicted to human dignity. In a certain sense, it is worse than inflicting physical death, than killing. 'Do not fear those who can kill the body,' said Christ, showing how much greater is the evil done to the human spirit and to human conscience. The principle of respect for conscience is a fundamental right of man."

.   .   .

Toward the end of Wyszyński's life, Wojtyła had decried "this old man's" lack of understanding of Solidarity at a crucial moment of the movement's history. Now he had to deal with the old man's protégé, who was even more insensitive.

Zbigniew Bujak, the senior Solidarity official underground, began writing Glemp a series of letters in the first weeks of martial law, appealing to him to act as an intermediary between Solidarity and the Church. Glemp never answered. "It was a general request," said Bujak, "in the situation that we each found ourselves in, to try to reach some agreement on Solidarity's operations, to link Solidarity and the Church. It was clear that as an institution, as a meeting point for the people, the Church would play an important role during martial law. . . . But we couldn't make decisions [until] a position was agreed upon between the Church and the underground. And there was no answer." Not from Glemp anyhow.

"However, I can say that . . . there were no disagreements between the pope and the underground as to the strategy."

Indeed, the pope's strategy was for Solidarity to remain alive underground, to resume publishing and broadcasting, and, somehow, through the Church and through his own person, to rally the spirits of the people. With that in mind, the pope (according to U.S. officials) began secretly sending money to the Solidarity underground out of papal discretionary funds and planning his own trip to Poland, which had been tentatively scheduled—before the imposition of martial law—for August.

A VATICAN SUMMIT

"Men of power mustn't give away their mystery," observed Edmund Morris, the biographer chosen by Ronald Reagan to write the history of his presidency. "As long as you are mysterious you can move any way. Leaders who are secretive and unknown do better than those who utterly reveal themselves. Reagan and the pope understood that."

President Reagan and John Paul II had secretly exchanged several letters in 1981 and early 1982, not only about Poland but about the prospects for broad arms agreements between the Soviets and the United States. Few things in his presidency had personally affected Reagan as much as the imposition of martial law in Poland. Holding the Soviets directly responsible, he promptly invoked disabling economic, cultural, diplomatic, and technological sanctions against both the USSR and Poland. Meanwhile, on Reagan's orders William Casey and Vernon Walters opened a whole new world of intelligence information to the Vatican, providing Karol Wojtyła information not only about Poland but also about every country and region the peripatetic pope visited and in which the Church wished to pursue its evangelical mission with special vigor.

Two weeks after martial law was declared, Reagan appointed William Clark as his national security adviser specifically to end all feuding and any disarray among his various foreign policy advisers. Clark, as biographer Edmund Morris notes, was "the Catholic conscience of the administration," and his mandate was to engage the Communists far more aggressively than Haig had, especially with regard to Poland. Indeed, his brief was to "Let Reagan be Reagan," in the words of the president's most ideological admirers.

On June 7, 1982, Reagan arrived in the Vatican for a summit meeting between these two very different superpowers that would personalize the remarkable secret alliance between them. Meeting alone without interpreters in the papal study for fifty minutes, two of the most powerful men on earth discussed in philosophical and practical terms a proposition so radical that no other leaders in the West had seriously considered it: that the collapse of the Soviet empire was inevitable, more for spiritual than for strategic reasons, and that the world built at Yalta not only should not but could not stand.

At Westminster Palace in London the next day, Reagan announced the end of the empire: The Soviet Union, he said, was gripped by a "great revolutionary crisis" in which Poland, then under martial law, but "magnificently unreconciled to repression," was the pivot. There would be "repeated explosions against repression" in Eastern Europe, he predicted, and "the Soviet Union itself is not immune to this reality." He and the pope had said as much to each other.

"I didn't cause this to happen," the pope would later say—at around the time when others began to guess at his singular role in the fall of communism. "The tree was already rotten. I just gave it a good shake and the rotten apples fell." Reagan would similarly insist that the Communist monolith was on the verge of implosion when he took office. Intolerable pressure had already built up from within; he had merely decided that the United States would apply additional moral and political force, hastening the inevitable. Doubtless the assessments of both men were right. But (as Mikhail Gorbachev would also soon recognize with regard to his own destiny) bureaucracies had to be overcome, basic instincts had to prevail over conventional wisdom, principle had to be asserted and upheld over comfort and convenience. Decisive actions had to be taken. The Reagan-Wojtyła summit cemented an understanding that each man would use the enormous power at his command to bring about in the world a fundamental change they both believed was intended by God: the eclipse of communism by Christian ideals.

President Reagan, the pope knew, had instant access to a kind of strategic (and covert) power that the Vatican lacked. Almost from its inception, Reagan believed that Solidarity was an elemental crack in the iron curtain and that Poland, the Polish pope, and Lech Wałęsa were the instruments that God had mysteriously chosen to shake the earth. He was determined to aid what he felt was a holy cause and instructed his deputies, especially after martial law was declared, to spare no effort or ingenuity in support of it. Immediately upon meeting the pope, he raised the subject of Walters's and Casey's visits and offered to send both men to the Holy See even more often—an offer the pope accepted on the spot. Moreover, Reagan declared, the United States was committed to keeping Solidarity alive, and he had already ordered more money and material to be funneled to the Solidarity underground.

Perhaps the greatest secret about the denouement of the cold war was that from shortly after the president's visit to the pope in 1982 until the Berlin Wall was dismantled in 1989, the United States government spent more than $50 million to keep the Solidarity movement alive. John Paul II, of course, was informed about the ambitious scope of this operation, conducted by the CIA (though he took care not to learn too many of its particular details).

Although intellectual opposites ("It's true that Ronald Reagan owned more horses than books," one of his aides once said), the pope and the president did find common ground. Both had been actors. Neither was moved quickly to anger. Both believed in the power of the symbolic act as well as in the role of divine Providence, particularly after both had been shot by assassins within six weeks of each other and survived. In the first minutes of their meeting both agreed that they had been saved by God to play a special role in the destiny of Eastern Europe. "Look at the evil forces that were put in our way and how Providence intervened," Reagan said, and the pope agreed.

Ronald Reagan's religiosity—like his evocation of the Evil Empire—has often been mocked or treated as evidence of cynicism or hypocrisy. (After all, he seldom attended church during his presidency). But those who knew him best had long understood and accepted the spiritual side of his character and the strength he drew from it.

His salvific Christianity was an essential part of his view of communism. He believed that the Union of Soviet Socialist Republics was fundamentally a Christian country, a part of Christian Europe. All the United States had to do was tip the balance toward Christianity and the USSR would revert to its natural Christian state. Ever since taking office he had wanted to talk to the pope about this, and about his overwhelming (some would say messianic) desire to bring about world peace. Knowing this, his wife, Nancy, had urged from the administration's earliest days that the pope be among the first foreign leaders the President met.

Very few people got Reagan right. Even after he left office, enjoying enormous popular affection yet held in considerable derision, he and his presidency remained a mass of contradictions, complexities, and myths. He was a believer in disarmament who presided over the costliest defense buildup in American history (with devastating effect on his country's economy), positive that he would be able to convince the Soviets of the futility of the arms race—which he did.

Widely perceived as absentminded and forgetful, he had a fine memory for odd pieces of information that interested him and a fascination for covert operations. Once he asked Casey, "What about the speedboats?" referring to a briefly considered and long-forgotten plan to use such craft to get printing supplies into Poland. "Special [covert] operations were a subject he understood," says Richard Pipes, who discussed them often with the president.

In the popular and journalistic imagination, his foreign policy became (understandably) identified largely with the Iran-Contra affair, an operation totally consistent with the darker character of his administration. Yet it was the Communist monolith of Europe—the Evil Empire, as he called it—that from his first days in the White House consumed his interest and attention.

In response to a question about the Soviets at his first press conference, Reagan said, "The only morality they recognize is what will further their cause, meaning they reserve unto themselves the right to commit any crime, to lie, to cheat." This response horrified Al Haig, the secretary of state, who saw his mission as improving East-West relations over the long haul. Haig was intent on drawing a line against the Communists in the Americas, on challenging and combating "Soviet proxies" in Central America and the Caribbean, and on "going to the source"—Cuba. And indeed, the parallel anti-Marxist goals of the United States and the Vatican were already being pursued in Central America. Reagan's gaze, however, was fixed on the lines drawn at Yalta in 1945, which he considered the most fundamental political fact of his adulthood and which he hoped to erase.

In February 1981, the pope had made a speech about the "artificial divisions" of Europe created at Yalta. At their Vatican summit, Reagan now raised the subject, and the two agreed that there was no reason to honor this "illegitimate concept," as Wojtyła called it. Europe was one entity. "We both felt a great mistake had been made at Yalta and something should be done,"

Reagan said many years later. "Solidarity was the very weapon for bringing this about."

"The Holy Father knew his people," noted the apostolic delegate in Washington, Archbishop Pio Laghi. "It was a very complex situation. How to insist on human rights in Poland, on religious freedom, and keep Solidarity alive without provoking the Communist authorities further. But [before the president's trip] I told Vernon [Walters], 'Listen to the Holy Father. We have two thousand years' experience at this.'" At the moment, the pope was still despondent over the current state of affairs in Poland, remarking to Reagan that his object was simply to open talks with the government so that Solidarity's gains could somehow be protected and martial law ended. Of late, he had noted small signs that Jaruzelski might be willing to enter into tentative discussions of some kind with the Church.

Reagan felt certain that the Communists had made a huge miscalculation in imposing martial law, that after allowing Solidarity to operate openly for sixteen months the authorities would only alienate the population further by cracking down. Reagan had always said that communism would eventually collapse from within. As he imagined it, first the people of the Soviet empire and then their leaders would come to see the error of their ways. As it turned out, he was right.

"His strength lay in understanding the crisis and vulnerability of the [whole] system, which all the academics were telling him was stable and solid and popular," said Richard Pipes. "And he would buy none of this. And that took a lot of courage . . . against the Allies, the Department of State." One person he didn't have to argue with was John Paul II, who eventually came to a very sophisticated understanding of Reagan's character and objectives. Surely the pope would have put more skeptical distance between himself and almost any other president or American administration, had he not been dealing with a leader as unconventional and charismatic as Ronald Reagan— or as generous with the gift of U.S. covert capabilities.

As former UN ambassador Jeanne Kirkpatrick noted, Reagan, in turn, saw the pope as a heroic figure, "an extraordinary man, learned and courageous, an indomitable kind of figure who had demonstrated this, and was really committed against Soviet control of Eastern Europe." He wanted to assure the pope that his intentions were good, that the media portrait of him as a dangerous warmonger was altogether wrong, and that lasting peace was the ultimate goal of his policies. From his first days in office, Reagan had also wanted to make it clear to Brezhnev that peace and disarmament were at the top of his agenda. This too had frightened Haig, who concluded that the only thing standing between the president's naiveté and the Soviets' cunning was himself. But at their first meeting the pope urged the president to pursue his own basic instincts in a search for peace.

"It wasn't very often that the president had the bit between his teeth on anything," Haig observed years later. "But he was steadfast in his assessment of the Soviet Union: He believed that if some particularly talented communicator could ever sit down with them, they would join us in a world order that would remove nuclear weapons from the earth and bring about a convergence of our mutual policies—and he literally believed that. I spent all my time implementing that conception, but I didn't share it.

"When I really saw the real Ronald Reagan, he handed me a draft of a letter to Brezhnev. He and Nancy [Reagan] had composed a letter that was weak-kneed. Had I been in the Kremlin I'd have laughed all the way to the bank. It was the most naive supplication of the two of them getting together and banning weapons of self-destruction. He thought he could sit down with any Soviet leader, from the beginning. And when I left, after eighteen months, he sent the letter. It took him two years and the Reykjavík summit before you saw the true Ronald Reagan and his assessment of Moscow: the height of naivete."

Within weeks of Reagan's visit with the pope, the letter to Brezhnev had been sent—and Haig (for many reasons) was gone. Flying in the face of American intelligence's best estimates of Soviet economic might, Reagan trusted his own instincts. He was certain that, as he told John Paul II, once the Soviets saw they could not keep pace with United States nuclear policies—particularly the introduction of cruise missiles in Europe and new anti-missile technology in the United States—they would sue for peace and disarmament.

"I couldn't believe that they were as strong as they were supposed to be in that kind of an economy," Reagan explained after he had left office. "How could you think that this was a solid economy when less than one family in seven owns an automobile, and if you set out to buy one you have to wait ten years for delivery? . . . When you see all of these news shots on the streets full of automobiles in the Soviet Union, those are government-owned automobiles that are provided to the bureaucrats." He pointed this out to the pope. If some of his formulations could be ridiculously simplistic, he nonetheless believed his own rhetoric, especially about the Communists.

"At this present moment in the history of the world," the pope said in his formal remarks after his meeting with the president, "the United States is called, above all, to fulfill its mission in the service of world peace. The very condition of the world today calls for a farsighted policy that will favor those indispensable conditions of justice and freedom, of truth and love that are the foundations for lasting peace."

Later the pope confided to Cardinals Casaroli and Silvestrini that he was moved and heartened by the private assurances Reagan had given him that he would pursue such a course. Reagan had spoken more about the Soviet people than the Soviet leaders, and this had also impressed John Paul II. Reagan had convinced him that he *was* a disarmer, that he believed nuclear weapons should be abolished, not just reduced in number.

The president's public remarks were intended for the Soviets: The administration, he said, would not withdraw its sanctions against the USSR or Poland until martial law was ended, political prisoners were freed, and dialogue had been resumed between the Polish government, the Church, and "the Solidarity movement that speaks for the vast majority of Poles."

The Vatican summit would be remembered by journalists mainly because Reagan fell asleep during the closing ceremonies. But in the mere fifty minutes that the pope and the president had been together, these leaders of two superpowers with quite different agendas had found important common ground.

CENTRAL AMERICA

The CIA's code name for the Roman Catholic Church of Central America was "the Entity." The Entity figured large in the Reagan administration's designs for fighting communism and Marxist-tinged movements in the Americas.

The administration had decided in its earliest days that the Marxist-leaning Sandinista government of Nicaragua must be overthrown. To carry out its plans, William Casey's CIA was funding a four-thousand-man "Contra" army, most of them partisans of the old Somoza oligarchy, supplanted by the Sandinistas in 1979 after almost forty years of U.S.-supported dictatorship.

In December 1982, responding to the overwhelming will of Congress, President Reagan had little choice but to sign legislation prohibiting the CIA and Defense Department from furnishing military equipment, training, or support to anyone "for the purpose of overthrowing the Government of Nicaragua." By law, the CIA was thereafter limited to trying to stop the flow of arms from the Sandinistas to rebels in neighboring El Salvador. However, neither Casey nor the president intended to be deterred by such legalisms, and the administration sought other means of funding and aiding the Contras—eventually leading to the Iran-Contra scandal.

With the administration restrained from operating freely in Nicaragua, the role of its principal moral and political ally in the country—the established Roman Catholic Church, the Entity—became ever more important.

But there was another Catholic Church in Nicaragua as well, the "Church of the People," which was aligned with the Sandinistas. Like the regime itself, this "popular church" commanded widespread support, especially among the poor. In 1981 the CIA began secretly funneling money to the senior officials of the established Church. The money was particularly useful in helping the Entity expand the operations of its Nicaraguan radio station and newspaper, both of which served as platforms for opposition to the Sandinista government.

When the Sandinistas accused the Nicaraguan archbishop Miguel Obando y Bravo (who had once warily supported their rebel movement as the only way to effectively oppose the Somoza oligarchy) of being a paid CIA agent, the Church adamantly denied the charges. Obando was not an "agent," but rather had come to be regarded by the CIA as one of its principal "assets," eager after Wojtyła's election to cooperate in agency-sponsored efforts to discredit the Sandinistas. According to Admiral John Poindexter, deputy director of the National Security Council at the time, "We would brief the bishops [in Nicaragua] on what we thought the Nicaraguan government was going to do, and what we thought the leftist organizations in El Salvador [where established church bishops also received funds] were up to. This would be done directly with the bishop in Nicaragua." Archbishop Obando was depicted in a cartoon in *La Barricada*, the Sandinista newspaper, twisting a cross into a Nazi swastika.

When senior members of congressional intelligence committees discovered early in 1983 that at least $25,000 in CIA funds had reached Obando's archbishopric, they were horrified, and—fearing public disclosure that would discredit both the Vatican and the United States—called Casey to the carpet. The CIA director dutifully pledged to cease paying priests and bishops from the agency's appropriations.

Soon after, Casey summoned a deputy, Alan D. Fiers, into his office and ordered him to "find another way to get it done." Fiers went to Lieutenant Colonel Oliver North at the White House, a member of the NSC staff, who gave him several thousand dollars to keep the cash pipeline to the Church open. Thereafter, Fiers arranged with a private contractor doing CIA business to overcharge the agency for legitimate work. The overage was then passed on by the contractor to a CIA agent in Nicaragua, who in turn arranged delivery to the Entity. It is unknown how many hundreds of thousands—or perhaps millions—of dollars reached the Entity through covert means during the Reagan years, but Wojtyła's Church became the administration's principal ideological ally in the struggle against the Sandinistas.

Meanwhile the popular church, without massive injections of cash but with support from much of the populace, was proving a powerful force. Moreover, Catholic clergymen from all over Latin America had moved to

Nicaragua to work with the Sandinista government, after years of the Somoza regime's oppression. Fearing that the popular church might prove too strong a counterforce to U.S. interests in Central America, particularly in Nicaragua and El Salvador, Casey and William Clark kept encouraging a papal visit to Nicaragua. They suggested to Pio Laghi, the papal representative in Washington, that the pope should demonstrate unequivocally that he stood with his bishops against the popular church; they also conveyed how important it was to the United States that John Paul II not condemn the Contras—revered by Reagan as "freedom fighters"—or Washington's covert war against the Sandinistas and its military aid to the government of El Salvador. Casey had also discussed these matters with Cardinal Krol.

"We shared an interest in discouraging Communist beachheads in this hemisphere," notes Jeanne Kirkpatrick, the UN ambassador under Reagan. "The pope is very anti-Communist; and he had a worldview not dissimilar to those of us in the Reagan administration about communism." As the pope prepared to travel to Central America in March 1983, both Vice President George Bush and Secretary of State George Shultz spoke out about what they described as Catholic support for Marxist revolutionary movements in Central America. Their statements drew a letter of protest from the U.S. bishops, who said the issues in Central America were not purely political, much less military, but essentially "human, moral issues" and that the Church's involvement "reflect[ed] its conscious 'option for the poor.' "

"The question of the popular church was very much an issue," Kirkpatrick says. "And the Vatican, including the pope and all his representatives, shared the view that the popular church denies effectively the authority of the pope. And that wasn't welcome. By us or the Vatican."

This then was the highly charged atmosphere that the pope entered when his plane landed in Managua on March 4, 1983. As far as the Reagan administration was concerned, "the pope was in Nicaragua to provide an alternative Catholic rallying point," according to Kirkpatrick. "And we encouraged this."

. . .

As the pope left Rome, President Reagan warned that if El Salvador fell to leftist rebels, other nations in the hemisphere would follow. He announced plans to increase the number of military advisers in El Salvador and to provide an additional $60 million in arms shipments to the Salvadoran army.

"If they get a foothold, with Nicaragua already there [in the hands of pro-Marxists], and El Salvador should fall as a result of this armed violence on the part of the guerillas, I think Costa Rica, Honduras, Panama, all of those would follow," Reagan predicted. All five of the countries he named—as well as Guatemala and Haiti—were on the pope's itinerary.

But the pope's words on the eve of his Lenten departure from Rome gave little hint that his journey was endowed with geopolitical meaning; in fact, they were disturbing to the administration's foreign policy architects, who were left unsure whether they could count on John Paul II to deliver the strong message they were hoping for.

"It is precisely that reality in which you are living that moved me to undertake this journey," the pope said in his message to the people of the Central American nations he would visit, "to be closer to you, children of the Church and of countries of Christian roots, who suffer intensely and who are experiencing the scourges of division, war, hatred, social injustice, ideological confrontations that beset the world and that expose to conflict innocent populations yearning for peace."

As usual, the pope had many audiences to reach. His words—and his itinerary—reflected concern not only with Rome's contest with the popular church, but also with fundamentalist Protestant sects that were evangelizing in Central America at a rate that was alarming the established Catholic Church.

. . .

The old man in blue jeans and paramilitary beret was a Trappist monk. He had a full beard, flowing locks, and childlike eyes. He loved poetry and dreamed, as he said, that the revolution would bring the people "bread and roses." He was waiting to be blessed by the pope. His name was Ernesto Cardenal and he was Nicaragua's minister of culture. At the Managua airport, as John Paul II greeted members of the Sandinista government, Father Ernesto quickly doffed his black beret, knelt down as the pope approached him, and seized the pope's hand to kiss it. But John Paul II quickly withdrew it, flushed red, raised his right index finger, and scolded him: "You must straighten yourself out with the Church; you must straighten out your position with the Church." Then, to avoid any contact with the minister-monk, the pope joined his hands, bent his head slightly, and moved on.

The Sandinista junta, led by Daniel Ortega and legitimized by popular elections, had initiated a broad program of social reform: free health care, a campaign against illiteracy, agrarian reform, and opportunities for housing ownership. The Sandinistas deliberately avoided the Soviet model of nationalization, but in their foreign policy they supported guerrilla organizations in El Salvador and maintained close military and economic ties with Cuba. Five members of the junta, including Father Ernesto, were Catholic clergymen or members of religious orders. The Vatican had insisted on their resignation from the government as a condition for the pope's visit. Then the demand had been withdrawn when the Sandinistas refused to capitulate, but John Paul II still wished the clergy to give up their civic positions or their religious status. Hence his rebuke to Father Ernesto.

The whole visit, from the moment of the pope's arrival, took place in a heated political context. "Between Christianity and the revolution, there is no contradiction," Sandinista supporters shouted at John Paul II after he had rebuffed Cardenal. Their words echoed Ortega's initial greeting to the pope at the airport: "Our experience shows that one can be both a believer and a revolutionary and that no unsalvageable contradiction exists between the two."

The junta leader continued by attacking the policies of the Reagan administration and reciting a bitter history of seven U.S. military interventions in his country. He quoted a letter from the bishop of León to an American bishop in 1921, at a time when Nicaragua was occupied by U.S. troops: "You haven't wept in pain," the Nicaraguan bishop wrote, "to see the flag of conquest flying on the spires of your cathedrals. . . . You haven't had your sanctuary turned into an armed camp, and the altar where the eucharistic bread is broken turned into a table where rations are handed out."

The pope listened without any visible show of interest. Nor did he respond to Ortega's other assertion at the airport: that over the past three years, 375 Nicaraguans had died from "outside aggression," including seventeen young people—killed by the Contras—buried only two days earlier.

John Paul II said only that he wanted to contribute "to ending the suffering of innocent people in this part of the world, to ending the bloody conflicts, hate and sterile accusations, leaving room for genuine dialogue."

But the Sandinistas weren't seeking dialogue. They wanted a cease-fire.

The conflict between the Church and the state echoed all the way to the altar. Saluting the crowd with clenched fists, the members of the Sandinista junta marched up to their seats at the open-air mass where half a million people were waiting in the vast space of July Nineteenth Square. Behind the altar a huge mural depicted Augusto César Sandino and other fallen Revolutionary heroes.

Archbishop Obando y Bravo had chosen a passage from the Gospel of St. John to be read by one of his priests: "I am the good shepherd. The good shepherd lays down his life for the sheep. He who is a hireling and not a shepherd, whose own the sheep are not, sees the wolf coming and leaves the sheep and flees; and the wolf snatches them and scatters them" (John 10:11–12). The priest declaimed the verses with an intonation and gestures that made it clear that the Gospel was alluding to the most current of current events, that Archbishop Obando y Bravo was the good shepherd and the Sandinistas were the fierce wolves. Sandinista militants and leftist Catholics began to grumble loudly.

John Paul II's homily was unusually harsh. It focused exclusively on the duty of submitting to the teachings of the pope and the bishops, even at the cost of renouncing one's own ideas. He attacked the people's church and ordered the faithful to obey their bishops.

"In effect, the unity of the Church is questioned when the powerful factors that constitute and maintain it—faith itself, the revealed word, the sacraments, obedience to the bishops and the pope, the sense of common vocation and responsibility in the task of Christ on earth—are opposed by earthly considerations, unacceptable ideological commitments, and temporal options, including the conception of a church which replaces the true one."

It was "absurd and dangerous to imagine that outside—if not to say against—the Church built around the bishops there should be another church, conceived only as 'charismatic,' and not institutional; 'new' and not traditional; alternative, and, as it has been called recently, a people's church." Hundreds of thousands cheered as he condemned government efforts to limit religious education and attempts to divide the Church.

Amid steady applause from a large contingent of nuns placed to the right of the altar, John Paul II insisted that for the sake of Church unity it was better "to forswear one's own ideas, one's own projects, one's own commitments, even the good ones." That remark provoked loud protests from the front rows of the audience. "We want peace," the Sandinistas and their supporters began to shout. "Popular power!" The pope, visibly irritated, called out "Silence!" once and then again, and again. Finally he raised his voice and declared, "The Church is the first to want peace."

He said not a specific word about the country's political situation, no mention of U.S. involvement, of the Contra war. When the pope launched yet another assault on Marxism, claiming that the Church's teaching had to be "free from the distortions due to ideologies or political platforms," the young Sandinistas in charge of crowd control began shouting, "Power to the people! Power to the people!" Others took up the chant for a full minute. In those sixty seconds, the area closest to the altar became bedlam. "Only one Church," yelled those of the right wing. "The church of the people," bellowed the leftists. In the shadows of dusk, his figure illuminated by a spotlight, John Paul II lifted his voice to make himself heard. At the audio console, government technicians spun the dials in a kind of surrealistic show—now cutting the pope's voice, now amplifying it, mixing the shouts of the activists with the cadences of Wojtyła. Farther back in the huge audience, there was confusion about what was happening. Decorum dissolved as the pope finished his remarks.

At the airport before the pope flew off to Costa Rica, Ortega explained that people had shouted for peace because "our people are martyred and crucified every day, and we demand solidarity with right on our side."

Meanwhile, the secretariat of the bishops of Central America issued a communiqué inviting prayers in "reparation for the profaning of the mass."

John Paul II likewise defined the episode as a profanation of the Eucharist and called for prayers for "the true Christians of Nicaragua."

So President Reagan and his aides could be confident: the pope's commitment to a course parallel to White House interests was secure. In El Salvador, Costa Rica, Guatemala, and Haiti for the next week, John Paul II would hew to an anti-Marxist line, avoiding departures that might be disturbing to the Reagan administration. In El Salvador, where Archbishop Oscar Arnulfo Romero had been assassinated in 1980 on orders of the Salvadoran military intelligence command because of his opposition to the brutality of the regime, the pope tamely praised him as a "zealous pastor," not as a martyr who had died like St. Stanisław. John Paul II would speak out for human rights—especially in Guatemala—but not against the authoritarian regimes that opposed communism. The American formula that Vernon Walters had outlined to Wojtyła for dealing with such regimes—encouraging a transition to democracy while seeking to block leftist forces aligned with Cuba or the USSR—was now the Vatican's policy as well.

THE GOLDEN CAGE

As comfortable as Karol Wojtyła felt taking up the role of world traveler, he felt equally uncomfortable in his other major role—Vatican bureaucrat. As much as he relished roaming the world as the central actor in a global spectacle, he hated being cooped up in the Vatican overseeing curial activities. In fact, his happiest times were undoubtedly those moments when he could steal away from the Apostolic Palace, unnoticed, in a black limousine with a discreet police escort, and head for the mountains of the Abruzzi.

If it was wintertime, he enjoyed his favorite sport, skiing. "He moves like a swallow," gushed Italian president Sandro Pertini, who accompanied the pope on one of his outings. Professor Jacek Woźniakowski, an old Kraków friend, offered a more sober assessment of Wojtyła's skiing skills: "He was always on the heavy side. He zigzags down, not especially fast or gracefully, but very competently."

John Paul II had a need for open spaces. Even back in Kraków he was known for not liking administrative chores and for escaping from the archbishop's palace whenever possible to hike in the woods or visit distant parishes. In the Vatican, his sense of being locked up only worsened after the assassination attempt. Before Agca's bullet, Wojtyła had at least managed to go on occasional long walks in the Vatican gardens. But the massive post-assassination mobilization of security personnel eventually brought an end even to these strolls. Now all life came to a screeching halt as the pontiff approached, something he found deeply bothersome. "It's a cage, a golden cage," he told a Roman monsignor, speaking of the Apostolic Palace.

His mentor Tyranowski had taught him to live every day to the fullest, and the pope's grueling schedule became evidence of how well he had learned his lesson. When his alarm clock goes off at five-thirty A.M. the pope gets up—though in the later years of his pontificate, he admits, with some difficulty—shaves, and dresses (all in white—boxer shorts, undershirt, socks, shirt with French cuffs, and cassock). His gold pectoral cross goes on last. Angelo Gugel, the valet he inherited from his predecessor, doesn't show up before breakfast: John Paul II insists that Gugel spend the early morning hours with his family.

Leaving his bedroom with its unadorned single bed (in which John Paul I died) and two straight-backed upholstered chairs, the pope begins his seventeen-hour workday. A typical day's schedule goes like this:

6:15 Solitary prayer in the papal chapel
7:00 Mass with fifteen to twenty guests, aides, and nuns from the papal household
7:30 Ten minutes of solitary prayer after others leave the chapel
8:00 Working breakfast in dining room with aides and guests
9:00 To private study to review schedule, read, and write for two hours
11:00 Nonstop formal audiences in the papal library with visiting bishops, foreign dignitaries, and guests

1:30 Working lunch in papal dining room

3:00 Fifteen-minute nap in armchair

3:15 Meditation while strolling on the terrace of the Apostolic Palace

4:00 Paperwork in study

6:00 Meetings with individual members of the Curia and Vatican staff

7:30 Supper—generally another working meal

9:00 Return to study for writing and reading

10:30 Prayer in the chapel

11:30 To bed

On Wednesdays the schedule calls for a general audience in Nervi Hall in the Vatican or, when the weather is fine, in St. Peter's Square. There he addresses thousands of the faithful on topics he considers especially urgent. Unlike his predecessors, John Paul II takes his responsibilities as bishop of Rome very seriously. On Sundays he often visits one of the 323 Roman parish churches. The week before, he will have invited the pastor of that parish to be a guest at his table and will have heard from him about the problems of his parish and its parishioners.

The workload of modern popes has always been heavy. The willingness of both Pius XII and Paul VI to slave away at their desks was legendary, but they were, by nature, Church administrators, insiders used to governing by pushing paper. John Paul II's peripatetic and absolutely personal style of administration stunned the members of the Roman Curia. It was through human relationships, not bureaucratic methods, that he meant, from the first, to rule the Church universal. Morning mass, for example, became an occasion for staying close to the faithful from all over the world. No one in the Curia could recall seeing the papal chapel so crowded day after day. The pope even used the occasion to brush up his language skills, often celebrating mass in the native tongue of his guests, even Korean and Japanese. After mass, John Paul II, usually joined by guests, takes not a light continental breakfast but enjoys an abundant Polish spread: ham, sausage, cheese, coffee, and sometimes eggs, preferably served soft-boiled, in a glass.

Wojtyła has also introduced the Curia to the working lunch. This is the main way the pope keeps in touch with his staff as well as with the bishops from throughout the world who come to Rome every five years for their traditional *ad limina* visits. Lunch at the pope's table has meant an unparalleled chance for most of the Church's four thousand bishops to talk to their pope in a fairly relaxed setting. The dining room is extremely simple, the atmosphere quiet and unassuming. There is an expandable table and, against the wall, a sideboard displaying some of the pope's Polish souvenirs. There is also a TV set where John Paul II sometimes catches a few minutes of the news, just enough to hear the lead stories of the day. Occasionally he will take in a soccer match.

Wojtyła has never paid much attention to food. Lunch, the principal meal of the day, consists of a first course (pasta if most of the guests are Italian, otherwise soup or an appetizer) followed by meat or fish with cheese. Wine is always served, and the pope often drinks half a glass or, more rarely, a beer. Whiskey may be served at meal's end, but only to guests. Mealtimes are not about gastronomy. Instead, the diners may join the pope in detailed discussions of plans for upcoming trips, or he will query the bishop of a diocese he plans to visit, or everyone at the table will consider the situation of the clergy, which always worries the pope. "Are the priests on good terms with the bishops?" he may ask his guest. "Are they obedient?"

In fact, John Paul II often leaves his plate almost untouched in his eagerness to ask questions. Appearing engrossed, he often looks away as if to concentrate better, or sometimes he leans on the table, his head in his hands, seemingly lost in another world as conversation swirls around him.

At mealtimes he also may tackle complicated doctrinal issues. When in the midst of preparing encyclicals or other important documents, he has taken up the habit of inviting Cardinal Ratzinger and his co-workers at the Congregation for the Doctrine of the Faith to lunch to follow up on discussions begun in the papal study. The cardinals tend to feel more comfortable speaking with the pope in this informal setting. "Especially if six or seven cardinals are invited, we talk with greater ease about certain topics, about problems facing the Church," says Cardinal Silvio Oddi, who for many years was prefect of the Congregation for the Clergy. "On these occasions the pope expresses his thoughts very clearly."

In turning lunches into symposia John Paul II has also carried on a tradition that he started at Kraków—of inviting scientists, economists, entrepreneurs, politicians, humanitarians, writers, and artists to discuss their areas of expertise; invitees may cover an impressive range of subjects, from philosophy to mathematics to quantum physics. In the summer at Castel Gandolfo he has organized similar meetings. Every other year an informal two-day seminar, attended by social scientists of every religious and philosophical stripe, gathers there with the pope in attendance.

During summer vacations at Castel Gandolfo John Paul II indulges in another of his favorite sports, swimming. It's been an important outlet for the pent-up energies of this latter-day "prisoner of the Vatican," but it gives him nothing like the sense of freedom he used to feel when he swam in Poland's lakes and then stretched out on the shore, covering his head with a big red handkerchief if the sun was too hot, laughing and joking with his friends and their children.

If there is one thing the pope has missed in the Vatican, it has been contact with children. He has always shown an enormous tenderness with children and teenagers. Professor Woźniakowski of Kraków describes how young Bishop Wojtyła would come to his home and roughhouse with his children on the carpet amid bursts of riotous laughter. Whenever he feels truly trapped and homesick, John Paul II invites over some of his old Polish cronies to unwind with him. Father Maczyński, the director of the Polish College in Rome, makes the pope laugh by doing impressions in a Russian, Polish, or Yiddish accent. Father Tischner, professor of social ethics in Lublin, is well known for his slightly risqué jokes. At Christmas and New Year's John Paul II likes to join the Polish nuns and other Polish guests in singing traditional carols. His specialty is rounds.

However ill at ease the pope may have initially seemed with bureaucratic strictures, members of the Curia quickly realized that he had an enormous capacity for work. The speeches he planned for his travels were routinely finished two months ahead of time. His yearly letter to priests on Holy

Thursday may well be written by November, to be delivered the following March or April. He is still a voracious reader, using every free moment, often while airborne, to catch up on books on history, anthropology, science, or the works of some great national poet or writer from a country he may be headed toward.

Upon arriving in his study after breakfast, the pope starts work by scanning two piles of press clippings put together by the Secretariat of State and his press spokesman, Joaquín Navarro-Valls. Twice a day the Secretariat of State sends him a black leather mailbag crammed with letters, files, draft reports from various Vatican departments, and documents awaiting his signature or approval. Methodically he plows his way through them. The first bundle arrives around one P.M., when aides from the Secretariat of State collect the paperwork he has finished the night before and that morning. Another black bag arrives around five-thirty in the afternoon, to be worked through in the evening.

The study where the pope does most of his writing—usually in Polish, in longhand or sometimes through dictation to a secretary—is part of the pope's private residence on the third floor of the Apostolic Palace. It is a simple room, dominated by a large, austere wooden desk, with a high-backed armchair on either side, covered in beige plush. On the desk are a small golden clock, a crucifix, and a matching desk set—blotter, holder for pens, and notepad. The pope's old white telephone, still with a rotary dial, is on a low table to the right of his chair. On the wall hangs an icon and a picture of the Madonna. The floor is carpeted with a simple Oriental rug. The study's window commands a vast Roman panorama. It is from this window that at noon on Sundays the pope prays the Angelus with the faithful gathered in St. Peter's Square below. From his desk, however, John Paul II can see only the sky. In any case, heavy curtains are often drawn while the pope works.

In this room, whose modesty always surprises visitors (particularly when compared with the great loggia on the second floor with its beautiful painted ceilings), the pope receives heads of the curial departments. These audiences follow a regular schedule: Mondays and Wednesdays it's the turn of the secretary of state (who has unlimited access to the pope, in any event). Under

John Paul I, the Secretariat of State definitively became the supreme body responsible for implementing the pope's decisions and coordinating the various departments of the Roman Curia. "We are the shadow of the pope," says Cardinal Angelo Sodano, appointed secretary of state in 1991. "He is the sole protagonist, and we all follow him and work for him." On Tuesdays the pope receives the Monsignore Sostituto, the second in command in the curial hierarchy, and on Wednesdays the Vatican minister of foreign affairs.

At six-thirty on Friday evenings, whenever he is in Rome, John Paul II meets before dinner with the prefect of the Congregation for the Doctrine of the Faith, which is responsible for all matters relating to official Catholic teaching and Church discipline. Each Saturday John Paul II confers with Cardinal Bernardin Gantin, the prefect of the powerful Congregation for Bishops. Here, Church appointments are discussed and the pope informs the cardinal of his final choices to fill vacant positions. Unlike his predecessors, Wojtyła often does not accept candidates chosen through the regular bureaucratic procedure (a preliminary investigation by the nuncios, followed by selection at a plenary meeting of the cardinals from the congregation). Instead, he may choose someone he knows personally, someone whose views he feels fit better with his own convictions.

In Rome, John Paul II largely shuttles back and forth between the second and third floors of the Apostolic Palace. At eleven A.M. the pope takes the elevator to the *appartamento nobile,* his formal apartments, which make a stunning contrast to his private quarters. Heads of state and important personages to whom he has given an audience there have invariably been impressed by their magnificent and ancient frescoes and friezes. The same floor also houses the papal library with its exquisite displays of objets d'art, its Renaissance bookcases and tables, and its splendid Oriental carpets on patterned marble floors. It is there that he often gives formal receptions for high-ranking visitors from foreign countries.

After supper the pope again goes upstairs, where he works until bedtime. His only relief is an hour-long stroll on the terrace, which he takes even in winter. As the years go by, it has become an increasingly common sight to see him praying and meditating on the terrace or in his chapel. Not far from the prie-dieu in the chapel, he has had a low table set up where he keeps letters from the faithful, who write him about their personal problems, asking for his prayers, or documents of his papacy for which he thinks it necessary to seek extra inspiration from God.

POLAND REDUX

No moment of his young papacy was as delicate, no problem as vexing, as the situation that faced Wojtyła in 1983 on his second trip to Poland. That winter had been an especially depressing one for Poles. Martial law seemed unrelenting. Dismissals, secret accusations, and acts of repression had poisoned the air. Many people, in despair, had given up and taken refuge in private life, creating the greatest baby boom in postwar Polish history.

The underground militants from Solidarity were having their own doubts—a general strike they called the previous November had failed dismally. The Polish Church was hewing to a very cautious line. The primate, Józef Glemp, worried endlessly that his priests might get involved in "extremist activities." The government, hemmed in by the Soviets, besieged by popular distrust, afraid of economic collapse, and facing an ongoing freeze on credits from the West, feared bloody uprisings like those of 1956, 1970, and 1976.

In such an atmosphere, the Church and the government approached the pope's arrival in a state of high tension. An agreement between the bishops and the government stipulated that the visit would be exclusively religious. The authorities in Warsaw insisted that the pope not mention the officially disbanded Solidarity. Jaruzelski himself had forbidden the pope to visit the Baltic cities of Gdańsk and Szczecin, the cradles of the Solidarity movement. A meeting between the pope and Wałęsa had been reluctantly granted only on the condition that it be kept strictly private. On the eve of his journey the pope commented that he would be arriving "at this sublime and difficult moment for my homeland." In an article entitled "Waiting for the Pope," the Warsaw underground weekly *Tygodnik Mazowsze* expressed the hope that John Paul's visit would "enable people to break through the barrier of despair, just as his 1979 visit broke through the barrier of fear." His actions on this journey, he was aware, would determine the way the Polish government dealt with martial law; they would send his countrymen a signal about whether to persevere or relent in their struggle; they would let the underground know whether it still had a champion in the Vatican; and they would determine whether Wałęsa continued to be a player or (as Primate Glemp hoped) part of Poland's past.

As he arrived on June 16, 1983, John Paul II did not hide his sadness at the condition of his country. It was evident in his first words at Warsaw's airport, after he had kissed the ground: "I ask those who suffer to be particularly close to me. I ask this in the words of Christ: I was sick, and you visited me. I was in prison and you came to me. I myself cannot visit all those in prison [the crowd gasped], all those who are suffering. But I ask them to be close to me in spirit to help me, just as they always do."

Later that same morning he held the first of two private meetings at Belweder Palace with Prime Minister Jaruzelski, sessions in which real negotiations finally began. The man who had crushed Solidarity looked stiff, correct, and expressionless as he greeted the pope. His pale face wasn't shielded by his usual dark glasses. His uniform gave him a certain patriotic elegance, but John Paul II noticed that when the general spoke, his right hand, which held his prepared remarks, trembled, and his left was clenched in a fist. Jaruzelski has since admitted that he felt extremely nervous and excited. Like every Pole brought up in the Catholic faith, he saw the pope as an almost mythic figure. "It was a very emotional moment," he said later about his first encounter with the pope. "I felt it was a great moment, [but] I noticed that he was rather cold toward me. He smiled at Professor Jabłoński [the Polish president, whom he knew], . . . while I was the man of martial law." When the time came for official speeches, the pope placed a microphone between himself and Jaruzelski, as if to distance himself as much as possible from the man in charge of martial law. Then the pope publicly addressed Jaruzelski and Jabłoński in a televised speech, asserting Poland's right to independence, "her proper place among the nations of Europe, between East and West." The path to true sovereignty and reform, he said, must take into account "social agreements stipulated by representatives of state authorities with representatives of the workers"—that is, the Gdańsk accords.

A few minutes later, pope, primate, Jabłoński, and Jaruzelski went to a small room, where immediately the pope raised the subject of martial law.

"He didn't deliver an ultimatum," Jaruzelski recalled. "He tried to convince, to persuade. He talked about the dignity of a human being. He said that the state must think of the individual, that dialogue is always needed, and that all trade unions have the right to exist."

"General," the pope told him, "for me the dissolution of the trade unions is more painful than the introduction of martial law in December 1981."

"I felt differently," the general said. He told the pope that the decision to impose martial law was "very dramatic for me, very painful; we were in a catastrophic situation which truly endangered Poland."

Jaruzelski had hoped that, with the Church in a position of unprecedented power (since the collapse of Solidarity, it had become the sole means of civic dialogue), the pope would, like Primate Glemp, seek to consolidate that power for the more limited objectives of the Church: new seminaries, access to the media, more church building, which was already proceeding at a pace that some critics found unseemly. More than two hundred permits for the construction of new churches had been issued since martial law began, while the country's economy and infrastructure continued to disintegrate.

"He didn't launch into any kind of polemics," Jaruzelski noted, but there was immediate and serious disagreement between the two on virtually every topic they discussed. Gradually the talks warmed somewhat on a personal level, though less rapidly on matters of substance. The general especially wanted the pope to "use his influence to help us isolate the most extreme wing within Solidarity [Wałęsa, KOR, and the underground], to help us lift the Western embargo, especially by the Americans."

"I am anxious to reach a certain state of normalcy as soon as possible," the pope declared, meaning, an end to martial law. "Then Poland will be regarded differently by other countries"—a reference to how the West could be persuaded to end its economic isolation of the country. The pope's message to the state was firm and unequivocal: The rights of the people must be restored; Solidarity must be reconstituted; martial law must end; eventually the Gdańsk accords must prevail. But he also took care not to offend the regime. He acknowledged its temporal power while charging it with moral responsibility. Nor did he say anything about the future of the churches and believers across Eastern Europe or (as in his first visit) proclaim the mission of the Slavic pope to unite all of Christian Europe.

Moscow followed John Paul II's arrival in Poland with reserve, but without visible threats or hysteria. The new Soviet leader, Yuri Andropov, had in fact ordered the Soviet media not to attack the pope. On the eve of his trip the newspaper *Sovietskaya Rossia* even published a remarkably favorable piece on the pontiff; lauding the pope's "position on halting the arms race, his support for the bishops of El Salvador and for a just solution of the conflict in the Middle East," which it claimed had "not only greatly irritated America but enraged Tel Aviv." Such deferential treatment by the Soviet press reflected, in part, Moscow's desire to defuse Western speculation about its involvement in the attempted assassination of the pope.

Over the next week, the pope honed a complex message. "Call good and evil by name," he preached at Częstochowa in perhaps the greatest homily of his pontificate. There, almost a million pilgrims waited expectantly for him to say the word *Solidarność*. But he didn't utter it in the manner expected by the huge gathering or by the Western press (which would spend much of the papal visit counting how many times he used the word). "It is up to you," he proclaimed, "to put up a firm barrier against demoralization," to assert the *"fundamental solidarity between human beings"*—something quite different from the Solidarity labor movement now crushed by the state.

On the first evening of the visit, tens of thousands of people had marched defiantly from the Warsaw cathedral past Communist Party headquarters, shouting "*Solidarność, Solidarność,* Lech Wałęsa, *Demokracja,* Independence," and already the authorities were on edge. Massive security forces had stood by. Now in the meadow at Jasna Góra, the Solidarity banner with its unmistakable red logo was flying everywhere. "You strengthen the students of Gdańsk," read one typical sign, with the word *students* spelled out in the familiar Solidarity script. Most of the crowd were young.

When the pope used the word *Solidarność,* the huge crowd responded with understanding and comprehension, not as a cheering throng but as a thoughtful community. "Mother of Jasna Góra," he appealed from the immense white and gold dais erected in front of the monastery fortress that shelters the Black Madonna of Częstochowa, "you who have been given us by Providence for the defense of the Polish nation, accept this call of Polish youth together with the Polish pope, and help us to *persevere in hope.*"

His idea, which he now passed on to a whole nation, was a variation of his own experience as a youth during the war: Victory was within. Spiritual victory forged from the suffering of their nation, the path of martyrdom, was possible. "Man is called to victory over himself," he declared. "It is the saints and the beatified who show us the path to victory that God achieves in human history." To achieve that victory requires "living in truth. . . . It means love of neighbor; it means fundamental solidarity between human beings." In a theme he repeated over and over in the following days, to the chagrin of the regime, he said that victory means "making an effort to be a person with a conscience, calling good and evil by name and not blurring them . . . developing in myself what is good, and seeking to correct what is evil by overcoming it in myself.

"You come to the Mother of Częstochowa with a wound in the heart, with sorrow, perhaps also with rage," he preached. "Your presence shows the force of a testimony, a witnessing which has stupefied the whole world: when the Polish worker made his own person the object of a demand, with the Gospel in his hand and a prayer on his lips. The images transmitted to the world in 1980 have touched hearts and consciences."

"Stay with us, stay with us," a million people in the meadow in front of the monastery chanted. They watched, spellbound, as he presented to the Virgin his bishop's cincture—with a hole in it from Ali Agca's bullet.

In his homily to another crowd of one million people in the steel town of Katowice (and to the Communist regime), he reiterated the basic rights of workers: "to a just salary," "to security," "to a day of rest." "Connected with the area of workers' rights is the question of trade unions," he said, "the right of free association," the right of all workers to form unions as "a mouthpiece for the struggle for social justice." Quoting the late Cardinal Wyszyński, he continued, "The state does not give us this right, it has only the obligation to protect and guard it. This right is given us by the Creator who made man as a social being." Each day his speeches alluded to these elements of the Gdańsk agreements.

He met privately with Lech Wałęsa on the last day of his visit, as well as with intellectuals who were secretly in contact with the Solidarity underground. He received from them copies of underground newspapers.

After eighteen months of martial law, Solidarity was no longer a mass organization of labor, with membership cards and a list of workplace demands. The state had destroyed that body, and its resurrection seemed almost inconceivable. But with the pope's second visit, Solidarity became an idea, a consciousness, a set of values, even a way of life "*in* solidarity." As such it would be no less a challenge to the state because in calling good and evil by name, in living in truth, in sharing communal values, the passivity that the pope had discussed with Geremek and his fellow intellectuals in the Vatican in 1981 would become a thing of the past.

Meanwhile, there existed a small but functional Solidarity underground whose leaders had met secretly with the pope's representative, Father Adam Boniecki, during preparations for the visit—an unmistakable sign that Wojtyła wanted them to persevere. Despite the fact that Solidarity's underground organization was initially weak, a support and supply network was developing with concerted help from the Catholic Church, the Western labor movement, and (unbeknownst to the underground) the CIA. This network was vital to internees, to members in hiding, and to their families. In addition, the underground had found a practical niche in which Solidarity could continue to function, inspire, and even flourish, and that was in publishing *samizdat* newspapers, magazines, factory bulletins, and in covert broadcasting. The CIA spent generously in this area (about eight million dollars in 1982–1983 alone), sponsoring activities that the government proved unable to smother. Printers were growing ever more skilled at covert publishing techniques and technology. One reporter counted 250 underground publications nationwide in August 1982. With large infusions of cash and the covert delivery of tons of equipment (the first fax machines in Poland, photocopying machines, inks), some 1,600 periodicals were soon in operation. William Casey had personally convinced Sweden's socialist prime minister, Olaf

Palme, to secretly allow Swedish ports, ships, and stevedores to be used for smuggling equipment to the underground. When Solidarity appeared to be doomed after martial law, Radio Free Europe, the Voice of America, Vatican Radio, and Solidarity's own underground transmitters (supplied by the CIA) punctuated the airwaves with messages from the underground, to the consternation of the authorities.* Thus Solidarity was surviving, its members living a jack-in-the-box existence, popping up with calls for resistance in print and at unexpected moments in unexpected places (even in rare pirate transmissions that interrupted programming on state-run television).

Before his trip, the pope had dispatched Father Adam Boniecki, editor of the Polish edition of *L'Osservatore Romano,* to meet with leaders of the underground and convey his gratitude and admiration. Boniecki, said Wiktor Kulerski, a Solidarity activist, "took down every bit of information concerning life underground, the activities we engaged in, the strategy we tried to carry out. . . . In these talks, there was something that really concerned him: He didn't want Solidarity to move toward the use of force. On this we were in complete agreement; and we told Boniecki that the movement underground was above all oriented toward the creation of a civil society and that its activity was aimed at building up the so-called social conscience so that citizens would not always obey all official orders—[through] nonviolent civil disobedience and also the creation of an independent culture and education." This too was a way of calling good and evil by name.

Kulerski said that through Boniecki, who brought a bound volume of all the copies of the underground weekly *Tygodnik Mazowsze* back to the pope, the underground was "certain of the pope's interest . . . and approval, and understanding. . . . More than once Boniecki said that the pope is anxious to get the information he brings him from Poland and that he [Boniecki] would like to have more facts, more information to pass on to the pope."

.   .   .

* Radio Free Europe and Voice of America were also used to send coded messages to the underground about deliveries of equipment and other matters, despite U.S. laws forbidding such activity.

The pope had four separate audiences to address during his visit—the people, the episcopate, the government, and the remnants of Solidarity—and all, even eventually the Communist leaders of Poland, were inspired to action by him.

At the close of his visit, the pope and Jaruzelski met again, this time alone face to face for more than an hour and a half at the Wawel, "a place of great symbolic importance," as Jaruzelski noted. The meeting, unscheduled, had been requested the night before by the pope.

The pope stunned Jaruzelski with his directness: "I understand that socialism as a political system is a reality," he said, "but the point is that it ought to have a human face."

The pope always spoke "in terms of human rights or civil rights," the general noted. "And when we discussed rights we naturally mean[t] democracy. If there is democracy, then you have elections; if you have elections, then you have power. But he never put it that way. It showed his great culture and diplomacy, because in substance he used words and phrases that you couldn't argue with. Because if he had said, 'You have to share power with Solidarność,' we would have argued about it, naturally. But when one simply mentions human rights, it's such a general term, such a general notion, that you can have a constructive discussion, which eventually brought us [the regime] closer to that goal without losing face. It's significant that soon after the pope's visit in 1983 martial law was lifted."

· · ·

Primate Glemp longed to see the strength of the Polish Church renewed, not squandered on a hopeless campaign for the demands and prerogatives of Solidarity. In Kraków, with the approval of the primate, a vicar was ordered to remove an altar dedicated to Solidarity inside his church and to stop worker education meetings held in the vestry. Many parish priests throughout the country, however, had been surprisingly forthright in their criticism of the primate and in their support both for the underground and for the broad program of "social renewal" that Solidarity represented.

During the pope's visit the episcopate had failed to schedule any meeting between the pope and Polish intellectuals who were in touch with the underground. Only after Father Boniecki brought back word of the underground's disappointment did Vatican officials hurriedly insert such a session into the pope's agenda.

In fact, Wojtyła had come to Poland as a "pope-primate" (in the phrase of Timothy Garton Ash), intent on giving clear instructions to the Polish Church, determined that he, not the primate, would lay down the doctrinal line that would guide the priests of Poland in the struggle to come. In Kraków, before two million people, the pope beatified two priests who had fought against the Russians in the unsuccessful Polish insurrection of 1863: Father Rafał Kalinowski and Brother Albert Chmielowski, about whom Wojtyła had written a play, *The Brother of Our God*. Noting their participation in the failed revolution, the pope not only praised the two priests for their "heroic love of the homeland" in that doomed struggle, but for their accomplishments, faith, and strength of character afterward. Kalinowski, who joined the Carmelites, became a teacher. Chmielowski founded the Albertine branch of the Franciscans and became a celebrated artist. The parallel to the experience of Solidarity was obvious. As he did throughout his trip, the pope called on Catholics and the Church itself to undergo an inner change, a kind of "inner conversion."

In his old archdiocese, the pope consecrated a new church in Nowa Huta to the memory of Maximilian Kolbe, following a big three-hour demonstration. "The pope is with us, the pope is with us, the Church is with us, God is with us. No freedom without Wałęsa. Free Wałęsa," chanted tens of thousands of people marching behind an enormous banner proclaiming "Solidarity fights and wins."

The next day the pope met with Wałęsa—a visit still surrounded by mystery and controversy. The authorities had at first resisted any meeting at all, but the pope insisted it take place as a matter of principle. Wałęsa, who had recently been released from custody but was denied the opportunity to return to work, was to meet with John Paul "as a private person" at a site selected by the regime, with no representatives of the press on hand.

Leaving Gdańsk by helicopter and accompanied by Bishop Tadeusz Gocłowski, who had been assigned to him by the episcopate, Wałęsa was expecting to meet the pope in Kraków but instead found himself landing far away in the Tatra Mountains. Six thousand soldiers and militiamen blocked the roads leading to the youth hostel that had been chosen as the site for the meeting. Bishop Gocłowski later wrote that the meeting, "which naturally concerned the situation in the country, the mood among the working people, and prospects for Solidarity's activities," lasted roughly forty minutes. Moreover, in their conversation there was an aura of "certainty about the victory of the ideal [of Solidarity], which had become so dominant all across Poland. They were in full agreement that, difficult as things might be, the facts were irreversible."

The pope and his spokesmen have always refused to discuss this meeting. Wałęsa's account in his autobiography says nothing of consequence about the meeting and is limited to two paragraphs in which he remembers mostly "the atmosphere of oneness and simplicity . . . [and] the pope's large feet."

According to Jaruzelski, the visit "lasted only twenty minutes; they got through with the introductions, there were heaps of [Wałęsa's] children about." The meeting occurred in a largely "symbolic dimension," but nothing of substance transpired. "Wałęsa wasn't happy about that, and I understand why," Jaruzelski says. "But it seems that at the time the pope thought that the most important thing was to preserve peace and calm in Poland. He perceived the goodwill of the authorities . . . and I think this was a sort of freezing, a hibernation of Wałęsa while waiting for future developments."

Indeed, the editor of *L'Osservatore Romano*, Monsignor Virgilio Levi, suggested in the next day's edition (under the headline "Honor to the Sacrifice") that Wałęsa had basically been put out to pasture by the pope, that he would be accorded "great honors" but would never return to the leadership of Solidarity. "My sources said that . . . Jaruzelski was to lift the state of emergency, but that [in exchange] Jaruzelski had asked [the pope] to give Wałęsa a lower profile," Levi recalls. "It was necessary. The pope wanted to see Wałęsa on the first day, then on the second day, then on the third day; and only on the seventh day did he meet with him in the Tatra Mountains." Meanwhile, Levi's colleagues at *L'Osservatore Romano*, who had been given advance copies of the pope's speeches, could see that when the speeches were finally delivered they had been toned down—apparently in deference to Jaruzelski and the promises he had made.

Many in the Vatican believe that Glemp or his personal aides were responsible for the account supplied to Levi. The primate may have hoped to remove Wałęsa from the political scene with an "authoritative" article in *L'Osservatore Romano* that—picked up by the world press—would result in a fait accompli. However, the day after the article appeared, the papal under-secretary of state, Eduardo Martinez Somalo, summoned Levi to his office. Without mentioning the contents of the article, he merely said that, given the reactions of media commentators, "we need a gesture." Levi, understanding exactly what was being asked of him, obediently turned in his resignation. In this way, a message was sent that the pope still supported Wałęsa's leadership.

Whatever the case, four months later, in October 1983, Wałęsa was awarded the Nobel Peace Prize. He eventually returned to head Solidarity and become the president of Poland.

In the end, the pope tried to help the government find a way out of its impossible predicament, and the people find a way out of their despair. Jaruzelski had become the first Polish leader since 1970 under whom Polish army troops fired on Polish citizens, and the legitimacy of his authority was anything but assured.

At Jasna Góra, the pope had said, "The state is firmly sovereign when it *governs* society and serves the common good of society and allows the nation to realize . . . its own identity." Then he had prayed for Poland's leaders: "Queen of Poland, I also wish to entrust you with the difficult task of those who wield authority on Polish soil." That authority was not God-given, he made clear. "The state gains its strength first of all from the support of the people."

"The pope wanted the visit to end on a positive note, with a compromise," Jaruzelski recalled in 1994. That was why he asked for a second meeting. "He knew that we were approaching the end of martial law—it was lifted a month later. He didn't want to disturb this atmosphere of reconciliation. . . . He said that many things had changed for the better in Poland."

The pope departed Poland feeling that the general was an estimable, ethical man, a religious man at heart, a Pole first and a Communist second, fearful of the Soviet Union. Part of the importance of Jaruzelski's and Wojtyła's second meeting lies in the personal bond of trust that developed between the general and the pope, despite their substantial differences. "It was a very important conversation," Jaruzelski later observed. The pope spoke of "his appreciation of the peaceful atmosphere of his visit and the cooperation of the authorities."

Jaruzelski thought of his dialogue with the pope as "split into two strata. One level was that of a friendly feeling; here I was welcoming a great man, a guest who was also our compatriot. But at the same time there was this other level . . . where we had to present our respective reasons which didn't always coincide. Sometimes they were totally different. . . . But these negotiations never closed on a brusque note of [total disagreement]. Even when we came to a controversial point that we couldn't resolve on the spot we decided to study it further in future meetings with the primate and the government, and try to find a good solution."

After a week in his homeland John Paul II departed in triumph, though outwardly the people's lives were no less dreary and deprived. "The most obvious and important" aspect of his pilgrimage, the editors of the underground bulletin *KOS* (number 35) concluded, was "that in the course of this historic meeting of the pope with millions of Poles we have again become visible to ourselves and others, that we have regained our voice and are able to stand straight again. A year and a half of terror have failed. We have become self-determining subjects again, something quite extraordinary in a totalitarian state. We should no longer consider ourselves objects of political bargains being struck above our heads."

This was exactly as the pope had hoped.

·   ·   ·

Brezhnev died on November 10, 1982. His successor as general secretary of the Communist Party, Yuri Andropov, former KGB head, wrote a furious letter to Jaruzelski in the wake of Wałęsa's receipt of the 1983 Nobel Prize. "The Church is reawakening the cult of Wałęsa, gives him inspiration, and encourages him. This means that the Church is creating a new type of confrontation with the Party." He was as spooked by the Church as his predecessor had been, and he perceptively analyzed the situation in Poland in the aftermath of the pope's visit:

> I want especially to speak of the Church [he wrote to Jaruzelski]. During the crisis [martial law] it received the greatest benefits and very seriously strengthened its political position and its material-financial base. . . .
>
> Today the Church is a powerful opposition force against socialism, appearing in the role of patron and defender of the underground and the idea of Solidarity. . . . In this situation, the most important thing is not to make concessions, but to draw the line by restricting the activity of the Church to the [Polish] constitutional framework, and narrow the sphere of its influences on social life.

Eighteen months later, in February 1984, Andropov died and was succeeded by Konstantin Chernenko. The old guard in the Kremlin was thinning. Suslov, the ideologist, was also dead. Jaruzelski's freedom of action was expanding. He increasingly saw the pope as a partner in Poland's future, not to the exclusion of the Soviets by any means, but as an essential element in any consensus that would allow the country to prosper socially and economically. Cautiously, the state-Church commission of Poland began discussing ways to relax the more draconian measures of martial law that still remained in the civil code.

Again Jaruzelski was summoned to a railway car meeting in Brest-Litovsk, in mid-April 1984, this time with Andrei Gromyko and Dimitri Ustinov. He was sternly warned about the dangers of such cooperation. "Jaruzelski evaluated the Church as an indispensable ally, without which at present it would be impossible to go on. Nothing was said [by Jaruzelski] about any decisive struggle against the machinations of the Church," Gromyko reported back to the Soviet Politburo.

Presiding over the review, Konstantin Chernenko noted grimly, "The counterrevolutionary forces continue their activities, the Church leads the offensive, inspiring and uniting the enemies of communism and those dissatisfied by the present system."

"Generally, if one may say so, the matter of building the [Communist] Party is out of line with Jaruzelski's soul," said Gromyko.

"I'm of the opinion that he was insincere with us," Ustinov added.

Mikhail Gorbachev had carefully studied the hundred or so pages of a report on the railway-car meeting.

"It turns out," he observed, "that Jaruzelski undoubtedly wanted to present the situation as better than it really was. It seems to me that we don't yet understand the true intentions of Jaruzelski." Gorbachev paused. *"Perhaps he wishes to have a pluralistic system of government in Poland."*

In eleven months Chernenko would be dead and Gorbachev would succeed him. Then both he and Jaruzelski would together discuss the idea of pluralism, for both Poland and the Soviet Union.

PART SIX

UNIVERSAL PASTOR

On Sunday, May 6, 1984, John Paul II celebrated a triumphal mass in Seoul for 103 Korean martyrs killed in the eighteenth and nineteenth centuries whom he had just declared saints. For the first time since the Middle Ages a canonization had been proclaimed outside of Rome.

Under John Paul II, the Catholic Church was becoming a saint factory. The pope was canonizing and beatifying Christian heroes at the rate of almost one a week. In the nearly two-thousand-year history of the Church, only three thousand men and women had previously qualified for sainthood. In his fifteen-year papacy, Pope Paul VI had made seventy-two new saints. By the twilight of his papacy in the mid-1990s, John Paul II had beatified (the last step on the road to sainthood) over seven hundred men and women (more than any other pope) and declared over three hundred saints. Until Wojtyła's papacy, the Congregation for the Causes of Saints had had to certify two miracles for each person beatified; John Paul II lowered the bar to one miracle.

The pope's purpose in creating so many new saints was to point up the fecundity of the Church, like a father proudly showing off his children. Among other things, saints are symbols of a flourishing religious life, role models for their cultures and communities—and a stimulus to overcome sagging priestly vocations. In announcing canonizations and beatifications abroad John Paul II was demonstrating that every province of the Christian empire could provide heroes for the Church universal.

Many of the saints canonized in his pontificate were chosen as examples of Christian courage for the modern world: Anuarite Negapeta, an African nun killed by a Simba soldier in Zaire while defending her vow of virginity; Peter ToRot, a catechist from Papua New Guinea, murdered in a Japanese POW camp in World War II because he refused to stop instructing the islanders in the Christian faith; Father Maximilian Kolbe and Edith Stein, both of whom died at Auschwitz; Gianna Berretta Molla, the Italian pediatrician who died because she refused to have an abortion.*

Sometimes John Paul II favored overtly political canonizations, like those of members of religious orders killed in the Mexican and French Revolutions or the Spanish Civil War. He saw them as symbolic victims of the evil produced by revolutions or by anticlerical and Marxist regimes.

The mass that John Paul II celebrated in Seoul for the Korean martyrs was one of those gigantic ceremonies that seemed designed by the pope and his aides to stun the world. A cross 130 feet high had been raised over the papal platform. A million faithful were present—in a country with barely 1.7 million Catholics. A fifteen-hundred-voice choir sang, while eight hundred priests and twelve hundred deacons and subdeacons went into the crowd to distribute communion. Amid this imperial pomp, the pope wore gold-colored satin vestments, embroidered with a white cloud and a dragon, the emblem of the oldest Korean royal dynasty.

In his homily John Paul extolled the Catholic Church of Korea, which had literally been born through martyrdom: "It bears forever the mark of blood. . . . Listen to the last words of Teresa Kwon, one of the first martyrs: 'Since the Lord in heaven is the Father of the whole human race and the Lord of all creation, how can you ask me to betray him? Even in the earthly world anyone who betrays his own father and mother will not be forgiven.' "

---

* The most controversial person beatified by John Paul II was Josemaría Escrivá de Balaguer, the founder of the mysterious Catholic lay organization Opus Dei. Escrivá's 1992 beatification was unusually swift—only seventeen years after his death, a modern record. It generally takes at least half a century to be declared "blessed." Moreover, many critics charged that Escrivá's case had been given special treatment. Important "hostile witnesses" were barred from the hearings (only eleven of ninety-two were allowed to testify), and when one of the eight ecclesiastical judges voted against Escrivá, the process was not halted, as Vatican rules demand.

John Paul II felt particularly close to Opus Dei and its 75,000 members around the world. They are almost all intensely orthodox in theology, blindly loyal to the pope, and highly influential in their home countries. Because of its great secrecy—and suspected power—Opus Dei was often accused of being a vast Catholic conspiratorial operation for world domination. As its membership lists were kept under lock and key, critics tended to call it the "Holy Mafia." Opus Dei had supported Karol Wojtyła since he was archbishop of Kraków. He had frequently been invited to address its members. In the days just before the conclave that elected him pope, Wojtyła went to pray at Escrivá's tomb in Rome.

Martyrdom was the sign of total dedication demanded of Christians by this pope. He regularly spoke about martyrdom to the cardinals, to the priests, and to the faithful to whom he addressed his encyclicals. He pronounced it "the highest witnessing of moral truth, to which relatively few are called." In his view betrayal was the dark side of martyrdom. For John Paul II, a man who wished to leave the priesthood wasn't an unfortunate fellow with problems, a tormented or a disappointed soul, but a traitor, a Judas, as Paul VI had once said. Martyrdom was the climax of readiness to die for the splendor of the truth. According to Wojtyła, every Christian must have this readiness. "The blood of the martyrs is the seed of Christians," he told the crowd in Seoul, quoting Tertullian.

Apart from Christ, the Virgin, and the Apostles, the Christian example most often cited by the Polish pope was St. Stanisław. When he spoke of martyrdom, there was no doubt among some in the Vatican that John Paul II was also thinking of his own willingness to die. By the time of his papacy, his growing mysticism had unquestionably readied him to face death for his mission. Indeed, many in the papal palace thought he was drawn to the idea of dying—of taking his place beside those men and women, of whatever confession, murdered by the totalitarian systems of the twentieth century, whom he celebrated as holy martyrs.

.   .   .

"I speak in the name of those who have no voice," the pope had proclaimed in Africa in 1980, "in the name of the innocent who are dying because they have neither bread nor water."

From the beginning, the pope's journeys were a continuous sermon on human dignity and the redeeming power of faith. The world became his pulpit in a way it had been for no other religious leader in history. This was the strategy on which he built his pontificate and sought to reanimate the Catholic Church: carrying the message of faith, social justice, discipline, and dogma to hundreds of millions of people around the globe.

In Korea, the pope spoke of the liberation of the worker. In the industrial city of Pusan, 300,000 laborers, peasants, and fishermen—far more than the 170,000 Catholics who lived in the Pusan diocese—came to hear him.

Korean workers toiled under brutal conditions: In the factories many were on their feet fourteen hours a day every day of the week, except for two Sundays each month, earning a monthly wage of two hundred dollars or less. They had no real unions.

"Man is often treated as a mere instrument of production," the pope told them, "as a raw material that should cost as little as possible. In situations like this the worker is not respected as a true collaborator with the Creator."

John Paul II became their voice.

His predecessor, Paul VI, had taken only eight foreign trips in the fifteen years of his pontificate, mostly to destinations with obvious religious or political symbolism: Jerusalem, Istanbul, Fátima, Bombay, the UN headquarters in New York.

John Paul II was a restless leader. In the first six years of his pontificate he visited Poland, Mexico, Ireland, the United States, Turkey, Zaire, Congo, Kenya, Burkina Faso, the Ivory Coast, France, Brazil, West Germany, Pakistan, the Philippines, Guam, Nigeria, Benin, Gabon, Equatorial Guinea, Portugal, Great Britain, Argentina, Chile, Spain, Costa Rica, Nicaragua, Panama, El Salvador, Guatemala, Honduras, Belize, Haiti, Austria, Korea, Canada, and South Africa.

He was systematically covering the globe, personally addressing multitudes of Catholics and non-Catholics. Literally billions of people had seen him on television. On the feast day of Saints Peter and Paul, June 29, 1982, he told the cardinals in the Vatican that his trips were an exercise of the "charisma of Peter on a universal scale." "If I stayed in the Vatican as the Curia would have me," he remarked to his friend Father Maliński, "then I'd be sitting in Rome writing encyclicals, which would be read by only a handful of people. If I travel and go to the people, then I'll meet lots of them, both simple folk and politicians. And they'll listen to me. Otherwise they'll never come to me."

As often as not, he visited parts of the earth where human beings live in terrible suffering—impoverished, oppressed, sick, and hungry. He sometimes jotted down the chosen destinations on plain white sheets of paper with a ballpoint pen during his morning meditation.

Whether in the First World or the Third World he preached that "the kingdom of God is also the kingdom of justice; and missionary activity throughout the world must go hand in hand with the introduction of conditions . . . that allow people to live with dignity."

He declared in Nigeria, "The cynical exploitation of poor and ignorant people is a serious crime against God's work." In Colombia he admonished "those who live in excess and luxurious abundance to shed their spiritual blindness."

"In the light of Christ's word," he told a Canadian audience, "the poor South will judge the rich North. The poor peoples . . . will judge the nations that have carried off their property, claiming an imperialistic monopoly over their goods and a political supremacy at other people's expense."

In Portugal he argued that justice requires peasants to be able to work their own land. In Spain he demanded that the state protect workers. "We can't just abandon the workers to their fate. This is especially true of those who, like the poor and the immigrants, have to rely on their hands in order to survive."

In Brazil, which has the largest Catholic population in the world, he defended the right of workers to form trade unions. In South Africa he condemned apartheid. In many newly independent African states he denounced authoritarian abuses. "How can we ignore the arbitrary arrests, the sentences, the executions with no real trial, the detention of dissidents under inhuman conditions, the torture, the persons who have disappeared?"

His very presence in the most desolate parts of the world provided a spark of hope for people in misery. For men and women trapped in the shantytowns and barrios of the Third World, the arrival of John Paul II sometimes offered the first significant testimony to their existence as human beings, the only time in their lives when their wretched living conditions were presented to the court of public opinion in their own countries and around the world.

People wept when they saw him. The arrival of the pope transformed (briefly, at least) their desperation and apathy. In Bolivia, a brown-skinned miner climbed up onto the papal platform and shouted with emotion, "Thank you, Holy Father, for accepting liberation theology. Thank you for your encyclical on work. They're closing the mines. Help us because we want them started up again. We're hungry, we don't have bread!" That John Paul II had condemned liberation theology was almost beside the point when all over the world millions of TV viewers could witness the *campesino*'s cry and see a Bolivian woman showing the pontiff her empty cooking pot.

Inevitably, there were critics in the Curia who saw the pope's trips as undignified road shows, theatrical displays of personal power and ambition and a drain on the already depleted finances of the Vatican. "Many people say the pope travels too much and at too frequent intervals," John Paul II noted in an interview given to *L'Osservatore Romano* and Vatican Radio in 1980. "I think that, humanly speaking, they're right. But it's Providence that's guiding us; and sometimes it prompts us to do things *ad excessum.*" He spoke of the opportunity to proclaim the Gospel and papal teaching on a "planetary scale."

And he meant *planetary.* He made no secret of his desire to be a world leader, a global prophet, the bearer of tidings of universal salvation. "I want to sensitize men and women of goodwill to the important challenges that the human family has to face in these waning years of the twentieth century," he proclaimed. If he struck some observers as a self-appointed messiah, constantly referring to providential guidance in his circumnavigation of the globe, he had a ready answer: "If God has called me with these ideas of mine, that was so they might resonate in my new universal ministry."

. . .

In asserting his global leadership John Paul II had a formidable ally in the media, which amplified his every phrase and gesture. No head of state enjoyed the kind of enthusiastic blanket coverage that he received. Not even the president of the United States, was followed by such an army of journalists from so many nations.

More alert than his aides, the pope quickly recognized the sheer dramatic power of his office. No other world leader celebrated open-air triumphs against such unabashedly theatrical backdrops. No secular leader could routinely address hundreds of thousands of citizens in mass meetings anywhere on earth. The forceful personality of John Paul II lit up the TV screen.

Images of him standing in the popemobile, arms extended in greeting, of him kneeling to kiss the ground of yet another country swept the television screens of the world. Without TV the "Wojtyła phenomenon" of the 1980s could never have existed.

The pope's great charisma, more than his doctrinal message, was his most formidable tool for keeping the Church together and shaping it in his own image—as one highly ranking monsignor noted at the time. No less an expert than Sir John Gielgud remarked that the pope had a great actor's sense of perfect timing. His message did not meet with universal approbation, however. Almost from the outset, many listeners were incensed by his regular condemnation of modern sexual trends, particularly by his unyielding opposition to abortion and birth control. His objectives were hardly limited to Christendom: He was determined to present to the whole world, secular and religious, an agenda based on moral and doctrinal principles that he was certain flowed from God.

Beneath the eye of the camera, his global evangelization came to life. John Paul II was the first pope to understand the television era, the first one who mastered the medium, who could handle a microphone, who was used to improvising, who wasn't afraid of performing in public. People watched him against the background of exotic panoramas: sailing down tropical rivers, standing on slopes of sacred volcanoes, or walking in the shadow of soaring skyscrapers—like some omnipresent Master of the Universe.

Inevitably (and to his great advantage) a war of one-upsmanship developed between a pope seeking to impress his audiences (aided by media advisers who were learning quickly) and TV reporters determined to make every broadcast an extraordinary event. Thus agents of the most skeptical and cynical mass media in the world wound up exalting the Roman pontiff in a manner previously unknown and on a scale unique to his person.

Masses celebrated by Pope Wojtyła became epic performances. He preached and prayed in stadiums and at racetracks, on the tarmacs of airports, and in meadows of clover. Wherever he appeared in cities, a Super Bowl atmosphere prevailed. "Juan Pablo Secundo, te quiere todo el mundo," they chanted in South America, "J.P. Two, we love you," in the United States. The pope acted like God's marathon runner. Local organizers felt compelled to create more and more fantastic stage designs for his open-air events, turning the papal platforms on which John Paul II celebrated masses into gargantuan Hollywood sets. Giant crosses and ever more elaborate constructions surmounted the altars. Sometimes the canopy above the tabernacle was shaped like a vast sail or an enormous stylized dove, or the walls to the side would form a pyramid, decorated with cultural symbols from whatever nation the pope was visiting. In his honor, bands played, choirs sang, dancers swayed.

Liturgical acts were transformed into spectacle. The long ranks of the local population marching in the offertory procession turned into a dazzling homage to the pontiff. Before his throne, bread, fruits, fabrics, arts and crafts, even babies in cradles passed in review. During the pope's visit to Madrid in 1982, an Italian writer noted that John Paul II "was seated on the terrace of the stadium like a satrap."

But the pope, fully aware of the profane elements surrounding his appearances (which in richer countries were partly financed through the sale of papal souvenirs), realized that all this was an opportunity for communication. He spoke in a dozen languages. He agreed to wear any of an incredible variety of hats that people offered him: student berets, Mexican sombreros, feathered Indian war bonnets, pith helmets. In Africa he put on goatskins and posed while grasping the spear of a tribal chieftain. In the American West he emerged from a tepee in a fringed chasuble; in Phoenix a group of Native Americans placed him on a revolving platform that turned him around like some sort of sacred wedding cake so that everyone in the audience could see and admire him.

The papal entourage quickly came to favor this kind of atmosphere and spectacular hype. In keeping with the strategy of Joaquín Navarro-Valls, hired as the Vatican spokesman in 1984—a former medical doctor, a correspondent for the Spanish newspaper *ABC*, and a member of Opus Dei—TV coverage was given preferential treatment. On the TV screen, as the pope and Navarro-Valls well understood, glory would invariably overshadow problems, emotion would overwhelm insight. Any uncomfortable questions from print reporters would be drowned out.

MARY

Wherever he went, in whatever the country, there was one appointment John Paul II never missed: a visit to a shrine of the Holy Virgin. The sight of him standing before statues and pictures of the Madonna and begging her protection for workers, nations, the sick, seminaries, universities, and hospitals—praying for her to bring peace to the world—became a trademark of his papacy. The Black Madonna of Guadalupe in Mexico was the first Marian shrine outside Italy he visited as pope. Inevitably, there was also the Virgin of the Apparition in Brazil, the Virgin of Perpetual Help in the Philippines, Our Lady of Luján in Argentina, the house of the Madonna at Ephesus in Turkey, the miraculous grotto of Lourdes in France, the sanctuary of Fátima in Portugal, the basilica of the Virgin at Mariazell in Austria.

He dedicated whole continents to the heart of Mary. "You know the sufferings and hopes of us all," he prayed. "As a mother, you know the struggle that is being fought in the world between light and darkness, between good and evil. O Mother of Mercy . . . keep us far from every injustice, division, violence, and war. Protect us against temptation and the slavery of sin and evil."

The legendary traditions bound up with each Marian sanctuary were sources of pride and inspiration for the pontiff. He reveled in the way they brought the Church—and the Mother of the Church—closer to the people. In Brazil he delighted in the tale of the fishermen who found a statue of the Madonna entangled in their nets. In Togo his presence recalled the first missionaries who passed on the myth of the "white lady." For John Paul II religious legends were faith turned into poetry.

At the time of Vatican II a majority of the bishops had not even wanted Paul VI to give Mary the formal title "Mother of the Church" lest ecumenical sensibilities be offended. But once Karol Wojtyła became Roman pontiff, he began to crack down on a recalcitrant Western Catholic community, imposing on it a systematic aggrandizement of the cult of Mary.

Many Catholics reacted with irritation to this mariolatric approach, this seeming obsession for presenting the Virgin Mary as the highest model of womanhood and the patron of whole nations. Some resented it as an attempt to impose a medieval religiosity on contemporary Catholicism and to export the Polish experience to the universal Church. The continuous references to the Madonna particularly disturbed leaders of many Protestant denominations, which have always insisted on putting Christ and the Bible at the center of Christian faith.

However, unlike God the Father, Jesus Christ, or the Holy Spirit, the Madonna has continued to make visible appearances throughout Christian history. And she has a unique relevance in the lives of hundreds of millions of Catholics: Many of them don't go to Church, don't accept the pope or his laws, but they turn to the Madonna-Mother because she, a woman who bore a child, seems to them to understand and help. John Paul II, a motherless child from age eight, gratefully identified with this image, which holds a supreme place in the Polish Catholic tradition.

The failed assassination attempt decisively convinced the pope that he was protected by the Madonna, and he serenely abandoned himself to her care whenever he sensed danger—to either his person or his goals. "We all remember," he has said, "that moment during the afternoon when some pistol shots were fired at the pope, with the intention of killing him. The bullet that passed through his abdomen is now in the shrine of Fátima [where the pope had it installed in a golden crown which he placed upon the head of the statue of the Virgin], his sash, pierced by this bullet, is in the shrine of Jasna Góra. . . . It was a motherly hand that guided the bullet's path and saved the agonizing pope at the threshold of death."

CERTAINTY

Pope Paul VI had spent his last years increasingly tormented by the dilemma of how to balance doctrinal continuity, the consensus of the faithful, and the dictates of his own conscience. John Paul II suffered no such conflict. "The Church," he declared, "doesn't depend on the criteria of numbers and fashion." Whether in the Vatican or on his travels, everything he did was aimed at building support for his leadership and his vision of a Catholic Church with no inferiority complex vis-à-vis modern society. He had always been certain that undiluted Catholicism was the only cure for contemporary evils.

As pope he demanded that, first and foremost, the Church's staff—priests, nuns, bishops, prelates, theologians—must obey papal teachings. In each country he visited, the pope hammered into the ears of the clergy his insistence on the value of celibacy. The clergy were to stay out of politics and revive the sacrament of penance; seminary training had to conform fully to the Vatican's rules.

"The Church of Vatican II, and Vatican I, and the Council of Trent are one and the same Church," he announced in West Germany in 1980. At a gathering of priests in France he said: "It is not the world that determines your role, but the Church." "Promise to obey me and your bishops" were his words in Spain.

His meetings with the clergy abroad were generally triumphalist affairs, conducted in an atmosphere of devotion and solemnity. Priests rarely got a chance to describe to the Holy Father the real problems and pressures they faced in their parishes, schools, and private lives.

However, in Switzerland, on a visit in June 1984, he was confronted with unusual frankness during a meeting with local priests. First, Father Mark Fischer requested a larger role in the Church for laypeople, including women. He proposed the ordination of *viri probati* ("tested" married laymen), and he suggested relaxing restrictions imposed by John Paul II to deter priests from leaving the priesthood. Father Giampaolo Patelli, who spoke after Father Fischer, expressed understanding and solidarity with those men who had left the priesthood to marry; then he raised the question of divorced and remarried couples who wanted to receive communion, suggesting that the time had come to end this Church prohibition, too. When the pope responded, it was with a flat-out refusal on all points, though he knew that the two priests had the backing of the Swiss bishops conference.

The duty of a pope, John Paul declared to the assembled priests, is "to confirm the brethren, to point the way, to teach the will of Christ and the

Church." The unity of faith and discipline, he emphasized, was essential. Nothing could justify "discord."

The headlong flight back to doctrinal conformity and away from the relative tolerance and flexibility that had marked much of the pontificate of Pope Paul VI was most emphatic in the area of sexual morality. Taking issue with the bishops, priests, theologians, and laypeople who had come to doubt the wisdom or relevance of some of the Church's basic teachings, John Paul II inexorably rejected every deviation from traditional doctrine. He forbade communion to Catholics who had divorced and remarried. He refused to lift the Church's ban on contraceptives. He insisted that artificial insemination for married couples violated the teachings of the Church. He forbade the use of condoms even as the world was reeling from the rapid spread of the AIDS virus. When theologians or Catholic health care workers talked about mercy and the possibility of using condoms as a lesser evil, he remained resolute. He vigorously reasserted the Church's condemnation of homosexuality.

"To me he seems to be obsessed with sexual issues," complains the Rev. F. X. Murphy, whose contemporaneous chronicles of the Second Vatican Council under the pen name Xavier Rhynne have been collected in several books.

Feminist criticism of the pope's view of sexuality became commonplace. "John Paul II always sees women in their biological dimension: either as mothers or as virgin who must follow the model of the Madonna," insists Ida Magli, an Italian anthropologist who has written several books dealing with women and the Church. "It's always the way they relate to their body: either they make children or they abstain from sexual intercourse. Wojtyła never sees women as persons in the same way he sees a male as a person. I think that deep in his heart he fears the rebellion of women. His harsh prohibitions, especially regarding abortion in whatever situation, betray a sort of unconscious hatred of the freedom of women."

Indeed, he blasted the recourse to abortion with a ferocity that seemed at odds with his temperment. Cardinal John O'Connor of New York was one of many prelates who were quick to realize that "this is the issue that concerns John Paul above all others in the world." The pope decried a "culture of death" that, he felt, increasingly encouraged abortion, euthanasia, and genetic engineering. Almost everything he published contained references to the sacredness of human life, to the privileged status of the unborn. "I think it is the one unifying theme of his papacy," says Cardinal O'Connor.

During his sermons at the Lenten retreat two years before his election, Wojtyła had shown the Curia a vision of the earth as a vast burial ground, a culture of death imposed by contraception and abortion. Now it was a papal vision. "Abortion is nothing but the assassination of an innocent creature," the pope maintained. "No human law can morally justify induced abortion," he repeated around the world. On the Mall in Washington, not far from where the Supreme Court had sanctioned abortion in *Roe* v. *Wade*, he told a crowd of several hundred thousand that "when life is threatened in the womb I will stand up for life."

Often he turned directly to a statue or picture of the Madonna when he wanted to complain about moral decline. "How can we not feel dismayed," he cried out in anguish at Fátima, "by the spread of secularism and permissiveness, which so badly undermine the fundamental values of the Christian moral order?"

From the first months of his papacy he realized that his stringent moral message had many critics inside and outside the Church, but he remained steadfast—and seemingly unconcerned. He could never compromise what he saw as the eternal truth of the Church's precepts. John Paul II felt obliged to teach the faithful and the clergy, not to let himself be influenced by their opinions.

"We're so used to politicians who take a poll, try to read the poll, and then want to be on the right wavelength, and he's so much the opposite of this that it's fascinating," observes one of his critics, Archbishop Rembert Weakland of Milwaukee. "He doesn't care what people think. He moves ahead. That's fine as a leader, but I think at a certain point you need some contact with what the grass roots are thinking and feeling, and how successful you are at reaching them."

This was the criticism most often heard from bishops and priests about the Wojtyła pontificate as its direction became clearer. They worried that the pope didn't sense the depth of alienation caused by his uncompromising stands, especially in the West among laywomen, women in religious orders, and young Catholics who chose to ignore the teachings of the Church.

That high degree of alienation had been accepted as fact by many bishops in the West, especially in the United States, where Catholic clerics tried to convince the pope that more attention had to be paid to dissent within the Church. But they soon saw that they were getting nowhere.

Archbishop John Patrick Foley, president of the Council for Social Communications—the Vatican's media office—makes the following distinction: "I don't think there was any uncertainty regarding what the teaching of the Church was before the election of John Paul II. I think there was uncertainty on the part of many in *perceiving* what the teaching of the Church was or what the limits were. . . . Good morals, like good art, begin by drawing a line. And I think this Holy Father has made it clear where the limits are. With regard to the mission of the Church, there are no limits. With regard to the teaching of the Church, limits are clearly defined."

Archbishop Weakland of Milwaukee is one of those who believes that Wojtyła was elected to play the role originally meant for Pope John Paul I. "There is validity to the critique that the Church needed direction. That this couldn't go on. Paul VI had great respect for people, for ideas, and he didn't like to clamp down on anything. He was not a disciplinarian. . . . He was eighty-three. And he was depressed by nature. It wasn't easy for him. So [the cardinals] wanted somebody energetic, somebody who could make decisions, somebody who could bring a little more discipline in the ranks. And kind of pull the Church together. And I'm sure that's what John Paul II saw his duty as, and he's been acting under that. The Church he took over was a Church that he felt might just disintegrate, fall apart, because of the lack of stability."

The late Cardinal John J. Wright of Pittsburgh, the highest-ranking American in the Curia at the 1978 conclaves, was among the cardinals believed to have supported Wojtyła's election as pope. Wojtyła and Wright often talked about the "drift in the Church" and shared a sense, says his former aide, now Archbishop Donald Wuerl, "that the leadership had to be clear and firm," that "there was certainly a lot of rough water, turbulence," and a need for "hearing a consistent, correct message. . . . That was the way you address some of the unrest in the Church, some of the dissent in the Church."

From the beginning the Wojtyła papacy was at odds with modernism, with "moral relativism," as he calls it, with liberalism, and "secularistic hedonism." "This clash, which some people would attribute to the pope, was coming anyway," says a highly placed curial monsignor. "There's no way around it, there's no doubt that certain aspects of modernity are a challenge to the Church. This clash was coming with the change that has come about in society. There's no way the Church could have lived comfortably with it. And somehow, whoever the pope was, he would have been called to take a stand against it."

This is a view widely shared by the pope's allies in the church hierarchy—a hierarchy that, by the end of the first five years of his pontificate, already bore the stamp of his appointments in the Curia and the bishoprics.

"If another pope had been guiding the Church in this conflict, between the Church traditions and modernity," the monsignor continued, "if you'd had a sick pope, for example, a pope who disappears, a pope who just stressed the negative side, the Church probably wouldn't have been able to stand up to this challenge, to this clash. . . . But by being such an assertive pope [Wojtyła] has done a lot also to somehow strengthen the Church, to be able to stand up for something."

As the monsignor watched the conflict heat up,

the thing that was going through my mind was: if we hadn't had this pope, if Pope Luciani [John Paul I] had lived, what would the Church be like? Would it be different? And that was the way to measure. . . . There's a certain sense in which the extraordinary strength of this pope's outgoingness, his constant traveling round, and the fact that he has maintained the presence of the papacy with great force on the international scene have probably also made it possible for him to carry out other aspects of his policy which might have otherwise completely divided the Church and disintegrated it. If an old Paul VI, or another pope, had tried, for example, to hold the doctrinal line with the same strength with which this man does in certain areas, the Church wouldn't have taken it.

Sister Theresa Kane, an American nun who personally confronted the pope by advocating the ordination of women, notes, "I've always felt that he sees us as kind of marching into battle or something, and he's at the head, and we're all kind of behind him. And the battle is the world and everybody else: the media, the government, politics, everything. He has that kind of air of 'we're going to go into battle and do all the right things.'"

Archbishop Foley of the Vatican media office believes that "the missionary journeys of the pope were giving people throughout the world a renewed sense of the universality of the Church. We didn't know there were so many Catholics; we didn't know they were so enthusiastic, we didn't have this sense of renewed pride in the Church."

Weakland and others, however, are convinced that John Paul's doctrinal rigidity has also driven out of the Church large numbers of Catholics who otherwise would have wished to remain in it. "A lot of people feel, rather than this heavy-handed dogmatic approach, he should take a pastoral approach," says Father Vincent O'Keefe, a former vicar general of the Jesuits who had his own struggles with Wojtyła. "In the United States we have a lot of Catholics who are divorced. The pope says the doctrine has to be clear. Well, the doctrine is too damned clear! That's not the problem. How do you deal with these people? How do you help these people? Is there no help for them? Do you say, 'Well, you can come to the Church but you can't partake in communion?' It's the same with people who practice contraception or abortion. How do you deal with these people? What kind of hope do you hold out to them?"

O'Keefe, like many American bishops, believes the pope has a cultural bias, that "he has a really deep antagonism to the West, certainly towards the United States. I think he feels we're too materialistic, we're too loud, we talk too much, we're spoiled." The Jesuit father asks, "How available is he for this universal Church that a lot of us are looking for? That was the great thing at Vatican II. That was the first time you had a universal Church in action."

But as the pope would make clear, he had a different view of the meaning of Vatican II.

. . .

Only once in his trips around the world did an audience dare to laugh at the pope's strenuous teachings on sex. It happened in Santiago de Chile. "Do you give up the idol of wealth?" John Paul II asked thousands of Chilean youngsters.

"Yes," shouted the audience.

"Do you give up the idol of power?"

"Yes."

"Do you give up the idol of sex?"

"Nooo," they roared.

The pope loves young people. They are his hope. For them he invented World Youth Day in 1986—a biannual pilgrimage in Europe, Asia, or the Americas, attended by hundreds of thousands of young Catholics from around the world, over which he has presided for days of masses and processions and homilies and workshops.

With young people John Paul II uncorks all his charm. He often has won them over with jokes and with straight talk. He got caught up in the shows they staged in his honor, he was even ready to hear things he would never have tolerated from older people. He summed up his attitude this way, during one of the World Youth Days: "What I am going to say to you is not as important as what you are going to say to me. You will not necessarily say it to me with words. You will say it with your presence, your songs, perhaps your dancing, your skits, and finally with your enthusiasm."

Later, when he had become old and frail and just keeping up with his schedule was obviously a burden, aides and reporters noticed how contact with young people seemed to rejuvenate him. With an adult audience, as the years went by, the pope sometimes seemed to be just going through the motions. There were times when his mind was somewhere else, when his patience was frayed. But that never happened with young people, with whom he demonstrated a physical closeness he offered few adults: He hugged them, he caressed them, he kissed their foreheads, he held their hands in his for minutes at a time. He fondled babies and focused entirely on them, ignoring the cameras. These weren't the gestures of an ordinary politician. They seemed to express a sense of (and perhaps a need for) authentic fatherhood. In those moments the force of his love made Karol Wojtyła a true "holy father." The pope showed a similar tenderness in the presence of suffering people: the way he embraced men crushed by poverty or kissed the heads of women bowed in exhaustion. In Calcutta, as he walked past the beds of the lepers, the sick, and the dying at Mother Teresa's hospice, a woman grabbed his hand and held it tightly to her face, while the pope looked at her with rapt intensity. Then seeming lost, he walked into the room where the day's corpses were laid out: two men, a woman, and a child. Even the cadavers received a gentle touch from him.

There were times when a simple picture summed up perfectly the universal mission that the pope wished to convey. In May 1984, in Bangkok, the pope went to meet the supreme patriarch of the Thai Buddhists in his monastery. Taking off his shoes, John Paul II walked gently up to a dais upon which eighty-six-year-old Vasana Tara was seated in the lotus position. The pope bowed and sat down in an armchair before a statue of the Buddha, looking the patriarch straight in the eyes—as custom demanded—for five long minutes of absolute silence.

Off to one side were the Buddhist monks in their saffron-colored robes facing the Catholic cardinals in their Roman collars and red skullcaps. All stood silently in the gilded hall with its heavenly blue walls. In the brief conversation that followed, with the aid of an interpreter, the pope smiled beatifically. The patriarch, motionless as a statue, pronounced a few short phrases. "We can bring happiness and peace to humanity," said Vasana Tara, "through our teachings and our exhortations to avoid evil, to do good, to purify our mind." John Paul II invited him to visit Rome. This was exactly what the pope believed.

REPRESSION

The black Volkswagen, license plate number SCV-201, arrived at the General Curia of the Franciscans at nine-forty A.M. on September 7, 1984. Two men dressed in black emerged from the car. The Franciscan friar who was waiting for them stretched out his crossed wrists and quipped: "You might have brought the chains."

The friar got into the black car. As the car drove down the Via Aurelia and slipped into the Vatican through a side entrance, the friar's thoughts went back to the early morning mass he had concelebrated with two cardinals. They had prayed that the Holy Spirit might "illuminate one and all." Their prayers didn't seem to be working.

Now forty-six years old, Brazilian Franciscan Leonardo Boff, one of the most brilliant liberation theologians, had been summoned by the prefect of the Congregation for the Doctrine of the Faith, Cardinal Joseph Ratzinger, to render an account of his latest book, *The Church: Charism and Power*. In it Boff analyzed the Roman model of the Church, which he reproved for being too turned in upon itself, too clerical and hierarchical. The Church, he said, had entered into a "colonial pact" with the ruling classes.

Using Marxist language Boff had written, "sacred power has been the object of a process of expropriation of the means of religious production on the part of the clergy, to the detriment of the Christian people." The core of the book consisted of a closely reasoned critique of the pyramidal system of Vatican power. The theologian was used to illustrating with a drawing the current views of the Church: a pyramid with God at the top, then Christ, Apostles, bishops, priests, and finally, at the bottom, the faithful. In this scheme, he explained, the clergy are in charge of everything, and the faithful have no rights except to take what they are given: "I'm not casting doubt on the authority of the Church, but on the way this authority has historically been exercised, with the goal of repressing all freedom of thought within the Church."

Boff insisted there was another way to organize the Church. He

411

sketched out another drawing: Christ, the Holy Spirit, the People of God, the bishops, the priests, and the lay coordinators of the community. A glimpse of this alternative model could be seen in any one of the 150,000 base communities in Brazil. Here the faithful gathered "around the Word [of God], the sacraments and the new ministries carried out by laypeople, men and women."

Cardinal Ratzinger's response was harsh and negative. In a confidential letter sent to Boff on May 15, 1984, he rebuked the theologian, accusing him of launching a "pitiless, radical assault" on the institutional model of the Catholic Church and of reducing its structures to an unacceptable caricature. "Is the argument that unfolds in these pages," the cardinal had asked of Boff's book, "guided by faith or by principles of an ideological nature, the product of a certain Marxist inspiration?"

The dispute between Boff and the Vatican was over more than just this new book. From the early 1970s, when Boff had written *Christ the Liberator*, the Congregation for the Doctrine of the Faith had been watching his ideas with suspicion. Now the moment for "clarification" had come. Boff was ushered into a room in the same palazzo where Galileo had been condemned by episcopal judges three hundred and fifty years before. But Cardinal Ratzinger greeted the defendant courteously: "Father, sit wherever you like; begin any way you want."

Boff began by reading a fifty-page defense in Portuguese, a translation of which he had sent to the cardinal. In his briefcase he also had photocopies of a petition signed by fifty thousand of his supporters in Brazil. The prefect of the Congregation for the Doctrine of the Faith had beside him a monsignor from Argentina, Jorge Mejia, who took a few notes but not regular minutes. Boff felt abandoned. He should have had with him Cardinal Aloisio Lorscheiter, former president of the Brazilian Bishops Conference, who had played a key role in the election of John Paul II, and Evaristo Arns, archbishop of São Paolo. They had specifically asked to be present, convinced of Boff's good faith and of his active Christian commitment to the poorest and most exploited classes of Brazil. But Ratzinger, with John Paul's approval, had turned down their request. The Vatican secretary of state, Cardinal Agostino Casaroli, had succeeded only in getting the two Brazilian cardinals

412

permission to come in at the end of the discussion, to help draft the final communiqué.

As Boff read his explanation, he couldn't shake the feeling that everything had already been decided. Back when he was writing his book, it struck him that the Church behaved like the Communist Party in the Soviet Union. Ratzinger and Wojtyła seemed to have no desire to understand what was really going on in the heads and hearts of liberation theologians. They both appeared to be immersed in the strategies of a great geopolitical game, where anything vaguely resembling socialism had to be checkmated.

In his travels Pope Wojtyła had repeatedly attacked liberation theology, but 1984 had been chosen as the year to unleash the Church's final offensive against it. On September 3, practically on the eve of summoning Boff, Cardinal Ratzinger had published a strict instruction (an explanation of church law) called "Certain Aspects of Liberation Theology." The document accused liberation theologians of "grave theological deviations" and, in the final analysis, of betraying the cause of the poor. It charged them with locating evil only in social, political, and economic structures, of radically politicizing the faith, and of dangerously confusing the poor of the Gospel with Marx's proletariat.

As far as Marx was concerned, the liberation theologians replied, some elements of his social analysis could be useful in the context of Latin America, "but Marxism as an ideology doesn't interest us." For Ratzinger, however, that distinction didn't hold up. He was afraid that the "Church of the People," the "popular church," was really a Church based on class.

In that case, the cardinal claimed, the whole sacramental and hierarchical structure of the Church was being called into question. Still, the greatest sin, in Ratzinger's eyes—and in the eyes of the pope, who had personally vetted the instruction—was that Catholic theologians might accept the theory and practice of the class struggle, "forgetting to notice the type of totalitarian society to which this process leads."

The congregation document couldn't help describing the situation in Latin America with almost the same dramatic language used by the liberation theologians: "In some regions of Latin America the monopolizing of most of the wealth by an oligarchy of owners devoid of a social conscience, military

413

dictatorships that despise elementary human rights, the corruption of certain rulers in power, the practical absence of, or gaps in, the rule of law, and the savage practices of foreign-based capital—all these constitute so many factors stoking feelings of violent rebellion in those who consider themselves the victims of a new technological, financial, and monetary or economic colonialism."

But when Boff and other liberation theologians read the document, they immediately recognized a crucial difference between John Paul II and Paul VI. The document forbade consideration of any violent response to injustice. In his encyclical *Populorum Progressio* the Italian pope, in keeping with an ancient Church tradition, had said that it was permissible to revolt against a "manifest, long-standing tyranny." But the Polish pope had abandoned this position. Ratzinger's instruction dealt with Latin America; but the target Wojtyła and Ratzinger wanted to hit was Moscow. The document contained the most hostile language about the Soviet empire heard since the days of Pius XII:

> The overthrow of the structures that cause injustice through revolutionary violence does not ipso facto mean the installation of a just government. All those who sincerely wish for the liberation of their brothers have to reflect on a fact of great relevance to our time: Millions of our contemporaries have legitimate aspirations to the fundamental freedoms they have been deprived of by totalitarian and atheistic regimes, which, in the name of liberating the people, have seized power by revolutionary and violent means. There is no ignoring this shame of our time: It is precisely through the pretense of bringing them freedom that entire nations are kept in conditions of slavery unworthy of human beings. Those who, perhaps out of thoughtlessness, become complicit in this sort of enslavement betray the poor whom they intend to save.

The expression "shame of our time"—no less than Ronald Reagan's invocation of the Evil Empire—was a slap in the face of the governments of Moscow and its allies. Even though Ratzinger's instruction claimed to be criticizing only "certain currents" of liberation theology, it was really a blanket condemnation. "When they talk about Marxism in the Vatican, they see a chain of images stretching to the Gulag, in Siberia," was one of Boff's first reactions to the document.

The discussion between the Franciscan friar and the cardinal went on for three hours, during which Ratzinger informed Boff that the Congregation for the Doctrine of the Faith was preparing a document on the "positive" aspects of liberation theology. (It appeared in 1986.)

At a certain point the prefect of the Congregation for the Doctrine of the Faith asked, "Aren't you tired? Would you like some coffee?"

They took a break, and Ratzinger, like a hostess praising the elegant dress worn by her guest, told the friar: "Your habit looks very good on you, Father. That's another way of sending a signal to the world."

"But it's very hard to wear this habit, because it's hot where we live."

"When you wear it people will see your devotion and patience, and they'll say: he's atoning for the sins of the world."

"We surely need signs of transcendence, but they're not transmitted through the habit. It's the heart that has to be in the right place."

"Hearts can't be seen, and yet one has to see *something*," the cardinal retorted.

"This habit can also be a sign of power. When I'm wearing it and I get on the bus, people stand up and say: 'Father, have a seat.' But we have to be servants."

Later Cardinals Arns and Lorscheiter were brought in while the text of a communiqué was prepared. Its terms were very mild. It said there had been a "conversation" between Leonardo Boff and Cardinal Ratzinger. The atmosphere was described as "fraternal." The friar had been called to explain some of the points in his book *The Church: Charism and Power* that had created "difficulties," but the Congregation for the Doctrine of the Faith would come up with a way to take Boff's explanations into account.

Boff was taken back to the Franciscan Curia in the same car, driven by Ratzinger's secretary, Joseph Clemens. The Vatican wanted to avoid questions from the journalists crowding around the entrance to the palazzo of the congregation.

On March 20 the Congregation for the Doctrine of the Faith made public a notification addressed to Friar Boff. His theses on the structure of the Church, the concept of dogma, sacred power, and the prophetic role of the Church were declared "untenable . . . and as such liable to endanger the sound doctrine of the faith."

Boff accepted the decision.

Nevertheless on April 26, 1985, he was condemned to a year of silence. He was not allowed to teach, lecture, or publish books. Boff accepted.

Eleven months later the Vatican lifted the ban, but in June 1987 Ratzinger stopped the publication in Italy of a new book by Boff, *Trinity and Society.* In 1991 the Vatican forced him to step down as editor in chief of the Franciscan review *Vozes.* The following year the Vatican banned him from teaching and imposed preventive censorship on all his writings. On May 26, 1992, Leonardo Boff left the Franciscan order and the priesthood. "Ecclesiastical power," he said, "is cruel and merciless. It forgets nothing. It forgives nothing. It demands everything."

· · ·

From the very beginning of his pontificate John Paul II decided to systematically crush dissent by Catholic theologians and to marginalize critics so they would no longer stir up unwanted discussion within the Church. With the appointment of Joseph Ratzinger as prefect of the Congregation for the Doctrine of the Faith in November 1981, it became clear that this was official policy.

The first to be struck by Wojtyła's policy was the French theologian Jacques Pohier, author of the book *When I Say God.* Pohier was forbidden to write, preach, or give lectures without specific authorization.

On December 15, 1979, it was the turn of Swiss theologian Hans Küng, who had been an influential participant at Vatican II and was a highly regarded lecturer at the University of Tübingen. The Vatican had first opened a dossier on Küng in 1967, when he published a book on the structure of the Church. But it was a subsequent book, *Infallible? An Inquiry,* that sent shock waves through the Vatican. That book called into question the dogma of papal infallibility proclaimed by Pius IX on July 18, 1870. Küng was warned "not to persist in the teaching of erroneous or dangerous doctrines." But the Swiss theologian always refused to go to Rome and submit to an interrogation, which he equated with a medieval trial. The Congregation for the Doctrine of the Faith relieved Küng of his teaching duties and took away his title of Catholic theologian.

Two days before Küng's condemnation, on December 13, 1979, the Flemish dogmatic theologian Edward Schillebeeckx, another protagonist of the Second Vatican Council, arrived at the congregation for questioning, the result of proceedings against him begun under Paul VI for his book *Jesus: An Experiment in Christology.*

On December 13 and 14, with John Paul II's approval, the Dominican priest was interrogated by three experts from the congregation under the direction of its secretary, Monsignor Jean Jérome Hamer. Before being questioned, Schillebeeckx had been attacked on Vatican Radio by Father Jean Galot, who was also to be one of his examiners.

The Schillebeeckx file became emblematic of John Paul II's attitude toward contemporary theological scholarship. The nine charges brought against the Flemish theologian challenged, among other matters, his opinions on the virgin birth of Christ, which he considered a relatively unimportant matter, the Resurrection, the institution of the Eucharist, and the founding of the Church. According to Schillebeeckx not everything in the New Testament was to be taken literally, nor was it a transcript of words that had been historically pronounced by Christ.

The Resurrection, Schillebeeckx said, was reality, but what kind of reality? What were those apparitions anyway: hallucinations? illusions? More important than the empty tomb or the apparitions of Christ after his death, the theologian felt, was the conversion of the Apostles after the crucifixion of their Lord.

As for the words repeated during mass—"This is my Body. . . . This is my Blood"—Schillebeeckx argued that they were part of liturgical tradition but that they had not actually been spoken by Jesus. Likewise, Christ had never made plans for founding a church, because, quite to the contrary, he had a sense that the world was coming to an end.

Nowadays no serious Catholic scholar is prepared to accept a literal interpretation of the Gospels, much less of the whole Bible. But John Paul II has always considered this trend of scriptural scholarship so great a danger that it might lead to the breakup of the Church—unless tightly controlled.

The pope found particularly dangerous Schillebeeckx's approach to the identity of Christ, who had been defined by the Council of Chalcedon (451) as "true God and true man." Hence, according to official Catholic teaching, Christ was *a person of the Trinity* who preexisted his incarnation. Schillebeeckx simply stated: "I accept the grand theological symbolism behind this affirmation that Christ is called the Son of God as Jesus, as a human being. But then do we have to say that the Son of God, before being Jesus, was in God? These are highly abstract speculations."

In 1980 the Vatican opened additional proceedings against Schillebeeckx, prompted by a book in which he claimed that in case of extreme necessity the Christian community could provide itself with extraordinary ministers for consecrating the Eucharist. On June 13, 1984, Cardinal Ratzinger issued an ultimatum, rejecting his thesis. On July 5, 1984, a few weeks before Boff was called on the carpet, Schillebeeckx went to Ratzinger with the general of the Dominicans, Damian Byrne, to settle matters. He promised to drop the question of lay ministers from his next book. The message of conformity that John Paul II and the cardinal wished to convey was not lost on the Church's priests and theologians.

∙ ∙ ∙

Cardinal Ratzinger and Pope John Paul II were just as determined to suppress dissent in the North American Church as in Europe and Latin America.

In 1986 Father Charles Curran was relieved of his teaching post at the Catholic University of America in Washington, D.C. On March 8, Curran too had gone to Rome for a "conversation" with Cardinal Ratzinger. The Congregation for the Doctrine of the Faith disagreed with practically all of Curran's views on sexual morality. Curran maintained that the use of contraceptives and sterilization was not always and everywhere wrong. He suggested that the Church recognize divorce and accept stable relationships between homosexuals as "morally justified."

Ratzinger invited Curran to reexamine his position and recant, threatening to forbid him from teaching. When he got back to the United States, Curran publicly refused to back down. Then in August he received a letter from the Congregation for the Doctrine of the Faith informing him that he was no longer suitable or eligible for teaching theology because of his dissent from the Church's teaching.

The Vatican also began to keep a close eye on the American bishops so that no prelates in individual dioceses would take contrary positions on issues considered crucial by John Paul II. Thus in December 1985, the Vatican assigned an auxiliary bishop to represent the pope's interests following an exhaustive investigation of Archbishop Raymond Hunthausen of Seattle.

Hunthausen's problems with the Vatican began when he allowed mass to be celebrated by members of the homosexual organization Dignity, which, unlike the Church-sanctioned organization Courage, did not advocate celibacy for Catholic homosexuals. Hunthausen had also used laicized priests to perform the mass. He had participated in antinuclear protests at the Bremerton, Washington, submarine base on Puget Sound and had withheld half his income taxes on grounds that they would be used for nuclear arms.

Officially, his antinuclear activities were not under investigation. In fact, Hunthausen had never been specifically informed about why he was being investigated, who had accused him, or what exactly he was accused of. Nonetheless, after two years of investigation, including a thirteen-hour interrogation (he called it a "grilling") and interviews with seventy priests, nuns, and laypeople in his diocese, an auxiliary bishop was assigned to him with "special responsibilities" in five areas: the liturgy, the role of ex-priests, the ethics of health care (including issues related to gays), seminary training, and marriage annulments.

Hunthausen's treatment was resented by many American bishops, and after two years his special auxiliary was sent to another diocese. Yet the Vatican insisted that a coadjutor monsignor be assigned to the Seattle diocese, and in 1991 Hunthausen retired at the age of seventy, five years earlier than usual.

The policy of closely monitoring doctrine culminated in a relentless campaign waged by John Paul II against the Jesuit order and its general Pedro

Arrupe. Pope Wojtyła used all his powers to bring to heel a socially committed and intellectually brilliant religious order that didn't fit his notion of a Catholic *reconquista*. Before withdrawing in silence, Edward Schillebeeckx had once remarked: "Rome puts the accent on restoring 'the Sacred' and hierarchical structures. It seems to me that they want to return to the Ancien Régime of sacrality without passing through the French Revolution."

The Jesuits *had passed* through the French Revolution and all the other revolutions of the modern era, including those of Marx, Freud, and Einstein. Despite the wish of Arrupe to remain faithful and loyal to John Paul II, it was inevitable that a profound intellectual rift would emerge between the order and a pope who harbored strong suspicions about modernity. As he said in his book *Crossing the Threshold of Hope*, Wojtyła is convinced that in the last three centuries, the history of the West has to a large extent been dominated by "a struggle against God, by the systematic elimination of all that is Christian."

Pedro Arrupe did not share such gloomy judgments. He did not even like to use the word *crisis* to refer to the postconciliar era. He was disturbed by the fact that the number of Jesuits was dropping. "I'm afraid," he said, "that we're about to offer yesterday's answers to address tomorrow's problems, that we're talking in such a way that people no longer understand us, that we're using a language that doesn't go to the heart of men and women. If that's the case, then we'll talk a great deal, but only to ourselves. In fact no one will be listening to us anymore, because no one will grasp what we're trying to say."

When Wojtyła became pope, the Jesuit order was already under fire from traditionalist circles in the Curia. Amid the turmoil of the 1960s and 1970s the Jesuits showed up at all the theological frontiers, in those no-(Church)man's-lands where people were looking for new ways to conceive of or adapt the Christian message. Jesuits had criticized *Humanae Vitae*, Paul VI's encyclical (to which Karol Wojtyła had made a crucial contribution) prohibiting artificial means of contraception. Jesuits, among them the editor of the French review *Études*, published articles maintaining that abortion was permissible in some cases, because an embryo could not yet be considered a person. A Jesuit, Father John McNeill, admitted he was a homosexual and argued that the Church had to change its attitude toward gays. In Latin America Jesuits were committed to opposing all military regimes. Jesuits, including Father Arrupe himself, maintained that some elements of Marxism were acceptable. A Jesuit professor at the Pontifical Gregorian University in Rome, José María Diez Alegría, challenged papal infallibility and some of the Church's strict attitudes toward sex. Father Vincent O'Keefe, one of Arrupe's assistants, had suggested revising the Church's opposition to birth control.

In the thirty-three days of his pontificate, Pope John Paul I had found time to write a tough speech against the Jesuits, admonishing them not to get involved with economic and political problems, to maintain discipline, and to cultivate a spiritual life. "Don't let Jesuit teachings and publications be a source of confusion and disorientation . . ."

General Arrupe didn't always agree with the positions taken by individual Jesuits. At times he rebuked or punished them, aligning himself with directives from the Vatican. But he had great respect for intellectual freedom and the conscience-driven choices of individuals. During a trip to the United States he had visited the Jesuit Daniel Berrigan in prison, where he was serving a sentence for destroying Selective Service records during the Vietnam War. "I went to meet him because he couldn't come to my place," Arrupe said simply when asked why he made the gesture.

One year after his election, on September 22, 1979, John Paul II addressed harsh words to a group of Jesuit provincial superiors at an audience, exhorting them not "to succumb to the temptation of secularism."

The Black Pope (as the general of the Jesuits is traditionally called) took great care to reaffirm his loyalty to Pope Wojtyła. (Arrupe, like the pope, was a devotee of St. John of the Cross and his mystical poetry.) But two years later John Paul II, intent on getting this unruly order back into line, blocked Arrupe from calling a general congregation, the congress where the Jesuit order makes its most important decisions. On August 7, 1981, when Arrupe suffered a stroke, John Paul II decided on a move absolutely without precedent in the four-hundred-year history of the Society of Jesus.

Left paralyzed, Arrupe had appointed the American Vincent O'Keefe vicar general of the order. On October 3, in a letter to the provincial superiors, O'Keefe gave advance notice of a general congregation to elect Arrupe's successor. Three days later, Vatican Secretary of State Casaroli arrived at the

Jesuit Curia, located a few steps from the basilica of St. Peter, and asked to speak in private with Arrupe. Even Father O'Keefe was invited to leave the room where the paralyzed Arrupe was propped up in a chair. Casaroli delivered a message from the pope and exited after a few minutes.

Reentering the room, O'Keefe saw a shattered man. The general was in tears and could only point to the letter from the pope lying on a small table. The pope had forbidden the calling of the general congregation and had suspended the constitution of the society. To govern the Jesuits, John Paul II appointed his own "personal delegate," eighty-year-old Father Paul Dezza, and a coadjutor, Father Giuseppe Pittau.

On September 2, 1983, the general congregation of the Jesuits, prepared by Dezza, elected as general the Dutch Jesuit Hans Peter Kolvenbach, a less socially engaged cleric than many of his predecessors.

Pedro Arrupe died in 1991.

Four years later, when John Paul II opened the session of the thirty-fourth general congregation, gathered in Rome to discuss the principal problems of the order, he was still admonishing the Jesuits to carry out theological research "in docile harmony with the directives of the magisterium." Speaking to Jesuit delegates from all over the world the pope felt it necessary to emphasize that "you must watch attentively lest the faithful become disoriented by doubtful teachings, by publications or speeches that are in open conflict with the faith and morals of the Church."

THE GREAT SYNOD

On January 25, 1985, twenty years to the day after the close of Vatican Council II, Pope John Paul II, accompanied by seven cardinals, went to the ancient basilica of St. Paul Outside the Walls. The day's agenda called for a mass, crowning a week of prayer for Christian unity. On hand were representatives of the Anglican, Orthodox, Lutheran, Episcopalian, Waldensian, and Methodist churches. They heard the pope maintain that "unity must not be confused with leveling the individuality of each legitimate Christian tradition." Then John Paul II made an unexpected announcement: Twenty years after the

Vatican Council, he had decided to convoke an extraordinary gathering of bishops—a synod—to look into the impact of Vatican II on the life of the Catholic Church.

This synod would be held from November 25 to December 8, 1985, with the patriarchs from the Eastern churches and all the presidents of the bishops conferences throughout the world taking part. The pope struck a personal note: "For myself, as someone who had the special grace of taking part and of actively collaborating in the running of it, Vatican II has always been and still is, especially in these years of my pontificate, the constant point of reference for all my pastoral activity."

The place chosen for the announcement—St. Paul Outside the Walls—was full of symbolism: In that same monastery on January 25, 1959, Pope John XXIII had first divulged to the world his intention of calling an ecumenical council.

Legend has it that John XXIII broke the news of the Council by some sort of happy inspiration. In fact, he had spent a long time pondering the project. Wojtyła's coup de théâtre was similarly well prepared. On January 21 John Paul II had already been given a complete preliminary working plan drafted by Bishop Józef Tomko, permanent secretary general of the synod. On January 26, Tomko published in *L'Osservatore Romano* a long article spelling out the limits of the assembly: "The Synod is not the Council, nor is it a mini-Council."

Despite the usually slow rhythms of the curial bureaucracy, the preparation for the synod was rapid. On March 14 the members of the ruling body of the synod gathered in Rome and were received by the pope in an audience the next day. John Paul II pointed out the road they were to take. He spoke of the need to reject inauthentic interpretations of Vatican II—both those based on a mistaken attachment to tradition and those that invoked the Council to justify the marriage of priests, the "ordination of women, and so on." The teachings of Vatican II, the pope declared, were not up for discussion.

"It's the postconciliar period that has to be revised," he said.

John Paul II was now entering on one of the most dramatic tests of strength in his pontificate. The "erroneous" positions that he sought to combat were not primarily those of the fanatical admirers of the preconciliar

Church, like the rebel French bishop Marcel Lefebvre, who championed the Latin mass and called Vatican II heretical. The pope thought the real enemy was the trend toward taking the Council as a point of departure for further changes within the Church. The real enemies were the theologians and bishops who wanted to democratize the Church by assigning greater powers to the bishops conferences. The real enemies were Catholics disposed to revising sexual morality, who favored a new place for women in the Church, and who argued that the Church still had something to learn from the modern world.

In one of his airborne press conferences John Paul II had told journalists: "I don't think the eminent cardinals knew what kind of personality I am, and therefore what kind of papacy they were getting." Now, at last, everybody would find out.

· · ·

Preparatory work was still being done when Cardinal Ratzinger appeared on the scene. The prefect of the Congregation for the Doctrine of the Faith was obviously speaking for the pope when he said:

> The last ten years have been decidedly unfavorable for the Catholic Church. . . . What the popes and the Council Fathers were expecting was a new Catholic unity, and instead one has encountered a dissension which—to use the words of Paul VI—seems to have gone from self-criticism to self-destruction. There had been the expectation of a new enthusiasm, but all too often it has ended in boredom and discouragement. There had been expectation of a step forward, and instead one found oneself facing a progressive process of decadence that to a large measure has been unfolding under the sign of a summons to a presumed "spirit of the Council" and by so doing has actually and increasingly discredited it.

The endless references to this spirit infuriated Ratzinger. He saw in them the emergence of a *Konzilsungeist*, a conciliar demon or "antispirit."

This gloomy picture painted by Ratzinger was contained in a little book by the Italian writer Vittorio Messori, entitled *Report on the Faith*, published in

May 1985. Rapidly translated into many languages, it was retitled *The Ratzinger Report.*

The book had an unusual origin. Messori, who wrote for the religious journal *Jesus,* had planned to interview the cardinal. In the spring of 1984 Messori's editor approached Ratzinger about the possibility of transforming the prospective interview into a book. The cardinal didn't respond. Then, out of the blue, Messori was invited to present himself on August 15 in the little town of Bressanone at the foot of the Alps.

There, in the episcopal seminary, Messori met a Ratzinger very different from the harsh Teutonic "panzer cardinal" often portrayed in the press. "He was," Messori writes, "an ascetical person but quite human; he could smile and trade jokes. He went about dressed as a simple clergyman, without the pectoral cross worn by all bishops."

The three days Messori spent with Ratzinger provided a systematic review of all the problems of the contemporary Church. The picture drawn by Ratzinger was unsparing and alarming. He thought that the faithful were gradually losing any authentic sense of the Church "as a mysterious superhuman reality." He bemoaned the decline of the principle of obedience and the loss of a sacramental and hierarchical vision of the Church. He lamented the spread of doubts about every aspect of doctrine, especially about the real presence of Christ in the Eucharist, the perpetual virginity of Mary, the physical resurrection of Jesus, and the resurrection of the body promised to all humans at the end of time.

Ratzinger was inexorably pessimistic. "In the culture of the 'developed' world," he said, "the indissoluble bond between sexuality and motherhood has been ruptured. Separated from motherhood, sex has remained without a locus and has lost its point of reference. . . . Motherhood and virginity (the two loftiest values in which [woman] realizes her profoundest vocation) have become values that are in opposition to the dominant ones." He added, "A feminist mentality has also entered into women's religious orders. This is particularly evident, even in its most extreme forms, on the North American continent."

Ratzinger charged that "the damage we have suffered in these twenty years is due not to the 'true' council, but to the unleashing within the Church of latent polemical and centrifugal forces; and outside the Church it is due to the confrontation with a cultural revolution in the West: the success of the upper middle class, the new 'tertiary bourgeoisie,' with its liberal-radical ideology of individualistic, rationalistic, and hedonistic stamp."

The Ratzinger Report alarmed Protestants who had begun a dialogue with the Vatican, and was read within the Church as a reflection of the pope's most sincere thoughts. Some observers coined the phrase "Wojtyła's Restoration," based on these words of the cardinal:

> If by restoration we understand the search for a new balance after all the exaggerations of an indiscriminate opening to the world, after the overly positive interpretations of an agnostic and atheistic world, then a restoration understood in this sense (a newly found balance of orientations and values within the Catholic totality) is altogether desirable, and, for that matter, is already at work in the Church. In this sense it can be said that the first phase after Vatican II has come to a close.

.   .   .

One man openly challenged the prefect of the Congregation for the Doctrine of the Faith, the archbishop of Vienna, Franz König, the popemaker in the conclave that elected John Paul II. As the synod was on the point of meeting, a book-length interview with König by the Italian journalist Gianni Licheri appeared. "Putting the accent on the word *restore*," König said,

> sounds very much like nostalgia for the past. The Church of the past looked with fear at every new thing in history. It felt detached from the world, which it saw as evil in itself. The Council has reversed that sort of position, introducing the openness we now have to history, to non-Christians, to the ecumenical movement. . . .
>
> How could we even think of a feeling of fear that would lead the Church to regret having opened up back then, and to take up

once again the weapon of condemnation? The Church has to go forward.

For König one of the major achievements of Paul VI had been the creation of three Vatican secretariats that would engage in dialogue with other Christian churches, non-Christian religions, and nonbelievers. They enabled the Church to meet humanity as it was.

Churchmen, almost invariably, speak the language of memory. To attack the problems of today they brandish quotations from yesterday: texts from the Bible, passages from the Church Fathers, lines from former popes. To confront Ratzinger and the man in the Vatican who stood behind him, König quoted the famous speech with which John XXIII had inaugurated the Vatican Council. On that occasion Pope John spoke out "against the prophets of doom, who announce ever more ill-omened events, as if the end of the world was upon us."

After Vatican II, the bishops conferences had begun to act as a counterforce to the monarchical government of the Roman Curia. Ratzinger was taking a hard line against the trend of power sharing in the Church. König countered: "Before the Council the bishops were considered little more than functionaries of the pope."

The two cardinals were at odds on another point as well. After Vatican II the old catechism of the Council of Trent had been shelved, and the bishops conferences had been encouraged to write their own manuals, to adapt the preaching of the Catholic faith to the cultural situation in their various countries. This alarmed Pope Wojtyła, who sensed the danger of heretical opinions infiltrating Catholic dogma.

"It was a mistake to begin with, and a serious one, to suppress the catechism and declare it obsolete," Ratzinger argued. He implicitly suggested going back to a manual put together in the Vatican that would catalog the core elements of the faith. König disagreed: "That [kind of] catechism served the past; today we have to look to the future."

The two champions had many partisan supporters, although, as usual, within the Catholic Church no bishop would even admit that two cardinals were fighting so fiercely. Good manners demanded that each be said to be merely voicing his opinion. John Paul II told a journalist that Ratzinger's book simply expressed the cardinal's opinion. But this was disingenuous: The pope had read the manuscript in advance and strongly approved of it. His secretary, Dziwisz, had congratulated Messori.

In the West especially, Catholic bishops were generally worried about the same things: a drop in attendance at mass, the aging of the clergy, the rapid loss of priests, nuns, and other members of religious orders, the disaffection of the faithful from confession, the tumultuous changes in moral thinking in society itself. Many bishops were ready to subscribe to König's assertion that "The Church must go forward and renew the spirit of the Council," but at the same time they shared some of Ratzinger's fears. He had touched a sore point when he said that the Church could be neither club nor party nor association. It had to remain the "Church of the Lord as a place for the real presence of God in the world." People listened when Ratzinger said that they must never lose the awareness of an essential core of faith, anchored in a grand synthesis of the Creed, the Our Father, the Ten Commandments, and the sacraments.

In preparing for the synod, the bishops hoped to reinforce Church unity. Still, two polarizing issues quickly emerged: What was to be the power relationship between the bishops conferences and the Curia, and what interpretation was to be given to the two decades of Church history since Vatican II?

On April 1 the Secretariat of the Synod had sent all the bishops conferences a questionnaire to help prepare a working paper for the assembly. The bishops were asked what had been done in their dioceses to make the Council known and accepted, what had been its positive effects, what errors and abuses had arisen in its wake, what remedies had been adopted, and what future steps would be useful in continuing to implement its teachings.

As soon as the replies began to come in, there was a whiff of gunpowder in the air.

The English bishops, led by Cardinal Basil Hume, were the first to enter the fray. In their official response sent to the Vatican in July, they attacked the "centralism of Rome" in the liturgy, in the appointment of bishops, and in some doctrinal interventions. With unusual frankness they accused the Vatican of mismanaging its bank, the Institute for Religious Works (IOR), which was directed by Monsignor Paul Marcinkus, one of John Paul II's close associates. The language of the document had a touch of British understatement: "It is felt that a clear presentation of the affairs of the Holy See is lacking." Finally the English bishops demanded a revision of the triennial synod's mode of operation—an elegant way of complaining that its role was insignificant. The document was made public, prompting some irritation in the Vatican.

The American bishops took the same line as their English colleagues. Bishop James Malone, president of the U.S. bishops conference, stated, "I don't share the view that the episcopal conferences ought not to play too large or active a role in the life of the Church." Malone boldly attacked Ratzinger (without naming him, of course). "The prophets of gloom, of whom John XXIII spoke, are still very much with us. They would have it that the last two decades have witnessed nothing but dissolution and collapse and that the Church can be saved only by returning to some earlier, fictitious golden age. While sympathizing with their undoubtedly sincere conviction, I don't believe that we can accept either their analysis or their prescriptions."

The preparatory document of the American bishops was also made public. A few days later the Vatican Secretariat of State issued a secret order to the nuncios (papal ambassadors) worldwide to tell the bishops of their countries not to publish their replies to the Holy See's questionnaire. The Vatican was getting nervous.

The Canadian and Dutch bishops didn't bow to the pressure, however. Holland directly challenged the Vatican: "Does the Holy See practice in sufficient measure the collegiality that it asks from others?" The bishops denounced as authoritarian behavior the imposition of Paul VI's *Humanae Vitae*. In addition, they lamented the intrusiveness of the nuncios in the affairs of national churches. According to the Dutch bishops, the nunciatures were no substitute for direct contact between the bishops and the Holy See.

The Canadians were even harsher. Their document assaulted the Curia's increasing tendency to centralization and uniformity. To counter it, the Canadian bishops asked the pope to create a permanent synod with adequate powers and responsibilities for real governance. From Belgium came support for the Canadian request. The Belgian bishops hoped that the jurisdiction of the synod would be widened. Even where the prelates were more cautious, as in France or Spain, criticism of the curial bureaucracy was undisguised.

At the Vatican this barrage of calls for a reduction in the Curia's power caused a good deal of indignation. One theologian very close to the pope, Hans Urs von Balthasar, commented, "They're hitting Ratzinger to get at the pope." Papal hard-liners didn't fail to make their voices heard, too. Monsignor Antonio Quarracino, president of the Latin American bishops conference and a bitter enemy of liberation theology, even invoked Satan, "who has doubled his efforts to create in the Church an atmosphere of uncertainty and disorder."

John Paul II liked that kind of language. He had never failed to put the faithful on guard against the "Great Dragon, the Ancient Serpent, him whom we call the Devil and Satan, and who seduces the whole earth." More than once he had explained that, "the gates of hell will not prevail, as the Lord has said. But that doesn't mean we are exempt from the trials from and battles against the Evil One."

.   .   .

For Karol Wojtyła, being pope meant demanding obedience—and vetoing any attempt to limit the supreme power given to him by Roman Catholic tradition. When John Paul II went to Holland for the first time just before the synod, he found himself being directly challenged by his own Church.

His arrival had been preceded by violent polemics over the selection of the new bishop of the diocese of Den Bosch. The pope had chosen a man far removed from the democratic and reformist tendencies of Dutch Catholicism, provoking demonstrations in the streets.

When his Holland tour brought the pope to Den Bosch, he found that most of the faithful and the clergy were bristling. They considered the new bishop, Jan Ter Schure, far too conservative, the complete opposite of his predecessor, Wilhelmus Bekkers, who had sometimes been called "the Pope John of the Netherlands." But above all Dutch Catholics felt that their sense of fair play had been violated. In accordance with ancient tradition, the chapter of senior prelates who administer the Den Bosch cathedral had given the pope a list of three candidates, from which he was to pick one. John Paul II rejected all three names and foisted Jan Ter Schure on the diocese. In so doing he was trampling on a vestige of ancient democracy within the Catholic Church. When the pope arrived for Ter Schure's installation and led a procession in honor of the Virgin, he found the streets practically deserted in silent protest.

During his sermon John Paul II tried to explain his choice: "I know you have been going through a difficult time in the last few weeks. Some recent appointments of bishops have deeply offended some of you." It was obvious that there was a chill among the audience as he spoke in the Gothic cathedral. "Every time he appoints a bishop the pope tries to understand the life of the local Church. He gathers information and seeks advice. You will understand that opinions are sometimes divided. In the final analysis, the pope has to make the decision."

Perhaps for the first time a modern Roman pontiff was obliged to justify himself. John Paul II even admitted to feeling grieved: "Brothers and sisters, be convinced that I have listened carefully and prayed. And I appointed the person whom I thought before God the most suitable for this office." The majority of Dutch Catholics were not moved.

•   •   •

On the morning of Sunday, November 24, a procession of more than four hundred patriarchs, cardinals, and bishops emerged from the shadows of Bernini's colonnade into the open space of St. Peter's Square. Lined up two by two, they had come directly from the Vatican Palace. They had descended the Scala Regia (Royal Stairs) and now, passing through the Bronze Door, they made their way toward the basilica.

Dressed in long white pontifical robes, they followed the crossbearer with a slow, deliberate pace, each holding a booklet with the special prayer for the synod: "Lord Jesus, enlighten your Church so that it may have no other desire but to hear your voice and to follow you. Keep watch over the pastors of your Church." From a distance on the almost empty square, the white miters and gold-embroidered robes seemed to sway gently in the breeze, shining against the dark pavement.

In his homily John Paul II evoked the spiritual climate of the Council and the richness of its teachings: "During the next two weeks all the synodal fathers, many of whom have lived in person the extraordinary grace of the Council, will walk with the Council once more, so as to revive the atmosphere of that great event." He didn't touch on the specific issues of the synod, but on one point he had already spoken out sharply. On the eve of the inaugural celebration a special meeting of the cardinals was held in the Vatican. While discussing the reorganization of the Curia, he had stressed that it was an instrument of the pope, bound to him by absolute obedience. He labeled as "aberrant" the critics who described the Curia as a parallel power or as a kind of barrier between the pope and his flock.

The real work of the synod began on Monday with the introductory report of Cardinal Godfried Danneels of Brussels, delivered to the 159 synod fathers who took their places in the Vatican Hall of Synods. There were thirteen patriarchs of the Eastern churches, three representatives of the religious orders, all the curial department heads, and twenty members appointed by the pope on his own authority.

The hall rose in semicircular tiers, like an ancient Greek theater. On the bottom level the bishops faced a table at which three cardinals chaired the extraordinary assembly. On the bottom too sat John Paul II, taking everything in.

. . .

Imagine a parliament that meets every three years but has no legislative powers, can't choose its own agenda, has no right to vote on a petition without the monarch's permission, and has only one chance to declare its view of the way its own community is being governed. Imagine the members of this parliament having only a few days to speak out in front of everyone else, with little opportunity for informal communication. Not surprisingly, the delegates to the synod threw themselves into the debate with a burst of energy. The fifteen speeches that followed one another in the synod's first few hours created a rich tapestry of the issues at stake, of the protagonists' intentions, and of the tensions rippling through the assembly.

Cardinal Juan Landazuri Ricketts of Peru confessed that in his country there was widespread ignorance about the Council. Its documents were either unknown or had had little impact on daily life. Speaking for clerics who were tired of reform, he claimed, "There are those who think everything has to be started over again, going beyond the Council, attributing to it things it never said, or unfairly using the Council to justify their own ideas and initiatives."

The Korean cardinal Stefan Kim contradicted Landazuri Ricketts: *"Aggiornamento* in the Church is an ongoing job. The reform of the Church is not exhausted in twenty years." Kim then launched a first strike at the Curia, citing the danger that "rigid interpretations, dictated by the longing for stability," could stifle the creativity of local churches.

Cardinal Eugenio Araujo Sales, from Brazil, replied, "Without Peter the bishops cannot maintain the unity of the Church. Without valid communion with the pope they are exposed to divisions, heresies, and apostasies."

Many delegates felt they were being treated like vassals. South African bishop Denis Eugene Hurley argued that in relations between the Holy See and the local churches the principle of "subsidiarity" had to be applied, meaning that the Roman Curia shouldn't interfere in issues that the local churches could resolve on their own.

Seated at the president's desk, John Paul II listened in silence, his chin propped up on his hand. He didn't guide or control the debate. At times he took notes, at times he closed his eyes, following his own train of thought or praying in silence. He never made a comment. Not even when the Ukrainian bishop of Winnipeg, Maxim Hermaniuk, dared speak a word—*power*—so seldom heard in debate in the Catholic Church. "At the end of every synod the bishops have noticed how totally inadequate their situation is and have expressed their strong desire to see the synod endowed with the power to make law," the bishop said. But it was all to little effect.

· · ·

The whole organization of the synod had developed under tremendous time constraints. About seven months had passed from the mailing of the questionnaire to the opening of the assembly. This, as the pope well knew, didn't really allow Catholic communities all over the world to do any in-depth consultation about the effects of the Council or work out proposals for consideration at the synod. In many places the bishops scarcely had a chance to meet. The faithful and the various Catholic associations had had no practical say in this crucial enterprise of evaluating one of the greatest religious revolutions of the twentieth century: Vatican II.

The bishops conferences hadn't even been able to contribute to the *lineamenta*, the working paper produced to prepare every synodal gathering. There was no working paper here; and the bishops found the introductory report of Cardinal Danneels in their Roman residences barely twenty-four hours before the assembly's opening. Finally, the synod itself had been scheduled to be exceptionally short: two weeks.

This hurried pace wasn't detrimental to everyone. It limited the formation of groups that might have altered the preconceived outcome of the deliberations, while it made it easier for the pope's co-workers to steer the synod toward his desired goals. Veterans of Vatican II were well aware that anyone who wants to reform existing structures or push forward new ideas needs time to form alliances among the bishops and to sensitize public opinion inside and outside the Church. The plenary debate lasted four days. During eight sessions, 137 bishops and cardinals took the floor. Other speeches were submitted in written form. It was a gigantic examination of conscience for a community of nine hundred million faithful.

Anyone following the debate in the plenary assembly, however, would have noticed that the persons named by the pope to key Vatican posts or long associated with Wojtyła often delivered the strongest denunciations of the errors and problems that had emerged in the years following the Council.

Polish bishop Jerzy Strzoba turned the synod's attention toward the crisis of European civilization and the "false interpretations" of theologians, which he claimed were preventing an authentic application of the Council's teachings. The bishop, who was very close to John Paul II, pointed to a key phrase of Vatican II, "People of God." With this term the Council Fathers had described the Church as a community of the faithful on the march through, but not above, history, a living community open to the world and not the perfect society imagined by the Council of Trent. "The doctrine of the Church as the People of God," Bishop Strzoba told his confrères, "has stirred up great anxiety and ambiguity." Wrongly interpreted, it might mislead Catholics into thinking that all the powers of the Church—priestly, magisterial, and pastoral—derived from the laity.

Instead Strzoba cited the concept of the Church as the Mystical Body of Christ: "The fundamental structures of the Church are willed by God himself," and hence they may not be touched, he said. "Behind the human façade stands the mystery of a superhuman reality, in which the reformer, the sociologist, and the organizer have no right to interfere."

Meanwhile, Monsignor Philip Delhaye, secretary of the International Theological Commission, appointed a member of the synod by John Paul II, did something that no one else dared: He directly attacked the Council itself, under the cloak of faulting some of its oversights.

Turning to the audience, he first said: "The Council was a thousand times right to speak of the greatness of the human person, of his rights and dignity, of the value of earthly realities." Then, amid the expectant silence, Delhaye asked the bishops: "But did the Council say enough about Christ the Redeemer, about the Cross, about grace?" Having launched his challenge, he cited the second oversight: Vatican II hadn't taken sufficient care in expounding the principles of moral theology. Third, Vatican II didn't pay enough attention to the priests: "We have noted a tremendous identity crisis in these same priests, an increasingly secularistic focus on the problems of priests, of their status, of their way of life. We have noted the discouragement, the deep sadness of many priests, the painful defections, the crisis in vocations."

But the assembly was not lacking in personalities ready to oppose such views. Bishop Ivo Lorscheiter, president of the Brazilian bishops conference, for instance, turned to the pope and exclaimed: "With all reverence, humility, and obedience we ask, Let the Council be considered a light, not a limit, to our future path."

John Paul II, closely following the assembly, was chagrined to note that key issues, which he thought he had resolved, kept popping up. In a speech that caused a furor in the Vatican, the president of the Austrian bishops conference, Karl Berg, argued that in the light of medical advances it was opportune to review the problem of the "responsible transmission of human life." Decoded, Berg's message meant that that it was high time to rethink the ban on contraception in Paul VI's encyclical *Humanae Vitae*. Forty-eight hours later, the archbishop was compelled to issue a press communiqué explaining that he hadn't been protesting against the teaching of the Church and the pope on the subject of procreation.

Berg also raised another delicate issue: allowing Catholics who had been divorced and remarried to receive communion. "Assuming a salutary repentance, a way ought to be found to give them the sacraments." Bishops from Africa and Japan supported him. Implicitly, Berg's speech had raised once again the question of the synod's real powers, of relations between the bishops and the Roman pontiff—in a word, of collegiality.

. . .

The bishops from the Third World had a different set of priorities. The issue closest to their hearts was the possibility of preaching the Christian faith in a way that suited the culture and mentality of their own people. They wanted to prevent the message of Christ from being perceived in Africa or Asia as something "Western." To express this need they used the word *inculturation*. Bishop Jean Marie Cissé of Mali explained how important it was for Africans that conversion to Christianity not amount to abandoning their original culture and community. The president of the bishops conference of Chad, Charles Vandame, proposed going back to the tradition of regional or continental synods, a usage from the first centuries of Christianity, and setting up an African synod. Indonesian bishop Francis Xavier Hadisumarta pointed out that new initiatives were required to make the Gospel more understandable to the people of Asia, who represented half of the world's population and most of whom adhered to other religions.

In one way or another, even when speaking of inculturation, the synod was returning to the mother of all questions: What real share do the bishops have in the decision making of the Church universal?*

---

* Not until the Middle Ages, with Gregory VII (d. 1085) and Innocent III (d. 1216), both extremely authoritarian popes, did the Catholic Church begin to develop along the lines of an absolute monarchy. In the first centuries of Christianity the bishops were chosen by the people. And as bishops of Rome the popes are still elected by the cardinals, who symbolically represent the Roman clergy. In the

Like background music, this theme accompanied all the plenary sessions. It was all for naught. Any reform proposals shattered against the will of the pope. John Paul II listened to everything, remembered everything, and favored the greatest freedom of discussion. But from the outset he had decided that papal power was not to be diminished, that all believers, priests, bishops, and the pope had to go back to recognizing the idea of the Church as the Mystical Body of Christ. The theology of the Cross, with its stress on sacrifice and redemption, had to be placed at the center of the faith, instead of the theology of the People of God and its ambiguous concepts of liberation. Also, the pope was convinced that it was essential to make a start on a new universal catechism, defined and written in Rome.

After the plenary debate, working groups got together to draft their papers. The request for a universal catechism was pushed through practically every group. All requests for a new balance of power between the bishops and the Holy See, however, were smothered by the supporters of the pope. A full thirty-five bishops, one-quarter of those present in the plenary assembly, had addressed the issue, but it was barely mentioned in the draft of the final document. John Paul II let it be known through his inner circle that he was satisfied with the progress of the synod. Notwithstanding some fears, a basically positive vision of Vatican II prevailed. The bishops were united in reaffirming that the Church's principal task was to evangelize the world. In the countries where Christianity had ancient roots, this actually meant reevangelizing millions of baptized persons who often just paid lip service to the Church's teachings. Hence, to bring the Gospel to modern man, the bishops concluded, a new approach was needed. The Church had to talk about everyday problems or the place of God would be taken by worldly goods with a resulting nihilism.

Squeezed between the limits dictated by John Paul II and working within a time frame designed to be as brief as possible, the synod got only one concession from John Paul II, a chance to vote on the final report

---

Orthodox churches, which invoke an extremely ancient apostolic tradition, the supreme authority is not the patriarch, but the synod, an organ that is substantially democratic because every national church enjoys uncontested autonomy.

prepared by Cardinal Danneels. The synod never got the freedom of the Council whose work it was theoretically judging. The synod didn't even have a chance to vote on a list of recommendations to be made to the pope. Even then there was a restriction in the way the votes on the final report were to be cast. The delegates could say only "yes" or "no," whereas traditionally in the Church's assemblies there is a custom of letting delegates also vote *placet juxta modum*, "Yes, but with emendations."

The final report of Cardinal Danneels came up for a vote on December 7 and passed almost unanimously. It was, in some ways, a balanced document that tried to address the main subjects discussed in the assembly.

John Paul II had achieved his goal of stabilization of the Church. "The Synod confirmed the Vatican Council as the Magna Carta of the Church and the greatest gift of God's grace for the twentieth century," observed the exiled theologian Hans Küng. "And that's among its positive aspects. On the other hand, the bishops' requests on the most burning issues were cast into oblivion. The bishops in general showed that they were more open-minded than the traditionalists in the Curia, but they had to face a pope who was not John XXIII. There was now sitting on the papal throne a Great Communicator and a Great Conservative."

John Paul II was quite satisfied with the report of the synod and the bishops' approval of it. He had never wanted to simply turn back the clock of history. His intention had been to institute reforms in the Church without shaking the structure and theological patrimony handed down through the ages. "The synod," he announced to the bishops, "has done a good job." It had advocated the Church's opening up to the world while avoiding a secular mentality and value system. It had preached the importance of inculturation and dialogue with the other religions and unbelievers. It had reaffirmed Catholic social doctrine, and quietly voiced its hopes for consultation at all Church levels.

In his whole concluding speech John Paul II never once mentioned the Church as the "People of God," citing once again the "Mystical Body of Christ," which happened to be the title of one of Pius XII's last encyclicals, the one Wojtyła himself had quoted in his preparatory paper for Vatican II.

When the assembly broke up after the singing of the Magnificat, the pope invited all the bishops and cardinals to dine with him in the Hospice of St. Martha in the Vatican. There he raised his glass as if offering a toast and asked ironically: "Why has the synod been extraordinary? It was called unexpectedly, it lasted only a short time, and it seems to have disappointed many people.

"Why disappointed?" he continued, his eyes scanning the waves of crimson and violet birettas crowded around the tables. "Because they expected a terrible struggle among the bishops, a conflict between them and the pope. And it never happened!" Beaming like a rector surrounded by his docile seminarians, John Paul II concluded amid the laughter of his audience: "Let's hope we haven't disappointed the Holy Spirit."

Seven months later, on June 11, 1986, *L'Osservatore Romano* published the list of the members of a restricted committee charged with drawing up a new universal catechism. Its chairman was Cardinal Joseph Ratzinger.

GESTURES

During John Paul II's papacy, conciliar reforms, however modest, spread throughout the Church and were realized in the daily practice of many Catholic communities: a modernized liturgy; improved relations with members of Protestant, Orthodox, and Jewish faiths; more frequent consultation between the Vatican and the bishops; increased (though still limited) roles for girls and women in the mass and other religious ceremonies; presentation of the Church as a community, not just a hierarchical, monarchical society.

Yet after the synod, John Paul II also blocked efforts to pursue many of the ideas and impulses of Vatican II; and in the ensuing years of his pontificate he virtually throttled discussion of all internal difficulties and tensions in the Church.

But Pope John Paul II had never concentrated exclusively on the internal workings of the Church. He had always seen the Church as a major factor in the world; not just a spiritual and diplomatic agency, but a huge social and humanitarian force: The Catholic Church educated more people than any other nongovernment institution in the world, cared for more refugees, ran more hospitals, sent out more missionaries, possessed more cultural treasures.

In 1985 he launched what curial prelates called a great "dialogue offensive" aimed at the believers of Allah. He had a high opinion of some aspects of the Muslim religion: its strong monotheism, its grand submission to a kind and compassionate God, its obligation of regular prayer, and, as he remarked more than once, its requirements of penitential fasts—a rapidly vanishing feature of Christianity in the West. But he also had a distrust of Islam that bordered on fear. "I'm very worried about fundamentalism, Islamic fundamentalism, Iran, Saddam [Hussein of Iraq], North Africa," he confided to Israel's ambassador to Italy, Avi Pazner.

It was above all in Africa that the pope was struck by the absolute necessity for a dialogue with Islam. In North Africa, from Egypt to the Maghreb, it was indispensable for the survival of the Catholic Church, whose members were very much a minority. The need for more extensive contacts, however, was also closely connected with the situation in the Southern Hemisphere, particularly in sub-Saharan Africa where the Church was rapidly expanding, but where Islam was growing even more quickly. In this struggle for believers, Islam had certain advantages: an uncomplicated creed with few precepts, no clerical apparatus or hierarchical structures, and a faith rather elastic in its treatment of traditional customs and favorable to polygamy. To avoid a disastrous clash between the two religions, it was vital, the pope thought, to create an atmosphere of coexistence, a task to which he applied himself vigorously.

It wasn't easy. In 1982, on a trip to Nigeria, he had planned a stop in the town of Kaduna, in a Muslim-dominated area some four hundred miles from Lagos, to meet a delegation of Muslim religious leaders. But when the pope arrived, they refused to see him. Instead, he was hurried into a little room at the airport where he delivered his prepared speech ("We can call one another brothers and sisters through our faith in one God") to an audience consisting of the governor and his entourage, before flying back to Lagos.

In 1985, when the pontiff returned to Africa, he made another overture to Islam in Morocco, where participants in the Pan-Arab Games had gathered in Casablanca. King Hassan II had tried to organize a large-scale meeting for the pope with representatives of the twenty-three countries taking part in the games. But they too refused to see him. To save the day, the king then called a meeting at the city stadium, where fifty thousand enthusiastic Moroccan youngsters had been summoned. The young people gave John Paul II a warm reception. "Dialogue between Christian and Muslims," he told his listeners, "is more crucial today than ever . . . in a world that is increasingly secular and, at times, atheistic. Young people can make a better future if they commit themselves to building this new world according to God's plan. . . . Today we have to testify to the spiritual values that the world needs."

But the pope's hopes for a common Christian-Muslim front against contemporary materialism and atheism collided with the surge of Islamic fundamentalism in the early 1980s. Several years later, visiting with the Italian industrialist Carlo De Benedetti at the Olivetti factory in Ivrea, the pope spoke with uncharacteristic harshness about Islam and the dangers he sensed in it. To counter fundamentalist influence and bring more stability to moderate Muslim governments, he suggested that De Benedetti and other Western capitalists invest in Islamic states, creating factories and jobs.

De Benedetti was somewhat taken aback by the conversation:

"You are familiar with our religion?" the pope asked him, apparently aware that De Benedetti was half-Jewish.

"Of course I know it."

"Ours is a religion of peace and love—and you don't have to tell me we don't always practice it." He paused. "Did you ever read the Qur'an? I recommend it. What the Qur'an teaches people is aggression; and what we teach our people is peace. Of course, you always have human nature, which distorts whatever message religion is sending. But even though people can be led astray by vices and bad habits, Christianity aspires to peace and love. Islam is a religion that attacks. If you start by teaching aggression to the whole community, you end up pandering to the negative elements in everyone. You know what that leads to: Such people will assault us."*

---

* De Benedetti was also dismayed to find he was required to make a contribution to the papal treasury before the pope would consent to visit the Olivetti factory. "How much?" one of his deputies asked

Despite such fears, John Paul II was always careful to distinguish in his public statements between Islam itself and Islamic fundamentalism. In the face of opposition from *Catholic* fundamentalists, he encouraged the construction in Rome of the largest mosque in Western Europe. But he insisted that Islamic countries be equally generous in allowing freedom of religion to Christians.

•   •   •

If dialogue with the Muslims was a necessity, John Paul II saw dialogue with the Jews as a duty, particularly because of the Holocaust. Two of the Vatican Council's premises had been that the Jewish roots of Christianity had to be acknowledged and that anti-Semitism was intolerable. John Paul II brought these ideas to fulfillment with a grand gesture on April 13, 1986.

On that day Wojtyła crossed the Tiber to enter the Synagogue of Rome on the Lungotevere dei Cenci, something no pope had ever done before. As Roman Jews know, their community is older than the oldest Christian church. When Sts. Peter (as tradition has it) and Paul came to Rome, the Torah was already being read and the Sabbath observed in the capital of the Roman Empire. When Christians went from suffering persecution to instigating it, among their principal victims were the Jews. During Easter Week Jews were forced to listen to sermons (they plugged their ears) and were jeered for having "assassinated Christ." It was only thanks to the unification of Italy, carried out by the king of Savoy Victor Emmanuel II (whom Pius IX excommunicated because the king's armies had invaded the Papal States), that Italian Jews acquired full freedom and civil rights. The imposing synagogues built in Turin, Florence, and Rome near the turn of the twentieth century thus bore double witness to the faith of the Jews and the defeat of the pope.

In June 1963, the chief rabbi of Rome had gone to St. Peter's Square to pray for the dying Pope John XXIII. John was revered as the man who had

the papal scheduler. A figure of $100,000 was suggested, and De Benedetti wrote a check for that amount to the pope himself. He presented the check to Wojtyła during a quiet moment on the pope's factory tour.

expunged from the Catholic liturgy for Holy Saturday the insulting reference to the Jews as "perfidious."

Now in April 1986, John Paul II arrived in the old Roman ghetto, seeking to ease painful memories. The largo from Handel's *Xerxes* played plangently as he stepped out of his limousine. But when he walked inside—the first Roman pontiff ever to enter a synagogue—a curtain of silence descended. A humble and respectful John Paul II exchanged an embrace with Chief Rabbi Elio Toaff. The pope wore a white zucchetto (skullcap) and his papal robes, the rabbi his eight-cornered hat and, draped over his shoulders, a white-and-blue-striped tallith. Together they walked down the Assyro-Babylonian nave of the synagogue and took their places on the teva—the platform where the cantor stands and the Torah is read.

Wojtyła listened to a speech by the leader of Rome's Jewish community, Giacomo Saban, who recalled how copies of the Talmud were burned on the Campo dei Fiori in 1553. The pope seemed pained when Saban alluded to the terrible silence of Pius XII, who never denounced Nazi atrocities against the Jews, and the deportations of Jews that were carried out in the heart of Rome: "What was happening on one bank of the Tiber [where the synagogue is located]," Saban noted, "couldn't be ignored across the river [where the Vatican is]."

That day the world saw a different Pope Wojtyła—not the master of the crowds, but a man who bore the weight of a tragic history, which the pope from Wadowice had dedicated himself to changing. Rabbi Toaff asked him to establish diplomatic relations between the Vatican and the state of Israel. (He did so in 1993, over the objections of his Secretariat of State, which was waiting for the government of Israel to reach an accord with the Palestinians first.)

When he delivered his speech in the synagogue, John Paul II's voice at times seemed close to cracking. He acknowledged the wounds endured for hundreds of years by Jews living in Christian countries, "acts of discrimination, unjustified limitations of religious freedom, and oppressive restriction of civil freedom as well. . . . Yes, once again, speaking through me the Church deplores, in the words of the [Council document] *Nostra Aetate*, the hatreds, the persecutions, and all the manifestations of anti-Semitism directed against the Jews at any time by whomever." The pope fell silent, looked straight at his audience, and said: "I repeat, *by whomever.*" Then he called the Jews the "older brothers" of Christians and, recalling the doors of convents and churches opened during World War II to Jewish victims of persecution, he pointed to future common goals: the end of all discrimination, the defense of human dignity, adhesion to individual and social ethics, peace, and coexistence between the two religions, "animated by brotherly love."

As a boy Karol Wojtyła had gone to the synagogue in Wadowice with his father to hear the celebrated cantor Moishe Savitski. Now, dressed in his satin papal robes, he sat hunched in a gilded armchair listening to a choir sing a hymn that had been chanted by condemned Jews in the death camps on their way to the gas chambers. As the voice of the choir swelled in the house of prayer, the pope bent further forward, his head bowed and his hand covering his mouth.

.   .   .

That same year, 1986, John Paul II went to India. Praying before the tomb of Gandhi in New Delhi, he brushed with his hand the black stone on which are inscribed the "seven social sins," as described by the founder of modern India: "Politics without principle. Wealth without work. Pleasure without conscience. Knowledge without character. Commerce without morality. Science without humanity. Religion without sacrifice." At Indira Gandhi Stadium, he addressed an audience representing the various Indian religions. "As Hindus, Muslims, Sikhs, Buddhists, Jainists, Parsees, and Christians, we are gathered here in brotherly love," he said. "In proclaiming the truth about man we insist on the fact that the quest for temporal and social well-being and for full human dignity corresponds to the profound longing of our spiritual nature."

Encouraged by his reception in India, he developed the idea of holding an international, interreligious assembly in Assisi, the city of St. Francis, the most peace-loving and most joyful of the Christian saints, to pray for world peace—another grand gesture of his pontificate. The pope had been discouraged by resumption of the arms race and the breakdown of negotiations in Reykjavík between Reagan and Gorbachev. And so he conceived the idea of an extraordinary initiative involving all the world's religions—a great common prayer to God, who would be invoked with all his names, in all languages, with the accent peculiar to each religious tradition to save the world from nuclear annihilation, end the cold war, and promote universal peace.

On the morning of October 27, 1986, in many spots around the globe, combatants momentarily stopped waging war. A few weeks before, in Lyons, Pope Wojtyła had launched an appeal for a "universal truce," a symbolic halt to all the armed conflicts that were staining the world with blood. He had made this request of military leaders and politicians in charge of nations and of revolutionary movements. He had also asked it "of those who are seeking to achieve their goals by means of terrorism and violence." Bishops and nuncios had contacted all warring parties that could be reached by the Catholic Church. Positive replies had come in from far and wide: from Ireland the IRA had given its assent; from Beirut so had the president of Lebanon, Amin Gemayel, and the country's Shiite and Sunni leaders; President Corazon Aquino of the Philippines, whose government was locked in struggle with the Moros, Muslim guerrillas, and Prince Sihanouk in Cambodia had both said yes. So had the Saharan guerrillas of the Polisario front, the Contras in Nicaragua, the guerrilla leaders in Angola and Sudan, the FARC of Colombia, the Frente Farabundo Martí in El Salvador, as well as the government of Sri Lanka and its opponents the Tamil Tigers.

In countries not at war, civil and religious authorities organized a moment of silent meditation. Meanwhile, in the plain at the foot of Assisi, John Paul II received long ranks of religious leaders: the Archbishop of Canterbury, the chief rabbi of Rome, the Dalai Lama, the metropolitan of Kiev (sent by the patriarch of all the Russias), the special representative of the patriarch of Constantinople, emissaries of the Buddhists, Muslims, Hindus, Zoroastrians, Sikhs, Shintoists, and traditional African and Native American religions.

Altogether, symbolically, the participants in Assisi represented four billion believers from sixty-five faiths and denominations. In the ancient cathedral of San Rufino, the pope prayed with the Christian delegates. In the church of St. Peter incense wafted through the air and Buddhists struck their gongs. In an old hall next to the Piazza del Comune Catholic priests prostrated themselves on the floor alongside Muslim imams. In the church of St. Gregory two Native Americans smoked a peace pipe. Not far away the Zoroastrians were lighting, with some difficulty, their sacred fire.

"The challenge of peace," the pope said, "transcends religious differences." On a note of self-criticism he added, "I am ready to acknowledge that . . . [we Catholics] have not always been builders of peace." For that reason, he added, his prayer was also an act of penance.

In the Roman Curia the whole day stirred up rumblings of discontent among the more traditional cardinals. The pope felt obliged to address the issue in his Christmas speech to the curial staff. Denying that the prayers at Assisi had either "hidden or diluted" the differences between religions, John Paul II defined the observance as a visible illustration of the meaning of ecumenism and of the effort to achieve the kind of interreligious dialogue promoted by Vatican II. The Holy Spirit, he stressed, grants all men and women access, in mysterious ways, to truth and salvation. Assisi had seen the manifestation of the "radiant mystery" of the unity of the entire human race.

John Paul II came to believe that the combined prayer by all the religious leaders that day was the turning point in the cold war and the beginning of the end of the arms race.

PART SEVEN

THE FALL OF COMMUNISM

The pope's first real sign of "socialism with a human face"—four years and three months after the declaration of martial law in Poland—came in the unlikely form of a visit to the Vatican on February 27, 1985, by Soviet foreign minister Andrei Gromyko. In Moscow, unbeknownst to the pope, Konstantin Chernenko was near death. Twelve days later Gromyko, who had served every Soviet leader since Stalin, would play a crucial role in the selection of Mikhail Gorbachev to succeed Chernenko as general secretary of the Communist Party of the USSR. ("Comrades," he would tell the Politburo, "this man has a nice smile but he's got iron teeth.")

Gromyko now let the pope know that the USSR might be interested in establishing diplomatic relations with the Holy See. When John Paul II voiced his concerns about world peace, particularly the need for progress at the stalled Geneva talks on arms control, and the plight of Catholics in the Soviet Union, Gromyko seemed unusually responsive. He suggested further explorations of such matters by representatives of the USSR and the Vatican. This overture took Wojtyła completely by surprise.

That spring, in May, he began receiving reports from Poland that Gorbachev might indeed be a different kind of Communist and that the Brezhnev era might finally be ending, two and a half years after his death. Gorbachev had traveled to Poland in late April to attend a meeting of the Consultative Political Committee of the Warsaw Pact. More consequentially, when the meeting adjourned, Gorbachev remained behind to speak with Jaruzelski. He had only an hour, the new general secretary said, but then the hour stretched into five as the two men conducted an exhaustive review of the situation in Poland and the USSR—and a long discussion about the pope and the Vatican.

From this discussion, Jaruzelski concluded that Gorbachev was a different kind of Communist and took steps, through the primate, to inform the pope of their meeting. "It was a critical moment," Jaruzelski disclosed almost a decade later (and Gorbachev too confirmed the portentous nature of their encounter): "Five hours of conversation face to face without an interpreter." Much of it centered on the Church and Wojtyła, but first "we spoke about the past, about the origins of the system, about the necessity for change."

Gorbachev had been general secretary for only a few weeks and he wanted to learn firsthand as much as possible about the internal situation in Poland and about the Holy See. Jaruzelski got the impression that, "though he was broad-minded" and had been a member of the Politburo for several years, "his knowledge of the Church and religion was superficial."

Jaruzelski clung to Gorbachev like a drowning man to a life preserver: Finally someone in the Kremlin was giving him a sympathetic ear—and not just anyone, but the general secretary himself.

"First of all I tried to explain the difference, the uniqueness of the Church's role in Poland, compared with that of the Church in other countries," Jaruzelski recounted. As rigidly controlled as conditions were then in Poland, the country had engaged in a bold experiment with human rights before the imposition of martial law, and both men agreed that Communist societies had to evolve in the direction of that experiment.

Gorbachev had yet to use the term *perestroika*—meaning "restructuring"—but this talk with Jaruzelski turned on some of the concepts he was later to introduce, including a broad guarantee of religious rights for Communist citizens. He asked Jaruzelski many questions about the failures of Poland's planned economy and about the moribund state of the Polish Communist Party. But the conversation kept returning to the Church, and eventually to the pope himself. Jaruzelski proposed that Gorbachev look at the Vatican as a power that shared some of the broader values of socialism and that wasn't necessarily an implacable ally of capitalism. He later recalled:

> I said that the Church is a great force in Poland. It favors the opposition, but it still takes a fairly rational stand. And I said that I wanted to build up the relationship with the Church, based on three principles: The first was settling disputes in the ideological and philosophical sphere; second, coexistence in the political

sphere, i.e., nobody gets in the other's way, give to Caesar what is Caesar's, give to God what is God's, etc.; third, cooperation in the social sphere, i.e., the commitment to fight existing social evils and pathologies, and to promote family policy, the younger generation, education: in short, the moral and educational issues.

It was very important for me that Gorbachev should understand better than his predecessors that the Church in Poland is a singular phenomenon, not only in the East, but from the Western perspective as well. It developed this way historically. And it also shaped our situation psychologically. . . . At that point I said that . . . the pope, despite his criticism of us, understood the nature of our country. He knew how this country functions, and he was interested in developing his East-policy [Ostpolitik]. Poland could become very important from this point of view, constituting a sort of a bridge.

"What kind of a man is he?" Gorbachev asked. "What is his intellectual training? Is he a fanatic? Or is he a man with his feet on the ground?"

Jaruzelski replied that the pope was "an outstanding personality, a great humanist, a great patriot," above all a man committed to peace.

Gorbachev now began talking enthusiastically about peaceful coexistence between East and West, arms reductions, even the radical elimination of armaments. Jaruzelski knew how important this was because he had heard the pope take a similar tack on such issues. When he did, Jaruzelski told Gorbachev, "it was not only as the leader of a great religion, a great Church, but also as the son of a nation whose lot had been particularly hard. When this particular pope spoke about peace, it sounded different than when, say, Pius XII talked about it."

It now occurred to Jaruzelski that he could become the intermediary between the pope and Gorbachev, that he could explain one to the other. Later, Gorbachev, like the pope, credited him with playing just such a role.

To what extent, Gorbachev wanted to know, could the Church "be helpful in the process of reform? To what extent would it act as a brake?"

"Everything indicates that the Church supports reforms and expects them," Jaruzelski said. The general then asked the general secretary about the situation of the Orthodox Church in Russia.

Gorbachev answered cautiously, and Jaruzelski could feel resistance.

"The pope," said Jaruzelski, "is interested in broadening the Eastern policy of the Church—in a rapprochement—but he can't do it without a gesture from Moscow, a move that would make it easier for him."

Though the pope was critical about martial law [Jaruzelski continued], just by coming to Poland in 1983 he made it somehow legitimate. However, this was possible only because we did a number of things to help the Church, including issuing construction permits for new churches, opening more seminaries, and various other privileges. Some moves like that by the Soviet Union would help establish good relations.

Years later, Jaruzelski elaborated:

I tried to explain why we had made these moves in Poland and what they would eventually yield us; that we were slackening our control over the souls of the people and winning in exchange some very important support from the Church. So I wasn't directly suggesting to Gorbachev, "Do it this way or that way," but rather, "This is how we are doing it, and our motivation is such and such." He was so intelligent—and perfectly capable of adopting any measure he thought right.

To Gorbachev, a Slav, Jaruzelski tried to illustrate the Slavic and Polish mentality of the pope, and "his great sensitivity to Poland's sovereignty . . . that this was a Slav pope who sensed better than others the realities of our region, our history, our dreams. . . . I said the pope is a man of universal thought who was not at all uncritical about capitalism and whose social teachings were rather close to some concepts of socialist and Communist ideology."

What Jaruzelski did not know was that Gorbachev had already decided never to threaten the use of troops again to maintain the Communist empire.

．　　．　　．

The advent of Gorbachev brought rapid changes to Church-state relations in Poland and created an atmosphere in which Jaruzelski felt safe to begin relaxing many of the restrictions that had accompanied martial law.

Jaruzelski gave an account of his meetings with the new Soviet leader to Primate Glemp, who passed the information on to the pope when he visited Rome. Gorbachev had also asked Jaruzelski about the character of the primate. The general spoke warmly of Glemp and his sympathy for the problems of the regime.

Then, on June 2, 1985, the pope issued one of his most important encyclicals, *Slavorum Apostoli* (Apostles to the Slavs), charged with both religious and secular significance. It was an invitation to ecumenical dialogue with the Eastern churches in the USSR.

With the coming of Gorbachev, the Kremlin would no longer automatically interpret such offers as insidious attempts to undermine the foundation of Communist legitimacy. Twice in the next year, at Jaruzelski's urging, Primate Glemp was permitted to visit Minsk and Moscow, where he met with Catholic and Russian Orthodox leaders and clergy, along with secular officials and scholars. Never before had a Polish cardinal visited the Soviet Union.

The "Slavic encyclical" commemorated the eleven hundredth anniversary of the evangelism of Sts. Cyril and Methodius, who brought Christianity to most of the Slavic peoples of Eastern Europe. In this document, the pope invoked the metaphor of Europe as one "body that breathes with two lungs." In 1980 he had made Sts. Cyril and Methodius co-patrons (with St. Benedict) of Europe.

Gorbachev, a Slav and a Communist, and Wojtyła, a Slav and a Christian, were moving toward each other, each increasingly aware of the other's power and potential for doing good. Later that month, the new general secretary propounded the economic changes that would come to be known as *perestroika:* He spoke of a humanism that united the aspirations of Europe for economic and political peace and security. Similarly, the pope's *Ostpolitik* was grounded in the belief that the Church must speak not just for Western Europe, but for a single undivided entity and culture, from the Urals to the Atlantic, "with a pan-European tradition of humanism that encompassed Erasmus, Copernicus, and Dostoevsky," in a historian's phrasing.

The pope was excited and hopeful about the changes Gorbachev was initiating. There was no doubt that Poland, the Communist nations of the East, and even the USSR were on the verge of a great transformation.

That spring, to the immense satisfaction of the pope, the USSR Council for Religious Affairs recommended Soviet participation in the interreligious convocation that John Paul had called for Assisi. But Wojtyła was also a realist; he had long years of experience dealing with Communist ideologues. Early in Gorbachev's tenure, the pope had a lengthy discussion about the new general secretary with Rocco Buttiglione, an Italian intellectual who frequently visited the Vatican. "Well, he's a good man, but he'll fail," the pope declared, "because he wants to do something that's impossible. Communism can't be reformed." The pope was never to change this judgment, though he hoped and prayed for Gorbachev's success. Gorbachev was already meeting resistance in the Soviet party and Politburo. *"Perestroika* is an avalanche that we have unleashed and it's going to roll on," the pope said to Father Mieczysław Maliński, his fellow underground seminarian. *"Perestroika* is a continuation of Solidarity. Without Solidarity there would be no *Perestroika."*

The avalanche was rumbling through Czechoslovakia. In the spring of 1985, in commemoration of the eleven hundredth anniversary of the death of St. Methodius, eleven hundred priests—one-third of the Catholic clergy in Czechoslovakia—concelebrated mass at the Moravian shrine of Velehrad. Cardinal František Tomášek, eighty-six years old, who had been imprisoned by the Communists, read a letter from the pope urging the priests "to continue intrepidly in the spirit of St. Methodius on the path of evangelization and witness, even if the present situation makes it arduous, difficult, and even bitter."

"We felt how strong we were," said Bishop František Lobkowicz, who was a thirty-six-year-old pastor at the time. Until then the Church had not figured conspicuously in the Czech opposition, though some prominent

Catholic intellectuals were affiliated with Charter 77, the umbrella organization of Czech resistance groups. Three months later, in "normalized" Czechoslovakia, 150,000 to 200,000 Catholic pilgrims marched to Velehrad for another observance in honor of St. Methodius. For months the government had tried to transform the event into a "peace festival." But when the Communist leaders took to the microphones, the pilgrims shouted back, "This is a pilgrimage! We want the pope! We want mass!" It was the largest independent gathering in Czechoslovakia since the Prague Spring of 1968.

•   •   •

The definitive sign that the era of martial law in Poland was finally ending came on September 11, 1986, when the regime announced a general amnesty and released the 225 prisoners who had been considered most dangerous to the state. The release of political prisoners had been the number one demand made by the underground since 1981.

For the first time in almost five years, all of Solidarity's leaders could meet freely. Polish jails were once more reserved for criminals, not political prisoners.

Among those given their unconditional release was Zbigniew Bujak, who had been arrested only two months earlier, after four and a half years of hiding and holding together the underground remnants of the union. While Solidarity's leaders and their intellectual allies were initially skeptical of the amnesty and feared that, as before, the government could jail them again at any time, it was clear that the regime had taken a big step. Solidarity, inspired by the pope and supplied largely by the CIA, had survived its long underground struggle.

Still, Jaruzelski wanted to prevent Solidarity from regrouping. It continued to lack any legal status, and censorship still prevailed, although *samizdat* publications, the Voice of America, Radio Free Europe, and Vatican Radio were now the most influential media in the country.

The state-Church commission, which had been the formal means of communication (most of it perfunctory) between the episcopate and the regime during martial law, finally began to discuss the substantive restoration of civil society. At Jaruzelski's suggestion, the commission began drafting plans for a Consultative Council of leading professionals, intellectuals, and other public figures to advise the government on matters of national policy. Though the regime professed its desire to include opposition writers, economists, and other intellectuals on the council, it forbade membership to Solidarity leaders.

As one commentator noted, "A group of people sitting around and talking to General Jaruzelski was not exactly what the opposition understood as political reform." Opposition leaders by and large boycotted the council. But several prominent figures did join, and its proceedings were avidly followed by the entire opposition and the Church. However inadvertently, the Consultative Council did become the precursor for the "Round Table" negotiations that would eventually lead to Polish democracy. Emboldened by Gorbachev, Jaruzelski made another significant gesture in the fall of 1987 when he created the Office for Civil Rights and appointed a nonparty member to prosecute abuses by the government.

Later, some revisionist historians and biographers would oversimplify this transitional period, as if the pope, Gorbachev, and Jaruzelski had been all calmly marching in lockstep toward the same goal. In fact, each had different objectives. As Adam Michnik has insisted, between the formal end of martial law in July 1983 and the revolution of 1989, Poland was not "socialism with a human face . . . [but] communism with a few teeth knocked out." These years remained overwhelmingly grim. Jaruzelski later observed:

> Well, yes, of course we all said it was impossible to go on like this, that we had to make sweeping changes, but they would have to be introduced gradually, without sending people into shock, without causing upheavals. You have to remember that though *perestroika* was there, so was the Warsaw Pact. If you read the speech of Gorbachev to our Tenth Party Congress, on the thirtieth of June 1986, you'd find some very orthodox language. . . . Or perhaps you remember the conversation Gorbachev had with Mitterrand? He went to Moscow in 1988 on a courtesy visit and timidly asked, "Mister General Secretary, wouldn't you give a little thought to this problem of the unification of Germany?" Gorbachev replied:

"I'll think about it in a hundred years' time." The next year the Wall was gone. . . . I know there are people who will tell you: "Oh, ten years ago I knew perfectly well, or I always believed . . ." They're lying.

On January 13, 1987, for the first time since their conversation in the Wawel in 1983, John Paul II and General Jaruzelski met, in the pope's study in the Vatican. Jaruzelski would later describe the visit as "historic," because of what he saw as a crucial meeting of minds. For different reasons the pope's closest aides have used the term "historic" for the session. The discussion lasted eighty minutes, during which Jaruzelski delivered a firsthand report on his conversations with Gorbachev and what the general secretary called his "new thinking."

"Yes, theirs was a historic meeting," said an intellectual with close ties to the Vatican. "Jaruzelski told him that he would share power without bloodshed. That was the point. He said, 'We are already defeated. There is no future for the party or the Communist system in Poland.' " The pace of reform, however, remained anything but certain, and the questions remained of just how much Gorbachev or the Soviet Politburo would tolerate, and how Solidarity would or would not figure in Poland's future. Jaruzelski later said:

I told the pope what I knew about Gorbachev and what role Gorbachev was playing, what were his intentions, what difficulties he faced, how important it was to support him, how to understand him, and what a great chance this was for Europe and the world—even if everything was not happening as smoothly as one may desire.

There is reason to believe that in their meeting at the Vatican the pope and Jaruzelski plotted out a future course for Poland, agreeing in principle to negotiations in which both the Church and the opposition would have a role. Jaruzelski, it seems, had arrived in a very conciliatory frame of mind. Certainly Jaruzelski was all too aware by then that the Polish Communist Party had no real popular support. Some new way had to be found to run the country—and the Church had to approve it. Otherwise, economic recovery was impossible, political healing and national self-esteem unthinkable.

By now, the regime was easing more of the restrictions on civil rights imposed during martial law: Travel in and out of the country was relatively easy, censorship had become less pervasive, the police less conspicuous; and some independent organizations were reinstated.

"I found that [the pope] had a complete understanding of the processes through which we were living," Jaruzelski said of their meeting. "I concluded that the pope saw in the trends and changes occurring in Poland a significance well beyond the Polish framework . . . that they [were], to a great extent, an impulse for the changes occurring in the other countries, especially in the Soviet Union."

By this time, Jaruzelski was openly courting the pope—and the forces of history. As usual, he sought the approval of those he admired, whether in the Kremlin or in the Vatican. In his (dubious) version of events, he claimed that, after imposing the brutal restrictions of martial law, he suddenly reversed direction out of a long-standing democratic impulse.

The pope's view of Jaruzelski, according to the people closest to John Paul II, was somewhat cooler than the general's perception of it, though there is no doubt that Wojtyła regarded Jaruzelski as above all a patriot. But in his dealings with Jaruzelski, the pope always tried to offer the general a vision preferable to Moscow's. This was one of his great accomplishments.

"The pope was aware," says Cardinal Deskur, "that Jaruzelski had a very strong religious background . . . Catholic school, Marian Fathers, etcetera. 'I think he is a man deeply *credente*—believing,' the pope said. 'He hasn't lost his faith.' " And Wojtyła intended to make the most of it.

•   •   •

What had been a ten-million-member trade union known as Solidarity emerged from the amnesty as a much smaller, politically centralized body run by Wałęsa, an organization that somewhat resembled a Western political party. But the former Solidarity still hovered over the nation as a kind of ethereal spirit combining properties of the mythical and the mystical. Despite the amnesty, Jaruzelski was adamant that Solidarity would never again be a trade union.

Wałęsa, on the other hand, aimed to create a powerful negotiating force, backed by the people and the Church. To this end, Wałęsa had a potent ally in Ronald Reagan, who had vowed not to lift American economic sanctions against Poland until the regime opened meaningful negotiations with the opposition. In his desperate need to end the disabling sanctions, Jaruzelski had hoped that the creation of a consultative council would satisfy U.S. demands. It did not.

The task facing Wałęsa was fraught with difficulty and required a delicate touch. In its underground existence, the opposition had become so decentralized, as one sympathetic historian of the movement wrote, "that there were now just too many groups to bring into any one coherent structure." A life of conspiracy did not foster trust. When Solidarity emerged from the underground it was torn by personal and ideological conflicts. Those who had been interned and arrested fought with those who had escaped capture. ("Lech Wałęsa deserves another Nobel Peace Prize," Jacek Kuroń wryly remarked, for his efforts at reconciling the factions within Solidarity.) Ultimately, Wałęsa decided against reconstituting the union's old national commission (which had been meeting when martial law was declared). Instead he handpicked members of a new body that became known as the Provisional Council of Solidarity.

Many of the disagreements in Solidarity were over economic policy, with Wałęsa's supporters advocating market reforms and his opponents decrying the hardships a market economy would inevitably bring. Poland's inflation rate was nearing one hundred percent annually, and real wages were fifteen to twenty percent lower than in 1980.

Given Jaruzelski's admission to the pope of the failures of party and regime, the real question was not whether negotiations would take place, but when and under what circumstances. In February 1987, at the urging of the Vatican (and with Archbishop Pio Laghi's private assurances to the White House that the Polish regime would eventually negotiate with the opposition), Reagan agreed to remove the economic sanctions.

. . .

In a visit to Prague that April, Gorbachev appeared to repudiate the Brezhnev Doctrine, declaring that "the entire framework of political relations between the socialist countries must be based on absolute independence. . . . Every nation is entitled to choose its own path of development, to decide its own fate, to dispose of its territory, and its human and natural resources"—words not unlike what the pope had been saying for the past eight years.

The other Communist leaders of Eastern Europe did not, however, share Gorbachev's enthusiasms. Their opposition ranged from Gustav Husak's passive resistance—during Gorbachev's visit to Prague, Husak echoed his rhetoric but opposed him in practice—to the defiant insistence of East Germany's Erich Honecker and Romania's Nicolae Ceauşescu that their nations had no need of economic "restructuring" or political opening. Even Hungary's János Kádár, who had already implemented more extensive economic changes than those now being adopted by Gorbachev, seemed disconcerted by the Soviet leader's advocacy of democratization.

During his visit to Prague Gorbachev hedged his bets a bit: "At present, several of the fraternal countries . . . have applied original methods and solutions. No party has a monopoly on the truth. We are far from asking anyone to copy us. At the same time, we do not hide our conviction that the process of reconstruction undertaken in the Soviet Union corresponds to the essence of socialism."

Husak, Honecker, Ceauşescu, and Bulgaria's Todor Zhivkov were all in their seventies and had come to power in the Brezhnev era. Gorbachev was unwilling (or unable) to force them to follow his example. Not implausibly, these leaders feared that the Gorbachev model and the kind of pluralism Jaruzelski was now talking about would spell the end of communism.

In Czechoslovakia, Gorbachev spoke openly of "the difficult period" of 1968 and the Prague Spring. "It was a crisis for you and for us," he told workers in one factory, making no attempt to defend or justify the Soviet invasion. This was precisely the sort of sign both the pope and Jaruzelski were looking for.

But when he briefly visited Moscow in late April 1987 to sign a declaration of Soviet-Polish cooperation—in "ideology, science, and culture"—Jaruzelski was told by Gorbachev that *perestroika* was encountering fierce resistance. Gorbachev later wrote:

> I candidly shared with Jaruzelski the difficulties facing *perestroika.* My hopes for support from the Party apparatus for democraticization and for overhauling the style and methods of the government had not been realized. Moreover, resistance to the changes was mounting from that direction. Jaruzelski listened closely to my reflections and told me about his own trials: even after the congress, the PUWP [the Polish Communist Party], especially on the local level, hadn't changed much. The Party apparatus was resisting reforms. In short, it was just like here.

THE DICTATORS

John Paul II's trip to Chile in April 1987 was part of his strategy for supporting the countries of Latin America in their peaceful transition to democracy. The pope wanted to secure, wherever possible, the political hegemony of Christian Democratic Parties or of a bloc of center-to-right-wing forces that, coincidentally or not, fit neatly with the vision of the Reagan White House. The victory by Christian Democratic leaders José Napoleón Duarte in El Salvador and Marco Vinicio Cerezo Arévalo in Guatemala seemed like early successes for this policy.

In Chile, contacts were under way among General Augusto Pinochet, the civilian national political parties, the Church, and Washington to negotiate an agreement in which Pinochet would call a presidential election or referendum. Part of this eventual deal (agreed to in 1989) provided that Pinochet, who in 1973 had led a coup crushing the elected government of Salvador Allende and presided over the brutal repression that followed, would be granted immunity for the crimes of his regime and that he would be allowed to retain his post as commander of the armed forces.

Pope Wojtyła facilitated his strategy by appointing Juan Francisco Fresno as the new archbishop of Santiago—a position of immense importance in a country whose population was eighty percent Catholic. Cardinal Fresno was much more diplomatic and flexible in dealing with Pinochet than was his predecessor, Cardinal Raul Silva Henríquez, who had become a dauntless critic of the Pinochet regime and a defender of its opponents and victims. He had created the Vicariate of Solidarity, which gave material help to individuals persecuted by the dictatorship and legal assistance to those who had been tortured and to the families of the *desaparecidos* (the thousands of persons who had "disappeared" at the hands of the army and the secret police). The vicariate had made the Church enormously popular. It was highly efficient at documenting for the United Nations and international humanitarian organizations the tortures, assassinations, and kidnappings committed by the regime. In the years preceding the pope's visit, the vicariate had documented 100 cases of torture and inhumane treatment in 1984, 84 in 1985, and 109 in 1986. Yet Cardinal Henríquez was packed off into retirement a few months after his seventy-fifth birthday—without getting the extension the pope often granted to especially important cardinals.

On the papal plane heading toward Latin America in April 1987, John Paul II made a statement that shocked liberals in the West. He claimed that the Chilean dictatorship, which had caused many thousands of deaths, could be considered less malign than its Polish counterpart. "In Chile there is a system that at the present time is dictatorial," he told a journalist who asked about the similarities between Chile and Poland. "But this system is, by its very definition, transitory." Questioned about whether there was a transition under way in Poland, the pope replied: "At least there are no grounds for hope on that score; so you can see that the struggle of the other people [the Poles] is much more difficult and demanding."

The Chilean people, meanwhile, greeted with spontaneous enthusiasm the coming of the pope, which they saw as a sign of hope for political change. In those April days hundreds of thousands of Chileans took up the cry *"Wojtyła hermano, llevate el tirano"* (Brother Wojtyła, get the tyrant out of here) and *"Wojtyła, Wojtyła, llevate el gorila,"* (Wojtyła, Wojtyła, get rid of the gorilla). When John Paul II arrived in Santiago on April 1, General Pinochet boasted that he had saved the country from "terrorism and atheistic, Marxist violence." Meanwhile, the pope presented himself as a messenger of peace, justice, truth, unity, and coexistence. He also voiced his hopes for "the victory of forgiveness, of compassion, of reconciliation." Throughout his stay in Chile—unlike his trips to Poland—he avoided saying anything that might heighten indignation and revulsion toward the dictatorship.

During one papal appearance, the Federation of Chilean Students managed to place among the pope's greeting party a nineteen-year-old girl named Carmen Gloria Quintana. Pinochet's soldiers, in the course of a demonstration, had doused her with gasoline and set her on fire. Her ears were now two holes, her face a patchwork of brown, pink, and white splotches. "I know all about it, I know all about it," murmured the pope as he brushed past her and sped on. In a meeting with the leaders of the Vicariate of Solidarity, who gave him an album with pictures of 758 *desaparecidos*, the pope declared: "I always bear in my heart the prisoners who have disappeared." But during his six-day trip he mentioned them only in passing and raised the issue of torture only once, during a stop in Punta Arenas, on the Strait of Magellan, fourteen hundred miles from the capital.

In Santiago, the day after he arrived, John Paul II became only the second head of state (after the president of Uruguay) to pay a visit to Pinochet at his official residence, where during the 1973 coup President Salvador Allende had been killed or (according to some) was forced to commit suicide. "I come as a priest," the pope said, "to give the blessing of peace to this house and to those who dwell in it." When the general invited the pope to step out onto the balcony to acknowledge the cheers of the pro-regime crowd—which had been bused into the square at dawn—John Paul II accepted. Obviously satisfied, Pinochet prayed together with the pope in the chapel of the palace.

The general capitalized on the pope's goodwill. On April 2, without batting an eye, he ordered the violent suppression by 600 soldiers of a demonstration of 250 homeless persons occupying a plot of ground in a Santiago suburb. In the course of the attack the soldiers killed a twenty-six-year-old man. The next day, during a papal mass at a park in the capital, Pinochet staged a massive intervention using armored cars, jeeps, policemen with nightsticks and shields, water cannon, and tear gas to combat 700 demonstrators shouting slogans against the dictatorship and throwing stones at police stationed on the edge of the park. The demonstrators, who belonged to the extreme left-wing party Mir and to organizations of young dissidents allied with the Chilean Communist Party, were a tiny fraction of the 700,000 worshipers present at the mass. But the general wanted to make a point. Police charged demonstrators, who were burning tires to shield themselves, and crashed through the crowd of the faithful. Beneath the altar where the pope was celebrating mass, soldiers in jeeps cut circular swaths. Journalists, pilgrims, and priests who tried to block them were run over and injured. The tear gas fumes even reached the altar, where John Paul II, his eyes red and his throat burning, skipped whole sections of his homily on reconciliation, while his personal physician gave him water and salt to fight off the poisonous air.

"Love is stronger than hate!" shouted John Paul II, while around him thousands of fear-stricken spectators cried out, "Save the pope!" Six hundred people were injured. All the political parties, including the socialists and Communists, denounced the actions of the security forces, calling their response a provocation. Cardinal Fresno and the president of the Chilean bishops conference, however, issued a communiqué identifying the police as the chief victims and blaming the demonstrators. It said the demonstrators had tried to prevent those in attendance from expressing their beliefs and had offended the pope. "We protest against this incredible assault, which meant blows and wounds to *carabineros,* papal guards, journalists, priests, and the faithful." Not a word was said about police brutality, which had been witnessed by the entire international press corps.

The organizer of the pope's trip, Monsignor Francisco Cox, hewed to the same line. When asked to comment on the death of Patricio Juica, the homeless man killed the day before, Cox declared: "The pope has prayed for him and has him in his heart. But it can't be forgotten that he died in a provocation caused by small groups of protesters."

All the principal parties opposed to the regime were in favor of a peaceful transition to democracy. But the pope, as if obsessed by the phantasm of a Marxist revoluton, asserted in his meeting with the bishops, "We must not confuse the noble struggle for justice, which is the expression of respect and love for man, with a movement that sees the class struggle as the only way to eliminate existing class injustices in society."

True to Wojtyła's strategy, Nuncio Angelo Sodano invited the leaders of all the political parties to a meeting with the pope. They were all welcome—provided they signed a letter committing themselves to work for the defense of every human life (the formula generally used to oppose legalized abortion); national reconciliation; the peaceful transition to democracy; and respect for Chile's Christian traditions. It was the first time since the death of Allende in 1973 that all the parties—from the rightists to the Communists—found themselves under the same roof. And before departing Chile—the pope disclosed privately, many years later—"I suggested to Pinochet that he step down."

. . .

The words condemning government violence that John Paul II had *not* spoken publicly in a Chile under the yoke of dictatorship he did pronounce in a country that had barely returned to democracy: Argentina. He arrived there on April 6, 1987, and lectured Raul Alfonsín, the first democratically elected president after the end of the military dictatorship. "Human rights had to be guaranteed," said the pope, "even in extremely tense situations, by avoiding the temptation to meet violence with more violence."

According to a public opinion poll, Argentineans responded to the pope with indifference or aversion. On the eve of his visit three churches had been the target of attacks. Argentina was a country where, under the previous military dictatorships, the struggle of the army against the *montoneros* guerrillas or any other kind of opposition had led to heavy casualties. The bishops had been deeply involved with the military regime. In March 1976 Cardinal Aramburu of Buenos Aires had given communion and his blessing to General Videla, the leader of a coup d'état. The head chaplain of the armed forces, Bishop José Miquel Medina, who was still in office when John Paul II arrived, had in the past gone as far as to justify torture—and he wasn't the only prelate to do so. On the whole the bishops conference had been very timid about criticizing the brutality of the dictatorship. The clergy had also kept silent when Bishop Enrico Angelelli, who was unpopular with the regime, died in a car crash that many people thought was a setup.

The winner of the Nobel Peace Prize in 1980, Adolfo Pérez Esquivel, held a news conference during the papal visit at which he denounced Bishop Medina, explaining, "There are those who were silent when, in the guise of defending Christian 'civilization' the dictatorship massacred the people." But the pope never said a word about the Church's involvement with the military, and he refused to meet with the Mothers of May Square, women who had had their relatives vanish, kidnapped by the military, and who for years had been calling for justice as they marched around the famous square in the Argentine capital.

In his appeals the pope again insisted on peace and reconciliation. In his speech to the bishops in Buenos Aires on April 12 he even implicitly seemed to defend their past approach: ("I know about your deeply felt interventions that have saved human lives.") Only on the seventh day of his stay in Argentina did he insert the briefest of allusions to the *desaparecidos* into a speech to young people.

In fact, the main goal of John Paul II's trip to Argentina seemed to be to prevent the passing of a law on divorce. In the city of Córdoba he said that denying the indissoluble bond of matrimony meant undermining the foundations of society.

The trip to Latin America in 1987 remains one of the most ambiguous moments in the career of John Paul II. Perhaps the most sincere priestly words heard in those weeks came from two bishops. At Concepción, in Chile, Bishop José Manuel Santos publicly denounced "state terrorism," lamenting that "people who committed horrendous crimes have still not been brought to justice." And at Viedma, in Argentina, Bishop Miguel Hesayne, speaking in the presence of the pope, said: "I ask the pope's forgiveness, because the Argentinean Church has not always identified itself with the poor and the persecuted."

· · ·

John Paul II arrived triumphantly in Warsaw two months later, on June 8, 1987, for his third pontifical pilgrimage to his homeland, this time to reclaim Solidarity. Though his visit came against the backdrop of profoundly disturbing privation and suffering, the expectant spirit of his first pilgrimage—the hope, the excitement, the defiance—was in the air. Moreover, Wojtyła was at the height of his global power and influence. In the Philippines, dictator Ferdinand Marcos had, for instance, abdicated the year before at the insistence of the United States and the Catholic Church.

Solidarity was now operating in the open, though tentatively, and its adherents understandably held the authorities in great suspicion. During the week of his visit, the pope had met privately with Wałęsa near the Gdańsk shipyard (after he finished his shift as an electrician) then served communion to him at a mass attended by hundreds of thousands. The pope made an unrelentingly emotional appeal to "the special heritage of Polish Solidarity," and each day his challenge to the regime became more overt.

At one of the most extraordinary masses of his pontificate, celebrated in Gdańsk before a crowd of 750,000 workers and their families, the pope invoked the 1980 accords, tracing their roots to the bloody events at the shipyard in 1970. The Gdańsk accords, he declared, "will go down in the history of Poland as an expression of the growing consciousness of the working people concerning the entire social-moral order on Polish soil." Looking out over a sea of Solidarity banners, the pope put aside his prepared text.

"I pray for you every day in Rome, I pray for my motherland and for you workers. I pray for the special heritage of Polish Solidarity." His audience was beside itself: weeping, applauding, praying, raising clenched fists.

John Paul II stood on a structure shaped like a gigantic ship, whose prow was in the form of St. Peter raising the keys to the kingdom and the Gospel in his hands. From his "ship," the pope told the crowd, "I'm glad to be here, because you have made me captain. . . . There is no struggle more effective than Solidarity!" He then asserted the workers' absolute right to "self-government." After the pope's speech in Gdańsk, Wałęsa said, "I'm very happy. Now even a fool can understand that finding a passage in this labyrinth . . . requires Solidarity. This is the only road."

John Paul II used almost every stop of his journey to widen the perceived gulf between his vision and that of the regime—to the increasing chagrin of Jaruzelski. The pope called for a rethinking of the "very premises" of Poland's Communist order. "In the name of the future of mankind and of humanity the word 'solidarity' must be said out loud," he told hundreds of thousands of seamen at the port of Gdynia, near Gdańsk, speaking from a towering altar set up near the harbor's gray waters. "This word was spoken right here, in a new way and in a new context. And the world cannot forget it. This word is your pride, Polish seamen."

The regime responded to the visit with television censorship, the deployment of tens of thousands of riot police, hundreds of detentions, and, finally, a bitter outburst by Jaruzelski at the farewell ceremonies for the pope at the Warsaw airport. Jaruzelski was angry and blunt, sounding as if he felt betrayed by the pope: "Your Holiness, you will soon bid farewell to your homeland. You will take its image with you in your heart, but you cannot take with you its problems." The pope grimaced and closed his eyes as Jaruzelski continued:

"Poland needs truth. But the truth about Poland is necessary too. How often in recent days has it been the victim of outside manipulation so offensive to the common sense of our people?" He referred sarcastically to the pope's repeated evocations of Solidarity both as an organization and as a concept: "May the word 'solidarity' be heard from this land by all people who continue suffering from racism, neocolonialism, exploitation, unemployment, reprisals, and intolerance." The audience was stunned by his disrespect.

It was one of the most aggressive public statements Jaruzelski made during his six years in power.

With this visit Poles could sense that the end of the regime was approaching. The party was shattered, the general and his minions obviously losing touch with reality. When Jaruzelski and the pope had met in private, the general seemed to take special pleasure in informing Wojtyła that, for the first time, bishops of the Church and local secretaries of the party had joined together all over the country to plan a papal visit.

It would be the last time as well.

.   .   .

Following the pope's visit, events in Poland moved with methodical swiftness: At each important turn, the regime responded with half-measures to the pressures from Solidarity, the people, and the pope, and became overwhelmed. Recognizing that the economic reforms of the past five years had failed, it scheduled a referendum that asked Poles to vote for or against a program of radical economic change, dramatic austerity, and limited steps toward political pluralism. Solidarity urged a boycott of the referendum on the grounds that the government would use it as a vote of confidence. The boycott succeeded. When it failed to attract a majority of eligible voters to the polls, the government announced that it had lost the referendum, the first time in postwar history that a Communist government admitted that it had failed to win an election.

Trying to avoid direct negotiations with Wałęsa or other Solidarity leaders, Jaruzelski reached out to the Consultative Council, whose members included Jerzy Turowicz and other Catholic intellectuals close to the pope. More than anything, Jaruzelski did not want to be the first Communist leader in the Warsaw Pact to be replaced by a non-Communist. There would be scores to settle. But his gesture was too little too late.

A series of spontaneous strikes in 1988 proved the turning point. Wałęsa had always warned that the workers would take matters into their own hands. The strikes, in April and May, turned into a tidal wave. But they weren't called by Solidarity. The strikers were almost all young, impoverished factory workers for whom the events of 1980 were the stuff of myth. They struck in anger because they were disgusted with their constantly eroding standard of living. Their raw emotions threatened chaos. The government flinched and turned to Wałęsa himself to coax the strikers back to work. But they refused—hundreds of thousands of them—until Jaruzelski and the regime promised that the government would begin talks about the country's future with an opposition that included Wałęsa.

Jaruzelski had imagined that a weakened Solidarity would allow him to implement reformist policies at his own pace and without organized opposition. Now, under duress, he agreed to the workers' conditions. Timothy Garton Ash wrote at the time:

For eight years now, Solidarity, the Church and Western politicians have said that the only way to secure popular support for such painful but indispensable economic reform is a dialogue leading to a historic compromise between the self-organized workers and a self-limiting Communist power. . . . For nearly seven years now, the Communist authorities have done almost everything except talk to Solidarity. . . . And after seven years, the workers in the country's great industrial strongholds stand up and say Solidarity! So the authorities do what they have so often said they would never do: They start talking to Lech Wałęsa. Wałęsa manages in return, with difficulty, to end the last strikes.

Wałęsa's four-hour discussion with government representatives on August 31, 1988, produced no startling breakthrough, but the fact that it occurred at all was highly significant. For six years, the government had written him off as "the former leader of the former Solidarity," in the words of Jaruzelski's press spokesman, Jerzy Urban.

On January 18, 1989, Jaruzelski announced that Solidarity would once again be legally recognized as a trade union. He had resigned as prime minister to become the president of Poland, with full executive powers. His successor as prime minister, Mieczysław Rakowski, formerly his deputy, made an official visit to Primate Glemp, as protocol dictated. Their conversation turned on the political situation, and Glemp now told the Communist Rakowski how essential it was to support Gorbachev's policies in the Soviet Union; he added that the pope was committed to those policies both in the USSR and in Poland.

On February 6, even as demonstrators around the country were protesting price increases, representatives of the government and the opposition sat down at what became known as the Round Table negotiations on the future of Poland. The end of an epoch was at hand.

The talks, quietly conducted under the aegis of the Church, lasted eight weeks and covered subjects ranging from economic policy to health care, from political reforms to the inalienable rights of Polish citizens. Wałęsa, General Czesław Kiszczak (the interior minister who had placed him under arrest in

1981), Politburo member Stanisław Ciosek, and a gaggle of party advisers carried out the most sensitive part of the negotiations themselves, with Cardinal Macharski of Kraków or his representatives in attendance. "If neither side gave in," said Ciosek, "we always knew we could go to the Vatican for help."

The crucial agreement reached by the Round Table mandated free and open elections in June for seats to a new body to be called the Senate. The full legalization of Solidarity was also agreed upon.

When elections were held on June 4, Solidarity won all but one of the 262 seats it was allowed to contest. Parish priests had called on the faithful at mass that Sunday to back Solidarity candidates against the Communists. "This is a terrible result," said Jaruzelski. "It's the Church's fault."

Jaruzelski, with unofficial support from the union, narrowly won the presidency. But such a shaky coalition of two old foes was bound to fail. On August 19, Jaruzelski asked Tadeusz Mazowiecki, a Catholic intellectual who had advised Wałęsa during the Gdańsk strikes of 1980, to form a cabinet, and on August 24 Mazowiecki became prime minister and Solidarity officially came to power.

Meanwhile, Wałęsa's first act after the Round Table accords were signed was to fly to Rome with five associates to thank John Paul II on behalf of Solidarity and the Polish people.

•　　•　　•

The reverberations from the fall of Poland shook the Eastern bloc for the rest of the winter, until there was no bloc left.

When Hungary opened its border with Austria in September (it had already struck the "leading role" of the party from its constitution around the time of the Round Table talks in Poland), tens of thousands of East Germans began streaming into the country, which became a jumping-off point for the West. Most went to West Germany, which by law guaranteed citizenship to all Germans.

Increasingly isolated, Erich Honecker, the East German Communist leader, protested the border opening to the Hungarians, but to no avail. Asked to intervene, Gorbachev politely refused. Soon East Germans were fleeing across the borders of Poland and Czechoslovakia as well. The West

German embassies in Warsaw and Prague were granting political asylum and free trips to the West.

Then in October, hundreds of thousands of people took to the streets of Leipzig and East Berlin, demanding Honecker's ouster. The police could not or would not contain the demonstrations and, finally, Honecker resigned. Egon Krenz, a younger Politburo member, assumed control of East Germany and on November 9 opened its border with West Germany. A day later, the Berlin Wall was opened, and workers began tearing it down.

The Communist dominoes were tumbling. On November 10, the thirty-six-year-old rule of Bulgarian President Todor Zhivkov ended with a party purge. In Czechoslovakia, huge crowds took to the streets, calling for multi-party rule and the resignation of President Husak. There were nightly vigils. Alexander Dubček, the leader of the Prague Spring of 1968, joined demonstrators in the capital, his first public appearance in twenty-one years. A month later, Husak resigned and a coalition government made up of Communists and Czech opposition members was established. Just seven months after being released from prison, dissident playwright Vaclav Havel was elected president.

Romania suffered the only truly bloody revolution of 1989. When the Romanian security forces attacked demonstrators in the city of Timişoara, the army rushed to the side of the people. Hundreds were killed—including despised party leader Nicolae Ceauşescu and his wife, gunned down by a firing squad.

And then there was the USSR.

•   •   •

On December 1, 1989, the sidewalks of the great avenue leading to the Vatican were thronged with tens of thousands of people in a state of anticipation and excitement. The general secretary of the Communist Party of the USSR and the supreme pontiff of the Roman Catholic Church were about to meet for the first time.

Virtually every monsignor and archbishop of the Curia had stopped work to witness, either from an office window or on television, the arrival of

Mikhail Gorbachev in his limousine (bearing the red flag with its hammer and sickle). For more than sixty years the Catholic Church and the Kremlin had struggled fiercely, and these men in black attire, trained in their seminaries to despise and fight the "enemies of God" throughout the world, had been in the front lines.

Yet the day before, in a speech in the Italian Capitol, the general secretary had spoken of the need for spirituality in the world. He had called for a "revolution in men's souls" while exalting "the eternal laws of humanity and morality of which Marx spoke."

"Religion helps *perestroika,*" he declared. "We have given up pretending to have a monopoly on truth. . . . We no longer think that those who don't agree with us are enemies." This was truly a "new world order."

Across Eastern Europe, the Communist empire was in collapse. In the Soviet Union, however, Gorbachev remained in full command. He had withdrawn the Red Army from Afghanistan (in implicit defeat) and was negotiating seriously with the United States on further reductions of nuclear and conventional armaments. The day after his meeting with the pope he was scheduled to fly to Malta to meet with President George Bush. He had allowed the countries of the Eastern bloc to go their own way, and the Soviet people by and large hoped that the attendant reduction in military expenditures would spur the Soviet economy and improve their lives. In March the first quasi-democratic elections in USSR history had taken place, and many of the old *nomenklatura* party bosses had been overwhelmingly defeated. Gorbachev and his foreign minister, Edvard Shevardnadze, were heralding an era of "democratic socialism."

With the liberation of Poland and the disintegration of communism west of the Ukraine, the pope saw himself and Gorbachev as kindred Slavic souls with surprisingly common objectives. Gorbachev agreed. Not the least of their shared goals was the cohesion of the USSR. Nationalistic tensions were rising (and blood had been shed) in Armenia, Azerbaijan, and Georgia, within the borders of the Soviet Union.

The pope's vision of Europe and the world made him feel closer in many ways to Gorbachev than to George Bush, whom Wojtyła saw in a very different light than he had Ronald Reagan. For the pope, Reagan had been, as Gorbachev still was, an instrument in the hands of God. For whatever reason, the pope had seemed untroubled by Reagan's unbridled commitment to Western materialism and capitalism.

As a result, at no point in the eight years of Reagan's presidency did the Vatican or the pope openly criticize the White House, though John Paul II didn't hesitate to confront the excesses of capitalism or materialism in global terms. He even prevailed on the U.S. bishops to water down their criticism of Reaganomics.

The pope had supported the anti-Marxist policies of the Reagan administration in Latin America (including in countries where Catholics were killing Catholics) and generally accepted its rationale for its military buildup in the 1980s, over the strong objections of his bishops in the United States. When the Vatican Academy of Sciences prepared a report sharply critical of Reagan's Strategic Defense Initiative ("Star Wars"), the pope—following heavy lobbying from Vernon Walters, Vice President Bush, CIA Director Casey, and Reagan himself—ordered the report buried. Not until the Persian Gulf War in 1991—after the fall of communism in Eastern and Central Europe—did the pope or his Church publicly oppose a single major feature of American policy.

John Paul II had met with Bush three times before his election to the presidency, and he didn't find in him much that was unconventional or selfless or farsighted or particularly principled. In fact, Wojtyła worried that Bush was a conventionally jingoistic leader at a time in history when such attitudes might prove dangerous and counterproductive. Unlike Reagan, Bush, as the pope saw it, was interested only in American strategic and economic advantage. At his meeting with Gorbachev, the pope said as much. Gorbachev was an altogether different matter, a man who had made possible many of the incredible changes then taking place in Europe. On June 13, 1988, Gorbachev had received Cardinal Casaroli in the Kremlin. "The most important thing is the human being," Gorbachev told Casaroli—sounding remarkably like the pope. "The human being must be at the center of international relations. That is the point of departure of our 'New Thinking.' " In Lithuania old Cardinal Vincentas Sladkevicius, who had been interned by the Communists for twenty-five years, described Gorbachev to intimates as "a tool of God" who was permitting Catholics in the USSR to worship freely.

True, the pope had told his closest associates that Gorbachev would ultimately fail, because of the impossibility of really reforming communism. And Gorbachev did remain committed to communism and the party, though in a radically altered shape. Gorbachev had envisioned *perestroika* sweeping across Eastern Europe, bringing down hard-line Communist leaders and paving the way for a new, reformed Communist rule. But he miscalculated.

That fall and winter, one after another, with lightning speed, the dictators of Eastern Europe were toppled—and democrats, not Communist reformers, assumed control, as citizens, inspired by Solidarity's victory, took to the streets, peacefully, by the millions. For decades, Soviet troops had formed a kind of dam against rebellion in the Eastern bloc, until Gorbachev proclaimed what his foreign ministry spokesman called the "Sinatra Doctrine," promising that the USSR would allow its satellite states to "do it their way" and that hundreds of thousands of troops would be withdrawn from the Warsaw Pact.

The first meeting between a general secretary of the USSR and a pontiff of the Roman Catholic Church was rich in symbolism for a new era. A member of the papal entourage observed:

> The pope knew what most Westerners did not know: that if you have destroyed the world order consecrated at Yalta, you go back to the world order consecrated at Versailles. And that's not a very good world order, because it contains all the seeds of the Second World War, that might lead to a third world war. Communism had brought a kind of violent suppression of a great quantity of conflicts, national conflicts, racial conflicts, and also class conflicts, and if you haven't got an adequate solution for these conflicts, if you don't have a new order for Europe, then it will explode.

There is evidence that not only the pope but the whole Vatican Secretariat of State was concerned about the forces unleashed by the fall of communism and that they were discussing these fears—and the desirability of the survival of a stable USSR—months before the arrival of Gorbachev in the Vatican.

Rocco Buttiglione, a philosopher and close friend of Wojtyła, who is also the author of a book on his thought and philosophy, remarked, "The Holy Father hoped that Gorbachev's attempts to keep together the Soviet Union would succeed, not to keep communism, but to keep [the center] together. . . . As a federation of free people." Immediately after the pope's meeting with Gorbachev, Vatican diplomats briefed White House officials and urged Bush to take a "prudent" course and support Gorbachev's efforts at cohesion—which the American president did at Malta.*

By the time of Gorbachev's visit to the Vatican, the basis for a relationship between the two men had been laid: through Jaruzelski as interlocutor; through secret correspondence between the pope and Gorbachev (the pope had praised *perestroika*, Gorbachev had admired the pope's writings); and through Gorbachev's visible commitment, in response to Vatican diplomacy, to increased freedom of religion in the USSR and to worldwide disarmament.

Wojtyła, wearing his white robes, greeted Gorbachev and his wife, Raisa, enthusiastically in the reception room of the papal apartments. Then the two men adjourned to the pope's study.

Speaking in his Polish-accented Russian, the pope noted that this was a meeting between two Slavs. The text of their private meeting, recorded by an interpreter and obtained by the authors of this book, underscores the personal regard that had developed between the two men. It also shows how the pope used Gorbachev's problems to win religious guarantees for believers in the Soviet Union more rapidly than otherwise might have been possible.

With the tearing up of the map drawn at Yalta, the pope saw the Vatican's and the Kremlin's interests as suddenly parallel on a whole range of international issues. This was underscored by his own beliefs in the shortcomings of capitalism and his comprehension of the social and economic rationale of socialism. Wojtyła and Gorbachev spoke of the Middle East, of

---

* Aides to both Bush and the pope have said that Wojtyła and the president spoke by telephone after Gorbachev left the Vatican.

poverty in the Third World, of a Europe aligned toward neither Washington nor Moscow, of Central America, of Indochina, and of the advantages of establishing diplomatic relations between the Vatican and the Kremlin.

"Generally speaking," the pope declared, "there are quite a few spots on this earth where peace is having a hard time. Perhaps we could act together in concert here." He was thinking particularly of regions with large Christian populations and historic Soviet influence.

Then John Paul offered the general secretary a homily on the subject of human rights:

> We have been waiting with great anxieties and hopes for the adoption, in your country, of a law on the freedom of conscience. We hope that the adoption of such a law will lead to a broadening of the possibilities of religious life for all Soviet citizens. A person becomes a believer by his own free will; it's impossible to force somebody to believe.

With such a law, the pope said, diplomatic relations between the Holy See and Moscow could move forward—something Gorbachev now desired more than the Vatican, owing to the need to strengthen his position at home and the pope's great international prestige. Gorbachev readily pledged that a law on freedom of conscience would soon be adopted by the Supreme Soviet.

The general secretary was keenly aware that freedom of conscience might have unsettling consequences—including calls for independence in the Baltics and in the Western Ukraine, where Catholic roots were strong. "I'm not going to give you any advice," said Gorbachev, "I'm just appealing to your experience and your wisdom . . . to avoid any politicization" of these questions.

Part of their discussion was philosophical. In the USSR, Gorbachev said, "we want to accomplish what we have planned through democratic means. But my view of events in the last few years suggests that democracy by itself is not enough. A code of morals is needed too. Democracy can bring not only good, but evil." This was consistent with Wojtyła's beliefs, as the general secretary well knew.

"You're right when you say that changes shouldn't happen too fast," the pope observed. "And we also agree that it's necessary to change not just the structures but ways of thinking. It's impossible, as someone [Bush] pretends, that changes in Europe and in the world will follow the Western model. This contradicts my deepest convictions. Europe, as a participant of world history, must breathe with two lungs."

With their substantive discussion completed, Gorbachev expressed his hope for "a new development in our relations. I expect that in the future you will take a trip to the USSR."

"I would be very happy if I were permitted to do so," said the pope. He then offered an insight into his heart and personal mission:

> I would be very happy to have the chance to visit the Soviet Union, Russia, to meet with the Catholics, and not only with them, to visit your holy places, which are for us Christians a source of inspiration. . . . You see, I don't know Eastern Europe well. I myself am a Western Slav. I never even knew those cities that were in Poland before the war and that are now part of the Soviet Union. I mean Lvov and Vilnius. But I would especially like to meet and feel what I call the "Genius of the East."

DEATH THROES

It was December 31, 1991. Red Square was full of excited people singing, shouting, dancing. They were shaking bottles of *sovietskoye shampanskoye*, stomping on beer cans, shattering glasses beneath their winter boots. Amid hugs and kisses the groups chaotically broke up and re-formed with a deafening roar. Meanwhile the honor guards in their heavy overcoats marched at the appointed hour toward Lenin's mausoleum, each holding his rifle steady with his right hand. In the clear bright night the rhythmic pounding of their goosestep, borrowed from the Prussians, was like an unreal dance, a disjointed ballet. Only thin metal chains separated them from the frenzied crowd on the square. When midnight rang out from the Spassky Tower, the crowd unleashed to the sky a shout of liberation and mad happiness.

Thousands of men and women had instinctively gravitated to the square to celebrate the demise of the Soviet Union. Russians and Americans, Italians and Kazakhs, Britons, Tartars, and Germans, people from every corner of the world, bureaucrats and prostitutes, businessmen and hooligans, toasted a future without the hammer and sickle.

The square, which had been sacred to the Communist regime, a taboo space where even smoking had been forbidden, was now swirling with activity, and all eyes were on Lenin's tomb.

A drunken kilted Scotsman danced up and down like a puppet. Several rancorous Communist Party veterans tried to push their way through the mob to place their red flags next to the mausoleum. The reek of alcohol was everywhere. Suddenly while soldiers still in the uniform of the former Soviet Union were changing the guard in front of the monument, a nondescript man rushed forward, in his arms a statue of Our Lady of Fátima. For more than half an hour he let the sad-eyed figure in the white gown and the blue mantle stare at the half-closed door of the mausoleum. It was a silent act of revenge.

Perhaps we'll never know who he was, that anonymous man carrying beneath the walls of the Kremlin a replica of the Madonna whose prophecy in 1917 had called for the conversion of Russia. But he couldn't have expressed more eloquently Wojtyła's most intimate feelings. The pope experienced the great upheaval in the Soviet Union as a kind of mystery play, in which, as he saw it, Our Lady of Fátima had played a major role. In March 1984, when Solidarity seemed doomed, the pope ordered that the original Fátima statue, three and a half feet tall, be specially shipped from Portugal to the Vatican. The pope had given orders to set it in his private chapel, where a picture of Our Lady of Częstochowa already hung on the wall. On the night of March 24–25, the feast of the Annunciation, he spent long hours in prayer before the statue. On Sunday, the 25th, in St. Peter's Square, he confided Russia and Eastern Europe to the care of the Virgin of Fátima, using language that insiders immediately understood: "We consecrate to you those men and those nations who have a special need to be entrusted to you in this way. Shed your light in particular upon those peoples from whom you yourself await our consecration." This last sentence wasn't in the prepared text. The pope had improvised it to fulfill a desire expressed by the White Lady, who, when she appeared to the three little Portuguese shepherds, had demanded the consecration of Russia so that the world might be spared terrible catastrophes. The eldest of the three children, who later entered the convent as Sister Lucia de Jesus Santos, had kept watch for decades for the Madonna's request to be carried out. But no pope had done what the Madonna required. After the consecration of March 25, Sister Lucia let John Paul II know that she accepted this ardent act of devotion.

Was it just a coincidence that the next year saw the death of Konstantin Chernenko, almost the last member of the Communist old guard, and the rise of Mikhail Gorbachev as general secretary of the Soviet Communist Party? The pope didn't think so. As Russia prepared to celebrate the thousandth anniversary of its acceptance of Christianity, the pope repeated the act of dedication: "To you, Mother of Christians," he proclaimed in 1987, "we entrust in a special way the people celebrating the six hundredth [Latvia] and the one thousandth [Ukraine and Russia] anniversary of their adhesion to the Gospel."

Even today John Paul II believes there is a very special link between the Holy Virgin and Russia. Father Werenfried van Straaten, who for decades helped raise funds in the West for the Church behind the iron curtain, discloses that the pope had brought to the Vatican the miraculous icon of the Madonna of Kazan, which had been lost after the October Revolution. The patriarch of Moscow, Alexis II, is convinced that it is only a copy, but that possibility does not seem to faze the pope.

Van Straaten, who has seen the pope regularly over the course of his pontificate, says, "He is firmly convinced that, with the icon of Kazan now in the Vatican, the Virgin will help him to get to Russia." But by mid-1996, the patriarch of Russia, fearful that the pope would successfully proselytize his own flock, was insistent that Wojtyła stay out.

John Paul II never imagined that the Soviet Union could come apart so quickly, nor did he wish it. Not even his closest Polish friend in the Vatican,

Cardinal Andrzej Deskur, ever heard him express such a desire. "He never said anything like that, not to me," Deskur says.

The pope's objective was the consolidation of the new freedoms won by Eastern Europe. During the months before the fall of Gorbachev, an accord had almost been reached with the Soviet president for the first trip to the USSR by a Roman pontiff. The Vatican secretary of state, Cardinal Angelo Sodano, confided to journalists in May 1991 that it was highly probable that in 1992 there would be a brief "symbolic visit" to Moscow and to Kazakhstan, the home of Catholic communities of Volga Germans deported by Stalin.

In August 1991, however, the Red Empire went into its death throes. At dawn on the 19th, in a coup d'état, conservative members of the Politburo seized power in Moscow and put Gorbachev under house arrest in his Crimean dacha, announcing that he had been taken ill. Boris Yeltsin, president of the Russian Federal Republic, rebelled against the coup and transformed the Russian parliament building (called the White House for its marble facing) into the headquarters of the resistance.

Thanks to a radio transmitter belonging to Father van Straaten, which was intended to broadcast Catholic-Orthodox religious programs and was smuggled into the parliament's kitchens in a vegetable truck, Yeltsin was able to maintain contact with the outside world. His resistance prompted the West to support him.

A sincere cry of joy can be heard in the telegram that John Paul II sent to Gorbachev on August 23, the day the coup leaders surrendered: "I thank God for the happy outcome of the dramatic trial which involved your person, your family, and your country. I express my wish that you may continue your tremendous work for the material and spiritual renewal of the peoples of Soviet Union, upon whom I implore the Lord's blessing."

John Paul II's hopes, like those of many other world leaders, were short-lived. Yeltsin's victorious resistance became a sign of the people's will to wipe out the Communist regime once and for all. On December 25 the man who invented *perestroika* left office, and in the afternoon the red flag was lowered over the green cupola of the Kremlin.

· · ·

Years later, much of the world came to hail Wojtyła as the conqueror of a war he had begun in 1978. The pope himself took a sober view. He expressly avoided parading as a kind of superman who had floored the Soviet bear. He urged his audience not to oversimplify things, not even to ascribe the fall of the USSR to the *finger of God.* When the Italian writer Vittorio Messori asked him about this, John Paul II replied: "It would be simplistic to say that Divine Providence caused the fall of communism. It fell by itself as a consequence of its own mistakes and abuses. It fell by itself because of its own inherent weakness."

John Paul II had experienced the crisis of communism from within, and above all he had meditated as a philosopher on the essence of communism's contradictions. Better than many Western politicians he understood that the Soviet system had collapsed through implosion. The external pressures had revealed the cracks in the system, but in the end the collapse had come from deep internal flaws.

In this collapse, economic and moral factors were interwoven. The economic resources of the USSR simply couldn't guarantee every citizen a secure existence, at however poor a level, while maintaining all the military apparatus of a superpower fighting a cold war. This was even clearer in the case of Communist East Germany, which, though far better organized than the USSR, was still facing economic bankruptcy on the eve of its collapse.

But it was above all ethical contradictions that had undermined the system. With Khrushchev the need for truth had stimulated an attempt to reform the system. With Brezhnev the denial of truth had produced stagnation and massive cynicism. With Gorbachev the thirst for truth, for *glasnost,* had become so intense as to overturn the system itself.

This theme of the truth and of the unsustainability of lies has always fascinated John Paul II in his thinking on totalitarianism. He read the works of both Andrei Sakharov and Aleksandr Solzhenitsyn and was moved by their moral conviction. Above all, Solzhenitsyn's booklet *Don't Lie* made a great impression on him, because he was convinced that the refusal to lie was the most powerful means of provoking a crisis in any totalitarian state. John Paul

II spoke at length about ethics when Solzhenitsyn came to visit him in the Vatican in 1994. Communism, the pope had said in his first visit to post-Communist Prague in 1990, had "revealed itself to be an unattainable utopia because some essential aspects of the human person were neglected and negated: man's irrepressible longing for freedom and truth and his incapacity to feel happy when the transcendent relationship with God is excluded."

PART EIGHT

THE
ANGRY POPE

Flashes of lightning illumined the altar. Beneath the grand papal canopy Karol Wojtyła stared out at a mass of dark umbrellas. To the crowd gathered at the clearing of the Kielce Flying Club, the pope looked like a strange figure conjured up from a distant world. The whiteness of his cope and the colors of his vestments underneath took on a lurid glare in the flashes of lightning. His face was distorted with anger. He raised his right hand in a clenched fist, while his left clutched the pages of the speech he had now thrust aside.

"Brothers and sisters," he cried out in a rasping voice. "There has to be a change in the way you treat a newly conceived child. While it may have come unexpectedly, it is never an intruder, never an aggressor. . . . You mustn't confuse freedom with immorality.

"I say this," he continued, as he faced the pouring rain and the gusts of wind raking the 200,000 spectators already numb with cold, "because this land is my mother; this land is the mother of my brothers and my sisters. This land is my home, and for that reason I allow myself to speak this way.

"All of you must understand," he shouted, still shaking his fist, "that the way you deal with these questions is thoughtless. These things cannot but cause me pain, and they ought to pain you too. It's easier to tear down than to build up. Destruction has been going on for too long; now we need to rebuild. You can't just heedlessly destroy everything."

Beneath skies darkened by rain-swollen clouds the crowd listened in silence. Perfunctory applause greeted John Paul II's address. He realized that he was out of touch with his audience. It was the first time this had ever happened with his compatriots.

He never imagined that his fourth trip to his homeland would turn out this way. He knew it wouldn't be easy to speak to people in a society lapsing into what he saw as selfish individualism, but he had somehow expected more fidelity from his compatriots—after all he *had* saved them from communism. With a leader's sharp eye and an actor's flair he noticed that his charisma was waning. The things that hurt him didn't seem to hurt the Poles. What he was stigmatizing as wrong struck many in the crowd as the very essence of what they had suffered so long for—the right to make their own decisions.

He had shown his ire in public, he had gotten angry. This was a rare event in his life. It was, in fact, almost unheard of. Among his Wadowice schoolmates, among the stone quarry workers in Kraków, among the professors in Lublin, the bishops in Poland, or the dignitaries in the Vatican, no one could ever recall seeing him explode with anger or lose his patience. He had always been calm, never shouting, always playing the mediator.

This time, however, he *had* shouted. At Kielce the crowd had withheld itself from him. John Paul II felt wounded and disturbed. "This people worships me with its lips, but not in the depths of its heart," he confessed afterward, unconsciously comparing himself to the God of Isaiah.

Was this how Moses felt when he came down from Mount Sinai and saw the Israelites dancing around the golden calf?

The end of communism marked the beginning of the Third Act of John Paul II's papacy. The First Act had been one of proud vindication for his Christian message after years of uncertainty—"Open the doors to Christ!" The Second Act, in the 1980s, saw the affirmation of a universal role for the papacy and the successful battle for the liberation of Poland from Soviet totalitarianism.

The Third Act opened in the 1990s, and it gave the pope an unexpected taste of solitude. Looking over the European scene, John Paul II's vicar for Rome, Cardinal Camillo Ruini, acknowledged, "The capacity of the Church to be a *Church of the people* seems to be in danger."

What is God to do without the Devil? For a century and a half the Catholic Church had battled against socialism and Marxism. For over seventy years it had fought the Communist system as its archenemy. The whole culture and social doctrine of twentieth-century Catholicism had been shaped by this tremendous duel. Now, suddenly, the stage was bare.

Nineteen ninety-one was a crucial year for the Church. At the point when the Soviet Union had not yet collapsed but had already lost its superpower status, John Paul II had to face the fact that the Church might also become *less* relevant, politically and socially. The first test came with the Gulf

War in January. Having decided to launch Operation Desert Storm, President George Bush paid no heed to the pope's urgent appeals to negotiate a last-minute Iraqi retreat from Kuwait. Bush treated the pope much as he treated Gorbachev: as a second-rate ally. He showered him with expressions of esteem and then ignored him.

A short time later the Holy See received another jolting wake-up call. The government of Israel vetoed the Vatican's participation in a conference in Madrid that was meant to pave the way for direct dialogue between Israelis and Palestinians. The reason cited was that the two states didn't have diplomatic relations, but such a rebuff would never have been dealt during the cold war.

John Paul II's bitterest surprise, however, was dealt to him by his own countrymen during his fourth trip there in June 1991.

．　　．　　．

For Karol Wojtyła travel has been what war was for Napoleon. The Pope has reigned not by staying at home in the Vatican, but by crisscrossing the world. And it was in these encounters with people from one nation after another that his battles had been won or lost. Arriving now in his post-Communist homeland on June 1, 1991, he was hailed by President Lech Wałęsa and Primate Józef Glemp as a new Moses, as the man who had freed his people from slavery and whose mission was to continue leading the Poles into the future. John Paul II meant to preach to his compatriots the Ten Commandments, the Law of Moses, the basic rules for building a state in accordance with God's will. What was new this time, however, was that the people showed little desire to be led, at least by the Church.

Poland had changed, and many of its people were taking an increasingly dim view of the clergy's desire to invade public life and of their authoritarian style of leadership. Many were getting tired of pharaonic churches and rectories built in the countryside, as if to mock the surrounding landscape of little poverty-stricken villages. The Church's building boom seemed a provocation to millions of Poles worried by the first brutal phase of their introduction to a free market economy, in which prices were being jacked up and salaries flattened in a way any previous Communist regime might have envied. People were getting tired of the imperial mode with which parish priests publicly demanded their flock pay a *voluntary tax* for the construction or repair of churches. People didn't like hearing stories about priests who drove around in Mercedes—or were caught by the police roistering at night in the company of half-naked women.

The clergy seemed to be blanketing the TV screens. They lobbied the media to promote "Christian values" (just as the Communist Party had once demanded that the media conform to Marxist-Leninist principles). The schools had brought back religious instruction thanks to a simple ministerial fiat. A proposed electoral law was blocked because President Wałęsa, under pressure from the Church, wouldn't accept a provision banning propaganda from the pulpit.

Furthermore, the Church was interfering in family life. To please the bishops the department for in vitro fertilization at the Center for Children's Health had been shut down. Divorce proceedings had been shifted from local to regional courts, thereby making the process more difficult and expensive.

Last but not least, a repeal of the law on the interruption of pregnancy, in effect since 1956, had been proposed in the Sejm by a small group of right-wing Catholics, the Christian National Alliance. The bishops backed it immediately. The new law would prohibit abortion except in the case of danger to the life of the mother. It called for a two-year prison sentence for the doctor who performed an abortion and in certain cases for the woman who received one.

The proposal had unleashed a wave of indignation among Polish women. Those belonging to Solidarity had even turned to the West, petitioning women in Italian trade unions to lobby in the international labor movement against the projected law.

The new climate was aptly symbolized by the remarks made on television some months before the pope's arrival by the deputy health minister, Kazimierz Kapera. He demanded a ban on all contraceptives, including condoms, and he labeled people with HIV "typical deviants." A popular outcry forced the deputy minister to resign, but Cardinal Glemp defended him as a victim of intolerance. The primate compared him to the late persecuted Cardinal Wyszyński.

All this had come to the attention of John Paul II, as he prepared for his trip to Poland. There had been few days in his pontificate when he hadn't been in direct touch with events in his homeland. He had a constant flow of information from reports and personal contacts with pilgrims, priests, bishops, and friends visiting the Vatican. He had been told that polls showed the Church slipping into second place behind the army as the country's most loved and respected institution. Sixty-seven percent of all respondents agreed that "the Church has too much power" and that "the Church shouldn't interfere in the political life of the state."

But the closest aides to the pontiff presented any and all criticism of the Church as maneuvers by ex-Communists or as the result of an anticlerical, atheistic trend that had to be thwarted—and the pope believed them. Catholics associated with the weekly *Tygodnik Powszechny* tried to give the pope a more balanced picture, but in Polish circles in Rome and among Polish bishops such moderates were a small and sharply criticized minority. In vain the pope's close friend the philosopher Józef Tischner had warned against a "republic of parish priests." In vain Czesław Miłosz, winner of the 1980 Nobel Prize for literature, had written, "People have begun to be afraid of priests. And that's certainly not a good sign." At this rate, Miłosz explained, Poland would become "a country no more Christian than France or England, with the added burden of an anticlericalism whose fury would be proportional to the power of the clergy and to the [clergy's] program of a confessional state." Adam Michnik, the dissident who had founded the Workers Defense Committees and who now was editor in chief of the powerful newspaper *Gazeta Wyborcza*, wrote: "It would be a good idea if everything would go back to the status quo ante, and if the Church would stop taking sides in political disputes."

The pope remained deaf to these signals. Although he maintained that the clergy shouldn't get involved in politics, he was convinced that his compatriots had to make a moral choice. The Polish way of life had to take its inspiration from Christianity; and it was the Church's duty to point the way. The state had to conform to the Truth as expressed by the fundamental values of the Christian faith. As he said in Kielce on June 3, Poles had to "examine their consciences on the threshold of the Third Republic."

The whole trip—2,850 miles in eight days—turned into a nonstop sermon, delivered with desperate fierceness. The pope plunged into the debate on the new Polish constitution, opposing the separation of Church and state: "The principle of absolutely refusing to admit the dimension of the holy into social or governmental life," he said, "means introducing atheism into state and society." He repeatedly raised the issue of abortion and stirred up protests from the tiny surviving Jewish community in Poland when he equated the Holocaust with "the great cemeteries of the unborn, cemeteries of the defenseless, whose faces even their own mothers never knew."

No day, no place passed without a harsh rebuke. In Łomża on June 4, while blasting adultery, he wondered out loud whether the seeds of fundamental principles hadn't been uprooted by the Evil One. In Białystok he announced that the economic crisis inherited from the past was marching in lockstep with an ethical crisis. At Olsztyn he attacked the media for "telling lies while pretending to present the truth." He denied that the Church had any aspirations to dominate society and claimed that such criticism was a new trial the Church had to endure.

In Włocławek he launched into violent invective against the secular culture of Western Europe: "We don't need to 'enter' Europe," he proclaimed, "because we helped to create it in the first place; and we went to more trouble doing it than those who claim a monopoly on Europeanism." Once again, before a rain-soaked crowd he spoke in anger: "And what should be the criteria for Europeanism? Freedom? What kind of freedom? The freedom to take the life of an unborn child?"

His outbursts were caustic, blending impromptu remarks with prepared speeches. He attacked utilitarianism and prevailing notions of sexuality in Western Europe: "As the bishop of Rome, I protest against the way they wish to reduce the concept of Europe." He condemned the "whole civilization of desire and pleasure which is now lording it over us, profiting from various means of . . . seduction. Is this civilization or is it anticivilization?"

"Pardon my burning words," he would say, his voice recovering its normal affability. "But I had to say them."

•   •   •

Ultimately his admonitions came to naught in the face of the new Poland, where the idea of free choice on sexual questions had already become so ingrained that most people saw no contradiction between calling themselves Catholic (ninety-five percent) and opposing a ban on abortion (sixty-nine percent). Even in rural areas, under the domination of parish priests, only thirty-six percent of those polled favored a strongly restrictive abortion law.

For Karol Wojtyła the experience of popular hostility in his own homeland was completely new. Father Tischner, who fully supported the pope's position, would later acknowledge that John Paul II's visit had been marked by a "certain emotional discord between him and his audience." The great majority of Poles were irritated by his sermons against consumerism at a time when families were wracked by the problems of simply making do. After all, for forty years people had dreamt of escaping the endless shortages; and now they were crushed by the burden of two million unemployed. Angriest of all were the women, especially the mothers, who felt the hardship of feeding the hungry children they already had. The idea of losing the right to choose whether or not to have more children only provoked rancor.

John Paul II left his country shocked and embittered. After everything the Church had done to bring down communism, he considered the criticism of the priests and the bishops by their flocks unfair. He was disappointed to see that some Catholic deputies in the Sejm, led by ex-premier Tadeusz Mazowiecki, the founder of the Democratic Union Party, didn't support the Church on the abortion issue. Returning to Rome, he felt troubled about the future. "Earlier," he had told the Polish bishops, "the Church received widespread recognition even from lay circles. But in the present-day situation there is no counting on such recognition. Instead we have to be ready for criticism and perhaps something worse."

Karol Wojtyła's bitterness lasted a long time. More than a year later, while spending Christmas in the Vatican with Sister Zofia Zdybicka and singing the nostalgic old songs of his childhood, he abruptly asked her: "Invite me to Zakopane." When Sister Zofia, his former student, now herself a professor at the Catholic University of Lublin, assured him that he was welcome, he pensively noted: "I was offended by the Poles." Then he stopped, looked at her, and added: "But I'm getting over it."

. . .

Yet the wound remained—and has never quite healed.

Seated at his desk in the Vatican and receiving reports on the slow, electoral reconquest of the countries of Eastern Europe by the reformulated and renamed Communist parties, John Paul II has often had to think back on his broken dream of a great spiritual renewal proceeding from the East. *"Ex Oriente lux,* light comes from the East," he had boldly announced in 1989 while flying over the Soviet Union for the first time, en route to South Korea. Both Catholic Poland and Orthodox Russia were to become an immense reserve of faith for the regeneration of the contemporary world.

Lost too was the vision he had nurtured of Poland as a special sign for all the nations—that old messianic dream of the poets of his youth, Mickiewicz and Słowacki. "He had hoped," recalls a close friend, "that his homeland would realize justice and freedom for the working people, as it built a society on the firm foundation of the truth, the truth about the human person." As one bishop noted, "He wanted to make Poland the bridge between the West and the East. He had the geopolitical view that as a Pole he could somehow play a part in this." For Karol Wojtyła Poland had suddenly turned into a showcase of defeat. The pope has become especially bitter about what he considered little less than a betrayal by leading Catholics like Jerzy Turowicz, the editor of *Tygodnik Powszechny,* who once had been his colleagues.

As a matter of fact, such people *haven't* changed. When totalitarianism fell, and with it the need for unity at all costs, already existing differences in evaluating modern society simply became more evident.

At a conference in Rome in 1994, a few hundred meters from St. Peter's, Professor Turowicz dared to break the most sacred of the pope's taboos: He said that most of the Polish Church hadn't really learned the lessons of the Second Vatican Council. Turowicz is an old gentleman with a quiet, intelligent air. Like all cultured Poles who grew up before World War II, he speaks fluent French. He and his family had been intimately acquainted for years with Cardinal Wojtyła, and he often visited Pope Wojtyła in the Vatican or accompanied him on his travels around the world.

His loyalty is beyond question, but there is no doubt that Turowicz sees Poland and the Polish Church differently from the way the pope sees them. He thinks that the Church shouldn't impose its beliefs on a pluralistic society: "The Polish Church is highly polarized nowadays. Preconciliar attitudes confront post-conciliar behavior," he reports. "And I'm sorry to say that most of the clergy are rather fundamentalistic and traditional, while the more liberal and open-minded ones are in the minority.

"Under communism," Turowicz continues, "the Polish Church was on the defensive; it saw danger everywhere. Somehow or other this attitude has persisted; and people in the Church think it's still in danger, which is not true in the sense that the Church enjoys full freedom. Of course, some values are in danger, but these are both civil and Christian values." Turowicz acknowledges that "some right wingers, in the Polish Church and in politics, wanted what for all practical purposes was a confessional state."

But Poland, and especially Polish youth, revolted. The Church-backed anti-abortion law, eventually passed by Parliament, was one of the main reasons for this popular reaction. In 1994 the voters gave a majority to center-left parties. In 1995 they elected as president former Communist Aleksandr Kwasniewski, defeating Lech Wałęsa—and Primate Glemp, who on the eve of the elections had tried to rally the faithful to support the former Solidarity leader, proclaiming that voters had to choose between Christianity and neo-paganism.

That same year, as if to show that everywhere in Europe even profoundly religious people would not put up with clericalism, voters in Ireland revoked the constitutional ban on divorce, defying their bishops and the pope, who had intervened in the referendum. For John Paul II it was yet another painful blow.

·   ·   ·

Thus his dream of a light from the East was shattered. Free from communism, Eastern Europe showed itself to be interested mainly in the quest for material well-being. To his old friend Juliusz Kydryński, who had stayed up all night with him back in Kraków as they kept watch over the body of his father, John Paul II again opened his heart. In a letter he wrote in 1994, shortly before Kydryński's death, Wojtyła shared some intimate reflections on what was happening in Poland and in the other countries of Eastern Europe.

He was deeply troubled that only a few years after the turn to democracy, the people were voting out the leadership that had opposed communism and choosing "old-time" politicians. How wise Moses was, the pope wrote to Kydryński, putting a new spin on the story of Exodus, how farsighted not to bring the Israelites into the Promised Land right after leaving Egypt. Instead he kept them in the wilderness for forty years so that all those who remembered being slaves could die off. Thus a completely new generation entered the land of Canaan.

Nowadays in the pope's vision of things another specter has begun to haunt the world: consumerism, a kind of virus (as he sees it) that is spreading from West to East. That was his message when he went to Prague for the first time after the fall of the iron curtain. "One ought not to underestimate the danger that the newly won freedom for contacts with the West can bring with it," he told the Czechs. "Unfortunately, not everything that the West offers by way of theoretical vision and practical lifestyles reflects the values of the Gospel. Thus it is necessary to prepare immunizing defenses against certain viruses, such as secularism, indifferentism, hedonistic consumerism, practical materialism, and the formal atheism that is so widely diffused today."

It's certainly a paradox of history that this great anti-Communist warrior should use language so similar to that of the Communist leaders who for decades used to warn the peoples of Eastern Europe and the Soviet Union against contamination by the "decadent" West.

Dining with his closest friends in the Vatican, John Paul II often analyzes the Eastern European situation. In many countries there, he says, beginning with Russia, civil society is poorly developed, democracy is fragile, the race to satisfy private interests is brutal. Thus the way is being paved for a *lumpenkapitalismus,* a wild and miserable kind of capitalism, a struggle of man against man.

When the pope traveled to the free Baltic countries in the autumn of

1993, he stunned his audience in Riga by declaring: "The exploitation produced by inhuman capitalism was a real evil, and that's the kernel of truth in Marxism." Some months later, in an interview with Jas Gawronski, a Polish-born Italian deputy to the Europarliament, John Paul II went even further: "These seeds of truth [in Marxism] shouldn't be destroyed, shouldn't be blown away by the wind. . . . The supporters of capitalism in its extreme forms tend to overlook the good things achieved by communism: its effort to overcome unemployment, its concern for the poor."

Upon hearing this statement, back in Moscow, Gorbachev cracked a smile: "Very interesting," he told an Italian friend. "It looks as if the pope is beginning to understand that there are positive values in socialism, and that they'll remain positive in the future too."

In recent years the pope has inveighed more and more forcefully against materialism in the West, his anger taking on global dimensions. He describes the twentieth century as an era in which false prophets and false teachers have won the day. On a visit to Denver in August 1993 he claimed that in modern societies life is often treated as, at best, a commodity and that Western culture, so used to dominating matter, also succumbs to the temptation to manipulate consciences. "The world," the pope declared, "is the theater of an endless battle that replays the apocalyptic conflict of death against life, as a culture of death seeks to impose itself on our desire to live to the full." Can it be, the pope asked, that "conscience is losing the ability to tell right from wrong? Truth is not a figment of the individual's imagination." In Germany, in 1996, his target was "radical capitalist ideology."

But it's not just Western materialism that Karol Wojtyła sees as the enemy. With increasing frankness the pope presents an apocalyptic vision of all Western culture. He views all the progenitors of modern thought—from Descartes and the Enlightenment to Nietzsche and Freud—as profoundly anti-Christian. In an interview with Vittorio Messori he reduced modern history to "the struggle against God, the systematic elimination of all that is Christian." His belief that such an assault "has to a large degree dominated thought and life in the West for three centuries" has been silently rejected by many in the Church and has caused problems for many non-Catholics who were interested in a Church open to dialogue with the contemporary world.

Materialistic Western society, the pope once explained to André Frossard, "aims to convince man that he is a complete being . . . definitively adapted to the structure of the visible world." That's the great danger, he added, "cutting man off from his own depths."

A LONELY PONTIFF

John Paul II's valet threw open the window and His Holiness went up the few steps to the parapet and leaned out over the piazza. Beneath him, clustered around the obelisk and the two great fountains, swarmed the cheering crowd of pilgrims. The recitation of the Angelus at noon every Sunday is a must for Catholics visiting Rome and for tourists curious to see the world's most powerful spiritual leader. Many Roman families as well have the habit of occasionally going to St. Peter's Square with the children to hear "their" pope.

John Paul II liked the motley, enthusiastic masses of humanity, ready to shout, applaud, and wave large flags from their home countries. They reminded him a little of the jubilant crowds he had met on the first trips of his papacy. They brought back memories of the evening when he gave his first speech as pope, from the loggia of St. Peter's. He had spoken confidently, though he didn't know yet how to hold his arms up and out, in the proper pontifical style: People thought he looked a little stiff and awkward.

That Sunday, July 12, 1992, John Paul II spoke once again of the Madonna. He had invented for his Sunday audiences a "spiritual pilgrimage" through Marian sanctuaries all over the world; this time the "stop" was at the Virgin of El Quinche, in Ecuador. Afterward he called for peace and justice in Bosnia-Herzegovina and made a point of saluting a group of Polish pilgrims, who were more excited than the others.

The pilgrims were just about to disperse when the microphone crackled with an unexpected announcement: "I would like to confide something to you. Tonight I will be going to the Gemelli Polyclinic to undergo some diagnostic tests." The astonished crowd looked up to the window of the Apostolic Palace where the small figure in white, no longer charismatic, was sharing all his human preoccupations: "I ask your prayers so that the Lord may be by my side with his help and support." Again he turned to the Mother who, he felt, had accompanied him ever since his earthly mother had died. "To the Most Holy Virgin I repeat, *Totus Tuus:* I am all yours—with complete trust in your motherly protection."

At seven-fifteen P.M. John Paul II, seemingly lost in thought, got into his car to head to the Gemelli Clinic, accompanied by his secretary, Don Stanisław. His personal physician, Dr. Renato Buzzonetti, had explained why he had to be hospitalized: It was a tumor, perhaps a cancer. The doctors had been slow to recognize this suspect growth in his colon. X-rays showed that the tumor apparently wasn't at a dangerous stage; but in any case it had gone farther than it should have, and it was urgent to operate.

When he got to Gemelli, John Paul II quickly went up to the eleventh floor where his room was ready. It was simple, like all the bedrooms in his life (except the one in the Vatican that he hadn't chosen himself). The pope cast a glance at—for him—the most important object in the room: a picture of the Black Madonna, the same one he prayed to in his long devotions in the chapel every morning. This was the room where he had stayed after the assassination attempt. From the corridor one could see the cupola of St. Peter's. A window opened out onto the courtyard of the hospital, where the faithful would soon gather to hear news about the pope's condition.

Only a handful of his intimates knew that this room hadn't been assigned him by accident on the day of the assassination attempt. In a sudden inspiration John Paul II had reserved it, along with another room for his secretary, on the same day that he left the Vatican as newly elected pope to visit his friend Andrzej Deskur in the hospital. John Paul II has always been convinced that the stroke Deskur suffered on the eve of the conclave in October 1978 was in some mysterious way linked to his election. He believed it a kind of "vicarious" accident, suffered on his account, woven into his destiny.

Despite the concern of his co-workers that he wouldn't be able to sleep, John Paul II had a totally peaceful night's rest. The nurse on duty, who kept watch next to the emergency signal, was never called. The next day, exchanging a few quips with his doctors, John Paul II was wheeled into the operating room.

Confusion continues to surround the details of the operation. "A modest and localized dysplasia" in the colon, said the official communiqué. (Dysplasia is an abnormal cellular growth, indicating the initial stage of a shift from a benign to a malignant tumor.) A Vatican statement stressed that the operation, which lasted almost four hours, was "radical and curative." The tumor, a villous adenoma of the colon, was the size of an orange. Later, word leaked out that it was "larger than expected" and that doctors hadn't performed the kind of routine invasive examination that might have resulted in early detection.

Since the operation, the health of John Paul II has been in steady decline. The athletic pope who had gone from youth to maturity hiking in the woods, climbing mountains, and kayaking on lakes, the pope who in his impatience at being cooped up in the Vatican had an Olympic-sized swimming pool built in his summer residence at Castel Gandolfo, and who, whenever he could, used to leave his desk to go skiing in the Apennines, has begun to return ever more frequently to his room on the eleventh floor of the Gemelli Clinic. Despite the Vatican's repeated affirmations that John Paul II is basically in good health, many observers suspect that the pope may have a new tumor.

Two more rooms have been added to his apartment in the hospital. His suite now includes a small living room for receiving guests and a kitchen. The small chapel has been completely remodeled. It is as if suffering was fated to become for Wojtyła a permanent sign of his pontificate.

On November 11, 1993, at an audience in the Vatican with a delegation from the United Nations Food and Agricultural Organization, the pope slumped backward and fell to the ground, causing a small fracture of his right shoulder. Official Vatican sources said that the pope had simply tripped on the steps of the little platform where his throne is placed in the Hall of Benedictions. But some people in the audience had the impression that the pope had passed out. On orders from the Secretariat of State, the film clip of the event, which the Vatican television crew was covering as usual, was never shown to the press. Journalists were told that at that moment the cameraman hadn't been focusing on His Holiness. A freelance photographer on the scene had his film confiscated by the Vatican staff.

For weeks afterward the pope had difficulty elevating the host during mass. He had hardly recovered when in early April 1994 he fell while skiing in the mountains of the Abruzzi. In an attempt to cushion his fall, his secretary, Don Stanisław, fell too, fracturing his arm.

On April 28 John Paul II had yet another fall, this time in the bathroom. It was reported that he had slipped while getting out of the tub after a shower. For several minutes he lay helpless on the bathroom floor with a broken thighbone. Finally he was taken to the Gemelli Clinic, where he was hospitalized for nearly a month. Ever since he has been forced to walk with a cane.

All these falls, though apparently unrelated, raised questions. Either the athletic pope has become more careless—which is hard to believe—or there was *something* that made him fall. Some prelates confidentially report that the pope has brief fainting spells, short blackouts during which his vision clouds over.

For diplomats and journalists accredited to the Holy See the state of the pope's health has become a recurrent topic of speculation. Nobody knows exactly what the pope has, but few doubt that he has a real disease, perhaps more than one. The situation resembles what used to happen with Communist leaders—officially sponsored optimism prevails until the last minute.

The most widely believed hypotheses are that he might have a slowly advancing tumor or that he is subject to transitory ischemic attacks (TIA). Official sources reject the hypothesis of Parkinson's disease, although the pope's left hand often shakes; and the trembling is so strong that when he tries to stop it by grasping his left hand with his right, both hands shake. Meanwhile some Vatican sources, in the strictest confidence, acknowledge that the pope has a disease of the nervous system.

"I'm a *biedaczek* [poor wretch]," said the pope, leaning on his cane one summer day in 1994, to a journalist who asked him in Polish how his health was.

Vatican propaganda tries to hide the pope's condition. On this score Vatican officials fit the well-known British description of diplomats: "Men sent abroad to lie for their country." Many people in the Vatican tell the tale of *L'Osservatore Romano* denying reports that Pope Pius X had a cold—and a day later he was dead.

In August 1994, when the pope went to Combes in the Italian Alps on vacation, the official statements by papal spokesman Navarro-Valls were bursting with optimism. Friday the 19th: "John Paul II took a walk for around two and a half hours." Saturday the 20th: "Yesterday he went on the longest walk since his femur was operated on. He left around 10 a.m. and returned after 5 a.m." Sunday the 21st: "Long walk." Thursday the 25th: "He went by helicopter to Le Petit Chaux, altitude 7,935 feet (after lunch and a nap) and began the descent to the valley." Friday the 26th: "The walk has been especially long."

But when the pope went on his trip the following month to Zagreb, the capital of Croatia, the whole world watched the agony of a man, his face contorted with suffering, who could barely walk down the ramp from the airplane. It was the first time that John Paul II, who was used to flinging himself to the ground to pay homage to his host nation, had to forgo kissing the earth. Two young people in Croatian national costume presented some soil to him in a wooden bowl, and the pope kissed it gently with a sad expression.

His fragility has reinforced his mystical convictions. Karol Wojtyła believes that there is always a reason for suffering; he sees pain as a lesser sort of martyrdom. "For me," he told his aides after he broke his shoulder in November 1993, "this is just another opportunity to join myself more intimately to the mystery of the Cross of Christ, in communion with so many suffering brothers and sisters." He is sure that his sufferings are a part of his mission as pope and have a special significance at a time when moral disorder and violence are so widespread. "The pope has a theological vision of painful events," a monsignor from the Curia explains. "In his mind there are two possibilities: either the forces of evil are in collusion to prevent him from doing what he wanted to do; or the Lord is asking him, in addition to his intellectual and physical commitment, to identify himself with the sufferings of others."

The struggle with his body seems to be encouraging his tremendous willpower. The later years of his pontificate have been characterized by a burst of activity: He has written *Veritatis Splendor* (The Splendor of Truth), regarded by many in his Curia as his most profound encyclical; *Evangelium Vitae* (Gospel of Life); and *Ut Unum Sint* (That They Be One). He has composed an apostolic letter, *Tertio Millenio* (Third Millennium), on the jubilee year 2000. He has continued to take long, tiring trips to the Far East and North America. He has even reorganized the conclave with a view to his own death. The cardinal-electors will no longer have to be locked up in the uncomfortable and antiquated cells in the Apostolic Palace. The next time they gather to elect his successor they'll sleep in the rooms of a modern residence in the Vatican, the Hospice of St. Martha.

.   .   .

Veritatis Splendor, published in the fifteenth year of his pontificate, is the encyclical of his maturity. In it he confronts what he considers the greatest danger of our times: moral relativism.

Rocco Buttiglione, one of the scholars whom the pope had called in for preparatory discussions about the document, notes, "This encyclical marks a new beginning. For the first fifteen years of John Paul II's papacy the problem was communism. Now the problem is the moral crisis of Western democracy. Freedom has to be related to truth. Democracy without truth is doomed to fail."

One bishop who helped draw up the encyclical recalls John Paul II's state of mind in one of the freewheeling group discussions that he likes to have after supper at Castel Gandolfo or in the Vatican to get ideas for his documents and strategies. At this session he was, as usual, listening in silence. Suddenly he interrupted the conversation and exclaimed, *"Ne Crux evacuetur!"* (Don't let the Cross go for naught—1 Corinthians 1:17).

As the pope sees it, a world without the Cross would be a desert; a world without the truth would be hell itself. It's crucial for the believer who wants to follow Christ to know what the truth is, what good and evil are.

The problem of the truth in a world he sees drifting toward ethical relativism is what he addresses in *The Splendor of Truth*. This encyclical took six years to write. One expert claims that a hundred people, one way or another, had a hand in it. The pope himself wrote the first draft in Polish, paying special attention to the first chapter, which is rich in biblical quotations and has more literary appeal than the rest. Then a second, alternative draft was produced by a number of committees; and on this basis the work continued through successive drafts.

As often happens with John Paul II, the main ideas were developed during the summer, when the pope donned a windbreaker and carried an alpenstock to hike the Italian Alps with Polish theologian Tadeusz Styczeń, his successor in the chair of ethics at the Catholic University of Lublin.

The encyclical expresses the whole range of John Paul II's humanism. It represents his attempt to draw up a moral summa and pass it on to the Church universal. Its centerpiece is human dignity and responsibility. *"Gloria Dei homo vivens"* (Living man is the glory of God), the pope stresses, quoting St. Irenaeus. He has been saying this throughout his pontificate.

Certain passages from the encyclical perfectly mirror the identity of Karol Wojtyła the pastor, the poet, and the philosopher. "If man does evil," he claims, "he still has the just judgment of his conscience to bear witness to the universal truth of goodness, as well as to the wickedness of his particular choice. But the verdict of conscience remains with him as a pledge of hope and mercy: While it attests to the evil committed, it also recalls the pardon he must beg for, the good he must do, and the virtue he must always cultivate with the grace of God."

Human reason is autonomous, the pope says, but it doesn't create ethical norms, which come from God. This is a problem that also fascinates nonbelievers: Vaclav Havel, for instance, has wondered recently whether the chief human values, in particular universal human rights, can really be considered binding on everyone unless it is admitted that they have a *transcendent foundation.*

There can be no question that many of John Paul II's concerns are also shared by non-Catholics. Nonetheless, this encyclical stirred up controversy within the Catholic world and beyond it because of its hostile attitude toward the intellectual freedom of theologians. The second part of the encyclical is a painstakingly detailed examination of certain contemporary schools of theology. In John Paul II's assault on these schools, which assert the importance of the historical, anthropological, cultural, and psychological conditions influencing the actions of the human person, John Paul II is implacable. He accuses them of undermining the doctrine of intrinsic evil. He wants them to be silent.

When the curial theologians, responding to the pope's wishes, included a declaration of papal infallibility in one of the drafts of *Veritatis Splendor,* a wave of muted resistance swept through the Catholic Church. In the final version, as Cardinal Ratzinger admits, the claim of infallibility was dropped; but the fact that it was ever introduced shows just how badly John Paul wanted, in his last years, to give a definitive—and binding—answer to the most intensely disputed questions facing the Church.

In *Veritatis Splendor* John Paul II eventually used the most authoritative language possible, short of a declaration of infallibility: "Brothers in the episcopate," he told the bishops of the world, "I intend to state the principles needed for discerning what is contrary to *sound doctrine.*"

The pope reminded the bishops of their "grave duty to be personally vigilant," so as to make sure that in their dioceses faith and doctrine were taught correctly. Should there be serious "failures" (that is, deviations from the Ratzinger-Wojtyła line), the title "Catholic" was to be taken away from schools, universities, hospitals, and family counseling centers associated with the Church. What the pope particularly had in mind were Catholic hospital and research institutes that encouraged in vitro fertilization and artificial birth control.

Dissenting theologians were ordered to keep silent about their controversial opinions. If they did, they might be granted forgiveness. Otherwise they were to be removed from their university chairs and forbidden to give lectures and publish books. The encyclical was, in part, an effort to wipe out dissent by decree: "Dissent, which consists of disputes and polemics deliberately aired in the mass media," the pope proclaimed, "is contrary to communion with the Church and to the proper understanding of the hierarchical structure of the people of God."

Hans Küng, the enfant terrible of German-speaking theology, reacted furiously: "The pope is convinced that his doctrine is the doctrine of Christ and of God himself. This is a messianism that does harm to the Catholic

Church. . . . The encyclical is rather an admission of failure. If the pope realizes that after fifteen years of speeches, after the trips, the encyclicals, and the catechism, Catholics are still not following his words, then *Veritatis Splendor* is the acknowledgment of a crisis: the inability of the pope to convince the Church."

The eighty-year-old Redemptorist priest Bernhard Häring, a leading moral theologian, was distraught: *"Veritatis Splendor* contains many beautiful things. But almost all the 'splendor' is lost when it becomes clear that the whole document has one supreme goal: to endorse total assent and submission to all the pope's utterances."

Even more surprising than these protests was the comment by the cardinal of Brussels, Godfried Danneels, whom John Paul II prized for the way he brought the 1985 Synod Bishops to a quiet and tame conclusion: "It's not the best of the papal encyclicals."

In the Catholic Church understatement is one of the subtler forms of opposition. Another is to praise an event—and quickly bury it. In a way this became the fate of *Veritatis Splendor.* Many bishops commented privately: "The encyclical says the right things, but what are we supposed to do with it? Our job is to find a way to bring people back into the churches."

· · ·

It's hard to say exactly when a pontificate begins to end. There are often no spectacular flourishes to announce the arrival of the Last Act. In the curial congregations it remains business as usual: The monsignors with their briefcases enter and leave the Vatican palaces as always. The vast machinery of bureaucratic meetings, the gatherings of bishops and cardinals, grinds on. Synods are convoked, consistories announced. The pope goes on trips; the pope publishes documents; the pope makes appearances, but . . .

But in the world of black robes and purple birettas there comes a day when the monsignors begin to talk in a peculiar tone about *him.* It's a barely perceptible way of distancing themselves from His Holiness, of only going through the motions of defending him or of forgetting to mention him. Subtle hints are dropped that no policy lasts forever. Wojtyła "is heroically preaching the Gospel *as he sees* it," an important nuncio said in 1996.

Romans have a coolly realistic saying: *"Morto un papa, se ne fa un altro"* (When a pope dies, they make another one). Nobody living within the walls of the Vatican ever forgets this.

In his last years John Paul II has begun to run into a kind of silent resistance inside the Catholic Church. People no longer accept his leadership without question. Although he has received more people in his private chapel or dining room than any other pope in this century, he has never made any close personal friends in the Curia. He has always been above it—but alone.

With the exception of Cardinal Ratzinger, the individuals he has named to the highest posts in the Curia are quicker to carry out orders than to confront him with dissenting or original opinions. "In certain areas he has a trusted team," confides a curial veteran, "but elsewhere his advisers are colorless, which is definitely one of the weaknesses of this papacy." Colorless men, this Vatican insider adds, tend not to be great thinkers—they are the kind of people for whom loyalty counts more than turning out provocative analyses that might run counter to the monarch's predispositions.

Thus Karol Wojtyła is more alone than ever; and from his throne he is forced to watch how in the Church and the Curia things are starting to slip away from him. The harsh decrees in *Veritatis Splendor* are the pope's attempt to preserve what he believes should be a changeless order. His concern to translate God's will into reality and his conviction that he was elected near the end of the millennium to carry out a specific plan of Providence have turned into a peculiar kind of imperiousness.

Over the last few years John Paul II has tried to find a way—beyond his papacy—to bind the Church to his view of divine will. He has declared that married men can never be priests. He has repeated his determination that the Church prohibit women from entering the priesthood. He has refused to consider allowing divorced and remarried persons to take communion.

Preventing the question of the ordination of women from even arising has become an obsession for him. His aim is to stop any discussion of the topic whatsoever. Specifically to force nuns not to bring up the issue at a synod on religious life planned for the autumn of 1994, a new papal document, *Sacerdotalis Ordinatio* (Priestly Ordination), was published to reinforce the old prohibition. Its argument was a traditional one that the Reformed churches and the Anglicans have long left behind: "Christ chose only men as his Apostles, and the Church has imitated Christ in its constant practice of choosing only men."

The tone of the document was most unusual: "In order to remove any doubt," John Paul II announced, "by virtue of my ministry of confirming the brethren, I declare that the Church has no authority whatsoever to confer priestly ordination on women and that all the faithful are definitively bound to this judgment." But doubts continued; and one year later, in November 1995, Cardinal Ratzinger was compelled to publish yet another instruction stating that the pope's pronouncement was "definitive and infallible" and that all the faithful were obliged to assent to it. As a matter of fact, the cardinal chose a highly contorted way of proclaiming the infallibility of a papal decision—something that had not happened since Vatican II. Ratzinger's new document decreed that the words of the pope referred to an already "infallible" doctrine.

"Roma locuta, causa finita" (Rome has spoken, the case is closed), St. Augustine used to say. In reality the more John Paul II surrounds the Church with barbed wire, the more glaring the cracks in the wall appear. Opposition keeps cropping up.

At the synod on Africa in 1994, Congolese bishop Ernest Kombo challenged the pope, who was present at the debate, when he voiced the hope that women could be named to the highest possible posts in the Church hierarchy, even as "lay cardinals." At the same synod the final document of the participating bishops expressed "horror [at] the discrimination and marginalization to which women are subjected in the Church and society" and voted for a provision declaring it imperative to include women on the various levels of decision making in the Church.

As sex in one form or another (divorce, married priests, the ordination of women, contraception) has become the battleground on which John Paul II exercises his will to command, the pope is increasingly confronted by opposition from the princes of the Church who are uneasy with what they regard as his cultural bias.

Cardinal Carlo Maria Martini of Milan (often mentioned as a *papabile*) proposed studying the possibility of women entering the diaconate, even though the Vatican had made it clear that such a question was *not* to be on the Church's agenda. Martini also defined priestly celibacy as a historical decision that could be changed. Asked in a BBC interview about the Vatican prohibition against communion for divorced and remarried persons, Martini made no secret of his discomfort.

Bishop Karl Lehmann of Mainz, president of the German bishops conference, even made a formal request of the Vatican to revoke the ban or at least to soften its absolute rigor, allowing couples to make their own decisions based on individual conscience. On orders from John Paul II, Cardinal Ratzinger prevented the German bishops from making any independent decision on the subject. At the consistory of 1995 Lehmann was punished for simply having tried to modify the pope's decree: He was denied the cardinal's biretta.

In Great Britain Cardinal Basil Hume (another *papabile* at the last conclave) spoke of homosexual love as an enriching experience—though *Veritatis Splendor* still lists sodomy as one of the mortal sins.

In January 1995 French bishop Jacques Gaillot was summoned to the Vatican and removed from his diocese with no prior warning because he had insisted on speaking out in favor of married priests, the use of condoms by people with HIV, and respect for committed homosexual relationships.

With large demonstrations breaking out in protest over his summary dismissal (Gaillot was given twelve hours to resign "voluntarily" but refused) the president of the French bishops conference, Joseph Duval, declared on public TV in Normandy: "This is an authoritarian act that can't be accepted by society, not even by the Church. People want consultation and dialogue. Authoritarian gestures on the part of Rome have multiplied in recent days: the Catechism of the Church Universal, the encyclical on morality (*Veritatis Splendor*), the ban on ordaining women, the impossibility of giving communion to divorced and remarried persons. These acts make the Church look like a rigid, closed organization."

One year later the French bishops issued a booklet about HIV which argues that condoms can be a "necessity," a position absolutely rejected by the Vatican. Even Dutch cardinal Adrianus Simonis of Utrecht, a well-known traditionalist, has come out in favor of this position as a "lesser evil."

And in 1996 a Wojtyła protégé, Archbishop Christoph Schönborn of

Vienna, chosen by the pope to preach the Lenten retreat in the Vatican, concurred: "Nobody can expect that love must bring death," he said.

A principal problem facing John Paul II's papacy continues to be democracy in his own house. As many French Catholics wondered during the Gaillot affair: Can a pope who championed democratic rights in Poland and all over the world continue to run the Church as an absolute monarchy? Bishop Rembert Weakland of Milwaukee, a former superior general of the Benedictines, maintains that Pope Wojtyła, "has this great fear that the whole question of freedom and democracy will somehow creep into the Church."

John Paul II refuses to address the issue. The new *Manual for the Clergy*, published in 1994, emphasizes that "false ideas of democracy corrode the hierarchical constitution [of the Church] willed by its Divine Founder." But the problem is becoming more and more acute, partly because the other Christian churches have addressed it so directly and often effectively. Many Catholics too are demanding a greater voice.

John Paul II's way of ruling has brought projects for unity with the other Christian churches—where democratic principles are put into practice by means of special assemblies—virtually to a halt. In his pontificate there have been many friendly gestures, but no real progress. It is above all within the Catholic Church itself, however, that ill feeling and resentment are piling up. Month after month the pope gets disturbing reports from the Secretariat of State. The Vatican's high-handed methods have prompted the emergence of broad-based opposition movements that air their discontent by collecting signatures. "We are the Church" is their battle cry. "What concerns everyone," they add, "should be decided by everyone." Such protests are unprecedented. In Austria, where John Paul II foisted the hard-line traditionalist cardinal Hermann Grör on Vienna as the successor of Cardinal König (and was forced to remove him in 1995 after accusations of pedophilia), a grassroots movement of 500,000 Catholics presented the bishops with a petition: They demanded a review of the issues of priestly celibacy, more democracy, and greater participation by the local Church in the appointment of bishops. (The bishops are picked by the pope on the basis of a secret list of candidates submitted by his nuncios.) The protest movement spread to Germany, France, Italy, Belgium, and the United States. In Germany, Catholic reformers collected 1.5 million signatures; and the Catholic theological faculty of Tübingen publicly appealed to the Vatican for an official rehabilitation of theologian Hans Küng, stressing that the faculty had never demanded his removal for alleged doctrinal deviations.

American Catholics made their objections heard at the highest level. In June 1995 more than forty bishops endorsed a twelve-page statement denouncing Vatican interference in the policy making of the American bishops conference. The signatories criticized the curial policy of weakening the role of all bishops conferences and the Vatican's custom of promulgating documents binding on almost a billion Catholics without prior consultation. "There is a widespread feeling," the American bishops said, "that Roman documents of varying authority have for some years been systematically reinterpreting Vatican II documents so as to present the minority positions at the Council as the true meaning of the Council." The villain of this piece was, undoubtedly, Karol Wojtyła.

The pope, comments Bishop Weakland, "is leaning further and further toward putting people against the wall, so that if he continues this line, he could easily begin to divide the Church."

In any event, unresolved questions keep resurfacing. The refusal to allow divorce, which is permitted by all the other Christian churches, has led to a boom in religious annulments, against which John Paul II vainly fulminates year after year during his audiences at the Sacred Roman Rota, the court that supervises church tribunals (and annulment proceedings) all over the world.

"The judge must not let himself be influenced by unacceptable anthropological concepts," he said in 1987. "The judge must always guard against the danger of sentimentalism, which only seems to be pastoral" (1990). "There can be no question of adapting the divine norm or even of bending it to suit the whim of a human being" (1992).

But the rate of annulments—in which the court declares marriages null and void from their beginning—has remained sky-high, with the United States leading the way. In 1989, 78,209 annulments were granted, 61,416 in the United States. In 1991, the figure was 80,712, with 63,933 in the United States. In 1992, there were 76,829, with 59,030 in the United States.

In 1995 John Paul II vented his anger at bishops in general "who might be tempted to fall behind in enforcing the procedures established and confirmed by canon law." This means that many bishops are effectively distancing themselves from rules they don't agree with.

The crisis—and it is a crisis, even in the view of many in the Church who admire John Paul II and agree with many of his pronouncements—can also be seen in the smaller crowds that show up in Europe when John Paul II returns to a country he has already visited. When he went to Prague in May 1995 the city ignored him. Only sixty thousand faithful appeared for the mass he celebrated at the city stadium—940,000 fewer Czechs than the number who attended during his 1990 visit.

A few weeks later, when he went to Belgium, no more than thirty-five thousand persons attended a mass in front of the basilica of Koekelberg. The Belgian bishops organized only a twenty-four-hour visit for him. On June 4, when the pope met in Brussels with some of his old classmates from the Belgian College in Rome (where he had lived between 1946 and 1948), Cardinal Jan Schotte bitterly complained to those present: "The Holy Father wanted to come to Belgium for three days, but the Belgian bishops didn't want him."

The sense of loneliness surrounding the papal throne is heightened by the behavior of the faithful, especially in Europe. Polls reflect a lack of consensus. In 1984 John Paul II was "very popular" with fifty-four percent of Belgians; the figure today is twenty-six percent. Only nineteen percent approve his ban on communion for divorced and remarried people; twenty-five percent approve the ban on contraceptives. The pope's ratings are high only when it comes to his trips abroad (sixty-two percent) and his role in Eastern Europe (fifty-four percent).

Even in Italy, the country most directly subject to the Vatican's influence, the faithful continue to go their own way. A poll taken in 1995 for the Italian bishops conference found that only twenty-three percent of Italians regularly attend mass; sixty percent never go to confession. More than half of Italian Catholics are in favor of divorce and premarital sex. About seventy percent favor the pill; fifty-three percent express no objections to homosexuality, and only fourteen percent think abortion should be illegal under all circumstances.

Polls, however, have never influenced John Paul II. In the pope's mind the fight to preserve moral and ecclesiastical laws as he knows them is his inescapable duty. All this is a heavy burden for him, but no one has ever heard him complain about the toils of his office. Sometimes when he returns exhausted from his travels, his guardian angel in the Vatican, Sister Eufrozja, will greet him by saying, "I'm worried about Your Holiness." To which he replies, with a roguish smile, "I'm worried about my holiness too."

EVE

The woman walked through the corridors of the palace, accompanied by a gentleman in a dark suit, but scarcely exchanging a word with him. The statues, tapestries, and frescoes seemed to whiz by her. In one room she glanced at an old Bible on a beautifully carved marble table; but, though these marvelous objets d'art stirred her curiosity, she wasn't impressed by them. She was used to the wonders of the world. Rome and New York, London and Geneva were as familiar to her as the great cities of Asia, Africa, or Latin America. Besides, she hadn't chosen that morning of March 18, 1994, to go on a cultural tour. She had come to talk business—about women, mothers, families. With sensitivity and delicacy, with frankness if she had to, but with steely toughness if it came to that.

She caught a glimpse of the throne in the Sala Clementina. Though empty, it looked majestic. But the gentleman in the dark suit quickly escorted her down another corridor.

John Paul II was waiting in his study. Through all the years of his pontificate women had been a problem—or at least the world press kept saying they were. Either the media talked about abortion and his refusal to grant women freedom of choice, or they talked about his ban on women priests. In either case he was constantly being accused of backwardness and insensitivity to the needs and aspirations of modern women. The pope met these charges with annoyance. When he read them in summaries of news reports he dismissed them with a twitch of his eyebrows.

John Paul II's sense of who he was in regard to women differed from his negative image in the media: He knew himself. He thought about women with feelings of infinite tenderness. Didn't he consider them irreplaceable, extraordinary beings? Hadn't he written a special apostolic letter, *Mulieris Dignitatem* (The Dignity of Woman), declaring, "A woman represents a particular value . . . by the fact of her femininity"? Hadn't he lyrically saluted "spousal love—with its maternal potential hidden in the heart of woman as a virginal bride"? He was convinced that "feminine genius," when joined to Christ, predisposed women to a special "openness to each and every person."

Radical feminism saddened Karol Wojtyła. When the subject came up during Zofia Zdybicka's visits to the Vatican, he used to say in bewilderment, "Sister, I have such respect for women, I have such a high opinion of them." He often told her: "I know that women have an enormous potential for doing good . . . it's just that right now they're under cultural constraints."

Once, in 1993, he had proclaimed his respect for women before the whole world, at the window of his study overlooking St. Peter's Square: "Mary, Virgin and Mother of the Redeemer, I wish to say a hearty 'thank you' from the entire Church to the Lord for the gift of woman, for each and every one of them."

But during his pontificate the tide of criticism against him would not abate—in and out of his Church. When it came to the idea of motherhood, a profound gulf separated him from the approach of feminists as well as many other women who would never have defined themselves as feminists. For Wojtyła pregnancy itself was an exalted symbol. For him, "the gestation of a baby is a metaphor for being a contemplative," explains David Schindler, American editor of the Ratzinger-sponsored theological journal *Communio*. "It's taking something in and being reflective. Dwelling within it, then comes the period of maturation, giving birth. And then concomitant with giving birth is the sense of suffering, of pain. . . . This view is fundamental with the pope."

But for feminists and others, who were suspicious of an overromantic or misleading vision of woman—as either Angel or Mother—it was essential to affirm the right to control their own bodies and not be treated as mere vessels, as flowerpots sheltering a precious plant. Thus the conflict was deepseated.

The pope was well aware that, on the subject of women, the spirit of criticism and opposition was widespread in the Catholic world, especially—as the Vatican departments never failed to remind him—in the United States. After all, it had been an American nun, a superior of the Sisters of Mercy, who dared to defy him just a year after his election. It happened in Washington, at the Shrine of the Immaculate Conception, on the last day of his first trip to the United States in October 1979. The shrine was thronged with around five thousand sisters. More than two-thirds of them had showed up without the veil or the religious habit, although immediately after becoming pope he had insisted on traditional attire for nuns—and continued to insist on it during his American tour. Disobedience irritated him.

Here and there in the neo-Gothic nave and aisles he could see some fifty sisters who stood out from the rest: They were wearing a strange blue armband, as if they were volunteers for some organization. When he asked his Vatican aides about it, they told him the nuns belonged to an opposition group advocating the ordination of women. Their motto was "If women can make bread, they can break bread."

The woman chosen to welcome him was Sister Theresa Kane, president of the Leadership Conference of Women Religious. She too had come in secular clothing. The pope looked at the diminutive woman in a blue tailored suit. She addressed her formal remarks to him for less than ten minutes; and at the end she declared over the microphone, in a resonant voice: "Your Holiness, the Church ought to respond to the sufferings of women by considering the possibility of including them in all the sacred ministries." Loud applause had greeted this remark, which was rebroadcast on TV all over the United States.

Afterward Sister Kane approached the papal chair and greeted the pope in an almost irreverent, democratic manner (compared with the submissive Polish and Italian nuns in the Vatican): "Good morning, nice to meet you." She shook his hand and asked for his blessing. She knelt down but didn't kiss his ring. John Paul II remembered this. By the time his turn came to address the sisters in the shrine, his usual amiability had vanished. He didn't smile once.

In later years Sister Kane would recall how swiftly the Vatican struck back. A few weeks after the episode, when she was in Rome for a meeting of the Congregation for Religious, she got a letter with the laconic message "We would appreciate a clarification of your greeting to the Holy Father at the Shrine."

At the Vatican she was met by a priest and not, as planned, by Cardinal Eduardo Pironio, prefect of the Congregation of Religious Orders. The scene, although vaguely intimidating, had a touch of the absurd. "Now that we have finished the other items on the agenda," the priest said, "I would ask you to clarify your greeting."

"I want to ask *you* what you want clarified," Sister Kane replied. There was a dead silence in the room. The priest turned to his colleagues and asked, "What is it we want clarified?" Nobody answered.

They obviously wanted her to say that in her speech to the pope she hadn't been referring to the ordination of women. But she insisted, "I want you to know: I did include ordination . . . ordination was included." Her punishment came at the end of Sister Kane's term of office as president of the Leadership Conference. When she asked to meet John Paul II, the Vatican informed her that a meeting would be "inappropriate."

Thus the protests by women had begun. Over the years, with rare exceptions, women had been the only ones to contradict John Paul II in front of large audiences, before the world press and television. They had used few words, but they never gave up on the issues, tenaciously passing the baton like relay runners.

The next year, 1980, in Munich, in heavily Catholic Bavaria, a young woman named Barbara Engel criticized the Church's attitude toward priestly celibacy and sexual problems. When the pope went to Switzerland it was once again a woman, Margrit Stucky-Schaller, who confronted him. "We regret that our work has so little importance for the faith and for the Church. We women have the impression that we are considered second-class citizens," she said.

In 1985, during the pope's trip to Holland and Belgium, the scene had been livelier. In Utrecht thousands of punk youths, anarchists, gays, and lesbians took to the streets in a loud, flamboyant protest against papal authoritarianism. They clashed with the police for three hours. Later that day Hedwig Wasser, the keynote speaker at the meeting of missionary organizations, quizzed him: "How can we possibly have any credibility when we proclaim the Gospel with a finger pointed in blame instead of a hand stretched out to help? When instead of making room for them, we exclude divorced couples, homosexuals, married priests, and women?" Unconcerned by the visible discomfort of the papal entourage, Wasser's gaze fixed on John Paul II as she calmly observed, "Recent developments in certain parts of the Church have forced many of us to disobey church authorities."

At Louvain-la-Neuve, a branch of the renowned old Flemish university, the attack had come from a young woman of Polish descent: Véronique Yoruba, the student body president. "We are disturbed," she said, "knowing that the use of contraceptives can place couples on the margin of the Church. Certain positions that you have taken concerning the nations of Latin America and liberation theology surprise us. We believe, in fact, that both Nicaragua and Poland, both El Salvador and Chile, are countries where people are struggling to affirm the very principles of justice, freedom, and democracy to which the Church is attached."

In the university lecture hall, pandemonium broke loose right in front of the pope. The applause from students favoring Yoruba was met by the roars from Wojtyła's fans, who tried to silence her, shouting, "Long live the pope!" Then she turned toward some of the more agitated members of the crowd and cried out sarcastically, "Thanks, Opus Dei." John Paul II's reaction was mild and paternal: He kissed the young student on the head.

Now, at the Vatican, in the spring of 1994, however, such conflicts couldn't be soothed with a little theatrical gesture. The woman coming to meet the pope was, in his eyes, an angel of death. John Paul II had begun the year by proclaiming that the United Nations was aiming to destroy the family and life and that the place where this crime was about to happen was Cairo.

The UN Conference on Population and Development, scheduled for September in Cairo, had to approve a Program of Action worked out in a number of preparatory meetings. The program focused on two principles: the reproductive rights of both couples and individuals and guarantees of reproductive health. It stressed the obligation of government to provide health services while granting the greatest possible freedom of contraceptive methods. This had already aroused Pope Wojtyła's suspicions: He feared a global policy encouraging massive distribution of birth control pills and condoms. But what alarmed him most was the program's insistence that abortions be performed under safe and legal conditions.

In the files prepared for the pope the Vatican Secretariat of State stressed how much political conditions had changed since the previous conference ten years before in Mexico City. During the Reagan administration the United States had pushed a "pro-life" policy with a view to pleasing the pope and reinforcing the strategic alliance with the Vatican. But now the winds in Washington had shifted. The Clinton administration favored a woman's right to choose and defended individual sexual rights, including those of homosexuals. It also favored the availability of safe and legal abortions.

The pope found this intolerable. He suspected that the United States and an American feminist lobby wanted to impose Western-style sexual lifestyles on the developing countries. In a letter to the families of the whole world, written a few weeks earlier, he had drawn the battle lines: on the one side the civilization of life and love, defended by the Church, and on the other a destructive anticivilization, permeated by utilitarianism, with irresponsible sexual education, abortion on demand, propaganda for free love ("which ruins families"), the destruction of marriage (leaving "orphans whose parents are alive"), and homosexual unions, following a trend that was "dangerous for the future of the family and society."

Just now John Paul II was working on the draft of his latest encyclical, *Evangelium Vitae* (The Gospel of Life). It was a withering attack on such "threats to life" as euthanasia and abortion.

The woman coming to see him had to realize that he would fight tooth and nail against a "new massacre, a true slaughter of the innocents, a new holocaust." The Holocaust was precisely the image that came to his mind every time he heard the word *abortion*.

The door opened.

The woman looked toward the desk in the center of the room. John Paul II was seated by himself, and only when she started to approach did he stand up as a sign of courtesy. He was alone. All the light in the room seemed to be focused on his white cassock and the gold of his pectoral cross.

The pope looked at his guest. Nafis Sadik, undersecretary of the UN Conference on Population and Development, was dressed in the costume of her native Pakistan: a long sari-like, pastel-colored top draped over similarly colored trousers. She was almost sixty years old with brown skin and hair that was still jet black. Her face had a calm and determined expression.

John Paul II exchanged a rapid hello and handshake with Sadik, and as he pointed out the chair she was to sit in, he began: "You know this is the Year of the Family." He paused for effect. Sadik, who had hardly taken her seat, was caught by surprise. Before she could reply, the pope continued: "But it seems to me the Year of the Disintegration of the Family."

The accusatory tone in the pope's words struck the UN representative. Immediately Sadik tried to point out that there are many kinds of families in the world: extended families, nuclear families, single-parent families, abandoned families. But the pope raised the index finger of his right hand and launched a tirade. "How do you think the populations of the world have grown? It is because of the family. A family is a husband, a wife, and their children. And marriage is the only basis for a family. Homosexuals and lesbians are not families."

The thought "You don't know the facts of life" flashed through Sadik's mind, but she simply told him that the conference's Program of Action dealt mainly with children and mothers, that is, the groups most vulnerable to the consequences of oversized families and sexual abuse.

Once again Wojtyła raised his right hand and announced: "The United Nations must speak out, the UN must provide moral and spiritual leadership." Sadik noticed that his hand kept trembling; the pope's whole face betrayed emotional strain. Sadik went back to explaining that the United Nations had to represent all the views of its members, that it had to reflect the cultures of 5.7 billion people. But it was hard to make her case, because the pope kept interrupting, jumping from one subject to another.

"Why is your approach different from the previous conferences?" he asked.

"Your Holiness, you should be happy," Sadik replied, "because with regard to the population problem we've chosen a person-centered approach. We never mention numbers. Everything is based on individual needs and individual choice."

In fact this was the great novelty of the Cairo conference's preparatory document. The question of population growth was primarily linked to the problems of development—to education, health, and the empowerment of women. Instead of recommending numerical limits that might encourage—as they had before—restrictions by the state on family size, the document insisted on the reproductive rights of women, on the free choice of family planning methods by each individual, and on safeguarding people's health. In the case of abortion—which the authors of the draft didn't advocate, but felt they had to confront—they asked for guarantees that it be made both safe and legal.

"Who does more for development than the Church?" the pope asked suddenly. He leaned forward and glowered at Sadik.

"I appreciate that," Sadik rejoined, adding that she had once studied in a nuns' school in Calcutta, "but not in the area of family planning."

Now she knew what line to take. The pope looked her right in the eye. She stiffened and returned his stare. This was a real fight, not some polite disagreement.

The voices went back and forth, the woman's warmer and lighter, the man's heavier and slower. Every now and then the pope raised his right hand like a preacher making a point. The UN envoy sat almost motionless. Sometimes her hand caught the slipping hem of her sari.*

"Family planning can be practiced only in accordance with moral, spiritual, and natural laws," said John Paul II.

"But natural laws make for unreliable methods of family planning," Sadik replied.

---

* Later, Sadik reconstructed the whole scene in a memorandum.

The conversation turned to the free choices of individuals in family planning. "In this area," the pope declared, "there can be no individual rights and needs. There can be only the couple's rights and needs."

"But 'couples' implies an equal relationship. In many societies, and not just in the developing world, women don't have equal status with men. There's a lot of sexual violence within the family. Women are quite willing to practice natural methods and abstain, because they're the ones who get pregnant and don't want to be. But they can't abstain without the cooperation of their partners."

She spoke to him about the approximately 200,000 women who die every year from self-induced abortions—a major health issue: "Religious leaders—and all of us, really—must address this very important issue."

"Don't you think," John Paul II interjected, "that the irresponsible behavior of men is caused by women?"

Sadik froze. "My jaw dropped," she reported afterward. John Paul II saw the shock etched on the face of his interlocutor and tried to change the subject.

But the woman in the sari stopped him. "Excuse me, I must respond to your statement about the behavior of women. In most of the developing countries men look on marital relations as their right, and the women have to comply. Men come home drunk, have sexual relations with their wives; and the wives get pregnant. Or they get HIV without having any control over their partner's behavior and their own situation."

Sadik wasn't finished. "Violence within the family, rape in fact, is very common in our society. The most upsetting thing about all this is that only women suffer the consequences. Many women, you know, wind up abandoned. Latin America is full of abandoned families, full of women who are left as the heads of households, with children to look after, while the men go off and start another family somewhere else."

The pope's look was stern; his eyes, usually so affectionate, had taken on a cold glitter. To Sadik, he seemed as taut as a spring. Nothing had prepared her for such a reception.

"Why is he so hard-hearted," she was wondering, "so dogmatic, so lacking in kindness? He could at least say, 'I really feel the suffering of these people; but the best way is the moral way.'" She told friends after the discussion, "He's not at all the benevolent person his image makes him out to be."

John Paul II felt no sympathy for his conversation partner either. To him Sadik's programs, despite her Pakistani heritage, were the product of American feminism, one of the worst features of the contemporary scene, a form of destructive cultural imperialism. Their talk showed him once again that the West had lost sight of the deep meaning of woman's mission, of her richest "treasure." What could be greater than to give life, to form the personality of a child, to guide him or her to adulthood?

The pope worried that even in the Church, even among theologians, one often found people who didn't fully understand the value of life and the unique role of women.

Now Sadik was telling him that the German bishops, while advocating the rhythm method of family planning, had admitted it wasn't always suitable. So they recommended that other methods be provided to let women safely decide on the number and spacing of their children.

The pope interrupted her in vexation. (It was clear that he didn't like being contradicted, nor was he used to it.) "I know the bishops' report, of course. It was the materialism of German society that pressured Catholics into making this report."

Sadik realized there wasn't much chance of finding common ground.

Again the pope changed the subject. "Teenagers must be taught responsible behavior, and that's the only way. Educate them."

"I don't think I have any problems with that." Still, Sadik stressed, one had to keep in mind the teenage pregnancies in the Third World.

"We can't condone immoral behavior," the pope objected.

But, as a woman and a gynecologist, Sadik insisted: "Even if you don't approve, you still have to treat patients for the consequences of their actions. You might even disapprove, but it's not for us simply to sit in judgment. We have to help if we can, help and provide . . ."

"The only way is to follow the moral, spiritual, and natural law. And you must educate, educate, educate," the pope shot back.

Stonewalled once more, Sarik recalls: "I got quite carried away. I was really trying to find a way to get to him, at least to strike a responsive chord, not necessarily to change his views. But his attitude was so harsh."

"How many Catholics do you think there are in the world?" Sadik suddenly asked. The pope was leaning toward her over the table. "How many Muslims are there?" he snapped.

"About 1.2 billion."

"And the same number of Catholics." (In fact, the correct figure was closer to 900 million.)

"Well, in fact, that wasn't the point of my question," Sadik resumed. "It was, how many Catholics do you think actually follow the teachings of the Church on this matter?"

"It's only the Catholics in those materialistic developed societies who don't," the pope insisted. "All the people in the poorer countries do."

"I am sorry to have to disagree with you, because in Latin America, for example, women have no access to contraceptives," Sadik noted "and so they resort to abortion. In fact, we find the highest rate of illegal abortion in many of the poorer Catholic countries in the world."

The pope rejoined that women were fully capable of deciding not to have sex if they wished to control a couple's sexual agenda.

"Well, I think that our experience is totally different. For the millions of women I've dealt with that's not how things are."

"The UN," he argued, "can't include compulsory sterilization, compulsory birth control, and abortion in its program."

"I'm sure there's nothing in our program on that," Sadik dryly observed. She sensed that the pope hadn't read the Cairo conference's preparatory document but was speaking only on the basis of some unrepresentative excerpts.

"You are a Muslim?" John Paul II asked Sadik out of the blue, then quickly added, "Islam is the fastest-growing religion in the world." Hardly pausing, he evoked for her his vision of a younger generation in the ex-Communist countries and elsewhere in the world discarding atheism and returning to embrace religion.

"The UN must promote ethical principles," he continued, "and it doesn't matter what the countries say. These Western societies are places where the family is disintegrating. Their ethical values are gone. I'm personally very concerned with this, and I take it as my personal mission. I'm going to the UN in October to give a speech about it."

The conversation lasted forty minutes. It took her a moment to realize it had ended. Suddenly Sadik found a silver medal placed in her hands. A monsignor came to alert the pope that he had other things to attend to. The audience was over. In the antechamber the photographer who routinely took pictures of papal audiences was strangely absent. Evidently, Vatican protocol dictated that Nafis Sadik wasn't worthy of a photograph.

Sadik walked out onto St. Peter's Square feeling disappointed by the lack of compassion in the man. "He doesn't like women," she commented later. "I expected a little more sympathy for suffering and death."

• • •

A week after the audience with Nafis Sadik, 140 nuncios from all over the world arrived in the Vatican for an extraordinary summit conference. John Paul II had decided to declare his own state of war against the United Nations. He was furious. His closest friend in the Vatican, Cardinal Deskur, had never seen the pope in such a rage. Usually John Paul II paid a visit every week to the ailing cardinal. Seated at the table where Deskur had arranged so many dinners to launch young Bishop Wojtyła, John Paul II spoke freely: "They are causing the shipwreck of humanity." His condemnation referred to both the UN and the Western democracies.

Once he had made his decision, John Paul II moved with a belligerence he had never shown before—not even when it was a question of saving Poland. The whole approach to the family by Western governments was contrary to reason and to God, the pope told Dominican Feliks Bednarski. He instructed his secretary of state, Cardinal Angelo Sodano, to personally mobilize all the diplomatic delegations of the Holy See to pressure the states friendly to the Vatican and to put together a lobby capable of blocking the UN program of action.

On March 25, 1994, the 140 nuncios summoned to Rome made their way through the great Bronze Door of the Apostolic Palace to hear from the secretary of state. They found themselves face to face with a real council of war. Apart from Cardinal Sodano there were the pope's minister of foreign affairs, the French Bishop Jean-Louis Tauran; Cardinal Roger Etchegaray, head of the Council for Justice and Peace; and Cardinal Alfonso López Trujillo, president of the Pontifical Council for the Family, the pope's closest and most loyal aide on issues of sexual ethics and marital problems.

In recent years meetings of this sort had been called on only three occasions: the Gulf War, the breakup of Yugoslavia, and the recognition by the Vatican of the state of Israel. The nuncios realized that the battle to defend life "from conception to death" would have to be fought with all the weapons of diplomacy. Some points of the UN Program of Action, they were told, contradicted "fundamental ethical principles" and favored abortion on demand, which would be used as a means of birth control. The pope was firmly convinced that the document was inspired by an individualistic vision of sensuality and that it regarded marriage as obsolete.

The effect was immediate. At the next meeting of the UN preparatory commission drafting the Program of Action, some Latin American delegations and the Greek one, representing the European Union, called for fresh debate on the text. The paragraphs on which there was disagreement were bracketed; before long the brackets had invaded the text and wrapped themselves like barbed wire around nearly one-third of it. At the Vatican there was rejoicing over the "stinging defeat" suffered by "Clinton and his feminist allies."

On April 28 the pope broke his thighbone, but that didn't stop him. In a mystical mood he told his aides, "Maybe this was needed for the Year of the Family"—meaning that his pain should be seen as a symbol of special sacrifice for the cause of family values. Encouraging this mystical atmosphere, Vatican Radio commented: "Once again the pope is a pilgrim in the world of suffering—of his own personal suffering—he who already bears on his shoulders the weight of the sorrows of humanity."

Now bedridden, in pain, and nearly immobile, John Paul II continued to lead the battle against the UN from the Gemelli Clinic. He pushed his co-workers to seek an alliance with Islam; and so Vatican diplomats began courting the most fundamentalist and extremist Islamic countries. The pope's foreign minister, Tauran, went to Libya and Iran. The risk that Islamic extremism might weaken secular and pro-Western Muslim states (generally more open to the Catholic Church) seemed irrelevant.

For the first time since Pius XII's struggle against Stalinism, the whole Church was being effectively mobilized all over the world to fight a political battle. All four thousand Catholic bishops were exhorted to lobby their governments and national political movements. Militantly pro-Wojtyła cardinals, such as John O'Connor of New York, were excited: "Let it be very clear to the world that the pope personally, and all of the pope's supporters, are all terribly distressed with the [UN] draft document." O'Connor was convinced that "the feeling is so strong that we might end up with something dramatic, if the Cairo conference goes through on the basis of the draft document, and the West goes along with it." With encouragement from Rome, he was thinking of a special trip to the UN by the pope to condemn the organization.

Bishops and cardinals who disagreed with this crusade took refuge in silence or merely gave it lip service. Many didn't share the impetuousness of the faithful cardinal of New York, the most important diocese in America, who proclaimed: "I see an alliance forming between the Catholic Church and the Muslim world against the West. It could really change an awful lot."

To the African bishops gathered for their synod in Rome, Monsignor Diarmuid Martin, a member of the Vatican delegation to the Cairo conference, sketched out the new strategy: "It is to be hoped that the pressure from the Islamic and African countries will be so strong that a positive solution can be found."

For the Vatican a "positive solution" meant that the Cairo conference should reject the proposal for safe and legal abortion. The diplomatic offensive on the Islamic front garnered some successes. On June 8 representatives of the Vatican Secretariat of State met discreetly in Rome with representatives of the Organization for the Islamic Conference, the Muslim World League, and the Muslim World Conference. The two sides, their joint communiqué declared, "are opposed to the individualistic orientation that characterizes the [UN] document. . . . Exacerbated and aggressive individualism ultimately leads to the destruction of society, bringing on a state of moral collapse, of libertinism, and the suppression of social values." In addition, the Vatican assumed the right to speak in the name of "believing Christians," even though the positions taken by the Reformed churches were a far cry from the fundamentalist Vatican strategy, and the Orthodox churches had never turned the question of abortion into a confrontation with civil authorities, as Karol Wojtyła had.

From Cairo came an official endorsement for the Catholic-Islamic holy alliance. The grand imam Haq Ali Gad el Haq, spiritual leader of Cairo's Al Azhar University, one of the most prestigious in the Muslim world, demanded that anything offensive to Islamic law and the "heavenly religions" (Judaism and Christianity) be struck from the UN program of action. Echoing the thesis advanced by the Vatican, the grand imam maintained that the UN document authorized abortion, homosexual relations, and free love. In consternation, the Egyptian minister for family affairs, Maner Mahran, was forced to issue a statement that his government would "not accept the adoption of any recommendation that violates the law of Islam."

At the height of the battle John Paul II appealed by letter to UN Secretary General Boutros Boutros-Ghali and to heads of state around the world, arguing that the Program of Action might bring on the moral decline of humanity. He personally phoned Bill Clinton and kept insistently making his case when the American president arrived for an audience at the Vatican on June 2. Cardinal López Trujillo then announced that the pope would go to the United Nations on October 20 to "raise a prophetic protest against the criminal assault being perpetrated against the family in the field of birth control." The ideas of the pope were elaborated in a pamphlet issued by Trujillo. It dealt, as John Paul II had ordered, with the "ethical dimension" of the population issue and made a frontal attack on the United Nations: "No international public institution has the right to bring pressure on the states to impose policies that are incompatible with respect for the person, for families, or for national independence."

Catholics all over the world were invited to be ready to bear witness, even if it meant martyrdom, to the value that every person has in the eyes of God. The Vatican's opponents in the struggle replied that the real martyrs were women abandoned to unsafe abortions and that the monsignors circulating such pamphlets weren't taking any risks.

As the September date for the opening of the conference grew near, the Vatican Secretariat of State, urged on by the pope, intensified its campaign. Fighting "demographic colonialism" was the watchword, aimed especially at the Third World. Apart from his Islamic allies, on every continent John Paul II could count on one or more nations that were sympathetic to his cause. In Europe there was Wałęsa's Poland; in Africa, Senegal, Benin, and the Ivory Coast; in Asia, the Philippines; practically all the countries in Central America; and in South America, Chile and Argentina. The president of Argentina, Carlos Menem, sent a letter to all the Latin American heads of state, proposing that they take a common position at the Cairo conference based on the "right to life."

Pope Wojtyła himself, released from the hospital, used his Sunday colloquies with the faithful from the window of his study to reaffirm that marriage was in danger, to condemn homosexual unions, and to evoke the threats facing all of humanity, especially from abortion. Sometimes he appeared to be in a towering fury such as the Italians had never seen before. If there was one issue that he took personally, it was women and reproduction. It seemed to Deskur that the pope's anguish had deep roots in his own life— and in that of Emilia, his mother, and also perhaps the story of Olga, the sister that Karol Wojtyła had never known.

. . .

On the eve of the Cairo conference the pope's spokesman, Joaquín Navarro-Valls, launched three public attacks on Vice President Al Gore, who was to head the American delegation. This was unprecedented—and counterproductive. In his press briefing Navarro-Valls also claimed that the conference was ignoring the real needs of development in the name of exaggerated individualism. The very presence of the pope's personal spokesman as a member of the Vatican delegation was itself a statement.

The Cairo Conference on Population and Development lasted from September 5 to 13, 1994. Sending in its shock troops—the representatives of nations with congenial views, among them Slovakia, Malta, Argentina, Ecuador, Chile, Peru, and Guatemala—the Vatican delegation repeatedly held up the working sessions by calling into question compromises that had already been thrashed out. It also stirred up hostility from nongovernmental women's organizations, because the Vatican refused to see that beneath the issue of reproductive rights and reproductive health lay a history of horror involving hundreds of millions of women forced to experience teenage pregnancy, clitoridectomy, abandonment, male domination, infectious diseases transmitted by their partners, and the deprivation of fundamental civil rights.

In the end, the alliance with Islamic fundamentalism broke down because Islamic religious law permitted abortion in the case of danger to the mother. Gradually even the opposition of Latin American countries that had been among the most confrontational slackened. As a result, for the first time the Vatican decided to approve "by consensus" (though with some reservations) a UN document on population issues.

Wojtyła's strategy, however, managed to get the conference to reaffirm that abortion was not an acceptable means of contraception. Language advocating access to legal and safe abortion everywhere in the world was excised. But it was a Pyrrhic victory. For the first time a UN document recognized the legitimacy of interrupting pregnancy and approved the principle that in those countries where abortion wasn't against the law (173 out of the 184 member nations), it should be made safe. But above all the Holy See found itself isolated in relation to the industrialized countries, whose delegations were highly irritated by the filibustering of the Vatican. It was a defeat for Wojtyła not just with regard to the women's movements in the West and in the Third World, but also with regard to a great many Catholic women, including those with no ties to feminist movements.

This moral isolation prompted some private rethinking of the issues. The next year, at the Beijing Conference on Women, the pope appointed American professor Mary Ann Glendon as the first woman ever to head a Vatican delegation. And when the debate on abortion came up again, the Vatican ultimately didn't oppose the adoption of a resolution asking all states to "review the laws that provide for punitive measures against women who have had an illegal abortion."

The Vatican had no intention of fighting the battle of Cairo all over again. Nor did John Paul II go to New York in October, officially for reasons of health. An appearance by the pope at the United Nations along the lines of his earlier ferocious attacks was judged to be inadvisable.

HERO

The faithful, about thirty strong, listened in dismay to the prayers for the repose of the soul of John Paul II. They had gathered at an altar in St. Peter's for the early morning mass when they learned the news. It was September 4, 1994. Word had reached the priest only minutes before the beginning of the service. The voice that made the announcement over the telephone sounded firm and official enough; moreover, there was no time to check. It was just past six-thirty A.M. *"Requiem aeternam dona eis, Domine . . ."* the priest began to recite in a loud voice.

But the pope wasn't dead—it was all a macabre joke. Similar calls kept coming in as John Paul II spent the last days of his vacation in his summer home at Castel Gandolfo. They came mostly at night, from persons who identified themselves as members of the Castel Gandolfo staff. Even a few cardinals were alerted: "Your Eminence, we wanted to inform you that . . ."

No one ever identified who was behind the calls. A maniac? A monsignor trying to frighten the cardinals on the eve of John Paul II's trip to Sarajevo? A prank?

The Vatican preferred to forget the whole embarrassing episode.

. . .

In the twilight of his pontificate, John Paul II is dogged by signs of his increasing frailty. On December 25, 1995, viewers around the world were shocked when on live TV from the Vatican an ashen Karol Wojtyła had to interrupt his Christmas sermon from the window of his study, shaken by a sudden fit of retching. Weeks later, he was tormented by an insistent, unexplained fever. But, as his old friend Maliński says, he continues to "look to the future with joy."

"The pope has a great faith in Providence," notes Cardinal Secretary of

State Angelo Sodano. "He doesn't care as long as the Lord gives him life. He has a great calmness that he doesn't lose even in the most difficult moments"—at least since Cairo. "He has the imperturbability as in the famous prayer of St. Teresa: 'Let nothing trouble you, let nothing scare you.' "

The pope still dreams of taking a great pilgrimage in the footsteps of Abraham. Retracing the path of Abraham means leaving Ur in Mesopotamia (modern-day Iraq) passing through Haran (Syria), Lebanon, Jordan, Israel, and Palestine, and going all the way to Egypt, the land of the Pharaohs. When John Paul II talks about this, his face becomes transfigured.

The footsteps of the patriarch frame the story of a dramatic conflict that has pitted Abraham's Jewish sons against his Arab sons, Islam against Christianity, East against West, fundamentalism against secular societies. The mystical pope continues to have a genuine ability to think in the language of politics. His campaign in support of Muslim Bosnia (and implicitly against the Christian Serbs), like his earlier opposition to the Gulf War, he sees clearly as an investment in the future.

John Paul II doesn't want the twenty-first century to proceed under the shadow of hatred between Muslims and Christians. He's aware of the dangers of Islamic fundamentalism and has denounced Muslim countries that promote "discrimination against Jews, Christians, and members of other religious families," who cannot so much as gather to pray in private. But at the same time he's persuaded that he has to take advantage of the message of tolerance that is part of Muhammad's legacy. He believes it would be a tragic error to make Islam the new international demon. That is why he sent Cardinal Achille Silvestrini, the prefect of the Congregation for the Eastern Churches, on a mission to Iraq, and why he supports ending the international embargo imposed on Baghdad.

The pope wants to see the Cross, the Crescent, and the Star of David reconciled. He feels that religion should never again serve as a pretext for war. He cautions believers against the verbal and physical violence of fundamentalism, of whatever stripe. On this score John Paul II has been quick to set an example. On July 1, 1995, during a trip to Slovakia, he stopped in the town of Prešov to bow his head and pray before a monument to twenty-four Protestant martyrs tortured and killed by Catholics during the endless inhuman battles over religion that became known as the Thirty Years' War (1618–1648).

The pope has another dream—a trip to Russia, to the far Solovetski Islands in the White Sea, where the Soviets built one of their most dreadful gulags—for Orthodox bishops, clergy, and religious dissidents. He would like to go there on a pilgrimage to honor the Christian martyrs of every denomination, thereby remembering all the victims of twentieth-century totalitarian systems that have tried to uproot Christ from human life. "Solovetski," he has told Father Werenfried van Straaten, "is for Russia what the Colosseum is for Rome."

The pope has one more vision—to cross the former bamboo curtain to permit the unification of Chinese Catholics with the Church of Rome and thus render the Chair of Peter more visibly universal. John Paul II's final struggle is to free Chinese Catholics from the chains of the Communist regime. "Millions of believers can't be constantly oppressed, placed under suspicion, and kept divided," he has said.

The harder the years press on Wojtyła, the more ambitious his schemes sometimes seem to become. He's anxious for the Church to be present "wherever things are happening," as he told Father Maliński. Even if his body is playing him false, he is not about to become one of those old men fixated on the past who want the world to end with them. Perhaps he *has* become more impatient and irritable. During overlong ceremonies he has been heard to mutter, *"Basta, basta."*

The final phase of Wojtyła's pontificate has been marked by pain and weakness. Suddenly his body has stopped obeying him. People in the Apostolic Palace see him walking down the corridors, bent over and looking old beyond his years. Reporters accompanying him on trips have seen his face swollen from the medication he has to take. "Sometimes I get scared. His face is so red," said Cardinal Silvio Oddi after leaving a papal audience. His eyelids are often half-closed, his step heavy, his movements uncertain. Often he speaks with difficulty; his voice sounds hoarse. There are times when the pope-actor, the unsurpassed master at stirring up crowds, can barely enunciate, when his intonation turns flat and dull.

Sometimes he loses the thread of a conversation. Journalists in the

Vatican press corps have observed that John Paul II, famous for his mastery of languages, occasionally has a hard time recalling the simplest Italian words.

Having to use a cane and discovering his own infirmity have been a tremendous blow to the mountaineering pope. After his election he compared himself to a fir transplanted from its homeland: sad at having to leave its native mountains, but still a mighty tree. Now behind every platform on which he celebrates mass there is a freight elevator to spare him the effort of climbing the stairs—a humiliating reminder of his helplessness. "His body isn't keeping up with his mind," says a prelate in the Vatican, "and that's his biggest problem."

With the passage of time the pope's own theology of suffering has undergone further development. Sister Zofia Zdybicka, who has known him since 1958, bears special witness to this: "He has always been a person of deep prayer," she says, "but now when I attend mass in his private chapel and I see him up close, I notice this difference: When he prays now, his face is full of pain."

Unless one understands this mystical connection between pain and mission there is no way to grasp the origin of John Paul II's desire—conscious or otherwise—to risk his life through excessive efforts or dangerous projects, like the planned trip to Sarajevo in the fall of 1994. The pope was ready to take the chance of being killed in the Bosnian capital, torn apart as it was by civil war. At the last minute, when the Catholics of Sarajevo were already waiting for him, the Vatican bureaucrats prevented him from leaving. He has never pardoned them for contributing to the impression of him as ineffectual and in irreversible decline.

In the face of his deteriorating health, John Paul II lives out his life more than ever in prayer. "No sooner does he pause than he starts praying," says a Curia veteran. His whole day marches to the beat of prayer. After getting up at five A.M. he prays for two hours in the chapel before celebrating mass. He prays before and after lunch, before and after dinner. He prays almost continuously in the course of the day. Even while riding in the popemobile he takes out his rosary, slowly fingering the beads till the last minute when he steps out of the car. *"Domine, non sum dignus"* (Lord, I am not worthy), he whispers when the applause around him gathers.

No one who has seen him is likely to forget the way he concentrates. He seems to be diving into the depths of his soul. "It's an amazing experience to see the pope on a prie-dieu, bending his head over his crozier," says Bishop Mariano Magrassi of Bari. "His brows are knit. During those moments of silence you can really see how his face is contracted in the effort to encounter God." In prayer the pope lets himself be swept away. "It's a quest to identify with God's will," says a monsignor who has often seen him in his private chapel.

· · ·

Though his hand is increasingly weary as he raises it to bless the faithful, it points to a wider horizon. The world has become aware that he is the last of the giants on the global stage—that there are no other great heralds of broad vision or principle, whatever their cause or ideology. He has defined his time as perhaps no other leader has, even while railing against the age itself. Meanwhile, John Paul II is left almost alone preaching the dignity of the worker and help for the unemployed, urging reconciliation and solidarity between the various strata of society, and exhorting the rich nations to care about countries stifled by poverty and foreign debt. Struggling against pain and fatigue, the pope continues to embark on long, exhausting trips to bring his message to the world, including a triumphant visit to the United States in 1995 that drew millions of Catholics and non-Catholics alike and an outpouring of adoring media coverage.

Suddenly on a world stage dominated by profound economic, national, and religious divisions, the pope stands out as the only international spokesman for universal values. He offers a gospel of salvation and hope in the face of the new idols—tribal egoism, exacerbated nationalism, fiercely sectarian and violent fundamentalism, profit with no concern for the quality of human life. "Something is owed to human beings, because they are human beings," he wrote in his social encyclical *Centesimus Annus* (The Hundredth Year, referring to the anniversary of Leo XIII's *Rerum Novarum*). His Catholic Church recognizes the role of profit but reminds everyone that justice demands the satisfying of certain fundamental needs.

To counter nationalistic extremism, which in recent years has led to bloody wars in the Balkans, in Africa, and in the former Soviet Union, he has delivered one of his most passionate speeches, condemning the worship of the nation. "This is not a question of legitimate love for one's homeland or respect for its identity," he told the diplomatic corps at the Holy See, "but of rejecting the *Other* in his diversity so as to impose oneself upon him. For this kind of chauvinism all means are fair: exalting race, overvaluing the state, imposing a uniform economic model, leveling [any] specific cultural differences."

John Paul II has committed the Holy See to an innovative concept of international law known as "humanitarian interference." The pope himself explained it with reference to Serbian aggression against Bosnia: "If I see my neighbor persecuted, I have to defend him. It's an act of charity. The international community has the same right and duty toward any nation that has been attacked—and as a last resort [to defend the innocent nation] by the force of arms."

Monsignors in the Curia report that in these last years John Paul II seems to be living beyond the world and viewing it from a transcendent perspective. *Evangelium Vitae*, his encyclical from the year 1995, can be read as Karol Wojtyła's last will and testament, a magnificent, desperate hymn to the sacredness of life. There are sentences full of poetic force addressed to all men and women, whether they live in skyscrapers or slums. "The primacy of persons over things . . . means passing from indifference to interest for the *Other*, and from rejection to welcome. The *Others* are not competitors to be warded off, but brothers and sisters to be united with. They are to be loved for themselves; they enrich us with their presence."

．　　．　　．

John Paul II's grandest project is to celebrate the new millennium with a jubilee to bring humanity closer to God and to launch a new evangelization of the world. The jubilee year is an ancient Israelite tradition adopted by the Catholic Church, which celebrates it every twenty-five years, instead of the original fifty, as a sign of spiritual renewal.

Some in the Vatican are convinced that the pope sees his own life span in terms of this goal—and that he perseveres from a deep conviction that he has been chosen to bring the Church into Christianity's third millennium. John Paul has conceived the vision of transforming the jubilee for the year 2000 into an occasion for purifying the Church of its sins. Millenarianism and messianism, rooted as ever in the piety of his native Poland, have been the sources of Wojtyła's faith since his youth. In his old age they are once again providing him with powerful inspiration for a project designed to shake the Catholic Church out of what he considers lethargy and lies.

The pope has urged all believers to ask forgiveness for the sins—and crimes—committed by Catholics in past centuries. When the proposal was made public in April 1994, in letters sent by the Vatican Secretariat of State to the 140 cardinals all over the world, many of the princes of the Church made no secret of their opposition to it.

The revolutionary invitation to a solemn *mea culpa* was contained in a seven-page memorandum: "How can we keep silent about all the forms of violence that have been perpetrated in the name of faith? About the wars of religion, the inquisitorial tribunals, and other ways of violating the rights of the individual? It is significant that these coercive methods, which violate human rights, have subsequently been applied by the totalitarian ideologies of the twentieth century. . . . The Church too must make an independent review of the darker sides of its history."

This notion of a global examination of conscience by the Catholic Church, a critical review of its entire history, is unprecedented. John Paul II is convinced that this massive act of spiritual renewal would give a strong impulse to the reconquest of souls in the contemporary world.

In floating the plan, John Paul II has had a hard time overcoming resistance within his own Church. When the College of Cardinals gathered in the Vatican on June 13, 1994, it gave the pope's proposal a chilly reception. Cardinals from the former Communist countries were especially hostile to the idea of any public act of repentance.

To acknowledge that a mistake had been made in the condemnation of Galileo, as the pope did some years before, may have been all well and good. But for the Church to beat its breast for two thousand years of history was just too much. Secretary of State Sodano, who had already taken the opportunity to sound out many of the cardinals, preferred not to mention the proposal in his introductory report to the gathering. The pope's press spokesman diplomatically noted the opposition in the College of Cardinals: "Some cardinals have already replied that a historical examination would be too complex, that it might be better to concentrate on analyzing our own time."

In the following months the pope began writing a document specifically devoted to his scheme for a grand act of repentance; then on November 14 he published the apostolic letter *Tertio Millenio Adveniente* (As the Third Millennium Approaches). "One painful chapter," he wrote, "to which the sons of the Church cannot fail to return with a mind open to repentance is the way [Catholics], especially in certain centuries, have acquiesced in methods of intolerance and even of violence in the service of the truth.

"Consideration of the attentuating historical circumstances," the pope went on, "doesn't free the Church from the duty to grieve profoundly for the weaknesses of so many of her sons who have disfigured her face." The time has come to repent, the pope proclaimed; every Christian should adhere to the wise words of the Second Vatican Council: "Truth cannot be imposed except by the force of the truth itself." Under orders issued by the pope in 1996, plans for the jubilee will focus on repentance for the Inquisition and the sins of anti-Semitism.

· · ·

Just before dying, Pope John XXIII whispered in Latin to his secretary Loris Capovilla, *"Ut Unum Sint"* (That they may be one—John 17:11). The last thoughts of the pope who had convoked Vatican II went out to the unity of Christians.

Echoing the words of his predecessor, Pope Wojtyła has dedicated an encyclical—perhaps his last—to this theme: The great jubilee for the year 2000 has to see the Christian communities draw closer together; the blood of Christian martyrs killed in the twentieth century should bind all the Christian churches in a special way and give a fresh impetus to the common witness to the faith, just as the martyrs in the Colosseum, Stanisław of Kraków, and Thomas à Becket assured the spread of Christianity in antiquity and in the Middle Ages.

Unity and conversion (the latter word recurs a full forty times in the encyclical) are the leading concepts of John Paul II as one epoch gives way to another. He is convinced that the Christian religion and religious feelings in general still have a great role to play in the future of the human race. The mind of the old pope intuitively grasps the weaknesses of our time: a lack of ethical sense, a spreading systemic relativism, which corrodes even secular values, a sense of fragmentation, an inability to lay the foundations for a meaningful life. He realizes that after decades of optimism contemporary men and women are once again asking questions about the reality of evil.

Many of John Paul II's actions and programs in recent years are meant as a legacy for his successors. He is ready to confess the guilt of the Catholic Church for burning at the stake men such as the great Bohemian religious leader Jan Hus (d. 1415), a forerunner of the Protestant Reformation, or the Florentine friar Girolamo Savonarola (d. 1498), who attacked the luxurious and anti-Christian lifestyle of the Renaissance pope Leo X.

After the harsh confrontation at the UN conference in Cairo, the pope silently examined his own conscience. Since then he has learned to appreciate better the historical importance of the women's liberation movement (a term he himself has been using of late). John Paul II was the first pope to address a letter to women all over the world, taking the blame for "not a few sons of the Church" who have hindered the emancipation of women. At last the pope seems to be acknowledging that women "have been misunderstood in their dignity, misrepresented in their prerogatives, marginalized and even reduced to slavery."

The constant pressure of women, especially from the Church's great women's religious orders, has forced the pope to admit that male-dominated Catholicism must address the question of power sharing. In March 1996 John Paul II issued a document stating that it is "urgent" that women be granted access to all levels in the Church where "decisions are worked out." Women, the pope said, help men revise their basic mental schemes.

But the most striking démarche of John Paul II was directed to the other Christian churches. Wojtyła has said he is ready to take a new look at the role of the Roman pontiff. He may even be opening the door slightly to the prospect of overcoming the absolutist structures of the Catholic Church in the next millennium. He has invited the other churches to join him in redefining the limits and modes of exercising papal authority. He has confessed: "Reforming the papacy, redefining its limits is an enormous task . . . which I cannot bear till the end all by myself."

Thus Karol Wojtyła, the bishop who went to school at Vatican II, could be the last pope in the absolutist spirit of Vatican I, the last sovereign of a Catholic spiritual monarchy that has endured for centuries. His reign, as Bishop Weakland observes, has been "highly centralized, with the pope as a great charismatic leader." It's likely to be the last of its kind.

· · ·

Every pope, wherever he comes from, ends up by becoming a Roman. Down through the centuries the Romans have praised and mocked, loved and hated their popes. They have borne them in triumph and thrown their corpses into the Tiber.

The Eternal City has seen the Polish pope ruling in St. Peter's, mixing affably with children in parishes around the city, staggering in the Colosseum under the weight of the wooden cross he carries in the Good Friday procession.

But there is one image of John Paul II that the Romans will not soon forget. On June 6, 1996, at nightfall, the Corpus Christi procession was winding down the ancient Via Merulana. The pope had decided to lead it despite his wretched condition.

Beneath the trees flanking the boulevard, thousands of Romans were marching: the confraternities with their banners, many middle-aged men and women, and quite a few young people. Most of them were carrying lighted candles. Amid this river of light a flatbed truck drove slowly along; on its back an armchair and a prie-dieu had been set up. And there was the old pope, on his knees, wearing his vestments, holding his head in his hands as he prayed—a gesture of weariness, abandonment, and trust.

In the shadows of the evening Karol Wojtyła sailed on in the mystic procession, like Osiris on his boat heading into the sunset.

SOURCES

The primary sources for the book are the authors' interviews with more than three hundred individuals, the vast majority conducted between 1993 and 1996.

In Part V, with the exception of Jeanne Kirkpatrick, Robert M. Gates, John McMahon, Vernon Walters, and Herbert Meyer, who were interviewed in 1994–96, all members of the Reagan administration and CIA officials cited—including the president—were interviewed in 1991. Cardinals Agostino Casaroli, John Krol, Pio Laghi, and Achille Silvestrini were interviewed in 1991, and Laghi and Silvestrini again in 1994–96.

Prologue

1–13   John Paul II's trip to Poland: Marco Politi, personal notes and reporting, *Il Messaggero*, June 2–11, 1979. *L'Osservatore Romano; L'Attività della Santa Sede.*

2   "I'm going back": John Paul II, quoted by Giulio Andreotti, interview with authors.

2   John Paul II to journalists: Marco Politi, personal notes.

4   Comments of future Solidarity leaders and activists: Zbigniew Bujak and Wiktor Kulerski, interviews with authors.

8   Reagan at watching trip on television: Richard Allen, interview with authors.

8–10   Communist leaders' reactions to papal visit: Wojciech Jaruzelski, Stanisław Kania, and Kazimierz Barcikowski, interviews with authors; Edward Rolicki, *Edward Gierek*; Kania, *Zatrzymac konfrontacje*; Jaruzelski, *Stan wojenny dlaczego*; Jerzy Ambroziewicz, *Znam was wszystkich.*

9   Situation in Lithuania: *Il Messaggero*, June 4, 1979.

9   Gromyko on Wojtyła's influence on Poland: Marco Politi, personal notes.

11–12   Casey's meeting with John Paul II: Robert Gates, Herbert Meyer, and Vernon Walters; Sophia Casey, interviews with authors; confidential CIA sources; confirmation of unspecified meetings by Joaquín Navarro-Valls and Pio Laghi in interviews with authors.

11   Satellite photograph: Herbert Meyer, interview with authors; confidential sources.

11–12   Religious aspects of Casey's discussions with John Paul II: Sophia Casey, interview with authors; some details confirmed by Joaquín Navarro-Valls; Gates.

12–13   Gorbachev and danger to socialism: Politburo minutes.

13   "One can say that everything that has happened": Mikhail Gorbachev, column in

SOURCES

La Stampa, in response to *Time* magazine cover story "Holy Alliance" by Carl Bernstein, February 24, 1992.

12   "breaking Poland out of the Soviet orbit": Ronald Reagan, interview with authors, 1991; William Clark and Richard Allen, interviews with authors.

Part I: Lolek

17   Account of Karol Wojtyła's birth: Andrzej Deskur, interview with authors.

17ff   Account of ancestry, birth, and childhood of Karol Wojtyła: Adam Boniecki, *Kalendarium*; George Blazynski, *John Paul II*; Maliński, *Pope John Paul II, Le radici, Il mio vecchio*; Offredo, *Jean Paul II*; Vircondelet, *Jean Paul II*; Lecomte, *La Verité*; Svidercoschi, *Lettera*; Szczypka, *Jan Pawel II*.

17   Triumph of Piłsudski: Szczypka, *Jan Pawel II*.

18   Austrian reports on Karol Wojtyła Sr.: Boniecki, *Kalendarium*.

19   Wojtyła on his mother: Andrzej Deskur, interview with authors.

19   Emilia's plans for her son: Szczypka, *Jan Pawel II*.

20–21   On Emilia's life: Bergonzoni, *Emilia Kaczorowska*.

21   Wojtyła's grades at school: Boniecki, *Kalendarium*.

21   Zofia Bernhardt: Szczypka, *Jan Pawel II*.

21   "the soul of home": Maliński, interview with authors.

22   Wojtyła to Carmelite priest: Władysław Kluz, interview with authors.

22–23   Beatification of Molla and Mora: *Washington Post*.

22   Wojtyła's envious comments on family life: Andrzej Deskur, interview with authors.

22   Emilia as "burned": Joaquín Navarro-Valls, interview with authors.

22   "total fidelity": *Mulieris Dignitatem* (On the Dignity of Women), papal encyclical.

23–24   Kalwaria ceremony: Władysław Kluz, interview with authors; authors' research in situ.

24–25   "On your white tomb": Written in Kraków, 1939; Wojtyła, *Opere Letterarie*.

25   Wojtyła after his mother's death: Juliusz Kydryński, *Quando Karol aveva diciott'anni*; Jan Kuś, Jerzy Kluger, and Halina Królikiewicz Kwiatkowska, interviews with authors.

25   "shadow of an early sorrow": Quoted in Boniecki, *Kalendarium*.

27   Episode with Helena Szczepańska: Szczypka, *Jan Pawel II*.

27   "My brother's death": Frossard, *Be Not Afraid*.

27   "With your weak, fading glances": Ibid.

28   Stethoscope: Andrzej Deskur, interview with authors.

28–30   Wojtyła's upbringing: Jan Kuś, Jerzy Kluger, Halina Królikiewicz Kwiatkowska, interviews with authors; Boniecki, *Kalendarium*; Blazynski, *John Paul II*; Maliński, *Pope John Paul II*.

28–30   On Wojtyła Sr.: Jerzy Kluger, interview with authors; Boniecki, *Kalendarium*; Blazynski, *John Paul II*.

28   Wojtyła and his father playing soccer: Kydryński, *Quando Karol aveva diciott'anni*.

29   Bohdanowicz recollections: Ibid.

29–30   Wadowice: Boniecki, *Kalendarium*; Szczypka, *Jan Pawel II.*

30–32   Jewish life in Wadowice: Jerzy Kluger and Regina Beer Reisenfeld, interviews with authors.

31–32   Wojtyła's friendship with Kluger: Jerzy Kluger, interview with authors; Svidercoschi, *Lettera*; Szczypka, *Jan Pawel II.*

32   "There will be a Jewish problem": Szulc, *Pope John Paul II.*

33   "his great composure": Blazynski, *John Paul II.*

34   Family roots: Boniecki, *Kalendarium.*

34   Description of Wojtyła Sr.: Jerzy Kluger, interview with authors.

35   Karol singing: Blazynski, *John Paul II.*

35   "His life took a new turn": Bohdanowicz, quoted in Kydryński, *Quando Karol aveva diciott'anni.*

35   Description of Wojtyła: Kazimierz Figlewicz, in Boniecki, *Kalendarium.*

35–36   Profile of Mickiewicz: Czesław Miłosz, *History of Polish Literature.*

36   Description of Beer: Jerzy Kluger, interview with authors.

36–37   Relationship of boys and girls in Wadowice: Jan Kuś, Jerzy Kluger, Halina Królikiewicz Kwiatkowska, interviews with authors; Kydryński, *Quando Karol aveva diciott'anni.*

37   "There were so many threads": Bober, quoted in Kydryński, *Quando Karol aveva diciott'anni.*

37   Wojtyła performing *Balladyna*: Szczypka, *Jan Pawel II.*

38   Wojtyła reciting *Promethidion*: Kydryński, *Quando Karol aveva diciott'anni.*

35–45   Wojtyła's social and theatrical activity: Regina Beer Reisenfeld, Halina Królikiewicz Kwiatkowska, Jerzy Kluger, and Jan Kuś, interviews with authors.

40–41   Description of Kotlarczyk: Largely drawn from Williams, *Mind of John Paul II.*

40–41   Wojtyła and Sapieha: Szczypka, *Jan Pawel II.*

42–45   Wojtyła and religious life: Jan Kuś and Władysław Kluz, interviews with authors; Frossard, *Be Not Afraid.*

42   "We begin with the impression": Quoted in Messori, *Varcare la soglia.*

43   Prus recollections: Władysław Kluz, interview with authors.

44   Beer recollections: Regina Beer Reisenfeld, interview with authors; Beer interview with North American Newspaper Alliance (NANA), 1979, cited by Szulc, *Pope John Paul II.*

44   Beer's meeting John Paul II: Jerzy Kluger and Regina Beer Reisenfeld, interviews with authors; Beer interview with North American Newspaper Alliance (NANA).

44–45   Wojtyła and chastity: Władysław Kluz, interview with authors.

46–63   Wojtyła's first university year in Kraków: Krystyna Zbijewska and Jan Kuś, interviews with authors; Boniecki, *Kalendarium.*

46   Wojtyła's radicalism: Krystyna Zbijewska, interview with authors.

46–48   Outbreak of World War II: Mieczysław Maliński and Jan Kuś, interviews with authors; Boniecki, *Kalendarium*; Maliński, *Pope John Paul II*; Svidercoschi, *Lettera.*

47   "We have to celebrate mass": Figlewicz, quoted in Szczypka, *Jan Pawel II.*

49   Deportation of Jagiellonian University professors: Ibid.

50–53   Tyranowski and the Living Rosary: Mieczysław Maliński and Franciszek Konieczny, interviews with authors; Boniecki, *Kalendarium*; Clissold, *Wisdom of the Spanish Mystics*; Maliński, *Pope John Paul II*. In 1949 Wojtyła wrote a remembrance of Tyranowski after his death ("To the Memory of John") that is included in Boniecki, *Kalendarium*.

53   "To drown, to drown!": Wojtyła, *Opere letterarie*.

53–57   Wojtyła's work at Solvay: Wojciech Żukrowski, Franciszek Konieczny, Józef Krasuski, and Franciszek Koscielniak, interviews with authors.

56–57   Episode with Dąbrowska: Józef Krasuski, interview with authors.

57–58   Kydryński's recollections of Wojtyła's father's death: Kydryński, *Quando Karol aveva diciott'anni*.

57   Wojtyła on his father's death: Szczypka, *Jan Pawel II*.

57   "I know I am small": Wojtyła, *Opere Letterarie*.

58   "These days I often think": Boniecki, *Kalendarium*.

58   "At twenty I had already lost": Frossard, *Be Not Afraid*.

58   Episode of Woltersdorf: Wojciech Żukrowski: W. Żukrowski, interview with authors.

59   Wojtyła and armed resistance: Ibid.

59–63   Wojtyła's life during World War II: Halina Królikiewicz Kwiatkowska, Danuta Michalowska, Wojciech Żukrowski, and Mieczysław Maliński, interviews with authors; Boniecki, *Kalendarium*; Maliński, *Pope John Paul II*.

60   John Paul II on saving Jews during war: Marek Halter, interview with authors.

60   Wojtyła on communism: Wojciech Żukrowski, interview with authors.

61   "Those Wednesdays and Saturdays": Blazynski, *Pope John Paul II*.

62   "It sounds like a paradox": Halina Królikiewicz Kwiatkowska, interview with authors.

62   "performance full of tension," "a great actor was born": Danuta Michalowska and Juliusz Osterwa, quoted in Boniecki, *Kalendarium*.

62–63   Wojtyła's vocation: Szczypka, *Jan Pawel II*.

63   Parable in Matthew 25, Norwid's paraphrase: Kydryński, *Quando Karol aveva diciott'anni*.

64   Pokuta recollections: Boniecki, *Kalendarium*.

65   Cieluch recollections: Ibid.

65   Wojtyła's theological studies: Mieczysław Maliński, interview with authors.

65–66   Wojtyła in hospital: Franciszek Konieczny, interview with authors.

66   Black Sunday: Szczypka, *Jan Pawel II*.

66   "The Germans were sure": Mieczysław Maliński, interview with authors.

66–68   Wojtyła and underground seminary: Mieczysław Maliński, Franciszek Konieczny, and K. Suder, interviews with authors.

68–69   Red Army officers in seminary: Franciszek Konieczny, interview with authors.

69   "The soldier knocked": From Lenten retreat given by Wojtyła, March 1976, the Vatican, quoted in Boniecki, *Kalendarium*.

70   Wojtyła's marks at university: Ibid.

70   Wojtyła on Poland's future: Mieczysław Maliński, interview with authors.

70   "With the war over": Władysław Kluz, interview with authors.

Part II: Father Karol

75   Catholic Church in Eastern Europe: Daim, *Il Vaticano*.

76   Wojtyła in Niegowić: Stanisław Wyporek and Maria Trzaska, interviews with authors; Boniecki, *Kalendarium*.

77   Wojtyła and bike riding: Stanisław Wyporek, interview with authors.

77–78   Wojtyła on communism: Stanisław Wyporek, interview with authors.

78–79   Wojtyła hearing confession: Karol Tarnowski, interview with authors.

79   "When we talk about confession": Szulc, *Pope John Paul II*.

79–80   Wojtyła's outings with youth: Mieczysław Malecki, Teresa Miesowicz, and Karol Tarnowski, interviews with authors.

80–81   Wojtyła and relations between men and women: Karol Tarnowski, Maria Bożek, and Teresa Miesowicz, interviews with authors.

81   "The surface of love": Wojtyła, *The Jeweler's Shop*.

81–83   Wojtyła on sexual relations: Wojtyła, *Love and Responsibility*.

82   Zdybicka recollections: Zofia Zdybicka, interview with authors.

83   Wojtyła on contraception: Karol Tarnowski, interview with authors.

83–84   Comments on KUL: Zofia Zdybicka, interview with authors.

83–84   Wojtyła in Lublin: Ibid.

84–85   Wojtyła on Catholic university and communism: Stefan Świeżawski, interview with authors.

86   Wojtyła on Mindszenty: Andrzej Deskur and Stefan Świeżawski, interviews with authors.

86–87   Wojtyła's meeting with Wyszyński: Władysław Kluz, interview with authors.

88   Wojtyła praying in Ursuline convent: Former Mother Superior Andrea Górska, interview with authors.

89–91   Preparation for Vatican II: Guasco et al., *La Chiesa del Vaticano II*; Poupard, *Il Concilio Vaticano II*.

90   Wojtyła and questionnaire: Hebblethwaite, *Synod Extraordinary*.

90–101 Wojtyła at Vatican II: Stefan Świeżawski and Jerzy Turowicz, interviews with authors; Maliński, *Pope John Paul II*.

91   Opening session of Council: Reporting in *Corriere della Sera* and *Il Tempo*, October 11, 1962.

92   "We shall be poor and naked": Wojtyła, *Opere letterarie*.

93   Wojtyła on criticism of Church: Karol Tarnowski, interview with authors.

96   "The Second Vatican Council": Frossard, *Be Not Afraid*.

96–99   Wojtyła's speeches at Council: Caprile, *Il Concilio Vaticano II*.

98   Wojtyła's habit of marking pages: Williams, *Mind of John Paul II*.

98   Wojtyła's contacts with bishops from other countries: Andrzej Deskur, interview with authors; Maliński, *Pope John Paul II*.

99   Data on Wojtyła's statements at Council: Boniecki, *Kalendarium;* Szczypka, *Jan Pawel II.*

99–100   Relationship between Wyszyński and Wojtyła: Kazimierz Kąkol and Jerzy Turowicz, interviews with authors.

100   Wyszyński and Wojtyła's appointment: Andrzej Bardecki, interview with authors.

100   Communist comments on Wojtyła's appointment: Andrzej Bardecki, interview with authors.

101   Wojtyła's inauguration mass: Szczypka, *Jan Pawel II.*

102   Wojtyła on the "concession and claim" of *Dignitatis Humanae:* The observation is from Hebblethwaite, *Extraordinary Synod.*

103   "We tried to avoid a dialogue": Stefan Świeżawski, interview with authors.

104   "The joys and hopes": Council documents.

106–7   Relation between Paul VI and Wojtyła: Andrzej Deskur and Tadeusz Pieronek, interviews with authors.

106–7   Wyszyński's encounter with Paul VI: Hebblethwaite, *Extraordinary Synod.*

107   "there is no appeal": Halina Bortnowska, quoted in Hebblethwaite, *Extraordinary Synod,* p. 22.

108   "You don't restructure": Andrzej Bardecki, interview with authors.

108   Black Madonna of Częstochowa: Marian Banaszak, *Historia kosciola katolickiego.*

109   Meeting between Zenon Kliszko and Wojtyła: Szczypka, *Jan Pawel II.*

109   Wojtyła's meeting with Communist leaders in Kraków: Ibid.

110–11   Polish secret police report: Cited in Szulc, *Pope John Paul II.*

111   Wojtyła's loyalty to Wyszyński: Andrzej Bardecki, interview with authors.

111   Wojtyła's refusal to travel without Wyszyński: Tadeusz Pieronek, interview with authors.

111   On popes choosing their successors: Andrzej Deskur, interview with authors.

112   "I know that I must prove myself": Boniecki, *Kalendarium.*

112–13   Paul VI's commission on birth control: Kaiser, *Politics of Sex and Religion.*

113   Wojtyła's influence on *Humanae Vitae:* Andrzej Bardecki, interviews with authors.

114–21   Wojtyła's Lenten retreat at Vatican: Wojtyła, *Segno di contraddizione.*

115   Wojtyła on his family: F. Bednarski and Andrzej Deskur, interviews with authors.

116   Wojtyła's manner with women: Krystyna Zbijewska, Zofia Zdybicka, Maria Bożek, and Maria Stadnicka, interviews with authors.

117   Kraków priest on *The Acting Person:* Tadeusz Pieronek, interview with authors.

119   "He's not a leftist": Jerzy Turowicz, interview with authors.

119   "Many a time": Quoted in Boniecki, *Kalendarium.*

120   Deskur's impressions of Lenten retreat: Andrzej Deskur, interview with authors.

121   "It is through the will": Wojtyła, *The Acting Person.*

121   Wyszyński's plans for Wojtyła: Romuald Kukołowicz, interview with authors.

121   "He quite obviously": Jacek Woźniakowski, interview with authors.

122   Events in Poland in 1968: Davies, *God's Playground.*

123   "When people are injured": Quoted in Boniecki, *Kalendarium.*

124   Wojtyła and politics: Jerzy Turowicz, interview with authors.

125   Wojtyła's daily schedule: Józef Mucha, interview with authors.

126   Wojtyła and Polish press: Andrzej Bardecki, interview with authors.

127   "St. Stanisław has become": Pastoral letter, May 8, 1977.

128   "Human rights cannot be given": Boniecki, *Kalendarium.*

129–47 Tymieniecka collaboration with Wojtyła: Anna-Teresa Tymieniecka, George Williams, Hendrik Houthakker, and Rocco Buttiglione, interviews with authors; acquisitions list, Widener Library, Harvard University; Wojtyła, *Acting Person;* records of International Phenomenological Society.

131   Navarro-Valls on the papal commission being "overprotective": Joaquín Navarro-Valls, interview with authors.

Part III: Conclave

151   Discovery of John Paul I: John Magee, interview with *Trenta Giorni,* September 1988. Other details, Cornwell, *A Thief in the Night.*

151–52 On John Paul I's last moments: Paolo Patruno, *La Stampa,* June 10, 1984.

152   John Paul I's family on his death: *La Stampa,* January 4, 1991.

152   John Paul I's psychological condition: Don Mario Senigaglia (John Paul I's secretary), interview with *Gente Veneta,* reported in *La Repubblica,* June 26, 1984.

152   "I've made all the arrangements": John Magee, interview with *Trenta Giorni,* September 1988.

152   John Paul I on his successor: Ibid.

152–53 Wojtyła's reaction in Kraków: Mieczysław Maliński, Józef Mucha, interviews with authors.

153   Votes for Wojtyła at August 1978 conclave: Kazimierz Kąkol, interview with authors.

154   Wojtyła's comments on election of John Paul I: Andrea Górska, interview with authors.

154   Wojtyła's comments leaving for Rome: Ibid.

154–69 Wojtyła and conclave campaign: Andrzej Deskur, interview with authors; Maliński, *Pope John Paul II.*

156–57 Maliński on future pope: Mieczysław Maliński, interview with authors.

157   Clarizio on Wojtyła: Ryszand Karpiński, interview with authors.

158   Meeting of Thiandoum and Luciani: Hyacinthe Thiandoum, interview with authors.

158   Statement of Nasalli Rocca: Andrzej Deskur, interview with authors.

159   Siri's comment about John Paul I: Zizola, *Il conclave.*

159   Meeting in French Seminary: Ibid.

160   Ratzinger on leftist danger: Joseph Ratzinger, interview with *Frankfurter Allgemeine Zeitung,* October 8, 1978.

161–62 König's campaign: Franz König, interview with authors.

162   Henríquez comment: Virgilio Levi, interview with authors.

162–63 Lorscheiter on future pope: Aloísio Lorscheiter, interview with Marco Politi, *Il Messaggero.*

163–64   Wojtyła at dinner with Cody: Virgilio Levi, interview with authors.

164   König's conversation with Wyszyński: Franz König, interview with authors.

165   Deskur's meeting with Wyszyński: Andrzej Deskur, interview with authors.

165   Villot's prophecy: Ibid.

166   Siri's statements: Licheri, *Quel conclave.*

166   Kąkol's dream: Kazimierz Kąkol, interview with authors.

167   Wojtyła's luggage: Maryśka Morda and Franciszek Konieczny, interviews with authors.

167   Journal on Marxism: Confidential sources.

167–68   Wojtyła in conclave: Donald Wuerl, interview with authors.

168   Ballots in conclave: Giulio Andreotti, interview with authors; Zizola, *Il conclave.*

168–69   Atmosphere in conclave: Franz König and Donald Wuerl, interviews with authors.

169   Wojtyła in arms of Wyszyński: Confidential sources.

169   "If they elect you": Cited by John Paul II during a meeting in the Vatican with Polish faithful, October 16, 1988, in *L'Attività della Santa Sede.*

170   "With obedience": *Redemptor Hominis* (The Redeemer of Man), papal encyclical, March 1979.

170   History of the crying room: MacDowell, *Inside the Vatican.*

171   Dziwisz's tears: Confidential sources.

    Other written sources about conclave: Reporting of Marco Politi, *Il Messaggero;* Maliński, *Pope John Paul II;* Blazynski, *John Paul II;* Frossard, *Be Not Afraid;* Murphy, *Papacy Today;* Hebblethwaite, *Year of Three Popes;* Andreotti, *A ogni morte di papa;* Lai, *Il papa non eletto;* Zizola, *Il conclave.*

Part IV: Il Papa

179   John Paul II in conclave: Franz König, interview with authors.

180   Inauguration mass: Marco Politi, *Il Messaggero,* October 23, 1978.

183   Canadian bishops: November 17, 1978.

183   John Paul II to woman journalist: October 21, 1978, Marco Politi, personal notes.

183   John Paul II to youth: Audience with Azione Cattolica, December 30, 1978.

183   Audience with journalists: Marco Politi, personal notes.

184   Trip to Assisi: Marco Politi, *Il Messaggero,* November 6, 1978.

185–86   Letter to bishops of Hungary: *L'Attività della Santa Sede,* 1979.

186   Wojtyła's passport: Ambroziewicz, *Znam was Wszystkich.*

186–87   Speech to Polish pilgrims: *L'Attività della Santa Sede,* 1978.

188   John Paul II and communism: Confidential sources.

188–89   John Paul II and foreign policy: Achille Silvestrini, interview with authors.

188–89   Vatican and socialist countries: Kazimierz Kąkol, interview with authors.

189–90   Bogomolov report: Institute for the Socialist System, *Bogomolov Report.*

191   Brezhnev and Gierek: Rolicki, *Edward Gierek.*

191–93   John Paul II and Villot: Wenger, *Le Cardinal Jean Villot.*

194–96   John Paul II's meeting with Gromyko: Gromiko, *Pamjatnoe.*

196   Benedetti's dream: Marco Politi, personal notes.

197   Vatican mediation between Chile and Argentina: *L'Attività della Santa Sede,* January 1979.

198–99   John Paul II and Latin America: Mieczysław Maliński, interview with authors.

198–215   John Paul II, liberation theology, and Puebla conference: Libanio Christo, *Diario di Puebla.*

200–2   John Paul II to journalists: Marco Politi, personal notes.

202   Flight attendant: Marco Politi, personal notes.

202–7   Mexico trip: Marco Politi, *Il Messaggero,* January 25–February 2, 1979.

208–9   CELAM pressure groups: Libanio Christo, *Diario di Puebla.*

209–13   Puebla conference and Lorscheiter's speech: *Puebla documenti.*

211–12   John Paul II and Indians at Cuilapán: Marco Politi, personal notes.

214   Synods on Dutch Church and Ukrainian Church: *L'Attività della Santa Sede,* 1980.

214–15   *Redemptor Hominis:* Tadeus Styczeń, *Le encicliche.*

217   Czech reactions: *Tribuna,* May 30, 1979.

217   Polish authorities and anniversary of St. Stanisław: Marco Politi, personal notes.

220–21   Communists' reactions to papal speeches: Stanisław Kania, Wojciech Jaruzelski, and Kazimierz Barcikowski, interviews with authors; Rolicki, *Edward Gierek.*

221   Kania's message to John Paul II: Stanisław Kania and Kazimierz Barcikowski, interviews with authors.

224   Dissidents' reaction to papal trip: *Głos* (Polish Catholic underground monthly), reported by J. Vinocur, *New York Times,* June 6, 1979.

226–28   John Paul II in Auschwitz: Marco Politi, personal notes and reporting in *Il Messaggero.*

228–30   John Paul II's sermon: *L'Osservatore Romano.*

231–33   John Paul II in Kraków: Marco Politi, personal notes and reporting in *Il Messaggero;* Wojciech Jaruzelski, Kazimierz Barcikowski, Bronisław Geremek, and Wiktor Kulerski, interviews with authors.

Other written sources on Polish trip: S. Viola, L. Accattoli, reporting in *La Repubblica; New York Times.* On Part IV in general: Del Rio and Accattoli, *Il nuovo Mosè;* Del Rio, *Un pontificato itinerante.*

Part V: Shaking the Empire

237   On Polish uprisings: Ash, *Polish Revolution, Magic Lantern, Uses of Adversity;* Ascherson, *Struggles for Poland;* Davies, *God's Playground;* reporting in *New York Times* and *Washington Post.*

240   John Paul II at Castel Gandolfo: Zofia Zdybicka, interview with authors.

243   John Paul II's public remarks: *L'Osservatore Romano* and other public sources.

244   Carter's letter to John Paul II: Zbigniew Brzeziński, interview with authors.

245   Wyszyński's actions about strike: Ash, *Polish Revolution, Magic Lantern, Uses of Adversity;* Szajkowski, *Next to God.*

SOURCES

245	"Oh this old man": Quoted in Szulc, *Pope John Paul II*, p. 347.
246	John Paul II's remarks to Brazilian workers: Marco Politi, *Il Messaggero*.
246–47	Casaroli's meeting with Soviet diplomat: Robert Gates, interview with authors; Gates, *From the Shadows*.
247–48	Politburo meeting, October 29, 1980: Politburo documents, obtained by authors in Moscow.
250	Warsaw Pact meeting, December 5, 1980: Stanisław Kania, Wojciech Jaruzelski, and Egon Krenz, interview with authors.
250–52	Politburo meeting, December 11, 1980: Politburo documents, obtained by authors in Moscow.
252–53	Ceremonies in Gdańsk: Ash, *Polish Revolution, Magic Lantern, Uses of Adversity*; Szajkowski, *Next to God*.
253–54	Central Committee document, January 31, 1981: Politburo records, January 12, 1981.
254–56	Wałęsa's visit to Rome: Wałęsa, *Way of Hope*; *L'Osservatore Romano*; Lech Wałęsa, interview with authors; Lech Wałęsa, interview with Oriana Fallaci.
255–56	Zimianian trip to Poland: Politburo minutes, January 22, 1981.
256–57	Politburo's treatment of Polish situation: various Politburo minutes, December 1980–March 1981.
257	Brzeziński's relations with Wojtyła, account of events of December 1980: Zbigniew Brzeziński, interview with authors.
257–71	Reagan's view of Vatican and Catholicism: Ronald Reagan, William Clark, Richard Allen, Jeanne Kirkpatrick, Alexander Haig, Vernon Walters, Robert McFarlane, John Poindexter, Richard Pipes, interviews with authors.
257–71	Reagan's view of Solidarity: William Clark, Richard Allen, Richard Pipes, Richard Perle, Robert Gates, John Poindexter, Robert MacFarlane, Caspar Weinberger, Jeanne Kirkpatrick, and Martin Anderson, interviews with authors.
258	Covert support for Solidarity: Zbigniew Brzeziński, Robert Gates, William Clark, interviews with authors.
259	Zagladin's mission to Rome: Gates, *From the Shadows*.
260–61	President's daily brief: Richard Allen and William Clark, interview with authors.
262	"It was there that we decided": Caspar Weinberger, interview with authors; also cited in Schweizer, *Victory*.
262	White House meeting, January 30, 1981: William Clark, Caspar Weinberger, Richard Allen, and Richard Pipes, interviews with authors; also cited in Schweizer, *Victory*.
263	"breaking Poland out of the Soviet orbit": Ronald Reagan, interview with authors, 1991; William Clark, Robert Gates, and Richard Allen, interviews with authors.
263–65	Covert aid to Solidarity discussed: Henry Hyde, Lane Kirkland, William Clark, Robert Gates, Bobby Inman, Richard Pipes, and Richard Perle, interviews with authors.
265	Casey and psy-ops: Richard Perle, interview with authors.
266–67	Casey and Clark preeminence with Reagan: William Clark, Alexander Haig,

Jeanne Kirkpatrick, Richard Allen, members of National Security Council staff, interviews with authors; Cannon, *President Reagan.*

266   Casey and Clark dealings with Laghi: William Clark, Pio Laghi, John Krol, Robert MacFarlane, John Poindexter, Richard Allen, interviews with authors.

267–68   Meetings with Krol: Krol, Richard Allen, William Clark, Edward Derwinski, interviews with authors.

268   Wojtyła's homily in church of Krol's father, speech about Krol: Boniecki, *Kalendarium.*

268–71   Krol/Wojtyła relationship: John Krol, Pio Laghi, and numerous American and curial bishops and monsignori, interviews with authors.

268–71   Relation between Wojtyła papacy and Reagan administration: Richard Allen, Vernon Walters, Robert Gates, William Clark, Jeanne Kirkpatrick, Robert Mc-Farlane, John Poindexter, Alexander Haig, Herbert Meyer, William Wilson, Zbigniew Brzeziński, Pio Laghi, John Krol, Agostino Casaroli, and Achille Silvestrini, interviews with authors; confidential sources—members of House and Senate intelligence committees and staff.

269   Walters meetings with John Paul II and subjects discussed: Vernon Walters, interviews with authors; cables sent by Walters from Rome to Washington between 1981 and 1988, obtained by authors under Freedom of Information Act and partially declassified.

270   Reagan administration's cancellation of family planning programs: William Wilson, interview with authors; confirmed by others.

271   Intercepted phone conversations: Confidential source.

271   Payments by North to priests in Central America: Confidential source, confirmed by John Poindexter and Robert Gates.

271–74   Jaruzelski's views: Wojciech Jaruzelski and Stanisław Kania, interviews with authors.

274–75   Reagan before AFL-CIO speech: William Clark, Richard Allen, interviews with authors.

275   Pope's letter to Brezhnev: Known to William Clark.

275   Reagan speech: Presidential documents, 1981.

276–80   Politburo meeting, April 2, 1981: Politburo minutes.

277   Margaret Thatcher: William Clark, interview with authors; Thatcher, *Downing Street Years.*

280–85   Jaruzelski and Kania's trip to Brest: Wojciech Jaruzelski and Stanisław Kania, interviews with authors; Jaruzelski, *Erinnerungen;* Politburo minutes, April 9, 1981.

280   "Jaruzelski had entrusted a pistol and a hand grenade": Jaruzelski, *Erinnerungen.*

281   Eastern bloc's weakest church: from Eric Hanson, *Catholic Church in World Politics.*

286   Suslov's arrival in Warsaw, report of Politburo Polish commission: Politburo documents.

286   Casey as clandestine minister of state and war: Persico, *Casey.*

286   Casey's letters to Reagan: Robert Gates, interview with authors.

287–88   Casey's discussions with John Paul II: Robert Gates, Herbert Meyer, interviews with authors; confidential CIA sources.

287–89 Details of Casey's meeting with John Paul II: Confidential CIA source; Sophia Casey; some details confirmed by Robert Gates and William Clark.

289–90 Casey's biographical details: Persico, *Casey;* Woodward, *Veil.*

291–93 Portrait of Dziwisz: Mieczysław Maliński, Rocco Buttiglione, Tadeusz Pieronek, Dominik Morawski, and Donald Wuerl, interview with authors; Boniecki, *Kalendarium;* confidential source in Vatican Curia.

294–96 Dziwisz's account of assassination attempt: Frossard, *Be Not Afraid.*

294 De Marenches warning to pope: Ockrent and De Marenches, *Dans le secret des princes.*

295 John Paul II and Virgin of Fátima: Frossard, *Be Not Afraid;* Andrzej Deskur and Mieczysław Maliński, interviews with authors.

296–97 CIA investigation and conclusions: Robert Gates, Herbert Meyer, Claire Sterling, John McMahon, interviews with authors; newspaper accounts of Gates's confirmation hearings as CIA director.

296–97 John Paul II's view of assassination: Andrzej Deskur, Giulio Andreotti, and Rocco Buttiglione, interviews with authors; confidential Curia sources.

296–97 Italian investigation: Reporting in *New York Times, Time, Washington Post;* Claire Sterling, *Reader's Digest.*

296–97 Deskur's accounts throughout: Andrzej Deskur, interviews with authors.

296–97 Various theories, including Bulgarian and Becket scenarios: Discussed with authors by members of American and Italian secret services.

297–98 Silvestrini and Casaroli's comments: Achille Silvestrini and Agostino Casaroli, interviews with authors.

298 Informal Vatican working group: Confidential Vatican sources.

299 John Paul II's view of Islam: Carlo De Benedetti, interview with authors; confidential sources.

299–302 Agca's actions before and after shooting: Trial accounts.

303 Scricciolo and lawyer's statements: *New York Times,* March 23, 1983.

303 NSA intercepts: Szulc, *Pope John Paul II;* confidential source.

305 Sterling's findings: Claire Sterling, interview with authors.

306 Clandestine source in Eastern Europe: Robert Gates, interview with authors.

307 Mantarov defection: *New York Times.*

308 Politburo "Decision" paper: Politburo minutes, November 13, 1979.

308–9 Reagan at Notre Dame: *New York Times;* presidential documents, 1981.

309 Reagan and reason he and John Paul II were spared: Reagan, William Clark, and Pio Laghi, interviews with authors.

310 Allen's letter to Wilson: Found in Wilson's papers at Georgetown University.

310–11 John Paul II's remarks to Polish pilgrims: *L'Osservatore Romano.*

311 Wałęsa remarks to Solidarity congress: Wałęsa, *Way of Hope.*

311 Brezhnev's and other Politburo members' comments on Solidarity congress: Politburo minutes, September 10, 1981.

311 Account of Solidarity congress: Wałęsa, *Way of Hope;* Ost, *Solidarity;* Weschler, *Passion of Poland;* Ash, *Polish Revolution.*

311   Glemp's meeting with Kania and Jaruzelski: Wojciech Jaruzelski, Stanisław Kania, and Kazimierz Barcikowski, interviews with authors.

312   Kukliński's information: Zbigniew Brzeziński, interview with authors; *Washington Post.*

312–13 *Laborem Exercens:* Marco Politi, *Il Messaggero.*

314   October situation in Poland: Wojciech Jaruzelski, interviews with authors; Ost, *Solidarity;* Ascherson, *Struggles for Poland;* Weschler, *Passion of Poland.*

314   Czyrek encounter with Gromyko: Cited in Spasowski, *Liberation of One.*

315   Brezhnev conversation with Jaruzelski: Politburo documents provided to and released by Polish post-Communist government.

315   Meeting of Jaruzelski, Wałęsa, and Glemp: Wojciech Jaruzelski, interview with authors.

316   John Paul II's meeting with Polish intellectuals: Bronisław Geremek and Jerzy Turowicz, interviews with authors.

317   Brezhnev letter to Jaruzelski: Politburo minutes.

317–18 Poland in 1981: Accounts of this period from Wojciech Jaruzelski, interview with authors; Ash, *Polish Revolution, Magic Lantern, Uses of Adversity;* Ost, *Solidarity;* Ascherson, *Struggles for Poland;* Szajkowski, *Next to God.*

318–19 Origins of Walters visits with pope: Confidential source, U.S. State Department (the deputy); Vernon Walters, Michael Ledeen, Alexander Haig, William Clark, Jeanne Kirkpatrick, and Pio Laghi, interviews with authors.

320–21 Walters profile: Vernon Walters, interview with authors; materials in *Time* library files.

322–29 Walters's visit with John Paul II: Vernon Walters, interviews with authors; Walters's cable to State Department, CIA, and White House, November 30, 1981, obtained under Freedom of Information Act and partially declassified.

322   Kukliński's escape: Confidential CIA source.

328   "When you greet him you are struck": Nikolai Lunkov, interview with authors.

329–30 Polish life, winter 1981: Ost, *Solidarity;* Ascherson, *Struggles for Poland;* Weschler, *Passion of Poland;* Walendowski, "Polish Church," "Controversy," "Pope in Poland"; *New York Times, Washington Post.*

330   Glemp meeting with Wałęsa: Wojciech Jaruzelski, interview with authors; Wałęsa, *Way of Hope.*

331–33 Politburo, meeting, December 10, 1981: Politburo minutes.

332–33 Solidarity commission meetings: Wałęsa, *Way of Hope;* Ost, *Solidarity;* Ascherson, *Struggles for Poland;* Ash, *Polish Revolution, Magic Lantern, Uses of Adversity, We the People.*

333   Jaruzelski expected in Moscow: Politburo minutes.

333   Jaruzelski timing: Zbigniew Bujak, Wiktor Kulerski, and Wojciech Jaruzelski, interviews with authors; Jaruzelski, *Erinnerungen.*

334   Jaruzelski's address to nation: Rosenberg, *Haunted Land; New York Times.*

335   Kania's comments: Stanisław Kania, interview with authors.

335   Jaruzelski's objectives vis-à-vis the Church: Wojciech Jaruzelski, interview with authors.

336–37   Notification of Glemp and Dąbrowski: Kazimierz Barcikowski, interview with authors.

337–38   Glemp's homily: Ash, *Polish Revolution;* Szajkowski, *Next to God.*

339   Bujak's comments: Zbigniew Bujak, interview with authors; Ost, *Solidarity.*

340–42   John Paul II's first reactions: Mieczysław Maliński, Rocco Buttiglione, Andrzej Deskur, Adam Boniecki, interviews with authors; *L'Osservatore Romano;* Vatican confidential source (a papal aide).

342–43,   Lewandowski's conversations with Pipes and John Paul II: Richard Pipes, Lewan-
347   dowski, interviews with authors.

344   Violence in Katowice and elsewhere: *New York Times.*

344–45   John Paul II's letter to Jaruzelski: Copy obtained by authors.

348–49   Wałęsa's meetings with Orszulik and analysis of Church objectives: Wałęsa, *Way of Hope.*

349   John Paul II at Christmas: Andrzej Deskur, interview with authors; confidential Vatican source; *L'Osservatore Romano.*

350–51   Poggi, Glemp, and Dąbrowski dealings: Andrzej Deskur, interview with authors; confidential Vatican source.

351   *"salvare il salvabile":* Wilton Wynn, interview with authors.

351   John Paul II's analysis of Jaruzelski: Mieczysław Maliński, Andrzej Deskur, Adam Boniecki, and Morawski, interviews with authors.

352   John Paul II's belief in power of prayer: Andrzej Deskur, Mieczysław Maliński, and others, interviews with authors.

352–53   Jaruzelski's letter to John Paul II: Obtained by authors.

353–54   John Paul II's response: Obtained by authors.

354   Bujak's attempts to reach Glemp: Zbigniew Bujak, interview with authors.

354   John Paul II's dispatch of funds to Solidarity underground: Confirmed by American intelligence sources.

355–61   Reagan's meeting with John Paul II: William Clark, Alexander Haig, Ronald Reagan, Pio Laghi, Agostino Casaroli, and Achille Silvestrini, interviews with authors.

355   Appointment of William Clark as national security adviser: Clark and Kirkpatrick, interviews with authors; Cannon, *Casey.*

356   Reagan at Westminster: Cannon, *President Reagan.*

356   "I didn't cause this to happen": Stated to Carlo De Benedetti; interview with authors.

357   CIA spending $50 million to keep Solidarity alive: Confidential sources—members and staff of congressional intelligence committees and CIA officials; confirmed in authors' interviews with Robert Gates and William Clark.

358–61   Profile of Reagan: William Clark, Richard Allen, John Sears, Edmund Morris, Lou Cannon, Alexander Haig, Martin Anderson, George Shultz, Jeanne Kirkpatrick, Richard Pipes, Robert MacFarlane, Stuart Spencer, and David Gergin, interviews with authors; Carl Bernstein, cover story in *New Republic,* January 20, 1985.

358–59   Reagan on Yalta: Ronald Reagan, interview with authors.

359–60   Reagan's view of pope as heroic figure: Jeanne Kirkpatrick, interview with authors.

360   Reagan's assurances of good intentions: William Wilson and Alexander Haig, interviews with authors.

360   Haig on Reagan: Alexander Haig, interview with authors.

360   Haig–Reagan relationship: William Clark, Richard Allen, Jeanne Kirkpatrick, Richard Pipes, and Robert MacFarlane, interviews with authors.

360   Reagan at Reykjavik: Cannon, *President Reagan.* Reagan was widely reported to be unprepared for his negotiation with Gorbachev at Reykjavik. On the final day, Gorbachev made an audacious proposal for major arms reductions, and Reagan would have accepted it, to the chagrin of his advisers, provided Gorbachev would have accepted SDI. This unscripted element of the summit, and Reagan's eagerness to embrace such deep cuts in armaments, unnerved many in the administration.

362   Reagan's view of Soviet economy: Ronald Reagan, interview with authors.

362   Reagan instructing Casey to take over coordination and funding of support for Solidarity: William Clark, Bobby Ray Inman, and Robert Gates, interviews with authors.

362   "The CIA's code name": Transcripts of trial of Alan Fiers, reports of trial in *New York Times.*

362   For a history of Casey and the Iran-Contra affair, see Woodward, *Veil.*

362   CIA funneling money to the church: John Poindexter, interview with authors.

363   Obando as CIA "asset": Ibid.

363   Discovery of CIA funds in Obando's archbishopric: Robert Gates, interview with authors; confidential source on intelligence committee staff.

363   Fiers's dealings: *New York Times* report of trial; confidential source on congressional intelligence committee.

364   Casey and William Clark encouraging papal visit to Nicaragua: William Clark, Jeanne Kirkpatrick, Pio Laghi, interviews with authors.

364   "We shared an interest in discouraging Communist beachheads": Jeanne Kirkpatrick, interview with authors.

364   "the pope was in Nicaragua to provide": Ibid.

365–69   Details of papal trip: Marco Politi, personal notes and reporting in *Il Messaggero.*

369   "He moves like a swallow": Confidential source in Italian politics.

369–70   "He was always on the heavy side": Jacek Woźniakowski, interview with authors.

370   "It's . . . a golden cage": Confidential source (Vatican monsignor).

370–71   John Paul II schedule: *Time* magazine private files.

371–72   John Paul II at meals and in meetings: Mariano Magrassi and Oddi, interviews with authors.

374   John Paul II's reading of press clippings: John Patrick Foley, interview with authors.

375   Meetings with Curia: John Patrick Foley, interview with authors.

376–87   John Paul II's 1983 visit to Poland: Wojciech Jaruzelski, Lech Wałęsa, Adam Boniecki, Virgilio Levi, Andrzej Deskur, Rocco Buttiglione, Mieczysław Maliński, and Zbigniew Bujak, interviews with authors; *Tygodnik Mazowsze;* Weschler, *Passion of Poland;* Ash, *Polish Revolution, Magic Lantern, Uses of Adversity;* Wałęsa, *Way of Hope;* *L'Osservatore Romano;* Marco Politi, reporting in *Il Messaggero;* KOS.

381–82   Solidarity's survival and underground activities: Robert Gates, Bobby Ray Inman, William Clark, Henry Hyde, Edward Derwinski, Wiktor Kulerski, Zbigniew Bujak, and Adam Boniecki, interviews with authors; Ash, *Polish Revolution;* Ost, *Solidarity;* Lopinski et al., *Konspira;* confidential sources (CIA and congressional intelligence committees).

381–82   Casey and smuggling equipment through Sweden: William Clark and Herbert Meyer, interviews with authors.

388   Andropov letter to Jaruzelski: Politburo minutes.

388   Jaruzelski meeting with Gromyko and Ustinov: Wojciech Jaruzelski, interview with authors; Politburo minutes, April 26, 1984.

Part VI: Universal Pastor

393–402   Details of the papal trips is from Marco Politi, reporting in *Il Messaggero.* Papal quotations are from official Vatican bulletins and from Politi coverage. Other printed sources: Del Rio, *Un pontificato itinerante;* Del Rio and Accattoli, *Il nuovo Mosè;* Luigi Accattoli, reporting in *Corriere della Sera;* Alceste Santini, reporting in *L'Unita;* Marco Tosatti, reporting in *La Stampa.*

393   Canonizations: Woodward, *La fabbrica dei santi.*

399   Gielgud's observation: Ash, *Uses of Adversity.*

404   Comments of F. X. Murphy: Murphy, interview with authors.

404   Comments of Ida Magli: Magli, interview with authors.

404–5   O'Connor comments: John O'Connor, interview with authors.

405   Weakland comments: Rembert Weakland, interview with authors.

406   Foley comments: John Patrick Foley, interview with authors.

406–7   Wuerl comments: Donald Wuerl, interview with authors.

407–8   Curial monsignor comments: Confidential source.

408   Kane comments: Theresa Kane, interview with authors.

410   John Paul II at Mother Teresa's hospice: Marco Politi, *Il Messaggero;* Del Rio, *Un pontificato itinerante.*

411–16   Boff case: Marco Politi, reporting in *Il Messaggero.*

411–16   Boff's meeting with Ratzinger: Reporting by Domenico Del Rio, *La Repubblica;* Luigi Accattoli, *Corriere della Sera;* Gianni Favarato, *La Repubblica;* Giovanni Gennari, *Paese Sera;* Giancarlo Zizola, *Panorama.*

417–18   Schillebeeckx case: Reporting by Gianfranco Svidercoschi, *Il Tempo,* Giancarlo Zizola, *Europeo,* Marco Tosatti, *La Stampa,* Henry Tanner, *New York Times.*

419–22   Arrupe case: Lamet, *Pedro Arrupe.*

422–39   Synod: Marco Politi, reporting in *Il Messaggero;* Caprile, *Il sinodo;* Hebblethwaite, *Synod Extraordinary;* Rhynne, *John Paul's Extraordinary Synod.*

425   Messori's meeting with Ratzinger: Vittorio Messori, interview with authors.

SOURCES

425–26   Quotations of Ratzinger: Messori, *Rapporto sulla fede*.

440   "I'm very worried about fundamentalism": John Paul II, quoted by Avi Pazner, interview with authors.

440–41   John Paul II's meeting with Islamic leaders: Marco Politi reporting.

441   John Paul II's conversation with De Benedetti: Carlo De Benedetti, interview with authors.

443   John Paul II in Rome synagogue: Marco Politi reporting.

444   John Paul II's trip to India: Marco Politi coverage.

444   John Paul II and Jews in Wadowice: Jerzy Kluger and Regina Beer Reisenfeld, interviews with authors.

444–46   Peace assembly in Assisi: Marco Politi coverage.

Part VII: The Fall of Communism

449   Gromyko's meeting at Vatican: from Gromyko memoir.

449   Gorbachev's meeting with Jaruzelski: Wojciech Jaruzelski, interview with authors; Gorbachev, *Erinnerungen*.

454   The pope's *Ostpolitik*: The description is from Weigel, *Final Revolution*, p. 98.

454   "*Perestroika* is an avalanche": John Paul II, quoted by Mieczysław Maliński, interview with authors.

454   The avalanche was rumbling through Czechoslovakia: The observation is from Weigel, pp. 174–75.

454   "We felt how strong we were": František Lobkowicz, quoted in Weigel, *Final Revolution*.

456   "A group of people sitting around": Ost, *Solidarity*, p. 173.

456   Poland was not "socialism with a human face": Weigel, *Final Revolution*, p. 152.

456   "Well, yes, of course we all said": Wojciech Jaruzelski, interview with authors.

457–58   Jaruzelski's meeting with John Paul II: Wojciech Jaruzelski, interview with authors; confidential source in papal entourage.

457   "I told the pope what I knew about Gorbachev": Szulc, *Pope John Paul II*, p. 406.

458   "I found that [the pope] had a complete understanding": Ibid., p. 405.

458   "The pope was aware": Andrzej Deskur, interview with authors.

459   "that there were now just too many groups": Ost, *Solidarity*, p. 162.

459   "Lech Wałęsa deserves another Nobel Peace Prize": Ash, *Uses of Adversity*.

459   Laghi's assurances to White House: William Clark and Pio Laghi, interviews with authors.

460   "At present, several of the fraternal countries": *Washington Post*, April 13, 1987.

460   Gorbachev's visit to Prague: *Washington Post*.

461   "I candidly shared with Jaruzelski": Gorbachev, *Erinnerungen*.

461–66   John Paul II's trip to Chile and Argentina: Marco Politi, reporting in *Il Messaggero*.

466–68   John Paul II's 1987 trip to Poland: Marco Politi, reporting in *Il Messaggero*; *Washington Post*.

469–71   Internal Polish situation and negotiations: Wojciech Jaruzelski and Stanisław Ciosek, interviews with authors; Wałęsa, *Way of Hope*; Ost, *Solidarity*.

471   "If neither side gave in": Stanisław Ciosek, interview with authors.

472–78   Gorbachev's visit to Vatican: Text obtained by authors.

473   John Paul II's view of Gorbachev: Achille Silvestrini, Virgilio Levi, Mieczysław Maliński, Wojciech Jaruzelski, Andrzej Deskur, and Rocco Buttiglione, interviews with authors.

474   Lack of Vatican criticism of Reagan: Reagan administration officials, confirmed by Vatican diplomats.

474   John Paul II's view of Reagan: Agostino Casaroli, Pio Laghi, Achille Silvestrini, and Andrzej Deskur, interviews with authors.

474   John Paul II's views of Bush: Privately confirmed by several Vatican officials.

475   "The pope knew what most Westerners did not": Member of papal entourage.

476   "the Holy Father hoped that Gorbachev's attempts": Rocco Buttiglione, interview with authors.

478–79   Scene in Red Square: Marco Politi, reporting.

479–80   John Paul II and Virgin of Fátima: Werenfried von Straaten, Andrzej Deskur, and Mieczysław Maliński, interviews with authors.

480–81   John Paul II and breakup of Soviet Union: Andrzej Deskur, Rocco Buttiglione, Mieczysław Maliński, interview with authors.

481   John Paul II and fall of Gorbachev: Werenfried von Straaten, Mieczysław Maliński, Wojciech Jaruzelski, Andrzej Deskur, interviews with authors.

Part VIII: The Angry Pope

487–92   John Paul II's 1991 trip to Poland: Reporting in *L'Osservatore Romano, Corriere della Sera, La Repubblica, Il Messaggero*, New York Times, International Herald Tribune, Time, Tablet; *L'Attività della Santa Sede*; Del Rio, *Un pontificato itinerante*.

488   "The capacity of the Church": European Synod of Bishops, Rome, November 28–December 14, 1991, *Holy See Bulletin*.

491   "People have begun to be afraid": Czesław Miłosz, quoted in *Corriere della Sera*, June 1, 1991.

491   "It would be a good idea": Adam Michnik, quoted in *Il Messaggero*, June 4, 1991.

492   John Paul II's comments during trip: press coverage; *L'Attività della Santa Sede*.

493–94   John Paul II's comments to Zdybicka: Zofia Zdybicka, interview with authors.

494   *"Ex Oriente lux"*: *L'Attività della Santa Sede*.

494   "He wanted to make Poland the bridge": Confidential sources.

494–95   Turowicz in Rome: Reporting by authors.

495   "The Polish Church is highly polarized": Jerzy Turowicz, interview with authors.

496   John Paul II's letter to Kydryński: Andrzej Bardecki, interview with authors.

496   John Paul II on Russia: Confidential sources.

497   John Paul II in Riga: Marco Politi, reporting in *La Repubblica*.

497   "These seeds of truth": Gawronski, *Il mondo di Giovanni Paolo II*.

SOURCES

497   Gorbachev's comment to an Italian friend: Giulietto Chiesa, interview with authors.

497   John Paul II in Denver: Marco Politi, reporting in *La Repubblica*.

497   "the struggle against God": Messori, *Varcare la soglia*.

498   "aims to convince man": Frossard, *Be Not Afraid, Portrait of John Paul II*.

498   John Paul II's announcement: *L'Attività della Santa Sede*.

499   John Paul II reserving room in Gemelli Clinic: Giulio Andreotti, article in *Aspenia* (Aspen Institute Review), no. 2, 1995.

500   John Paul II's colostomy: *Bulletin of the Holy See*.

500   John Paul II's shoulder fracture: Marco Politi, reporting in *La Repubblica*.

501   Skiing accident: Stanisław Dziwisz; reporting by authors.

501   Accident in bathroom: Marco Politi, reporting in *La Repubblica*.

501   Illness hypotheses about John Paul II: Confidential sources.

501   "I'm a *biedaczek*": Marco Politi, reporting in *La Repubblica*.

502   Pius X's cold: Zizola, *Le Successeur*.

502   Navarro-Valls's reports on John Paul II: *L'Avvenire*, August 19–26, 1994.

502   John Paul II in Zagreb: Marco Politi, reporting in *La Repubblica*.

502   John Paul II on his sufferings: Reporting by authors.

502   "The pope has a theological vision": Confidential sources.

503   Buttiglione on *Veritatis Splendor*: Rocco Buttiglione, interview with authors.

505–6   "The pope is convinced that his doctrine": Hans Küng, quoted by Alessio Altichieri, *Corriere della Sera*, October 6, 1993.

506   "*Veritatis Splendor* contains many beautiful things": Bernhard Häring, interview with Marco Politi, *La Repubblica*, October 7, 1993.

506   Danneels on *Veritatis Splendor*: Marco Politi, reporting in *La Repubblica*.

507   "In certain areas he has a trusted team": Confidential source.

508   African synod: Marco Politi, reporting in *La Repubblica*.

508–9   Martini, Lehmann, and Hume on *Veritatis Splendor*: Marco Politi, reporting in *La Repubblica*.

510   "false ideas of democracy": *Direttorio per il ministero e la vita dei presbiteri* (Manual for the Clergy), April 1994.

510   Reform movements in Church: Marco Politi, personal notes and reporting.

511   Weakland comments on John Paul II: Rembert Weakland, interview with authors.

511   John Paul II to Sacred Roman Rota: *L'Attività della Santa Sede*.

512   John Paul II's trip to Prague and Belgium: Marco Politi, reporting in *La Repubblica*.

512   Behavior of faithful in Italy: *"La religiosità" in Italia*.

514   John Paul II's comments to Zdybicka about women: Zofia Zdybicka, interview with authors.

514   "the gestation of a baby": David Schindler, interview with authors.

515–16   Kane's encounter with John Paul II: Theresa Kane, interview with authors; Marco Politi, reporting in *Il Messaggero*.

516–17   Criticism of Church by women in Germany, Switzerland, Holland, Belgium: Marco Politi, reporting in *Il Messaggero*; *L'Attività della Santa Sede*.

SOURCES

519–24   Sadik's meeting with John Paul II: Nafis Sadik, interview with authors; Marco Politi, reporting in *La Repubblica*.

524   Vatican preparation for Cairo Conference: Marco Politi, reporting in *La Repubblica*; other reporting by authors.

524   Deskur's comments: Andrzej Deskur, interview with authors.

526   O'Connor's comments: John O'Connor, interview with authors.

526   Diarmuid Martin's comments to African synod: Marco Politi, reporting in *La Repubblica*.

526–27   Islam and Cairo conference: Marco Politi, reporting in *La Repubblica*.

527   López Trujillo's announcement and pamphlet: Marco Politi, articles in *La Repubblica*.

528   Navarro-Valls's attack on Gore: Marco Politi, reporting in *La Repubblica*.

528–29   Cairo conference: Reporting in *La Repubblica*.

529   Beijing conference: Marco Politi, reporting in *La Repubblica*.

530   Mass on September 4, 1994: *Il Messaggero*, *La Repubblica*.

530   Phone calls to cardinals: Confidential sources.

531   John Paul II and Abraham's pilgrimage: Marco Politi, reporting in *La Repubblica*.

532   John Paul II's dream of Russian trip: Werenfried von Straaten, interview with authors.

532   John Paul II and Chinese Catholics: Speech to the diplomatic corp, Vatican, January 13, 1996.

532   John Paul II's comments on Maliński: Mieczysław Maliński, interview with authors.

532–33   John Paul II's health condition: Confidential Vatican sources; Marco Politi, personal notes.

533   Zdybicka's comments on John Paul II's health: Zofia Zdybicka, interview with authors.

533   John Paul II and suffering: Confidential Vatican sources.

534   "It's an amazing experience": Mariano Magrassi, interview with authors.

536   Memorandum about public repentance: Marco Politi, reporting in *La Repubblica*.

538   Document on women: Libreria Editrice Vaticana, June 29, 1995.

BIBLIOGRAPHY

Books

Ambroziewicz, Jerzy. *Znam was wszystkich.* Warsaw: Polska Oficyna Wydawnicza, 1993.

Andreotti, Giulio. *A ogni morte di papa.* Milan: Rizzoli, 1982.

Ascherson, Neal. *The Struggles for Poland.* London: M. Joseph, 1987.

L'Attività della Santa Sede, 1978–1995. Città del Vaticano: Libreria Editrice Vaticana.

Ash, Timothy Garton. *Polish Revolution: Solidarity.* New York: Scribner's, 1983.

————. *The Magic Lantern.* New York: Random House, 1990.

————. *The Uses of Adversity.* New York: Vintage, 1990.

————. *We the People.* Cambridge: Granta Books, 1990.

Arias, Juan. *L'enigma Wojtyła.* Rome: Borla, 1986.

Banaszak, Marian. *Historia kosciola katolickiego.* Warsaw: Accademia di Teologia Cattolica di Varsavia, 1992.

Bergonzoni, Luciano. *Emilia Kaczorowska in Wojtyła.* Edizioni Carroccio, Vigodarzere, 1988.

————. *Edmondo Wojtyła.* Padova: Centro Editoriale Cattolico Carroccio, 1992.

Berry, Jason. *Lead Us Not into Temptation.* New York: Doubleday, 1992.

Blazynski, George. *John Paul II: A Man from Krakow.* London: Weidenfeld and Nicholson, 1979.

Bokenkotter, Thomas. *A Concise History of the Catholic Church.* New York: Doubleday, 1990.

Boniecki, Adam. *Kalendarium zycia Karola Wojtyła.* Krakow: Wydawnictwo-Znak, 1983.

Briggs, Kenneth. *Holy Siege: The Year That Shook Catholic America.* San Francisco: HarperSanFrancisco, 1992.

Brumberg, Abraham. *Genesis of a Revolution.* New York: Random House, 1983.

Brzeziński, Zbigniew. *Power and Principle: Memoirs of the National Security Adviser, 1977–1981.* New York: Farrar, Straus and Giroux, 1982.

Cannon, Lou. *President Reagan: The Role of a Lifetime.* New York: Simon and Schuster, 1991.

Caprile, Giovanni. *Il Concilio Vaticano II.* Rome: La Civiltà Cattolica.

————. *Il sinodo straordinario, 1985.* Rome: La Civiltà Cattolica, 1986.

Carter, Jimmy. *Keeping Faith: Memoirs of a President.* New York: Bantam, 1982.

Catechism of the Catholic Church. San Francisco: Ignatius Press, 1983.

Chelini, Jean. *La vita quotidiana in Vaticano sotto Giovanni Paolo II.* Milan: Rizzoli, 1986.

Clissold, Kenneth. *The Wisdom of the Spanish Mystics.* New York: New Directions, 1977.

Cornwell, John. *A Thief in the Night: The Death of John Paul I.* London: Viking, 1989.

Daim, Wilfried. *Il Vaticano e l'Est.* Roma: Coines Edizioni, 1973.

BIBLIOGRAPHY

D'Amato, Al. *Power, Pasta, and Politics.* New York: Hyperion, 1995.

Davies, Norman. *God's Playground: A History of Poland.* Vols. 1 and 2. New York: Columbia University Press, 1982.

De Montclos, Christine. *Les voyages de Jean Paul II.* Paris: Centurion, 1990.

Del Rio, Domenico. *Wojtyła: Un pontificato itinerante.* Bologna: Edizioni Dehoniane Bologna, 1994.

————, and Luigi Accattoli. *Wojtyła: Il nuovo Mosè.* Milan: Mondadori, 1988.

Falconi, Carlo. *Popes in the Twentieth Century.* Boston: Little, Brown, 1967.

Frossard, Andre. *Portrait of John Paul II.* San Francisco: Ignatius Press, 1988.

————, and Pope John Paul II. *Be Not Afraid.* New York: St. Martin's Press, 1982.

Gates, Robert. *From the Shadows.* New York: Simon and Schuster, 1996.

Gawronski, Jas. *Il mondo di Giovanni Paolo II.* Milan: Mondadori, 1994.

Ginsborg, Paul. *A History of Contemporary Italy.* New York: Penguin, 1990.

Gorbachev, Mikhail. *Erinnerungen.* Berlin: Siedler Verlag, 1995.

Gromyko, Andrei. *Pamjatnoe.* Moscow: Izdatel'stwo Politicheskoi Literatury, 1988.

Guasco, Maurilio, Elio Guerriero, and Francesco Traianiello. *La chiesa del Vaticano II.* Milan: San Paolo, 1994.

Haig, Alexander. *Caveat: Realism, Reagan, and Foreign Policy.* New York: Macmillan, 1984.

Halter, Marek. *La force du bien.* Paris: Robert Laffont, 1995.

Hanson, Eric O. *The Catholic Church in World Politics.* Princeton: Princeton University Press, 1987.

Hebblethwaite, Peter. *The Year of Three Popes.* Cleveland: William Collins, 1979.

————. *In the Vatican.* New York: Oxford, 1986.

————. *Synod Extraordinary.* New York: Doubleday, 1986.

Herman, Edward S., and Frank Brodhead. *The Rise and Fall of the Bulgarian Connection.* New York: Sheridan Square Publications, 1986.

Institute for the World Socialist System. *Bogomolov Report.* Moscow, 1978.

Jaruzelski, Wojciech. *Stan wojenny dlaczego.* Warsaw: Polska Oficyna Wydawnicza, 1992.

————. *Erinnerungen.* Munchen: Piper, 1993.

Kaiser, R. B. *The Politics of Sex and Religion.* Kansas City, Mo.: Leaven Press, 1985.

Kania, Stanisław. *Zatrzymac konfrontacje.* Warsaw: Polska Oficyna Wyadawnicza, 1991.

Karolek, Tadeusz. *John Paul II: The Pope from Poland.* Warsaw: Interpress Publishers, 1979.

Kelly, George A. *Keeping the Church Catholic with John Paul II.* San Francisco: Ignatius Press, 1990.

Kydryński, Juliusz. *Quando Karol aveva diciott'anni.*

————, et al. *Mlodziencze lata Karol Wojtyła.* Krakow: Oficyna Cracovia, 1990.

Lai, Benni. *Il papa non eletto.* Bari: Laterza, 1993.

Lamet, Pedro Miguel. *Pedro Arrupe.* Milan: Editrice Ancora, 1993.

Lecomte, Bernard. *La Verité l'emportera toujours sur le mesonge.* Paris: J.-C. Lattes, 1991.

Lernoux, Penny. *People of God: The Struggle for World Catholicism.* New York: Viking Press, 1989.

Libanio Christo, Carlos Alberto. *Diario di Puebla.* Brescia: Ed. Queriniana, 1979.

Licheri, Gianni. *Quel conclave e poi Wojtyła jet.* Brescia: Queriniana, 1979.

Livingstone, E. A. *The Concise Oxford Dictionary of the Christian Church.* New York: Oxford University Press, 1990.

Lopinski, Maciej, Marcin Moskit, and Mariusz Wilk. *Konspira: Solidarity Underground.* Berkeley: University of California Press, 1990.

MacDowell, Bart. *Inside the Vatican.* Washington: National Geographic Society, 1991.

MacEoin, Gary. *The Inner Elite.* Kansas City: Sheed, Andrews, and McMeel, 1978.

Maliński, Mieczysław. *Il mio vecchio amico Karol.* Rome: Ed. Paoline, 1980.

———. *Pope John Paul II: The Life of Karol Wojtyła.* New York: Seabury Press, 1980.

———. *Le radici di Papa Wojtyła.* Rome: Borla, 1980.

Melady, Thomas P. *The Ambassador's Story.* Huntington, Ind.: Our Sunday Visitor Publishing Co., 1994.

Messori, Vittorio. *Rapporto sulla fede.* Rome: Ed. Paoline, 1985.

———. *Varcare la soglia della speranza.* Milan: Mondadori, 1994.

Murphy, Francis X. *The Papacy Today.* New York: Macmillan, 1981.

Nichols, Peter. *The Pope's Divisions.* Boston: Faber and Faber, 1981.

Ockrent, Christine, and Alexandre De Marenches. *Dans le secret des princes.* Paris: Edition Stock, 1986.

Offredo, Jean. *Jean Paul II: L'aventurier de Dieu.* Paris: Carrere-Michel Lafon, 1986.

Ost, David. *Solidarity and the Politics of Anti-politics: Opposition and Reform in Poland since 1968.* Philadelphia: Temple University Press, 1990.

Persico, Joseph E. *Casey.* New York: Viking, 1990.

Pieronka, Tadeusza. and Romana M. Zawadzienkego. *Karol Wojtyła: Jako Bishup Krakowski.* Kraków: Papieska Akademia Teologiczna, 1988.

Pontifical Council for the Family. *Marriage and Family.* San Francisco: Ignatius Press, 1987.

Poupard, Paul. *Il Concilio Vaticano II.* Edizioni Piemme, 1987.

Puebla documenti. Bologna: Editrice Missionaria Italiana, 1979.

Rachwald, Arthur R. *In Search of Poland: Solidarność.* Stanford, Calif.: Hoover Institution Press, 1990.

Reese, Thomas J. *Archbishop.* New York: Harper & Row, 1989.

———. *A Flock of Shepherds.* Kansas City: Sheed and Ward, 1992.

Rhynne, Xavier. *Letters from Vatican City.* New York: Farrar, Straus and Company, 1963.

———. *The Third Session.* New York: Farrar, Straus and Giroux, 1965.

———. *John Paul's Extraordinary Synod.* Wilmington, Del.: Michael Glazier, 1986.

Rolicki, Janusz. *Edward Gierek.* Replika, Warsaw: Polska Ofycyna Wydawnicza, 1990.

———. *Edward Gierek: Przerwana dekada.* Warsaw: Polska Oficyna Wydawnicza, 1990.

Rosenberg, Tina. *The Haunted Land.* New York: Random House, 1995.

Schweizer, Peter. *Victory.* New York: Atlantic Monthly Press, 1994.

Spasowski, Romuald. *The Liberation of One.* New York: Harcourt Brace Jovanovich, 1986.

Sterling, Claire. *The Time of the Assassins.* New York: Holt, Rinehart and Winston, 1983.

Styczeń, Tadeusz. *Le encicliche di Giovanni Paolo II.* Milan: Mondadori, 1994.

Svidercoschi, Gianfranco. *Lettera a un amico ebreo.* Milan: Mondadori, 1993.

Szajkowski, Bogdan. *Next to God—Poland: Politics and Religion in Contemporary Poland.* New York: St. Martin's Press, 1983.

BIBLIOGRAPHY

Szczypka, Josef. *Jan Pawel II: Rodowod.* Warsaw: Instytut Wydaniczy Pax, 1991.

Szostak, John. *In the Footsteps of John Paul II.* New Jersey: Prentice-Hall, 1980.

Szulc, Tad. *Pope John Paul II.* New York: Scribner's, 1995.

Thatcher, Margaret. *The Downing Street Years.* London: HarperCollins, 1993.

Thomas, Gordon, and Max Morgan Witts. *Averting Armageddon.* New York: Doubleday, 1984.

Uboldi, Raffaello. *Vita di Papa Wojtyła.* Milan: Rizzoli, 1983.

Vircondelet, Alain. *Jean Paul II.* Paris: Julliard, 1994.

Wałęsa, Lech. *Way of Hope.* London: Collins-Harvill, 1987.

Weigel, George. *The Final Revolution: The Resistance Church and the Collapse of Communism.* New York: Oxford University Press, 1992.

Wenger, Antoine. *Le Cardinal Jean Villot.* Paris: Desclée de Brouwer, 1989.

Weschler, Lawrence. *The Passion of Poland.* New York: Pantheon Books, 1984.

Willey, David. *God's Politician.* New York: St. Martin's Press, 1992.

Williams, George H. *The Mind of John Paul II: Origins of His Thought and Action.* New York: Seabury Press, 1981.

Wills, Garry. *Reagan's America: Innocents at Home.* Garden City, NY: Doubleday, 1987.

Wojtyła, Karol. *Segno di contraddizione.* Milan: Vita e Pensiero, 1977.

———. *The Acting Person.* Analecta Husserliana, Volume X. Boston: Reidel Publishing Co., 1979.

———. *Pietra di luce: Poesie.* Città del Vaticano: Libreria Editrice Vaticana, 1979.

———. *The Jeweler's Shop.* San Francisco: Ignatius Press, 1980.

———. *Love and Responsibility.* San Francisco: Ignatius Press, 1993.

———. *Opere Letterarie: Poesie e Drammi.* Città del Vaticano: Libreria Editrice Vaticana, 1993.

Woodward, Bob. *Veil.* New York: Simon and Schuster, 1987.

Woodward, Kenneth L. *La fabbrica dei santi.* Milan: Rizzoli, 1990.

Wynn, Wilton. *Keepers of the Keys.* New York: Random House, 1988.

Yallop, David. *In God's Name: An Investigation into the Murder of Pope John Paul I.* New York: Bantam, 1984.

Zizola, Giancarlo. *La restaurazione di papa Wojtyła.* Bari: Laterza, 1985.

———. *Il conclave.* Rome: Newton Compton, 1993.

———. *Le successeur.* Paris: Desclée de Brouwer, 1995.

Articles

Alexiev, Alex. "The Kremlin and the Vatican." *Orbis* (Fall 1983): 554–65.

Bernstein, Carl. "Holy Alliance." *Time,* February 24, 1992.

———. "Reagan at Intermission." *New Republic,* January 20, 1985.

Brumberg, Abraham. "The Achievements of General Jaruzelski." *New Leader* (Dec. 26, 1983): 6–8.

———. "A New Deal in Poland." *New York Review of Books* (Jan. 15, 1987): 32–36.

———. "The New Opposition." *New York Review of Books* (Feb. 18, 1988): 23–27.

———. "Poland: State and/or Society—The See-Saw between Government and Solidarity." *Dissent* (Winter 1989): 47–55.

———. "Poland: The Demise of Communism." *Foreign Affairs* (Winter 1989–90): 70–88.

Civic, Christopher. "Czechoslovaks Find Faith." *Tablet* (Sept. 3, 1983): 840–42.

Darnton, John. "60 Days That Shook Poland." *New York Times Magazine* (Nov. 9, 1980): 39–41, 109–18.

Epstein, Edward J. "Did Agca Act Alone?" *New York Times*, January 15, 1984.

Gage, Nicholas. "The Attack on the Pope: New Link to Bulgarians." *New York Times*, March 23, 1983.

Hebblethwaite, Peter. "Major Religious Demonstration Pits Catholic Muscle against Czech Regime." *National Catholic Reporter* (July 19, 1985): 1, 10.

———. "Hungarian Prelate Lauds Regime That Jails Catholics." *National Catholic Reporter* (Feb. 14, 1986): 56.

Hemphill, Clara. "Disorder in the Court." *New Republic*, September 16/23, 1985.

Kaminski, Tadeusz. "Poland's Catholic Church and Solidarity: A Parting of the Ways." *Poland Watch* (Summer 1984): 73–91.

Latynski, Maya. "The Church: Between State and Society." *Poland Watch* (Spring 1984): 12–24.

Medek, Ivan. "Roman Catholic Church in Czechoslovakia: Danger of Disunity." *Religion in Communist Lands* (Spring 1980): 44–48.

Milewski, Jerzy, Krzysztof Pomian, and Jan Zielonka. "Poland: Four Years After." *Foreign Affairs* (Winter 1985–86): 337–59.

Stehle, Hansjakob. "The Ostpolitik of the Vatican and the Polish Pope." *Religion in Communist Lands* (Summer 1980): 13–21.

Sterling, Claire. "The Plot to Murder The Pope." *Reader's Digest*, September 1982.

———. "Bulgaria Hired Agca to Kill Pope, Report of Italian Prosecutor Says." *New York Times*, June 10, 1984.

———. "The Great Bulgarian Cover-Up." *New Republic*, May 27, 1985.

Tomsky, Alexander. "John Paul II's Ostpolitik?" *Religion in Communist Lands* (Summer 1980): 139–40.

Tymieniecka, Anna-Teresa. "Feature Study." *Phenomenology Information Bulletin* (published by the World Institute for Advanced Phenomenological Research and Learning), October 1979.

Walendowski, Tadeusz. "The Polish Church under Martial Law." *Poland Watch* (Fall 1982): 54–62.

———. "Controversy over the Church." *Poland Watch* (Winter 1982–83): 39–45.

———. "The Pope in Poland." *Poland Watch* (Spring-Summer 1983): 1–10.

ACKNOWLEDGMENTS

This book could not have been written without the collaboration of Paul Lipkowitz. Paul, our principal research associate, has been involved in every phase of the book's preparation. His intelligence, dedication, tenacity, and professionalism are reflected on every page. We cannot thank him enough and, as he leaves to pursue his own journalistic career, we wish him Godspeed.

·   ·   ·

Lynn Nesbit, our agent, first suggested bringing the book to Doubleday; her counsel and friendship have been with us every step of the way. From the time *His Holiness* was an idea taking shape, it has had the encouragement and support of a wonderful group of people at Doubleday who have also become friends. Tom Cahill, distinguished author and former vice president of religious publishing, guided us through the first draft of the manuscript. Trace Murphy assisted in every phase, and his dedication has been a gift. Steve Rubin and Bill Barry welcomed us to Doubleday, and for that we are especially grateful. Arlene Friedman, who became Doubleday's president and publisher later in the project, brought her ebullience and intelligence to matters at just the right moment. To succeed Tom Cahill, she chose Eric Major, whose guidance and good nature could not have been more welcome. There are others at Doubleday whose commitment to this book has made a huge difference: Suzanne Herz, Jennifer Daddio, Robin Swados, Jean Anne Rose, Stuart Applebaum, Ellen Sinkinson, Christian Schoenberg, and Herman Gollub.

We have been the beneficiaries as well of those who have worked with us side by side in the preparation of the manuscript: Allesandra Scanziani, who traveled to the Soviet Union and assisted us there; Ewa-Joanna Kaczynska, whose expertise in matters Polish was only part of her contribution; Allesan-

ACKNOWLEDGMENTS

dra Todisco; Ottavia Fusco; Tamar Gargle and Jennifer Glaisek, whose patience and friendship are treasured; Irena Morecki, who diligently translated the *Wojtyła Calendarium* from the Polish.

A special word about Peter Heinegg, who both translated from the Italian and reviewed the manuscript with an acuity and insight. His contribution to the book is enormous. Tom Englehardt, a brilliant editor, was invaluable; likewise Barbara Flanigan, a copy editor whose role was much more.

Others who reviewed parts of the manuscript and whose counsel and support were lovingly offered were Bob Woodward, Cheri Kaufman, Jacob Bernstein, and Susan Cheever.

Max Bernstein was, as always, a delightful presence.

Other friends and colleagues were especially helpful and generous: Wilton Wynn, Faye Wattleton, Giovanni Volpi, Camilla McGgrath, Tim Hayes, Richard McDermott, Adele-Marie Stan. Special thanks to the American Academy in Rome, particularly Pina Pasquantonio, Caroline Bruzelius, and Adele Chatfield-Taylor.

INDEX